Get off the Interstate

by

Valerie Evans
Goddard

Best Wishes –
Valerie Evans
Goddard

For more information please contact
Valerie Evans Goddard
Verita Publishing
PO Box 498
St. Marys, Georgia 31558
1st edition, Second Printing

Dedication

To Bill

Your love and support
make all my dreams
possible.

Table of Contents

ACKNOWLEDGMENTS

Get off the Interstate would not have been possible without the love and support, first and foremost, of my family. Bill, Jason and Rusty, life would be impossible without my men, I love you. Thanks to my Dad, who continually offers his support. One of my greatest supporters, my sister Cindy, who means the world to me ~ I love you Sister; thanks to Cooper and Tucker for being the light of my life and to Tim for taking care of them all. To my father-in-law, Joe Goddard who amazed me with his encouragement and all four of my sisters-in-laws and their families ~ Thanks! Last but certainly not least; in memory of two women who shaped my life, offered me unconditional love always and made me the woman I am today ~ Hazel Evans, my Mother and Blanche Goddard, my Mother-in-law. I miss them both every day.

Thank you is not enough for all that my editor has done to make this book a reality. Christine taught me so much and was the driving force behind my developing writing skills. I could never have completed this book without you; and a big thanks to the men in her life who loaned her to me and kept her reasonably sane. Thanks to Mary Lynne and Jeff, who assisted in the birth of this project and have seen it through to the end with encouragement, love and unending support. Mary Lynne is my rock and my touchstone. She has always been there to remind me to take my medicine and rest when deadlines were coming quickly and the work could not wait. I love ya, Buddy!

To the best graphic design man in business. Johnny you created what I saw in my mind's eye without my ever having voiced it. Thank you from the bottom of my heart. Betty, what can I say, you have been a second Momma to one of the most precious things I have - Thank you.

I wish to thank the following people who have assisted with the research phase of this work, those who have offered words of encouragement and told me fascinating stories: the staff of the Camden County Library, who let me check out lots of books on the same subject and didn't yell too loud when I didn't return them on time!; the Bryan-Lang Historical Library and Darren Harper; Orange Hall Visitors Center, thanks for all of the wonderful stories.

Thanks go out to the St. Simons Island Visitors Center; the Jekyll Island Authority and guide, John Hunter who didn't mind sharing a few secrets hidden in the cellar; the Darien Visitors Center, who shared their tales of McIntosh and the Altamahaha; the staff at Fort King George; Ann Davis and Buddy Sullivan, who are a wealth of knowledge on McIntosh County and coastal Georgia.

I appreciate the assistance and support of the Midway Museum and Mrs. Clark; Fort McAllister, Danny Brown - thanks for your assistance, your notebook saved me days of research; Terry Trobridge, the Georgia Regional DNR Office, thanks for taking pictures and the personal tour; Mrs. Helen Szmyd of the Garden Club of Georgia, thank you so much for all of information you provided.

Thanks to Jerry at the Bryan County Historical Society Museum, your stories are great, keep the faith you'll get that book out there someday; Joe Thompson at Wormsloe, whose endless knowledge of his post and Georgia History is amazing; Tom Alligood at Skidaway Island; the Pirate House for a host turned tour guide that told me a pirate story. Last but certainly not least, the Georgia Historical Society and the Georgia Historical Library Staff, the assistance you provided is without equal. There are so many others that related old family stories, historical information and gave me insight on references when I was stuck on a story; Thanks to you all!

INTRODUCTION

Writing and researching *Get Off the Interstate* has been pure fun and a historian's dream. I could spend the remainder of my life and never completely cover everything wonderful there is about the Coastal Georgia area, I realize that I have only skimmed the surface. Yet as I traveled the coast, I have found interesting and amazing facets in each and every county not addressed on a historical marker.

One unsuspected but fulfilling reflection emerged during the research phase of the book. As I explored Coastal Georgia, invariably I would be accompanied by friends and family who wanted to tag along. After spending a little time with me, the most frequent response I received was: "I never really noticed historical markers until you brought them to my attention, now I see them everywhere." I hope once you read these pages that you too will not only see them but stop and take a moment to read them. Represented is one of Georgia's most valuable resources, her history. My hope continues that as adults, we pass along the stories, tales and legends to our children so that history continues to live in the hearts and minds of our future. If we fail to pass along these stories a part of history, which can never be recovered, dies and our children are the poorer for it.

An abundance of little known history is contained in the following pages of this book. The following is a sampling of information and wonderful historical tales from each county not yet detailed on a Georgia Historical Marker.

CAMDEN COUNTY

I would be remiss if I did not take a moment to mention one of Camden County's most valued treasures, Cumberland Island National Seashore. Though Cumberland does not have a marker detailing her history, the island is teeming with wonderful stories.

Georgia's coastline is bordered by a group of barrier islands, Cumberland Island being the southernmost and largest in the chain. Cumberland spans a length of seventeen miles and width of approximately one mile. The Island is bordered on the western side with saltwater marshes and on the eastern shore with a pristine, white sugar sand beach and the blue water of the Atlantic Ocean. The interior of Cumberland Island offers the tightly woven branches of a maritime forest and provides a wonderful haven in the midst of summer heat. Wild horses freely roam the island as well as other abundant wild life from armadillos to feral pigs. The island is host to all manner of bird life with shellfish and sea life in abundance on the shores and into the depths of the Atlantic. Cumberland Island was once owned by the prestigious Carnegie family and the history of the island is rich with stories of their relations. The ruins of Dungeness can be seen along with the island's focal points of Plum Orchard and Greyfield Inn. Plum Orchard, built in 1898, as a Georgian Revival style mansion and the home of Carnegie's son was donated to the National Park Foundation in 1971. Greyfield Inn, built in 1901, is still owned and operated by members of the Carnegie family. Opened in the 1960s as an inn, Greyfield provides an elegant stay amidst rustic, semi-tropical surroundings.

St. Marys is known as the gateway to Cumberland Island National Seashore. The Cumberland Queen greets visitors at the St. Marys waterfront and transports them to another world of peace, where the silence is only broken by a call of a sea bird or the splash of dolphins and manatees rolling in the surf. St. Marys and Cumberland Island National Seashore are the perfect cure for the stresses of a busy lifestyle.

St. Marys has much to offer from the historical Oak Grove Cemetery to her quaint shops, lodgings and restaurants downtown. Nearby Kingsland offers more commercial fare, lodging and each year entertains thousands with her Labor Day Catfish Festival. Woodbine, the Camden County seat, is approximately ten miles to the north. Woodbine's Crawfish Festival is the highlight of the year.

The following legend has been passed from generation to generation and I close the introduction to Camden County with,

The Legend of Sweetwater Creek

It is told that one day Withlacooche, an aged chieftain, was seated by the road trying to extract a thorn from his foot. Pretty Mary Jones, seeing the man in pain, offered her help and was able to extract the thorn. The chieftain was grateful and promised to help her if she ever needed his assistance. Soon after, Withlacooche saw Mary crying. Her fiancé, Ben Johnson, had enlisted in the Navy. Mary felt that if he went on a long cruise, he would never return. Remembering her kindness to him, the old chief came to her aid. He gathered red berries and green leaves and scattered them on the waters of Sweet Water Branch. He told Mary that he had cast a spell on these waters and whosoever drank of them would return, so she took Ben to the branch to drink. The spell brought him back to Mary and they were happily wed. This spell still holds true! Most people, after visiting in our town, usually come back to the "Beautiful Little City by the Sea" if they ever leave.[1]

GLYNN COUNTY

I didn't have far to look when trying to decide on an introduction to Glynn County. One of the greatest features of the county is in plain sight of all who pass, though they most often go unnoticed on Glynn Counties' St. Simons Island. I had visited the island hundreds of times and I never knew of the existence of "Tree Spirits" until this book. What, you might ask, are tree spirits? That question is best answered in the voice of a gruff old man who speaks with a distinct Gullah dialect and this was his story:

> "Tree Spirits, they are all over the island. Hundreds of ships were built from St. Simons oak. But the sea winds were unkind to the ships. The faces in the trees are the faces of the tree spirits who never wanted to leave the island. They grieve for those lost at sea. They are a warning. If you take wood away from St. Simons, the wind will make you pay.

> Watch for the face carved in the tree, but do not look back. It is bad luck to look back at the face of a tree spirit."

The carvings are the creations of North Carolina sculptor, Keith Jennings. The faces are carved into tree hollows, onto the stumps of long ago severed branches and into the heart of the live oak. The images immortalize sailors lost at sea on board mighty sailing vessels constructed of St. Simons oak. The resigned expressions of doomed men peer sightlessly from the branches and leave haunting images etched in your memory. The Tree Spirits can be found at the following locations: Demere Road at Skylane Drive, 2012 Demere Road, across from the farmer's market; Redfern Village (off Frederica Road) at the Wine & Cheese Cellar; 3305 Frederica Road; Demere Road at the Island Arts Center; and On Mallery Street next to Murphy's Tavern in the Village.

Keith Jennings is also the sculptor of an amazing life sized head of a right whale cow and her calf located at Neptune Park on the south end of St. Simons. St. Simons Sound was called, during the early 1700's, the Bay of Whales due to their abundance. Hunted beyond their ability to recover most whales are now listed on the endangered species list.

McINTOSH COUNTY

Like the Cumberland Queen to the south, the Sapelo Queen departs each morning laden with her human cargo of visitors bound for the peace and solitude of another of Georgia's barrier islands, Sapelo. Sapelo is an unheralded treasure of McIntosh County, which can not be overlooked for neither her historical value or the beauty that lay between her shores.

Though most of Sapelo today belongs to the State of Georgia approximately one per cent of the island remains in the hands of Hog Hammock citizens, a village set on the south end of the island. These people are the descendants of the slaves who once worked Sapelo plantations and who still hold tightly to a way of life that has long since faded into history on the mainland.

Sapelo has been owned by a string of wealthy men though the years, the last of which was R. J. Reynolds. He was responsible for the creation of the University of Georgia's Marine Institute in 1950 on the island. The research conducted there concentrated on the ecology of the saltwater marshlands. That research has revealed the effects of the marsh on commercial fishing industry, vital to the economy of McIntosh County.

Sapelo Island has been the lifelong home of author, Cornelia Bailey. Her stories of growing up on the island, its history, culture and legend bring to life a time that can only be known through the eyes of someone who has lived it. Noted author, Buddy Sullivan, whose works on Sapelo, McIntosh and Bryan Counties have been invaluable to researchers, including myself, is a native of McIntosh County.

Those who visit Sapelo are treated to a sense of cultural history that gently emerges during the thirty minute ferry ride and becomes evident upon arrival. Guided island tours bring visitors to the community of Hog Hammock, the University of Georgia Marine Institute, the Reynolds Mansion and the restored lighthouse. The lighthouse was built in 1820 and continued to serve the island until 1905 when it was deactivated. Restored in 1998, the Sapelo Lighthouse once again became an active aid to coastal navigation.

The Sapelo ferry dock and Visitor Center are located in Meridian, eight miles northeast of Darien, off of Georgia highway 99. Guided tours are available and reservations are required. The Visitor Center is open Tuesday through Sunday.

I suggest that while you take that ferry ride you keep an eye trained on the murky intercoastal waters. The waters beyond McIntosh County are known for a prehistorical beast known as the Altamaha-ha. Laugh if you will but sightings have been spoken of since the days when the Creek called the banks of the Altamaha River home. Since that time sightings of the mysterious creature have been recorded as far south as Jacksonville, Florida.

E. Randall Floyd, author of *Great Southern Mysteries*, wrote an article featured in the *Augusta Chronicle*. Floyd, a professor of journalism at Augusta College, quotes sightings which have occurred north of Darien in Appling, Tattnall and Wayne Counties where the Altamaha is no longer brackish.[2] Randall reports that a legend of a giant sea serpent was passed down by the Tama Indians, early settlers wrote of encounters and that the creature was described as being a giant snake which hissed and bellowed when frightened.

In 1969, McIntosh County began keeping a record of the mysterious sightings. *The Darien News* on February 3, 1983, reported:

> After two years of lying low, Altamaha-ha was sighted. This sighting reported Jan 16, 1983, Wednesday morning, 8:15 a.m. Tim Sanders, who worked as a car salesman at Darien Motor co., was traveling to work from Brunswick. Crossing the Champney River Bridge, looked east and spotted what he thought to be porpoises playing near the river bank about 100 yards away. Tim parked the car on the side of the road and watched. He soon realized that there was just one animal in the water - not a porpoise, but it rose from the water like a porpoise. The creature began swimming across the river. Tim estimated the creature to be about 20-25 ft long. As the creature swam at its leisure, his long body would crest the water with 6 - 7 ft between the humps. His body described by Tim as being about the size of the torso of a man, the color only "dark". Regarding the creature's head, Tim said he saw "what I thought was a snout". After the creature swam across the river, it went into a little cove. Tim drove over the bridge and walked down the Butler Island diked roadway to check for it but it was not around. "The thing that threw me, is I've never seen a fish that big", Tim said. It could have been a sturgeon, "but sturgeons never looked or swum like that", he said.

Obviously, the Loch Ness Monster of Scotland has an American cousin. McIntosh County is offering a reward for definitive proof of the existence of Altamaha-ha.

LIBERTY COUNTY

Liberty County has produced more historical leaders during the formation of our country than any other place in America. It is obvious as one visits most notably the eastern portion of the county that history and preservation of historical facets of the community are a priority. The care that has been taken with history in Liberty County is evidenced in the *Historic Liberty Trail*.

The Liberty Trail is a driving tour that leads from one historic sight to another marked along the way with signs baring the Liberty Bell symbol. The tour meanders through marshland and ancient oaks telling the stories of history from the founding days of the colonization until the modernization of today. Many of the sights have been recognized through the historical marker program, to find out more about those sights refer to the Liberty County chapter within these pages, those sights include: The Midway National Historic District, Dorchester Academy, Fort Stewart, LeConte Woodmanston and Fort Morris.

Seabrook Village is four miles east of I-95 on Trade Hill Road. The village is an excellent example of colonial life and is featured on the Liberty Trail. Seabrook is a colonial village with historical interpreters in period garb. The day to day activity of the community is as it would have been during colonial times. Guests are invited to grind corn, make candles or try out a scrub board used to wash laundry. Included is the grave art of Cyrus Bowens and various period antiques. Unfortunately, Seabrook Village is often closed to the public.

Historians continue to flock to Liberty County for information and research. Home to Lyman Hall and Button Gwinnett, signers of the Declaration of Independence and George Walton, who lived there for a number of years. Liberty County is a dose of yesteryear, easily taken.

BRYAN COUNTY

One of the many things I found fascinating about Bryan County was the Richmond Hill Fish Hatchery. The "Fish Farm", as locals call it, raises more than thirty million fish of various species and sizes each year, in forty-one different ponds. The fish are used to stock reservoirs, lakes and streams throughout Georgia. The hatchery is also involved with saving the rare Robust Redhorse from extinction. The Robust Redhorse is a sucker fish that was believed to be extinct only to be found again a few years ago in the Oconee River.

The Richmond Hill Fish Hatchery was the gift of Henry Ford to the State of Georgia in 1936. Civilian Conservation Corps workers performed initial construction under the direction of J. O. Bacon, and in 1938, the hatchery was opened and operated by the Georgia Game and Fish Division. The hatchery produced the first farm raised American Shad that same year. The hatchery has been renovated and modernized over the years and today is a state of the art facility.

The Richmond Hill Hatchery is striving to bring back from extinction the very rare Robust Redhorse, *Moxostoma robustum*. This thirty inch long fish can grow up to and often surpasses seventeen pounds and provided a plentiful source of food for the Indians which inhabited Georgia before colonization. The Robust Redhorse is a white flaky fish when cooked and was to southeastern Indians what salmon was to Indians of the Pacific coast; a dependable food source. Damming, siltation and pollution diminished the Robust Redhorses numbers and the loss of suitable bedding habitats, the extinction of mussels, which was a food source and the introduction of predatory species such as the flathead catfish eventually brought about their demise. In

iv

1991, five large Robust Redhorses were brought the Richmond Hill Fish Hatchery collected from the Oconee River by Jimmy Evans and technician Wayne Clark of the Georgia Department of Natural Resources. The fish were unidentified until Dr. Byron Freeman of the University of Georgia finally recognized it as the Robust Redhorse. Some of these reproducing fish have been captured, thanks to fishery science and a grant funded by Georgia Power. Techniques were developed, which eventually produced eight to ten-inch juveniles. These fish were released into the Broad River to see if they could survive. Only time will tell if the Robust Redhorse will recover or be lost again, this time forever.

Visitors may tour the Richmond Hill Fish Hatchery at no charge. The facility is located on Georgia 144, approximately one miles east of I-95.

CHATHAM COUNTY

Last, but certainly not least in any category is Chatham County. Savannah is covered with historical markers, justifiably so with the extraordinary history represented there and in the county. Even with one hundred and twenty-nine markers which were currently in place throughout the county, I managed to find a few fascinating facts which were not represented by markers.

The World War I casualties are honored by a long avenue of palmetto trees embracing Victory Drive. The trees were planted to honor those lost during World War I between the years of 1914 and 1918. The Savannah Women's Federation placed a stone monument at Daffin Park on the corner of Victory Drive and Waters Avenue to explain the significance of the palmetto trees and commemorate the observance. To find the next unmarked point of interest, travel further along Victory Drive until you arrive at its intersection with Whitaker.

There at Whitaker and Victory, looking east, you will see a tall unassuming stone fountain located in the center of the median. The simple fountain was placed in this spot in 1934 by Savannah resident, Percival Cohen. The fountain's purpose was to quench the thirst of Savannah's horses and dogs. Everyone needs a cool drink from time to time. Next up on the tour, travel to Whitaker where the block is bordered by York, Bull and Oglethorpe Streets.

The intersection where York, Bull, Oglethorpe and Whitaker meet was the site of Savannah's first Burial Ground. Before Colonial Park Cemetery was established this site was the city cemetery for seventeen years. Once identified by a plaque next to the RAF Gallery, the sign has since been removed and few are aware that a historic cemetery still occupies the spot. Unless another sign is placed or citizens continue to hold the site sacred, eventually Savannah's first Burial Ground will be lost with time. Continue to Abercorn and Drayton, there you will find the Marshall House.

It was where the Marshall House now stands that Savannah's first newspaper, the *Georgia Gazzette,* was printed under the watchful eye of Georgia's official printer, James Johnston. The Gazzette also provided paper currency and it was here that the laws pertaining to the newly established Georgia colony were printed.

From Camden County in the south to coastal Georgia's northern most coastal county, Chatham, the area is steeped in rich history. My hope is to bring a little of Georgia's coastal history to those that might not have found it otherwise; to have a reader say, "I didn't know that;" and to pass on a story, legend or old folks tale which might have otherwise died.

I have included within these pages every Georgia Historical Marker standing during the time of my research, no matter which organization placed the marker, as I covered the six coastal Georgia counties. I am sure that you will find markers that are not in the book that are now in place, unfortunately markers are often removed for maintenance, painting or repair; I did not intentionally leave any marker out although eventually the book had to go to press with what I had.

One last note: Included here are Atlantic Coastal Highway Commission or ACH markers. These markers are quickly deteriorating and unfortunately are no longer being maintained. This text will likely be the last recording of many of those markers, however, thanks to the Georgia Historical Society much of the history will be incorporated into newly posted markers.

I truly hope you enjoy reading about coastal Georgia's amazing history as much as I have enjoyed writing it. Begin your journey on Interstate 95 at Georgia Exit 1 near the Florida state line, Camden County is your first stop, now *Get Off the Interstate* and discover what you've been missing.

Endnotes

[1] Baker, Dot. *Historical Tour of St. Marys* The Earl of Camden Chapter Daughters of the American Revolution. 1970

[2] A mixture of salt and fresh water.

PREFACE

Get Off The Interstate is a quite simply a combination of two things that I love, history and travel. Writing this book has been an adventure. Even though I have lived in Georgia my entire life and thought I knew a great deal about her history, I have learned so much more. The study of history doesn't have to be about dry facts and dates. People make history and all of them have failings and triumphs. That's what makes history interesting. What I've tried to do with this book is to show you the human side of history. Behind every significant event is a story and most historical figures don't achieve that pinnacle without stumbling along the way. It is those stories that I have included here.

First of all let me say that I have done extensive research to make sure that the facts I give here are historically accurate. However, when dealing with history a certain amount of legend always creeps into the mix. Events, reactions, stories and even dates are altered over the course of time. I am certain that imperfections in the facts I relate here can be found. Even with careful attention to every detail in an attempt to attain historical accuracy, time changes things. The facts accepted today as truth, may come into question tomorrow from a new perspective.

The idea for this book happened quite by accident. Bill, my husband, and I joined our friends, Jeff and Mary Lynne for a much needed weekend away. We "camped," if you can call it that, in their luxurious RV at Belle Bluff Campground near Darien, Georgia. Jeff and Mary Lynne had arranged for an early tee time at Sapelo Hammock Golf Club the last morning of our wonderful weekend away. Bill and I aren't golfers, so we decided to go exploring. I think we were born explorers, we enjoy traveling the back roads just to see what we will find.

Darien is a lovely place. A remnant from times long past, one of the last few old fishing villages that has maintained its quiet Southern charm over the years. I won't go into the details of the history of Darien and McIntosh County, you will have to read the book for that, but suffice it to say that the area is filled with captivating history!

Bill and I drove around the rambling roads, imagining the histories of the beautiful old houses situated on the bluffs overlooking the Altamaha River. The sun was shining, a faint scent of jasmine and gardenia filled the air, ahead an armadillo scurried off the road to safety. What a way to spend a lazy Sunday afternoon in May. As we drove along, each of us lost in our own thoughts and enjoying the day, we saw a marker in the distance and I asked Bill to stop. We were in the middle of nowhere, what could possibly have occurred here to warrant a marker? The Georgia Historical Marker briefly told the story of a long ago plantation and the Georgia military hero who had once owned it. Of course, the writer in me sat up and took notice. The first thought I remember having is, "Wow, I didn't know that. That would make an interesting story!" I read the marker to Bill and we discussed the plantation and the people who once inhabited the land all around us. Back in the car, we were on our way again. A few miles down the road we noticed another marker and again we stopped to read. This marker was dedicated to a Revolutionary War hero, a descendant of the first marker subject, and sat in the edge of a park that was once his plantation. Bill was quiet for a few minutes, then said, "You know, nobody ever sees these things. I bet most people don't even know they're here." My response was true to form, I can be rather opinionated, and said, rather sarcastically, "Sometimes you have to *Get Off The Interstate*." Bill responded, "That's a book, you know." Well the ideas began to flow.

I could write a travel book and talk about all the Georgia Historical Markers. I could tell people where they are and write stories about them, I know there is more to the story than that! You drive by markers all the time, do you ever stop? Almost no one does. The only time anyone reads the markers is when they're visiting a historic site. You know touristy things. Then I thought, if people read a funny story, an interesting tidbit or a scandalous tale connected with these markers it would be fun to learn about the area. Thus, *Get Off The Interstate* was born.

Of course, as always, life happens. I became distracted with work, writing several short stories, articles and I even have a novel that needs to be developed a little more, the house, the kids and on and on. Even still my mind kept returning to the travel book thing. On a whim, I pitched the idea to my editor. My editor and friend, Christine has more enthusiasm than any ten people I know put together. Of course, she supports me and has a "can do" attitude about everything. She was all for it. When I rattle off my ideas and tell her, "I want to do this and this and this..." Christine always reels me in and puts me back on track. So after much discussion and some pouting on my part, we decide which direction to go with this. I thought, "This would be a leisurely process, I would get to do some traveling around coastal Georgia that I love so much and it would be an easy project to complete," boy was I wrong! About a week after pitching the idea to Christine, she called as she does every day to kick my butt and to make sure I stay on track with the pieces I'm writing. She said, "Where are we on that travel book thing?" My first response was, "HUH?" So far the book was just an idea in my head, I hadn't committed one word to paper and had no clue where to start. Christine outlined for me the what we were looking at and again she asked, "Can you do it?" Confidently, I said, "Yes."

I immediately began to research, I like that part, then soon realized that a research trip was needed and very soon! Then the unexpected. Of all things, I get sick. Not just your garden variety sick, I get really sick. I won't give you all the gruesome details of the horrors my very wonderful doctors put me through, ugly antibiotics that make you feel even worse than you did before and nasty tests that you have to submit to and so on. After much medicine and a couple trips to the hospital, I'm almost say...60 percent.

Christine, Bill and Mary Lynne kept me going the entire time. I get no sympathy from Christine mind you, she still kicks my butt every day and won't let me slack off. Bill took over everything in the house, the cleaning, cooking, everything without a word. Mary Lynne calls to make sure I'm taking my medicine and Christine wants to know if I finished sixty stories in two days.

Finally we get to do our research trip. Christine and I were off to Glynn County. She's a great editor and true friend but a lousy navigator, let me tell you. We drove all over Glynn County and I think we went the long way around every time. To be honest it wasn't her fault, I marked the map and neither of us had any clue where we were going in the beginning, but soon we found our way and were really excited when we got everything done in one day. Well almost. We did run into one or two road blocks and "No Trespassing" signs. We discovered right away that one area, in the interest of restoration and authenticity, had removed most of their historical markers. The area provides guided tours and does a wonderful job of maintaining the historical district and its artifacts. But the great markers with all that interesting history are stored away in a basement and you'll have to take the tour to learn more there.

Then we discover the mystery of the disappearing markers. First of all we have a listing of all the markers for each county, the directions to each marker are included but are written in a short hand code, once you get the hang of is quite easy to follow. I am an organizer so I prepared the lists of markers, sat down with the map and routed our course to make the most of out limited time. Well, the list says a marker is there, but believe me it isn't there. Ok, so double check the directions, nope the marker is gone. So fine, on to the next one. We noticed several markers had been removed due to road work or construction. Then you find in two weeks when you go back to take a few more pictures or pick up a marker you've overlooked or whatever, that suddenly the marker you couldn't find is right where it was supposed to be. I know I'm not imagining this... We did find out later that markers in bad shape are often taken in for repainting and repair, therefore, if you're traveling around and following my routing remember if the marker isn't there you're not lost. It will probably return at a later date!

After our research trip we were so excited to get home and get our pictures developed. We went right away. Another surprise. One entire roll of film was over exposed. We lost an entire roll. Ok, so back to the drawing board. We were all set to make our second trip and it began to rain and rain and rain. I couldn't go during the week so Christine had to make this trip alone. Finally, all the pictures are done, well, except one. It seems there is always one more.

Then tragedy strikes again. I saved all of my copies both on my computer hard drive and a floppy disk so that it could travel with me whenever I was able to work for a bit. I had a few minutes during the day and popped in the disk into my laptop to finish a story I'd been working on when...the messages said, "disk corrupt." NOOOO! My first thought was, "Ok, I have a back up at home on my hard drive." I called Bill and told him to email the story so that I could finish it up. I had worked late into the evening the night before and I guess I was slightly befuddled. I didn't save my work on the hard drive. The whole first section was gone. We tried every way possible to recover it. Nope, just gone. I called Christine and explained. I think she was more heart broken than me. Again we recovered. I started from scratch with the writing.

Over the course of one of our morning encouragement sessions Christine happened to mention, "by the way..." "By the way," when anyone says, "by the way," run in the other direction, someone is about to mention a tidbit of information that is going to ruin your day. Christine said, "how many entries do you have in your 'bib'?" My eyes opened wide, "excuse me?" I am new to the nonfiction world. I have written a good deal of fiction work but as you know, writers dream that stuff up! A 'bib' as in bibliography, I was supposed to be keeping that? Well, it was back to the drawing board again. After some effort I did get my 'bib' written, I kept a few notes along the way so it wasn't quite as hard as I thought it would be. And the only sympathy I got from my friend, the editor, was "Welcome to the writer's world!"

Now we have pictures, I have written most of the historical pieces and soon we go into layout! I'm so excited. It's been such fun, I've learned stuff and I'm a much better writer for it. As the book has progressed I've notice a writing style develop that I never knew existed, what an amazing discovery. We have one more edit and the book goes to print. Maybe I'll be in bed before 1:00 a.m. Well, maybe not, I'll be starting a new book soon. The next book is entitled, "*Get Off the Interstate, The Stories Behind the Historical Markers of East Coast Florida.*"

I hope you enjoy this book. I hope it brings you new insight into how much fun you can have exploring history and still learn something. I have been told that I am truly the epitome of Southern womanhood and I took that as the compliment it was meant to be. I love this area and can't imagine living anywhere else at this time in my life. I hope I have been successful in passing along a part of the feeling I have for coastal Georgia. Take it along on the journey through the saw grass marshland stirring in breeze as the voices of history introduce you to the Georgia coast. Remember, to find the really amazing sights and places when you travel, you've got to *Get Off the Interstate*!

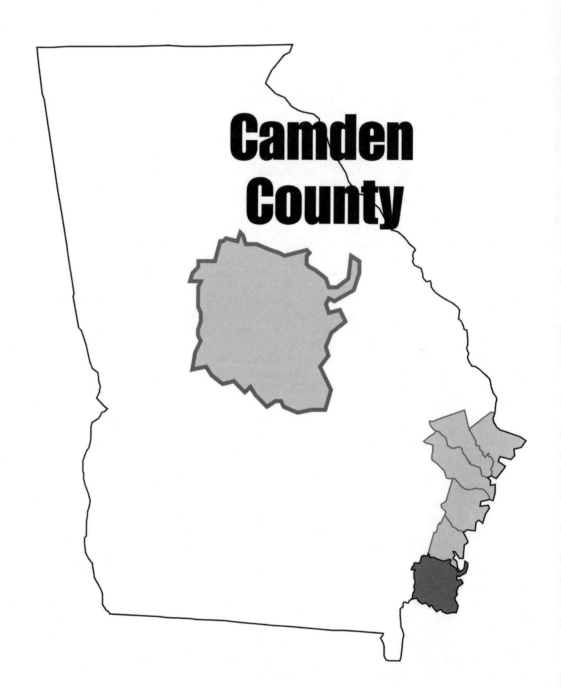

Camden County

CITY OF ST. MARYS

This town was built on the north bank of the St. Marys River at a place called Buttermilk Bluff. The original tract of land, containing 1620 acres, was purchased by the proprietors for laying out the Town of St. Marys for Jacob Weed for thirty-eight dollars each on Dec. 12, 1787. The city was first laid out by James Finley, county surveyor, in August 1788 and recorded Jan. 5, 1789. The twenty proprietors were: Isaac Wheeler, William Norris, Nathaniel Ashley, William Ashley, Lodowick Ashley, James Seagrove, James Finley, John Alexander, Langley Bryant, Jonathan Bartlett, Stephen Conyers, William Ready, Prentis Gallup, Simeon Dillingham and Richard Cole.
The city was laid out a second time as authorized by Act of Dec. 5, 1792. Map of town drawn by Parker, Hopkins, and Meers, certified by James Parker, surveyor, Jan. 3, 1792. The Town of St. Marys was incorporated by an Act passed Nov. 26, 1802.
St. Marys was the temporary county seat until the first courthouse and gaol was erected at Jefferson (Jeffersonton) as authorized and named in Act passed Nov. 29, 1800. Jeffersonton was the permanent county seat for sixty years (1801-1871).
An election held Jan. 3, 1871 authorized by an Act passed Oct. 27, 1870 for removal of county seat from Jeffersonton to St. Marys. St. Marys was the permanent county seat for fifty-two years (1871-1923). An act of Aug. 11, 1923 authorized the removal of the county seat from St. Marys to Woodbine.

Osborne and Dillingham Streets, St. Marys
GPS reading: N3043.5605, W08132.8375

In 1787, the proprietors[1] signed Articles of Agreement purchasing 1620 acres north of the St. Marys River and south of the Satilla for the establishment of a town to be called St. Marys. The property was owned by the brothers of Georgia's Royal Governor James Wright. The land deal was very lucrative, in addition to the price per acre, the brothers were given a Kings Grant of equal property further north along the St. Marys River.[2]

The St. Marys property was divided into squares and each proprietor was sold a block of four squares for the fee of forty-eight dollars. Each square equaled one acre and all excess lands were to be jointly owned. The proprietors agreed that anyone outside their close knit group must adhere to certain conditions in exchange for ownership of a St. Marys' lot. The stipulations were that the buyer had six months from the date of purchase to construct a business or dwelling on the lot and the structure would be assembled of logs or brick. Only after these conditions were met would the title of the lot be transferred. Although it might seem strange to insist on these stipulations, the proprietors believed they would eliminate the risk of the town coming under the ownership of any one individual by implementing these restrictions.

The Georgia Legislature acknowledged St. Marys in 1792, although the city was not incorporated until 1802. St. Marys was prospering and the city's population had grown to exceed 1600 inhabitants. Streets were developed and named in honor of the city's original proprietors. The main thoroughfare was named for perhaps the most colorful of her benefactors, Henry J. Osborne.

Henry Osborne was born in Ireland in 1752 and as a boy dreamed of the American colonies. He was certain that the New World would offer him a more profitable future. Henry kissed his Irish wife goodbye and sailed for Philadelphia. It was there he earned his law degree and eventually married for the second time. Henry became a dedicated civil servant and a highly regarded individual in Pennsylvania. During an investigation in 1783, Philadelphia's Supreme Executive Council found that Henry Osborne was guilty of bigamy. He was removed from all state posts and quietly disappeared from Pennsylvania in disgrace. Henry traveled south to Camden County, where he again ascended the ranks of political office.

Eventually, the aggressive politician was named as a delegate to the Continental Congress in 1786. Henry declined to attend the proceedings, which were held in Philadelphia where he was no longer welcomed. He was appointed Justice of the Georgia State Supreme Court the next year and retained the appointment until 1789.

Henry Osborne's redeeming historically significant claim was his electoral vote. He cast the determining ballot for the first President of the United States, George Washington. Perhaps his deciding vote was Henry's only good work during his time as a public servant.

In 1791, while serving as a Superior Court Justice, Henry certified an illegal voter count for Camden County. The race involved the election to Georgia's Congress with General Anthony Wayne and General James Jackson battling for the seat. When the polls closed General Wayne had received fifteen votes to General Jackson's ten, two hours later Henry summoned Camden County's Sheriff Samuel Smith to his residence and presented him with a totally different election return. It seems Judge Osborne and several of his cohorts had reopened the polls. The new count was much more impressive, with General Wayne winning the election by a decisive margin. The Sheriff was at once suspicious and sealed the election results. The Savannah Gazette reported on August 4, 1791, that the Grand Jury of Chatham County handed down indictments against Judge Henry Osborne and his accomplices for reopening the 1791 Congressional election. Henry did not contest the unfavorable verdict and was subsequently allowed to resign.

Henry married for the third and final time in 1791 to a St. Simons Island socialite, Miss Catherine (Kitty) Howell. All the while, Henry remained married to his wives in Ireland and Philadelphia; no record of dissolution of these marriages exists.

It was during this time that Henry became deeply involved in the Yazoo land fraud. The Yazoo land fraud case involved an act passed by the Georgia legislature in 1795 in which numerous government representatives were bribed to falsify property bids and the selling of vast amounts of Georgia territory that did not exist. A disputed land contract led to a duel between Henry and James Jackson. Henry refused to discharge his weapon and instead stood while his opposition took aim and squeezed the trigger. The shot missed and the duelists returned home. For his involvement in the Yazoo case, Henry was stripped of his citizenship, although it was reinstated in 1798. Henry Osborne faded into private life until his death in 1800 on St. Simons Island.

St. Marys began to flourish in the late 1700s, it was during this time that a group of displaced settlers were allowed to join the St. Marys community, French Acadians. St. Marys gained popularity as a port city; crops, lumber and live stock were exported from her busy wharf. A series of yellow fever epidemics ravaged the region over the next several years, taking a tremendous toll on the Acadians. Oak Grove Cemetery, located on Bartlett Street, is crowded with the head stones representing two-thirds of the St. Marys population who had succumbed to the deadly disease. Many of the graves at Oak Grove are carved with the French epitaphs of the Acadians.

The city had recently entered a rebuilding phase when the War of 1812 brought St. Marys to her knees. The border city was easily accessible to the British, who occupied northeast Florida. St. Marys' military protection had been recalled to join the action, leaving her defenseless. British blockades allowed very little food and scarce supplies to be delivered into the city. St. Marys was being starved into submission, but she remained resilient.

In spite of the poor circumstances, one of the most impressive dwellings of the city was completed on Osborne Street during this time. A perfect example of Greek Revival architecture, Orange Hall, was constructed for the Pratt family. The mansion acquired its name for the grove of citrus trees, which graced the lawn. Today, the estate serves as the St. Marys Welcome Center, filled with period antiques and open for self guided tours.

The mid 1800s brought civil war and many of St. Marys' citizens were lost. Although the city did not remain untouched, St. Marys was never burned like so many of her sister cities. The South's reconstruction was difficult, the era of great plantations was over, the population declined. St. Marys' tenacity prevailed and after the War she searched for a means to attract settlers and business.

The St. Marys City Council decided to offer free land to anyone willing to clear and plant crops or build a factory. The land would remain with the settler for ten years and at that time the settler would have first opportunity to purchase the property. Samuel L. Burns and Company Sawmill was the beginning of big business in St. Marys, many others would follow.

Today, St. Marys continues to thrive. The city was named *Money Magazine's* Number 1 Small Town in America in 1996. The population growth stems largely from nearby Kings Bay Naval Submarine Base and the military and civilian work force assigned there. St. Marys is also regarded as the Gateway to Cumberland Island National Seashore, which is a pristine pearl in the chain of coastal Georgia islands. History, museums, water sports and golfing are but a few of St. Marys attractions. Visitors enjoy the quiet little fishing village that speaks volumes of history and offers a moment to reflect in the waters of the Atlantic Intercoastal Waterway.

FIRST PRESBYTERIAN CHURCH

Built by public subscription as a place of divine
worship for inhabitants of St. Marys and its vicinity.
Reverend Horace Southworth Pratt was ordained
and installed as the first pastor by the Presbytery
of Georgia in June, 1822.
Incorporated under the name of the Independent
Presbyterian Church of St. Marys Dec. 20, 1828.
On Dec. 5, 1832 the Independent Church was
incorporated as the First Presbyterian Church of
St. Marys in the Georgia Presbytery.

Osborne and Conyers Streets, St. Marys
GPS reading: N3043.5035, W08132.8623

Initially called the St. Marys or Union Church when it was constructed in 1808, the church provided an interdenominational place of worship, housing the first organized school and the town meeting hall. Horace Southworth Pratt was conscripted as the first pastor. In 1822, the church joined the Georgia Presbytery and was renamed the First Presbyterian Church.

Orange Hall was built as the parsonage for the First Presbyterian Church in 1829 for Reverend Horace and Jane Pratt, by her father. The caretakers of Orange Hall say that the Pratt's young daughter Jane, who died in early childhood, still plays amid the rooms of the mansion. Toys are moved from the child's bedroom to other rooms and beds are left in disarray. Even though young Jane did not die in St. Marys, it is said that she has returned to the home she knew best.

Many stories concerning the church have been passed down through the generations. A story that is particularly interesting concerns smugglers unable to get their cargo ashore because of the local customs officer. The men were said to have stolen the minister's horse under a cover of darkness and hoisted it into the church belfry (though in reality they only tied the horses tail to the bell pull). The entire St. Marys population gathered the next morning and gazed up at the belfry, where the terrified animal voiced his turmoil. While the town's people figured out a way to get the horse down, the smugglers brought their ill gotten goods ashore to an eagerly awaiting merchant. The smugglers were then off to sea again with the ebb tide.

During the Civil War, federal troops threatened to burn the church. The towns people gathered as troops placed a ring of dry wood and brush around the sanctuary. The fire was set as many of the congregation looked on while the dancing, orange flames grew closer to the white washed wooden structure. Observers related that "distant rolls of thunder could be heard as if God was greatly dismayed." The sky darkened and a huge rainstorm erupted. Within minutes the fire was doused.

Fire did damaged the church in 1956, when the bell tower burned, and extensive renovations were necessary. The church appearance remains today much the same as the day it was built. The First Presbyterian Church continues to host an active congregation and remains the oldest church in continuous service in the state of Georgia.

The First Presbyterian Church

WASHINGTON PUMP & OAK

There were originally six wells one in each square, the
only source of pure water for St. Marys,
(until the tidal wave of 1818).
On the day that the Father of His Country was buried at
Mt. Vernon local services were also held throughout the
nation. St. Marys citizens marched to the dock to meet a
boat bearing a flag- draped casket, bore it up Osborne St.
and with due ceremony and firing of guns, buried it where
the Well known as the "Washington Pump" now is.
To mark the spot, four oaks were planted and have since
been known as the "Washington Oaks". Only this one
remains, This well was driven the year of Washington's
burial and has ever since been called
the "Washington Pump".

Osborne and Conyers Streets, St. Marys
GPS reading: N3043.4765, W08132.8539

Afterhaving worked in his Mount Vernon garden for the better part of the day in the wind and rain, George Washington entered the house for his evening meal. Washington was so weary from his labor that he did not bother to change into dry clothes, the rainwater still matted his hair. Later that evening, while he sat reading with Mrs. Washington and Tobias Lear, his secretary, Washington began to grow hoarse and complained of a sore throat. After retiring to bed, he woke Mrs. Washington saying he was experiencing a severe ague.[3] Mrs. Washington quickly roused the household and summoned Mr. Lear to her husband's side. Mrs. Washington and Lear begged to send for the doctor, but Washington would not hear of it. Instead, the overseer was fetched who had experience bleeding the sick. The bleeding had no effect.

The following morning, the doctor was called to Washington's side. Doctor Craik was well aware when he entered the room that the situation was dire. The doctor requested two more physicians be in attendance and all conferred. Washington was bled several times, while different concoctions of chamomile and vinegar were used. It was obvious that the former President was not responding to any treatment. Washington's breathing became labored and his throat swelled shut.

Washington submitted to the ministering from the trio of doctors much more for their sake than his own. He realized from the onset that this sickness was fatal and accepted the fact with quiet dignity. Finally, late into the evening he requested to be left in peace. Honoring his wishes, Tobias Lear assisted Washington in arranging several matters to ease the probate of his estate. He asked for Mrs. Washington and requested she retrieve two wills in his desk. Looking over both of them, he had her burn the rejected one.

A short time later he quietly slipped away. Mrs. Washington, Mr. Lear and Dr. Craik were at his side. Mrs. Washington was quoted as saying, "Is he gone? Tis well all is now over, I shall soon follow him! I have no more trials to pass through."

Congress issued resolutions stating that a mock funeral procession would be held in Philadelphia, the Nation's Capital, on December 26, 1799 and further requested that all citizens wear black armbands for thirty days. A proposed marble monument for Washington's remains at the new Capitol building was made. General George Washington, first President of the United States was memorialized on the floor in Congress with these words, in part,

> "The melancholy event which was yesterday announced with doubt, has been rendered but too certain. Our Washington is no more. The hero, the patriot, and the sage of America; the man on whom in times of danger every eye was turned, and all hopes were placed, lives now only in his own great actions, and in the hearts of an affectionate and afflicted people."

The Washington oaks and wells are no longer evident in St. Marys, merely the remnants of what once was. The historical marker stands in memory of the first president.

"First in war, first in peace and first in the hearts of his countrymen. . . ."

—Henry "Light-Horse Harry" Lee, from his eulogy delivered before Congress.

ST. MARYS METHODIST CHURCH ESTABLISHED 1799-1800

This church is the oldest religious organization in city, although not oldest church building. George Clark served as first missionary to people here in 1792. John Garvin was first appointed pastor to St. Marys in 1799. Methodist services were first held in the building erected for a Courthouse. In 1812 City of St. Marys deeded Methodists a lot 200 x 200 ft. still in use at this time. Church built after 1812 was in use until a few years before the Civil War when the old church was moved to another site and given to the Negro Methodists. Present chapel built before Civil War. While St. Marys was occupied by Federal troops in 1862, this chapel was used as a Quartermaster's Dept. where animals were butchered.
A deed was granted the church in 1878. The building was renovated on several occasions.
Between 1792-1935, 103 Pastors have served this church. It was the first church of Bishop Arthur J. Moore in 1909.

Conyers Street east of Osborne Street, St. Marys
GPS reading: N3043.4810, W08132.8118

There were fourteen members of the congregation at St. Marys Methodist Church when John Garvin was appointed pastor in 1799. Having no permanent facility, the assembly congregated in various public buildings. The city government deeded Public Square 9 to the church trustees and the church finally was constructed in 1812. The St. Marys Methodist Church congregation, at last, had a home.

The church was a simple wooden structure with double doors on the southern end. A door to the right was the men's entrance and to the left, the women's. During that time, the men and women were not permitted to "mix" at the services. The pastor's salary was a mere sixty-four dollars annually. James Osgood Andrew[4] said, "If our poverty were our purity, some of us ought to be purified ere long…"

Sabbath School, sponsored by the church, had sixty-four students in attendance and eleven teachers in 1841 and was flourishing, church membership was dwindling. Church members were being cast aside for infractions such as profanity, general immorality, lying, intemperance and adultery.

By 1858, a new sanctuary was necessary and the new edifice was constructed for $695.00, this building is still used today as the chapel for the St. Marys United Methodist Church.

Federal troops ordered the church closed during their occupation. The town was inundated with Yankee soldiers, and St. Marys Methodist Church was used as a butcher's shop. St. Marys and the church were fortunate, when federal troops withdrew, the town was intact. Services resumed in 1866, answering the need for revival within the congregation created by the Civil

War. The church began to prosper by 1872, the pastor's salary was increased to $250.00 annually, a cabinet organ was purchased, and the membership grew to eighty-five parishioners.

St. Marys Methodist continued to grow and change with the times. It has seen difficult years and often the regrowth paralleled that of the history of St. Marys. New brick buildings were added to house classrooms, a social hall and a kitchen. A new parsonage was built in 1958. Increased membership led to a larger, more modern sanctuary in 1966. Built along side the older structure, the current sanctuary has a seating capacity of 360 members and guests.

Recognized as a historical site in 1981, St. Marys United Methodist Church continues to grow. A new social hall has been built and the classrooms have been renovated. The Sabbath School is now called the Happy Apple Academy. A new parsonage was constructed in 1999. Today, membership exceeds 700 parishioners.

St. Marys United Methodist Church

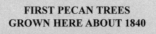

**FIRST PECAN TREES
GROWN HERE ABOUT 1840**

Grown from pecan nuts found floating at sea by Captain
Samuel F. Flood and planted by his wife nee: Rebecca
Grovenstine on Block 47. The remainder of these nuts
were planted by
St. Joseph Sebastian Arnow in
the north half of Block 26.
These first plantings produced large and heavy-bearing
trees, as did their nuts and shoots in turn. Taken from St.
Marys to distant points throughout southeastern states,
they became famous before the Texas pecans were
generally known.

**200 block of Weed Street, near Ready Street, St. Marys
GPS reading: N3043.3702, W08132.7603**

Pecans have been traced to the 16th century and the name was derived from a Native American word meaning, "all nuts requiring a stone to crack." The nut producing trees are the only ones growing wild in North America, often reaching heights of 150 feet, and many living in excess of 150 years. Older pecan trees have been measured to a diameter of over three feet.

The wild trees produced a plentiful supply of the nuts, coming to maturity in the fall, the natives stockpiled them for the lean winter. Native Americans utilized the versatile nuts for everything from flour to a fermented drink called *powcohicora*. The hickory tree is a close relative of the pecan and the word hickory is derived from *powcohicora*.

American colonists were first to export the pecan during the eighteenth and nineteenth centuries. Quick to realize the demand, orchards began to appear. Planters of this era began to experiment with the production of various sizes, shapes, shell formations, flavor and growing cycles.

Today, seedlings of the trees once planted by Rebecca Grovenstine Flood can still be seen along East Weed Street in St. Marys. The seedlings are approximately seventy years old and continue to produce nuts in the fall of the year.

Pecan production has become a billion-dollar a year Georgia enterprise. The United States is responsible for over 80 percent of the world market and the United States Department of Agriculture has estimated that an excess of 350 million pounds of pecans are produced each year. Albany, Georgia has the largest orchards in the United States, claiming more than 600,000 trees.

POINT PETER

East of here, at the junction of Peter Creek and St. Marys
River, the British built Fort Tonyn in 1776, controlling the
southern part of the Colony of Georgia for two years.
In 1778 American Revolutionary forces, both land and water,
forced evacuation of the exposed position. The English
retreated northwest along the North River into Pagan Creek
Plantation, home of the Tories, Charles and Jeromyn Wright,
brother of Royal governor James Wright. On high land
along Alligator (now Borrell) Creek, they built log and sand
breastworks and repulsed the American cavalry under
Colonel Elijah Clark. It appears that in the War of 1812,
Fort Pickering was built on the Fort Tonyn site.

**Osborne Street and Point Peter Road, St. Marys
GPS reading: N3044.5924, W08133.2318**

The attack by the South Carolina militia on British held Fort Tonyn had two objectives: (1) to protect Georgia from infiltrating British forces and (2) to keep the British guessing the American militia's intent.

American General Robert Howe had been encamped with his contingent of 2000 men near Savannah for six months by the summer of 1778. Very few of his men were experienced soldiers, most were planters from South Carolina and Georgia. A quick, decisive attack on the British forces was necessary to take Fort Tonyn and eventually move into northeast Florida, General Howe patiently waited for reinforcements from Colonel Williamson, who led the South Carolina Militia. Colonel Williamson arrived with his contingent of 800 men on July 5th and General Howe petitioned Governor Moultrie of South Carolina to allow him to proceed with the attack on the fort.

The British hastily erected Fort Tonyn near St. Marys on a little peninsula of land called Point Peter. Howe's battalion met with little opposition. When the small British force saw the strong front of American militia bearing down on them, they destroyed the fort and withdrew to St. Augustine.

The British proved to be a minor problem compared to the fighting between the American officers that discredited General Howe's entire command. Colonel Charles C. Pickney, serving under General Howe, wrote to Governor Moultrie to advise him of his situation. Pickney stated that his three company commanders refused to take orders from him. Colonel Houston refused to take any order given, Colonel Williamson hinted that his men answered to no one but himself and Commodore Bowlan flatly established that in the Naval Department, he was supreme. Pickney beseeched Governor Moultrie saying, 'With this divided, this heterogeneous command, what can be done?'[5]

With the British fort taken, the American forces waited for new orders. When no word came, the officers decided to follow their own agendas. The debilitating summer heat and disease claimed nearly 750 American soldiers and General Williamson, recently promoted, withdrew with what remained of his battalion. Colonels Williams and Pickney determined that the Native Americans would assist the British in Florida and marched their regiments into Native American territory, decimating the corn harvests of eight settlements. The American forces pushed the Native Americans into remote locations, hoping to avoid their alliance with the British. The Cherokee retaliated a year later. They massacred several families and burned a number of homes. Pickney, now a General, responded by annihilating thirteen Cherokee villages.

TABBY SUGAR WORKS OF JOHN HOUSTOUN MCINTOSH

These are the ruins of a tabby sugar works built by John Houston McIntosh at New Canaan Plantation soon after 1825. In his sugar house McIntosh installed what was, according to Thomas Spalding, the first horizontal cane mill worked by cattle power.

McIntosh, born in 1773 in what is now McIntosh County, settled in East Florida as a young man and became the leader of a group of American citizens who, during the War of 1812, plotted the annexation of East Florida to the United States. This plot crushed by the Spanish government, McIntosh removed to Georgia and acquired two plantation in Camden County, Marianna, where he built a home, and New Canaan, where he began the

cultivation of sugar cane under the influence of Thomas Spalding, who had experimented in sugar production and seen the use of steam-propelled horizontal cane mills in Louisiana.

After McIntosh's death in 1836, New Canaan was sold to one Col Hollowes, who changed the name of the plantation to Bollingbrook and lived there until after the Civil War. During the war, Hallowes planted cane and made sugar in the McIntosh sugar house. He also used the tabby sugar works as a starch factory, producing arrowroot starch in large quantities.

GA 40 Spur 2.9 miles north of GA 40 at Kings Bay Submarine Base
GPS reading: N3047.5905, W08134.6387

John Houstoun McIntosh was born in nearby McIntosh County and following in the footsteps of his elder relations, he distinguished himself in the War of 1812. After the war, John Houstoun purchased two plantations in Camden County, New Canaan and Marianna, choosing Marianna as his home in 1819. The McIntosh Sugar Works originated around 1825 at the site of the New Canaan Plantation.

Marianna included 800 acres of what is now known as the Kings Bay Naval Submarine Base. Just after the Civil War, the house burned and all that remained was the tabby foundation. When the United States Army purchased the property, all known plots in the family cemetery were disinterred and the remains were placed in Oak Grove Cemetery at St. Marys.

New sanctions imposed on imports following the War of 1812 made it impossible to acquire sugar, creating an excellent opportunity for Georgia planters. Thomas Spalding, a McIntosh cousin, began producing sugar on Sapelo Island in 1805. After realizing an admirable profit, Spalding proposed to other planters including John Houstoun, that sugar cane would boost the profits for the area plantations. Spalding introduced his cousin to the process and provided McIntosh and other planters with the necessary sugar cane plants to begin cultivation.

John Houstoun used an innovative design for his mill, much different from Spalding's or any other traditional cattle powered operation. His design left open the option to expand production and the ability to upgrade his operation to steam, if it proved profitable. The mill was constructed of tabby, created by mixing equal amounts of oyster shells, sand, lime and water. The outer walls are fourteen feet tall and fourteen inches thick. There were three rooms, each with a specific purpose, the milling room had an additional second floor constructed of wood.

The milling room was to the west. The second floor housed the power source, cattle and drive mechanism. The central room was for clarification and boiling the sugar cane. The Jamaica train[6] was installed on the north wall, it was designed to evaporate the sugar cane juice safely and less costly than using the open-kettle system. The furnace was located on the north porch with a fire door through which the bagasse[7] could be burned.

The mill had a very innovative recycling process. The burned bagasse provided heated air. The air then passed through the flue beneath the boiling pans and heated the cane juice contained in the Jamaica train. Once the liquid was reduced to its final form, sugar was the result. In the curing room and two warehouse areas to the east, the sugar was finished and prepared for shipment.

Many factors prevented the expansion of the sugar mill, a lack luster sugar crop, experimental technology and most importantly, the death of John Houstoun in 1836. After John Houstoun's death the sugar mill and New Canaan Plantation were sold to Colonel Hallowes and combined with another plantation known as Bolingbrook. Hallowes lived there until after the Civil War. He continued to produce sugar and at one time, manufactured a great deal of arrowroot starch at the Mill.

Today, the site of John Houstoun McIntosh's Sugar Works is an impressive example of early 19th Century tabby. The area has been well preserved as a historic site by St. Marys and Camden County. Picnic tables are in place for a quiet place to have a bite and explore the ruins and many very nice bicycle paths have been built to provide hours of safe family entertainment without a penny spent.

John Houstoun McIntosh's Sugar Works

POST ROAD

This road, formerly an Indian trail which parallelled the coast was used by the Spanish and the British. In 1778 it was travelled by Revolutionary soldiers who marched against Fort Tonyn at Point Peter. Albert Gallatin while U. S. Secretary of the Treasury in 1805 recommended the Old St. Marys Road, a portion of the Post Road, as one of seven principal routes that were important to U. S. defense and postal service.

US 17 at Kinlaw Road, 4.4 miles north of Kingsland
GPS reading: N3051.6940, W08142.1562

The Georgia Legislature decreed in 1792 that a road be built from Liberty County through Glynn and Camden Counties ending in St. Marys. Royal Governor James Wright issued the Road Act with instructions concerning how the road was to be completed and appointed a commission that would be responsible for overseeing the construction. The commission included Sampson Ball, William Armstrong and Jeromyn Wright, the Governor's brother.

The commission was to design the road and enlist a surveyor to finalize the plans. The Road Act stipulated that all tenant workers and slaves were to be engaged as road workers until the project was completed. The Act's use of tenant workers and slave labor was the basis for the use of prisoners as "Chain Gang" highway workers in the late 19th Century.

The commission elected to follow William Bartram's research as recorded in his book, *The Travels of William Bartram*. The book details Bartram's exploration through coastal Georgia and the Post Road would follow virtually the same route.

William Bartram was a distinguished botanist that traveled on horseback throughout the eastern United States, initially with his father, who was connected to the Royal Court of England. William Bartram's travels led him throughout Georgia and near St. Marys. Bartram diligently recorded all that he saw[8], later his accounts were compiled and published.

The Old Post Road was completed in 1802. The route was described as traveling "southwesterly from Brunswick, continuing near Waynesville, then onward by Wayside Plantation, past Bickley's Chapel, passing Oak Hill cemetery, through Jerusalem to Brown's Ferry, across to Jefferson, through the woods to Seals and finally on to St. Marys. Today, the Old Post Road has virtually disappeared from existence along with most of the places along its route. Portions were incorporated into other roads and Georgia historical markers have been placed, as closely as possible, to mark the original route.

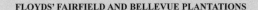

FLOYDS' FAIRFIELD AND BELLEVUE PLANTATIONS

Charles Floyd and son John moved to Camden Co. and
established rice plantations on the Satilla River
about 1800.
John Floyd (1769-1839) was a noted general and hero in
War o 1812; a state legislator, U. S. Congressman and
presidential elector. Outer walls of Bellview plantation
home were built in shape of anchor, and still stand.
Charles Rinaldo Floyd, son of Gen. John Floyd, filled
many military positions of high trust. Was a Georgia
legislator and talented artist.
Burial ground for members of family is on plantations.
Handsome U. S. monuments mark the graves of Charles,
John, and Charles Rinaldo.

US 17 at Billyville Road in Colesburg
GPS reading: N3055.9445, W08142.9656

C harles Floyd was orphaned at the tender age of seven. With no one to take him in, he was sent to serve as a cabin boy on a merchant ship until he reached his majority. When Charles came of age, he settled in southern Carolina and married Mary Fendin in 1768. The couple had one child, John, born at Hilton Head, Carolina, in 1769. As Captain Floyd, he fought admirably during the Revolutionary War. Charles was taken prisoner during a battle outside of Charleston, his home was burned, and still he held fast to his convictions. The Commodore of the prison ship was so impressed at Captain Floyd's unwavering ideals that he was allowed privileges not extended to the other prisoners.

John Floyd was apprenticed at the age of sixteen to a master carpenter. He became so accomplished, the carpenter offered to release him of the obligation. John refused and fulfilled his remaining commitment as agreed. He married Isabella Maria Hazzard in 1793, the couple had twelve children.

John and Isabella moved with his parents to McIntosh County in 1795 and then to Camden County in 1800. They purchased a substantial amount of property later known as Floyd's Neck. The Floyd men were accomplished planters and John applied his considerable carpentry skills to building boats. He built schooners, merchant vessels and racing boats.

Like his father before him, John Floyd was called to serve his country. When the War of 1812 began, John was given the rank of Brigadier General and led troops against Fort Tonyn at Point Peter. John distinguished himself in a number of fierce battles.

When the war was over he was persuaded by the Georgia legislature to lead a survey of the Georgia/Florida state boundaries. John's dedication to civil servitude led him to become an advocate for the States Rights Party, Justice of the Peace, Georgia Representative, and later, Senator. John Floyd's contribution to the state of Georgia were recognized when Floyd County was named in his honor.

John Floyd created Bellevue Plantation for his father and Fairfield Plantation for himself, occupying Bellevue Plantation after his father's death and expanding it with an additional story made from native cypress. Bellevue was built in the shape of an anchor to acknowledge the fortune that the sea had provided for the Floyd family. Both glorious plantations were completely destroyed during the Civil War. All that remains of either majestic dwelling are the thick tabby walls in the shape of an anchor that was once Bellevue. The family cemetery still remains near the site of the former Fairfield plantation. Fifteen graves are cradled by a short brick wall and protected by a wrought iron gate.

The Floyd lineage was teeming with highly successful and most interesting personalities. The following are mentions of John and Isabella's children that managed to reach adulthood:

MARY HAZZARD FLOYD married EVERARD HAMILTON, they had eleven children. Colonel Hamilton served in the War of 1812 as aide-de-camp to his father-in-law, General John Floyd. He was elected Secretary of State for Georgia and served for ten years. Mary wrote: *A Little Family History* - copies are still available in archival libraries including, the Georgia Historical Society Library, Savannah and the Bryan-Lang Historical Library, Woodbine, Georgia.

CHARLES RINALDO FLOYD married CATHERINE SOPHIA POWELL, they had two children. After Catherine's death, Charles Rinaldo married JULIA ROSS BOOG, they had seven children. General Charles R. Floyd led troops in the relocation of the Cherokee Indians and fought Native Americans in the Okefenokee Swamp. He was an accomplished duelist, poet and artist and kept a detailed diary. Copies can be seen at the Georgia Historical Society Library in Savannah, Georgia. The United States Government placed a marble monument to acknowledge his patriotism at his gravesite near Fairfield Plantation.

SARAH CATHERINE WIGG FLOYD married AIME DeLAROCHEAULION, they had three children. Sarah had a double wedding ceremony with her sister, Susan. Aime was an accomplished French physician and Sarah was an extraordinary pianist and taught music.

SUSAN LODVISKI DIXON FLOYD married BENJAMIN HOPKINS, they had ten children. Colonel Hopkins served in the Florida militia during the Seminole Indian War and volunteered for duty during the Civil War. Benjamin was a lawyer and planter in Florida.

JOHN FENDIN FLOYD married ANN H. ALSTON, they did not have any children. Just over a month after their marriage, John was shot to death in Darien, Georgia, over a political disagreement.

CAROLINA ELIZA LOUISA FLOYD married JAMES HAMILTON BLACKSHEAR, they had four children. Major Blackshear was a planter and though odd for day, Carolina owned land in Laurens County, Georgia.

RICHARD FERDINAND FLOYD married MARY ANN CHEVALIER, they had three children. Colonel R. F. Floyd commanded the local militia, Camden Chasseurs of Horse. He served as sheriff, lived at Hermitage Plantation and owned Brookfield Plantation. Richard was an accomplished draftsman and artist, his primary topic being horses. He was appointed Brigadier-General of the State of Florida during the Civil War.

MALINDA ISABELLA FLOYD married WILLIAM PROCTOR HOPKINS, no children. Her maid at Baisden's Bluff[9] murdered her by poison only six weeks after her marriage.

SAMUEL AUGUSTUS FLOYD never married. Samuel lived with a mulatto female and the couple had six children, all baring the name Floyd. He was an invalid and sold Bellevue Place to a former slave, Pompey Floyd, in 1877 for $100.00.

HENRY HAMILTON FLOYD married MARGARET ANN BOOG, they had one child. After her death he married her younger sister, MORDINA JANE BOOG. They had twelve children. Both sisters were of Jamaican decent. Henry was a surveyor and kept an extensive journal, which can be seen at the Georgia Historical Society Library in Savannah, Georgia.

If you weren't counting, the Floyds were blessed with 59 grandchildren!

CAMDEN COUNTY

Formed from old Colonial parishes: St. Mary and St Thomas. Camden one of eight original counties of Georgia created by the State Constitution of 1777. County named for Charles Pratt, Earl of Camden, Chief Justice and Lord Chancellor England. Camden County gave territory to Wayne in 1808 and 1812 and to Charlton in 1854. St. Marys was temporary County Site until Jefferson (Jeffersonton) was named as first permanent county site by an Act of Nov. 29, 1800. Jefferson seat of government sixty-nine years (1801-1871). Election held Jan. 3, 1871, authorized county seat be removed from Jefferson to St. Marys. St. Marys county seat for fifty-two years (1871-1923). Act of Aug. 11, 1923 authorized removal of county seat from St. Marys to Woodbine. Present courthouse here erected 1928.

Some of the first and early settlers of the county were: Talmadge Hall, James Woodland, Thomas Stafford, David & Hugh Brown, John King, John Hardee, Henry Osborne, Jacob Weed, John Webb, Abner Williams, Charles & John Floyd, Nathan Atkinson, Isaac & Richard Lang, Joseph Hull, William Berrie, Thomas Miller, John Bailey, Sr., and nephew, John Bailey, and Lewis DuFour.

First County offices were: Alexander Semple, Clerk of Court; Wilson Williams, Sheriff; John Crawford, Coroner; Nathaniel Ashley, Tax Col.;
Robert Brown, Register of Probates.

A number of the early settlers of this county came from Acadia, San Domingo, Minorca, and Spanish East Florida.

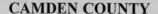

US 17 at 4th Street in Woodbine
GPS reading: N3058.0724, W08143.4005

When Europeans adventurers arrived at the Georgia colony, they were met by a proud group of bronzed warriors belonging to the Lower Creek Indian Nation. The Native Americans, who had been ill treated at the hands of the Spanish Franciscan priests, were apprehensive of the British. They slowly developed a trusting friendship and a pact was made, setting aside land, essentially creating what would become Camden County. In 1733, they smoked the pipe of peace[10] with the Great White Chief, General James Edward Oglethorpe, thus adopting The Treaty of Savannah. The treaty is beautifully written with five most important points detailing the conduct of the British soldiers and the Creek Indians.

First, the English encouraged its settlers to trade with the Creek. The Creek leaders and General Oglethorpe agreed to a schedule of prices. Five buckskins could be traded for one blanket, while fifteen buckskins would buy a rifle with flint, powder and shot. Secondly, the British pledged that any man guilty of molesting the Creeks would be tried and punished according to British law. Likewise, the Native Americans were to trade fairly and should any Native American brave accost the settlers, those offenders would be subjected to the penalties dictated by British law as well. Third, the Creeks demanded that as the population of settlers grew, settlements would remain within the established boundaries and not expand into Creek territory. Fourth, the Native Americans agreed to apprehend escaped African slaves and deliver them to the garrison commander. They would be paid four blankets or two guns for each live capture. If the slave was killed during their apprehension, the payment was one blanket. The head of the escaped slave had to be returned to the commander as proof. Finally, the Creek elders took an oath against the Spaniards and French. The treaty closed with this:

> "And to show that we, both for the good of ourselves our wives and children do firmly promise to keep this talk in our hearts as long as the sun shall shine or the waters run in the rivers we have each of us set the marks of our families."

The treaty was later expanded and then abandoned as the struggle for control of the American colonies increased.

In 1758, the Colonial Legislature in Philadelphia divided the Georgia colony into twelve parishes. The American Revolution brought more reorganization and in 1777, the parishes became counties. St. Thomas and St. Marys parishes were united, becoming Camden County. In 1923, the county seat was moved from St. Marys to Woodbine due to a shift in county population. In 1928, the present Camden County courthouse was built in Woodbine. It is the only courthouse built in the Gothic Revival style in the state.

Today, Camden County spans 782.5 square miles. This makes it the sixth largest county in the state. Its population was 43,664 as recorded in the 2000 census.

REFUGE PLANTATION

On the Satilla River 2.8 miles from here, was one of the largest rice plantations in the South. Originally a crown grant of 500 acres to George McIntosh in 1765 It passed to his son, John Houston McIntosh. In 1836 Gen. Duncan Lamont Clinch, U. S. Army hero of the Seminole War and husband to Eliza Bayard McIntosh, daughter of John Houston McIntosh, settled here. He farmed until 1844, then entered politics. Elected to Congress on the Whig ticket in 1844, he served through 1845. Born in Edgecombe Co., N. C., Apr. 6, 1787. Gen. Clinch died Nov. 27, 1849 in Macon, GA. His plantation remained in the family until 1905.

US 17, 1/2 mile north of Satilla River
GPS reading: N3059.1230, W08143.6982

King George I awarded George McIntosh a 500 acre land grant, which he named Refuge Plantation. The grant was issued in memory of his father, John McIntosh Mohr's service to the Crown against Spain. Refuge Plantation became the home of George and Ann McIntosh until his death in 1780. The plantation was then left to his son, John Houstoun, who was only seven years old at the time of his father's death.

Refuge Plantation was the temporary location for the county courthouse and a militia drilling field. The plantation was christened Refuge because it was often a rest stop for wayfarers traversing the state and many coastal inhabitants sought a safe haven there in times of war and Native American uprisings.

John Houstoun McIntosh was only a boy when Refuge Plantation became his and by the time he settled down to have a family, he was living in north Florida. When his youngest daughter, Eliza, came of age and intended to marry, her father presented her with Refuge Plantation as a wedding gift. The Reverend Raphael Bell conducted the ceremony joining Eliza Bayard McIntosh and Duncan Lamont Clinch in marriage on December 8, 1819, in St. Marys.

Duncan was a soldier, much like his father-in-law. By the time of his marriage to Eliza, Duncan was Colonel of the 8th infantry, eventually attaining the rank of Brigadier General. When the Seminole war began in Florida around 1835, General Clinch was placed in command of that district. He commanded the battle of Withlacoochee with exemplary courage. By September of 1836, General Clinch resigned his commission due to ill health and retired to Refuge Plantation. He was elected to Congress in 1844 and served for approximately a year. General Duncan Lamont Clinch died in 1849 at the age of 62.

For his distinguished service during the Seminole War in the 1830s, a fort built on the south side of the St. Marys inlet at Fernandina was named in his honor. The federal government began construction on Fort Clinch in 1847 and continued throughout the Civil War. Yet, strangely enough when the war began in 1861, the fort was occupied by Confederate forces. The fort was taken by federal troops when a withdrawal was ordered by General Robert E. Lee the following year. The garrison operation was substantially reduced in the years following the Civil War and eventually ceased altogether. In 1898 the fort was again activated for several months during the Spanish American War.

The state of Florida purchased the abandoned fort in 1935 to develop one of the first state parks. The park was opened in 1938. Today, the park offers picnicking, camping, saltwater fishing and swimming as well as a wonderful example of a Civil War era fortification. Throughout the year on the first Saturday of each month, Civil War reenactors and historical interpreters in full regalia host a day as it would have been in the 1860s. Candlelight tours are also done on Saturday evenings for an unforgettable glimpse into life as it was nearly one hundred and fifty years ago.

After the death of General Clinch, Refuge Plantation passed to his daughter, Elizabeth, who had married a well noted soldier named Robert Anderson. By the time the couple married Captain Anderson had endured an illustrious military career. By 1860, Major Anderson assumed command of the Union forces at Fort Moultrie in the Charleston Harbor. Major Robert Anderson was a pro-slavery southerner serving as a Union Officer. Because Major Anderson was Southern by birth, the Union felt he would tread carefully and not provoke the South into war. Southerners assumed Major Anderson would be sympathetic to their demands that the fort be turned over to the Confederacy. Major Anderson wanted more than anything to avoid the war completely and prayed constantly that the seceding states return peaceably to the Union.

As his situation at Fort Moultrie deteriorated, Major Anderson considered evacuation both necessary on military grounds and desirable in terms of avoiding provocation. These sentiments raised some doubt in Lincoln's mind about his loyalty. However, Anderson held firmly to the Union and to his responsibilities as an officer. Major Anderson was greatly disturbed at having to choose between war and peace. On December 26, 1860, he moved his two company garrison from the barely defensible Fort Moultrie to unfinished Fort Sumter in the middle of the Charleston harbor.

Major Anderson withheld fire until he had no other alternative. In April, Fort Sumter came under thirty-six hours of constant bombardment and was forced to return fire. By April 13, he was forced to surrender his post. He marched out, with his seventy men on April 14th, saluting his flag as it was hauled down. The following day Major Robert Anderson sailed for New York with a heavy heart and a sense of failure in not having prevented Civil War. The ordeal at Fort Sumter crushed Robert Anderson, he was never the same man again.

He retired to New York City, briefly emerging from private life to attend the ceremony at Sumter in April 1865 to raise the flag he had watched being lowered in surrender four years before. After the war, he and his wife left for Europe, hoping to improve his health. However, in 1871, Major General Robert Anderson died in Nice, France. He was brought home for burial at West Point. Elizabeth Bayard Clinch Anderson return to her family home at Refuge Plantation to live out her remaining days.[11]

After one hundred and forty years of family ownership, Refuge Plantation was sold in 1905.

Endnotes

[1] Founding fathers of St. Marys

[2] The transaction was filed in Camden County Deed Book A.

[3] fever and chills

[4] The first Methodist Bishop born in the American colonies.

[5] Colonel Charles C. Pickney informed Governor Moultrie of his situation and the diversity in his ranks, in a letter dated 10 Jul 1778

[6] A vacuum evaporation system.

[7] plant residue

[8] Bartram noted foliage, gathered plant samples, recorded animal species, settlements, trails, etc..

[9] The Hopkins family home in McIntosh County, Georgia.

[10] The direct translation from the Creek language to English.

[11] Interesting note: Robert and Elizabeth Anderson were the great grandparents of the 1940's popular movie actor Montgomery Clift.

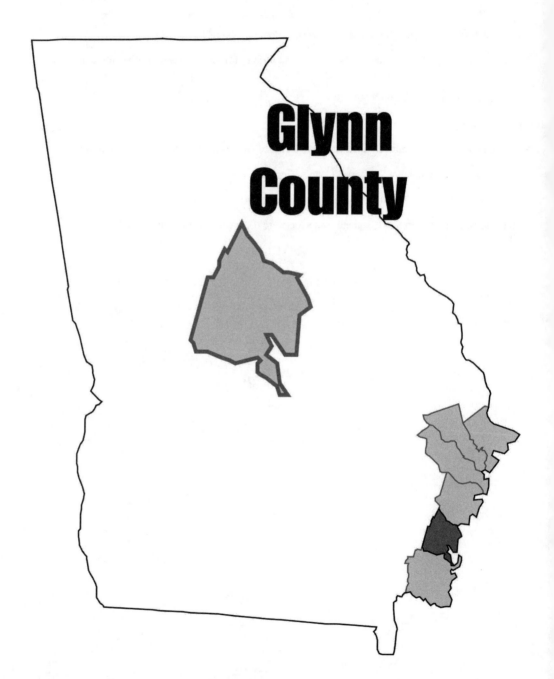

Glynn County

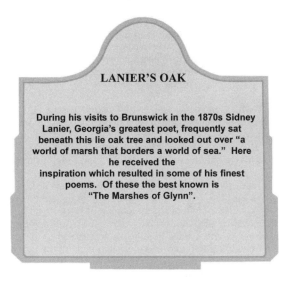

LANIER'S OAK

During his visits to Brunswick in the 1870s Sidney Lanier, Georgia's greatest poet, frequently sat beneath this lie oak tree and looked out over "a world of marsh that borders a world of sea." Here he received the inspiration which resulted in some of his finest poems. Of these the best known is "The Marshes of Glynn".

US 17/GA 25, 0.4 miles south of the road to St. Simons Island
GPS Coordinates: N31.15549, W81.479051

Sidney Lanier was inspired to write the following verses while admiring the marshes that adorn the shores of Glynn County. Standing near this historical marker one has but to turn and gaze upon the wonder of the soft stirring sawgrass in the embrace of a gentle breeze to understand Lanier's inspiration. The marsh is so serene, spending a few moments observing the landscape will bring calm to ones soul.

The Marshes of Glynn
Sidney Lanier, Baltimore 1878

Glooms of the live-oaks, beautiful-braided and woven With intricate shades of the vines that
myriad-cloven
Clamber the forks of the multiform boughs,—
Emerald twilights, — Virginal shy lights,
Wrought of the leaves to allure to the whisper of vows, When lovers pace timidly down through the green colonnades Of the
dim sweet woods, of the dear dark woods,
Of the heavenly woods and glades,
That run to the radiant marginal sand-beach within
The wide sea-marshes of Glynn; –

Beautiful glooms, soft dusks in the noon-day fire, — Wildwood privacies, closets of lone desire, Chamber from chamber parted
with wavering arras of leaves, — Cells for the passionate pleasure of prayer to the soul that grieves, Pure with a sense of the
passing of saints through the wood, Cool for the dutiful weighing of ill with good; –

O braided dusks of the oak and woven shades of the vine, While the riotous noon-day sun of the June-day long did shine Ye
held me fast in your heart and I held you fast in mine; But now when the noon is no more, and riot is rest, And the sun is a-wait
at the ponderous gate of the West, And the slant yellow beam down the wood-aisle doth seem Like a lane into heaven that leads
from a dream, –
Ay, now, when my soul all day hath drunken the soul of the oak, And my heart is at ease from men, and the wearisome sound
of the stroke
Of the scythe of time and the trowel of trade is low, And belief overmasters doubt, and I know that I know, And my spirit is
grown to a lordly great compass within,
That the length and the breadth and the sweep of the marshes of Glynn Will work me no fear like the fear they have wrought
me of yore When length was fatigue, and when breadth was but

bitterness sore, And when terror and shrinking and dreary unnamably pain Drew over me out of the merciless miles of the plain,—

Oh, now, unafraid, I am fain to face
The vast sweet visage of space.
To the edge of the wood I am drawn, I am drawn, Where the gray beach glimmering runs, as a belt of the dawn,
For a mete and a mark
To the forest-dark: —
So:
Affable live-oak, leaning low, — Thus—with your favor—soft, with a reverent hand, (Not lightly touching your person, Lord of the land!) Bending your beauty aside, with a step I stand On the firm-packed sand
Free
By a world of marsh that borders a world of sea.
Sinuous southward and sinuous northward the shimmering band Of the sand-beach fastens the fringe of the marsh to the folds of the land.
Inward and outward to northward and southward the beach-lines linger and curl As a silver-wrought garment that clings to and follows the firm sweet limbs of a girl. Vanishing, swerving, evermore curving again into sight, Softly the sand-beach wavers away to a dim gray looping of light.
And what if behind me to westward the wall of the woods stands high? The world lies east: how ample, the marsh and the sea and the sky! A league and a league of marsh-grass, waist-high, broad in the blade, Green, and all of a height, and unflecked with a light or a shade, Stretch leisurely off, in a pleasant plain, To the terminal blue of the main.

Oh, what is abroad in the marsh and the terminal sea?
Somehow my soul seems suddenly free
From the weighing of fate and the sad discussion of sin, By the length and the breadth and the sweep of the marshes of Glynn.

Ye marshes, how candid and simple and nothing-withholding and free Ye publish yourselves to the sky and offer yourselves to the sea! Tolerant plains, that suffer the sea and the rains and the sun, Ye spread and span like the catholic man who hath mightily won God out of knowledge and good out of infinite pain And sight out of blindness and purity out of a stain.

As the marsh-hen secretly builds on the watery sod, Behold I will build me a nest on the greatness of God: I will fly in the greatness of God as the marsh-hen flies In the freedom that fills all the space 'twixt the marsh and the skies: By so many roots as the marsh-grass sends in the sod I will heartily lay me a-hold on the greatness of God: Oh, like to the greatness of God is the greatness within The range of the marshes, the liberal marshes of Glynn.

And the sea lends large, as the marsh: lo, out of his plenty the sea Pours fast: full soon the time of the flood-tide must be: Look how the grace of the sea doth go About and about through the intricate channels that flow
Here and there,
Everywhere,
Till his waters have flooded the uttermost creeks and the low-lying lanes, And the marsh is meshed with a million veins, That like as with rosy and silvery essences flow
In the rose-and-silver evening glow.

Farewell, my lord Sun!
The creeks overflow: a thousand rivulets run 'Twixt the roots of the sod; the blades of the
marsh-grass stir; Passeth a hurrying sound of wings that westward whirr; Passeth, and all is still; and the currents cease to run;
And the sea and the marsh are one.

How still the plains of the waters be! The tide is in his ecstasy. The tide is at his highest height:
And it is night.
And now from the Vast of the Lord will the waters of sleep Roll in on the souls of men, But who will reveal to our waking ken
The forms that swim and the shapes that creep
Under the waters of sleep?
And I would I could know what swimmeth below with the tide comes in On the length and the breadth of the marvellous marshes of Glynn.

CONFEDERATE BATTERY

In 1861, Confederate battery positions on Jekyll Island were equipped with one 42-pounder gun and four 32-pounder navy guns en barbette, each having about 60 rounds of shot and shell.

Casemates, hot shot furnace and magazines are recorded, also. Of greater strength than batteries on St. Simons Island, the earthworks of palmetto logs, heavy timber, sandbags, and railroad irons were mounted for the protection of Brunswick.

February 10, 1862, Gen. Robert E. Lee requested permission from Gov. Joseph E. Brown to dismantle the stronghold as "the inhabitants of the island and Brunswick have removed themselves and property" to inland points.

Maj. Edward C. Anderson removed the guns, sending them to Savannah. March 9, 1862, Lt. Miller of the USS Mohican landed a rifle company and marines, hoisting the Union flag over the island. In January 1863, to strengthen fortifications at Port Royal, S.C., a Federal force was sent by flatboat to seize the railroad irons. Some of the men who had helped build the defenses guided the detachment to them and "the men enjoyed demolishing them far more than they had relished their construction."

Riverview Drive, south of Horton house near airport, Jekyll Island
GPS Coordinates: N31.07061, W81.426147

Governor Joseph E. Brown ordered the construction of the Confederate Batteries on Jekyll and St. Simons Islands in 1861. The batteries, built of earth, wood and iron, were heavily fortified with enough artillery to protect inland Brunswick from a Union attack by sea. The iron was taken from railway tracks at Brunswick, which were dismantled to prevent their use by the Union Army.

During the blockade of the Southern coastline as many as 1,500 Georgia troops manned the batteries. On April 10, Union General Quincy A. Gillmore attacked Fort Pulaski near Savannah. Confederate General Robert E. Lee demanded that Brunswick and the surrounding area be evacuated and every available soldier was ordered north to Savannah. Brunswick, Jekyll Island and St. Simons Island were left in smoldering ruins, nothing of use was left for the Union Army to plunder. The St. Simons Lighthouse was destroyed, the wharves were burned, and a good portion of the structures in the city, including the luxurious Oglethorpe Hotel, which would have made an excellent hospital or headquarters for the Union Army. Most of Brunswick's citizens fled to Waynesville approximately forty miles inland.

When the Union warship USS *Mohican* arrived with her company of marines off the coast of Georgia, they met with little resistance against taking what they wished, actually receiving the cooperation of the few men left to defend the area. Though taking Brunswick was no prize, the town was completely stripped and nothing of value or use remained. The USS *Mohican*'s marines were ordered to take Brunswick due to its proximity to Fort Clinch on the south side of the St. Marys inlet.

While heavily ensconced near Fort Clinch, the USS *Mohican*'s marines were ordered to put a halt to the blockade runners delivering arms, ammunition, food and supplies to the Confederacy. Most runners were extremely fast ships that carried no weapons, though it might seem strange that the blockaders had no arms, the odds weren't with the runners and most were readily captured. If they were captured with weapons, the crew could be tried for piracy; if convicted, the sentence was death. Most blockade runners, when captured, either bought their way out of convictions or went to prison camps. Though prison camps were awful, certain death was not worth the risk. Once the USS *Mohican* was in place to halt the blockade runners, displaced slaves had to be settled.

Five hundred contraband[1] were settled by the Union Army at Retreat Plantation and Gascoigne Bluff. The area around Christ Church at St. Simons was used to train African American men for service in the Union Army. The Union forces were eventually ordered back to South Carolina to join the fighting and the contraband colony was broken up.

The Brunswick and coastal islands saw very little action during the final days of the Civil War; most of the activity centered around General Sherman's coastal target, Savannah. By 1864, many of the former slaves began to drift back to their former plantations, when the guns of the Civil War fell silent, many of the former owners returned as well. Reconstruction brought a new way of life to the South and her recovery would be a long arduous process.

JEKYLL ISLAND CLUB WHARF

Here anchored the most luxurious pleasure craft in the world during the existence of the Jekyll Island Club 1886-1942.

No other yacht was comparable to John Pierpont Morgan's several Corsairs. Corsair II, too large to dock, anchored in the channel. Morgan was escorted ashore by a flotilla of small craft, after a cannon had sounded off his arrival in these waters. Corsair II was 304 ft. overall, beam 33 ½ ft., draft 17 ft., speed 19 knots, tonnage 1,600. About this Corsair Morgan, when asked how much it cost, made his classic remark: "If you have to consider the cost you have no business with a yacht."

Other palatial yachts owned by Jekyll Island Club members were: Pierre Lorillard's Caimen, James Stillman's Wanda, Astors' Nourmahal, Vanderbilt's Alvah and Valiant, H. Manville's Hi Esmaro, Jr., Pulitzer's Liberty, George F. Baker's Viking, E. T. Stotesbury's Castle, Cranes' Llyria, Theodore N. Vail's, Speedwell and Northwind, Commodore Frederick Bourne's Marjorie, Goulds Hildegards, Saono, and Ketchum. Edwin Gould built a private dock in front of his cottage, "Chichota." Andrew Carnegie, whose family owned Cumberland Island, visited Jekyl on yachts, Skibo and Missoe.

Off Riverview Drive at the wharf, Jekyll Island
GPS Coordinates: N31.05828, W81.423122

Jekyll Island became a playground for the rich and famous in 1886. The South still bore the scars of the Civil War, but the wealthy seemed not to notice. The island's only connection with the mainland was by ferry boat during the early years, although most of the millionaire businessmen simply arrived aboard their impressive yachts and were ferried to the Jekyll Island Club Wharf.

The *Corsair II*, owned by financier John Pierpont (J. P.) Morgan, was so immense that it was impossible to bring her into the wharf. The *Corsair II* was anchored out in the river and her dinghy, a thirty foot boat, brought the Morgan party ashore. It must have been a spectacular sight to see; Pulitzer's *Liberty*, Vail's *Northwind* and Carnegie's *Missoe* with perfectly oiled teak gleaming in the sun.

J. P. Morgan's ship *Corsair II* was by far the most elaborate, rivaled only by the original *Corsair*. The yachts were named in honor of J. P.'s grandfather who was a Corsair.[2] The original *Corsair* eventually became the *Gloucester* in 1898, the *Corsair II* was sold to the Coast and Geodetic Survey fleet of National Oceanic and Atmospheric Administration and was renamed *Oceanographer*.

The days of opulence soon came to an end. By the early 1900s, membership began to dwindle, the Stock Market crash in

1929 sounded the death knell. When the United States joined World War II in 1942, the government asked the membership to suspend use of the island for the duration of the war. The membership never returned and the doors of the Jekyll Island Club were closed permanently.

The Jekyll Island Club was declared a National Historic Landmark in 1978, and in 1985, work began to restore the club to its original glory. A $20 million restoration project was undertaken and today, the club has been completely renovated. The Jekyll Island Club offers all of the opulence and amenities expected of a grand four star hotel. J. P. Morgan would be pleased.

M. E. THOMPSON AND
THE PURCHASE OF JEKYLL ISLAND

Melvin E. Thompson, Acting Governor, 1947-1949, was born in Millen, Jenkins County, Georgia, in 1903. After a career as educator and public servant, Thompson was elected Lieutenant Governor for the term beginning January, 1947. Following the death of Governor- Elect Eugene Talmadge, shortly before his inauguration, Thompson became Acting Governor until the next schedule general election. During his term as Acting Governor, one of his contributions to the state was the acquiring of Jekyll Island for $675,000. The state acquired Jekyll Island by a court condemnation decree, a bargain in which has been compared to the original purchase of Manhattan Island. Jekyll Island has proved to be one of Georgia's greatest assets as a year round resort area.

Near junction of Riverview Drive and Stable Road, Jekyll Island
GPS Coordinates: N31.05502, W81.421775

S o you thought the 2000 presidential election was controversial. Let me tell you about the Georgia governor's election of 1946. Eugene Talmadge won; of that, there was no doubt. Unfortunately, during the Democratic Convention, Eugene developed a stomach aneurysm and things did not look good. The Georgia constitution stated,

> "The Georgia General Assembly, in the event of an elected Governor's death before he assumes the office, will appoint the second place electorate."

The Talmadge camp spread the word to all their supporters to write in the name Herman Talmadge, Eugene's son, just in case. When the results were tabulated, though gravely ill, Eugene Talmadge won the governor's race as expected and Herman, a not so close second, managed 675 write-in votes. Herman visited his dad in the hospital and gave him the results of the election. Eugene responded with:

> "Son, there was a fellow in here the other day. He told me, 'Gene, you know every man, woman, and child in the state of Georgia is praying for you. Even folks who have never prayed before in their lives."
> Eugene grinned and said, "Half of them are praying I'll recover and half of them that I won't."

He didn't.

Mr. Arnall, the sitting Georgia Governor, made a statement that he was entitled to remain Governor until a special election could be held to fill Eugene Talmadge's unassumed term. He further stated that after he was sworn in, he would turn the governorship over to Melvin Thompson, who had been elected Lieutenant Governor. The Talmadge people yelled foul. The Talmadge group quoted the Georgia Constitution allowing for the legislature to select the second place winner as Governor. Of course, Herman was second. The Attorney General decided in favor of Arnall, pending a resolution by the courts.

After a recount, it was found Herman had in fact finished third and couldn't be considered. Mysteriously fifty eight new votes were found in Telfair County, Mr. Talmadge's home district, Herman was in second place again! The Georgia General Assembly overturned the Attorney General's decision. January 15, 1947 at 1:50 a.m., Herman Talmadge assumed the office of Governor. He quickly had the oath of office administered and delivered his inaugural address. Talmadge headed straight for the Governor's office and found his entry barred. Two of his supporters busted down the door and found former Governor Arnall. Talmadge and Arnall passed heated words, Arnall refused to relinquish the office.

Herman realized his supporters were quite angry and to avoid having anyone hurt, thought it best to leave. Herman returned in the early morning hours armed with a .38 caliber Smith and Wesson, took possession of the office and changed the locks. Mr. Arnall, in retaliation, set up his office in the capitol rotunda. The rotunda office only lasted a short time, someone dropped a huge firecracker from the stairs above and an assassination attempt was reported in the local newspapers. Mr. Arnall moved his headquarters to his Atlanta law office.

The Georgia Attorney General administered the oath of office to Lieutenant Governor Melvin E. Thompson on January 18, and during the same ceremony appointed him acting Governor. All three Governors began making appointments to key offices and "acting" as Georgia's Governor. Shortly after the appointment of Thompson, Arnall resigned as promised. Georgia was down to only two sitting Governors, which was still one too many. Herman Talmadge was appointed by the Georgia General Assembly and M. E. Thompson was appointed by the Georgia Attorney General. Both Talmadge and Thompson had legitimate claims to the office. Herman, under questionable circumstances, had received enough votes to be second in the election and M. E. Thompson, the Lieutenant Governor, who by law succeeds the Governor in the event of his death while in office. Will the real Governor of Georgia please stand up?

Georgia's Supreme Court decided on March 19, in a five to two vote, in favor of M. E. Thompson; thus, ending sixty three days of dual governorship. Thompson was only governor for two years, during that time he negotiated the purchase of Jekyll Island for $675,000.

Herman Talmadge was later elected as Governor in a special election. He won reelection against Thompson two years later in the general election for good measure. Neither Mr. Arnall nor Mr. Thompson won an elected office ever again. Herman Talmadge went on to become a United States Senator.

Herman Talmadge outlived both Arnall and Thompson, he passed away March 21, 2002.

FIRST TRANSCONTINENTAL CALL

First Transcontinental Telephone call was submitted by a telephone of this type January 25, 1915. Mr. Theodore N. Vail, President American Telephone and Telegraph Company talked from Jekyll Island, Georgia to Mr. Alexander Graham Bell inventor of the telephone in New York; Thomas A. Watson, assistant to Mr. Bell in San Francisco; and to President Woodrow Wilson in Washington, D.C.

Riverview Drive south of the hotel near Indian Mound, Jekyll Island
GPS Coordinates: N31.05785, W81.422408

Atlantic Telephone and Telegraph (AT&T) Company began building the long distance link across the United States in 1885. The lines started in New York and reached Chicago in 1892. AT&T President Theodore Vail made the development of the transcontinental telephone line a priority in 1908. He realized that the technology was not in place at that time but hoped that it would catch up as his telephone line stretched across the nation. AT&T's ambitious Chief Engineer John J. Carty announced in 1909 that the transcontinental line would be in place and working in time for San Francisco's 1915 exposition to celebrate the opening of the Panama Canal. Unfortunately, there were still problems with the amplification and sound could barely be heard through the muffled static of the lines. In the summer of 1913, AT&T tested high vacuum tubes on the long distance lines and their problems were solved. On June 27, 1914, the transcontinental telephone line was completed; the last pole was erected at Wendover, Utah.

AT&T faced one other problem, they had managed to complete the Atlantic to Pacific telephone line before the Panama Pacific exposition was ready. AT&T waited, and in January 1915, everything was in place.

Not only was this the first transcontinental telephone call, it was the first conference call. The call was placed long distance from New York to San Francisco. Imagine doing your job with not only your boss but the President of the United States listening in as well. That's exactly what happened to Alexander Graham Bell.

Bell was ready to test his invention. The call was routed from New York by way of Jekyll Island, where Theodore Vail was vacationing at the Jekyll Island Club, then through to the White House so that President Woodrow Wilson could listen in, and finally, the call reached its ultimate destination, San Francisco. Thomas Watson, assistant to Alexander Graham Bell, was quite literally waiting for the phone to ring. The call took five operators and twenty three minutes to process.

The conversation was brief and to the point. Bell said, "Mr. Watson, come here. I want you." To that Watson replied, "It will take me five days to get there now."

The demonstration was a success, as was the telephone.

THE BOAT HOUSE SITE

This is the site of the Jekyll Island Club Boat House where the 100 foot steamer The Jekyll Island was stored during the off season. (The Club season was usually from after New Years until before Easter).
There was no Jekyll Creek bridge (dedicated 1954), no Sidney Lanier bridge (opened 1956) in the Jekyll Island Club Era. Many Club members entrained to Brunswick on their plush private railroad cars. There they were met at the wharf by the steamer The Jekyll Island; The Hattie; The Sybil (45 foot Naphtha Launch named for Sybil Brewster); The Kitty (named for Kitty Lawrence, niece of Charles Lanier, a President of The Club). These launches were used as pleasure craft at the convenience of the Club members for fishing, excursions, and to bring supplies and mail from Brunswick.
Other members arrived by yacht at the dock or, if the craft was too large for the shallow water there, anchored in the channel and were brought to shore by smaller craft.
James A. Clark was Captain of Boats and summer manager of the Jekyll Island Club for over forty years.

Riverview Drive south of Stable Road, Jekyll Island
GPS Coordinates: N31.05253, W81.42155

The Georgia Historical Marker for the Boat House Site is off the main road but quite visible. The Boat House site itself can only be seen by going to the edge of the marsh. Most of the Boat House has been washed away by storms and worn away by time. Concrete pylons continue to stand fast and mark the area where the Boat House of The Jekyll Island Club once stood.

During the heyday of the Club, the only transportation available to and from the island was by boat. The Club provided a launch to it members for both transportation and entertainment. The large 100 foot steamer, The *Jekyll Island* or the smaller, *Sybil* provided these services and was captained by James A. Clark for over forty years.

The Boat House site provides a beautiful view of the Intercoastal Waterway.

The Boat House Site

BROWN COTTAGE CHIMNEY

McEvers Bayard Brown, New York Banker This chimney is all that remains of the cottage of Bayard Brown, original member of Jekyll Island Club. In his gay, young days, he built this cottage at Jekyll, overlooking the marshes. He erected a bridge to reach the isolated house, built stables for his horses, and furnished the cottage elegantly for his bride-to-be. But the wedding never came off. The house deteriorated and was torn down. This eccentric millionaire was known as "The Hermit of the Essex Coast" in England. At the age of 37, he became an exile from America, sailing on his yacht Valfreyia. "Unrequited love" is said to be the cause of his renouncing his native land to become a legendary port-bound yachtsman for 36 years. On the Essex Coast, his yacht engines were always in readiness for a sea voyage.

His crew of 18 waited in vain for the order to put to sea. One thing was certain, Mr. Brown had plenty of money — a million dollars a year, according to one account. Sometimes he would toss gold sovereigns from his yacht for anyone to pick up. Anyone who mentioned "America" in his presence was dismissed. He died in 1926 requesting that his body be returned to America on the Valfreyia.

Riverview Drive at the south edge of the airport, Jekyll Island
GPS Coordinates: N31.06889, W81.425997

McEVERS BAYARD BROWN, millionaire and eccentric. Reports were that Brown, a New York Banker, received a million dollars annually, which qualified him as one of the wealthiest men of his time; certainly, his lifestyle supported the supposition. He was a founding member of the Jekyll Island Club and grew to love the area so much that he decided to build a permanent home there.

He began construction of what was laughably called, "Brown's Cottage." Cottage gives one the impression of a quaint little dwelling. This was hardly the case, it overlooked the marshes and when finished, would be a grand estate. Brown built the home as a bridal gift for his fiancé who planned to join him for their wedding on the island. Unfortunately, the fiancé had second thoughts, and Brown, quite plainly put, was left standing at the altar. McEvers Brown was completely heartbroken, he went into a self imposed exile and in 1890 sailed for England, vowing never to return to America.

After arriving on the Essex coast of England, Brown sold his sixty-three ton yacht and purchased a 1,000 ton sloop, originally built for the Prince of Wales. McEvers Bayard Brown pouted for 36 years. He lived aboard the huge vessel, never leaving it, and the yacht never left wharf. The engines were kept in a constant state of readiness and employed a full time crew of eighteen. Although, the crew was never allowed to sleep onboard the yacht, they were to be prepared to depart in a moment's notice. Brown was so disillusioned and bitter that anyone mentioning America in his presence was dismissed on the spot.

Brown Cottage Chimney

Even as World War I blazed away in Europe, Brown stayed aboard the yacht, either anchored just off the coast or up one of the nearby rivers. McEvers Bayard Brown died in 1926, he was 73. His will stipulated that $250,000 was to be divided among various charities, with the bulk of his wealth bequeathed to the Jekyll Island Club. The club had fallen on hardtimes and the funds greatly reduced the club's liability.

McEvers Brown never saw the "cottage" after completion, although he did allow employees of his beloved Jekyll Island Club to live there. It was McEvers Brown's dying request that his body be returned to America aboard his yacht, *Valfreyia*. When Brown's body was returned to New York, a long faded and somewhat charred photograph of a young woman was found among his possessions.

LE SIEUR CHRISTOPHE ANNE POULAIN DU BIGNON
(1739-1825)
HORTON - DU BIGNON HOUSE
DU BIGNON BURIAL GROUND

Beginning with Poulain du Bignon, five du Bignon generations made Jekyll Island one of Georgia's most romantic Golden Isles. This tabby ruin and burial ground alone remain from Jekyll Island's century (1794-1886) as the du Bignon Plantation. Christophe Poulain, native of Lamballe, Brittany, was a much-decorated French naval captain whose loyalty to Louis 16th in the French Revolution forced him to flee his patrimonial lands. In 1792 on his ship, the Sapelo, he brought his family to the hospitable Georgia Coast. With four other French royalists, he purchased first Sapelo Island and then Jekyll. By 1794 he acquired Jekyll as his own plantation and enlarged Major Horton's house as his manor. Sea Island Cotton recouped his fortunes and supported a Georgia dynasty of landed aristocracy like that established by his forebears. In 1814 Poulain was buried near du Bignon Creek with a live oak tree as his monument. His son Henri added honors to the island plantation as he made the Goddess of Liberty reigning queen of coastal racing boats. And when Henri's grandson, John Eugene du Bignon, sold Jekyll to a group of millionaire capitalists, with them forming the Jekyll Island Club, Poulain du Bignon's island began a new chapter in its fabulous history.

Riverview and Major Horton Drives, Jekyll Island
GPS Coordinates: N31.10203, W81.414882

While serving under General Oglethorpe at Fort Frederica, Major William Horton applied for and received permission to establish a plantation on nearby Jekyll Island. As one of Oglethorpe's most dedicated men, Horton distinguished himself at the battles of Gully Hole and Bloody Marsh. Horton was also well know as the founder of Georgia's first commercial ale distillery; he was very popular among the men at Fort Frederica.

After Spain's defeat, they burned everything that would catch fire and Horton's plantation was left in ruins. Major Horton was undaunted, he rebuilt in 1746. Major William Horton died in 1749 and the plantation was left to his son. Horton's son cared little for the property, eventually allowing the property to be sold for nonpayment of taxes.

Christophe Poulain du Bignon, a Frenchman escaping the horror of his homeland's revolution, bought the former Horton plantation in 1800. Du Bignon raised sea island cotton until his death in 1825. Cotton proved to be the economic answer with the help of slave labor. The plantation was a success and eventually, passed to a third generation of du Bignon family, Henri Charles du Bignon. It was to Henri du Bignon that the slave ship *Wanderer* delivered the last slave cargo accepted in the United States.

The Civil War began and with it the decimation of the plantation system. It was no longer feasible to grow cotton without free labor to care for and harvest it. The du Bignon plantation was like most others without cotton, they were no longer able to pay their debts. The du Bignon's were forced to sell the plantation a section at a time. Eventually, the Horton-du Bignon plantation home fell into ruin, though the shell of the house still stands. Descendant John Eugene du Bignon retained one parcel of the plantation for himself.

John Eugene eventually sold the property to a group of wealthy businessmen for the establishment of a playground for the rich known as the Jekyll Island Club. The club operated on the island for fifty-six years. The exclusive club was one hundred members strong and the list was like a *Who's Who* of influential men in the United States.

The manicured landscape was designed by noted architect H. W. S. Cleveland and the clubhouse, completed in 1887, was built by architect Charles Alexander. The clubhouse featured sixty rooms of opulence. Many of these men were so taken with the island that they built "cottages," which were actually palatial mansions, to reside in during their winter sabbaticals at the Jekyll Island Club.

**du Bignon Family
Burial Ground**

**MAJOR WILLIAM HORTON
Born in England
Came to Georgia in 1736
Died at Savannah in 1748**

These are the remains of Horton's tabby house. Major Horton of Oglethorpe's Regiment, the first English resident of Jekyll Island, erected on the north end of Jekyll a two-story dwelling and large barn. He cleared fields her for cultivation of crops which supplied the settlers at Frederica on St. Simons Island, a neighboring island, who would have suffered except for this assistance. Major Horton cut a road across the north end of Jekyll, running east and west from this tabby house to the beach. This road is still known as the Horton Road.

Major Horton was a trusted officer chosen by James Oglethorpe for important missions. Upon Oglethorpe's final return to England in 1743, Major Horton succeeded his as commander of the military forces of the Colony of Georgia.

Poulain du Bignon, owner of Jekyll Island after the Revolutionary War, repaired the Horton tabby house and made it his home. As the du Bignon family grew, wooden wings were added to the house.

**Riverview Drive, Jekyll Island
GPS Coordinates: N31.10203, W81.414882**

Major William Horton was the subsheriff of Hertfordshire, England, when he joined General James Edward Oglethorpe as second in command to settle the Georgia colony. Horton proved to be one of Oglethorpe's greatest assets, his leadership at the battles of Bloody Marsh and Gully Hole against the Spanish ensured a victorious day.

Distinguished service earned Major Horton a tract of land on Jekyll Island. He became the first permanent white settler on

Jekyll Island and built his home there in 1743, a two story wooden framed structure with tabby walls.

Horton planted barley, rye and hops as well as vegetables. It was rumored that his malt was imported from Pennsylvania Quakers. He provided supplies to the soldiers of Fort Frederica from the harvest of his fields. Probably, the most important export from Horton's plantation, at least for the soldiers, was the yield of the brewery. The brewery was built approximately one hundred yards from Major Horton's home. A huge copper kettle was shipped from England for the brewing and news of Horton's ale spread quickly. Soon it was in great demand.

Today, the ruins of Major Horton's home are still standing. It is one of only two surviving examples of an 18th century two story colonial construction. This site is one of the most impressive remnants of tabby structure on the Georgia coast.

When General Oglethorpe returned to England in 1743, Major Horton assumed command of military forces in Georgia and remained at the post until his death. The plantation was left to Horton's son who cared little for the place, which was eventually sold for nonpayment of taxes. The du Bignon family bought the property and remained as its owner for nearly a century. Across the street is the du Bignon burial ground and just a few yards down the road are the ruins of the brewery. The brewery is no longer marked. Although at low tide on du Bignon Creek, the remains of the tabby walls can still be seen.

As for Major Horton road: we laughed ourselves silly on Major Horton's road to no where. The road, when it was built, led to the beach. Houses now impede the way; the only place the road does lead to is an abandoned electrical station and a gated path. One would have expected Major Horton's home to possibly be on Major Horton Road. Well, that is not the case here. The ruins are located at the corner of Riverview Drive and Maurice (not a paved road), if you turn onto Maurice from Riverview Drive, it will take you to Beachview Drive on the other side of the island.

The Horton House

TABBY

Tabby was the building material for walls, floors, and roofs widely used throughout coastal Georgia during the Military and Plantation Eras. It was composed of equal parts of sand, lime, oyster shell and water mixed into a mortar and poured into forms.

The limed used in tabby was made by burning oyster shell taken from Indian Shell Mounds, the trash piles of the Indians.

The word tabby is African in origin, with an Arabic background, and means "a wall made of earth or masonry." This method of building was brought to America by the Spaniards.

When the Coquina (shell rock) quarries near St. Augustine were opened, hewn stone superseded tabby for wall construction there. Coastal Georgia has no coquina, so tabby continued to be used here even as late as the 1890s.

Riverview and Major Horton Drives, Jekyll Island
GPS Coordinates: N31.10203, W81.414882

Evidence of the oldest colonial tabby in Georgia can be seen at Fort Frederica. The fort was first constructed around 1730. Later abandoned, the fort eventually fell to ruin. Many archaeological excavations have been done there and only sparse remnants of the original tabby remains. The Horton du Bignon House at Jekyll Island was built shortly after Frederica, the structure remains today as a two story tabby ruin and with a chimney on the west side. Several other Horton structures are nearby, these structures and parts of the original house were constructed later as the consistency differs from the earlier structure. The later structures have much more evidence of erosion.

After the town of Frederica was deserted, the use of tabby declined sharply. It was not until well known planter, Thomas Spalding, living on Sapelo Island, started construction using tabby that a resurgence of the durable "concrete" occurred. Much of the tabby on Sapelo has been lost over time. The Spalding home was eventually purchased by R. J. Reynolds, who apparently did extensive renovations so that no tabby remains visible on the mansion.

A number of other tabby ruins and structures are still in evidence in Glynn County: Cannon's Point once the home of John Couper; Pink Chapel constructed in 1838; Hampton Plantation, much of its ruins have been made into a community park and the Slave Cabins of Hamilton Plantation, which were given to the Cassina Garden Club in 1931. These structures have been beautifully preserved and the forms remain intact. All of these structures are located on St. Simons Island.

The most current uses of tabby can be dated to the early twentieth century. Tabby during this time was often mixed with cement and only two of these structures remain in Glynn County, the Jekyll Island Dairy Barn Silo and Hollybourne Cottage.

POULAIN DU BIGNON AND
DU BIGNON BURYING GROUND

This burying ground contains the bodies of several members of the du Bignon family, descendants of Le Sieur Christophe Poulain de la Houssaye du Bignon, native of Saint-Malo in Brittany. One of four Frenchmen, former residents of Sapelo Island, who purchased Jekyll Island in 1791. Poulain du Bignon became the sole owner a few years later.

In his youth du Bignon was an officer in the French army in India and served for years fighting against the domination of Great Britain. Later he commanded a vessel of war sailing under the French flag. He died in 1814 and was buried here near du Bignon Creek with a live oak tree as his only monument.

Sea Island cotton was the principal crop planted on the du Bignon plantations on Jekyll Island and a large acreage was devoted to its cultivation.

The du Bignon family owned Jekyll Island until 1886, when they sold it to a group of millionaires who immediately formed the famous Jekyll Island Club.

Riverview and Major Horton Drives, Jekyll Island
GPS Coordinates: N31.10203, W81.414882

Christophe Poulain du Bignon immigrated to America to escape the French Revolution in 1789. He and several other wealthy French royalists settled on Sapelo Island.

Sapelo was one of three barrier islands along the Georgia coast that General Oglethorpe had promised to the *Guale* (*whal'li*) Indians. General Oglethorpe had sworn an oath that these islands would not be taken by the White Man and would be left as hunting grounds for the *Guale*. Eventually, white settlers migrated to the coastal islands regardless of the *Guale* pact. Plantations were built on Sapelo and stood until the Revolutionary War, when the British raided the island, took everything of value and burned the remainder.

Christophe and the other French noblemen had their slaves build a large mansion on Sapelo called "Chocolate." It was their intent to raise and sell African slaves as if they were cattle. However, the Frenchmen quarreled among themselves over issues concerning the operation and the heinous scheme failed miserably. The Sapelo partnership was dissolved in 1793.

The du Bignon family and several others joined together and purchased Jekyll Island. Eventually, Christophe became the sole owner of the island shortly after the American Revolution.

Christophe du Bignon had his slaves plant sea island cotton on as much of the 3,000 acres of Jekyll Island as possible. The older portions of the island were clear cut of its live oak timber. Christophe continued to dwell on the island until his death in 1825, his son Henri Charles du Bignon inherited Jekyll Island.

In 1858, Henri Charles was the recipient of the last major cargo of slaves to land in the United States. The slave ship, *Wanderer* landed on the island in the midst of a storm, under a cover of darkness without even the light of the moon to guide their way. The slaves were herded onto the beach and huddled near fires built to warm the shivering group.

The du Bignons became wealthy from sea island cotton by means of the backs of their slaves until the Civil War ended the plantation era in the South. They found it impractical during Reconstruction to continue a cotton plantation on the island without slave labor, so section by section the land was sold.

One parcel was purchased by John Eugene du Bignon, a descendant of Christophe Poulain du Bignon. John Eugene, with his brother-in-law Newton Finney, had a plan to gain their fortune, Jekyll Island was the key.

It was fashionable in the late 1800s for wealthy northern businessmen to gather in very private, exclusive clubs. They could retire with their families from the hectic burden of their wealth and socialize with their peers. Finney and du Bignon saw Jekyll as a place these men would find hard to resist considering its mild climate and abundant hunting opportunities.

John Eugene secretly continued to acquire land on the island; meanwhile, Finney used his position as a member of the prestigious Union Club in New York to sell his wealthy business associates on the idea of starting a hunting club on Jekyll

Island.

By 1885, du Bignon had acquired the entire island; he and Finney negotiated a purchase price of $125,000. The property had been purchased at a cost of only $13,000, leaving a tidy profit for du Bignon and Finney. In 1886, the Jekyll Island Club was officially incorporated. Jekyll Island brought wealth to the du Bignon family once again.

THE SPANISH ON JEKYLL ISLAND

Within sight and sound of St. Simons Island, Jekyll Island was ideal for entertaining Spanish visitors to the settlement at Frederica.
Major William Horton, resident of the island, received the guests while Oglethorpe on St. Simons, with cannon booming and his few soldiers appearing and reappearing on the south beach, professed a strength he did not have.
In 1736, Spanish Commissioners Don Pedro Lamberto and Don Manuel d'Arcy, sent by Governor Sanchez of St. Augustine to discuss rival claims to the Georgia coast, were feted on Jekyll.
On board the Sloop Hawk in Jekyll Sound, kilted Highlanders from Darien with clanging broadswords, Tomo-Chi-Chi and Hyllispilli with about 30 of their "chiefest" Indians in war paint and regella loudly denounced the Spanish and helped Oglethorpe impress the visitors with strength and good will of the colonists. Agreeing to leave all questions to the courts of Spain and England, the emissaries returned to St. Augustine pleased with their mission. Angered by the decision, Spain recalled and executed Governor Sanchez.
After the Battle of Bloody Marsh, the Spaniards burned the buildings on Jekyll Island.

Beachview Drive at Clam Creek Road, Jekyll Island
GPS Coordinates: N31.10784, W81.412602

While Major William Horton entertained the Spanish with folk tales and ale from his brewery, General James Edward Oglethorpe attempted to intimidate their guests. Governor Sanchez of St. Augustine sent his representatives, Don Pedro Lamberto and Don Manuel d'Arcy, to Frederica to make clear their claim on Florida and Georgia lands. General Oglethorpe tried mightily to convince the Spaniards that his forces were ten times the number he actually commanded.

The ruse worked in part. Oglethorpe had his men light off canon, run in and out from different directions, all the while Major Horton was offering the utmost in hospitality to the concerned duo and acting as though nothing was happening in the forest all around them. Meanwhile, John McIntosh Mohr, his band of Scottish Highlanders and their Creek Indian allies were shouting and portraying their own illusion of bloodthirsty savagery. The Creek would run into the group covered with war paint and scream unknown threats. The Spaniards were clearly shaken.

When the two Spanish representatives departed, all parties agreed to leave the division of property to the English and Spanish courts. Spain wanted blood. When news of the agreement arrived, they ordered Governor Sanchez to return to Spain and answer for his inability to take what they perceived as Spain's territory by force. Sanchez was given no time to explain, he was executed upon arrival.

The Spanish soldiers attacked at what was later called the Battles of Gully Hole and Bloody Marsh, they were met by an unexpected force. When the smoke cleared, after two days of battle, Spain had lost over a third of its men. They no longer had the will to fight and retreated back to St. Augustine. The Spanish never attempted to fight on Georgia soil again.

CAPTAIN WYLLY ROAD

There were two Captain Wylly's in the history of Jekyll. It is believed the road was named for Charles Spalding Wylly (1836-1923). Captain in the Confederate Army, 1st Georgia Regulars, a descendant of Clement Martin, who was granted on April 5, 1768, Jekyll Island by the Crown. His grandfather, Captain William Campbell Wylly, remaining loyal to the British in the Revolution took part in the campaign when the British General Prevost crossed the St. Marys and marched on Savannah. After the Revolution he moved to Nassau and was made Governor of New Providence. In 1807 he returned to Georgia, lived first on Jekyll, then St. Simons. Captain Alexander Campbell Wylly was born in Belfast in 1759, moving to Savannah from there.

This road is one of the few that now bear names given by the Jekyll Island Club members. What is now Beachview Drive consisted of three shell roads: Morgan (for John Pierpont Morgan); Bourne (for Frederick G. Bourne, Director of Singer Sewing Machine Company and President of Jekyll Island Club 1914-1919); Lanier (for Charles Lanier, original member of club, and President of Jekyll Island Club 1897-1913). He was a kinsman of Sidney Lanier poet author of "Marshes of Glynn."

Beachview Drive and Captain Wylly Road, Jekyll Island
GPS Coordinates: N31.21871, W81.384305

The original roads of Jekyll Island were little more than rough pathways carved into undeveloped landscape. The early owners of the island had little desire to construct roads other than those required to travel between their homes and the water's edge, where they were ferried to Brunswick for supplies and socializing.

Jekyll Island was purchased by a group of wealthy investors in 1886 from John Eugene du Bignon, whose family had owned the property since 1800. The island now belonged to a contingent of men whose names are readily recognized, such as Astor, Rockefeller, Morgan and Pulitzer. Their purpose was to establish a resort to which the men and their families could escape the immense burden of their wealth and prestige.

The Jekyll Island Club was completed in 1887 and soon the island visitors began to construct "cottages" that afforded additional privacy. As the cottages were built, roads became necessary to travel about the island. The narrow paths paved with crushed shells were cut into the undeveloped scenery by servants with as little disturbance to the natural surroundings as possible. The owners had no wish to completely disturb the island habitat and even today, two thirds of the island is set aside by the Jekyll Island Authority to remain undeveloped.

The roads were named in honor of Jekyll Island Club members. Captain Wylly Road is one of the original roads, which existed during the early years of the club. The road is believed to have been named for Captain Charles Spalding Wylly.

Charles Spalding Wylly was the fourth child born to Elizabeth Sarah and Alexander Wylly at St. Simons in 1836. His maternal grandfather was the much acclaimed Thomas Spalding of Sapelo Island. Charles Wylly served the Confederacy with distinction during the Civil War and worked diligently to recover his families' wealth during the South's reconstruction. Obviously, he was successful to be included among the membership of the Jekyll Island Club.

Captain Wylly's occupation after the Civil War was listed as philanthropist. It was in this vocation that he worked with the Brunswick Chapter of the Daughters of the American Revolution to erect a monument in honor of General James Edward Oglethorpe. General Oglethorpe had designed the old city of Brunswick in a grid pattern much the same as the design of Savannah. A cross was set at Queens Square in Brunswick to commemorate General Oglethorpe's devotion to the poor and down trodden citizens seeking a new life on Georgia's shores.

The shell roads of Jekyll Island were eventually "improved" and paved with asphalt. Unfortunately, the improvements resulted in the loss of many of the original roads. Gradually the Jekyll Island Authority is reclaiming the old roads and replacing much of asphalt with oyster concrete, closer to the original surfaces. Because these restored roads will only accommodate pedestrians, bicycles, trams and horse carriages, only the historic areas have been refurbished.

GASCOIGNE BLUFF

Throughout the ages Gascoigne Bluff has been the gateway to St. Simons Island. An Indian Village was located here. Capt. James Gascoigne of HM Sloop-of-war, Hawk, which conveyed the Frederica settlers on their voyage across the Atlantic in 1736, established headquarters for Georgia's naval forces and had his plantation here. In the invasion of 1742 the Spaniards anded at this Bluff.
Live oak timbers for the building of USS Constitution, better known as "OLD IRONSIDES," and the other vessels of our first shipment North where the vessels were bluff.
During the Plantation era these lands became the sea island cotton plantation of James Hamilton. A wharf here was the shipping center for the St. Simons plantation.
1874-1902 this Bluff was lined with great mills, where cypress and long leaf yellow pine timbers were sawed into lumber and shipped to all parts of the world.
The causeway built in 1924, connecting St. Simons with the mainland has its terminus here.
In 1949 the Methodist Church acquired the upper part of the Bluff and established EPWORTH- BY-THE SEA as a conference center.

Hamilton Road and Arthur J. Moore Drive, St. Simons Island
GPS Coordinates: N31.16963, W81.407619

Pronounced "*Gas'co-neeze*," Gascoigne Bluff was originally a Creek Indian village. The area was named for Captain James Gascoigne, commander of the *Hawk* which led a flotilla of ships that delivered settlers to Frederica in 1736. The most notable settlers included General James Oglethorpe, John and Charles Wesley.

The first British naval base was established here, during the War of Jenkins' Ear. The naval base at Gascoigne provided a deep water harbor to port large warships for sea battles against Spain. The war began in 1739. The war's name was attributed to Captain Robert Jenkins who claimed that a Spanish guard cut off his ear in 1731. He displayed the severed appendage for the House of Commons and spoke so vehemently against Spain that the British Prime Minister was forced to declare war. The Spaniards accused British sailors of smuggling and they were tortured until they admitted guilt, the torture included severed appendages such as Robert Jenkins' ear. The points that Jenkins brought to the House of Commons were that Spain had broken the Treaty of Utrecht, which ended Queen Anne's War in 1713. The treaty allowed Britain to work the slave trade along with Spain. Second was the controversy surrounding the borders between Spanish Florida and Georgia. When war was declared General Oglethorpe responded by attacking the Spanish at St. Augustine, he captured two forts on the San Juan River but failed to take Castillo San Marco. Spain retaliated by attacking Fort St. Simons and Fort Frederica. The Spanish were beaten soundly during battles at Gully Hole and Bloody Marsh. These battles ended the Spanish threat to Georgia.

Gascoigne Bluff continued to prosper and during the plantation era, sea island cotton production soared and was shipped to ports all over the world. During the Civil War all exports of cotton came to a halt and the area was once again used as a naval facility.

The war years were hard and the cotton industry was all but dead, a new endeavor was needed to replace it. The answer came in the form of the vast expanse of live oaks, which grew in abundance all over St. Simons Island. The oaks brought renewed hope to the area and with it the emergence of the sawmill industry. Emancipation unwillingly supplied cheap labor, freed slaves needed jobs to provide for their families.

The oaks were cut and milled at Gascoigne Bluff. The lumber was used in the construction of a number of warships including the USS *Constitution*. She was called "*Old Ironsides*" because canon fire tended to bounce off her sides rather than penetrate the St. Simons oak planking. The Brooklyn Bridge was also built of St. Simons' lumber, milled at Gascoigne Bluff.

Telephone service connected the bluff with the rest of the world in 1878. St. James Union Church, now Lovely Lane Chapel, was constructed in 1880 to serve the spiritual needs of the mill community. Although the mail had been delivered daily from Brunswick via a small rowboat, in 1912 the first post office on the island was opened.

**CASSINA GARDEN CLUB
HOUSES**

These houses were slave cabins on the Gascoigne
Bluff section of Hamilton Plantation which was
developed in 1793 by James Hamilton into one of the
largest estates on St. Simons Island.
Eventually the Gascoigne Bluff area was given to
Glynn County for a park honoring the first naval site in
America. These cabins were given to the Cassina
Garden Club in 1931 for preservation purposes.

**Arthur J. Moore Drive, St. Simons Island
GPS Coordinates: N31.17066, W81.407088**

James Hamilton established Hamilton Plantation in 1793. Hamilton, a Charleston merchant who eventually settled at St. Simons, planted cotton as the plantation's primary crop. It was shipped from the Hamilton dock at Gascoigne Bluff to ports around the world. The plantation was eventually divided into smaller tracts and given to freemen of color after emancipation.

Two tabby cabins remain on what was once described as "by far the finest place on the island." The cabins were donated to the Cassina Garden Club in 1931and placed on the National Registry of Historic Places in 1988, preserving them for future generations. They are the best examples of tabby on any of Georgia's developed islands. Today, the cabins are well preserved and beautifully landscaped, thanks to the efforts of the Cassina Garden Club.

Not far from the slave cabins is the largest southern red cedar in Georgia, as judged by the Georgia Forestry Commission. In 1989, the tree measured 15'6" in circumference, its height reached 59'6", the width of its branches measured an impressive 74'.

Cassina Garden Club Houses

**The largest southern red oak
in Georgia**

A MISSION BY THE SEA

In 1949, the South Georgia Conference of the Methodist Church
purchased 43.53 acres of the Hamilton Plantation from the Sea Island Company for a Christian conference center. They named "Epworth" after the Wesleys' English village home. "By The Sea" suggests the pines and palms running in rows with the Atlantic ocean only a short distance away. Opening day, July 25, 1950, brought 800 Methodists to the banks of the Frederica River, where Bishop Arthur J. Moore preached under the moss draped live oaks (Quercus Virginiana) in the tradition of John and Charles Wesley. In 1962, Epworth By The Sea was designated an official Methodist shrine. Across the river lie the marshes of Glynn made famous by Georgia poet Sidney Lanier.

**At Epworth By The Sea, St. Simons Island
GPS Coordinates: N31.17225, W81.406315**

YOUNG AND OLD TARRY AMID THESE
SACRED SURROUNDINGS AND GO FORTH
TO FACE THE MORNING.

*E*pworth By The Sea recently celebrated thirty years as a Christian retreat. On July 25, 1950, Bishop Arthur J. Moore led the opening ceremony, dedicating the facility to John and Charles Wesley and their life long devotion to Methodism. The crowd gathered after the heartfelt services to have a barbeque dinner on the ground, a long held tradition of southern Christian congregations.

The retreat was named for the Wesley's childhood home of Epworth, England. The town is located in Lincolnshire about one hundred miles to the north of London. Samuel Wesley, the family patriarch, was the Rector of the Church of England parish at Epworth.

Epworth by the Sea is today a Methodist Conference Center situated on the banks of the beautiful Frederica River. The retreat covers eighty-three acres of manicured lawns and well tended gardens. A fountain at the heart of the gardens provides a quiet place to reflect on the day.

Lovely Lane Chapel, originally built in 1880, is a grand sanctuary with amazing stained glass windows accenting the edifice. The chapel has been chosen as the perfect location for an untold number of weddings, christenings and various religious services over the years.

The center provides accommodations consisting of motels, family apartments and youth dormitories that can house up to 1000 people. The Conference Center features auditoriums and meeting rooms, which have hosted a wide variety of events. Youth assemblies, the Fellowship of Christian Athletes Camp and Christian concerts are scheduled yearly as well as nonsecular activities including the Amelia Island Quilters retreat and the Annual Georgia Writer's Conference. *Epworth by the Sea* also provides a preschool and nursery.

The center offers various amenities including a swimming pool, lighted tennis courts, a gymnasium with half basketball court and open fields for baseball, football and soccer. Whether there for a conference, retreat or a renewal of spirit, Epworth has much to offer. Epworth is a place for Christians to meet, enjoy outdoor activities and explore their spiritual needs.

EPWORTH BY THE SEA

John and Charles Wesley were born in a parsonage with thatched roof and solidly built walls in Epworth, England. This home was destroyed by fire when John was six years old. All the family were able to escape except John. From an attic window the little boy's face shone in the reflection of the flame. A human ladder was formed and the life of him who later "put his hands under the civilization of England and lifted it up toward God" was saved.

Epworth By The Sea has been built with the hope that through Christian atmosphere, friendly fellowship and spiritual dedication there may be a place where many shall purpose to make Jesus Christ supreme.

Epworth By The Sea, St. Simons Island
GPS Coordinates: N31.10203, W81.414882

John and Charles Wesley were born to a huge family of nineteen children, only ten of the children survived to adulthood. Their parents, Susannah and Samuel Wesley were considered eccentric. Samuel Wesley was the Epworth parish Rector, and Susannah managed their home with an iron fist.

Samuel believed himself to be a poet. The only collection of his poetry ever published bares an illustration of Samuel with a maggot clinging to his forehead. The volume was entitled simply, *Maggots*. The verse it contained was a morose collection of drivel. The prose, for example, "The Grunting of a Hog" and "The Tame Snake in a Box of Bran" was not well accepted. He did not attempt to publish poetry again.

Although the Wesleys had nineteen children, their efforts were dangerously close to an end with the fourteenth child. Had that have been the case, John Wesley and Methodism would never have been born. The reason for the discord lay in the differing political views in the Wesley household. Susannah supported James II as the rightful heir to the thrown of England, while her husband felt William, Prince of Orange, was the rightful heir. Susannah and Samuel argued the subject vehemently. Finally Samuel retorted, "If we are going to have two kings in this home then we shall have two beds!"

Samuel and Susannah did not share a bed for well over a year. Meanwhile, Susannah complained to the bishop of Lincolnshire and the archbishop of York that she was 'maritally' deprived. Neither bishop would interfere. Finally, husband and wife reconciled and very first the night of their reunion, John, their fifteenth child was conceived. Charles arrived four years later.

Epworth By The Sea, St. Simons Island
GPS Coordinates: N31.17225, W81.406315

HER CHILDREN RISE UP AND CALL HER BLESSED

Susannah Annesley, youngest of twenty-five children and product of a second marriage, was just thirteen when she announced to her Puritan minister father that she intended to become an Anglican, giving no explanation for her conversion. She stated that she had her reasons and had detailed them in her diary. The diary was later lost when the family home was destroyed by fire. Susannah spoke to no one of her decision, she claimed it was between herself and God. Her decision placed her life in grave peril, this was a time when ones' religious leanings could result in death. When she married, her father was unable to officiate because he was a not an Anglican minister and could not conduct services in a state church by law. Minister Annesley was deeply hurt.

The marriage between Samuel and Susannah was strained for many of their forty-four years. They were plagued with illness, disease and the childhood deaths of nine of their children. Twice fire destroyed their home and at one time Samuel was sentenced to prison for unpaid debts. Susannah accepted the difficulties with little complaint and placed the well being of her family in the hands of God.

The strength and openness of Susannah Wesley was extremely unusual during a time when women were not allowed any freedoms. Susannah was not only out spoken, but political and stubborn. Her children were raised strictly, taught to cry softly, eat what was prepared for them and never to raise their voices. Susannah believed in the use of the rod but the confession of transgressions could avoid it. Susannah taught all of her children, including the girls, to read at the age of five and she made it her priority of spend at least one hour alone with each child every week.

Susannah Wesley is noted as one of the great mothers in history. An example of her guidance came one day when one of her daughters wished to do something that was not altogether bad, but not exactly proper. When she was told not to do it, the girl remained unconvinced. In the kitchen of their family home, late into the evening, as mother and child sat beside a dead fire, Susannah said to her daughter,

> "Pick up that bit of coal."
> "I don't want to," said the girl.
> "Go on," said her mother. "The fire is out, it won't burn you."
> "I know that," said the girl. "I know it won't burn me but it will blacken my hands."
> "Exactly," said Susannah Wesley. "That thing which you wish to do won't burn, but it will blacken. Leave it alone."

John, the Wesleys' fifteenth child, was almost lost in a fire that consumed the Wesley home in 1709. After the event Susannah paid special attention to the child, who she believed had been saved for a special purpose. John was known to have commented in his youth that he would never marry "because I could never find such a woman as my father had."

Susannah, after the death of Samuel, spent her remaining years living with her children and the last year of her life under John's care. Samuel Wesley once said of his wife, "Some of the truly great people are the ones who were faithful in doing simple things."

EPWORTH PIONEERS

In 1945, South Georgia Methodists resolved to establish a religious center. After searching four years for a site, the Sea Island Company offered to sell them 43.53 acres of Hamilton Plantation. Because the Conference did not have the $40,000, Bishop Arthur J. Moore asked nine laymen to join him in signing a bank note for a tenth of the purchase price. Not one refused. Since D. Abbott Turner never signed a note, he gave $4,000 in cash. Later known as the Epworth Pioneers, they were A. J. Strickland, Jr., Alfred W. Jones, Sr., Walter Blasingame, J. Slater Wright, Ben J. Tarbutton, Sr., Leo B. Huckabee, Jerome Crawley, George T. Morris and D. Abbott Turner. On July 25, 1950, in the Wesley tradition, almost 800 Methodists met under moss draped live oaks for the formal opening. Churches and individuals responded, paid the debt and began a tradition of love, prayers and financial support which makes God's ministry at Epworth possible.

Epworth By The Sea, St. Simons Island
GPS Coordinates: N31.17225, W81.406315

Methodists of southeastern Georgia, in 1945, felt the need to provide a facility where Christians could congregate for seminars, spiritual revival and wholesome recreation. Unfortunately, the need was there but the funds were in short supply. Finding suitable property at an affordable price also appeared to be impossible. The answer to the Methodists' prayers was delivered by Bill Jones and the Sea Island Company.

Bill Jones and his cousin, business tycoon Howard Coffin, were owners of the Sea Island Company, which developed numerous properties along the Georgia coast in the 1920s and 30s. Howard Coffin was a visionary and taught his younger cousin Bill very well. The Cloister on Sea Island was perhaps their most noted joint venture. Coffin would develop an idea, sketch the plans, arrange for financing and turn the project over to Bill, who would make it happen. The Cloister opened on October 12, 1928, the hotel received a very modest reception. Over the next year Howard Coffin suffered one blow after another. The death of his beloved wife Matilda started the descent, the stock market crash of 1929 was followed by the Great Depression. Coffin was forced to sell his holdings on Sapelo Island to tobacco magnet, R. J. Reynolds Jr. in order to hold onto Sea Island. Depressed and suffering from poor health, Coffin killed himself with a single rifle shot in 1937.

Bill Jones was left to struggle for the survival of Sea Island alone. After much sacrifice and hard work turned a profit for the first time in 1941, The Cloister became one of the few five star resorts in America. Bill Jones' creation of Sea Island and The Cloister was soundly eclipsed by his dedication to the natural and historic preservation of coastal Georgia. His acts of philanthropy are evidenced in more than seven churches to which he donated property on St. Simons Island.

In 1945, Bill Jones offered a portion of what was formerly Retreat Plantation to the south Georgia Methodists at a price well below market value. Unfortunately, even at the discounted price, they could not afford to purchase the property. Bishop Arthur J. Moore turned to his parishioners. Even though times were hard and many were struggling to survive, nine men took on the debt. Each signed a bank note, indebting themselves for $4,000. Although, today, four thousand dollars seems to be a minuscule sum, when compared to 1945 dollars it would be equivalent today to ten times that amount. Only one man out of the ten was able to offer the $4,000 in cash, he is listed as Alfred W. Jones, Sr., we know him as Bill. The notes were quickly repaid and over the years the parishioners have contributed tens of thousands of dollars for buildings, restorations and expansions.

Today, the manicured lawns of Epworth are as inviting as the facility itself. The peaceful surroundings are accented by monuments to benefactors who have made not only financial contributions to *Epworth By The Sea* but personal commitments as well. Lovely flower gardens and fountains bring a sense of invitation and welcome. *Epworth By The Sea* is a state of the art facility, one has but to wander around the grounds to appreciate the sacrifices made to build this magnificent place of spiritual renewal. Bill Jones' influence continues as his son and grandson preserve his legacy of conservation and wise development along the Georgia coast.

A MAN NAMED WESLEY PASSED THIS WAY

On October 21, 1735, John and Charles Wesley and General James Oglethorpe (founder of the colony of Georgia) and eighty-four other passengers sailed from England on the ship "The Simmonds". After a hundred and fourteen days they sailed into the Savannah River (February 14, 1736). In March of 1736, Charles Wesley accompanied General Oglethorpe to Fort Frederica; soon after John Wesley joined his brother Charles, Benjamin Ingham and Charles DeLamotte, two other members of the "Holy Club", also lived and labored on this island. No other place in America has been the scene of the labors of so many who by heroic endeavor created the Methodist Church which today numbers many millions.

At Epworth By The Sea, St. Simons Island
GPS Coordinates: N31.17225, W81.406315

HERE WE HAVE BUILT A MEMORIAL

The Wesley Brothers were extremely intelligent boys. Charles, while still a youth, competed in a "Challenge" or known today as debating. The subject was Greek grammar. The challenge began early each morning and continued until late into the night, three or four nights a week and continued for eight weeks. Charles won the competition. The prize was to be named as King's Scholar and admittance into either Oxford or Cambridge. Charles chose to follow his brother John to Oxford.

While at Oxford the Wesley brothers began a religious support group called, The Holy Club. Several Oxford classmates joined the endeavor and each Sunday evening the club met. The young college men read the Greek New Testament and classical literature, they agreed to fast each Wednesday and Friday. The membership acted as a conscience, gauging the conduct of each young man individually. The group penned a list of questions for each person to address during his daily devotionals. The questions concerned all aspects of life from the very simple, "Do I get to bed on time and get up on time?" to the profound, "Is Christ real to me?"

The club had quite an impact on Charles, who was a fun loving soul. His peer's influence changed his focus to more ecclesiastical thoughts and acts. It was during this time that his gift for music began full force. Charles was quite a prolific lyricist and with the guidance of the Holy Club his tunes began to bring a religious message. He wrote more than 6,500 spiritual hymns during his lifetime, familiar songs of devotion include: Christ From Whom All Blessings Flow, How Sweet Thou Art and Hark! The Herald Angels Sing. These vocal praises and many more of his verses are intoned in churches all over the world after more than 250 years.

Various members of the Holy Club joined the Wesley brothers as they traveled to the Georgia colony, arriving in 1736. Their purpose was to convey Christianity to the colony at the request of General James Oglethorpe.

The Wesley's believed in a system of Christian perfection, which led them far from the popular Calvinist beliefs of the time. Georgia colonists finally ostracized the pious Wesley brothers and their followers. When no church welcomed their preaching, they conducted services for any small gathering "under the trees." Charles finally threw up his hands in frustration and returned to England. Less than one year later, the ever faithful John followed his brother home.

LOVELY LANE CHAPEL

Built by Norman W. Dodge in 1880 and named St. James
Union Church, the chapel is now the oldest church building
on St. Simons Island. Repair following a
hurricane in 1897, deconsecrated in 1911 and used as a
recreation center, the chapel was reconsecrated after the
Methodists purchased the property in 1949. Restored under
the leadership of Bishop Arthur J. Moore, the chapel is now
a favorite place for worship, weddings,
baptisms and prayer. The magnificent stained glass
windows are irreplaceable pieces of Old English Art Glass.
The Methodists renamed the church Lovely Lane Chapel
after the site of the 1784 founding conference of American
Methodism in Baltimore, Maryland.

Epworth By The Sea, St. Simons Island
GPS Coordinates: N31.17225, W81.406315

Norman White Dodge was one of four sons born to New York industrialist, William Earl Dodge. Norman joined the family business and soon assumed a dominant position in the Georgia Land and Lumber Company branch. The central enterprise was known as St. Simons Mills at Gascoigne Bluff.

Eventually, the area became a settlement and claimed a post office, company store and offices, telephone and telegraph services and a water system fed by artesian wells. The public wharf was called "Steamboat Landing," and was located at the old Hamilton Plantation dock. Today, Steamboat Landing is still in use as a marina. St. Simons Mill, by 1880, employed over three hundred workers.

The mill's success prompted the building of a church to meet the needs of the growing community. In 1880, Norman Dodge built St. James Union Church. For thirty-one years the sanctuary served the Gascoigne Bluff community. By the early 1900s, the bottom fell out of the lumbering business. Most of the hard wood timber had been clear cut and nothing remained of the dense forests. The workers of St. Simons Mill began to seek employment in other places and soon the mill was forced to close.

St. James Union Church was converted to a recreation center in 1911 and the irreplaceable Old English Art Glass windows were removed to Christ Church for safe keeping. The windows remained in storage until 1947.

The property on which St. James Union Church was situated was sold in the 1920s to the Sea Island Company and in 1947, was again sold for the construction of a Methodist conference center. The center was called *Epworth By the Sea* and St. James Union Church was renamed Lovely Lane Chapel.

Lovely Lane Chapel was named for a Baltimore edifice built in 1774. It was there that a new religious denomination was created, the Methodist Episcopal Church. John Wesley had reluctantly agreed to the American Methodists' desire to organize their own church. Wesley sent Thomas Coke from England to supervise the development of the Methodist Episcopal parish and to consecrate Francis Asbury as the General Superintendent, the consecration was held at Lovely Lane Meeting House in Baltimore. Today, nothing remains of the original Lovely Lane Meeting House. A bronze plaque was placed at the International Culinary College, which occupies the original location of Lovely Lane.

When Lovely Lane Chapel was reconsecrated in 1947as a part of *Epworth By the Sea*, the breathtaking stained glass windows were returned to their rightful home. Today, the chapel provides a beautiful backdrop for weddings and baptismals as well as a place of spiritual renewal.

The Lovely Lane Chapel

MILITARY ROAD

This Military Road, built in 1738, connected Fort Frederica and Fort St. Simons.
Near this point the road passed the tabby cottage where General Oglethorpe established the only home he had in America. This cottage, shaded by great live oak trees, was surrounded by a garden and an orchard of oranges, figs and grapes.
During the Spanish invasion of Georgia in 1742 a battle was fought here. On the morning of July 7th approximately two hundred Spanish soldiers reached this place, where they were met by Oglethorpe with four platoons of his regiment and the Highland Independent Company from Darien. In this engagement the Spaniards were routed, "upwards of 100" being killed and sixteen taken prisoner. Oglethorpe took two prisoners with his own hands.
The Spaniards, pursued by the British, retreated to their camp at the south end of St. Simons. In the afternoon of the same day, at a place five miles south and on this same road, another battle, known as the Battle of Bloody Marsh, was fought. This, too, was a British victory, ending the threat of Spanish domination of Georgia.

Frederica Road, 0.4 mile south of Christ Episcopal Church, St. Simons Island
GPS Coordinates: N31.21723, W81.379863

General Oglethorpe had only recently returned from England when his country declared war against Spain, beginning the War of Jenkins' Ear. Oglethorpe with a force of one thousand men set out to attack Fort Mosa, near St. Augustine, in May of 1740. He divided the men into battalions but failed to establish a chain of command, fighting erupted among the British regulars, Creek Indians and Scottish Highlanders. Orders were ignored, inadequate guards were posted and when three hundred Spanish soldiers attacked at dawn on June 15, Oglethorpe's men were unprepared. Virtually, the entire command was killed, wounded or captured. The Highlander Company alone buried thirty men that day in Florida. John McIntosh Mohr, the

Highlander Captain, was captured and sent in chains to Spain.

Oglethorpe, in retaliation, laid siege to St. Augustine but failed to take the impregnable Castillo de San Marco. Spanish reinforcements managed to slip through the British naval blockade and Oglethorpe was outnumbered. The Royal Navy removed any chance of triumph when the commander of the fleet instructed Oglethorpe that he would leave by July, due to the impending storm season. Reluctantly, Oglethorpe ordered a withdrawal in early July and admitted defeat. He retreated with his men to Frederica and prepared for the Spanish assault that he knew was imminent.

During the conflict at St. Augustine, Oglethorpe suffered from a incapacitating fever, the sickness lingered for several months after his return north. He agonized over the defeat at St. Augustine more so than the fever itself. After his recovery, Fort Frederica was strengthened and increased companies were stationed at Delegal's Fort and Fort St. Simons. The forts were connected to Fort Frederica by a crude path called Military Road. Huts were built to house the soldiers and their families, but disease and desertion eventually weakened the regiment until it was little more than half strength.

Lieutenant William Horton was dispatched to England to request more funds to increase the regiment. The government agreed to fund an additional grenadier[3] company and Horton was named its captain. General Oglethorpe also commissioned Mark Carr as a Captain of a marine company of boatmen.

While Oglethorpe was attempting to shore up his little army after the defeat at the gates of St. Augustine, events outside of Georgia had shifted the momentum of the war to Spain. King Philip was encouraged by British defeats and ordered Governor Montiano of Florida to take Fort Frederica. On June 20, 1742, the Spanish fleet sailed from St. Augustine with fifty-two men onboard warships, schooners, sloops, galleys, half galleys, piraguas[4] and other small boats. The fleet became scattered en route and one of the Spanish galleys almost captured Oglethorpe as he led a watch battalion to Cumberland Island.

The Spanish fleet gathered at St. Simons Sound on July 4th. The flotilla of thirty-six ships struck fear in the hearts of every man, woman and child. Oglethorpe immediately assembled his men and bribed the Creek Indians to join the battle, only a few chose to fight. General Oglethorpe's force numbered five hundred men. The Spanish attacked the British ships on the incoming tide the next morning. The cannons of Fort St. Simons thundered propelling their round iron missiles into the attacking force. The fighting progressed to hand to hand when the Spanish attempted to board British ships. Several other Spanish ships slipped to the northwest of Fort St. Simons and began landing troops.

Oglethorpe ordered that Fort St. Simons be evacuated as the Spanish landed. The cannons were destroyed and the ships too damaged to set sail were put to flame. It was a mass exodus as the soldiers retreated with their families up the Military Road to safety at Frederica.

BATTLE OF GULLY HOLE CREEK

During the late morning of July 7, 1742, Georgia Rangers guarding the military road approach to the town of Frederica sighted a force of over 100 Spanish soldiers and their Indian allies. James Edward Oglethorpe, founder of Georgia, quickly organized a force composed of the Highland Independent Company, Rangers and Indian friends and courageously led the assault on the Spanish at a place near this marker. The fighting was fierce and lasted almost an hour as Frederica's defenders routed the invaders. Spanish losses numbered more than one-third of their force. One Spanish captain was killed and another was captured in the intense fighting. Oglethorpe's losses were light. Although the battle was brief, it turned out to be the heaviest fighting on the St. Simons Island campaign. Oglethorpe's victory settled the question over ownership of this disputed territory between Spain and Great Britain. It also signaled the end of Frederica's existence since its regiment was disbanded in 1749.

Frederica Road, 0.2 mile south of Christ Episcopal Church, St. Simons Island
GPS Coordinates: N31.21871, W81.384305

The Spanish quickly took unoccupied Fort St. Simons on July 7, 1742. Spanish Florida Governor Don Manuel de Montiano sent out two reconnaissance patrols that eventually found nothing more than each other and joined together to explore the Military Road. Near Frederica, at Gully Hole Creek, the patrols were spotted by Oglethorpe's rangers. One of the rangers was killed by the Spanish and the others raced back to warn Oglethorpe. Oglethorpe mounted his horse, commanded the Highlander company to follow and charged out of the gates of Fort Frederica.

Oglethorpe boldly wielding his sword with a few Scottish Highlanders and Creek Indians, road directly toward the Spanish patrol and captured two soldiers. The remainder of the troops were chased about three miles down Military Road. Oglethorpe reigned in his horse and waited for reinforcements. During this brief encounter, the Spanish counted losses of thirty-six men.

Oglethorpe positioned a detachment across Military Road to delay the advancing Spanish soldiers, in order to assemble his forces for the imminent battle at Fort Frederica. Captain Demere's British regulars, numbering sixty men and forty-five Scottish Highlanders with rangers and Creek Indians assumed either side of Military Road at the point where it met the marsh. The British threw up piles of brush and logs and waited.

Spanish Captain Antonio Barba was ordered to lead three companies of grenadiers, two hundred men, and remove the British. When the grenadiers reached the marsh, the camouflaged British troops opened fire. Several Spaniards were killed in the first volley, Barba coolly formed his men into a battleline at the edge of the marsh and began unloading heavy fire into the tree line. The smoke and noise caused confusion within Captain Demere's ranks and most of his regulars broke and ran, abandoning the Highlander company to their fate. Oglethorpe rushed toward the battle, meeting Demere and the fleeing regulars, he immediately ordered them to return to the marsh, ignoring their cries that all was lost.

When Oglethorpe reached the battle site, the fighting was over. Lieutenant Sutherland's platoon and Lieutenant John Mackay's Highlanders had held fast and won the day. The Spanish had fought bravely but retreated when they ran out of ammunition. Spanish losses numbered a dozen men, Oglethorpe had no casualties. Governor Montiano was stunned by the second defeat that day, along the same narrow pathway called Military Road. The morale of the Spanish soldiers collapsed.

Understandably, Montiano was hesitant to attack Fort Frederica again by way of the Military Road and decided that a river attack best suited his needs. He sent two half galleys, which were immediately driven back by cannon fire from the fort. Oglethorpe attacked Fort St. Simons with five hundred men on July 12. The attack was betrayed when one of his own men fired a warning shot and deserted to the Spanish camp. A livid Oglethorpe returned to Fort Frederica with his men.

Oglethorpe initiated a clever deception by sending a message to the deserter implying that he was a spy and reinforcements were on the way. The letter was turned over to Montiano, as Oglethorpe had anticipated and although the trick did not entirely fool the Spanish Governor, it made him overly cautious. When ships appeared on the horizon, Montiano assumed they were the fresh soldiers arriving to aid Oglethorpe and the fleet might trap them on the island. Montiano ordered an immediate retreat. As the Spanish withdrew, they destroyed everything in their path. Fort St. Simons was leveled, Major Horton's plantation on Jekyll Island was burned and Fort Prince William was bombarded on Cumberland Island.

This was Spain's final attempt to gain control of lands to the north of Florida. The War of Jenkins' Ear would eventually be settled on the battlefields of Europe and within two decades Spain would lose her tenuous hold on Florida itself. Over time the skirmishes that day on the Georgia coast became known as the Battle of Gully Hole and the Battle of Bloody Marsh, recalled long into history that on that day the marsh ran red with Spanish blood.

THE WESLEY OAK

Not far from this spot stood the "great tree" under which Charles Wesley had prayers and preached. March 14, 1736, the first Sunday after his arrival. There were about twenty people present, among whom was Mr. Oglethorpe. A year later, George Whitfield, appointed by the Bishop of London to serve as Deacon at Savannah and Frederica, wrote in his Journal (August 8, 1737): "In the evening we had publick Prayers, and expounding of the second Lesson under a large tree, and many more present than could be expected."
A wooden Cross made from a tree long designated as the Wesley Oak hangs on the wall of Christ Church near the pulpit.

Frederica Road at Christ Episcopal Church, St. Simons Island
GPS Coordinates: N31.21966, W81.386971

Visitors to coastal Georgia are always captivated by the majestic, natural canopy provided by the ancient live oaks prevalent in the area. The oaks' name is attributed to the deep green leaves that retain their color throughout the year. Known for their enormous size and thick intertwined branches they often create a natural shelter. While many trees in the area are older, legend says that the life span of the live oak is three hundred years. The timeline details one hundred years of growth, one hundred years of mature existence and one hundred years of decline. It was a live oak which sheltered Charles Wesley in 1736 during his first sermon underneath the "great tree."

Charles Wesley arrived in Georgia, three years after General James Oglethorpe founded the colony and for a time served as his secretary. It was clear that the primary mission for Charles was ministering to the citizens and soldiers of Frederica. Unfortunately, Charles' exuberance and youthful enthusiasm was not well received by the parishioners. He sent pleading messages to his brother John in Savannah to direct him in the leadership of his flock.

Even with John's intervention, Charles was unable to lead the congregation at Frederica. Suffering from ill health and a dejected spirit, Charles left Frederica for England. He had spent one year in Georgia.

Charles' devotion and dedication were applauded in England. Friends told how Charles would be so absorbed with his work, he would run into trees, walls and trip over fences. He rode horseback from one town to the next, would often stop along his way and barge into the home of an acquaintance yelling, "quill, paper, quickly," jot down a few lines, shove the paper into his pocket and depart without another word.

Charles Wesley, his preaching, his music and his poetry touched the lives of so many during his lifetime and beyond. His legacy will be forever remembered in the voices that rise up to Heaven in song.

CHRIST EPISCOPAL CHURCH

This congregation was established as a mission of the Church of England in February, 1736. The Rev. Charles Wesley, ordained priest of that Church, conducted the first services in the chapel within the walls of Fort Frederica. The Rev. John Wesley, Rector of Christ Episcopal Church, Savannah, also served this mission. Under the name of St. James, this was one of the eight original parishes established in 1758. After the Revolution, this and other churches which had been served continuously by clergymen of the Church of England formed the Protestant Episcopal Church in the United States of America. Christ Church was incorporated by the State Legislature in 1808 and given a glebe of 108 acres; and in 1823 was one of the three parishes organizing the diocese of Georgia. The first Church built on this property in 1820 was almost destroyed during the War Between the States. The present building was erected on the same site in 1884.

Frederica Road at the church, St. Simons Island
GPS Coordinates: N31.21966, W81.386971

C hrist Episcopal Church is the second oldest Episcopal Church in the state of Georgia, the origin of the church can be traced to 1776. The present church has graced this property since 1820, when the congregation was awarded a grant of 108 acres. Preceding the donation, services were conducted beneath the shade of massive oaks by John and Charles Wesley.

The original edifice was terribly ill used as the headquarters for occupying Union forces during the Civil War. Showing no respect for the long standing sanctuary, the soldiers smashed the organ, broke the windows, burned the furnishings and used the altar to butcher game and chop wood for their cook fires.

Anson Green Phelps Dodge, Jr. arrived at St. Simons to visit his father, who was supervising the family lumber business at Gascoigne Bluff. The wealthy young man was immediately enchanted by St. Simons and determined to spend his life there. Called to the ministry, Anson Dodge, returned north to attend the seminary. While there he married his childhood sweetheart, unfortunately she died in India on their wedding trip.

Devastated by his loss, Anson returned to St. Simons, and in 1884, built Christ Church in his young wife's memory. The beautiful white, wood sided church was built in a cruciform design with a trussed Gothic roof, wooden interior having beautiful stained glass windows. The oldest of these windows is the Confession of St. Peter, which was created by Mayer & Company of Munich, Germany in 1899. Another window is attributed to Louis Tiffany. A picturesque cross style brick fortification fence surrounds the church property and is an original structure.

Reverend Dodge spent the reminder of his years attending to the spiritual needs of the islanders and his final resting place is beside his beloved young wife in the shadow of the church to which he dedicated his life.

The Christ Church was used as the backdrop for the late Eugenia Price's *The Beloved Invader*, the first book in her trilogy of historical fiction. Reverend Anson Green Phelps Dodge Jr. serves as the central character.

The church and grounds are open for public viewing during daylight hours.

Christ Episcopal Church

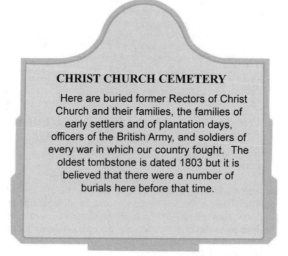

CHRIST CHURCH CEMETERY

Here are buried former Rectors of Christ Church and their families, the families of early settlers and of plantation days, officers of the British Army, and soldiers of every war in which our country fought. The oldest tombstone is dated 1803 but it is believed that there were a number of burials here before that time.

Frederica Road at Christ Episcopal Church, St. Simons Island
GPS Coordinates: N31.21966, W81.386971

Lying peacefully beneath the protective branches of ancient oaks is the Christ Church Cemetery. The cemetery is a serene walk through the history of St. Simons, shaded by the extended boughs of great cedars, massive oaks and fragrant magnolia trees. The light fragrance of climbing jasmine scents the air filled only with the sounds of the distant whippoorwill call.

The carefully tended grounds are safely held within the embrace of a cross style fortification while ancient tombs are

surrounded by iron forged guardianship. The gravestones bear the names of individuals who have defined St. Simons and Georgia history. Among them lay the remains of soldiers representing every conflict engaged in by the United States.

Captain Miles Hazzard led a reconnaissance mission in 1863 during the Civil War to St. Simons Island, particularly of interest to Hazzard because this was the land of his birth. When Captain Hazzard and nine Confederate soldiers of the 4th Georgia Cavalry reached Christ Church, he was angered to find that his family's graves had been desecrated. He wrote a note to the Federal Commanders and placed it on a stick planted in the middle of road in front of the church. The note was addressed to the Federal Commanding Officer and read in part,

"...let me tell you, Sir, that beside these graves I swear by heaven and to avenge their desecration. If it is honorable for you to disturb the dead, I shall consider it an honor and will make it my ambition to disturb your living."

Never again were the graves molested.

**Christ Church
Cemetery**

Locals tell a story of a young woman who was terrified of the dark and after her untimely death, her husband would light a candle beside her grave each evening to ease her fear. Eventually the husband died and was buried by her side. It is said, during the dark of the night, that a light can be seen flickering beside the graves. True love lives on.

Across the street is Wesley Garden with a simple marker that reads:

WESLEY GARDEN

This walk leads to the Wesley Memorial monument and garden. It was dedicated June 12, 1966 to commemorate the ministries of John and Charles Wesley in Georgia and particularly at Frederica.

The focal point of the Wesley Garden is an eighteen foot Celtic cross weighing fifteen tons. The garden is in a natural setting of great trees and planted in azaleas and shrubs native to this area. During the spring and summer the paths through the garden are alive with color and provide a cool walk beneath the shade of ancient trees.

Wesley Garden's Celtic Cross

ST. SIMONS ISLAND

From March 9 – May 12, 1736, Charles Wesley, secretary to James Oglethorpe, was Anglican cleric to the founders of Fort Frederica. His stern discipline earned disfavor among the colonists and Oglethorpe. John Wesley, religious leader to the colony of Georgia, visited Charles in April 1736, preaching in the storehouse, Charles returned to England, John ministered to the Fredericans in four trips before leaving "with an utter despair of doing good there" on January 26, 1737.

After John's return to England, in May 1738 the brothers had "heart warming experiences" and later founded the Methodist movement.

Opposite Fort Frederica entrance, St. Simons Island
GPS Coordinates: N31.22067, W81.386751

John and Charles Wesley sailed for Georgia in October of 1735, at the insistence of General James Oglethorpe. The trip was a four month long ordeal. During the sailing a vicious storm tossed the ship and as the wind whipped a horrendous crack was heard, the main mast toppled as if a lumberjack had felled the beam with his axe. The Englishmen aboard were shaking with fear and all the while the Moravians, a Czechoslovakian people, remained calm while they prayed and sang hymns. John Wesley was greatly impressed with their faith and knew he had much to learn from the Moravians.

Upon arrival, John was appointed rector at Savannah. Charles was to be the chaplain and secretary for General Oglethorpe at Frederica. John and Charles were high born[5], although never wealthy, were well educated. Their strict religious beliefs held little value for the working class people of the Georgia colony and to the Native Americans who believed in nature's spirit. These were the people to be their parishioners.

John's parish was so vast that, even for the most devoted cleric, it was much more than one man could handle. He faced a language problem as well. To overcome these barriers he began teaching himself Spanish. The local languages were so varied that sermons had to be repeated in Spanish, French, German and English everyday. His schedule was filled each day from 5:00 a.m. English prayers until 4:00 p.m. evening devotionals. After reading prayers in the morning, John would join the Moravians at Ebenezer where he studied their philosophies.

Meanwhile, Charles was experiencing troubles of a different kind at Frederica. Quarrels and problems arose between Charles and his parishioners, causing John to make the long tiresome journey to the small town for mediation. One argument involved two women, of questionable character, the women begged sympathy from the church for repentance concerning their loose morals. When Charles attempted to convert the women to Christianity, General Oglethorpe misinterpreted the situation and had words with Charles over his involvement with them. To punish Charles, Oglethorpe removed all comforts and Charles was forced to sleep on the ground. Eventually, General Oglethorpe did allow Charles to explain, but by this time he was sick and disillusioned with the Georgia colony. Charles longed for England and in May 1736, Charles Wesley submitted his resignation. Oglethorpe persuaded him to stay, reasoning that there was no replacement available to care for the spiritual needs of the soldiers. Charles remained until August, then sailed first to Charleston and on to England, never returning to Georgia.

All the while, trouble was brewing in Savannah as well. Thomas Causton was a local political leader and first chief magistrate for Savannah. There was a constant battle for leadership between Oglethorpe and Causton. Word reached London that Causton was intent on court martialing General Oglethorpe for some unknown infraction, John Wesley sided with Oglethorpe, which was to be his downfall.

Causton was corrupt and John Wesley had found proof. John publically reported that Moravians were not being credited for work performed, thus, their indenture was never decreased. Causton had applied the Moravian's credit to workers on his own plantation. Causton's guilt was without question and he was removed as chief magistrate. John had made a mortal enemy and all of Causton's hatred toward Oglethorpe was now directed at John. Soon Causton found the perfect outlet to discredit John and exile him in disgrace from the Georgia colony.

John was tutoring a young lady named Sophia Hopkey, who was a fellow passenger on the voyage from England. After their arrival in Georgia, their friendship blossomed. Sophia believed it was John's intent to ask for her hand, but on the advice of a local Bishop, John broke his association with Sophia without a word. Sophia complained to her uncle over John's sudden coldness and as a result the tension between John and Causton escalated, Sophia was Thomas Causton's niece. Sophia ran away and married a shopkeeper.

Local gossips described John as a jilted lover. Rumors circulated that he had begged a promise of Sophia never to marry another and then failed to propose. John's troubles increased in August when Sophia returned to his church and requested the sacrament of Holy Communion, John refused. A warrant in John Wesley's name was issued the following day by Causton on behalf of Sophia. The charge was defamation based on his refusal to grant Sophia the sacraments in public without due cause. Causton requested restitution in the amount of one thousand pounds sterling for damages. Upon Wesley's refusal to answer the charges, stating that this was a church matter, he was ordered to Savannah to stand trial.

Causton, unwilling to wait for the court's decision, challenged John to settle the matter with swords. John Wesley refused to fight Causton and instead wrote a letter to Sophia explaining why he had refused the sacraments. John explained that she had not attended church since her marriage, she had not offered her name to the Curate[6] as required for partakers of Holy Communion and she had not repented before God for her transgressions. After repentance, John Wesley said he would, with a clear conscience, administer Holy Communion. John Wesley's trial began in August 1737. Causton hand selected the jury. The trial ended in a mistrial, Causton's jury refused to return an indictment against Wesley.

John Wesley was never able to reestablish his reputation with the people of Frederica. The parishioners began to regard him as a Roman Catholic heretic, which was against the charter of the Georgia Trustees. The attendance in church dwindled to only a faithful few.

By November 1737, John found himself in court again. Causton was determined to prove his case and John realized it was time to leave the Georgia Colony. John publicly announced his intention to leave. Mr. Williamson, Sophia's husband, issued a warning that John Wesley was indebted to him for one thousand pounds sterling awarded by the court and anyone assisting his departure would stand in court beside him.

John Wesley sailed away from Georgia in December 1737, never having paid the restitution. He felt as though his attempts to bring religion to the colony was a complete failure. John and Charles Wesley never realized the impact of their ministry on the Georgia colony.

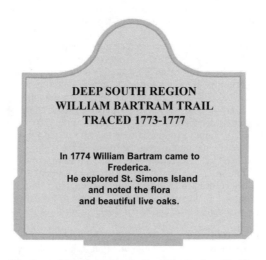

DEEP SOUTH REGION
WILLIAM BARTRAM TRAIL
TRACED 1773-1777

In 1774 William Bartram came to
Frederica.
He explored St. Simons Island
and noted the flora
and beautiful live oaks.

Frederica Road past the entrance to Fort Frederica, St. Simons Island
GPS Coordinates: N31.22313, W81.387186

W illiam Bartram was a Quaker and a naturalist who journeyed throughout the eastern seaboard exploring, collecting plant samples and observing the land. After having written about his exploration of coastal Georgia in his book, *The Travels of William Bartram*, surveyors used his route as the basis for establishing road ways. The Old Post and Military Roads were routed based on Bartram's exploration of the area.

Bartram spent time exploring the sites of the deserted fort and town of Frederica in 1774. The following is a description, in Bartram's own words, of what he found there:

> *"The fortress was regular and beautiful, constructed chiefly with brick, and was the largest, most regular, and perhaps most costly of any in North America, of British construction: it is now in ruins, yet occupied by a small garrison; the ruins also of the town ownly remain; peach trees, figs, pomegranates, and other shrubs grow out of the ruinous walls of former spacious and expensive buildings, not only in the town, but at a distance in various parts of the island; yet there are a few neat houses in good repair, and inhabited: it seems now recovering again, owing to the public and liberal spirit and exertions of J. Spalding, esq., who is the president of the island, and engaging in very extensive mercantile concerns."*

HARRINGTON HALL

Capt. Raymond Demere,
a native of France, served many years in the
British army at Gibraltar before coming to
Georgia in 1738 as
an officer in Oglethorpe's Regiment. His home,
Harrington Hall, was located at this site.
Later generations of the Demere family lived at
the south end of St. Simons Island where their
plantation was called Mulberry Grove.

Lawrence Road, 0.6 mile north of Frederica Road, St. Simons Island
GPS Coordinates: N31.22192, W81.368818

Captain Raymond Demere fought along side General Oglethorpe at the battles of Gully Hole and Bloody Marsh. Commanding a company of the 42nd Regiment with sixty British Regulars, Demere deployed his men to the eastern side of the trail to await attacking Spanish troops. Demere's men, confused by the smoke and musket fire retreated toward Frederica and during their flight met Oglethorpe. They could hear the sounds of fierce fighting in the distance and feared the worst. Demere turned his troops around to rejoin the fighting and arrived in time to watch the Spanish retreat. Demere, regardless of his untimely retreat,was given a tract of land just outside the walls of Fort Frederica. It was there that he chose to build his plantation called Harrington Hall becoming a St. Simons planter.

Demere, originally from France, became a member of St. Simons society, a diverse group with varied interests. Although never wealthy, he maintained a European refinement and courtesy blended with the simplicity that was demanded of the rugged environment. Though Harrington Hall was isolated, the Demere family kept abreast of current events by traveling to fashionable vacation spots and making sojourns abroad uncommon.

Harrington Hall was left to Raymond Demere, Jr. after the death of his father and remained in the family until the Civil War. When the Demere family returned after the Civil War, they were greeted by utter desolation. The fields were overgrown, the house was uninhabitable and former slaves had claimed the land taking several years for the land titles to be restored to the family. Meanwhile, the Demere tried to resurrect Mulberry Grove Plantation. Freed slaves were unaccustomed to working for wages and the family had little money or access to credit to pay them. Harrington Hall was eventually abandoned and fell to ruin.

Many of St. Simons' former slaves congregated at the center of the island along Frederica Road and eastward to the marsh. They called their community "Harrington," after the old Demere homestead nearby. Harrington has the island's largest concentration of residents that can trace their proud lineage to the slaves of St. Simons.

GERMAN VILLAGE

Here in 1736, Oglethorpe settled a group of German Lutherans, known as Salzburgers, and their settlement was called the German Village. These Salzburgers made their living by planting, fishing, and selling their products to the Frederica settlers. When Oglethorpe's regiment was disbanded in 1749 the Salzburgers left St. Simons Island. During the Plantation Era, the Wylly family lived here, their plantation being called "The Village."

Lawrence Road at Village Drive, 1.2 mile north of Frederica Road, St. Simons Island
GPS Coordinates: N31.2287, W81.362767

The ship *Two Brothers*, commanded by Captain William Thomson, arrived at Frederica in October 1738. The official records say 116 "head" of Salzburg Germans were aboard the ship, the actual number was greater because children did not count as a full "head." The Salzburgers indentured themselves, promising to become servants to the British crown until the price of their passage was reimbursed.

The Salzburgers, a hard working and industrious people, were not treated fairly. Once they arrived the cost of their housing, food and other necessities of life were added to their debt. Many of these people died never having repaid their indenture.

The German population settled in a place known as the German Village or Village Bluff. The Salzburgers planted orchards, which provided dates, limes, figs, peaches and pomegranates. They grew cotton in small quantities and hay was cut and stacked in the meadows adjacent to the town. Thousands of mulberry trees were planted at the south end of St. Simons in an effort to fulfill the Trustee's elusive quest for a silk industry.

After Frederica was deserted, the Salzburgers dispersed into different areas of the state. The property changed hands often over the years and eventually was sold to Captain Alexander Wylly, a former British officer who built Sinclair Plantation. His plantation of over a thousand acres became known simply as "The Village." In 1838, Dr. Thomas Hazzard of Pike's Bluff Plantation killed Wylly's youngest son, John, in a boundary dispute. A broken pediment[7] marks Wylly's grave in the Christ Church burying ground, symbolic of his tragic death in the prime of life.

Later the plantation house served as a meeting place for the Sinclair Club. Today, a housing development has been constructed on the site. Nothing is left noting the existence of the original German Village except the historical marker denoting the site.

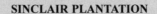

SINCLAIR PLANTATION

This was the plantation of Archibald Sinclair, tything man of the town of Frederica. In 1765 it was granted to Donald Forbes as bounty land for his services in Oglethorpe's regiment. Forbes sold to Gen. Lachlan McIntosh of Revolutionary fame, whose son, Major William McIntosh, lived and died in the old plantation house. Here, in the family burial plot, lie the bodies of Major McIntosh and his two children. The Agricultural and Sporting Club of St. Simons Island, an organization of plantation owners founded in 1832, used the old tabby home as their clubhouse.

Lawrence Road, 1.8 mile north of Frederica Road, St. Simons Island
GPS Coordinates: N31.23638, W81.355096

Sinclair Plantation, known as St. Clair Plantation, was granted to Archibald Sinclair in 1740. It has been speculated that Sinclair's name has been Americanized over time or perhaps the man himself shortened the name, which was quite common during that time. In 1745, the plantation was noted as one of the most successful on St. Simons Island. However, ten years later the property is not listed in the 1755 Entry of Claims, which indicates that the family had left the island and that the Sinclair grant had been vacated.

In 1765, the land was granted to Donald Forbes. Forbes sold the plantation to Lachlan McIntosh whose son, Major William McIntosh, lived in the old plantation house until his death in 1799. Headstones placed by the Daughters of the American Revolution mark Major McIntosh's grave and nearby are the little brick tombs of his two children.

Sinclair Plantation changed hands again in 1805, when the property was purchased from the McIntosh estate by George Baillie, who then sold it to his cousin, Alexander Wylly. Sinclair was included as a part of Wylly's Village Plantation, which was once the old German Village of the Salzburgs. When Mrs. Wylly's mother, Mrs. Ann Armstrong, arrived from the Bahamas to make her home on St. Simons, she lived in the old Sinclair house and died there in 1816. The Wylly's daughter Frances, married Dr. William Fraser and lived as a young married couple for a time at Sinclair. They eventually moved to Darien, where Dr. Fraser was elected Mayor.

Sinclair Plantation was eventually sold to Major Pierce Butler, who leased the house for a nominal rent as a meeting place for the St. Clair Club. In 1832 the house became the headquarters for the Agricultural and Sporting Club organized by island planters. The old plantation house burned in 1857. In 1954, the property's historical significance was recognized when the Georgia Historical Commission erected a bronze marker.

Frederica and Demere Roads, St. Simons Island
GPS Coordinates: N31.1592, W81.388376

Retreat Plantation was located adjacent to Hamilton Plantation on the southern tip of St. Simons Island. The tract was originally settled by James Spalding and in 1804, Major William Page purchased the property. Page, a South Carolinian who had managed the Hampton estate for Pierce Butler, saw great potential in the property. He named the plantation Retreat and moved his family into the small cottage that overlooked St. Simons Sound and Jekyll Island.

William and Hannah Page had only one child, a daughter they named Anna. She grew to become a beautiful young woman whose hand was won by Thomas Butler King, a lawyer from Massachusetts. The couple inherited Retreat Plantation at the death of Anna's parents in 1827. King became an accomplished lawyer and planter but his ambition was political. He spent six terms as a Congressman in Washington and as much time traveling throughout the country to promote his business ventures.

One of the earliest proponents of the transcontinental railroad, King helped organize the Brunswick Altamaha Canal and was appointed Collector of the Port of San Francisco. For three years, Thomas King did not come home at all. Even so, he and Anna managed to have ten children. The tasks of raising a family and running the plantation fell to Anna while she suffered through her husband's frequent absences.

The Kings planned to build a fine mansion at the end of an avenue of oaks that Anna had planted in 1848, but the right time never quite arrived to construct it. They continued to live in the little cottage of hand hewn timbers with a shuttered veranda and gabled roof. Anna's gardens surrounded the house, she refused to grow any flower that did not possess a pleasing fragrance, calling them "plants without souls." Anna nurtured as many as ninety-six varieties of roses, among the other flowering plants. In the springtime sailors approaching St. Simons often said they could smell Retreat Plantation a dozen miles from shore. John James Audubon paid homage to Retreat, when enroute to St. Augustine his ship put in at St. Simons to escape a storm. He was entertained by Thomas Butler King at Retreat and was enthralled by the ambiance.

Anna King died in 1859 on the verge of the Civil War, which would claim one of her children. Henry King marched to the war at the first signs of conflict, taking with him Neptune, a faithful slave to serve as his manservant. It was very common for wealthy young men to have their manservants to care for their needs during the war. Neptune had long been responsible for the care of the King children and when Henry left to serve felt it was his place to go along. During the battle at Fredericksburg on December 13, 1862, Henry King was killed. Neptune braved the battlefield, retrieved Henry's body, and returned him to St. Simons, where he was buried in Christ Church Cemetery beside his mother.

Neptune was under no obligation to return to the war, however, he accompanied the King's younger son when he too joined the Confederacy. The loyal caretaker stood by as the Confederacy surrendered in 1865. Neptune was freed after the war and chose the surname "Small" as his own, referring to his petite stature. The King family gave Neptune Small a tract of land on St. Simons for his years of loyal service. Neptune died in 1907 and was laid to rest on the grounds of Retreat Plantation, where a bronze marker recounts his bravery.

Neptune Park was built in the memory and recognition of Neptune Small. The park is located in the Village on St. Simons Island, near the pier overlooking the ocean.

The slave cabin once provided shelter for slaves of Retreat Plantation. Only a handful of these early 1800s structures still remain and there are fourteen of these located on St. Simons Island. The dwellings were usually home for two families. The former Retreat Plantation cabin has a tabby foundation covered with stucco and was lined[8] to give the appearance of expensive building material, brick.

OLD SPANISH GARDEN

Spain maintained missions along the coast for more than a century. Beginning in 1568 Jesuit and, later, Franciscan missionaries labored to Christianize the Indians and cultivated in the mission gardens figs, peaches, oranges and other plants introduced from Europe. Due to Indian uprisings, pirate raids and British depredations these missions were removed further south in 1686. A map of St. Simons Island made in 1739 by Capt. John Thomas, engineer of Oglethorpe's Regiment, locates an "Old Spanish Garden" near this site. In this area materials from the Spanish mission period have been found.

Demere Road and Ocean Boulevard, St. Simons Island
GPS Coordinates: N31.13535, W81.390372

*G*uadalquini (*Guadal qwin-e*), the Native American name for St. Simons Island, was used in the 1500s when a tribe of Mocama inhabited the land. The Spanish attempted to bring Catholicism to the Native Americans and in the early 1600s reestablished missions that had previously been deserted. The missions were deserted as a result of the Mocama uprising of 1597, which led to the deaths of five members of the Spanish Franciscan clergy. The priests were killed in an attempt to force the Mocama to practice Christianity. The Mocama balked when part of the conversion to Christianity meant losing their ancient customs of dance, celebrations, warring and multiple wives. The spirits of nature and healing had no place in the Christian world. The Spanish retaliated by burning the Mocama villages and destroying their food crops. Those clergy are now known as the Georgia Martyrs and a relief[9], in tribute, hangs in the St. Williams Church on St. Simons Island.

The Spanish mission *San Buenaventura de Guadalquini* was established in 1605 in an area called the Spanish Garden of St. Simons. The mission was in place to convert the Gualeans (*Gwi`-le-ens*).[10] The area experienced a time of prosperity and many additional missions were erected to house newly arriving Franciscan priests. The new arrivals brought fruit trees and vegetable seeds, hence the name, Old Spanish Gardens.

This time of abundance and peace was short lived. Spain not only offered religion, they also brought diseases for which the Gualeans had no defenses. The British arrived in 1670 and became yet another threat to the Native American way of life. Other Native American tribes aligned with England's forces and attacked the fragile Guale settlements. The settlements and missions were deserted one by one. The Native Americans loyal to Spain and the Franciscan priests retreated to the missions of St. Augustine. The battles between Spain and England over the Georgia territory soon began.

DELEGAL'S FORT

The first fortification built by the British on the South End of St. Simons Island was erected near this site in April, 1736, by soldiers of the South Carolina Independent Company under command of Lieutenant Philip Delegal. Before coming to St. Simons these soldiers had been stationed at Fort Frederick, near Port Royal, South Carolina.

The fortification erected here, known as "Delegal's Fort at Sea Point", commanded the entrance to the harbor, being located "so that all ships ... must pass within shot of the point."

In 1738, when a regiment of British soldiers was brought to St. Simons Island, Lieutenant Delegal and his soldiers were taken into Oglethorpe's Regiment. Fort St. Simons was then built taking the site of Delegal's Fort. Most of the area covered by this fortification has been washed away.

Ocean Boulevard, 0.1 mile north of Demere Road, St. Simons Island
GPS Coordinates: N31.13554, W81.38799

Delegal's Fort was built in 1736 by Carolina soldiers to serve as the southern defense for Charleston. The fortification was renamed Fort St. Simons in 1738, but was only used for six years after the Spanish suffered their defeat at the battles of Bloody Marsh and Gully Hole. As the Spanish retreated, they paused long enough to burn the fort in retaliation for their sound lashing.

John Couper purchased the land in the early 1800s and sold four acres to the federal government for one dollar. The area was to become the site for the first St. Simons lighthouse. Construction began in 1807 and James Gould of Massachusetts was hired to build the structure. Although the original plans called for brick, Gould decided to use the "coastal concrete" known as tabby.

Upon completion of the lighthouse, President James Madison appointed Gould the first Light Keeper in 1810 at a salary of $400 per year. The lantern was powered by whale oil and continued until the majestic animals were hunted to near extinction. The light was then converted of kerosene.

During the Civil War, the Confederates dynamited anything that might aid the advancing Union forces, including the lighthouse. The federal government replaced the beacon in 1872.

New technology brought electricity to the light in 1934 and when the last lighthouse keeper retired in 1950, the United States Coast Guard fully automated the light. Today, the Fresnel lens is illuminated by a one thousand watt mogul lamp, which rotates once every minute. The Coastal Georgia Historical Society restored the keeper's house in 1972 and since 1984 visitors have been welcomed to the site.

The lighthouse is a romantic symbol as the steady, rotating light scans the St. Simons sound. It brings assurance to sailors traversing these waters and is a landmark linking days long gone to future generations.

The Lighthouse, written by the late Eugenia Price, is the second book in her coastal Georgia trilogy. The novel was inspired by the history surrounding St. Simons and her luminescent beacon.

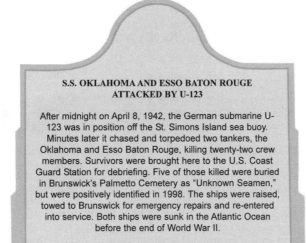

**S.S. OKLAHOMA AND ESSO BATON ROUGE
ATTACKED BY U-123**

After midnight on April 8, 1942, the German submarine U-123 was in position off the St. Simons Island sea buoy. Minutes later it chased and torpedoed two tankers, the Oklahoma and Esso Baton Rouge, killing twenty-two crew members. Survivors were brought here to the U.S. Coast Guard Station for debriefing. Five of those killed were buried in Brunswick's Palmetto Cemetery as "Unknown Seamen," but were positively identified in 1998. The ships were raised, towed to Brunswick for emergency repairs and re-entered into service. Both ships were sunk in the Atlantic Ocean before the end of World War II.

**Old Coast Guard Station, 4201 First Street, St. Simons Island
GPS Coordinates: N31.1456, W81.487495**

There are two parts to this story, one, the obvious sinking of the SS *Oklahoma* and the Esso *Baton Rouge*, the other of the men who risked their lives, just as any soldier did, only to be ignored by their country. During World War II we often thought that the fighting was all "over there." We think of Germany and Japan, the closest we think of home is the devastation at Pearl Harbor. Eighty-two American vessels carrying war supplies were sunk by German submarines between January and May 1942, six of those ships were off the coast of Georgia and Florida.

The SS *Oklahoma* was an oil tanker. German *U-boat 123* sent her to the shallow, sandy bottom off the coast of Georgia in April 1942. Her crew consisted of thirty-eight merchant mariners, nineteen of these men gave their lives in the darkened hours of that spring morning.

The United States Merchant Marines were a part of the Naval Auxiliary by law. Merchant mariners were private citizens, employees of independent companies contracted by the government to deliver oil, gasoline, munitions and food. Those who weren't classified unfit for duty for one reason or another were exempted from the draft while serving as merchant mariners. Everyday that these men were in danger on hostile wartime waters and everyday they risked their lives for their country. Yet, these men were not entitled to any veteran's benefits, not even a flag to cover a fallen man's coffin, or a burial befitting one who gave all for his country.

The United States fleet at Pearl Harbor was demolished in December 1941, leaving the nation reeling in its wake. The public never thought of submarine activity in mainland waters. Enemy submarine sightings and reports of their demise were spoken of in local Georgia newspapers almost daily. These reports proved to be more fiction than fact. In fact, few U-boats were sighted, however, three German submarines were actually sunk during the winter and spring of 1942.

The torpedo blasts resulting in the sinking of the SS *Oklahoma* and Esso *Baton Rouge* hit with such impact that window panes were shattered in the city of Brunswick and the reverberation could be heard as far as eighteen miles inland. Many area citizens assisted in the rescue and recovery efforts. When the sun broke the horizon that April morning, all that could be seen of the two merchant ships was their bows breaking the waters surface.

Twenty-two merchant marines were killed that night. Nineteen men aboard the SS *Oklahoma* and three on the Esso *Baton Rouge* gave their lives. Five men listed as casualties were burned beyond recognition and were buried in Brunswick's Palmetto Cemetery in graves marked "Unknown seamen —1942." The ships were raised and towed to a spot near the King and Prince Hotel. The bodies were removed on April 20. The unknown seamen were buried on April 26, 1942.

Through the perseverance of a group of caring individuals, the mystery of the unknown seamen has been solved. A year long investigation, beginning in 1998, was launched; headed by Michael P. Higgins and Don Robertson both members of The Propeller Club of the United States - Port No. 91, Brunswick, Georgia; Bill Chubb, a retired Coast Guard commander, and Terrence Logan, who ran a veterans' program at the University of Minnesota. The Propeller Club of the United States raised the funds and placed a proper memorial for the five Merchant Mariners. The club dedicated the monument on National

Maritime Day, May 22, 1999.

These are the five SS *Oklahoma* Merchant Mariners:

Alfredo Carmona, 46, (Wiper) He was born in San Juan, PR, he listed a wife in NYC and a friend, Elozia Torres in Tampa, FL. It is possible he has relatives in the coastal southern part (Cape May vicinity) of New Jersey.

Joseph Geary[11], 37, (Cook) of Boston, MA, Father: William Geary, Providence, RI

Arthur James Genter, 42, (Oiler) born in New Orleans, LA; Sister: Mrs. M. Meyers lived in Evansville, Indiana. A private detective in New Orleans voluntarily located an 80 year old niece, Mrs. Frances Hahn living in Evansville, Indiana and his sister in a nursing home in Evansville, Indiana.

Charles Rivette, 20, (Ordinary Seaman) Father: Port Arthur, Texas. Family identified.

Osswald Ryder, 21, (Messman) Father: John Ryder, Ville Platte, Louisiana. On 6/24/99, sisters and nieces saw the story in the newspaper and arrived from Louisiana to pay their respects at his grave.

Congress recognized the contribution of merchant seamen of World War II in 1988, awarding them the status of military veterans. The recognition only applied to those serving between December 1941 through December 1945. Former President Bill Clinton later signed a resolution extending the date to December 1946, the same as those serving in the armed forces.

ST. SIMON'S TROLLEY STOP

1 ½ Hour Historic Island Tours
Leaves from this point
(Daily at: 11:00 am 1:00 pm
Winter Hours
(Labor Day thru March 15th)
1:00 pm (only)

Historic site of 1800's mule drawn Trolley Stop. It met passengers from the steam ships and transported them to the St. Simon's Hotel, which was located at what is now Massengale Park.
It was later motorized and operated for many years.

Near wharf on St. Simons Island
GPS Coordinates: N31.13454, W81.396262

Without slave labor the vast amount of cotton produced before the Civil War was no longer possible. Sharecropping and tenancy arrangements began to take over as immense plantations were carved into smaller farms. The plantation era was over and the short lived lumber industry began. However, by the 1920s, raw pulp wood had been clear cut and the lumber industry dwindled to an end. In the mid 1900s, tourism became the newest industry in coastal Georgia.

The St. Simons Trolley has provided the definitive historical tour of St. Simons since 1991. The tour includes the lighthouse, one of only three working lighthouses in Georgia; the sites of Gully Hole and Bloody Marsh, where the battles against Spain was fought for control of the Southern colony are also presented. The military fortress of Fort Frederica, the colonial town and fort settled by General James E. Oglethorpe, Retreat Plantation, where relics from the era of slavery can be seen, and a walking tour of Christ Church and Cemetery, where a number of the island's most notable citizens were laid to rest.

Professional guides continue to provide glimpses into the 400 year history and folklore surrounding St. Simons Island.

GLYNN COUNTY

Glynn County, one of the eight original Counties of Georgia, was organized under the 1777 Constitution of the State of Georgia. It was named in honor of John Glynn, a member of the British House of Commons who defended the cause of the American Colonies in the difficulties which led to the Revolutionary War.

Glynn County contains the lands formerly included in the Colonial Parishes of St. David, St. Patrick, and St. James, which had been organized in 1785. Among the early officials were the Hon. George Walton, Signer of the Declaration of Independence, Judge of the Superior Court; James Spalding, Alexander Bissett, Richard Leake, and Raymond Demere, Justices of the Inferior Court; John Goode, Clerk of the Inferior and Superior Courts; John Palmer, Sheriff; John Burnett, Register of Probates; Richard Bradley, Tax Collector; Martin Palmer, Tax Receiver; Joshua Miller, Surveyor; Jacob Helvestine, Coroner; George Handley (who in 1788 was elected Governor of the State of Georgia) and Christopher Hillary, Legislators; George Purvis, Richard Pritchard, Moses Burnett, John Piles, and John Burnett, Commissioners of Glynn Academy.

Glynn County Courthouse, G and Union Streets, Brunswick
GPS Coordinates: N31.15227, 81.494522

Glynn County was established in 1765 as one of the eight original Georgia counties, it wasn't until 1777 that the legislature officially incorporated Glynn County. The land was native to the Creek Indians and expanded over approximately 423 square miles. Brunswick is the county seat.

The history surrounding Brunswick's name is a long and detailed diatribe. Suffice it to say that the town derived its name from the German ancestry of the Hanover line of George II. The monarchy can be traced to Braunsweig Lunenburg, Germany, and Brunswick is the Anglican form of Braunsweig.

The first settlement of Glynn County was located on St. Simons Island in 1738, known as Frederica. The town was initially created to house the fighting men of John McIntosh Mohr's 42nd Regiment of Foot made up of Scottish Highlanders and Creek Indian natives. McIntosh's troops joined General Oglethorpe in defeating the Spanish at the battle of Bloody Marsh. These soldiers were later given land grants and many established vast plantations in the area.

At the end of the Revolutionary War, Glynn County prospered. The population increased and newly built plantations required slave labor to farm tobacco and rice. The lumber industry was booming, largely due to the constant construction, expanding the economic base. From 1794 through 1797, cypress timbers taken from Cumberland and St. Simons Islands were sent to Boston to build the greatest warship of its time, the USS *Constitution*.

Peacetime was not good for all areas of the county, Frederica was in the death throes of her final hour. Without the military, houses were vacated, merchants closed their shops, and the streets were deserted. Within fifteen years Frederica was a ghost town.

The Honorable George Walton, a founder of Glynn County, was a signator of the Declaration of Independence, a judge of the Superior Court and Governor of Georgia. Though Walton's term was short, his tenure was not without scandal. He bestowed so many land grants that had he remained in office just a few additional months, no property east of the Mississippi River would have gone unclaimed. An extensive investigation resulted in the *Yazoo Land Fraud* case, brought in 1795.

The basis of the land fraud case was Walton, along with other southern Governors, had abused the Head Right Laws. The Head Right Laws stated that each man returning from the Revolutionary War was entitled to purchase two hundred acres of land plus fifty acres for each dependent, not to exceed one thousand acres for any single family. Walton bent to the pressure of wealthy men, some of them legislators, was swayed by the vast amount of money that could be made. Large companies knew that the ownership of vast quantities of land also brought great political power. One grant, to a single company, totaled 2,664,000 acres. However, the county from which the property was granted contained a total of only 407,680 acres.

Three companies, the South Carolina Yazoo Company, the Virginia Yazoo Company and the Tennessee Company formed an alliance to purchase land from the Georgia Assembly. In December 1789, a bill was signed into law approving the sell of 20,000,000 acres of Georgia land. The deal fell through when the companies tried to pay with worthless currency. Five years later, the Georgia, Georgia-Mississippi, the Upper Mississippi and the Tennessee Yazoo Companies bribed the assembly to sell them forty million acres for $500,000. The bill passed by a narrow margin several months later. The Georgia Union Company had placed a bid of $800,000 with an additional $40,000 deposit. This bid was ignored. Several United States Senators were stockholders in the Yazoo companies, so it was certain from the start that Yazoo would win the bid. The public balked when word of the questionable dealings was spread. The Reformer Political Party sent United States Senator James Jackson to investigate.

The legislators tried to hide their involvement by gathering all contracts concerning the land deals and torching them in what was known as the Holy Fire. The Holy Fire was given its name because land speculators did not start the fire with flint, the fire descended straight from the Heavens and ignited the offending documents. Of course, it was aided by a somewhat powerful magnifying glass. The Holy Fire did not save them.

Public outcry forced the resignation of the legislators involved in the land fraud. James Jackson was appointed to fill one of the vacated seats and vowed to bring down those involved in the scandal. Sources say that Jackson swore to call out[12] every person involved. He did challenge former Governor Walton, but Walton refused.

Georgia refunded the money for the land. Some of the land had already been sold to other people. Those who refused to take the money kept the land but the state refused to acknowledge the claims of the owners and did not turn over the titles. The land owners brought suit against the state of Georgia in 1810 and the United States Supreme Court decided in *Fletcher vs. Peck* that the state had infringed on a valid contract and must turn over all titles.

Former Georgia Governor George Walton moved to Augusta, where he was appointed Judge of the Superior Circuit of Georgia and served from 1799 until his death. He died at his home near Augusta in 1804 and was buried at Rosney Cemetery until 1848. It was then that his remains were re-interred beneath a monument commemorating his signature on the Declaration of Independence at the courthouse in Augusta.

The Glynn County Courthouse

MARK CARR

Brunswick's first settler came to Georgia in 1738 with Oglethorpe's regiment. He was granted 500 acres at this place, on which he established his plantation.
Several tabby buildings erected by him stood nearby and a military outpost was maintained here. In 1741 Indians from Florida raided his plantation, causing 750 pounds damage. The Indians killed or wounded some of the soldiers, while others were taken prisoners.

Union Street and First Avenue, Brunswick
GPS Coordinates: N31.13744, W81.489002

General James Edward Oglethorpe, Georgia's founder, selected Brunswick for his headquarters. Brunswick did not prosper for the next thirty years. Mark Carr was granted 500 acres for his service and became in essence Brunswick's first European citizen around 1738. He was Captain of Oglethorpe's Marine Boat Company and led his company in the defense of Fort Frederica against the Spaniards. Carr built a plantation known as Carr's Fort on the bank of the Turtle River near Plug Point. The town of Brunswick was not established until 1771, when the British purchased some of Carr's holdings that lay on the fringes of town. Frederica was named the first county seat and in 1797 the General Assembly selected a more populated Brunswick as a replacement for the dying military town. George Washington designed and surveyed Brunswick's town squares in 1778. There were only five ports of entry in the United States during that time, Brunswick was one of the five.

Glynn Academy[13] opened its doors in 1819, but due to lack of attendance did not thrive. It was reopened in 1840 with more success. By 1825, the courthouse, a jail, mercantile and thirty residences occupied Brunswick. Three local men were deeded undeveloped sections of town with the intent to build a canal to the Altamaha River. The canal would connect the inland plantations to Brunswick's port.

The Oglethorpe House Hotel was built in 1836, the same year that the Georgia General Assembly incorporated Brunswick. Two years later Brunswick saw the construction of a bank, newspaper and plans for establishing the Brunswick and Florida Railroad. Glynn Academy then instructed eighty-five students with four teachers. Timber and cotton prices had begun to wan and the lack of funds delayed both the canal and railroad. The Cotton Crash of 1839 brought a halt to all construction. The canal was finally opened in 1854, and two years later, the railroad. The census of 1860 noted the population as 468.

The Civil War began in 1861 and Brunswick's Confederate protectors were ordered to the northern front. The Confederate soldiers were determined to leave nothing of use to the Union Army and they burned the lighthouse and wharf, even the Oglethorpe House. Citizens were ordered to evacuate, Brunswick became a ghost town. At the end of the war in 1865, the city leaders feared the Brunswick would never recover. Nothing was further from the truth. The citizens did return and brought with them, affluence. Brunswick had the largest lumber operation in America and massive quantities of heart pine lumber was produced from 1874 through 1908. The lumber supplied wood for planking all over the world. The canal and river traffic was now secondary travel to the railroads, which joined all corners of Georgia. The rails connected Brunswick's port to the rest of the United States.

Brunswick withstood yellow fever, hurricanes, U-boats during World War II and fire. The Naval Air Station Glynco was founded in 1943, it has boarded every type of aircraft in operation and was the largest blimp base in the world. Brunswick's ship building industry manufactured over ninety-nine ships during the World War II era.

Brunswick is home to numerous manufacturers and suppliers, most in the lumber or seafood industries. Brunswick has, to this day, the deepest natural harbor on the Georgia coast and is still a bustling port. Her number one industry is tourism and over 1.5 million tourists per year vacation in Brunswick and on the Golden Isles.

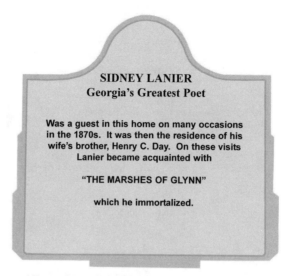

SIDNEY LANIER
Georgia's Greatest Poet

**Was a guest in this home on many occasions
in the 1870s. It was then the residence of his
wife's brother, Henry C. Day. On these visits
Lanier became acquainted with**

"THE MARSHES OF GLYNN"

which he immortalized.

Albany Street just off George Street, Brunswick
GPS Coordinates: N31.14479, W81.487495

Sidney Lanier was born in Macon, Georgia on February 3, 1842. It was at an early age that his love for verse and talent for taking pen to paper emerged. After college, he joined the Confederate Army and served in the Civil War until he was captured and imprisoned in Maryland. While in a Union prison he contracted tuberculosis, the disease continued to plague him for rest of his life, eventually complications of the illness led to his death.

Lanier married Mary Day, and his first novel, *Tiger Lilies*, was published in 1867. The volume contained stories of romance, war recollections and German philosophy. The years after the war saw Lanier wander from one vocation to another. He worked in his father's law office, taught school, and finally, accepted a position as first flutist for the Peabody Orchestra in Baltimore, Maryland.

He was an accomplished musician and, in many circles, was considered a genius for both his musical talents and ability to write prose. Tuberculosis or consumption, as it was known then, dictated most of his actions. Lanier was constantly seeking locations that might ease the constant lung congestion and prolong his life. Even during his search, Sidney Lanier was driven by his life's work. He wrote, lectured and performed whenever invited. There were many times he was unable to stand for a lecture but continued in spite of his frailty.

Sidney Lanier was noted as Georgia's Poet Laureate. It was during a trip to Brunswick, where physicians felt the coastal salt air might ease his breathing, Lanier found serenity, though only for a short time. *The Marshes of Glynn* was inspired here and is still considered one of his most beautiful works.

Sidney Lanier died Sept. 7, 1881, in Lynn, North Carolina. Three years later Mrs. Lanier published an expanded edition of his poetry. The complete edition of his compositions, ten volumes, was printed in 1945. Sidney Lanier's impressive body of work ensures that his name will long be remembered.

US 17/GA 25 at junction with GA 99 near the Altamaha River 1.4 miles
GPS Coordinates: N31.3081, 81.460458

John Couper was the first large planter to take permanently residence on St. Simons Island. He left Scotland at the age sixteen "for the good of his native land," he often said and to find his fortune in America. He became an apprentice to the Savannah branch of a Scottish mercantile firm and moved to Florida during the Revolution with his loyalist employers. After the war, he became a successful merchant in the once-thriving but now extinct coastal town of Sunbury, where he married Rebecca Maxwell in 1792. The following year Couper began purchasing scattered tracts of land on St. Simons Island.

In 1796, Couper moved his family to St. Simons into a modest one and one half story cottage built by Daniel Cannon, who was a carpenter of old Frederica. Meanwhile, a handsome mansion was in construction. In 1804, the Coupers moved into the beautiful home. The ground floor was built of tabby with a wooden upper story, painted white with green blinds. Broad steps led up to a wide piazza that surrounded the second story and provided a magnificent view of the Hampton River and the distant marshes. The plantation was called Hopeton-on-the-Altamaha at Cannon's Point.

John Couper's interest in horticulture was reflected in the beautiful grounds of Hopeton. Shrubs, trees and flowers of every description grew in profusion alongside groves of lemons, oranges and Persian date palms. It was at the request of President Thomas Jefferson that Couper imported two hundred olive trees from France, which soon yielded a superior quality oil.

The Coupers were gracious hosts and the plantation was rarely without guests. Visitors often stayed weeks or months on end; one young couple came to spend their honeymoon on the plantation and stayed until the birth of their second child. It was said that the Hopeton Plantation slave cook, Sans Foix, was unequaled in the entire colony.

John Couper earned the respect of his peers through his experiments with various seeds of sea island cotton that improved its yield. He served as a member of the Georgia legislature and a delegate to the state constitutional convention. When he saw the need for a lighthouse on the southern end of St. Simons, John Couper sold the tract on which it stands today to the United States government for the sum of one dollar.

The accomplishments of John Couper were secondary to the man himself. He said to be an individual of uncommon courtesy with a sharp mind and a quick wit. Couper's genuine love of life was shared with all who knew him. The tall, red-haired Scotsman could laugh at adversity as readily as a well told story and was said to have never been guilty of taking himself too seriously.

James Hamilton, his son, studied at Yale, graduating in 1814. He then travelled to Holland to study water management and land reclamation. Upon his return in 1827, James took over management of the plantation.

James Hamilton Couper was a renaissance man, an archaeologist, a geologist, a conchologist[14], an architect and a historian, though the occupation James most preferred was that of a simple planter. He expanded the family holdings to include the Altama and Elizafield plantations and all prospered. Among the things that can be attributed to James Hamilton Couper was the first scientific production of cottonseed oil and Bermuda grass.

Even though planting was his passion, many architectural designs of James Couper still exist. One site that is certainly breathtaking is the classic Greek temple design of the Mother Church of Georgia in Savannah. Here Couper installed an 1819 Revere and Son bell, from the foundry of revolutionist Paul Revere. The bell still chimes before services and bears a wonderful inscription:

"The living to the church I call, and to the grave I summon all."

Hopeton-on-the-Altamaha at Cannon's Point was left in ruins during the Civil War. James Hamilton Couper died in 1866.

**NEEDWOOD BAPTIST CHURCH
AND NEEDWOOD SCHOOL**

Needwood Baptist Church was organized in 1866 on nearby Broadfield Plantation as Broadfield Baptist Church of the Zion Baptist Association. This structure, built in the 1870s, was redesigned in 1885 when the church moved its congregation here. Its formation and history are representative of religious development in the context of plantation rice culture. The nearby one-room Needwood School provided elementary education for this community from 1907 until desegregation in the 1960s. Both structures are examples of early African-American vernacular architecture.

**At the church 2 miles south of Hofwyl Broadfield Plantation on US 17
GPS Coordinates: N31.28215, W81.440637**

Needwood Baptist Church is said to be the first African American Baptist church erected by free people of color before emancipation. The reference further states that Sherman made his famous promise here to the newly freed slaves of "forty acres and a mule," however, this is likely an error.

General William Tecumseh Sherman torched Atlanta and proceeded with his legendary March to the Sea. Along his route to Savannah, thousands of former slaves joined his expedition walking alongside the troops. Secretary of War, Edwin M. Stanton, was there to greet him and asked if Sherman would take the time to address the African American leaders. General Sherman agreed, the meeting was slated for January 1865. Historians have said that the gathering was held at Needwood Baptist Church, the only reference I have found states that the meeting was south of Savannah, which Needwood certainly is.

The leaders representing the African American community had been slaves themselves, many had purchased their freedom and a number of them were ministers. During the meeting Sherman asked Pastor Garrison Frazier to tell him what freedom meant to him. Garrison's response was very simple. He said, "placing us where we could reap the fruit of our own labor, to have land and turn it and till it by our own labor." Garrison further voiced a concern that a prejudice against his people in the south existed, there was a need of separation because "the prejudice will take years to get over."

Four days later, Sherman responded with Field Order Number Fifteen. The land set aside would be the Sea Islands and a thirty mile portion of property on the South Carolina coast near Charleston. The order stated that each family would receive forty acres of land and later he added the loan of an army mule. Sherman assigned General Rufus Saxton to execute the order. Lands confiscated or abandoned during the Civil War would be turned over to the Freedman's Bureau headed by General Oliver Otis Howard.

Cautiously 1,000 African Americans, former slaves, stepped forward to receive the promised property. Minister Ulysses Houston led the group and the liberated people were given plots on Skidaway Island. They regulated themselves without a need for law enforcement, Minister Houston acted as governor for the community. By summer the group had planted and harvested an abundance of crops.

The order was to grant "temporary provisions for freedmen and their families during the rest of the war." Saxton had erroneously informed the people that "they would be put in possession of lands." Abraham Lincoln, the Great Emancipator, overturned Sherman's Field Order only a month later. Lincoln would not live to regret the action, by April 1865, John Wilkes Booth shocked the nation by assassinating the President.

President Johnson assumed office upon Lincoln's death and during the following summer and fall issued special pardons returning the lands to the former Confederates. Ironically, General Howard was ordered to issue the proclamation returning the lands.

The Needwood Baptist Church School was in operation from 1907 through 1962, when integration was implemented, and the doors were closed forever. The school was probably first owned by the community and later solely supported by the Needwood Baptist Church.

OLD POST ROAD

This road, formerly an Indian trail which paralleled the coast, was used by the Spanish and British. In 1778 it was traveled by Revolutionary soldiers who marched against Fort Tonyn. The first mail service south of Savannah was established over this road in 1763. Later it became a regular stagecoach route.

At Coleridge, a short distance north of the present Waycross Highway, Job Tyson maintained a tavern for travelers along the post road. It was the only hostel between the Altamaha and Satilla rivers and was a regular stagecoach stop.

GA 32 and Post Road at Brantley County line
GPS Coordinates: N31.31137, W81.732718

The stagecoach route between Charleston and Savannah provided the only public conveyance during the waning 1700s between these two cities. By 1800, the route was extended, from Charlotte to New Orleans.

Stagecoaches were little more than covered wagons until 1830, when they began to appear as we see them in the old western movies. Stagecoach travel was not a comfortable experience. Usually, twelve people crowded into a wagon were jolted over rough roads, their luggage stuffed on the floor of the coach allowed no leg room. The only protection from the heat, cold, dust or rain were the leather shades buttoned to the roof and sides of the coach.

The average settler in 1830 could not afford to take the stagecoach and any wealthy traveler would ride in a private carriage. Stagecoach travel was not a popular conveyance during this time, the only saving grace for these coaches was the United States Mail. Carrying the mail was the only way they made a profit at all. By today's standard the cost would be about ninety cents per mile.

Stagecoach travel was slow. It took three days and nights to travel across Georgia from east to west and four days and nights north to south. Accommodations along the route were sparse and did not have the best of reputations. Rooms with private beds were uncommon and passengers often had to bunk together. The food was plentiful enough, the menu usually consisted of salt pork, vegetables and cornbread.

Though stagecoach travel was uncomfortable, the accommodations barely adequate, accidents occurred quite frequently, though passengers were in very little danger. One would survive the bruises from being bounced about on the rutted roads, lice was probably the worst of the amenities at the boarding rooms. Accidents were seldom fatal and contrary to the movies, robberies were virtually unknown.

In 1867, the *Omaha Herald* printed the following rules of etiquette while traveling by stagecoach:

> "STAGECOACH ETIQUETTE: If a team runs away, sit still and take your chances; if you jump; nine times out of ten you will be hurt. In very cold weather abstain entirely from liquor while on the road; a man will freeze twice as quick while under the influence. . .Don't smoke a strong pipe inside especially early in the morning; spit on the leeward side of the coach. If you have anything to take in a bottle, pass it around...Don't swear, nor lop over on your neighbor when sleeping...Never attempt to fire a gun or pistol while on the road...Don't discuss politics or religion, nor point out places on the road where horrible murders have been committed...Don't grease your hair before starting or dust will stick there in sufficient quantities to make a respectable 'tater' patch."

Stagecoaches soon disappeared with the advent of trains. Trains were much more comfortable and faster to one's destination. The Civil War brought much damage to the train tracks all over the nation, but they were quickly repaired, and within a few years travelers could go from one coast to the other in only one week.

Visitor's Center, I-95 South between exits 38 and 42
GPS Coordinates: N31.16469, W81.29223

Honoring Lieutenant David Anderson Everett,
United States Navy returned Prisoner of War from Vietnam

The National Council of State Garden Clubs initiated a campaign to pay tribute to the nation's armed forces by designating state and national highways as "Blue Star Highways." The Blue Star Highway Program began in 1945 subsequent to World War II.

David Anderson Everett was born in Brunswick on January 24, 1947. He earned a bachelor's degree in Forestry from the University of Georgia and enlisted in the Navy that same year. He was selected to the Aviation Officer Candidate program in Pensacola and was commissioned Ensign in 1970. He was eventually promoted to the rank of Lieutenant.

Lieutenant Everett was shot down August 27, 1972, while on a photo escort mission over North Vietnam. He was flying an F4 Phantom belonging to Fighter Squadron 151, operating from the USS *Midway*. Lieutenant David Everett remained a prisoner of war until his release March 29, 1973.

In an interview concerning what sustained him during his trying days in captivity, Lieutenant David Anderson Everett stated:

> "It would have been simple to state that my faith in God sustained me during the ordeal. I well remember my painful first night in Hanoi and finding a cross etched in the plaster wall of my cell. Certainly the crude reminder lifted my hope and religion was a fundamental component of what sustained me in the days that followed. But it was not religious conviction alone that saw me through the crisis, rather a synthesis of my 25 years of living in America. I am grateful for having had the opportunities afforded me. To those many persons who helped so much to lighten the dark days in the prisons of Southeast Asia we remain forever indebted."

The Georgia House of Representative passed House Bill 294 on November 19, 1999, which requires the Department of Transportation to fly the POW-MIA flag year round at each of the rest areas along interstate highways in the state. The bill further states that the Department of Transportation place a plaque at each rest area to indicate Georgia's appreciation of the sacrifices of prisoners of war, those missing in action and their families. The measure passed unanimously.

Endnotes

[1] Freed slaves

[2] Privateer or a pirate with a license to plunder opposing countries sailing vessels.

[3] Soldiers specializing in projectile weaponry.

[4] A dugout or canoe like boat.

[5] Their family held a respected place in the community.

[6] The rector's assistant in the parish.

[7] spade or tool

[8] Indentions etched in the tabby surface.

[9] relief - a wooden carving in the form of a portrait of the Georgia Martyrs.

[10] The name given to the Native American Indian tribe inhabiting the area, in honor of the San Buenaventura de Guadalquini mission.

[11] Missing, his body was never recovered.

[12] Challenge to a duel.

[13] First public building built in Brunswick in 1819, a public school

[14] A scientist who studies shells.

McIntosh County

BUTLER ISLAND PLANTATION

Famous Rice Plantation of the 19ᵗʰ century, owned by
Pierce Butler of Philadelphia. A system of dikes and
canals for the
cultivation of rice, installed by engineers from Holland,
is still in evidence in the old fields, and has been used
as a pattern
for similar operations in recent years.
During a visit here with her husband in 1839-40, Pierce
Butler's wife, the brilliant English actress Fannie
Kemble, wrote her "Journal of a Residence On A
Georgia Plantation," which is said to have influenced
England against the Confederacy.

US 17-GA 25, 1.3 miles south of Darien
GPS Coordinates: N31.35446, W81.445336

The story of Pierce and Frances Anne Kemble Butler has all the ingredients of a thrilling movie of the week and in fact, the story was eventually depicted in a movie. The fifteen year marriage was filled with intrigue, betrayal and in the end, all out war. Neither of the combatants walked away from the marriage unscathed.

Pierce (Butler) Mease was born into the elite of Philadelphia society. He descended from wealth and was in line to inherit the family fortune upon the death of his grandfather, provided he changed his family name to "Butler," which he did without a moment's hesitation. Pierce passed his time following a popular young English actress named, Frances Kemble, around the theater circuit throughout England. He constantly sought out the beautiful young girl, securing employment as a flutist in her orchestra. He showered her with lavish gifts and accompanied her family on various outings and holidays. His purse was always welcomed among her family and friends.

Frances Anne Kemble was born to a much different life. She was born, as they say in a trunk, to a London theatrical family. Her father, Charles Kemble, was a well known Shakespearean actor and her aunt, Sarah Siddons was an extremely popular actress of her day. Fanny, as she was called, began her acting career at age 19, playing Shakespeare's Juliet. She made her United States theatrical debut in 1832, touring from Boston to Washington. She was accompanied by her father and aunt, Miss Adelaide DeCamp and of course, Pierce Butler. Fanny was a huge success. Like the starlets of today, young ladies copied her hairstyle, her image appeared on plates, scarves and souvenirs. Meanwhile her father's investment in the Covent Garden Theatre failed miserably, the Kemble family was near destitute. Financial hardships and Charles Kemble's delicate sensibilities, left Fanny as the sole source of income for the family. Pierce Butler's undying devotion and perseverance combined with the emotional stress of financial responsibility for her family, led Fanny to believe that she had few alternatives but to accept his repeated proposal of marriage. Fanny agonized over the separation between herself and the theatre. She expected that her marriage would allow her to become a financial benefactor of the arts and perhaps, take small parts from time to time. However, Fanny's future husband knew nothing of these ideas.

Frances Anne Kemble and Pierce Butler exchanged vows in a lavish ceremony at Christ Church in Philadelphia on June 7, 1834. From the start, the bride had an unrealistic view of marriage and the groom's attitudes were unwavering. Pierce expected the new Mrs. Pierce Butler to host tea parties and entertain society's elite, becoming an extension of himself and an ornament on his arm. Mrs. Fanny Butler, on the other hand, expected to travel about the United States following a play or theatre company. Fanny's life became much different than she had anticipated. As Miss Fanny Kemble, acclaimed theatrical success and celebrity, Philadelphia society flocked to her side, begging for her attention; as Mrs. Fanny Butler, former actress would be society wife, the same blue blooded Philadelphia socialites snubbed her at every turn. Popular opinion was that a former actress was little more than a common streetwalker.

The newlyweds began housekeeping at the Walnut Street address of Pierce's brother, John. In 1835, the couple moved to a Branchtown, Pennsylvania farm. Fanny and Pierce called the farm Butler Place. The couple spent five years at Butler Place and although they were not happy years for Fanny, she did try to adjust to life as Mrs. Butler.

The marriage began to deteriorate shortly after the vows were spoken. Fanny attempted to make the farmhouse a home by introducing all of the things she loved, such as great literature, music and art. She encountered a cool reception of Pennsylvania society and was soon discouraged. She set aside the effort, keeping to herself and refusing to associate with any of her neighbors. Stories of Fanny's aloofness were whispered throughout the community. When the Reverend George Bringhurst, the rector of the Episcopal House of Prayer in Branchtown, paid a visit, Fanny remained concealed behind a screen during his entire stay. Fanny felt her actions were justified because Reverend Bringhurst appeared without invitation. A local newspaper defined her character by reporting, "nearly all local traditions allude to her haughty demeanor and the scorn with which she regarded the people of her region."

To add to their bitter problems, Pierce expected Fanny to be a gentle, submissive wife supporting his ideals. Fanny views were contradictory, she supported Women's Equal Rights; thus, their conflicting views on a woman's place in society led to vicious battles. Pierce had numerous affairs with many different women. Oddly enough, Pierce's trysts were considered just by the town gossips. People believed that Fanny deserved whatever treatment she received for daring to act superior. Evidence of Pierce's infidelity was revealed when he reportedly participated in a duel with James Schott, who caught Pierce in a very compromising position with Schott's wife.

Fanny and Pierce had two daughters. Sarah, born in 1835, and three years later, Frances Ann. Pierce hired a governess, Miss Amelia Hall, to care for the girls. She was described as having taken over everything in the household, except for the name Mrs. Pierce Butler. When trouble within the marriage could no longer be denied, Pierce used the children as weapons in his battles with Fanny. She was forbidden to care for them, talk to them or have any kind of interaction with them. Amelia was given complete control. Pierce forbid Fanny any communication with her closest friends, Charles and Elizabeth Sedgwick. In fact, he tricked her into breaking this rule by presenting her with a letter from Elizabeth. Fanny assumed that she had been granted permission to open the letter, since Pierce himself had given it to her. Pierce seized this opportunity to say that she had disobeyed him when the letter was opened.

Pierce's grandfather died in 1838. When the will was read, Pierce had inherited two Georgia plantations with a full compliment of slaves. Pierce initially made several trips alone to the Georgia plantation known as Butler Island. He did not allow Fanny to accompany him largely because he did not wish to endure her wrath over the slave issue. Pierce was now a wealthy slave owner, Fanny considered herself a staunch abolitionist. The chasm between the two had widened, creating a marriage in name only.

Rumors that her husband was living with a slave woman during his visits to the Georgia plantation were repeated to Fanny. She was livid over the latest infidelity and in an effort to rekindle their relationship, Fanny begged to accompany her husband to Butler Island in late 1838. Fanny remained at Butler Island a little over a year.

Fanny was both enthralled by the natural beauty of the landscape and horrified over slavery. She found the landscape to be lush and green, even in the depths of winter. But even the splendor of her surroundings was not enough to shield her from the cruelty of human bondage. Though Butler Island Plantation slaves were dealt with fairly and for the most part, compassionately; Fanny was aghast at their human condition. She was looked upon by the slaves as a sympathetic emissary from the day of her arrival. Fanny became a mediator between the slaves and Pierce Butler. They begged clothing, food and additional medical care and Fanny took their requests to Pierce. To his credit, Pierce acted on the requests. Butler Island slaves were among the most well cared for in the area.

Butler Island was a very successful rice plantation, the slaves worked under a task system that was common for plantations of this type. They were assigned certain tasks to be completed over the course of the day. Upon completion of those tasks, the slaves were free to pursue endeavors of their own. If they chose to sell wares they had created, the slaves were allowed to keep the majority of the profits.

Fanny despised the very thought of slavery, although she thought of the slaves as little more than pets. They were creatures who deserved no more than they received and she was very content to have them serve her. Fanny's elitist attitudes were evenly distributed to those she considered beneath her including her neighbors. She was a walking contradiction, Fanny expected to be independent, yet well care for; she wanted all the best things of life and abhorred materialistic people. Fanny embraced the abolitionist cause and expected slaves to cater to her every whim. She concluded that, even though, she was unwilling to give up the comforts that slavery afforded her, slavery for the sake of supporting a vast plantation was wrong. Obviously, slavery became a very hypocritical issue for Fanny.

A story related later in her memoirs told of how mutton was served at the Butler table. Although she thought the meat was very tasty, Fanny was astonished to find that no recognizable cut of meat was brought to them, no shoulder or leg of mutton. When she inquired, Fanny was told that the carpenter was also their butcher. He knew but one way to cut the meat, in squares. Because of this, one sheep only provided for dinner four times rather than the standard six.

Fanny often summered by herself in Massachusetts and spent one year in Europe alone. After a series of separations over the next eight years, Fanny finally left her husband for good in 1844. Fanny traveled to England alone, returning to the theatre to support herself. Pierce filed for divorce in 1845 alleging that Fanny had "...willfully, maliciously, and without due cause deserted him." Fanny at first denied the desertion, then stated that the separation had been by mutual consent. She stated that if desertion had indeed occurred, that it was justified by the insufferable treatment from Pierce. Fanny wrote a sixty page book entitled *Narrative,* which was referred to in the divorce court as "a historical sketch of matrimonial discord." The court threw it out as prejudicial.

The divorce of Pierce Butler and Fanny Kemble was finalized in 1849; litigation was long and drawn out because Fanny refused to appear in court. The decision, made by Judge King, established a precedent concerning spousal desertion in Georgia. It has since been referred to in hundreds of cases since that date. After the divorce, Fanny resumed her maiden name and returned to England. She was granted an allowance of $1500 per year, the mortgage to Butler Place and permission to see her daughters two months each summer. As a result of the divorce, Pierce wrote *Mr. Butler's Statement* in response to Fanny's earlier diatribe.

Fanny kept a journal of all she had witnessed at the Butler Island Plantation. The result was a much noted work of historical literature, *Journal of a Residence on a Georgian Plantation in 1838-1839.* Largely due to pressure from the Butler family, she refrained from publishing her text, although the manuscript was repeatedly revised and circulated among her friends. During the Civil War, Fanny decided she had waited long enough and published the journal she had kept twenty-five years earlier. Her vivid descriptions of the treatment of slaves were credited with ensuring British neutrality during the Civil War, although it is not known how much credence can be placed on this claim. The bombing raids of the German blitz during World War II destroyed most official documents in Britain, Fanny's influence on Britain's neutrality during the Civil War remains a mystery.

Fanny gave dramatic Shakespearean readings to support herself in both the United States and England after the divorce. She lived in Lenox, Massachusetts, in a cottage next to her once forbidden friends, Elizabeth and Charles Sedgwick. After her daughters were married, she lived periodically with each of them. She came back to Philadelphia often. On July 14, 1860, she traveled to see her grandson, Owen Wister, who had just been born to her daughter Sarah. In the autumn of 1872, she vacationed in Rome with the Wister family. It was during this particular trip that she met and befriended Henry James. The two remained close friends throughout their lives. James wrote that Fanny, who was ever the temptress, was "...one of the consolations of his life." After Pierce's death in 1867, Fanny returned to Butler Place. Butler Place, consisting of 83 acres, was sold in 1916 for $800,000. The house was torn down in 1925 to make room for 500 rowhouses.

After the divorce, Pierce gambled away his fortune. He was forced to sell much of his Philadelphia property and most of his Georgia slaves with auctioned off in 1859. After losing the respect of Philadelphia society during the Civil War for his southern sympathies, U.S. Marshals arrested him under the suspicion of gunrunning for the Confederacy. He was later released on the condition he kept his Southern sympathies quiet. After Lincoln's death, Pierce refused to drape his windows in black crepe as instructed by the city government. This defiance of Union authority was the final straw, a raid was planned against his house. Oddly enough, the attack was averted by the abolitionist Morris Davis. Pierce Butler contracted malaria in 1867 and died alone.

Frances Anne Kemble died at the age of 84 in London on January 15, 1893, while being helped to bed by her maid. In a letter to her daughter, Henry James wrote a tribute to his dear friend:

> *"She went when she could, at last, without a pang. She was very touching in her infirmity all these last months—and yet with her wonderful air of smouldering embers under ashes, she leaves a great image—a great memory."*

The Butler Island Plantation

FAMOUS BUTLER AUTHORS

Pierce Butler and his daughter, Frances, who shared his interest in the South, returned to Butler Island in 1866, and worked to rehabilitate the plantation. Pierce Butler died in 1867 but Frances continued for several years to manage the island acreage. She wrote a book "Ten Years on a Georgia Plantation," an interesting and valuable account of life in this section during Reconstruction. Owen Wister famous author of "The Virginian" and other novels was the son of Sarah Butler, sister of Frances. He often visited Butler Island Plantation.

US 17-GA 25, 1.3 miles south of Darien
GPS Coordinates: N31.35446, W81.445336

No discussion of Famous Butler Authors would be complete without beginning with Frances "Fanny" Kemble Butler, the matriarch of the Butler Family. Fanny Kemble was the mother of writer, Frances "Fan" Butler Leigh and grandmother of Owen Wister, son of her daughter Sarah.

Although Fanny was never allowed to publish during her marriage to Pierce Butler, *Journal of A Residence on A Georgian Plantation*, her most notable work, was written while she was married on any scraps of paper she could find and in letters to Elizabeth Sedgwick. Pierce forbid Fanny to publicly release any of her works, her abolitionist views contradicting Pierce's pro-slavery stance. Pierce inherited the vast rice plantation on which Fanny's book depicted the lives of Butler Island plantation slaves, discrediting the Butler family name. Pierce, with his wandering eye and gambling habits, was fully capable of tarnishing the family name with no help from Fanny.

Fanny did not publish until fourteen years after her divorce. During the marriage, Pierce used access to their daughters to keep his wife silent and later, threats from the Butler family frightened her into submission. It was England's support of the cotton producing South that finally drove Fanny to keep quiet no longer. It is said that her book turned the tide in England against the South and kept England out of the war. The book had little effect in America during the war largely because by the time the book was released the war was all but over. The work is written as a series of letters to Elizabeth Sedgwick, a close friend and Philadelphia neighbor.

These letters detailed Fanny's view of the thoughts and feelings of slaves while going about the daily course of their lives. Many chapters of her most famous work were written on a singular aspect of a slave's life and how the author was affected. Fanny Kemble Butler wrote a number of other works. Her *Journal of Frances Anne Butler,* published in 1835, was her first work to bring scandal to the Butler name. Fanny went on to publish other works of less notability including: *Records of a Girlhood* in 1878, *Records of a Later Life* in 1882, *Notes Upon Some of Shakespeare's Plays* in 1882, *Far Away and Long Ago* in 1889 and *Further Records* in 1891. Fanny died in London on Jan. 15, 1893.

Frances Butler, born to Fanny and Pierce Butler in 1838, married the Reverend James Wentworth Leigh, Dean of Hereford. Fan, as she was known, was much more sympathetic to the southern cause than either her mother or sister Sarah. Fan lived in the North for the majority of her life; thus, romanticizing her view of slavery and southern traditions. Her father exercised great influence over the young girl, slanting her views toward the South. When Fan arrived at Butler Island Plantation, her first images as an adult were of a defeated South with freed slaves that had no idea how to or the desire to live apart from the land on which they were raised.

Fan worked very hard to ensure the former slaves were treated fairly, educated and cared for. It was during this time that Fan wrote, *Ten Years on a Georgia Plantation*. Fan wrote a passage that sums up her thoughts of slavery and though she never spoke of it specifically, her view of the book authored by her mother.

"The accounts which have been written from time to time have been written either by travellers, who with every desire to get at the truth, could but see things superficially, or by persons whose feelings were too strong

either on one side or the other to be perfectly just in their representations. I copy my impressions of things as they struck me then, although in many cases later events proved how false these impressions were, and how often mistaken I was in the opinions I formed. Indeed, we very often found ourselves taking entirely opposite views of things from day to day, which will explain apparent inconsistencies and contradictions in my state-ments; but the new and unsettled condition of everything could not fail to produce this result, as well as the excited state we were all in."

Writing formats were in a transitionary period during this time. The use of letters was fading. Journals concerning the thoughts and impressions were now being bound, composing most books. Narratives were becoming increasingly more popu-lar.

In the end, Fan was very accepting of the changes that befell the South, even though understanding the newly freed man's actions and motivations came with more difficulty. The fact that the majority of the freed slaves returned to their Butler Island home to work as share croppers spoke volumes as to their treatment there. A reflection of how much the former Butler Island plantation slaves cared for the only home most had ever known was revealed when, after the Civil War, the furnishings, live-stock and effects of Butler Island, left in the care of slaves, were in perfect condition. Those holdings left in the care of the white overseer were either ill-used or sold for his personal benefit.

Fan cared for the former slave's medical needs, saw to their education and provided religious ministering to all of the "Butler" people. However, now that the freed men were sharecroppers, they felt they only were responsible for a 'share' of the work. The former slaves were unable to view the entire process of crop production. Without specific guidance for their day to day tasks, the sharecroppers were unable to understand that each day's work was progressive and each step must be followed to gain a successful harvest.

It became painfully obvious that Butler Island Plantation would no longer be successful. The toll was finally too much for Fan Leigh. Fan, her husband and family left to live in England in 1877. The plantation was again in the hands of an overseer. Owen Wister was the last member of the Butler family to live at Butler Island Plantation.

Owen Wister was born to staunch abolitionists, Dr. Owen and Sarah Butler Wister, in 1860. The family harbored much interest in the pursuit of art. Wister's mother was an accomplished pianist and the family frequently traveled to Europe from their Pennsylvania home. Owen attended private schools in Switzerland and England, studied at St. Paul's School in Concord, New Hampshire, finishing his education at Harvard University.

After graduating from Harvard in 1882, Wister studied music for two years in Paris, eventually giving up the idea of a musical career due to poor health. He returned to the United States, where he worked as a bank clerk in New York. He spent time, on the advice of his physicians, in the West to restore his health in 1884. Owen Wister became enamored with that part of the country. He entered Harvard Law School in 1885, graduating in 1888, and for a short time, practiced law in Pennsylvania before devoting himself to writing. He married his cousin, Mary Channing in 1898, the couple had six children.

Owen Wister spent time in the late 1800s at his families' Butler Island plantation. However, in 1901, it became apparent that the family could no longer maintain the property and it was leased to William and Emma Strain. The Strain's purchased the property in 1805. Butler Island Plantation had belonged to the Butler family for over 110 years. By 1923, the descendants of the Butler family sold all its remaining property in Georgia.

Owen Wister took summer sabbaticals to the West and based on these travels, he wrote numerous stories of Western fic-tion. His first story, *'Hank's Woman,'* published in *Harper's,* launched his career as a writer. Beginning with his first experi-ence in Wyoming in 1854, he kept detailed journals and notes. These were published as *Wister Out West* in 1958, posthumous-ly.

After a conversation with Theodore Roosevelt, a classmate from Harvard, in 1891, Wister began writing stories of America's last frontier. These stories paved the way for his novel, *The Virginian: A Horseman of the Plains* published in 1902. The book is dedicated to Theodore Roosevelt and was later illustrated by Frederic Remington. The story tells of a modest, quiet hero, who is more comfortable with his horse than people. The tale was a great success and has been retold four times in film. *The Virginian* displayed a picture of the West as heroic and awe inspiring. However, in modern times the work has met with criticism as being too wholesome and patriotic.

The Virginian was Wister's only western novel. Instead he began writing short stories of cowboy fiction. Over the next two decades, Wister produced a variety of different works from *Philosophy 4*, about his life at Harvard, to *Lady Baltimore*, a novel addressing the aristocracy of Charleston, as well as several children's stories. In 1930, Wister penned *Roosevelt: The Story of a Friendship, 1880-1919,* his most notable work. The work was lovingly written about his friend Teddy Roosevelt. A compilation of his works was published in 1928, comprising eleven volumes.

Owen Wister died on July 21, 1938, at Kingston, Rhode Island. His works of the American West did much to popularize cowboy stories so widely read during this era. Owen Wister was the last of the Butler Authors and the end of an era.

As the Revolutionary War grew near the land holdings of General Lachlan McIntosh expanded. Named General's Island in honor of Lachlan's military rank, the island is located directly adjacent to the town of Darien. The location was ideal, there was enough water to flood the fields during the various stages of rice cultivation, the rich soil proved ripe for growing and transportation was easily accessible.

Lachlan McIntosh was granted 500 acres of General's Island and purchased an additional 500 acres. Together with sixteen slaves, he developed the land into one of the most productive rice plantations of the area. His mentor, financial backer and friend, Henry Laurens of Charleston, purchased 900 acres on the adjoining Broughton Island. Laurens was an absentee plantation owner. Lachlan kept a watchful eye on the Broughton Island Plantation.

The rice plantation slaves worked on the task system. The driver assigned each slave the tasks to be completed that day. The driver was usually a dependable slave, who had proven himself worthy of a leadership position, keeping the work moving, his importance was second only to the manager. The driver's job was particularly important because each step of the planting, growing and harvesting process was crucial to the success or failure of the year's crop.

The land was plowed and harrowed to prepare for spring planting. The seeds were dropped by hand in April and covered with the aid of a small hoe. During sprout flow, the first field flooding, the water level would cover the seeds. The water level would remain constant until the seeds began to sprout. The fields were then drained and the grain was allowed to develop. In May, when the rice was well established, the fields would be weeded and flooded again with the point flow, increasing the water level so that it covered to tops of the plants. After a few days, the water was gradually drained until it half covered the plants this was known as the long flow. The long flow remained until the plants were able to stand firm, then the water was slowly drained away. The slaves would carefully loosen the soil around each plant to encourage maturity. After the fields were weeded again, the lay-by flow began until the plants were completely underwater. The rice would remain submerged for about two months. Occasionally, the water would be drained away and clean water allowed to flow in through trunks or flood gates. This process prevented the water from stagnating.

Harvesting of the April rice began in September. The lay-by flow was completely drained away and the grain was cut with rice hooks or sickles. The rice was left to dry overnight, then gathered and tied into sheaves. The sheaves of rice were then threshed to remove the grain, during this period threshing was done by beating the stalks with flails.[1] If the rice was to be sold rough, it was then shipped to the agent. If the rice was to be sold clean, it was husked and strained for debris. After cleaning, the rice would be packed in tierces or barrels and shipped to market at Charleston.

In addition to rice, Lachlan also operated a sawmill that produced lumber and shingles. By 1776, he included a mercantile in his endeavors, again backed by Henry Laurens. Lachlan had amassed property amounting to about 14,000 acres by this time; however, the Revolution was upon them and with it came near disaster.

Lachlan suffered great financial hardship due to the war. He discovered that in addition to his financial straits, Lachlan was about to lose General's Island and Henry Laurens was in danger of losing Broughton Plantation as well. The properties had not been registered at the conclusion of the war and were about to be declared vacant. Lachlan used every political tie he had to preserve the properties. Eventually, he was able to gain the renewal certificates and the ownership of both Broughton and General's Island was secured.

Lachlan's finances never recovered. Taxes and debts from attempting to maintain the vast land holdings was a constant strain. Notices began to appear selling parcels belonging to Lachlan McIntosh. By 1799, both his sons, John and William had died; so too had his mentor Henry Laurens. Georgia mourned frequently as its honored war heroes died one by one. In February 1806, Lachlan McIntosh was given a full military funeral with all of the honors due him.

General's Cut, named in honor of Lachlan McIntosh, was dug using slave labor in 1808. The canal went through the marsh grass, crossed the river at Darien's wharf and connected the Darien and Butler Rivers. The canal decreased the time it took to travel from Darien southward to St. Simons. A ferry began providing public transportation between the two ports. In March 1919, a project was undertaken to clear *General's Cut*.

DARIEN

This is Darien, in the heart of the historic Altamaha delta region. Settled in 1736, by Scottish Highlanders under John McIntosh Mohr, it was named for the ill fated settlement on the Isthmus of Panama. The first military parade in Georgia was held in Darien, February 22, 1736, when Gen. James Edward Oglethorpe reviewed the Highland Company in full regalia, with claymores, side arms and targes. The Highland Company supported Oglethorpe in all his campaigns, and won everlasting fame on the field of Bloody Marsh. During the Revolution, Darien men again came to the front - Gen. Lachlan McIntosh, Col. Wm. McIntosh and Col. John McIntosh were among the heroes of that War. In 1818 the City of Darien was chartered, and became the County Seat. The Bank of Darien, chartered in 1818, was the strongest Bank south of Philadelphia, with branches in 7 Georgia cities. Huge mills sawed into lumber millions of feet of timer rafted down the river. Darien was one on the great ports of the Eastern Seaboard. It was burned in 1863 by Northern troops stationed on St. Simon's Island. Rebuilt in the 1870s. Darien again became a great port, and the mills sawed lumber to be shipped all over the world. Depletion of the forests brought this era to an end in the early 1900s.

US 17-GA 25 at the Altamaha River Bridge, Darien
GPS Coordinates: N31.36925, W81.434859

John McIntosh Mohr[2] and Hugh Mackay gallantly led 177 men, women and children to Barnwell's Bluff, site of Old Fort King George, in January 1736. The resilient band of Scots were to settle on the banks of the Altamaha River. General James Edward Oglethorpe had handpicked these people known as the "World's Finest Fighting Force." Their purpose was to man an outpost, defending the newly founded colony of Georgia against the Spanish army. The Scottish Highland Soldiers would succeed where many English soldiers before them had fallen.

The Scots began building their settlement and Captain Dunbar, who had sailed with the band from Inverness on the *Prince of Wales,* wrote to the Georgia Trustees, "The Scotts have settled at Barnwell's Bluff on the Altamaha and desire their town shall be called Darien." The name was taken from the disastrous Darien Scheme.

The Darien Scheme was masterminded by William Paterson in 1693. Paterson had acquired great wealth through the East

Indian Company and was the founder of the Bank of England. The scheme included a group of Scotsmen who were to establish trade with Africa and the Indies, route a course from the Atlantic to the Pacific and make a fortune while maintaining Scottish independence from England. The Scots were so enamored by Paterson's Darien Scheme that they sank over half of the country's funds into the endeavor. By July 1698, five ships set sail from Leith, Scotland. The venture was doomed from the start. Paterson had not understood the vast expanse of the Pacific Ocean and the trip, which was planned for three months, actually took four. When the sick and starving Scotsmen arrived in Caledonia, they found Paterson's worst mistake, the Spanish were already there.

The Scotsmen built a rough settlement and named it Darien. The first fighting began between the Scots and Spanish only two months after the Scottish ships landed, one of the Scottish ships was taken. A report was dispatched to Edinburgh begging for supplies, the English issued a proclamation that no one was to trade with the Scots. The desperate situation escalated to unbearable by June. The Scots were plagued by disease and finally made the decision to abandon their settlement and return home. Paterson, the only dissenter, was forced to relent, being very ill himself.

The return journey was no easier, another 150 people died. They were forced to abandon one ship in Jamaica and another in New York, a third ship was abandoned at sea. When the sick and weary band of Scotsman reached their homeland, only one ship remained. A second expedition had been dispatched before the first group arrived in Scotland. However, this group lasted less than a year before they too were forced to retreat by the Spanish. The Darien Scheme resulted in over 2000 lives lost and devastated the economy of Scotland. In the end, Scotland had no choice but to bend to England's rule and the Act of Union was signed.

When General James Oglethorpe began recruiting settlers and soldiers in 1732 to colonize Georgia, the Scots quickly accepted the offer. A new brave band of Highland warriors had high hopes for the "New World." The Highlanders arrived on the banks of the Altamaha River in 1733 and named their settlement, New Inverness, with much hope for the future. Cannon were placed at Fort King George, huts were built for the soldiers and their families and a small kirk or church for their newly ordained minister, Reverend John McLeod of the Isle of Skye.

Oglethorpe made his first visit to New Inverness in February 1736. He wore the Highlander garb to honor his hosts and was presented with the first military parade in Georgia. The proud Scottish Highlanders were quite impressively displayed in full uniform and weaponry. General Oglethorpe would return again that summer to survey the area and lay out the town squares. The District of Darien was created to encompass what is now known as McIntosh County.

The Battles of Gully Hole and Bloody Marsh distinguished the Scottish Highlanders in battle. Oglethorpe's substantial contingent consisted of a small force of British soldiers, the fierce Highlanders and their Native American allies. The Spanish were soundly defeated, never to threaten Georgia territory again. Oglethorpe lost only one man on the field of battle, his death was a result of the intense July sun.

New Inverness became Darien and was incorporated in 1816. The county seat was established there two years later, after it was moved from Sapelo Bridge. Darien experienced a period of profound growth during this time, the city was renown as a great port of export. Regular steamboat service had been established by 1819 between Darien and the interior Georgia capital of Milledgeville.

Timber export managed to sustain the town of Darien. Huge rafts of timber were floated down the Altamaha from the state's interior. The sawmills were producing over 20 million board feet of lumber per year during the boom time. However, by the early 1900s, the forests were depleted and the lumber industry gradually died.

Today, Darien is a relaxed community with a population of approximately 1,800 people. It is a self proclaimed "Fisherman's Paradise," with fish camps scattered along the coastline. Darien has a rich historical feel about it as visitors wander along the waterfront park among the tabby ruins, which have graced her shores for over two hundred years. Tied along the city dock are shrimp boats with their nets hanging high. The call of sea birds can be heard as they swoop to feed on the remains of the days catch. Darien's history remains a vital part of her present and has much to offer; from picnicking, walking the quaint town, biking on her endless bike paths or simply relaxing in a place that has withstood the test time.

Darien Waterfront

FORT DARIEN

Fort Darien, laid out by General James Edward Oglethorpe in 1736, was built on this first high bluff of the Altamaha river to protect the new town of Darien. It was a large fortification, with two bastions and 2 half bastions, and was defended by several cannon. From the time of its settlement by Scottish Highlanders in 1736, until after the Battle of Bloody marsh in 1742, the town of Darien was in constant danger from the Spaniards of Florida. Often for weeks at a time the Highland soldiers were absent from home on military campaigns, with only a few men left to guard the women and children who, for safety, lived within the walls of the fort. On several occasions the post was fired upon by Spaniards or their Indian allies. After the War with Spain was ended, the fort, no longer needed, fell into ruins, but was rebuilt and armed during the Revolutions, when it again saw action, this time against British forces.

US 17-GA 25 at the Altamaha River Bridge, Darien
GPS Coordinates: N31.3686, W81.434859

General James Oglethorpe, realizing that the women and children of Darien would be alone in the settlement much of the time, built Fort Darien for their protection. The fortification, on a high bluff overlooking the Altamaha River, was built with thick tabby walls to withstand considerable punishment. The thick tabby construction was fortified with two bastions, two half bastions and ten cannons. The women and children of Darien would be safe within the fortification's walls.

While Darien's men were away fighting the Spaniards, French or Native Americans, the women of Darien quite literally held the fort. Colonial women were thought of little more of than property, however, the Highlanders held different beliefs. The Scottish Highlanders felt that it was a woman's right to own property and protect that which was hers. To this end, the Scottish women were fierce in defense of things dear to them. They were able to shoot muskets, fire cannons and wield a sword or dagger if necessary. The pride and bravery of the Scottish soldier was meek compared to that of the Scottish woman protecting her home and family. The women of Darien planted, cared for and harvested gardens to feed the city, tended the cattle that would be eventually sold to provide meat for the soldiers at Frederica and protected their homes in the absence of their men.

After the Spanish relinquished Florida, the fort saw only limited use. Although the fort was restored during the American Revolution, shortly after the war, Fort Darien soon fell to ruin. The only remains of Fort Darien's short life are tabby ruins. Today, the Darien Welcome Center occupies the site. Behind the Welcome Center on the north bank of the Altamaha River is a beautiful waterfront park built by the city of Darien. There, visitors can enjoy the serenity of the river as the current pulls it along the shore.

FORT KING GEORGE
- 1 mile-

The site of Fort King George first fort on Georgia soil built by the English. Erected by the colony of South Carolina in 1721, 12 years before the Georgia Colony was founded.
This fort served as a barrier against the Spanish in Florida, French in the interior and their Indian allies for about a decade.
Soldiers who died in service are buried nearby in a graveyard lost for 200 years. Some of the graves are marked now. Others are on the site of a 16th century Spanish Mission.

US 17-GA 25 0.8 mile at the Altamaha River Bridge, Darien
GPS Coordinates: N31.3686, W81.434859

After the founding of Charles Town, Carolina, in 1670, the English settlers began to venture south. The Spanish, who had long before established missions to convert the Native Americans to Christianity, were forced further south to St. Augustine. Fearful of being surrounded on all sides by hostile forces, Colonel John "Tuscarora Jack" Barnwell was dispatched to England to request the establishment of a post on the Altamaha River. The French were established along the Mississippi River and on the Gulf of Mexico and to the south, the Spanish, both were decisive threats. The French had begun to infest the Altamaha shores and the Spanish were ready to battle for control of the territory. The English Board of Trade approved the establishment of a field fortification at the mouth of the Altamaha River; thus, Fort King George was born.

The Altamaha River protected the fort from invasion to the north, while a moat encased the remaining three sides. Inside the moat were palisades or sharpened posts to ward off a land attack and a third line of defense was six foot tall parapets or an embankment made of rocks and soil, providing additional protection to the soldiers within. Steps leading to the tops of parapets were in place to provide a safe haven for the loading and firing of handheld weapons.

Along the fort's riverside were fascines or sheaves of wood to serve as a barrier of defense. A sentry box or centinel contained a posted guard with a bell to warn of invasion. Nine large bore cannons faced the river for long range targets and

Fort King George reconstructed

several small bore cannons were in place to destroy targets within a shorter range. The fascines held an opening called a water gate to bringing fresh water into the fort. The fort's major line of defense was the blockhouse, a gabled, three storied structure. Weapons, ammunition, gun powder and supplies were housed on the first floor, a gun room with cannon ports on all sides encompassed the second, the third level was used as a lookout post. The other buildings within the palisade walls were a hospital, guard house, officer's quarters and barracks for the enlisted men. A brick kiln used for baking was near the enlisted barracks as well as a pillory and stock[3] used for discipline. A supply boat provided food, rum and news from the outside world every ten days.

For seven agonizing years, the English Independent Company withstood the hardships of their remote post. Disease, threats from the Spanish, French, Native Americans and fear of the unfamiliar territory were the hazards constantly faced by the Fort King George soldiers. In 1727, the garrison abandoned the fort and returned to Charles Town. Only two lookouts were left behind to man the post and warn of an assault from the south. Though the fort was abandoned, it served as the first established British domain of what would become known as Georgia.

Today, the fort has been reconstructed to appear as it did in 1721. Visitors may take a self guided tour of the fort and other displays depicting the early days of Darien.

MCINTOSH COUNTY

This county, created Dec. 19, 1793 from Liberty county was named for the McIntosh family, early settlers, whose name was associated with most events in Georgia history for many years. John McIntosh, with 170 Highlanders, came to Georgia in January 1735 and founded Darien. George N. Ragan was made Tax Collector of McIntosh County Dec. 23, 1793. County officers, commissioned March 25, 1794 were: William Middleton, Sheriff; John Baillie, Clerk of Superior and Inferior Courts; John Richey, Coroner; George N. Ragan, Surveyor. Joseph Clark was commissioned Tax Receiver on Dec. 21, 1794.

Courthouse on US 17-GA 25, Darien
GPS Coordinates: N31.37028, W81.434178

Before General Oglethorpe established the colony of Georgia, Colonel John Barnwell lobbied the English Crown to establish a fort along the coast between what would eventually be the colony of Georgia and Spanish Florida. Carolinians struggled to maintain a settlement at Charles Town and feared trouble from the French in the west and Spain to the south. Fort King George was established along the Altamaha River in 1721, twelve years later General Oglethorpe landed at Savannah. Life was not easy at the fort. The soldiers detailed there were older men. Disease was rampant, supplies were difficult to obtain and the isolated post was lonely. The death toll was very high and by 1734, the fort was completely abandoned.

General James Edward Oglethorpe founded the colony of Georgia at Savannah in 1733. It was not long before he reached the same conclusions as Colonel Barnwell before him. The need for an outpost at the mouth of the Altamaha River was great. General Oglethorpe convinced a band of Scottish Highlanders, known for their courage and grit, that the lands along the Altamaha could be tamed. By 1735, 177 men, women and children began the arduous journey led by John McIntosh Mohr and Hugh MacKay.

The Highlanders developed their settlement called New Inverness, later to be known as Darien. They placed cannons at Fort King George, built a chapel for worship and public meetings and constructed huts for the women and children. For seven years, they protected and maintained the fortification, until General Oglethorpe called on their services once again.

The Highlanders were called to arms in July 1742, when the Spanish boldly sailed into Georgia waters. General

Oglethorpe stated on numerous occasions, "As Georgia goes, so will all of British North America." He knew that once Spain took the infant colony, like dominoes, the other colonies would eventually fall. Spain would not rest until her flag flew from St. Augustine to Cape Cod.

General Oglethorpe decided that Fort Frederica on St. Simons Island was the place to make a stand. Having spent a good deal of time with the Highlanders and their Creek allies, he learned much about guerilla warfare. He recognized that traditional military manuals detailing formation and stance had no place in the battles they were about to face. The Scottish Highlanders style of attack was to pick a target and charge forward until the target no longer stood. Although the Highlanders fought as a unit, their strike force was completely unorthodox. They did not form lines and neatly march forward, they gathered in a huddled mass then broke and ran as fast as their legs would carry them wielding a broad sword and yelling like a banshee. It's quite possible that the Highlanders would frighten their enemy into submission without engaging them in combat at all.

The Spanish approached Fort Frederica with confidence, their informants relayed that the little settlement was not heavily fortified and could be easily taken. General Oglethorpe had plotted the Spanish course and knew they would have to pass through the marsh in single file to reach the fort. The Highlanders, Creek Indians and a few British regulars waited silently for the Spanish soldier's approach. As they approached, the column was taken in ambush. The leaders of the column were massacred, the rest fled for their lives in retreat. This engagement is known as the Battle of Bloody Marsh. Only one British soldier was lost, he succumbed to heat exhaustion, another deserted to the Spanish forces.

General Oglethorpe knew that the Spanish would regroup and attack again, so he devised a ploy using the deserted soldier. A message was sent in the hands of a Spanish prisoner with his vow to deliver the draft directly to the deserted soldier. The confidential message stated that the entire British fleet was within hours of the Georgia coast and Spain would surely meet its demise. Of course, as Oglethorpe planned the message reached the hands of the Spanish Commander.

The Spanish realized they were no match for the British fleet and when masts appeared on the horizon, they retreated in fear. The day was won. Spain never threatened the Georgia colony again. The masts on the horizon were a mere coincidence, belonging to ships transporting goods to the colony.

The McIntosh Clan distinguished themselves during the American Revolution. William McIntosh was a Colonel of Light Horse; Lachlan McIntosh served as Brigadier General of the Continental Army and led the Georgia forces; John McIntosh, grandson of John McIntosh Mohr, commanded the troops at Fort Morris, and when told to turn over his fort in surrender replied, "Come and take it," and the list goes on.

At the conclusion of the Revolutionary War, Darien became a part of Liberty County, which was created in 1777. McIntosh County, named for the McIntosh Clan which continued to contribute so much to the area, was established from part of what was Liberty County. The McIntosh county seat was established at Sapelo Bridge and John McIntosh donated property for the construction of a County Courthouse.

Darien became a bustling port, first with cotton and later with timber. The city on the Altamaha River became a very favorable port of call. Like the phoenix rising from the ashes Darien and McIntosh County have experienced grave times and managed to resurrect itself to become the pretty little city beside the Altamaha River once again.

**McIntosh County
Courthouse**

ACH
Oglethorpe Oak
1736

**Traditional site of Oglethorpe's shel-
ter in 1736 upon occasion of his
visit to Darien, a town founded that
year by Scotchmen under his direction.**

Courthouse on US 17-GA 25, Darien
GPS Coordinates: N31.37028, W81.434178

In 1969, a living historical marker fell, the proud Live Oak standing on the Courthouse Square of Darien had sheltered many generations of Georgians over the vast expanse of time. Founding Scottish Highlanders to the current citizens, all enjoyed a moment in the shade of her enormous branches.

During General Oglethorpe's visit to Darien in 1736, the protective oak sheltered his command from the sun and rain; thus, it became "Oglethorpe's Oak." After generations of hurricanes, lightning strikes and destruction by fire, the oak finally succumbed. Only a stump marks the spot of the majestic oak where James Edward Oglethorpe, founder of the state of Georgia, once stood.

THE BURNING OF DARIEN

On June 11, 1863 the seaport of Darien was vandalized and burned by Federal forces stationed on nearby St. Simons Island. The town was largely deserted, most of its 500 residents having sought refuge inland. Lost were public buildings, churches, businesses and most private residences. Conducting the raid were units comprised of among the first African-American troops to serve the Union cause, the 54th Massachusetts Volunteers under Col. Robert G. Shaw, and the 2nd South Carolina Volunteers under Col. James Montgomery. The burning of Darien, undefended and of little strategic importance, was one of the most controversial events of the Civil War.

Darien City Hall, Darien
GPS Coordinates: N31.22093, W81.29039

The day of June 11, 1863, was clear and hot in south Georgia. By 8:00 a.m., the sun would scorch exposed skin to a rosy pink. Colonel James Montgomery, leading the 2nd South Carolina and Colonel Robert Gould Shaw, in command of the 54th Massachusetts, sailed down the Altamaha River to Darien.

Three boats carried the detachments of the 2nd and 54th followed by the gunboat, *Paul Jones.* As the soldiers made their way toward Darien, Colonel Montgomery directed the random shelling of the plantations situated along the banks of the Altamaha as they passed. No regard was given to the number of women and children who occupied the residents and no homesite was spared.

By the time that the detachments reached Darien, the sun was directly overhead and sweltering. The soldiers marched into Darien and found the town virtually deserted. Two women and two slaves were the town's only citizens. Some were said to have watched the plunder from the safety of the nearby forest, while others escaped the grisly scene traveling to inland towns untouched by General Sherman's flanks.

Colonel Montgomery ordered the men to remove everything of value from the town; household furnishings, livestock, food, anything that might bring a price or be of use, was loaded onto the waiting ships. Montgomery then gave the order to burn the town. Colonel Shaw momentarily protested, but after realizing that nothing could be done to bring a halt to the destruction, he sadly watched as the pretty little town of Darien was reduced to ashes. Colonel Montgomery set the final blaze with his own hand.

Montgomery's reasoning for burning a town that offered no threat, discharged no arms against the Union and was virtually barren of all inhabitants,

> '...the Southerners must be made to feel that this was a real war and that the hand of God would wipe them
> from the face of the earth, like the Jews of old.'

Colonel Shaw was disgusted by the act and described it to his parents as a "dirty piece of business." Shaw knew that only two courses were available to him, to keep his opinions to himself and live with a troubled conscience or to refuse to participate in further raids and face a certain court martial. Colonel Shaw chose to keep quiet and obey orders.

Less than one month after the burning of Darien, Colonel Shaw led the 54th Massachusetts Volunteers on an attempt to breach the walls of Fort Wagner. The mission failed and the fort was never taken. Colonel Robert Gould Shaw and more than two hundred of his men were killed.

After the Civil War, Shaw's mother and her friends sent $1,400 to the Darien Episcopal Church in memory of her son. She called the disaster an "unjustifiable and cruel deed" and offered her son's correspondence as proof that he detested the incident.

West of US 17-GA 25 at Jackson and West Third Streets, Darien
GPS Coordinates: N31.37174, W81.436554

The Scottish Highlanders were so devoted in their beliefs that when they sailed for the American colonies with them was their minister, the Reverend John McLeod. One of the first structures built in 1736 was a small Presbyterian chapel or kirk, as they called it, where they would hold their services. In 1741, a disillusioned Reverend McLeod left the Georgia colony for Carolina.

The Meeting House was built about 1750, serving dual purposes as a Presbyterian place of worship and a place to conduct governmental affairs. Spiritual services were held only when a Circuit Rider was available or a laymen took the pulpit. The Meeting House provided services until the early 1800s.

In 1809, the Presbyterian congregation began to gather at the Courthouse at Sapelo Bridge. The parishioners still had no full time minister; however, over the next twenty years Reverend William McWhir served as itinerant minister whenever he traveled through the area. If Darien was the cradle of Presbyterianism in Georgia, then Reverend McWhir should be known as "the hand that rocked the cradle." He kept the Darien congregation active as well as providing a guiding hand for all South Georgia Presbyterians. Reverend McWhir died in 1851.

The Georgia Legislature granted a charter to "The Independent Church of Darien, Georgia" in 1820, and a year later amended the charter to read, "First Presbyterian Church of the City of Darien." During this time, the congregation moved their services from the Sapelo Courthouse into the city of Darien. The First Presbyterian Church was the first church built in Darien and was constructed at the center of town. The Reverend S. S. Davis became the first full time minister and ordained Ruling Elders of Session including General John McIntosh, James Nephew, John McIntosh Kell and Ebenezer Rees.

A devastating blow struck the Darien Presbyterians, when in 1826, during the span of one year, three of the Ruling Elders died. General John McIntosh, James Nephew and John McIntosh Kell's loss was lamented in the church records. In 1828, the deceased Elders were replaced, but within the next five years, they too would move to other cities or die. Even though the loss-es were deeply felt, the congregation continued on and slowly began to prosper.

By 1861, the First Presbyterian Church recorded a membership of 120 people. It is interesting to note that of that 120 members, sixty-one were listed as African Americans, concluding that both White and African Americans attended services together. Churches of this time had balconies that the slaves were allowed to sit in for worship service, many times the white children of the congregation were cared for in those balconies by the slaves.

One itinerant minister of the Presbyterian church was Joseph Williams. Joseph Williams was a free African American and through his work, he successfully brought a considerable number of African American slaves into the Presbyterian church. He was also responsible for the mission at Ebenezer church, founded in 1857.

Entries in the Minutes of Session reveal the discipline that the Presbyterian church demanded of its members. White as well as African Americans were excommunicated for transgressions such as neglect of Christian duty, drinking, fighting, swearing, gossip or immorality.

The First Presbyterian Church suffered yet another devastating blow when Montgomery's Raiders and Robert Gould Shaw's 54th Massachusetts Volunteer Infantry of freed African American troops burned the city of Darien. Along with the Episcopal and Methodist churches, the Presbyterian church was burned. Montgomery was known to be ruthless and this was well emphasized when he ordered the destruction of Darien. Shaw, having little choice, followed the orders given by Montgomery.

The city of Darien was little more than a ghost town after the fire. It would be eight years before the Presbyterian church was rebuilt. In 1870, on a lot donated by General John McIntosh, a new wooden church was built. The cost of the construction was approximately $4,100.00 and the funds were raised by church women selling dinners and ice cream. The Reverend John Quarterman served as minister during this time.

A neighboring home caught fire in 1899, the sparks quickly spread to the Presbyterian church and other nearby buildings. Some of the furniture and church records were saved, but the building itself was a complete loss. The Session met immediately and began to make plans for the construction of a new sanctuary. The construction would consist of tabby and stone with a Gothic design. The tabby and stone were less prone to the hazards of fire. The church was completed in September of 1900 and dedicated by former pastor, Reverend A. B. Curry. This edifice is still in use today.

Darien Presbyterian Church

SAINT ANDREW'S EPISCOPAL CHURCH

Saint Andrew's Episcopal Church in Darien received its charter in 1843, under the Rt. Rev. Stephen Elliott, first Bishop of the Diocese of Georgia. The church edifice, a large wooden building with a belfry, erected on a lot a short distance North of this site, was completed in 1844. The Rev. Richard Brown was the first Rector. This building was burned in 1863, when Darien was put to the torch by Federal troops stationed on St. Simon's Island, and for several years after services were held in a little church on The Ridge.
In 1872, James K. Clarke, Mr. Langdon and Donald Munroe headed a movement to rebuild Saint Andrew's in Darien. Other members of the church assisted with money and with work. Plans were secured from England, and the edifice as it now stands, a copy of a little church in Britain, was built.
The church was opened in January of 1879, with the Rev. Samuel Pinkerton as Rector.

Wayne Street at Vernon Square, Darien
GPS Coordinates: N31.36861, W81.432359

St. Andrew's Episcopal Church was chartered in 1843 with the Right Reverend Stephen Elliott, first Bishop of the Diocese of Georgia, officiating the consecration. The original sanctuary was situated to the north of where the church now stands. Reverend Elliott addressed the thirty-ninth Annual Convention of the Protest Episcopal Church in March 1861 with a very eloquent speech. Reverend Elliott's spoke of the unity within the church with regard to the unrest between the northern and southern states. He maintained that, although their membership was dedicated to the church as a whole, they were also citizens of their communities and bound to defend them. He requested that each of the Diocese within the Confederate States meet in Montgomery to discuss the changing civil affairs. Within two years of Elliott's speech, St. Andrew's Episcopal Church of Darien would lay in ashes as a result of the Civil War.

June 11, 1863, Colonel James Montgomery with his 2nd South Carolina Volunteers and Colonel Robert Gould Shaw with his 54th Regiment of Massachusetts Volunteer Infantry, a predominately African American regiment, landed gunboats on the shore of the Altamaha River and began shelling the small city of Darien. After the initial attack, the troops marched into the town and finding it all but deserted, save the infirmed and a few women and children, pillaged everything they could carry and torched the remainder.

The Civil War left the residents of Darien in financial ruin. The parishioners of St. Andrew's were unable to raise the needed funds to rebuild their sanctuary. The parishioners had retreated to inland locations all over the state and beyond. For a time, the Episcopal services were held at the Ridge until the church in Darien could be rebuilt.

In 1869, the Reverend Robert F. Clute took charge of the ministry at St. Andrew's. Reverend Clute and Senior Warden William R. Gignilliat were sent to raise money to rebuild. The two appealed publically in "*Harper's Weekly*" magazine for donations. The article did not portray Colonel Shaw kindly. It was widely thought that Colonel Shaw had been in command on that fateful day when the Union torch was put to Darien.

An unlikely source read the article and responded. Mrs. Sarah B. Shaw of Boston wrote a letter to Reverend Clute in an effort to clear the name of her son. Mrs. Shaw included exerts from correspondence received from her son concerning the "unjustifiable and cruel deed." Great pains have been taken to absolve Colonel Shaw of any wrongdoing in the destruction of Darien. Through letters made public by his mother, his enormous regret and guilt over the matter was revealed. Colonel Montgomery gave the order and although as second in command, Colonel Shaw vehemently voiced his reluctance to bring to ruin a city that held no combatants; however, under the threat of a court marshal, Colonel Shaw complied. After the fact, Shaw wrote two letters disavowing any responsibility for the burning of Darien and questioning the authority of Colonel Montgomery to do so.

The Reverend Clute, in an attempt to make the matter right, issued a retraction in "*Harper's Weekly*" along with his apology to Mrs. Shaw. Family and friends of the late Colonel Robert Gould Shaw, through his mother Mrs. Sarah B. Shaw, donated $1,400.00 toward rebuilding St. Andrew's Episcopal Church in Darien.

Plans for rebuilding began in 1872. Reverend James W. Leigh, husband to Frances "Fan" Butler of nearby Butler Plantation, gathered the plans of an English church that the new sanctuary would emulate. Mr. James K. Clarke, Mr. Langdon and Mr. Donald Monroe, all of Darien, joined together to export the timber for construction. However, it is noted that both Mr. Langdon and Mr. Monroe were financially unable to continue the project. Mr. James K. Clarke, a parishioner of the Methodist church, carried the burden alone.

Construction began in 1876 and was completed in 1879. The church was constructed at the site of the old Bank of Darien at south Vernon Square and Green Street, where it still proudly stands today.

SITE OF BANK OF DARIEN

The old Bank of Darien, in its day the strongest Bank South of Philadelphia, was organized in 1818 with a Capital Stock of $1,000,000. The first Directors on the part of the State were: Thomas Spalding, Scott Cray, John McIntosh, James Troup, James Dunwoody; for the stockholders: Calvin Baker, Barrington King, John Kell, Henry Harford, Jonathan Sawyer.
With Branches in Savannah, Macon, Milledgeville, Marion, Dahlonega, Auraria and Augusta, the Bank of Darien was a powerful force in Agricultural and Commercial activities in Georgia. It also financed the gold fields of North Georgia and North Carolina. An important factor in the economy of the South, the Bank was at one time the depository for $1,400,000 in Federal Revenues. The Bank of Darien became deeply involved in politics, and during the latter years of its operation was the center of bitter controversy. Its charter was terminated by the State Legislature in 1841.

Wayne Street facing Vernon Square, Darien
GPS Coordinates: N31.36861, W81.432359

The Bank of Darien was built on Vernon Square in 1818. Conceived and built largely due to the efforts of Thomas Spalding, the bank's first president. The bank was jointly owned by the state of Georgia and private stockholders. The first bank of Georgia, Planter's Bank, had opened in Savannah only eight years before, but the need for a local bank to serve the citizens of McIntosh and Glynn counties had become obvious. The Board of Directors read like the Who's Who of McIntosh County. Such names appeared as McIntosh, Spalding and Troup among others. Coastal planters needed supplies to maintain their vast plantation and they needed credit.

The Bank of Darien was hugely successful for a short period of time. Branches were opened in all of the notable Georgia cities and the gold fields of both north Georgia and North Carolina received backing from the bank. During the most successful years, the Bank of Darien boasted $1.6 million in revenues. Banks during this time printed their own currency and the coins were minted by the federal government. The bank notes were backed by *specie*[4], the paper notes could be exchanged for gold. Forgery became a major problem because the paper notes were easily copied.

The branch in Dahlonega was built to support the northern Georgia gold rush as miners poured into the area in hopes of that "One Big Strike." The miners needed money for supplies and to stake their claims. Like many things during this era, the gold rush did not last.

Almost from its inception the Bank of Darien experienced fighting among its Board of Directors. Thomas Spalding realized that his days as President were numbered, although it did take time to remove him from office. Anson Kimberly was supported by the state's five directors and Thomas Spalding was supported by the local board. The directors were at an impasse. It was only a twist of fate that one of Spalding's supporters became ill and the state directors called for a vote for the bank presidency. One vote away from maintaining the split decision, Spalding lost his seat.

The nation was in the grips of the National Panic of 1837, Darien's economic condition was no better. By 1839, the Bank of Darien did not have enough *specie* to back the notes in circulation. Disaster struck when the bank discovered the theft of $23,000.00 in gold. The theft forced the bank to withdraw all of its notes and replace them with new currency. The Bank of Darien had suffered a fatal blow.

Governor Charles McDonald notified the Board of Directors that they should withdraw their application for a renewed charter or the state would take action. When the charter came up for renewal in 1841, no one was surprised when the state refused the request. The state of Georgia saw to the liquidation of all bank assets. In 1842, the citizens of Darien saw the end of an era. The Bank of Darien was no more.

Standing in the lobby of the McIntosh County courthouse are two safes that held vast wealth in the lucrative days of the Bank of Darien.

Bank of Darien safe

1836
METHODISTS AT DARIEN

John Wesley, founder of Methodism, spent January 2
& 3, 1737, among the Scots in Darien, where he first
prayed extempore.
In 1836 after many efforts, circuit riders aided by lay-
man F. R. Shackelford organized a Society. On
November 29, 1841, the cornerstone was laid for
Darien Methodist Church on Vernon Square. This
church, set afire twice by Federal troops in 1863 did
not burn and became the rallying site for the rebuilding of Darien. Destroyed in 1881 by a hurricane, it
was replaced in 1883 by the present sanctuary. The
Women's Society, begun in 1878, raised funds for
rebuilding.

Darien United Methodist Church, Vernon Square, Darien
GPS Coordinates: N31.36884, W81.433105

Darien was celebrating the settlement's first anniversary when an unexpected group of visitors arrived, including the Reverend John Wesley. Reverend Wesley, whose journey was waylaid by lack of provisions, was travelling from Savannah to the outer post of Frederica to visit his brother Charles. The trip proved to be longer than anticipated and the group was forced to make an unanticipated stop in Darien. Due to the ongoing celebration, the visit was extended, and Reverend Wesley spent the day at the side of the Scots minister John McLeod.

Reverend McLeod led services as Reverend Wesley looked on with skepticism for the extempore[5] style sermon. Reverend Wesley was asked to lead the benediction and it was there in Darien that he first prayed extempore at a public gathering. Reverend Wesley found it exhilarating to speak as his heart led him and would continue the practice throughout his long and dedicated career.

Reverend McLeod soon left the city of Darien and religious teachings were left to circuit riders for a time. The idea of circuit riders was first promoted by Reverend Wesley in the early days of the colony. These lay preachers were responsible for many churches, travelling on horseback or by mule from site to site. The sites were sometimes so remote that it would take days to reach the settlement. Circuit riders were expected to visit each congregation in his charge at least once during the year and start new churches at settlements where no organized worship existed.

Circuit riders carried all of their meager belongings in their saddlebags. They preached wherever a group would gather and then were on their way to the next needy community. The life was so difficult, that few of these devout souls lived to reach their 30th birthday. Although compensation was barely enough to keep them in basic supplies, such was their devotion that monetary reward was of no consequence. Bishop Asbury, the founding bishop of American Methodism, stated, "Grace here and glory hereafter, if he is faithful, will be given" in regard to the lack of wages and life of hardship that circuit riders endured.

Soon the Methodists of Darien could afford the construction of a permanent place of worship in 1841. For more than twenty years, services were held in the church and then the Civil War reeked havoc on every corner of the south. The raid on Darien left the Darien Methodist Church damaged but still standing. Although the fire was set in two different sections, the church refused to succumb to the flames. Area citizens believed this was a sign from God and used the steadfast Methodist Church as their inspiration to rebuild the city. The Women's Society began selling ice cream and

Darien Methodist Church

chicken dinners while county court was in session, raising the funds required to rebuild the devastation left behind by the Union Army. Even with their resilient Darien spirit, more troubles for the struggling settlement were yet to come.

Darien and McIntosh County suffered the effects of three devastating hurricanes within five years. Over that period not one building was left unscathed. The damaging storms led to the rebuilding of the Methodist Church once again in 1884. The church was completely rebuilt using timbers from the old structure when possible.

The church still stands today as it did in 1884 with the addition of an educational wing completed in the 1950s. Neither fire nor flood could destroy the Methodists at Darien.

DARIEN'S RAILROAD AND DEPOT

In 1889, the Darien Shortline Railroad was organized to transport yellow pine timber to the Darien sawmills from Georgia's interior. Originating in Tattnall County and continuing through Liberty County, the Darien & Western line was completed in 1895 to its terminus near this site where a passenger depot was built, now marked by the gazebo. In 1906 the line was bought by the Georgia Coast & Piedmont Railroad, which extended the line 18 miles south to Brunswick in 1914. The train depot was then moved from Columbus Square to the riverfront near the present U.S. Highway 17 bridge. The depot burned in 1971.

Columbus Square, Franklin and Madison Streets, Darien
GPS Coordinates: N31.37115, W81.432483

Timber was transported along the Altamaha River until 1889. Great rafts of logs could be seen floating down the Ocmulgee and Ohoopie rivers and onto the Altamaha for processing at the sawmills of Darien. In February 1890, the Darien Shortline Railroad began offering limited lumber transport services from the interior lands of western McIntosh, Liberty and Tattnall counties.

By January 1895, the tracks were finally completed. The railroad ran from Belleville to the depot constructed at Columbus Square in Darien. The Darien Shortline Railroad had financial difficulties leading to the creation of the Darien & Western Railroad, still the only connection to points south of Darien was by water. The Darien & Western merged with two other rail systems in 1906, becoming the Georgia Coast & Piedmont Railroad.

Georgia Coast & Piedmont brought many improvements. By 1914, steel bridges fording the south Altamaha and Darien rivers, had been completed. Rail transportation was now available to Brunswick and other southern Georgia towns.

During this time, the lumber industry in Darien was waning. The inland forests had been harvested to a point where only smaller timbers were left standing. The Georgia Coast & Piedmont Railroad went bankrupt in 1919. The bridges and trestlework, however, found a new purpose in 1921, the new highway system was born. Now, an overland paved highway was available to connect Brunswick and Darien. The popularity of the automobile would eventually make rail travel obsolete. Automobile travel was faster and not dependent on steel tracks, only roads which were being built at an amazing pace.

Eventually, the railroad depot was moved to the Darien waterfront, but train travel was virtually a thing of past. Some goods transportation was still done but that too was soon to be overtaken by trucks. The Darien depot burned in 1971 and was never rebuilt.

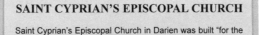

SAINT CYPRIAN'S EPISCOPAL CHURCH

Saint Cyprian's Episcopal Church in Darien was built "for the Colored People of McIntosh County," through the efforts of the Rev. James Wentworth Leigh, D.D., F.S.A., Dean of Hereford, England.
It was named for the martyred African Bishop.
Contributions toward the building of the church edifice were received from England, Philadelphia and from local citizens.
Members of the congregation led by the Senior Warden, Lewis Jackson, gave directly of their time and labor.
Saint Cyprian's church edifice was consecrated, Sunday, April 30, 1876, by the Rt. Rev. John W. Beckwith, bishop of Georgia, and placed under the guardianship of Saint Andrew's Episcopal Church in Darien, of which the Rev. Robert Clute was then Rector.

Fort King George Drive and Rittenhouse Street, Darien
GPS Coordinates: 31.36658, W81.431383

The little tabby church named Saint Cyprian's Episcopal was built in 1876 by former slaves, who worked the nearby plantations. Its construction was attributed to Reverend James Wentworth Leigh. Leigh was an Englishman, married to Frances "Fan" Butler. Reverend and Mrs. Leigh were known to be pro-slavery sympathizers. During the 1870s, Reverend Leigh was the pastor of both the white St. Andrew's Episcopal congregation and St. Cyprian's, which served African American parishioners.

The church's namesake came to the Christian calling at the age of 25. He was so sincere in his belief that he pledged a vow of never ending chastity before his baptism. In 249 C.E., he became a priest and a bishop of Africa.

Bishop Cyprian of Carthage was known for his particular devotion to the Pope during a time when it was not popular. The Bishop wrote many letters of encouragement to the Pope and worked detailing the importance of unity within the church. Pope Cornelius died in exile in 253 C.E. and Bishop Cyprian was beheaded five years later for refusing to denounce the church. Suffering for their beliefs brought Pope Cornelius and Bishop Cyprian sainthood. They share a feast day to remind followers that unity within the church is of utmost importance.

In 1876, St. Cyprians was consecrated by Right Reverend John W. Beckwith, a Confederate Chaplain during the Civil War and aide to General William Joseph Hardee. After the war, he served as a priest in North Carolina, Maryland, Mississippi, Alabama, Louisiana and Bishop of Georgia.

The church operated until 1896, when it sustained significant damage by a hurricane. St. Cyprian's was restored within several months, services were never suspended. St. Cyprian continues to this day to have an active congregation.

St. Cyprian's Episcopal Church

200 YEARS OF SAWMILLING

For nearly two centuries the story of sawmilling in the Southeast was enacted on this point on the Altamaha River. In the summer of 1721, men from South Carolina sawed the 3-inch planks to build Fort King George. In 1736, indentured servants of the Scottish Highlanders set up pit saws here and sawed lumber for the permanent houses of Darien and for public buildings in Savannah and Frederica. This was the first commercial manufacture of lumber in Coastal Georgia. Through the years, sawmilling continued on this site.

In the latter part of the 18th century, a large water mill was constructed and used here, operated by impounding tidal water in a basin on flood tide and sawing with the ebb.

In 1816, the Darien Eastern Stream Sawmill was built here. Designed by an engineer from London, the mill had five gang saws. In use, with brief interruptions, until about 1905. It was then dismantled because of lack of large timber. A circular sawmill, built alongside the same basin, took its place, to be used until the end of the sawmill era in Darien.

Fort King George Historic Site, Darien
GPS Coordinates: N31.3649, W81.417199

Can you imagine the sight of huge cypress and yellow pine rafts drifting down the Altamaha river during the height of the sawmilling era in 1818? The virgin timbers were cut from the forests of inland Georgia and transported on the murky waters of the Ocmulgee and Ohoopie rivers, bound together creating enormous rafts. The rivers would be so thick with cut timber that a man could walk from shore to shore without getting his feet wet. The timbers eventually reached the Darien Eastern Steam Sawmill at Lower Bluff, one mile east of town, where they would be cut into lumber and loaded aboard schooners for delivery as building materials.

Sawmilling began in Darien in 1720. The construction of Fort King George created a need to establish the industry. It would last until the early 1900s when industrious mill owners realized that they had depleted the raw timber resources of Georgia's forests and raw materials were no longer available. During that two hundred year span, the saws of Darien were silenced only once as a result of the devastation that was the Civil War. The saws were reawakened with the boom of Southern Reconstruction in 1870.

Pit saws were first used to produce planking for the construction of Fort King George. As the name implies, huge timbers were rolled lengthwise across a pit in the ground or onto the wooden supports. The operation required the efforts of two men, the man below pushed the thick six to ten foot blade down through the log using the removable lower handle and the man above pulled the saw on the up stroke by a permanently fastened handle called the tiller. The lower handle was removable, so that the saw could be easily removed after the cut was made. The process was slow and labor intensive, by the late 1700s, pit saws gave way to water powered mills.

Tidal mills were utilized during the late 1700s and early 1800s. They employed the use of water to replace the manual labor of men. The incoming tide was held by a gate. When the gate was opened, the rushing water powered a wheel that moved the saws. Innovation again brought forth change, by 1816, steam power replaced the tide dependent water system and a new system of sawmilling was born.

The steam powered gang sawmills of Darien were among the first built in the south. The Darien Eastern Steam Sawmill was established by Jacob Rokenbaugh in 1816, east of Darien at the Fort King George site. The development of steam powered sawmills allowed the lumber industry to grow to its most prosperous, which oddly enough, led to its eventual demise. The steam plant was driven by boilers equipped with grates to burn sawdust and other scrap wood. The tubular boilers produced steam pressure that ran the mill engines and pumps. The engines supplied power to the circular saws, which efficiently cut the timbers into lumber.

The Civil War years brought a halt to the lumber industry, but only for a short time. The South's Reconstruction after the war again propelled Darien to become the leading producer of lumber for the east coast. Lumber warehouses built of tabby were abundant along the Darien waterfront.

A hurricane struck Darien in 1898, scattering timber for miles. The town never completely recovered. The Hilton Lumber Company supplied a new circular saw in the early 1900s to handle the smaller logs that were now being processed. The timber was in such demand that smaller trees were not allowed to grow to their full potential and eventually, the forest was depleted. The 1920s saw the end of the Georgia timber industry, the forests had been virtually clear cut. With the advent of World War I, the timber industry faded into history.

The remnants and artifacts of the three noted methods of sawmilling can be seen at the Fort King George historical site in Darien. Ruins of the steam powered circular sawmill, the mill pond which held tidal waters and the log basin where pit saws produced lumber for the construction of Fort King George are shown in example at the sawmilling site. Along the Darien waterfront are the tabby remains of structures that once warehoused the city's greatest industry.

OLD FORT KING GEORGE

Site of old Fort King George, built in 1721 by Col. John Barnwell, of South Carolina, under British Royal orders. This tiny cypress blockhouse, 26 feet square, with 3 floors and a lookout in the gable from which the guard could watch over the inland Waterway and St. Simons Island, was flanked by officers quarters and barracks, and the entire area was surrounded on all but the river side by a moat and palisades. Garrisoned by his Majesty's Independent Company, with replacements of Colony scouts, the fort was occupied for six years. During that time more than 140 officers and soldiers lost their lives here and were buried on the adjacent bluff. The first of the British 18th century scheme of posts built to counteract French expansion in America. Fort King George was also a flagrant trespass upon Spanish territory, and during its occupation Spain continually demanded that it be destroyed.

The troops were withdrawn to Port Royal in 1727, but until Oglethorpe arrived in Savannah in 1733 South Carolina kept two lookouts at old Fort King George.

At Fort King George Historic Site, Darien
GPS Coordinates: W31.3649, N81.417199

The site Colonel John Barnwell chose for construction of Fort King George had been a well occupied locale for over 200 years. The first tenant was the Spanish Mission, *Santo Domingo de Talaje* Mission, followed by the *Guale* Native Americans tribes, pronounced *Wally*.

Santo Domingo de Talaje was established during the late 1500s. Archeologists have recovered two olive jars, *majolica*[6], a musket butt plate, sword fragments, rosary beads and a Spanish coin. All of the artifacts have been authenticated as belonging to the mission during this period.

The *Guale* Village obviously housed a large tribe. Fifteen huts constructed of wattle and daub, a framework of woven twigs covered with clay, have been unearthed. A clay pit[7] with clumps of clay still intact, a small clay pot with several tiny ears of maize or corn and numerous shards of *Guale* pottery were also found. Warring northern tribes attacked the village in 1661 and the village was burned. The *Guale,* already suffering from disease brought by European immigrants, were in no condition to fight the stronger group of Native Americans. They escaped to nearby Sapelo Island and never returned to the village by the Altamaha River.

Colonel John Barnwell and his garrison built Fort King George, in 1721, with permission of England's Board of Trade. Colonel Barnwell recanted that the marsh appeared as "resembling meadows" with "vast cypress swamps." This cypress swamp proved to be quite useful. He sent his garrison into the swamps to cut cypress for the construction. The group of hired English soldiers, after gathering the timber, refused to begin construction until higher wages were promised. Colonel Barnwell had little choice but to agree.

The Englishmen were fine salary negotiators, but the remote location and harsh conditions were intolerable. The Independent Company of soldiers were middle aged, war weary veterans oriented to milder climate and the comforts of a soft bed. Two-thirds of the company were known to have met an untimely death in one year. They were plagued by extreme heat, biting flies, mosquitoes, malaria, malnutrition and relentless attacks by the Native Americans. Excavation of the site has revealed more than sixty-five graves and fifteen gravestones. It is recorded that more than one hundred and forty officers and soldiers died at Fort King George, without a shot ever having been fired.

At Fort King George Historic Site, Darien
GPS Coordinates: N31.3649, W81.417199

Fort King George was built on the site of this early mission called *Santo Domingo de Asao* or *Talaje* by the Spanish. Missions were established in the primary chiefdoms of the villages, where the chief and his council house were located. Each mission served a much larger American Indian community within the tribe. The average mission housed a chapel and a convent or friary, where only one nun or friar lived. The missions provided religious services and education and were a governmental and economic link between the American Indians and the Spanish.

The *Talaje* mission was established at the mouth of the Altamaha River in 1595. Five other missions were also built amid the *Guale* chiefdoms along the Georgia coast. The *Guale* tolerated the friars for two years, until their interference in tribal matters grew tiresome. Although it was allowable for the friars to command religious affairs, in matters of tribal government, the friars were clearly subordinate to the *Guale* Chiefs. In 1597, the *Guale* rebelled. All of the residing friars were killed with the exception of one, who managed to escape. The missions were burned and the sites were abandoned by both the Spanish and the *Guale*.

The *Guale* chiefs sent a messenger to the Spanish village and requested that the missions be reestablished in 1605. Several original missions were rebuilt and many inland missions were established from the forks of the Altamaha across the wetlands of the Okefenokee Swamp to the Alapaha and Withlacoochee Rivers. The *Guale* chiefs found that association with the Spanish brought many benefits and it was in their best interest to renew the relationship.

The Chiefs governed their tribes with the help of a hereditary counsel, their noble relatives. Villages sent headmen for representation and all met in the counsel house of the primary Chief. The friars acted as agents relaying messages to and from the Spanish and *Guale*. The chief maintained autonomy over his own society. The *Guale* people were greatly impressed when the Chief returned from a visit with the Spanish and distributed ornate clothing, beads, iron tools and the like, compliments of the Spanish government. The friendship and gifts from Spain did not come without a price. The Spanish government at St. Augustine expected the alliance of the *Guale* against their English and French enemies. However, the *Guale* were soon to find that the price for Spanish allegiance was much higher.

Their incorporation in the Spanish mission system, required the *Guale* to participate in the *repartimiento*.[8] The Spanish insisted that a certain number of unmarried male *Guale* were sent to St. Augustine each year to work the cornfields and maintain the Spanish fortifications. The primary *Guale* Chiefs were allowed to select the individuals, who would be drafted to work from March until June each year. The warriors were paid with trade goods that could be exchanged for one real[9] or an eighth of a Spanish *peso*, per day.

Over 300 warriors were sent each year, many died from exhaustion and overwork. A number of the *Guale* chose to or were forced to remain with the Spanish permanently. The loss of the young men and women was devastating to the tribe.

Without the young to procreate and bring children, eventually, the old would die and with them, the tribe. Others brought back European diseases to which their people had no immunity. The very old and very young were the weaker, therefore, in the most danger of dying from disease. The threat of the *Guale* extinction was a very real possibility. The *Guale* homeopathic medicine were of no use to fight the dreadful fevers and pox. Nothing was available to fight the dreaded diseases, where only one in thirty survived.

The *Repartimiento* system took a great toll on the mission villages. There were very few eligible marriage partners and the population began to decline. Forced resettlements began during 1656-1657 due to the Timucuan Indian warring and the Spanish destruction of several interior missions. The English began slave raids of the decimated villages, by 1659, the *Guale* retreated to the safety of Georgia's barrier islands.

Excavation of the Fort King George site, where the *Santo Domingo de Asao* mission once stood, revealed olive jars, glazed pottery, a musket buttplate, rosary beads and a coin. Also found was a tiny pot with several small ears of corn or maize. These artifacts are on display at the Fort King George Historic Site Visitor's Center.

BIRTHPLACE OF
JOHN MCINTOSH KELL

Laurel Grove, at the end of this avenue, was the birthplace of John McIntosh Kell, 1823-1900, distinguished Naval officer. He was a member of the expedition of Commodore Matthew C. Perry to Japan in 1853, and was Master of the flagship *Mississippi* on the homeward cruise. When Georgia seceded from the Union, John McIntosh Kell resigned his commission to join the Confederacy. He was Executive Officer of the *Sumter*, then of the *Alabama* throughout her brilliant career on the seas, and in her final battle with the *Kearsarge* off Cherbourg. Later in life, John McIntosh Kell served for several years as Adjutant General of the State of Georgia.

GA 99, 0.8 mile east of US 17, near Fort King George, Darien
GPS Coordinates: N31.3649, W81.417199

John McIntosh Kell was born in McIntosh County, son of John and Margery Spalding Baillie Kell. John Kell descended from the founding fathers of McIntosh County, his ancestors included the famed Scottish Highlander John McIntosh Mohr and Thomas Spalding of Sapelo Island. At the age of 19, John Kell applied for and received an appointment to the Navy. He entered as a midshipman and served on numerous vessels during his years of service. John engaged in combat in California during the war with Mexico.

John McIntosh Kell was given orders to accompany Commodore Matthew Perry on a goodwill tour of Japan. Their mission was to convince the Japanese government to allow American ships access to the Japanese harbors for trade, fueling and supplies. John worked as liaison for Commodore Perry, whose mission was a tremendous success. He earned the rank of lieutenant for his part in the Japanese trade agreement and was given the choice assignment as Master of Commodore Perry's flagship *Mississippi* on the return voyage.

Upon his return from Japan, John McIntosh Kell married Julia Munroe and returned to McIntosh County. His stay would last only for a short time, the flames of Civil War were beginning to ignite and John had made a momentous decision concerning his career. In January 1861, Georgia seceded from the Union, Civil War was on the horizon, and Lieutenant Kell resigned his commission to serve the south. Given command of the Georgia state gunboat *Savannah*, he was soon reassigned as Executive Officer onboard the CSS *Sumter* at the request of Commander Raphael Semmes. The Confederate States Navy promoted him to First Lieutenant and awarded him command of the CSS *Sumter* during her commerce raiding cruise in 1861-62. The CSS *Sumter* was decommissioned in 1862.

John McIntosh Kell was devoted to Commander Semmes and at Semmes' request, continued to serve as his Executive Officer on the CSS *Alabama*. His career on the *Alabama* was exemplary. The *Alabama*, under John's command, was responsible for sixty-five Union vessels captured or sank within two years. In June 1864, the *Alabama* finally met her match, she was in desperate need of repair, her crew tired and battle weary, they were challenged by the USS *Kearsarge*. Commander Semmes could have chosen to retreat and fight another day, but did not. The battle weary CSS *Alabama* was in no condition for the fray, the *Kearsarge* was undefeated, her crew was fresh and rested. After receiving several devastating blows below the waterline, the CSS *Alabama* sank. John McIntosh Kell stood his post until the final moments before the *Alabama* went to her watery grave. Along with other survivors, John was rescued by the British yacht *Dearhound* and taken to England.

John McIntosh Kell, upon his return from England, was promoted to the rank of Commander for his bravery under fire and given command of the ironclad CSS *Richmond* in 1865. It was here that he served the remainder of his naval career. At the end of the Civil War, John McIntosh Kell retired his commission and returned home to Georgia.

John was touted as the reason for the many successes of the CSS *Alabama*, however to his dying day, he remained loyal to Commander Semmes, who was forced into retirement after the loss of his ship. John Kell defended the reputation of Commander Semmes and refused to acknowledge any praise, recounting that he did only what was his duty to his Commander and his ship.

John McIntosh Kell was appointed Georgia's Adjutant General after his retirement from the Navy. Life in the Georgia capital was vigorous and he enjoyed his time there. John and Julia spent many hours with their friend, Sidney Lanier. Lanier made frequent visits to the Kell home in Sunnyside, Georgia, entertaining everyone present with renditions from his flute or readings of his poetry.

John McIntosh Kell was content during the waning years of his life. A man who had accomplished all he set out to do and had lived life to its fullest. He had traveled all over the world, served his county, state and nation with honor and spent the last years of his life making up for time lost with his beloved Julia. When he died in 1900, John McIntosh Kell left a legacy that most men could only dream of, a legacy of no regrets.

ST. ANDREW'S CEMETERY

At the end of this avenue, on high land overlooking the creeks and marshes, Thomas Spalding of Sapelo established his family burial ground. For many years the Spaldings and their kinsmen were buried there. In 1867, Charles Spalding, son of Thomas Spalding, gave to Saint Andrew's Episcopal Church in Darien the land surrounding the family plot, to be used perpetually as a cemetery. On February 20, 1876, the Right Reverend Dr. Beckwith, Bishop of Georgia, consecrated the ground now known as St. Andrew's Cemetery.

GA 99, 1.4 miles east of US 17-GA 25, Darien
GPS Coordinates: N31.22463, W81.25016

The St. Andrew's Cemetery began as the Spalding family plot. Thomas Spalding was noted in E. Merton Coulter's *Thomas Spalding of Sapelo* to have said of the cemetery,

> "there to sleep the long sleep beneath the giant old oaks draped with the funereal moss - and there to followed by other Spaldings until there should grow up a veritable Spalding city of the Dead"

Thomas Spalding, age 77, died at Ashantilly, the home of his son, Charles. He was laid to rest in the Spalding family plot along side his wife, Sarah. The Ashantilly property joins that of the St. Andrew's Cemetery. During their 48 years of marriage, Thomas and Sarah Spalding knew an abundance of grief. The couple bore sixteen children and of those only five were preceded in death by their parents.

James, the couples' eldest son, died of influenza at the age of twenty-three. James had served in US Navy and later was elected as a state representative for two terms. He was buried in Milledgeville, then the state capital of Georgia. Hester Margery, followed her brother in death a mere four years later, she was also in her early twenties. Before James and Hester, the Spalding's had lost five offspring in early childhood and four at birth.

Charles Spalding, the oldest surviving child of Thomas and Sarah, donated the land to St. Andrew's Episcopal Church in 1867. Since that time, the burial ground has expanded until St. Andrew's was forced to add another section to the existing cemetery. Crypts, stone urns, angels and the like are thickly spread across the vast internment of the original property.

Grave stones have changed over the centuries and the meaning of many monument carvings have been lost. The stones of St. Andrew's reflect the changes of two hundred years. Hourglasses represent the passage of time until loved ones can join the dearly departed in heaven and trumpets signal "the call to the Christian Resurrection." During the Victorian era, the willow tree signified a sentiment of sorrow carved on tombstones, but legend tells us, the willow tree continued to flourish and remain whole, no matter how many branches the tree lost. Tiny lambs, cherubs and angels often appeared on children's graves representing the lamb of God, the cherub appearing as the child given wings and the protective hand of angels caring for the child. Hearts standing for the love of God were also common, as were pomegranates because of the many seeds in each piece of fruit. Birds are one of the most frequently seen symbols on graves, mythology considered the bird as a messenger to Heaven. Another common marking is the Bible or a hand with the index finger, pointing toward the hereafter.

"THE THICKET"
SUGAR MILL - RUM DISTILLERY RUINS

On the banks of Carnochan Creek, a short distance
East of here, are the ruins of a famous Sugar Mill
and Rum Distillery operated early in the 19th century.
These buildings, constructed of tabby by William
Carnochan on his huge sugar plantation at "The
Thicket," followed closely plans laid out by Thomas
Spalding of Sapelo. The sugar works and rum distillery were operated successfully on a commercial
scale until 1824, when a hurricane tore off the roof
and upper story of the mill and cane barn, and
destroyed other buildings.

GA 99, 5.4 miles east of US 17-GA 25 near Ridgeville
GPS Coordinates: N31.25523, W81.23393

*T*he Ticket was long said to be the remains of the old Spanish *Tolomato* Mission. Many notable publications carried features extolling the wonderful Spanish ruins, including the *Atlanta Constitution*, the *New York Times*, *National Geographic* and educational publications from the University of California and Duke University. It was not until Ellis Merton Coulter edited a volume called *Georgia's Disputed Ruins,* that the true identity of the glorious tabby structures was revealed. Published in 1937, the book contained definitive proof that the ruins were, in fact, William Carnochan's sugar mill and rum distillery. The final evidence came from a letter penned by Mrs. Kate McKinley Treanor of Athens, Georgia, to Isaac Flood Arnow of St. Marys and written in 1932. Mrs. Treanor, the niece of Thomas Spalding, lived in the area and once owned the property in question. Mrs. Treanor lived in the old sugar house at the Thicket until 1912 when she sold it to Howard Coffin.

The original owner, William Carnochan was a local businessman owning an interest in the Darien Eastern Steam Sawmill. Originally from Jamaica, he relocated to the Georgia coast, where he learned to manufacture the sweet intoxicate liquor, rum. *The Thicket* is located five miles northeast of Darien along the banks of Carnochan Creek.

The buildings there were a tabby octagonal sugar mill, a boiling and curing house that occupied a single building and four wooden slave houses. It is safe to assume that the business of selling rum to the public began in 1816. An advertisement in a Savannah newspaper in 1817 read,

"14 puncheons or large casks of 4th proof Georgia Rum, equal in flavor and quality to Jamaica. A constant supply of the above can be had here (Savannah) or at the Distillery, Darien, on very accomodating terms to country merchants and others."

Rum is made from the juice of sugarcane. Originally planted on Columbus's third voyage on the island of Hispaniola, Spanish colonists discovered that fermented sugarcane produced a sweet liquor by distilling the cooked down molasses. Sailors soon made the same discovery; because the sweet tasting liquor was cheap to produce, it became the drink of sea going men. Colonists considered rum the drink of ruffians and the lower class. Rum was not widely used as a cocktail drink until the 1900s.

The distillation process is basically the same today as it was 200 years ago. Traditionally aged in charred oak casks[10], rum should be aged for approximately three years, but often in the 1800s it was aged for a few months or weeks. Today, premium rums are aged as much as 20 years. The liquor ranges from smooth amber to nearly black. Each Caribbean Island produces

Remains of *The Thicket*

its own rum, only a few of which are available for export. The Virgin Islands are famous for their "over-proof" rum[11] and Puerto Rico produces the world's most widely consumed rum today, *Bacardi*.

William Carnochan's sugar mill and rum distillery pursuit last only a short time. In 1824, a calamitous hurricane tore through the area and demolished the enterprise. Carnochan never rebuilt.

Charles Spalding lived and cultivated the property before the Civil War and T. P. Pease clerked a plantation store in a wooden second story above the octagonal sugar mill. Erosion from Carnochan Creek began to compromise *The Thicket's* foundation. Pease had numerous loads of oyster shells brought in the stabilize the area, the shells are still scattered about the site today.

After the Civil War, Pease's former slaves lived in the tabby cabins. A number of the wooden structures were beginning to decay and were sold to the newly freed African Americans. Joseph Mansfield bought the property in 1884, the old wooden cabins were torn down leaving only four tabby buildings standing. Those prime examples of colonial tabby construction can be seen at the site of *The Thicket*.

OLD RIVER ROAD

The River Road has changed but little in location since its beginning as a Military Route in 1739. Scottish Highlanders first marched over it on their way to invade Spanish Florida, and troops have used it in three wars ~ the War with Spain, the Revolution, and the War Between the States. As a civilian highway, this served first as the road to Fort Barrington and the Ferry, later as an important link in the old Macon to Darien highway, over which planters in their carriages, stage coaches, and riders carrying the U.S. mail, travelled during the early 19th century.

US 17-GA 25 at the GA 251 Junction, 1 mile north of Darien
GPS Coordinates: N31.23101, W81.25596

The Old River Road was established to provide an inland link along the Altamaha River from Darien to Fort Barrington and was later extended to Macon. The road was little more than a sandy pathway. It has bore the footprints of Scottish Highlanders defending the colony against Spanish dominance, the War with Spain, the Revolutionary War and the Civil War when northern aggressors followed the road to pillage and burn the coastal Georgia communities along its route.

In 1773, naturalist William Bartram traveled along the Old River Road as he progressed inland by means of the "high road" toward Fort Barrington, which was described as "the sudden transition from rich cultivated settlements to high pine forests." The pine forests would eventually disappear as sawmilling increased in the area and by the 1920s little more than stubble would mark the land.

Almost any type of landscape could be seen as one traveled the Old River Road. Dense forest filled with ancient oaks, fragrant magnolias on the flat lands, sandy bluffs near the river and cypress swamps in the wet lands between gently rolling hills. The hills were capped with pines reaching straight and tall toward the sun.

George M. Troup, Governor of Georgia, built his plantation called *Valdosta* along the Old River Road about 40 miles southeast of Macon in Laurens County. The road gave him easy access to the place of his childhood in McIntosh County.

In the days following General Lee's surrender at Appomattox southern soldiers traveled the Old River Road making their way back to families they prayed were safe and homes still standing, wondering what the future held for them.

Jefferson Davis, President of the Confederacy, found himself to be one of those travelers as he attempted to escape capture by the Union forces. His family and the members of the Confederate Cabinet traveled in a wagon train along the Old River Road. At Ball's Ferry, Jefferson Davis learned of a plot to rob the wagon train. He traveled down the Old River Road, frantically searching for his family. They met near Springfield at the home of E. J. Blackshear. After a short rest and breakfast, the wagon train crossed the Oconee River at dawn. Jefferson Davis moved down the east bank of the river and crossed at Dublin. Confederate Postmaster General John Reagan stopped the train in front of F. H. Rowe's store on the courthouse square. Rowe, a native of Connecticut and a loyal Southerner, directed the Confederates along the Telfair Road. Davis spent that night at the southern tip of Laurens County between the forks of Alligator Creek. That same night the Wisconsin Calvary reached Blackshear's Ferry. Colonel Henry Harnden, a Union Officer, was sent east from Macon in hopes of picking up Davis' trail. He was informed by former slaves of a small wagon train crossing the ferry earlier in the morning. The slaves related that one of the men was addressed as "Mr. President." When the cavalry arrived in Dublin, they were misdirected by Rowe, who sent them down the Old River Road east of the Telfair Road. Had the cavalry been sent a day earlier, Jefferson Davis would have been captured along the Old River Road; a day later and Davis might have escaped capture entirely. Davis and his party were apprehended two days later in Irwinville, Georgia, on May 10, 1865.

Later, the road served as the route that the raftsmen used to return to their inland Georgia homes after floating their timbers down the Altamaha River. The road connected McIntosh to Glynn and Liberty Counties, where travel by rail was not yet possible. The railroad did not extend into McIntosh County until the early 1890s.

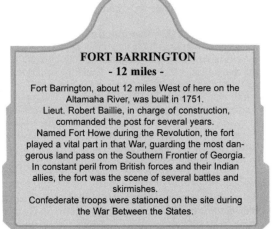

US 17-GA 25, 1.3 miles south of Darien
GPS Coordinates: N31.23101, W81.25596

General James Edward Oglethorpe's plan for the city of Darien, in 1736, followed the same design used for the city of Savannah three years earlier. However, Darien had a point of vulnerability. The land area to the south of the city was open for invasion. Would be attackers could ford the Altamaha River and approach the city without notice. The need to protect Darien's southern exposure led to the construction of Fort Barrington.

The area west of what is now the community of Cox was chosen for the site of Fort Barrington and was considered a remote post. The fort was named for a favored relative of General Oglethorpe's, Lieutenant Colonel Josiah Barrington. Lieutenant Robert Baillie was chosen to oversee the construction and to command the fort in 1761. Lieutenant Baillie married Anne McIntosh, daughter of famed Scottish Highlander John McIntosh Mohr.

The British funded construction and British engineers designed the exceptional fortification. The fortification was built on a sandy ridge overlooking the Altamaha River at a shallow ford slightly north of where the river divides into four channels.

The area surrounding the fort consisted of a mix of sandy slopes, river swamps and dense bay forests that were natural barriers against attack. The square structure was protected by seventy-five foot walls and manned by twenty-five rangers. The structures within the walls included a tower bastion for protection, officer lodgings, a store and a munitions magazine.

When the American Revolution began in 1776, Colonel Lachlan McIntosh was placed in command of the Southern Colonial forces. The British first attacked Savannah in March of that year. Although their mission failed to take the city, the British did manage to escape with a vast quantity of rice and other supplies.

Colonel McIntosh's troops concentrated on taking possession of Fort Barrington from the British. The soldiers forded the Altamaha River at the shallow crossing and surprised the unsuspecting British soldiers. The fort was easily taken and never fell under British control again. The post was now called Fort Howe, in honor of Robert Howe, who commanded the Southern area of Colonial operations.

Once the Americans had taken Fort Howe. The Creek Indians, who allied with the British, continued to lay siege to the fort throughout the remainder of the Revolutionary War. Colonel William McIntosh's Light Horse troop repulsed the attackers during each raid. In 1777, Colonel William McIntosh was given Command of the Southern forces.

The fort fell into disrepair and was vandalized for many years after the Revolution. During the Civil War, Colonel Charles H. Spalding ordered that the Liberty Independent Troop be assigned to Fort Barrington. The detachment was ordered to blockade the Altamaha River against Union gunboats and defend the Railroad Bridge. Neither objective was successful. After the war, Fort Barrington/Howe was abandoned and left to fall into ruins.

Today, nothing is left of the wooden fort, and the river has reclaimed half of the earthworks that once protected it. A local hunting club purchased the property and a private boat ramp was put in where the fort once stood. Near the location of the old fort is the Barrington County Park. Opened to the public, the remote Barrington County Park offers a boat launch, camping or a place by the Altamaha River for a quiet picnic.

Note: On a balmy summer afternoon, my editor and I went in search of the ruins of Fort Barrington. We had become such accomplished trackers of historical markers, if it was there, we would find it. Based on the directions posted on the marker and following the road signs that were few and far between, we drove out on our quest. We arrived at the spot where our directions had led us and parked near the Altamaha River, between two sandy embankments. There was no sign of a fort or where one might have been, so we proceeded on foot.

We hiked along trails, knowing that if this weren't the middle of the summer, the two of us might not be safe here. Evidence of the active hunting club was vividly apparent with colorful ribbons marking the well worn paths. The two of us ambled through the gently rolling hills in the most serene Georgia forest, filled with ancient oaks and magnolias, sweet bay, hickory and the occasional tall pine. We struggled through the muddy wetlands with its bald cypress, her knees poking up here and there.[12] Deer and wild pig tracks in mud told us that this trail was frequented by man and beast. Still, we found no sign of the fort.

We had hiked about two miles into the forest, when the lack of water and the presence of biting flies convinced us that we had traveled far enough. We headed back to the truck. We drove around the sandy roads barely big enough for my small SUV with the air conditioner blasting in our heat reddened faces and eventually found the Barrington County Park. Still no sign of the illusive Fort Barrington. One more trip along the sandy path to river to make sure we had not missed any sign of the remains of the fort built in 1751. Defeated for now, we realized that we had spent enough time on this one particular historical marker and it was time to move on.

Several days later as I read through my reference materials again, I came upon a passage that detailed the location of Fort Barrington, "built on a sand ridge in McIntosh County to control the best place to cross the broad Altamaha River in its southern section, a shallow ford north of where the river divides into four channels." Fort Barrington was once located where we had initially parked near the Altamaha River, between the two sandy embankments.

ARDOCH

Ardoch, fronting on the old Stage Road from Savannah to Darien where it traversed this Swamp, was the plantation home of the McDonalds from Colonial Days through the early 19th century.

During the Revolutionary War, members of this branch of the McDonald clan were Loyalists, as were many families of Coastal Georgia. In a skirmish fought in this home in Ardoch, only a short distance from this spot, Robert McDonald was killed in the presence of his wife and children, and the Ardoch house burned.

US 17-GA 25, 6.9 miles north of Darien
GPS Coordinates: N31.27543, W81.26180

Ardoch Plantation, located slightly north of Darien, was the home of Scottish immigrants, Charles and Margaret McDonald. As the Revolutionary War raged around them, the McDonald family vowed to remain neutral; unfortunately, the war did not leave them untouched. The fighting around their Ardoch Plantation was escalating and Charles McDonald opened the door to view the action. As his family looked on, Charles took a British musket ball to the chest. While he lay dying, Margaret and her children watched in horror as British soldiers ransacked their home. The soldiers burned what they did not take, leaving nothing for the devastated McDonald family, but shock and disbelief. True to their Scottish heritage as survivors, the McDonald family managed pulled themselves together and bravely rebuilt their lives.

Mary McDonald married Gilbert Gignilliat in 1806 and they continued to live at Ardoch for the rest of their lives. During their lives together, the couple had two sons. Norman Page, named for Mary's brother, was born in 1809, and five years later, William Robert Gignilliat was born. Mary McDonald Gignilliat died shortly after the birth of her second child, leaving an infant son and young Norman. The loss of their mother was compounded a year later when their father died suddenly. Mary and Gilbert Gignilliat died December 10, 1814 and 1815, respectively, exactly one year apart to the day. Perhaps, Gilbert died of a broken heart, no longer having the will to live without his loving wife. The children continued to live at Ardoch and were raised by a servant of their mother's, Jane McLeod. Jane McLeod later married Robert McDonald, who resided on the lands adjoining Ardoch. The relationship between Robert and Charles McDonald, the original owner of Ardoch Plantation, is not known; it has been said that the men were cousins, but that can not be confirmed.

Norman Gignilliat became one of the most successful planters and businessmen in McIntosh County before the Civil War. He amassed more than 10,000 acres of land, owning not only his family home at Ardoch, but nearby Windy Hill plantation as well. William became a noted plantation owner and planter in his own right. He purchased Greenwood Plantation in northern McIntosh County and through his efforts, the property became an abundant rice plantation.

Norman Gignilliat enlisted in the McIntosh Guards as a captain, prior to the Civil War. However, when the fighting began he was forced to resign his commission. Norman was physically unable to serve the Confederate forces due to his extreme bulk. He contributed the only way he could by equipping the McIntosh Guard throughout the war. After the Civil War, Norman Gignilliat moved to Marietta, Georgia, where he spent the remainder of his life. Norman McDonald became a distinguished McIntosh County Justice of the Peace and later served two terms as a Georgia State Representative.

An interesting note to the Ardoch Plantation story; due to his vast land holdings, Norman Gignilliat required a substantial number of slaves to work the plantations. He was said to be a very benevolent master. A number of years after emancipation freed Gignilliat's slaves, a group of them purchased his McIntosh plantation with the desire to replenish it to its prewar splendor. Though the former slaves gave the plantation every effort, times were hard in the south for everyone. Eventually they were forced to sell.

OLD MEETING HOUSE

Two hundred yards west of this spot stood the "Old Meeting House," built before 1750 to serve the Scottish Presbyterians of the District of Darien. A landmark in Colonial days, it was in use until after the Revolutionary War, both as a church and as a meeting place for the citizens of St. Andrew's Parish on important occasions. It was here that the "Darien Committee" met on January 12, 1775 to choose their delegates to the Provincial Congress at Savannah, and to adopt the six Resolutions which are today among our treasured Revolutionary documents.

US 17-GA 25 8.1 miles north of Darien
GPS Coordinates: N31.28548, W81.26399

The Old Meeting House was one of the first structures the Scottish Highlanders built, just north of the Altamaha River. It stood as a place of worship and the center of government for the St. Andrew's Parish.

As the air of discontent grew heavy over the American colonies, it was becoming obvious that war with England was inevitable. It was a cold winter day in January 1775 when the Darien Committee met at the Old Meeting House. Lachlan McIntosh headed the committee, which decided to join the American Congress in Philadelphia. The "Intolerable Acts" gave the Royal Governor the power to issue limited land grants, raised quitrents[13] and given this power, the Crown controlled offices began exercising excessive authority. The Acts resulted in the decision that American rights would be best served by representatives responsible to the colonies and not the Crown.

To that end, the Darien Committee adopted six resolutions. The committee first expressed their approval of "the unparalleled moderation, the decent, but firm and manly, conduct of the loyal and brave people of Boston and Massachusetts Bay, to preserve their liberty."

The resolutions addressed British colonial policies such as excessive authority, limited land grants and excessive quitrents. The fifth resolution detailed "our disapprobation and abhorrence of the unnatural practice of slavery in America" and further urged "the manumission or emancipation of our slaves in this colony, upon the most safe and equitable footing for the masters and themselves." The final resolution named delegates Archibald Bulloch, Noble W. Jones and John Houstoun McIntosh to represent Christ Church Parish, Savannah and the surrounding areas at the Provincial Congress in Georgia. These delegates were sent to convince Congress of the necessity to appoint delegates to the Continental Congress scheduled to meet in Philadelphia in May.

The fight for American independence had begun.

CAPTURE OF 23 OLD MEN IN 1864

Near here, in Ebenezer Church, 23 old men were captured by Federal troops on the night of August 3rd, 1864. These civilians, too old for military service, were the sole protection of McIntosh County, which was constantly being plundered by forces from blockade gunboats.

Advised of the meeting by spies, Federal troops surrounded the church in the darkness and opened fire. The old men were captured and marched overland to Blue and Hall landing near Darien, where they were put on board ship and taken to Northern prisons.

US 17-GA 25 8.8 miles north of Darien
GPS Coordinates: N31.29335, W81.26422

Union Officer, George M. Colvocoresses, Commander of the *Saratoga* during the Civil War, gathered intelligence off the Georgia coast by the simplest of means, he read the local newspaper. Through his reading, he learned that the men of McIntosh County too old, young or infirmed to go to war, were to meet at Ebenezer Church, the temporary county seat and courthouse. The purpose of the meeting was the establishment of a Coast Guard.

Commander Colvocoresses' intent was to surprise and capture these men. He met his goal with ease and in broad daylight. The Union troops lay in wait for the men all through the night of August 2, 1864 and when all had assembled at Ebenezer at the appointed time, the Union troops surrounded the church. Commander Colvocoresses reported that during the seizure they had taken twenty-six prisoners, twenty-two horse and carriages, fired two bridges and destroyed a large post. Three of the men were able to escape. It was further reported that the mission was accomplished with no "unpleasantness" or loss of life. Commander Colvocoresses marched his prisoners, with lines of mounted troops on either side, to waiting ships. The prisoners were then transported to northern prison camps.

Colonel William B. Gaulden, who was to be the Commander of the Coast Guard to be formed on that fateful night, was late for the meeting. Colonel Gaulden later admitted that he had an idea that the Union planned a raid. Unfortunately, Colonel Gaulden had this realization too late to move or cancel the meeting.

In an article for the Savannah newspaper, Colonel Gaulden detailed the capture of his men. He issued the following challenge to Commander Colvocoresses in the article, "...when he (speaking of Colvocoresses) calls to see me again, I shall be at home, and will try and give him a more respectful reception."

Captain Armand Lefils, who was captured and later released, told Colonel Gaulden the facts of the capture. Even the Union troops had no desire to imprison Captain Lefils, who was 71 years old. It is not known how many of the men survived to return home. What is known is that William J. Cannon, who was captured that day, lived to see the South surrender but in his weakened state died on the long walk home, before he could once again stand on McIntosh soil.

OLD BELLEVILLE
OR TROUP CEMETERY

Within these walls are buried Captain Troup, British
Naval officer, and his wife, Catherine McIntosh
Troup. They were the parents of George M. Troup,
Governor of Georgia 1823-1827;
U.S. Senator 1829-1833.
It was on this plantation that George M. Troup
spent his early boyhood.
Ten other graves lie within this enclosure; the
inscriptions on the marble slabs which marked
them were effaced by time before 1850.

In Crescent, 1/2 mile left of road from GA 99, follow the signs to Pelican Point
GPS Coordinates: N31.53497, W81.363705

Belleville Plantation, located on a bluff beside the Sapelo River, was granted to Captain John McIntosh, father of Catherine McIntosh Troup, as a reward for his loyalty to the English crown. Catherine met Captain George Troup, a British Naval Officer, on a trip to England and soon the couple was married. The Troups had two sons, who were raised at Belleville Plantation, George Michael and James.

George was born at McIntosh Bluff on the Tombigbee River, the area once a part of Georgia is now part of the state of Alabama, on September 8, 1780. Initially, Troup was educated at home, then in the schools of Savannah when his parents went to live at Belleville Plantation. He attended Erasmus Hall in Flatbush, New York and graduated from the College of New Jersey, now Princeton, in 1797 with a degree in law.

George practiced law for a short time in Savannah, then became a member of the State House of Representatives in 1803. That same year, Troup married Anne St. Claire McCormick of Bryan County, she died within one year of their marriage. He was elected to Congress in 1807 and continued to be reelected until 1815, when he chose not to run. During his terms in Congress, George advocated the removal of Creek Indians from the remaining Georgia territory.

George Troup moved to his peaceful Laurens County plantation named *Valdosta* in 1816; however, he did not rest for long. In March 1817, he was elected to the United States Senate until 1818, when he again resigned; this time to run for the office of Georgia Governor. George Troup's first two attempts for the highest office in the state were unsuccessful. During that time he remained at his Laurens County plantation. During his time in Congress, George married again. Ann Carter of Albemarle County, Virginia, became his bride in November 1809. The couple had four children.

In 1822, George Troup was finally elected Governor of Georgia. This election was the last regular election by the legislature. Two years later, George Michael Troup became the first Governor of Georgia to be elected by popular vote. During his term as Governor, Troup oversaw the acquisition of the last remaining Native American lands in Georgia. His policies to expand Georgia territory brought the threat of military action by the United States against the Creek Indians, who were struggling to hold on to the land that was rightfully their own. Governor Troup sought the counsel of his first cousin, William McIntosh, in order to obtain the Native American lands. William McIntosh, half Creek Indian and half Scottish, was Chief of the Lower Creeks and a military leader who fought with the Americans against the British in the War of 1812. Chief McIntosh visited Governor Troup often, staying at the home he kept for his wife Peggy, about eight miles south of Laurens County. Governor Troup directed the Secretary of War to appointment of a commission that eventually signed the Treaty of Indian Springs with Chief William McIntosh and other representatives of the Creek nation. Chief McIntosh believed, in agreement with his cousin Governor Troup, that the Creek Indians would be much better served away from the influence of the "white people." Other factions of the Creeks did not agree and vowed to kill anyone signing a treaty giving up Native American lands. Chief McIntosh signed the treaty despite the warning, receiving $27,491. In exchange, the Creeks ceded to the state all of their lands. Chief McIntosh beseeched Governor Troup to send soldiers for his protection; however, the force was too late. Chief William McIntosh was attacked at his home and murdered for his part in the Treaty of Indian Springs.

George Troup returned to the United States Senate in 1828, but retired before the expiration of his term; at the age of 48, his health had begun to fail. He was a staunch advocate of State's Rights and believed during his term in the Senate that these rights were in grave danger.

The Central of Georgia Railroad planned to expand the railroad from Savannah to Macon in the 1830s. The most direct route ran through Laurens County. Local residents led by former Governor Troup forced the railroad to the north. This decision proved to be a double edged sword. The scattered plantations of Laurens County were the only communities outside Dublin, the county seat, and having no railroad to connect the city to the outside world. Dublin virtually faded away before the Civil War. Ironically, their actions kept Dublin and Laurens County away from the route of immeasurable devastation of General William T. Sherman's army during his "March to the Sea."

Former Georgia Governor George Michael Troup died on April 26, 1856, while visiting one of his plantations in Montgomery County. George Troup was buried at Rosemont Plantation, Montgomery County.

The overgrown enclosure called Troup Cemetery holds, among others, the graves of Captain George Troup and Catherine McIntosh Troup. The graves are hidden from sight by lush weeds sprouting pretty yellow blooms in the spring and summer. Hidden amid the vegetation, one can barely see a small American flag marking the memorial to the parents of Georgia's former Governor.

BAISDEN'S BLUFF ACADEMY

Located a short distance East of here, near the River, Baisden's Bluff Academy was the main educational institution in McIntosh County in the early years of the 19th century. A Boarding School, operating the year round, its roll held the names of prominent families of this county and from adjoining areas. "Mr. Linder" was Principal. General Francis Hopkins, Wm. A. Dunham, James Dunwoody, James Smith and Jacob Wood were Commissioners.
In 1823 torrential rains washed the dormitory into the river, leaving a ravine which can still be seen. The school never recovered.

GA 99, 12.2 miles east of US 17-GA 25 near Crescent
GPS Coordinates: N31.30353, W81.21598

Students, before the advent of formalized education, were primarily males of wealthy families. Their education was largely focused on religion and if the young men were to benefit from higher education, they were sent abroad. Upper class colonial families began to realize in the early 19th century that male children required more than the core classes to be well educated. Wealthy young ladies still did not receive education beyond the basics of reading, sums, writing, needlepoint and etiquette.

Education, in the early 1700s, was left to individual parishes and communities. It was in 1783 that the Georgia Legislature passed laws encouraging individual counties to establish academies. The coffers of America were drained during the Revolution and as a result, there was only a minimal amount of state funding available for the construction of public schools. The same year, the Assembly of the State of Georgia passed an Act of Attainder, Banishments and Confiscation against Loyalists, men who remained loyal to the English crown during the Revolutionary War. The Act provided that confiscated lands would be used as sites for public academies and other properties would be sold with the proceeds used to fund construction of the facilities.

Baisden's Bluff Academy was the first source of public education in McIntosh County. Baisden's Bluff was located in, what is today, the community of Crescent approximately 12 miles northeast of Darien on the southern side Sapelo River. Four other "free" public schools were built in McIntosh County, which included Darien, Lower Sand Hills, Upper Sand Hills and Harris Neck. Baisden's Bluff was the first and most notable.

The Baisden's Bluff Academy was a boarding school; however, in order to "board" the student was required to provide his own bed. Tuition was set between $6 to $8.00 per term and board was a hefty $130.00 per year. The Baisden Bluff school operated year round with only a two week break in December and a week long break in the spring.

The eighteenth century school system put a much stronger emphasis on science than ever before. Students were beginning to find the traditional religious explanations of their environment unconvincing. It was the famous inventors, such as Benjamin Franklin, that encouraged the study of science. Conversely, the fine arts movement was barely beginning to emerge during this time.

The first Headmaster of Baisden's Bluff Academy was Matthew "Mr. Linder" Lindon. In July 1823, torrential rains flooded the area surrounding the academy. A new dormitory had recently been constructed on the bluff overlooking the Sapelo River. When the flooding began the soft earth gave way and although Mr. Linder and others desperately struggled to save the dormitory, it slowly slid in a wash of mud into the Sapelo River. Mr. Linder became critically ill as a result of exposure and died shortly after the incident.

Horace Belknap became the new Headmaster upon Mr. Linder's death. However, little more than a year after his appointment, in September 1824, a horrific hurricane swept into McIntosh County. The heavy tabby walls of the academy's main building, already weakened from the torrential rains the year before, began to crumble and were considered beyond repair. Horace Belknap resigned his position.

The Baisden's Bluff Academy Commissioners decided to relocate the school closer to Darien. Nothing could save the institution, by 1834, the ruins of Baisden's Bluff Academy were sold. Today, no sign of the old academy buildings exist; however, a ravine where the dormitory once stood marks a path to the river.

**OLD COURT HOUSE
AT SAPELO BRIDGE**

Sapelo Bridge, on the old Savannah to Darien Road 200 yards east of this spot, was the seat of McIntosh County from 1793 to 1818. Here the Court House and other public buildings stood; here, too, were the Armory and Muster Ground for the McIntosh County Calvary Troop, and here the Stage Coaches stopped to refresh the passengers and change horses.

**US 17-GA 25 0.8 mile north of Eulonia
GPS Coordinates: N31.32094, W81.25335**

McIntosh County was created from a portion of what had previously been Liberty County to the north in 1793. The county seat was established at a small community called Sapelo Bridge, which is now known as Eulonia.

Until a permanent courthouse could be constructed, the seat of government resided at Fairhope Plantation, home of Colonel John McIntosh. The township of Sapelo Bridge and Fairhope Plantation was located at the headwater of the Sapelo River. The area began to develop as homes were constructed, a parade ground was laid out and an armory was built. The troops of McIntosh County Calvary utilized the parade ground for their frequent inspection of the guard. The small community gained further notoriety when the stagecoach began make regular stops on its route between Savannah and her southern neighbors of Darien and St. Marys.

Darien began to develop in the early 1800s, due to its prime location on the Altamaha River. Exports of rice and cotton from the Darien wharves promoted the rapid growth of the small town and later the lumber industry made it a boomtown. What had once been only the site of Fort Darien and a few small buildings was now a flourishing city.

The development of Darien spurred county officials to poll its citizens on the question of moving the county seat. The people voted in favor of bringing the county government from Sapelo Bridge to Darien. In 1818, Darien became the McIntosh County seat. The Sapelo Bridge community faded into history.

JOHN HOUSTOUN MCINTOSH

John Houstoun McIntosh, son of George McIntosh, was born at Rice Hope, May 1, 1773. When a young man, he settled in East Florida and became a leader of the U.S. citizens living there. He was appointed "Governor or Director of the Republic of Florida" in 1812. After a stormy career in Florida, he returned to Georgia, and in 1818 served in the Seminole War as General in the Militia.

In 1825, he began intensive cultivation of sugar cane on his plantation in Camden County, and there installed the first horizontal sugar mill ever worked by cattle power.

US 17-GA 25 2 miles north of Eulonia
GPS Coordinates: W31.33084, W81.25203

B orn to George and Anne Priscilla Houstoun McIntosh in May 1773, John Houstoun McIntosh descended from a long line of Scottish Highlanders. His grandfather was the famed John McIntosh Mohr, who founded the city of Darien with his band of Highlander Soldiers and fought bravely against the Spanish in the Battles of Gully Hole and Bloody Marsh.

John Houstoun settled in northeastern Florida as a young man and began to amass considerable property. In 1811, President James Madison felt that the time had come to take Florida from Spain. To this end, he dispatched a messenger to seek the aid of John Houstoun, because he was the wealthiest American living in Spanish territory and owned the most property. President Madison sweetened the deal by establishing the Independent Republic of East Florida and appointing John Houstoun as Governor. John Houstoun accepted the appointment and began organizing a militia known as the Patriots. The group of Protestant farmers saw the rebellion against Spain as a chance to expand their land holdings and become wealthy.

The Patriots marched toward St. Augustine, the Spanish stronghold. Along the way, they took Fernandina with little effort. John Houstoun and his men knew the British fleet gave additional protection to the Spaniards and lay in wait off the Florida coast, this knowledge left the group undaunted. What they did not expect were escaped slaves and displaced American Indians, who had been driven into northern Florida. The slaves and American Indians fiercely fought the Patriots in order to remain free in Spanish territory. The attack on the besieging Americans was successful and for a time Florida remained in the hands of Spain.

After being repulsed at St. Augustine, John sold his holdings in northeastern Florida and returned to Georgia in 1814.

Joining the militia in 1818, he served with General Andrew Jackson in the First Seminole War. The campaign's objective was to stop the Seminoles from attacking border settlements and harboring escaped slaves. The drive was more successful than General Jackson had hoped it would be. General Jackson's victories forced Spain to relinquish their hold in Florida. The Seminole were driven deep into the everglades of south Florida.

Shortly after returning to Georgia, John Houstoun purchased two plantations in Camden County. Marianna Plantation became the location of his home and New Canaan was a sugar cane plantation. These plantation lands were bordering and inclusive of what is now known as Kings Bay Naval Submarine Base.

John Houstoun McIntosh died in 1836 at the age of 63.

RICE HOPE

Famous Rice and Indigo Plantation of Colonial and Revolutionary times, Rice Hope was the home of George McIntosh, son of John McIntosh Mor of Darien, and brother of General Lachlan McIntosh. George McIntosh was Official Surveyor for St. Andrew's Parish, Member of the Commons House of Assembly, Member of the First Provincial Congress of Georgia, Member of the Council of Safety. During the Revolution, the home of George McIntosh at Rice Hope was burned and his slaves and stock run off by the British.

US 17-GA 25 2 miles north of Eulonia
GPS Coordinates: N31.33084, W81.25203

George McIntosh was born in 1739, the youngest surviving child of John McIntosh Mohr. George, at the age of eleven, accompanied his oldest brother, Lachlan to Charles Towne. George was educated and later, given over to an architect as his apprentice.

The McIntosh brothers returned to Georgia in 1758. George, due to Lachlan's connections, was appointed as Commissary of Supplies for Fort Frederica. He was soon appointed as a delegate from St. Andrew's Parish to the Commons House, along with Robert Baillie who married McIntosh sister, Anne. Lachlan held various posts including official surveyor, tax collector and Justice Of The Peace. With George and Robert providing a McIntosh link to the royal government and Lachlan in a key position, the McIntosh Clan was able to control the affairs of the entire parish.

In 1768, George and Robert Baillie's election victories were challenged. However, before the matter could be concluded, Royal Governor James Wright decided to dissolve the Commons. Neither George nor Robert Baillie returned to the Commons House for the next assembly.

During this time George McIntosh was granted a 1,500 acre plantation that he dubbed Rice Hope. The plantation was north of what is now Eulonia, where the muddy waters of the Sapelo River become saw grass filled marshland. The name proved prophetic. The plantation became a very successful producer of rice and indigo.

Lachlan served as a delegate for the Commons House in 1770, however, it was not long before Governor Wright again dissolved the assembly. Wright was angered because the delegates demanded more local authority rather than the royal declarations allowed. George was reelected to the Commons, this time representing St. Marys Parish, having purchased property in the parish shortly before Lachlan's term. It was intentional that George purchased the St. Marys property and became the representative for St. Marys Parish. The strategy allowed the McIntosh family to maintain a strong influence in the Commons House.

George married Ann Priscilla Houstoun in 1772, and the couple had one child, John Houstoun McIntosh that same year. With the colonial unrest intensifying, George along with his brothers, Lachlan and William, served as delegates to the Provincial Congress in Savannah.

Rice Hope became the victim of the Loyalists, when shortly after the Revolutionary War began, it was destroyed. The house was burned, the livestock and slaves were scattered. Several factors were prerequisite to the decimation; the McIntosh family's influence and the Continental forces had used Rice Hope as a waypoint while marching their troops against the British held Fort Barrington. The fort was eventually taken and held by the colonials for the remainder of the war.

In March 1777, George McIntosh was placed in irons and jailed. The charge was treason. He was accused of supplying rice to the British, a clear violation of the Continental Association. George had joined in a venture with his two brothers in law, Robert Baillie and Sir Patrick Houstoun, to sell a shipment of rice to Dutch Guiana. Shortly before the shipment left the harbor, another partner joined the venture, William Panton. The Continental's suspected both Baillie and Houstoun had Tory leanings; however, William Panton was a known Tory. Panton took the shipment to St. Augustine, where he altered the shipping documents and sold the cargo in the British West Indies.

Although the circumstances of the accusations reveal only guilt by association, Button Gwinnett pursued the charges against George. He was determined to ruin the McIntosh name by whatever means necessary. Perhaps Gwinnett's almost obsessive hatred of the McIntosh clan stemmed from the fact that George's was the only dissenting vote when Button Gwinnett was appointed as President of the Council of Safety.[14] It was the general consensus of the McIntosh family that Button Gwinnett was an inept leader and corrupt politician.

The Continental Congress eventually found that there was not enough evidence to pursue a conviction against George. George, neither cleared of the charges nor convicted, was simply released from jail. He returned to Georgia a broken man. George McIntosh died in December 1779 leaving behind his wife and son, John Houstoun, who was only seven years old.

John Houstoun McIntosh inherited his father's entire estate, which remained under the care of his Uncle Lachlan until he reached his majority. Rice Hope Plantation remained in the hands of John Houstoun until 1834, when it was sold to a cousin, Alexander McIntosh. The deed, detailing the sale of Rice Hope Plantation, is one of the few early historical documents of McIntosh County remaining. Devastating courthouse fires obliterated most county records in 1863 and 1873.

MALLOW PLANTATION

This plantation was a Crown grant to Captain John McIntosh, a British army officer who served in Florida during the War with Spain. Later, when this officer went into the Indian country, his brother, the eccentric Captain Roderick (Rory) McIntosh, with their sister, Miss Winnewood McIntosh, occupied the home which was built upon this bluff in the 1760s.
The exploits of the redoubtable Rory have filled pages of pre-Revolutionary Georgia history.
After the Revolution, Mallow became the property of Captain William McIntosh, a son of Captain John. He, too, was a British Army officer, and was the father of the Indian Chief, General William McIntosh.
Early in the 19th century, Mallow was purchased by Mr. and Mrs. Reuben King, and they were living here when the plantation was raided by forces from a Federal gunboat anchored in nearby Sapelo River, in November, 1862.

At Pine Harbor, 2.8 miles east of US 17, 2.2 miles north of Eulonia
GPS Coordinates: N31.32498, W81.22279

The British crown granted Captain John McIntosh several plots of land due to his distinguished service during the War with Spain. One of these land grants was known as Mallow Plantation and served as his residence. After the war, John decided to move to the Alabama territory, where the tribes of the Lower Creeks made their home. William, son of John McIntosh, accompanied his father.

Mallow was left in the hands of John's brother and sister, Captain Roderick "Rory" and Winnewood McIntosh. In all probability, John McIntosh left his sister, Winnewood, in charge of the running and management of the plantation. Rory, an eccentric, was always intent on storming any fortress that proved a nuisance to his Majesty, the King, and placed no importance on matters of money.

Rory was never a rich man, but he lived comfortably and at ease. During a trip to St. Augustine, while the city was in Spanish possession, Rory sold a herd of cattle and received payment in gold. He wrapped his earnings in a canvas bag. Along the way, the canvas tore and many of the gold dollars fell along the road. Rather than dismount and gather the coins, he tied up the hole in the canvas and continued his journey. Years later, when Rory found himself short of funds he returned to place along the road and retrieved the coins he had dropped.

Rory loved dogs and kept English Setters that he trained to track. He once made a large wager that he could hide a coin three miles from where he stood and his dog would retrieve it. Luath, his dog, was sent out and returned panting without the coin. "Treason," yelled Rory and set out to find what problem Luath had met. When he arrived on the spot, Rory found the log where he had hidden the coin, the earth around the site had been dug up but the coin was obviously missing. Rory looked up to see a man in the distance splitting rails. Rory approached the man with his dagger drawn. He threatened the man with his life if he did not reveal the location of the gold piece. The man, clearly afraid, produced the coin. He had watched Rory place something underneath the log, when he walked away the man had gone to investigate and found the gold. Rory tossed him back the coin and said, "Take it, vile caitiff[15], it was not the pelf[16], but the honor of my dog, I care for."

After the death of Captain John McIntosh, William decided to return and stake his claim for Mallow. He left in his wake two American Indian wives, one Creek and the other Cherokee and two sons. One of his sons, William McIntosh, eventually became known as Chief of the Lower Creek and the other, Roderick or Roley, became a lesser Chief in his own right.

Once Captain William, known as Captain for his brief service to the crown, returned to Mallow he married Barbara McIntosh of the adjoining Fairhope Plantation and daughter of his cousin, Colonel William McIntosh. Captain William lived out his days at Mallow Plantation and was buried under the Great Oak at Mallow Plantation in 1794.

Mallow was sold to Rueben King after the death of Captain William McIntosh. It was the King family who was in residence when Federal troops looted the plantation. Eighty-five year old Rueben and Sarah Amanda Walker, his daughter, watched as the soldiers plundered everything of value. Mallow was fortunate that day, it was left virtually untouched, while flames lit the sky as neighboring plantations burned.

Today, nothing is left of Mallow Plantation except for the old family burial plot surrounded by a high tabby wall, though time and nature have taken a toll on the epitaphs. Other family members were buried outside the plot and it is suspected that numerous graves lay unmarked in the shady grove oaks that was Mallow Plantation.

COLONEL JOHN MCINTOSH

About one mile from this spot at Fairhope, the adjoining plantation, Colonel John McIntosh, a hero of the American Revolution, was buried in 1826. It was Colonel McIntosh, in command of Fort Morris at Sunbury, who, when the British Lieut. Col L.V. Fuser demanded the surrender of the fort on Nov. 20, 1778, replied: "Come and Take It." A member of the family of Scottish Highlanders who led in the settlement of Darien and for whom the county of McIntosh was named, Col. McIntosh had a long and distinguished military career, serving throughout the Revolution and the War of 1812.

South of Pine Harbor, 2.8 miles east of US 17, 2.2 miles north of Eulonia
GPS Coordinates: N31.32451, W81.22338

Colonel John McIntosh became a Revolutionary War hero with the words, "Come and take it!" His challenge to Colonel L. V. Fuser confused the British commander enough to gain Fort Morris a six week reprieve. During the second assault, Colonel McIntosh was captured and held at Sunbury, which federal forces were using as a prisoner of war camp for Continental officers. Colonel McIntosh was later exchanged for a British officer and lived to fight another day. He gained the respect of those in higher authority and was later presented with a sabre baring the words, "Come and Take It!"

Eight years after the war, John McIntosh moved with his wife, Sarah Swinton McIntosh, to the banks of the St. John's River in Florida. During a visit to St. Augustine, he was seized and taken prisoner. He remained in the custody of Spain at Moro Castle in Havana for nearly a year accused of moving against the Spanish government. Through the efforts of George Washington and others, McIntosh was finally released to return to his beloved Sarah. During his absence Sarah who had gradually lost her sight, would never see her husband's face again. Sarah died in 1799 on St. Simons Island.

John McIntosh was called to service again in defense against the British in the War of 1812. He commanded three regiments of infantry and a battalion of artillery at Savannah. Promoted to General, McIntosh was reassigned with his troops to the Gulf Coast area where the British threatened. He marched a thousand miles through the wilderness of Georgia to defend Mobile from attack. Upon his return in June 1815, Mayor Thomas U. P. Charlton wrote the following:

"You had devoted the vigor of manhood in combating for the liberty and independence of your country, and when that liberty was again menaced by the same foe, an advanced period of life did not prevent you from again unsheathing the sword of seventy-six in defense of the same righteous cause. This consistent patriotism and bravery of conduct exhibits the true features of a character in which love of country and freedom predominates over every other consideration."

General John McIntosh died in 1826, a hero.

CAPTAIN WILLIAM MCINTOSH

In this plot under the "Great Oak at Mallow Plantation,"
Captain William McIntosh father of the Indian chief,
General William McIntosh, was buried in 1794. Captain
McIntosh, an officer in the British army, when stationed in
the Creek country, married two Indian women and their
sons, William and Roderick,
became chiefs among the Creeks.
Gen. William McIntosh was killed by his own people on
May 1, 1825, for signing the Treaty of Indian Springs.
Later his sons and his half brother, Roderick (Roley) led
the great Creek trek to Old Indian Territory. They and
their descendants have been distinguished lawyers, ministers, statesman, artists, soldiers - noted leaders in the
building of the West.

South of Pine Harbor, 2.8 miles east of US 17, 2.2 miles north of Eulonia
GPS Coordinates: N31.33084, W81.25203

C aptain William McIntosh descended from an illustrious military line: Benjamin McIntosh, one of the original Scottish Highlanders, who founded McIntosh County, and his father, Captain John McIntosh, who fought bravely against the Spanish in Florida. For his services, Captain McIntosh was awarded two land grants from the crown; the first of which was called Belleview Plantation, today known as the Belleview Community; the second grant became Mallow Plantation.

Mallow Plantation was the primary family home. The plantation bordered that of Fairhope Plantation owned by Colonel William McIntosh, son of John McIntosh Mohr, and John's cousin. In 1760, when Captain John decided to leave Mallow for the Indian country of Alabama, he turned over control of his plantation to his brother Roderick, nicknamed Rory, and sister, Winnewood.

William accompanied his father to Alabama. There William met and married Senoya Heneha. Senoya was a member of the Wind Clan of the Lower Creeks. She gave birth to a son, who she named William for his father. Among the Creeks, family virtue is derived from the mother's lineage; therefore, the fact that young William was half Scottish went unnoticed as he grew to be a young brave within the tribe. Following the Creek tradition, William took a second wife. The second wife bore him another son, named for William's brother Roderick and called Roley.

William, Sr. eventually left the Creeks after the death of his father, John. He petitioned and received the patriarchal inheri-
tance of Mallow Plantation. Upon returning to Mallow, William married Barbara McIntosh. Barbara was the daughter of his cousin William of the adjoining Fairhope Plantation. William and Barbara lived at Mallow until his death in 1794.

Young William was a renaissance man of two worlds. His time was divided between the Creeks, where he was taught how to survive in the wilderness, and at Mallow, where he was given the benefits of a European education. He has been described as a man who was graced with handsome features, intelligence, bravery and a commanding manner. William's business sense served him well and he acquired quite a fortune. Like his father before him, William had three wives. Each wife was afforded her own plantation to live and raise her children. Susanna Coe was Creek; Peggy was Cherokee; and Eliza Grierson was Scottish.

Young William joined the American forces and fought valiantly in the War of 1812, distinguishing himself at the battles of Autossee, HorseShoe and during the Florida campaign. At the war's end, William McIntosh was one of the signators of the Treaty of Fort Jackson, was promoted to the rank of Brigadier General and eventually, became the speaker for the Lower Creek villages. His work with the Creeks earned him the title, Chief of the Lower Creek.

Chief McIntosh served the Creek Nation well. He believed he could elevate the condition of the American Indian with warm homes, abundant food and peaceful living; specifically, the Creeks. He supported the move west into new territory, feeling that it would take the people away from the bad influences of the "white man." Chief McIntosh felt he was doing what was best for his people when he signed the Treaty of Indian Springs in 1825. The treaty gave over a vast amount of land in return for a substantial amount of money. Chief McIntosh knew that for the Creek tribes to survive, they would have to make peace with the white man; if not, they would slowly fade into extinction. The treaty infuriated the Menawa, a group of Creek leaders who had vowed that the next Chief to sign away Creek lands would die.

Hearing rumors of threats against his life, Chief McIntosh sent dispatches to his cousin, Georgia Governor George Troup, asking for support. Seventy-seven days after signing the treaty, Chief McIntosh was in the house of his wife Susanna when the Menawa set it ablaze. McIntosh quickly sent his son, Chilly, for help. As Chief McIntosh opened the door to escape the flames, bullets tore through his body, his blood cascaded down the steps of his home. Chief William McIntosh was dragged into the yard, his lifeless body was scalped. The plantation slaves were scattered, crops were burned and the livestock was slaughtered.

Susanna, grief stricken, threw her body over her dead husband and remained there for three days until the troops sent by Governor Troup arrived. The troops buried Chief William McIntosh in the blood soaked ground of his home.

The Creeks did their best to fight the enforcement of the Treaty of Indian Springs. Yet in the end, the Government upheld the treaty and forced the Creeks from their lands. Chilly McIntosh, son of Chief William, and his uncle, Roley McIntosh, now a Chief in his own right, led the weary people to Oklahoma. Almost half failed to survive the journey.

SUTHERLAND'S BLUFF

Sutherland's Bluff, about 1.5 miles South on this road, overlooks the Sapelo River and the Inland Waterway. The site was named for Lieut. Patrick Sutherland, to whom it was granted upon recommendation of General James Edward Oglethorpe in recognition of the Lieutenant's service at the Battle of Bloody Marsh. At the beginning of the Revolutionary war, a shipyard was laid out at Sutherland's Bluff, moulds were made at Philadelphia, and live oak timbers were cut at the Bluff for the building of gunboats and four frigates for the Continental Navy. The British blockade of 1778 prevented the completion of the work. In the late 18th and 19th centuries, Sutherland's Bluff was a regular stop for ships sailing the Inland Waterway, and a store and livery stable kept there for the convenience of outfitting passengers disembarking for overland travel.
In 1954 archaeological investigations disclosed evidenced of ancient Indian and Spanish occupation of the bluff.

7 miles east of US 17 toward Shellman Bluff then bear right 0.7 mile
GPS Coordinates: N31.33495, W81.19302

Sutherland Bluff Plantation, located on the Sapelo River, was a Crown Grant issued to Lieutenant Patrick Sutherland for his distinguished service during the Battle of Bloody Marsh. During the battle, three platoons of British regulars retreated in the face of the enemy fearing they were outnumbered. Lieutenant Sutherland and one platoon held the entire left flank, while the Scottish Highlanders and their Creek allies commanded the remainder of the field. For this, General Oglethorpe recommended Lieutenant Sutherland receive a grant of Georgia lands.

The property later came into the hands of Robert Mackay who, in turn, sold the plantation to Thomas Spalding in 1810. Spaulding presented Sutherland Plantation as a wedding gift to his daughter, Jane Martin Leak Spaulding, when she married Daniel Howard Brailsford. Brailsford was a state legislator and McIntosh County Commissioner of Roads. The couple had two children, Sarah and William. Sarah later married Richard L. Morris, a rice planter. William ran Sutherland Plantation and served the Confederacy.

William became the master of Sutherland Plantation at the tender age of seven when his father was brutally murdered. In August 1833, Daniel Howard Brailsford was attending his duties as Commissioner of Roads when he was approached by his former overseer, John Forbes. Forbes had been dismissed two years before according to Brailsford, because he no longer required his services. The parting was said to have been amicable; however, the newspapers of the time claimed the dismissal was the motive behind Forbes' assault.

The reports say that Forbes attacked Daniel Brailsford during the morning hours, wounding him in the jaw with a double barreled gun. Obviously, the wound was not too severe because later in the afternoon as Daniel Brailsford was giving instructions to road workers for the next day's work; Forbes returned. The lead, this time, struck a fatal blow to the abdomen and Daniel Howard Brailsford died there on the road, one hundred yards from the Sapelo River. Forbes was immediately apprehended. A more plausible motive is suggested in Robert Manson Myers' *The Children of Pride*. Myers states that Daniel Brailsford was "allegedly" focusing his attentions on Forbes' wife.

The McIntosh County Superior Court met in November. The trial only lasted for two days, it took a jury fifteen minutes to decide Forbes' guilt. He was sentenced to death and the hanging took place shortly thereafter.

William Brailsford, under the tutelage of his grandfather, eventually took over management of Sutherland Plantation. William became one of the wealthiest Sea Island cotton planters of coastal Georgia. He was known as an aggressive sportsman, who enjoyed horses, racing, betting, hunting and other outdoor sports.

William's constant companions were James Hamilton Couper, Randolph Spaulding, his uncle, only four years William's senior, and Charles Augustus Lafayette Lamar. The reputation of this group was known far and wide as carousers, wealthy young men who, without concern, spread their money around to the most unseemly places. William, in particular, was noted as having an extremely volatile temper.

Charles Lamar enjoyed great influence over William and it was with Lamar that he allied himself during the early days of the Civil War. Sutherland's Bluff Plantation became headquarters for the Lamar Rangers commanded by Charles Lamar. From the bluff overlooking the Sapelo River, the Rangers could observe Yankee vessels traversing the water below. The fact that Sutherland Plantation was the principal picket[17] station in McIntosh County led to its eventual destruction and devastation by the invading federal forces.

William Brailsford joined the Confederate Army as a First Lieutenant in Savannah, June 1861. In September 1861, William Brailsford succeeded Captain Lamar as commander of the company. The company then became known as Captain Brailsford's Company, Lamar Rangers of the 1st Georgia Cavalry Battalion. In addition to picket duty, the unit served also as the Fugitive Slave Recovery Unit. Promoted to Captain, Brailsford commanded the unit through some of the most fierce fighting of the war. While fighting in the Tennessee/Virginia Incursion, Captain Brailsford was captured by federal forces near Murfreesboro, Tennessee. He was confined at Johnson's Island Ohio Union Prison Camp, where he spent the remainder of the war. Captain Brailsford was released in May 1865 and returned to Georgia.

He returned only to find the Sutherland Bluff Plantation had been devastated by Union troops. William Brailsford would never live on the plantation again and instead, settled in Bryan County on his Retreat Plantation. William Brailsford died in June 1887. He is buried in the family cemetery at Retreat.

Another cemetery lies on the edge of the Sutherland Bluff Plantation property. Some of the ancient stones there bare the surnames of Spaulding, Thorpe and Wilson, memorials to those whose labor and enslavement served to bring success to the coastal Georgia plantations.

The Sutherland Bluff Plantation eventually fell to ruin and was used as a refuse site. Mr. Elwood Harper purchased the property and has developed the Sapelo Hammock Golf Club. The home sites and championship golf course are perfectly placed among the towering live oaks that have stood through generations of history. Traveling down the path, the original road through Sutherland Bluff Plantation, transports you back to a time long ago.

THE MCINTOSH FAMILY
OF MCINTOSH COUNTY

The service of this family to America, since the first of the Clan, with their leader, Captain John McIntosh Mohr, came from the Highlands of Scotland to Georgia, in 1736, forms a brilliant record. The roll of distinguished members of this family includes: Gen. Lachlan McIntosh, Col. William McIntosh, Col. John McIntosh, Maj. Lachlan McIntosh - officers in the Revolution: Col. James L. McIntosh, killed in the Mexican War; Maria J. McIntosh, authoress; Capt. John McIntosh, Capt Wm. McIntosh of Mallow. Capt. Roderick (Rory) McIntosh - British Army officers serving in the War with Spain and in the Indian country; George M. Troup, Governor of Georgia; John McIntosh Kell, Second Officer of Alabama; Thomas Spalding of Sapelo; Creek Indian Chiefs - Gen. Wm. McIntosh, Roley McIntosh, Judge Alexander McIntosh. Aces Blue Eagle ... and many more.

US 17-GA 25, 1.7 miles south of the South Newport River, South Newport
GPS Coordinates: N31.37076, W81.24040

The American McIntosh Clan was founded when brothers John McIntosh Mohr and Benjamin McIntosh joined General James Edward Oglethorpe to establish and defend the English colony of Georgia. The Highlanders were known for their bravery and perseverance in battle, making them a valued group in General Oglethorpe's ever expanding colony.

The McIntosh's contribution to the city of Darien, McIntosh County, the state of Georgia and the developing nation were extraordinary. A member of this family has distinguished himself in every war this country has ever fought. They were pioneers, soldiers, sailors, Native American chiefs, lawyers, elected officials, doctors, planters, bankers, authors, the list goes on and on. Most importantly, they were colonists.

They suffered a great many tragedies along the way and celebrated each others triumphs. One line about the family summed up what the family meant to each other and it said, in part, "when one McIntosh prospered the entire family benefitted." They were devoted to one another as a family.

A rogue or two in the mix proved to keep the family interesting. A story is told of the Highlanders upon encountering the Roman legion during the ancient Scottish wars. It is as follows:

A great big hairy kilted Scotsman jumps up on a hillock "Aye so you're Romans eh? - gie me yer ten best men then." Ten legionnaires were dispatched. Bang, crash, wallop! . . None returned. A hundred soldiers are sent up. Five minutes later a lone survivor struggles back, but drops dead before he can say a word. Risking all, the commander sent his whole legion up the hill. Screams, shouts and the commotion of battle followed. Then on the sky line a lone Roman officer approaches. "Sir. Sir. They've cheated. They lied! There were two of them all the time . . ."

I conclude this section with a family history of both lines of the McIntosh Clan. I have done my best to provide an accurate accounting of the family tree, however, it may contain mistakes, because early McIntosh County records were burned in various courthouse fires, much of the information is no longer available. Please understand that this is a representation of what this author believes to be fact. I apologize for any family member, I might not have included or placed incorrectly. What follows is my best effort to represent the distinguished McIntosh Family of McIntosh County.

JOHN MCINTOSH MOHR   married   **MARJORY FRASER**
1698 - 1762   March 3, 1725   1701 - ?

Children

1. Colonel William (1726 - 1801) married Mary Jane Mackay

    Children
    1. Lieutenant Colonel John (1748 - 1786) married   (1) Sarah Swinton
                                                      (2) Mrs. Stevens
                                                      (3) Mrs. Agnes Hillary

    2. Major Lachlan (1750 - ?)
    3. William (1752 - ?)
    4. Marjery (1754 - 1818) married   James Spalding

        Children
        1. Thomas Spalding (1774 - 1851)

    5. Barbara (1760 - ?) married   Captain William McIntosh
                                                      (her cousin)

    6. Hester (1765 - ?) married   Alexander Baillie
    7. Donald (1770 - ?) never married

2. General Lachlan (1727 - 1806) married   Sarah Threadcroft

    Children
    1. John Hampden married   Charlotte Nephew
    2. George
    3. Catherine McCauley
    4. Lachlan married   Mary Perisana Donnom
    5. General John (1754 - 1826)

3. John (1728 - 1796) never married
4. Alexander (did not survive to adulthood)
5. Mary (did not survive to adulthood)
6. Phineas (1732 - did not survive to adulthood)
7. Lewis & Janet (twins 1733 - did not survive to adulthood)
8. Anne (1737 - 1761) married   Robert Baillie
9. George (1739 - 1779) married   Ann Priscilla Houston

    Child
    1. John Houston (1773 - 1836)

BENJAMIN MCINTOSH   **WIFE UNKNOWN**

1. Captain John married   Wife Unknown

    Children

    1. Catherine married   George Troup

    Children
    1. George Michael (Governor of Georgia)
    2. James

2. Captain William married   (1) Creek wife - Senoya Heneha
                                            (2) Cherokee wife
                                            (3) Barbara McIntosh

Captain William's child with Senoya
1. Brigadier General - Chief William married   (1) Creek wife - Susannah Coe
                                            (2) Cherokee wife - Peggy
                                            (3) Barbara McIntosh

      Captain William's child with Cherokee wife
2. Roderick

2. Captain Roderick (Rory) McIntosh
3. Winnewood McIntosh

WILLIAM BARTRAM TRAIL
Traced 1773-1777

Donald McIntosh welcomed William Bartram to his home in 1773, giving him shelter from "A Tremendous Thunderstorm."

US 17-GA 25, 1.7 miles south of the South Newport River, South Newport
GPS Coordinates: N31.37076, W81.24040

No one could better describe William Bartram's travels through the marshes, forests and swamps of coastal Georgia better than the man himself. The following excerpt was taken from his own text, entitled, *Bartram's Travels*.[18]
William Bartram passed the first night in Georgia under the roof of the Honorable B. Andrews, Esquire of Savannah. He then departed and stayed the next evening in a home along the Sapelo and Newport Rivers, no other clues to his location are given.

      "THE next morning I took leave of this worthy family, and sat off for the settlements on the Alatahama, still pursuing the high road for Fort Barrington, till towards noon, when I turned off to the left, following the road to Darian, a settlement on the river, twenty miles lower down, and near the coast. The fore part of this day's journey was pleasant, the plantations frequent, and the roads in tolerable good repair. But the country being now less cultivated, the roads became bad, pursuing my journey almost continually, through swamps and creeks, waters of Newport and Sapello, till night, when I lost my way; but coming up to a fence, I saw a glimmering light, which conducted me to a house, where I stayed all night, and met with very civil entertainment.

Early next morning, I sat off again, in company with the overseer of the farm, who piloted me through a large and difficult swamp, when we parted; he in chase of deer, and I towards Darian. I rode several miles through a high forest of pines, thinly growing on a level plain, which admitted an ample view, and a free circulation of air, to another swamp; and crossing a considerable branch of Sapello river, I then came to a small plantation by the side of another swamp: the people were remarkably civil and hospitable. The man's name was M'Intosh, a family of the first colony established in Georgia, under the conduct of General Oglethorpe. Was there ever such a scene of primitive simplicity, as was here exhibited, since the days of the good King Tammany! The venerable grey headed Caledonian smilingly meets me coming up to his house. "Welcome, stranger, come in, and rest; the air is now very sultry; it is a very hot day."

I was there treated with some excellent venison, and here found friendly and secure shelter from a tremendous thunder storm, which came up from the N. W. and soon after my arrival, began to discharge its fury all around. Stepping to the door to observe the progress and direction of the tempest, the fulgour and rapidity of the streams of lightning, passing from cloud to cloud, and from the clouds to the earth, exhibited a very awful scene; when instantly the lightning, as it were, opening a fiery chasm in the black cloud, darted with inconceivable rapidity on the trunk of a large pine tree, that stood thirty or forty yards from me, and set it in a blaze. The flame instantly ascended upwards of ten or twelve feet, and continued flaming about fifteen minutes, when it was gradually extinguished, by the deluges of rain that fell upon it.

I SAW here a remarkably large turkey of the native wild breed: his head was above three feet from the ground when he stood erect; he was a stately beautiful bird, of a very dark dusky brown colour, the tips of the feathers of his neck, breast, back, and shoulders, edged with a copper colour, which in a certain exposure looked like burnished gold, and he seemed not insensible of the splendid appearance he made. He was reared from an egg, found in the forest, and hatched by a hen of the common domestic fowl.

OUR turkey of America is a very different species from the mileagris of Asia and Europe; they are nearly thrice their size and weight. I have seen several that have weighed between twenty and thirty pounds, and some have been killed that weighed near forty. They are taller, and have a much longer neck proportionally, and like wise longer legs, and stand more erect; they are also very different in colour. Ours are all, male and female, of a dark brown colour, not having a black feather on them; but the male exceedingly splendid, with changeable colours. In other particulars they differ not.

THE tempest being over, I waited till the floods of rain had run off the ground, then took leave of my friends, and departed."

JONESVILLE
- 6 miles -

This Site of the village of Jonesville, so named for its first settler, Samuel Jones, is about 6 miles West on this road. There, early in the Revolution, McGirth with British forces attacked a small garrison at Moses Way's stockade and a fierce battle took place, ending in the defeat of McGirth. In 1843 a Congregational Church was chartered at Jonesville with Nathaniel Varnedoe, Wm. Jones and Moses L. Jones, Trustees. The village became a refuge for women, children and invalids from the Coast when that area was blockaded by federal gunboats during the War Between the States.

US 17-GA 25 0.6 mile south of the South Newport River, South Newport
GPS Coordinates: N31.38020, W81.23477

Samuel Jones was issued a land grant from the English Crown in 1768. Jones built his home there and the settlement of Jonesville was established. The small community was set at the headwaters of the South Newport River in the further northwestern corner of McIntosh County.

During the Revolutionary War the small settlement saw fighting when the notorious Colonel Daniel McGirth, sometimes spelled as McGirt, and his brother, Captain James McGirth stormed through. Colonel McGirth commanded the Florida Rangers, a band of cutthroat marauders, who served the British as Royalists.

In 1776, the First Florida Expedition from Georgia was responsible for building a line of defense against British attack. The expedition built forts including Fort Howe[19], McIntosh, Darien and Beard's Bluff. When McGirth and his men attacked Jonesville at Moses Way's Stockade, they met an unexpected force and were defeated.

The settlement was never large, only inhabiting eighteen families at its population's height. However, it was known to be a pleasant inland escape that coastal plantation families retreated to during the sultry malarial season. In 1843, the Congregational Church was chartered in Jonesville to give both the full time and seasonal residents a place to worship.

Jonesville played a small, but important, part in the Civil War for the citizens of McIntosh County. When federal gunboats threatened their shores and troops raided the coastal regions, Jonesville was a place to hide. The elderly, infirmed, women and children of the coastal plantations found a safe haven there to remove themselves from the Union assault until the worst was over.

After the Civil War, Jonesville began to decline. Soon only sparse recollections were left of the little settlement. The name was changed several times, it was known as Jones's Station because mail was posted there and later, simply Jones as it appears on detailed maps today.

SOUTH NEWPORT
BAPTIST CHURCH

This Church was organized by the Rev. Charles O.
Screven at Harris Neck, 7 miles West of here, during
the early 1800's. As the Harris Neck Baptist Church, it
was admitted to the Sunbury Baptist Association
November 12, 1824.
In the early 1830's, the Church was moved to this site
and became the South Newport Baptist Church. On
December 9, 1841, the South Newport Baptist Church
was chartered, the Trustees named: Charles W.
Thorpe, Gideon B. Dean, Thomas K. Gould, William J.
Cannon, Henry J. White. The present edifice is the
second
erected on this site.

US 17-GA 25 at GA 131 Junction, 0.4 mile south of South Newport River.
GPS Coordinates: N31.38140, W81.23439

The South Newport Baptist Church, once known as the Harris Neck Baptist Church, began through the efforts of Reverend Charles O. Screven. Although Screven organized the church in the early 1800s, it was not chartered until 1841, eleven years after his death. Known then by the name of South Newport Baptist, representing its new location. The sanctuary that now stands is the second building on the current site, its congregation continues to grow.

About one-tenth of a mile north of South Newport Baptist Church stands a remarkable little chapel, known as "The Smallest Church in America." Although the distinction was most likely true in 1950, when the tiny chapel was built, others have taken the title since that time. The Chapel is certainly the smallest in Georgia.

Mrs. Agnes C. Harper, a rural grocer, wanted to give travelers along the highway (US 17) a quiet place for meditation, reflection and interdenominational worship. The charming little sanctuary has a high pitched roof supported by exposed rough beams, small stained glass windows and a glass star in the ceiling to illuminate its interior. The petite cathedral measures ten by fifteen feet, with room for twelve parishioners and a clergy. Yet, the slight dimensions speak nothing of the incredible warmth one feels when only walking through the door.

The church is located in a shaded grove dubbed Memory Park. The park and chapel were legally deeded to Jesus Christ preventing the property from ever being sold. Upon the pulpit lays a child's plain school notebook. Within the pages are the troubles, hopes and praises of travelers who have happened upon the little sanctuary and those that bring their prayers purposely to the blessed little church.

The haven, known as Christ's Chapel, is supported by donations. Sadly, a sign had to be placed requesting that the lock on the tithe box not be broken. The landmark is open to the public 24 hours a day. From time to time weddings and special services are held in the little church with just enough room for Jesus.

CONFEDERATE POST IN 1864

Near this spot, Company F of the Third South Carolina Cavalry, Lieut. W. L. Mole commanding, was stationed during the summer of 1864. The Company was on Patrol duty, guarding the Coast of McIntosh County.

On the night of August 18th, the post was attacked by Federal Troops coming up the South Newport River. Of Company F, less than 20 men escaped death or capture. Five civilian prisoners were taken also, and the Bridge over the South Newport River was burned.

US 17-GA 25, 0.2 miles south of the South Newport River, South Newport
GPS Coordinates: N31.38040, W81.23439

Two weeks after the capture of twenty-three old men at Ebenezer Church the same federal soldiers from the USS *Saratoga,* under the authority of Commander George M. Colvocoresses, faced the Third South Carolina Cavalry. The *Saratoga* slipped into the South Newport River with darkness as her camouflage. As the sun broke the horizon on August 18, 1864, at South Newport, the skirmish began.

Lieutenant W. F. Mole commanded one hundred men assigned to the Confederate Army, Company F. Twenty men out of the original one hundred were left standing, the rest were captured or lay in crumpled heaps across the battle ground. Not even the innocents were spared, five noncombatants were also taken prisoner. The bridge over the South Newport River, which was the only crossing for miles, was burned. The road to Savannah was cut off and with it the supply lines.

Soldiers protecting Savannah depended on inland supply routes for food, ammunition and medical supplies. When Commander Colvocoresses cut off those lines from both the inland routes and the waterways, Savannah was completely isolated. Unless Union troops were driven back, Savannah would eventually be forced to surrender or starve. By December 1864, Savannah was taken by General Sherman's men virtually without a fight.

Endnotes

[1] A hand threshing implement consisting of a wooden handle at the end of which a stouter and shorter stick is so hung as to swing freely.

[2] Mohr was Scottish title signifying head of the clan.

[3] A wooden framework with holes for the head and hands, in which offenders were once locked to be exposed to public ridicule as punishment.

[4] Gold

[5] Extempore is a method in which a sermon is delivered without a written script to guide the minister.

[6] Glazed pottery

[7] A 16th century kiln

[8] *Repartimiento* was a system of forced wage labor.

[9] Pieces of eight, gold

[10] Oak was and is still used, because it doesn't leave an offensive odor or taste to the rum. The casks were charred to deodorize the liquor and bring color with a distinctive flavor.

[11] 150 proof

[12] Cypress knees are actually part of the tree's root that emerges from the water or the mud in which the tree is growing.

[13] The fees charged by the crown to occupy granted land.

[14] This office was later changed to Governor of the State.

[15] A Scottish curse word

[16] coin

[17] A detachment of soldiers guarding the main body of the army.

[18] No corrections to the text have been made in regard to spelling, punctuation or content.

[19] Initially called Fort Barrington

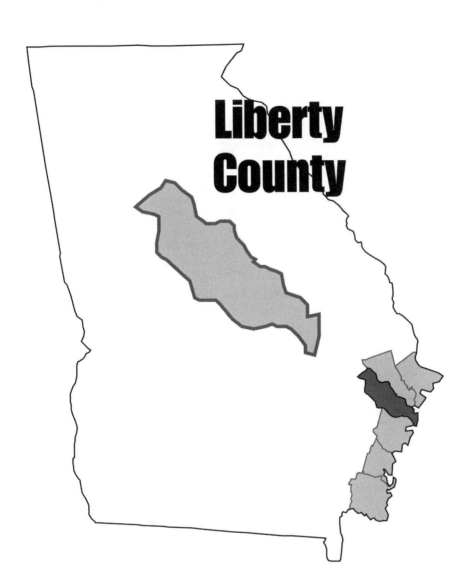

Liberty County

SKIRMISH IN BULLTOWN SWAMP

In November of 1778, Lieut. Col. James Mark Prevost, with 100 British Regulars, and 300 Refugees and Indians under McGirth, crossed the Altamaha River and moved into Georgia, killing or taking prisoner all men they found, and ravaging the plantations. Continental troops and Militia marched against them. Near this spot, where the old Savannah to Darien road crossed Bulltown Swamp, a small detachment of Mounted Militia, Col. John Baker commanding, met and fought a
delaying action with the invaders. Colonel Baker, Captain Cooper and William Goulding were wounded.

US 17/GA 25, 6 miles south of Riceboro
GPS Coordinates: N31.66167, W81.398027

Colonel John Baker received his commission as Captain of the St. Johns Riflemen at St. Johns Parish in January 1776 and led his men valiantly in battle over the next two years. In November 1778, Baker's command was ordered to delay the British forces marching into Savannah for as long as possible. Colonel Baker collected whatever Continental Army troops he could find to increase his numbers and traveled along the Fort Barrington Road engaging Colonel Prevost's British Regulars at Bulltown Swamp. Prevost, commander of all British forces in East Florida, led 100 British Regulars, 300 Loyalists and a contingent of Creek Native Americans under the command of Daniel McGirth. McGirth was known to be ruthless and cruel, he spared nothing or no one that crossed his path.

Colonel Baker realized at the onset that his sparse forces were extremely out numbered and had little chance against the superior force, this did not deter their attack. Baker, along with Captains Cooper and Goulding, was wounded in the fighting, and the Continentals were forced to retreat to Riceboro Bridge. At the bridge they once again encountered the British and another skirmish ensued. Increased losses forced Baker's detachment to retreat again.

Baker was a man of compassion, who believed strongly in his cause. He cared for his men and they fought as much for him as they did duty to their country. One example of his concern was displayed on a cold rainy night. Baker encountered a young fifteen year old soldier shivering as he lay curled on the muddy ground beneath a tree. Baker recognized the young man as one of his Continental Light Horse Regiment assigned to drive the British from East Florida. He took off his woolen cloak, draped it about the boy and walked away. The young man, having lost so much at his young age, was a widower with a infant son and never forgot the kindness of his superior officer. This young man eventually distinguished himself during the Revolution and rose to the rank of Colonel by the end of the war. The man's name was Colonel Daniel Stewart. He returned, a hero, to his home in Liberty County.

RICEBOROUGH

Near the old North Newport Bridge, a short distance
East of here, the Court House square for Liberty
County was laid out by Act of the Georgia Legislature
of February 1, 1797. Riceborough was then the Seat
of Justice for Liberty County, and a Court House and
Public Buildings were erected her on land given by
Matthew McAllister, Esq. Thomas Stevens, Daniel
Stewart, Joel Walker and Henry Wood were named
Commissioners.
Riceborough was for many years an important port for
the shipping of rice and other agricultural products
from this area.

US 17/GA 25 near the junction with GA 119, Riceborough
GPS Coordinates: N31.74516, W81.43988

From the time of its conception in 1777, the Liberty County seat was Sunbury. The public meeting house was the center of government and no courthouse was ever constructed. In 1791, the Georgia Legislature appointed commissioners in order to build a courthouse and jail, no such public buildings ever materialized. The commissioners did not follow through with the legislative edict largely due to the decline in population. It had become apparent that Sunbury was in decline. Sunbury remained a resort area to the wealthy for several years until hurricanes, disease and lack of use left the town virtually deserted.

The Georgia Legislature stepped in and moved the county seat to North New Port Bridge. Matthew McAllister, Esquire, donated a plot of land two hundred-thirty feet in length and one hundred-fifty feet in width, near the North New Port Bridge in 1797. This property became the site for the first Liberty County Courthouse and Jail. The settlement was renamed Riceborough. An act was passed by the legislature stating that all public business including elections and matters for the courts would now take place there. Riceborough was centrally located within the district and near Savannah, which had become the most important Georgia port.

After almost forty years, the Liberty County seat was moved again. The population had shifted and settlements had became more populated inland. In 1836, the Georgia Legislature moved the Liberty County seat to the town of General Parade Ground and made provisions for the sale of the jail at Riceborough. No mention in county records was made concerning the disposition of the courthouse. General Parade Ground was renamed Hinesville in 1837 and replaced Riceborough as the Liberty County seat that same year.

Today, Riceborough is no more than a tiny dot on a well detailed Georgia map. Following Sunbury into the annals history, Riceborough was eventually deserted and became little more than a sparsely populated subdivision.

LeCONTE BOTANICAL GARDENS

Five miles west of here on the old Post Road, the southern most postal route in America, is the site of the home and botanical gardens of Louis LeConte, naturalist, mathematician and scholar, for whom the famous LeConte Pear was named. A native of New Jersey, Dr. LeConte was married to Ann Quarterman, a member of Midway Church in 1812. He established his famed botanical gardens on his extensive plantation. In his attic he fitted a chemical laboratory which included novelties of a botanical garden in which he cultivated rare plants, which came from all parts of the world. Although the modest Dr. LeConte did not exploit his achievements, it was nothing unusual for visitors from foreign lands to view his gardens.
Dr. LeConte's internationally known sons, Dr. John LeConte, born in 1818 and Dr. Joseph LeConte, born in 1823, at the family plantation, were two of the most distinguished scientific scholars of the nineteenth century. They made the University of California famous.

US 17/GA 25, 2 miles south of Riceborough at Retreat
GPS Coordinates: N31.70276, W81.413938

Woodmanston Plantation, a thriving rice plantation, at its peak encompassed over 3,000 acres. The home site was built by the LeConte brothers, John Eatton and William, in 1760, and was noted as one of the largest in the South. Located in the Bulltown Swamp off of the South Newport River, Woodmanston Plantation came to international fame for the botanical gardens grown there.

Louis, like his father John Eatton LeConte, was a physician. He used his skills on the plantation nursing his family and slaves. Physicians of the 19th century were known to concoct their own medicines from plants and herbs, Louis was no different. The attic of the house at Woodmanston became his laboratory.

By 1813, Louis began to develop the garden. His love of flowers and shrubs cultivated at Woodmanston expanded to an intense interest in botany and horticulture. The garden measured over an acre and in addition to native plants included many new and exotic species. Louis had a special love for camellias and his collection was extraordinary; some reached fifteen feet high with trunks over a foot in diameter. Flowering bulbs were another of Louis' specialties, he cultivated over forty different variety in his garden. Some of these bulbs were brought from such faraway places as Barbados, Mexico, Portugal and Spain.

Louis LeConte's children inherited his love of science and natural beauty. Of the six offspring, this was especially true of his two sons, John and Joseph. They both became professors working to establish the University of California at Berkeley, where John served as the University's first president. Joseph gained an international reputation for his works in physiological optics, evolution and religion, and geology. Joseph is most remembered as one of the founding members of the Sierra Club.

Louis, after the death of his wife Ann, devoted most of his time and energy to the garden where he passed the time until he again could lay beside his beloved wife. His son, Joseph, recalled in his autobiography that,

> 'Every day after his breakfast... he walked about the garden, enjoying its beauty and neatness and giving minute directions for its care and improvements.'

Ironically, the LeConte garden reached its peak at the time of Louis' death in 1838. While the garden contained a wide variety of plants and shrubs, it is noted that no finer specimens of *Camellia Japonicas* (Camellias) and bulb type plants could be found in any single garden in America. Joseph LeConte journeyed one last time to the place of his childhood in 1896. He was astonished to find Woodmanston and her garden in state of complete abandon and disrepair.

Today, thanks to the efforts of the LeConte Woodmanston Foundation, the plantation and gardens are being restored. The sixty-four acre historic site is surrounded by pine forests and the Bulltown Swamp, protecting the heart of the plantation where the main house and gardens were located. A nature trail has been constructed leading through the former rice fields and cypress swamp. The former fields, with the use of restored trunk gates, can still be flooded using gravity flow and the management have plans to grow rice utilizing methods reminiscent of 19th century cultivation. Eventually, the historic plantation site and gardens will be opened to the public as both a tribute to the great scientific minds that created and maintained Woodmanston Plantation and Botanical Gardens with a reminder of days long past.

SIMON MUNRO

In the family cemetery on this plantation, Westfield, Simon Munro, donor of the silver communion
service used for many years in old Midway Congregational Church, is buried. Early in the Revolutionary War, Simon Munro, a resident of St. John's Parish, was banished from the State of Georgia, and forbidden to set foot within its borders, because of his Tory activities. After repeated petitions from his friends and neighbors, the banishment was lifted and he was allowed to return to his home and family.

5.6 miles west of US 17 on Sandy Run Road, south of Riceborough
GPS Coordinates: N31.72397, W81.500825

P resident John Adams was quoted as saying in 1776,

"only one-third of the people supported the Patriot Cause. A second third wished to remain loyal to 'King and Country'."

Loyalists, also known as Tories, were the men and women who refused to renounce the British crown even after the Declaration of Independence was signed on July 4, 1776. Twenty per cent of the population of the British controlled American colonies opposed separation from England. Loyalists were most common in the southern colonies because these were the last areas settled and the newly founded colonies had little experience with the restrictive resolutions and exorbitant taxes. Even the most avid patriots had kinsmen who embraced British rule, including such noted government figures as Adams, Washington, Franklin and Jefferson. Loyalists felt that a compromise could avoid a revolution, grievances between the Colonists and the Crown could be resolved through diplomacy.

The defeat of Britain left over 100,000 Loyalists stripped of their possessions and they were forced to escape the American colonies with only their lives. They dispersed to various places such as, Great Britain, Canada, Florida, the West Indies and the Western Frontier. Some were not as fortunate and like the patriots, gave their lives for their beliefs.

Simon Munro was a Loyalist. His name appeared, along with those of prominent citizens, on the list of treasonous individuals subject to the antiloyalist laws enacted at the conclusion of the Revolution. He was forced from his home and banished from the State of Georgia. If he was found on Georgia soil, his sentence was death.

When Munro knew his days as a citizen of Georgia were numbered, he donated a silver communion service to the Midway Congregational Church. There he had worshiped alongside the most avid of patriots in the parish that would one day be called, "Liberty." His association with the Midway Church proved to be Simon Munro's saving grace. Church members, friends and neighbors gathered Simon's belongings and stored them until he was allowed to return to his home.

The Treaty for Peace of 1783, enacted by Congress, recommended that the thirteen colonies allow the Loyalists one year to return and obtain restitution for their losses. Further confiscation was to be illegal. However, confiscation and persecution often continued. Most Loyalists could not regain their lost property, many feared for their lives and refused to return home. By 1790, antiloyalist laws no longer existed.

The British government continued, at great expense, to reimburse many Loyalists with pensions and compensation for confiscated property. Assistance was given to those that applied. Simon Munro applied for restitution of the slaves that were killed or captured. His claim amounted to 540 British pounds for thirteen lost slaves. Although that doesn't sound like much, converted to the funds of today the claim would be equivalent to approximately $60,000.00.

The affect of the Loyalists on American history are a mystery, most Loyalists were soon forgotten. The long held belief that the American Revolution was a unanimous effort among the colonies is a myth that we as citizens choose to hold dear. However, patriots that fought for independence from England penned another document called the United States Constitution, which contains a Bill of Rights protecting those, like the Loyalists, whose opinions differ.

The Canadian government in 1789, the same year the Bill of Rights was proposed, created a hereditary organization called The United Empire Loyalists. The organization was established to honor those who supported the crown before the Treaty for Peace of 1783. The organization is still in existence today.

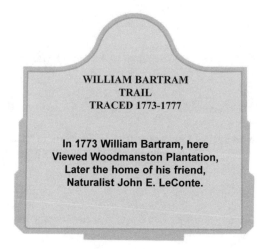

WILLIAM BARTRAM
TRAIL
TRACED 1773-1777

In 1773 William Bartram, here
Viewed Woodmanston Plantation,
Later the home of his friend,
Naturalist John E. LeConte.

Barrington Ferry Road, south of Sandy Run Road, south of Riceborough
GPS Coordinates: N31.70546, W81.487854

The well reknown American naturalists, John and his son, William, passed by Woodmanston Plantation on their trek to Florida in 1765. The father and son described and collected a plant they named the Franklin tree or *Franklinia Alatamatha* in honor of their friend, Benjamin Franklin. These specimens were found growing on the banks of the Altamaha River only fifteen miles south of Woodmanston Plantation. The Franklin tree is now thought to be extinct and the only specimens we have today are the descendants of those collected by the Bartrams.

By the early 1800s, botanists from around the world were flocking to the region in search of the *Franklinia* and other rare or unknown plants. Many of these plants, were found growing at Woodmanston under the meticulous care of Louis LeConte. For the next twenty-eight years, Louis conducted many plant finding expeditions in the undeveloped areas surrounding his plantation and built an extensive botanical garden at Woodmanston Plantation.

William Bartram spoke of Woodmanston in his book detailing his travels south to Florida. The passage beautifully states[1],

"The extensive plantation of rice and corn, now in early verdure, decorated here and there with groves of floriferous and fragrant trees and shrubs, under the cover and protection of pyramidal laurels and plumed palms, which now and then break through upon the sight from both sides of the way as we pass along; the eye at intervals stealing a view at the humble, but elegant and neat habitation, of the happy proprietor, amidst arbours and groves, all day, and moon-light nights, filled with the melody of the chearful mockbird, warbling nonpareil, and plaintive turtle dove, altogether present a view of magnificence and joy, inexpressibly charming and animating."

William Bartram, traveler and naturalist, is noted for his meticulous recordings of his travels. Many roads, postal routes and ferry ways were created based on findings during his travels. William Bartram died in 1823. Death came suddenly and kindly to the aged naturalist, as he would have wished, while strolling through his beloved garden.

WOODMANSTON PLANTATION

Established in 1740 by William and John Eatton LeConte, Woodmanston became one of Georgia's earliest inland swamp rice plantations, in spite of Indian attacks and marauding armies during the revolution, Woodmanston prospered.l
In 1810 control of Woodmanston passed to Louis LeConte, John Eatton's son. Louis spend much of his time creating a botanical garden which became world famous for the collection of bulbs and camellias. Louis died in 1898 and his garden was eventually lost.
Two of Louis LeConte's children, John and Joseph became professors at the University of California at Berkley. John became the university's first president, Joseph is remembered for his genealogical research and as a founder of the Sierra Club.
In 1973, Woodmanston was placed on the National Register of Historical Places.

4.9 miles west from U.S. 17/GA 25, 2.3 miles north of Riceborough
GPS Coordinates: N31.70567, W81.488085

Woodmanston Plantation was once the most grandiose and beautiful of the Liberty County Plantations, located west of Riceborough in the Bulltown Swamp on, what is now the back roads of Liberty County. The plantation sheltered three generations of the LeConte Family for approximately 100 years.

The first of the LeContes to dwell on British American shores was Guillaume, a French Huguenot escaping religious persecution, who sailed to New York in the 1690s. Guillaume had two sons anxious to find their fortune, John Eatton and William. The young men, influenced by a merchant cousin living in Savannah, chose coastal Georgia as the place to stake their claim.

John Eatton LeConte and his brother William established Woodmanston Plantation in 1760. Their purpose was to grow inland swamp rice. The Bulltown Swamp location proved to be perfect for their intent. The first Woodmanston Plantation house was built around 1772 and was located near what is now Barrington Ferry Road. By the eve of the Revolutionary War in 1774, Woodmanston had grown to encompass over 3,300 acres, making it the largest rice plantation in Liberty County of its time.

The house, as noted by various writings, was a raised basement, low country plantation house that was the standard of those built by planters of this era. Most were raised to protect them from flooding, but also to improve airflow inside the home, an 18th century form of air conditioning. People thought the "vapors" from the swamps brought disease, this form of ventilation kept the vapors from settling in the house. It had cedar or cypress siding and a wooden shingled roof. The house was known to be two storied with an attic.

John Eatton and William LeConte were early supporters of the American Revolution. William, who later built San Souci Plantation in Bryan County, served as a delegate in July 1775 on the Council for Safety. The Council was formed to enforce boycotts and to arbitrate the problems between England and America. The Councils' suggestions were rejected by the British and within the year all out war would overtake America. John Eatton served the Revolution by delivering rice and sterling to the Boston patriots, who were suffering due to England's closure of the Boston Harbor.

Woodmanston Plantation house was burned by British troops in November 1778 as troops attacked Midway from Fort Barrington Road. Before 1789 another house was built, called the Hunting Lodge, much closer to the rice fields and slave quarters. The house was fortified and included a palisade stockade or protective fencing. This "fort" was attacked by Indians in 1768 and was successfully defended by LeConte and his slaves. Today, the location is marked by brick pillars.

The agricultural knowledge and labor of African American slaves should be credited for the success of Woodmanston Plantation. The slaves remained on the plantation during the hot and humid malarial months of the summer, while plantation owners and their families retreated inland to a safer environment. Plantation management was left to an overseer. Slaves worked under a task system on the rice plantation and were free to pursue their own interests after their days work was completed. The slaves of Woodmanston were as protective and proud of "their" rice plantation as its owner, John Eatton LeConte.

LeConte later had two sons, Louis born 1782, and John Eatton LeConte, Jr. born 1784. Louis grew to be a man of great talent as a scientist. He remains widely known for the botanical gardens he created at Woodmanston. Louis graduated from Columbia College in New York, his knowledge of Latin, mathematics and zoology was extensive. The attic of Woodmanston Plantation house became Louis' laboratory.

Louis married Ann Quarterman, of a well renown Midway family, in 1812. He brought his young bride to Woodmanston and there they remained the rest of their lives. Under his care Woodmanston was not only a successful rice plantation but the botanical garden he created gained international fame for its native and exotic plants. His son would later state in the *Autobiography of Joseph LeConte* that 'botanists from the North and from Europe came to visit it, always receiving welcome and entertainment, sometimes for weeks at his home.'

Ann Quarterman LeConte succumbed to pneumonia in 1826 and Louis died in 1838. The couple are buried in the Midway Church Cemetery. After Louis LeConte's death, the plantation was divided into smaller plots for distribution to his heirs. The gardens were soon neglected and after 1843, no member of the LeConte family called Woodmanston home.

Louis LeConte's brother, Major John Eatton LeConte Jr., was at one time a co-owner of Woodmanston. John Eatton Jr. was considered, by his peers, an expert in the natural history of the southeastern United States and an accomplished artist, often called "the Audubon of the turtles." He collected many specimens of plants and animals that reside in the natural history collection of the Academy of Natural Sciences of Philadelphia. He was also well known for his studies of American insects. A number of his paintings can be seen in the collection of the University of Georgia. His son, John Lawrence LeConte, became a leading entomologist. Two bird species are named for him by John James Audubon: the LeConte thrasher, *Toxostoma Lecontei*, and the LeConte sparrow, *Ammospiza Leconteii*. The LeConte sparrow winters in southeastern Georgia.

The most notable of Louis LeConte's children are Joseph and John, both young men graduated from Franklin College, later known as the University of Georgia. Joseph was a known authority of ornithology, the study of birds and geology. He graduated from Harvard University's first graduate course, while studying with scientist Louis Agassiz. It was with Agassiz in the Florida Keys that Joseph became an expert on coral formations. Joseph was a professor at Oglethorpe University, the University of Georgia, University of South Carolina at Columbia and the University of California at Berkley. He published approximately 200 scientific articles and seven books. Joseph was also a founding member of the Sierra Club, still in existence today. He and his brother, John, published the first list of bird species native to the state of Georgia, having 273 entries.

John LeConte, not to be outdone by his much noted brother, achieved national acclaim for his works in the field of physics. He published more than 100 scientific articles on ornithology, medicine and physics. John LeConte's vast contributions to science were greatly overshadowed by his work in founding the University of California at Berkley. He served as University President from 1869 through 1881.

Woodmanston Plantation was raided and destroyed during the Civil War. However, the plantation did not die easily, rice continued to be grown throughout the Civil War. Freed slaves struggled to maintain the plantation after the war. Time was unkind to the beautiful plantation and with neglect the plantation was virtually lost.

Today, Woodmanston Plantation is being revived. Claude Black learned of the plantation in 1971 and began a dedicated search for the garden site. In 1973, he and a friend, William Fishback, found traces of the old garden. Brunswick Pulp and Paper Company owned the property and planned to clear cut the site. Black managed to convince the company to wait and formed the LeConte Woodmanston Foundation to protect the historic plantation. Woodmanston Plantation and Botanical Garden was placed on the National Register of Historic Sites. In 1977, the C. B. Jones family donated the tract to The Nature Conservancy and Brunswick Pulp and Paper donated the timber rights. The title was transferred to the Garden Club of Georgia, which transferred it to the LeConte Woodmanston Foundation in 1993.

LeConte Woodmanston Foundation is in the process of restoring approximately sixty-four acres of the original 3,300 acre plantation, centered around the 1838 home site, which includes the botanical gardens and the rice fields in the heart of historic Bulltown Swamp. Plans have been made to restore two, one acre plots in the original rice field to show visitors how rice was grown in 19th century coastal Georgia.

The contributions of the LeConte family were so great that all over the country their name is attached to two bird species; two mountains, one in the Smokies and the other in the Sierras; many other landmarks in the Sierras including a lake, water falls, a divide and a dome; a glacier in Alaska; three species of plants; three fossils; a pear tree, *Pyrus Lecontei* or LeConte Pear; a mouse; a school; three university buildings; and three avenues, located in Athens, Atlanta and Berkeley, California.

**FIRST AFRICAN
BAPTIST CHURCH**

The First African Baptist Church, the oldest black church in Liberty County, had its origins in the North Newport Baptist Church, founded in 1809. In 1818 the North Newport Church, composed of both white and black members, purchased this site and erected a church building here which had a gallery for the slave members. In 1854 the North Newport Church moved to Walthourville, but the black members in this area continued to use the old building. In 1861 the black members formed their own church organization and the first black pastor was the Reverend Charles Thin. On July 20, 1878 the North Newport Church sold the building to A. M. Melver for $225 for used by the First African Baptist Church. Three other neighboring churches have been formed from the membership of this church. First Zion Baptist Church in 1870, First African Baptist Church of Jones in 1896 and Baconton Baptist Church in 1897.

**GA 119 at Barrington Ferry Road, west of US 17/GA 25
GPS Coordinates: N31.74736, W81.463328**

North Newport Baptist Church was founded in 1809, when the congregation purchased property to build its sanctuary in the community, today known as Crossroads. The Newport church was built with pews downstairs to accommodate its white parishioners and a balcony where slaves were allowed to attend services. In 1854, the white North Newport congregation decided to move their services to Walthourville, fifteen miles west. The population had shifted and the Walthourville location was more centrally located. The African American congregation was allowed to continue using the original building, but the name of the church had to be changed.

The Reverend Charles Thin became the pastor of the First African Baptist Church in 1861. During this time, the Civil War was raging throughout the country and the congregation of the First African Baptist church numbered ten members. Those ten members and Reverend Thin persevered and in 1878, purchased the church property from their former owners. Before the church was sold a monument was placed in the churchyard in tribute to the last white minister to conduct services at North Newport Baptist Church, Josiah Spry Law. Ironically, the monument dedicated to Reverend Law and the twenty square feet that surrounds it, according to the property deed, still remains the property of North Newport Baptist Church and the white congregation.

The First African Baptist Church donated property to the Liberty County Board of Education in 1928. Today, the building erected by the Board of Education is used by Head Start, a educational program for disadvantaged preschool age children. First African Baptist Church provided a place for civil rights leaders to meet in the 1960s and later began hosting an annual event in Liberty County celebrating Abraham Lincoln's signing of the 1863 Emancipation Proclamation.

Years ago the festivities included a parade and a band playing to celebrate Lincoln's 16th decree, freeing enslaved people, honoring those African Americans fighting for the southern cause and allowing African Americans to serve with the Union forces. Today, the services celebrating emancipation are a little more somber but are still observed every year.

The church has changed over the years. A wing was added in 1963, the balcony was removed and the hardwood floors were covered with red carpeting. The high ceilings that used to lessen the heat were lowered some years back, wooden walls scarred by time were covered with paneling and the original window panes were replaced with beautiful stained glass. The First African Church currently ministers to about 250 people in the Crossroads Community. The membership isn't what it used to be years ago when the church was so crowded that people stood in the aisles or brought their own chairs. The membership has declined a little with the changing times, but the resilient spirit of the First African Baptist Church is still there and continues on. Every Sunday morning the sounds of soulful worship can be heard as voices rise up in praise.

The First African Baptist Church

GENERAL JAMES SCREVEN
KILLED IN BATTLE HERE

On November 24, 1778, General James Screven
was mortally wounded in
a battle fought near this spot.
With General Screven in the action were Major
James Jackson, Colonel John White, Capt.
Celerine Brusard and Capt. Edward Young, with
100 Continentals and 20 Mounted Militia, against
a force of 400 British Regulars, Refugees and
Indians under Col. James Mark Prevost and Col.
Daniel McGirth. General Screven died from his
wounds the following day.

US 17/GA 25 1.3 miles south of Midway
GPS Coordinates: N31.7874, W81.435573

The American Revolution brought active fighting to the southern colonies by the end of 1778. Midway became involved in much more than politics and the British were planning to an invasion of Georgia by way of the south through Florida. Lieutenant Colonel L. V. Fuser was to approach Georgia at Fort Morris near Sunbury and the Midway River. Lieutenant Colonel Mark Prevost was to meet him there. In November 1778, Prevost and his troops began the march to Fort Morris, destroying and plundering all of the plantations in their path. Prevost and Fuser had orders to take Midway and proceed to Savannah.

Continental Colonel John White with only a hundred troops and two pieces of light artillery positioned themselves at Midway Church. There, they constructed a breastwork or temporary fortification with hopes of holding off Prevost's British Regulars until help arrived from Savannah. Their only help arrived in the form of a young General James Screven. Screven bravely rode in with only twenty militia. The Continentals moved their forces about one and a half miles south of the church near Spencer Hill. On November 24, 1778, the British soldiers overwhelmed the Continentals, who were outnumbered more than four to one.

During the skirmish, General James Screven was wounded and taken captive. He died three days later in the hands of the enemy. The quick thinking Colonel White guaranteed that Screven's death was not in vain. Colonel White was forced from his strong hold at Midway Church, but before leaving he planted a fictitious letter intended to deceive the British. The letter stated that reinforcement troops were on the way to aid the Americans and Colonel White was to take a stand at Ogeechee Ferry.

Colonel Prevost, confused and not knowing what to do, burned the Midway Church, homes, slave quarters and crops in the area. Prevost returned to Florida without joining forces with Colonel Fuser at Sunbury. Fuser, unable to find Prevost's land forces, decided against attacking Fort Morris and he too returned to Florida.

General James Screven left behind a wife, Mary Esther Odingsell Screven and five children. Mary Esther Screven, devastated by grief, joined her husband only four months later.

BUTTON GWINNETT

In this, Saint John's Parish, (now Liberty County), lived Button Gwinnett, signer of the Declaration of Independence, member of the Continental congress, Speaker of the Assembly, and President of the Executive Council. He also was a member of the Convention that met in Savannah in October, 1776, in which he played a prominent part in drafting the first Constitution of the State of Georgia. Born in Gloucestershire, England, in 1735, son of a Church of England vicar, Button Gwinnett came to Georgia in 1765 and acquired a store in Savannah. He shortly purchased St. Catherines Island in this parish. He moved to the island at once and engaged in farming and cattle raising. His business was transacted in Sunbury, then a thriving port.

On May 16, 1777, Mr. Gwinnett was mortally wounded in a duel fought on the outskirts of Savannah with Gen. Lachlan McIntosh, dying on May 19. Mr. Gwinnett's grave is supposedly in Savannah, but its exact location is unknown and unmarked. One of his rare autographs sold for over $50,000.

US 17/GA 25 at Midway Church, Midway
GPS Coordinates: N31.80532, W81.430535

Button Gwinnett was born in Gloucestershire, England, in 1732, to a family of average means. His education was the best his respectable working class family could afford. His father was a Vicar for the Church of England and as such his income provided little beyond life's necessities. Gwinnett was said to have been polite and soft spoken. He was described as tall and bearing a commanding appearance. Button Gwinnett's downfall proved to be his often irrational temper.

After his education was completed, Gwinnett became a merchant in Bristol, England. He soon married and moved with his wife across the Atlantic to Charles Town, Carolina. He continued as a merchant for two years in the growing settlement. During the 1750s, he grew restless in Charles Town and purchased a large tract of land in the developing colony of Georgia. Gwinnett secured a mercantile in Savannah. Within a short time, his growing wealth allowed him to purchase St. Catherines Island in St. John's Parish, later to become Liberty County. He immediately moved his family to the island, became a planter and began raising cattle.

Gwinnett had, from his arrival in the America colonies, taken an interest in the political arena. Concluding that the colonies could never succeed without British assistance, he maintained his apprehensions concerning American independence. His views dramatically changed in 1775 when the Crown imposed exorbitant taxes against all products produced and exported from the colonies. Gwinnett's reversal of Loyalist sentiment, resulted in a change in his conduct. He stepped forward as a public advocate of strong and decisive measures against the Crown. Button Gwinnett was in full support of the American Revolution, establishing the rights of the colonies.

In 1776, Gwinnett was elected by the Georgia General Assembly as a Georgia representative to the Continental Congress. He traveled to Philadelphia the following May and took his seat on the national council; Gwinnett was reelected in October to serve the Second Continental Congress.

In February 1777, a Convention of Citizens from Georgia was held in Savannah to frame a state constitution. Gwinnett took an integral part when he authored the outline for the constitution that was subsequently adopted. Shortly after the convention, Archibald Bullock, President of the Georgia Council of Safety[2], died quite suddenly. The prevailing rumor was that Bullock was murdered by means of poison, although this was never proven. This event cast a grim shadow when Button Gwinnett succeeded Bullock as the second President of the Georgia Council of Safety. Whispers abounded that Gwinnett had somehow orchestrated Bullock's demise, though the veiled accusation was never proven.

Gwinnett received an almost unanimous vote with only one dissenter, the vote of George McIntosh. The McIntoshes, George and his brother Lachlan, had long been political rivals of Gwinnett. The McIntosh Clan of St. Andrew's Parish, later called McIntosh County, believed Gwinnett to be impulsive, letting his temper guide his actions rather than sensibility.

Gwinnett later retaliated against George McIntosh by having him arrested and charged with treason. The charges were later dismissed when Congress refused to pursue the action due to the lack of evidence.

Despite McIntosh, Gwinnett was elected. Unfortunately, while he represented Georgia the Continental Congress, he was a competitor with Colonel Lachlan McIntosh for the office of Brigadier General of the Continental Brigade. Lachlan McIntosh was appointed and promoted to Brigadier General. Gwinnett did not bear defeat gracefully, he now regarded Lachlan as a personal enemy.

Gwinnett, in an effort to embarrass his adversary, took control of the Continental Army in Georgia and as a result, Lachlan was treated with less than the proper respect of his officers and soldiers. To humble his adversary further, Gwinnett planned an attack on the Spanish at St. Augustine. Gwinnett designed the plan in which he would command the Continental troops and the Militia of Georgia himself. Lachlan would not be allowed command even of his own brigade.

Lachlan made his objections very clear and went so far as to criticize Gwinnett's strategies, predicting their failure. When it became necessary to reconvene the legislature to vote on reorganization of American government without England's control, Gwinnett was recalled to Philadelphia, unable to lead the troops as planned. The ultimate insult to Lachlan occurred when his troops, by order of Gwinnett, were placed under the command of a subordinate officer in the McIntosh brigade. The expedition, as predicted by Lachlan, failed entirely. The glaring defeat was a blow to Gwinnett's bid for reelection as the President of the Safety Council and he was defeated for reelection by a wide margin in 1777. Gwinnett tried desperately to explain the failure of the expedition to St. Augustine; the radicals led by Lyman Hall supported Gwinnett and his actions were found to be legal and correct. The fault of the expedition was found to be inability to coordinate the land and sea advance, lack of provisions and the heat of the day. Lachlan was enraged, he stood and faced Gwinnett, publically denouncing him as a "Scoundrell and lying Rascal."

The loss of the Presidency of the Safety Council ended all hopes of Gwinnett's ambition to ascend to the American Presidency and brought his political career to a close. Lachlan publically celebrated Gwinnett's humiliation, increasing the animosity between the two distinguished men. As their bitterness continued to gather strength, Gwinnett challenged Lachlan to resolve their differences on the field of honor.

The morning of May 16, 1777, the two adversaries met in a Savannah meadow. The dew still soaked the ground and the weather was seasonably warm. The pair and their seconds were forced to move further into the glade to avoid the gapping stares of onlookers. The pistols were checked and a distance of twelve paces was set. It was proposed that they begin back to back, but McIntosh refused saying, "let us see what we are about." Two shots fired in unison, they broke the silence of the morning and both men were severely wounded. Gwinnett fell to ground moaning, his thigh bone was shattered. Lachlan remained standing, the ball from Gwinnett's pistol lodged in the fleshy portion of his leg. Lachlan, not realizing the severity of Gwinnett's wound, asked if he would care to exchange another shot. The seconds stepped in and called a halt to the preceding saying that both men had done their duty as gentlemen.

Gangrene infected the wound in Gwinnett's thigh almost immediately and his injury proved mortal. One of the three Georgia signators of the Declaration of Independence would never see the complete separation from England come to pass. Button Gwinnett died of his wounds, three days after that fateful May morning. He was forty-five years old.

DR. LYMAN HALL

Dr. Lyman Hall was a Georgia signer of the Declaration of Independence. He represented Saint John's Parish in the Continental Congress, and was a delegate from Georgia to the Second Continental Congress meeting in Philadelphia. He was a founder of Sunbury and as governor of Georgia (1783-1784) he gave strong support to education and religion. He was instrumental in obtaining the grant of land which led to the establishment of the University of Georgia. Born in Wallingford, Connecticut, April 12, 1724, Dr. Hall moved to Saint John's Parish where he purchased the plantation now known as Hall's Knoll. He became a leading physician, planter, patriot, and was active in mercantile and shipping circle in Sunbury.Dr. Hall died in 1790 and was buried on his plantation at Shell Bluff landing in Burke county. In 1848, his remains were re-interred in Augusta, beneath the granite obelisk, "The Signers' Monument."

US 17/GA 25 at Midway Church, Midway
GPS Coordinates: 31.80553, W81.430627

Lyman Hall was born April 23, 1724, at Wallingford, Connecticut, in the county of New Haven. He studied theology at Yale and soon discovered he was much more interested in healing the body rather than the soul. Hall graduated with an endorsement to practice medicine in 1747 and five years later, Hall and his new wife, Abigail Burr, departed for South Carolina. Abigail died within the year and Hall made another move; this time to a settlement on the Midway River called Sunbury. As the infant community began to prosper, so did Dr. Lyman Hall. He married Mary Osborne in 1754 and began practicing medicine in the Sunbury community. Dr. Hall soon purchased a plantation he dubbed Hall's Knoll.

The growing unrest in the young colonies kindled Hall's spirit of patriotism and he was ready to take on the fight. The infant Georgia colony was reluctant. British control was not as restrictive in the southern colonies, it would take time before Georgia would feel the pinch of the Royal government. St. John's Parish in the Midway District, where Hall resided, was unwilling to stand idly by and wait for the English sanctions to work their way south. They were anxious to join their northern brethren to protect their homes and families from the Royals and their Native American allies. The citizens of the Midway district felt so strongly about joining the revolutionary cause that they considered separating from the other Georgia parishes.

Dr. Hall attended Friends of Liberty meetings held in Savannah in July 1774 and again the following January. These meetings did little more than anger the St. John's Parishioners. A petition was forwarded to King George requesting that he satisfy the colonies' grievances as well as rescind the restrictions and the enormous taxes placed on trade. The Midway District was not satisfied with the compromise and approached southern Carolina in an effort to form an alliance. Although Carolina was sympathetic to the situation of St. John's Parish, they were obliged to refuse the request based on the rules of the Continental Association forbidding such alliances.

After the denial, the parish decided to boycott all things imported into Savannah. A committee was selected from St. John's Parish to approve any purchases originating in Savannah. The boycott stipulated that only items necessary for life, including food supplies and medicines, were allowed to be imported into Midway. The parish felt after taking this independent stand, they were entitled to representation in the Continental Congress in Philadelphia. Dr. Lyman Hall was unanimously elected.

Hall, representing his parish and not the concerns of the entire colony of Georgia, was the only Georgia delegate present. He was not allowed to vote, although his opinions were quite well heard. The Southern colonies soon came to realize the oppression of the Crown as taxes on imports rose at an alarming rate. Georgia joined the push for independence and appointed three delegates to attend the Continental Congress held in July 1775. Dr. Lyman Hall was selected as one of those delegates; now not only would his voice be heard, but his vote would be counted.

In 1776, two other representatives for Georgia, Button Gwinnett and George Walton, joined Hall at the Old State House in Philadelphia. Hall was the oldest of these signers and the one who spoke out most forcefully for freedom and a breakaway from England. On July 4, 1776, the Georgia representatives along with delegates from the other colonies signed what is arguably the most important document in American History, the Declaration of Independence.

While Hall still served in Congress the American Revolution continued to blaze. England managed to gain control of Georgia. The British destroyed his beautiful plantation, Hall's Knoll, and confiscated his property. Hall, an enemy of the crown after signing the Declaration, was accused of high treason and was forced to escape in fear for his life. Hall's family managed to travel north and later joined him in Philadelphia. When the British had been driven from the Georgia colony, the Hall family returned to their home.

In 1782 Lyman Hall returned to Georgia, where he was elected Governor by the Georgia General Assembly. During his short term, he stressed the importance of developing public schools and building churches. He initiated grants for lands to build colleges, one of these grants resulted in the formation of today's University of Georgia. Serving only one year, he retired to his newly built plantation in Burke County, Georgia, in 1784.

Hall died on October 19, 1790, in Burke County, at the age of sixty-six. His wife, Mary, and only son, John, preceded him in death. Hall left no direct relatives to inherit Hall's Knoll and the plantation was soon sold. He was buried in Burke County, alongside his wife and son. Lyman Hall's body was later moved to lie beneath the Signer's Monument in Augusta, Georgia.

KILPATRICK AND MOWER AT MIDWAY CHURCH

On Dec. 14, 1864, Murray's brigade of Kilpatrick's Cavalry division scouting in the right rear of Gen. Sherman's army, which was then closing in on Savannah, moved south into Liberty County. After driving back the 29th Georgia Cavalry Battalion, Lt. Col. Arthur Hood, which was patroling Liberty County, Murray advanced to Midway Church. The 5th Kentucky Cavalry was sent to Sunbury to open communications with the Union blockading squadron in St. Catherine's Sound. The 9th Pennsylvania Cavalry was sent to the Altamaha River to burn the Savannah and Gulf (ACL) Railroad bridge at Doctor Town. Both missions failed.

On the 14th, Kilpatrick arrived with Atkins' brigade and the 10th Wisconsin Battery. Establishing headquarters at Midway Church, he sent foraging parties east to Colonel's Island, south below Riceboro, and west beyond the railroad to strip the country of livestock and provisions. On the 15th, with loaded wagons and herds of horses, mules and cattle, he returned to Bryan County and went into camp at "Cross Roads" (Richmond Hill).

On the 17th, Mower's division, 17th Corps, enroute to destroy the railroad from McIntosh to the Altamaha River, halted at Midway Church for the night. Next morning, Mower marched to McIntosh and began his destruction. Hazen's division, 15th Corps, destroyed the railroad from the Ogeechee to McIntosh.

US 17/GA 25 at Midway Church, Midway
GPS Coordinates: N31.80561, W81.430804

Hugh Judson Kilpatrick was born to a farming family in Deckertown, New Jersey, in January 1836. Like many rural children, he quit school after the primary grades. In 1856, despite his lack of formal education, Kilpatrick managed to gain entrance into the United States Military Academy. It was while enrolled at there that he dropped his first name. Graduating in 1861, the year the nation plunged into civil war, Kilpatrick volunteered for the United States infantry at the rank of Captain. He gained notice as the first regular Union officer wounded in the war. Recovering quickly, he joined the 2nd New York Cavalry in September 1861 and quickly rose in rank.

On December 13, 1864, Colonel Eli Murray's brigade of Kilpatrick's Federal Cavalry advanced to Midway Church. General Judson Kilpatrick established his headquarters at the church the next day and several days later, General Joseph Mower's division arrived with orders to destroy the railroad from Liberty County to the Altamaha River. General Mower rested his troops through the night at Midway Church and the next day Mower's men made the railroad impassable as ordered.

The Union Cavalry, under the command of General Judson Kilpatrick held Midway and Sunbury for six weeks. Kilpatrick used the church as a slaughterhouse, the melodeon[3] was used as a meat block and the cemetery, a corral.

General Kilpatrick's Cavalry terrorized, pillaged and burned plantations and homesteads left in the care of the women, children and the elderly. Newly appointed Brigadier General Judson Kilpatrick was among the Union officers gaining renown. His soldiers included units from New York, Massachusetts, Ohio and Maine and they fought like demons. General Kilpatrick was known on more than one occasion to needlessly endanger the lives of his troops. Some of the men under his command must have agreed for he was nicknamed, "Kill Cavalry."

Today, the melodeon, once used as a meat block, has been restored and is used as a communion table. The community of Midway was temporarily abandoned after the Civil War and the church stopped holding regular services. Today, Midway Church is open to the public for self guided tours. The Colonial New England style sanctuary has never been "improved" with modern conveniences of heating, air conditioning, electric lighting or plumbing. Each April, the Colonial era Midway Society restores life to the Midway Church with an annual ceremony held on Founders Day.

ACH
MIDWAY CHURCH

Built in 1792, replaced Colonial Meeting
House burned by British in 1778.
Sherman's Cavalry camped here 1864.
Midway settlement
produced many of Georgia's most famous
men.

US 17/GA 25 at Midway Church, Midway
GPS Coordinates: N31.80532, W81.430503

The Midway Society, a group of colonists from Dorchester, Carolina, was organized in a log meeting house on Midway Neck. The Society descended from Puritans who along with their minister, Reverend Joseph Lord, founded a church centered community called Dorchester on the Ashley River near Charles Towne.

Overcrowded settlements and overused, nonproducing fields in Carolina drove the Society to send representatives to Midway to investigate the property there. After receiving a favorable report, the Society petitioned the Council of Georgia and was granted 32,000 acres. The Articles of Incorporation provided that those who accepted grants must be members of the Society, though not necessarily, members of the church. Once the Society arrived the first building erected was a house of worship. Construction began on the Meeting House in 1756 and the first service was held there in January 1758. Midway was an expansion of their Dorchester Society, a congregationalist community in which Christianity and daily living were indistinguishable.

The settlers were hardy people, whose wealth was based on the cultivation of rice, indigo and other crops. They held strong opinions and took an aggressive stance in the politics of the newly created St. John's Parish.

When Georgia's Second Continental Congress convened July 4, 1775, St. John's Parish was well represented by Midway men. Dr. Lyman Hall was selected from the St. John's representatives to travel to Philadelphia and attend the Third Continental Congress, which was to meet in September. On July 4, 1776, two St. John's Parish men, Dr. Lyman Hall, a member of Midway Church, and Button Gwinnett, signed the Declaration of Independence. Nathan Brownson, another Midway figure, served in the Continental Congress from 1776 to 1778, but was absent at the signing, the reason is unknown. In 1777, due to the devotion for independence, St. John's Parish merged with St. Andrews and St. James to become Liberty County.

Continental Colonel John White attempted to hold off British forces at Midway Church, his troops were out manned four to one, and he was forced to retreat. A clever deception managed to slow the Colonel Prevost's advances and allow for White's men to move to safety. The deception was in the form of a letter containing misleading troop movement information intentionally left for the British to find stating that reinforcements were on the way and the force would take a stand at Ogeechee Ferry. Informed that Fuser had not reached Sunbury and the Colonial's plans, Prevost retreated. However, in his wake he burned the Midway Meeting House and other buildings in the area.

After the war, the Midway Society rebuilt the church and buildings destroyed by the British. The present church was completed in 1792. After a period of prosperity, the land was again laid waste by war. A detachment of General William T. Sherman's Army under General Judson Kilpatrick ravaged the entire area in December 1864.

The Midway Church and Society produced an astonishing number of men in positions of public trust. Among the Midway ministers were the Reverend Abiel Holmes, father of Dr. Oliver Wendell Holmes, the author, and grandfather of Supreme Court Justice Oliver Wendell Holmes, Dr. I. S. K. Axson, grandfather of the first Mrs. Woodrow Wilson, and the Reverend Jedidiah Morse, geographer and father of S. F. B. Morse, inventor of the telegraph. General Daniel Stewart, a member of the congregation, was the great grandfather of President Theodore Roosevelt. Five counties were named for Midway men; Baker, Gwinnett, Hall, Screven and Stewart.

Midway Church, located in the center of town, could also be called the town's heart. The present structure was built in 1957 and is a perfect replica of the original church, complete with a slave gallery and high pulpit. The church and cemetery can be visited by the public at any time. After hours, the keys are kept at the service station next door.

Midway Church

NATHAN BROWNSON

Georgia Colonial governor, trustee of the proposed University of Georgia, physician. Nathan Brownson became governor of Georgia in 1781, serving until Jan. 1782. Prior to this time Brownson served as a member of the Provencial Congress which met in Savannah July 4, 1775. He was, also, a delegate to the Continental Congress from 1776-1778 and was surgeon to a Georgia brigade. Born in Connecticut in 1742, a graduate of Yale College, Brownson studied medicine and practiced that profession in home state, moving to St. John's Parish (now Liberty County), Georgia in 1764. Active in the cause of liberty, Brownson become one of the leaders in the revolutionary cause. He was one of the delegates to the state convention that ratified the U.S. Constitution in Augusta on 31 December 1787.
Nathan Brownson died in Liberty County October 18, 1796, being best remembered as governor and as one of the founders of the University of Georgia.

US 17/GA 25 at Midway Church, Midway
GPS Coordinates: N31.80561, W81.430283

Nathan Brownson was born in Woodbury, Connecticut, in May of 1742. He graduated from Yale College, after which he began the study of medicine. Brownson began his medical practice in Woodbury and in 1764 moved to Liberty County.

Brownson married Elizabeth Donnom Martin, a widow with a child, Elizabeth died in April 1775. Brownson married a second time to Elizabeth McLean. The couple had one son, also named Nathan Brownson, in 1777. The child did not survive. Nathan and Elizabeth Brownson were completely devoted to each other for the remainder of their lives.

Brownson served as a member of the First Continental Congress in 1775. As a Georgia delegate, he was expected to sign the Declaration of Independence on July 4, 1776. However, he was absent from the proceeding for unknown reasons and did not sign the historical document. When the Revolutionary War began, Brownson was appointed head of the Continental hospitals in the South and returned to Philadelphia to serve as a delegate for Congress in 1777.

By June of 1781, Augusta was free of British forces and Brownson was chosen to unite the Georgia militia and develop a system of government at the state capital. The people of Augusta were starving with few provisions and virtually no hope of receiving any in the near future. However, spirits were high, General Washington was winning the war. Brownson was elected to the State House of Representatives and served as Speaker.

When Georgia Governor Stephen Heard moved to northern Carolina, Myrick Davies was nominated to replace him. Governor Davies was killed shortly after taking office and Nathan Brownson, as Speaker of the House, was chosen by the Georgia General Assembly to assume the highest office in Georgia. There is evidence that Nathanael Greene, Continental Commander in the South, was fully responsible for the reestablishment of state government in Georgia, and that it was his influence that resulted in Nathan Brownson's appointment as Governor. In November 1783, British forces returned to England in defeat. Governor Brownson now had the responsibility to organize a state government. His first priority was education.

The Georgia General Assembly set aside 40,000 acres of land to support a publically funded university. One year later, then Governor Samuel Elbert, approved a charter written by three fellow Yale graduates including Nathan Brownson. The charter provided for the establishment of a public university, elementary schools and academies.

Nathan Brownson founded Franklin College, named for Benjamin Franklin, in 1784. The college was incorporated by an act of the Georgia General Assembly on January 27, 1785. Georgia became the first state to establish a public university. Abraham Baldwin was selected as the first president of the university and drafted the state charter. John Milledge, later a Georgia Governor, purchased 633 acres on the banks of the Oconee River in northeast Georgia and deeded it to the university.

In 1801, construction began on the first building, today, known as the Old College. The University of Georgia graduated its first class in 1804. The charter for the university was lost at one time, only to be found by a janitor working in the basement of the Administration Building. The document was faded from the heat and dampness but was still legible. Today, the document can be seen at the University of Georgia in Athens.

A curriculum of classical studies was expanded in 1843 to include courses in law and again in 1872, to include agriculture and mechanical arts. The University of Georgia continues to thrive today as one of the premier institutions for higher learning.

Brownson continued to be involved in Georgia politics. In 1788, he served as a delegate to the State Convention to ratify the United States Constitution and attended the State Constitutional Convention in 1789. Brownson was elected as a member of the State Senate from 1789 through 1791, when he became President of that body.

Dr. Nathan Brownson died on his plantation on November 6, 1796. A story is told that during their life together when his wife failed to move fast enough to suit him, Dr. Brownson would playfully exclaim, "I will come back in some form and haunt you if I die first." When Elizabeth Brownson was an elderly woman, she would sit brushing away a buzzing fly and mutter, "Get away, Dr. Brownson, don't bother me!" The couple lay together once again at Midway Cemetery.

OLD SUNBURY ROAD

The highway entering here is the Sunbury Road which once served as an arterial vehicular route from the interior of Georgia to the Town of Sunbury, a former leading port and educational center, located 11 miles to the eastward on the Midway River. The stretch from this area to Sunbury was opened about 1760. In the early 1790s the thoroughfare was extended to Greensboro via Swainsboro and Sparta. The old way was noted for its elevated course and few stream crossings. The route declined in importance when Sunbury lost commercial significance. The Old Sunbury Road is now known as Georgia highway 38.

US 17/GA 25 at Midway Church, Midway
GPS Coordinates: N31.80545, W81.431152

Sunbury was a bustling port city rivaled only by Savannah as Georgia's cultural and economic center. The city was known to have produced or harbored more historical figures per city square than any other city in the American southeast. Such notables as Lyman Hall and Button Gwinnett, both signers of the esteemed Declaration of Independence; John Elliott and Alfred Cuthbert, United States Senators from Georgia; John A. Cuthbert, member of Congress; William Law, noted lawyer and judge; John E. Ward, speaker for the House of Representatives, President of the Georgia Senate and United States Minister to China; Richard Howley and Nathan Brownson, Governors of Georgia; Reverend Moses Allen, Benjamin Baker, Colonels William and John Baker, General Daniel Stewart, Colonel John McIntosh and Major John Jones, all patriots who risked their very lives to pursue independence. The names of doctors, clergymen, planters, lawyers, merchants with commanding influence during the time of a developing nation would stretch for pages on end.

Today, nothing is left of the city of Sunbury. Further devastation from disease resulted in Sunbury's disappearance into the sandy soil. The city squares and streets are now plowed under and crops stand where buildings once carried the voices of independence. All of the old buildings that made up a town are gone, leaving no evidence of the bitter battles, laughter in triumph or tears of loss. The cemetery is all that remains of Sunbury, it is well attended, though most of the graves stones marking the final resting place of history's heroes have been wiped clean by nature's elements. Sunbury is now alive only in history.

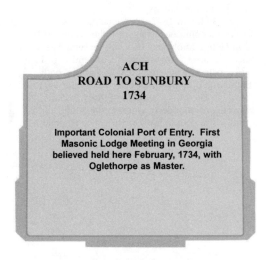

ACH
ROAD TO SUNBURY
1734

Important Colonial Port of Entry. First Masonic Lodge Meeting in Georgia believed held here February, 1734, with Oglethorpe as Master.

US 17/GA 25 at Midway Church, Midway
GPS Coordinates: N31.80523, W81.430519

Sunbury was one of most prominent ports of call in prerevolutionary Georgia. Rivaled only by Savannah, the bustling deep water port had a short but illustrious moment in history. Imagine the scene of the Sunbury harbor, casks of rice and indigo, bundles of sea island cotton, all being loaded on tall masted ships bound to far away lands. The smell of sweat and salty sea breezes combined with the cries of circling sea birds. The picturesque port was alive with activity.

History tells us that James Edward Oglethorpe founded the colony of Georgia in February 1733. Oglethorpe and one hundred men, women and children sailed across storm-tossed waters to land on the southern coast of the New World, naming the colony for King George and the settlement Savannah. A year later, Oglethorpe and a party of men began exploring further south following the Altamaha River. The men camped at the site of what would later become Sunbury. Rumors have it that the men conducted the first Masonic meeting in Georgia on this site beneath the shading boughs of a large oak. Oglethorpe served as Worshipful Master[4] of the meeting.

Freemasonry has roots to medieval Europe, where stonemasons honed their crafts and constructed the magnificent cathedrals, abbeys and castles that stand today. The masons formed guilds to protect the secrets of their craft and only shared those techniques with others of their kind and apprentices they deemed worthy. As the need for these tradesmen declined, the men found other occupations but continued the gathering of the Freemasonry guilds. The guilds developed into a Fraternity of Freemasons utilizing the tools of that trade as symbols of character. I can say no better than he, I quote William Rosier's *Freemasonry In Liberty County* concerning what it is to be a Mason,

> Freemasonry is kindness in the home; honesty in business; courtesy toward others; dependability in one's work; compassion for the unfortunate; resistance to evil; help for the weak; concern for good government; support for public education; and above all, a life-practicing reverence for God and love of fellow man. It encourages good citizenship and political expression but is not a political organization. Its charitable activities are manifold, yet, it is not a welfare or benefit organization."

The square and compass were the most important tools of a masons trade, together the two implements form the familiar Masonic "trademark." The letter "G" at the center of the symbolical triangle represents the Mason's belief that God is the center of life. The qualities required of a man to become part of the select fraternity are,

> " . . . We receive none, knowingly, into our ranks who are not moral and upright before God and of good repute before the world . . ."[5]

The Masons of Georgia are the product of thousands of years of history. No other organization today can boast the tradition and pride that belongs solely to the Freemasons. An example of this history occurred during the Revolutionary War. Sunbury was used as a prisoner of war camp for American soldiers by the British after the fall of Fort Morris. A group of these men belonged to the Union Society of Freemasons from Savannah. According to their charter, if a meeting was not held annually on March 21, they would forfeit their charter. Four of the prisoners, all Masons, approached a British Officer, also a member of the fraternity and requested permission to hold a meeting. They were granted permission and conducted the meeting underneath the same oak that had watched over Oglethorpe as he conducted his first Masonic meeting in Georgia. The charter never lapsed and the Union Society continues to exist.

After the Revolution, Sunbury eventually dwindled away until the town was no longer viable. The oak tree, which proudly stood in the midst of Sunbury remained even after the town's demise. For over a century, the majestic tree stood proud in its historic significance until one young man brought the towering oak to its untimely death. It seems the young man was chasing a rabbit, which hid in the hollow of the historic oak. The boy, knowing nothing of the significance of the tree, built a fire at its base to smoke out his prey. The fire was the death blow for the ancient oak, it died in 1840.

A local resident, John Stephens, was aware of the history of the great tree and managed to save a portion of it from the flames. A gavel was carved from the hardy oak and presented to Solomon's Lodge in Savannah along with an alms[6] box, which was presented to the Bethesda Home for Boys. In 1853, another small block was placed in the cornerstone of the Pulaski Monument in Savannah Monument noting the occasion of "The First Masonic Meeting in Georgia."

THE REV. MR. JOHN OSGOOD

This is the grave of the Rev. Mr. John Osgood, who came to Midway with the first settlers in 1754 from Dorchester, S.C., and served them faithfully as their minister and friend until his final sermon, May 5, 1773. Born in Dorchester, one of their own people, Mr. Osgood received part of his education from their old pastor, the Rev. Mr. Fisher, and was graduated from Harvard in 1733. Ordained to the pastoral charge of the Congregational Church November 24, 1735, the Rev. Mr. Osgood ministered to these people, in Dorchester and in Midway, for 38 years. He died on August 2, 1773.

US 17/GA 25 in the cemetery at Midway
GPS Coordinates: N31.80602, W81.430809

In the mid 1700s, a mass exodus occurred in the towns of Dorchester and Beech Hill in southern Carolina. The Congregationalists'[7] population had grown so large at Dorchester and Beech Hill that no more land was available for farming or for young families to settle. The lack of available property, coupled with disease and nonproductive farm lands, made the decision to move the congregation imperative.

A delegation was sent to view the land of coastal Georgia. A favorable report was given and in 1752, the group acquired two grants encompassing 32,000 acres along the Georgia coast. Many members of both the Dorchester and Beech Hill churches led by their minister, Reverend John Osgood, moved south.

The effect of the move was devastating for the Congregational Church in St. George Parish, Dorchester. Osgood's defection left them without a minister and the existence of the Dorchester Congregational settlement perished. The structure that housed the Beech Hill Church soon fell to ruin and Dorchester became known as only a village in the parish of St. George.

Reverend John Osgood was selected to lead the district and his parish swelled to three hundred fifty white followers and fifteen hundred African Americans. Although Sunbury was a thriving port city, Midway was much more centrally located and it was chosen as the center of the district, site for the Midway Congregational Church.

Reverend John Osgood served his faithful parishioners for thirty-eight years and died in August 1773. The grave of the esteemed first minister of Midway Congregational Church lies in the Midway cemetery among those he guided to heaven for so many years.

**SAVANNAH NEW
INVERNESS ROAD
1736**

This highway follows an old colonial road constructed in 1736 as a measure of defense against the Spanish and Spanish Indians by connecting the fighting Scotch Highlanders at New Inverness (now Darien) with Savannah. It was surveyed and cleared by soldiers and Indians furnished by Tomo-chi-chi under the direction of Capt. Hugh MacKay by order of Gen. James Oglethorpe. The road was traveled by such famous Georgians as Button Gwinnett, Dr. Lyman Hall, and John and Joseph LeConte.

**US 17/GA 25 opposite Midway Church, Midway
GPS Coordinates: N31.80506, W81.430922**

Serviceable roads were a major concern to most growing settlements; travel until 1736 was concentrated on the various rivers and intercoastal waterways. The Scottish Highlanders knew that should the Spanish to the south attack, they would travel by sail. The settlers knew they would never out run nor out maneuver the Spanish; therefore, an inland road was necessary to evacuate their families in case of invasion.

Roads connected the political centers of the era included churches and meeting houses. These were the centers that towns eventually developed. In 1736, Captain Hugh MacKay was instructed by General Oglethorpe to build a road to Savannah. With the assistance of their Native American allies led by Tomo Chi Chi, a great friend to Oglethorpe, the Savannah-New Inverness Road was built. The emergence of a road also meant that wheeled carts could have easy access, making transportation somewhat simpler. The roads also brought forth another problem, fording the rivers between Savannah and New Inverness, later called Darien. Bridges were still considered the highest form of architecture and were not common during this time. Ferries soon began to appear at large waterway crossings.

The Savannah New Inverness Road remains today, known as US Highway 17.

MIDWAY MUSEUM

Established by South Carolina Calvinists of English and
Scottish extraction in 1752, the small settlement of Midway
became "the cradle of Revolutionary spirit in Georgia". Two
of Georgia's three signers of the Declaration of
Independence,
Lyman Hall and Button Gwinnett, were sons of Midway,
as were four Revolutionary Governors of the young state.
Exhibits, documents and furnishings housed in the Midway
Museum commemorate and reanimate the love of liberty
which distinguished the Midway Society from the Colonial
period through its last meeting in December 1865.
Built in 1957, the Museum is owned and administered by the
Midway Museum, Inc., organized by the Saint John's Parish
Chapter, Daughters of the American Colonists and by the
Liberty County Chapter, United Daughters of the Confederacy.

US 17/GA 25 at Midway Museum, Midway
GPS Coordinates: N31.80676, W81.43273

Midway Museum was built as a raised cottage, a style commonly seen along coastal Georgia during the 1700s. The house was constructed to represent homes of the 18th century era, which graced the knolls of Sunbury and Riceboro. A typical coastal home was sketched by Basil Hall in 1828; it was his vivid description that was used as an example for the construction of Midway Museum in 1957. The detailed depiction stated:

> "a frame-house, being made of timbers squared and fastened together, and afterwards covered with planks at the sides and ends, while the roof is either boarded or protected by shingles, a sort of wooden slate, two feet in length, and six inches wide. Almost all the houses in that part of the country have verandahs, or what they call 'piazzas'."

The museum houses a collection of items including documentation and donated furnishings representative of "the cradle of Revolutionary Spirit," so apparent in Midway. A settee that once belonged to President Thomas Jefferson sits in the parlor, among other antiques gracing the varied rooms. The Midway Society, whose last annual meeting took place in December 1865, is distinguished among the Museum's holdings. The public is welcomed at the museum, Tuesday through Sunday. A small fee is charged for the self guided tour, which is used to maintain the Midway Colonial Museum.

Across the street from the Midway Museum, you will find among the giant oaks the Midway Cemetery. Approximately 1200 graves are held within the boundaries of the brick walls that surrounds the two acre cemetery: Two Revolutionary War Generals and Governor Nathan Brownson lie peacefully here.

A story is told concerning two slaves who were given the job of constructing the brick walls that encases the cemetery. It seems that the two men argued and one hit the other in the head with a brick, killing the man on the spot. To cover his crime, the slave placed the dead man within the wall and laid brick entombing him within the wall. He told his owner that the man ran off to escape his bonds. Filled with guilt, the slave eventually confessed his crime. To this day, the wall continues to crumble and crack at the spot where the slave was buried.

The Midway Museum

During the Civil War the cemetery was desecrated by General Kilpatrick's Union cavalry. While General Kilpatrick waited with his men at Midway to join General Sherman on his march into Savannah, he corralled calvary horses and livestock in the walled cemetery.

The Cemetery is open at all times. Stop in at the Midway Museum for a pamphlet that can be used as a guide through the history burial ground. The pride and care taken to maintain not only the cemetery but the historic city of Midway is obvious to visitors and a credit to all those responsible.

"HALL'S KNOLL"
Home of Dr. Lyman Hall

Home-site of Dr. Lyman Hall, signer of the Declaration of Independence, member of the First Continental Congress, Governor of Georgia, member of Midway Congregational Church near here. Graduate of Yale University. (1747) Born in Wallingford, Conn. April 12, 1724, Dr. Hall moved to the Puritan Colony at Dorchester, S.C. in 1757 and after those Puritans had established themselves here in Saint John's Parish in the Province of Georgia, he moved to this place and became the leading physician of his time. He died Oct. 19, 1790, and was buried on a bluff overlooking the Savannah River. In 1848 his body was re-interred in Augusta with that of George Walton, another Georgia signer of the Declaration of Independence, beneath the Signers Monument, a granite obelisk.

Saint John's Parish was later named Liberty County in commemoration of the patriotism of the Midway Colonists here, who, from the passage of the Stamp Act, became the most uncompromising champions of liberty, and, who, in advance of the remainder of the Province, took radical action by sending Dr. Lyman Hall to the Continental Congress in Philadelphia as a delegate before the Province at large could be induced to join the federation.

US 17/GA 25 1 mile north of Midway Church
GPS Coordinates: N31.81965, W81.430004

D
r. Lyman Hall, born in Wallingford, Connecticut, immigrated south with fellow parishioners of the New England Congregationalists, where he served occasionally as their minister. Hall, a physician by vocation, became a rice planter and later a politician when his radical blood was stirred by the British.

Restless from the start, Hall found it hard to decide where he would choose to reside. Migrating between southern Carolina and Georgia several times, he finally joined the New Englanders' and their quest to develop a settlement at Midway in St. John's Parish. Hall purchased a rice plantation, he referred to as Hall's Knoll, near the settlement of Sunbury. From Hall's Knoll, he cared for the medical needs of his neighbors and made a success of the rice plantation.

Georgia was slow join her northern neighbors against England. The youngest of the colonies, settlers of Georgia felt that they had no cause to join a rebellion against the mother country. Georgia was far removed from the northern uprisings against England, which was trying desperately to maintain control over her wayward brood.

There were actually three factions that divided Georgia colonists during this time; one saw Royal Governor Wright as a benefactor to the colony; the second were aristocrat supporters of the Whigs[8] of Christ Church, and the third was the far more radical New Englanders of St. John's Parish. Wright's supporters chose to ignore the problems steadily arising with England. As supporters of the Royal Governor, they were given annual grants and lucrative trade agreements; therefore, they had no complaints concerning the status quo. The faction supporting the Whigs felt that the Royal government should have limited powers and the wealthy should control the Colonial government. The third faction believed that the people should determine their own destinies in a democratic society.

Lyman Hall belonged to the third faction. Hall paid close attention to the growing unrest in the colonies to the north and the increasing restrictions placed on the American colonies. Even with the rumblings of trouble, Georgia refused to send delegates to the First Continental Congress of 1774 held in Philadelphia. St. John's Parish was not pleased with this decision, and decided to send Lyman Hall to represent their interest in the Continental Congress. Hall refused. However, when threats of boycotts failed to sway the other Georgia parishes, Lyman Hall agreed to travel north, primarily to carry his community's appeal against the patriot-ordered trade boycotts. Hall took two hundred barrels of locally grown rice with him, a donation for the patriots in the North. Interestingly enough, during this period there were discussions of St. John's aligning themselves with the patriot groups in Charleston and seceding from the rest of the Georgia settlements. Of course, this never came to pass.

For four months, beginning in May 1775, Lyman Hall represented Georgia alone at the Second Continental Congress. He shared official duties with delegates from all of the remaining colonies including such notables as; Virginia's fiery Patrick Henry, Pennsylvania's legendary Ben Franklin, as well as John Adams from Massachusetts.

The Second Continental Congress gathered in Philadelphia in May 1775, after the bombardment of Lexington and Concord. The group decided to relocate its meeting place from the tight fitting Carpenter's Hall to the grander Pennsylvania State House, known today as Independence Hall.

Early changes included the resignation of Virginia's Peyton Randolph as presiding officer, to be succeeded by John Hancock of Massachusetts. The major issue of discussion by this Congress, now that shooting had begun, would be a choice between declaring full independence or seeking a reconciliation with England.

Before the matter of independence could be addressed, other issues took precedence. The Congress issued a resolution for all colonies to prepare for possible war, they appropriated funds to purchase military supplies, announced the formation of six rifle companies from Virginia, Pennsylvania and Maryland to assist the New Englanders holding Boston under siege and appointed Virginia's George Washington as commander of the Continental Army.

Congress turned to British controlled Canada to join in the American Revolution for freedom and in July 1775, adopted John Dickinson's Olive Branch Petition, addressed to King George III, seeking reconciliation on the colonists' terms.

The Congress, contradictory to the Olive Branch Petition, adopted the Declaration of the Causes and Necessity for Taking Up Arms, a decree by Pennsylvania's John Dickinson and Virginia's Thomas Jefferson. The document accused Parliament of using force to enslave the colonies and sought to justify their use of force to meet force.

Congress also created a colonies wide postal system during this session. Ben Franklin was appointed as the Nation's first Postmaster General. On August 2, Congress rejected an early British effort at reconciliation, considering the compromise inadequate.

By now, events were escalating back home in Georgia. There, in early 1776, local patriots arrested Royal Governor Wright; he was later paroled and allowed to escape to the British warships harbored in the Savannah River. The first revolutionary battle of Georgia erupted on the Savannah River when British soldiers attempted to seize Georgia grown rice. The Georgia Provincial Congress met and having no choice, selected representatives to travel to the Continental Congress at Philadelphia in July 1776. Those chosen were Lyman Hall, Button Gwinnett and a young Savannah lawyer named, George Walton. As destiny would have it they would be witness to the momentous event when John Adams called for consideration of the proposed Declaration of Independence.

Adams wrote to Archibald Bulloch, president of Georgia's Provincial Congress, stating,

"A declaration, that these colonies are free and independent states, has been reported by a committee appointed some weeks ago for that purpose, and this day or to-morrow is to determine its fate. . . ."

By July 1776 Georgia would claim full representation in Congress along with their brethren from the other twelve colonies, all would be the signers of the Declaration of Independence. What an unusual trio they were!

Lyman Hall was by far the oldest of the Georgia delegates. He was one of only five doctors to sign the Declaration. George Walton, at age twenty-six, was one of the youngest signers. Last, but certainly not least, Button Gwinnett whose signature, due to its rarity, would become the most valuable of all the document's signators.

Two months later, on November 19, Congress was informed that King George III had not only rejected the Olive Branch Petition, but had declared the colonies to be in a state of rebellion. Still seeking reconciliation, Congress moved on December 6 to send England another statement of loyalty to the Crown, but not to Parliament.

As 1776 came to a close, the Continental Congress called for real independence rather than an accommodation. England's King George responded by ordering the closure of American ports to normal commerce. The act only intensified the American mood in favor of total and irrevocable separation from England. The colonies declared war and the American Revolution began in full force.

LAMBERT PLANTATION

Just east of here was the 863 acre plantation of John Lambert which he purchased in 1784.

John Lambert was born in South Carolina in 1716 and died at his plantation here in December 1786. He is buried in the Midway Cemetery. He never married and, having no family, left his entire estate in a perpetual trust with the stipulation that the income be applied "to the support of the gospel, for the relief of the poor and distressed, or whatever pious and good purpose may be answered." The executors sold the plantation and slave in 1847 and invested the capital in securities. The Estate of John Lambert exists to this day, using the yearly income for "pious and good purposes."

US 17 at Bill Carter Road, at road leading to LeConte Gardens
GPS Coordinates: N31.76664, W81.448683

John Lambert's early years are shrouded in mystery and many stories have been repeated over the years since his birth. The most intriguing of the stories relates that as an infant he was found swaddled in a basket on Lambert Bridge in southern Carolina. A local family came upon the babe and brought him into their home to raise. Although the family searched for the parents and waited for someone to claim the infant, no one came forward. They named him John, a common name, and Lambert because of the bridge where he was found. The foster parents soon died, leaving young John an orphan once again. Planters in the area cared for the child, each taking a him in for a year until he reached his majority.

Contrary to the first story, the other concerns his death, rather than his mysterious birth. The tale concerned a suit filed in Liberty County Superior Court by persons claiming to be relatives in an attempt to protest John Lambert's will. The testimony given during the trial stated that John's parents were Jeremiah and Leah Lambert of St. James Parish, southern Carolina. John's mother was reported to have died as a result of his birth and his father i supposedly passed away in 1792, six years after John. The petitioner's case was dismissed and John Lambert's will was left unaltered.

Regardless of the circumstances involving his birth and parentage, John was a self made entrepreneur. As a boy, while searching for fish bait, he found a piece of American Indian pottery, he traded the pottery for chickens. He sold some of the eggs and with the rest his flock grew. He began to sell chickens. Later, John had enough money to expand his animal husbandry to include pigs then cows. He amassed enough money to buy a mule and one slave, applied for a land grant and became a planter. When John arrived in Liberty County in 1784, he was wealthy. Within three years he had built a large plantation and acquired numerous slaves, becoming a prominent citizen and serving as a Selectman[9] for Midway for three terms. John Lambert, however, lived alone his entire life never marrying or fathering an heir. The man, who was a well respected Midway citizen in life, became a benefactor to her residents in death.

John made a few simple bequeaths, excused two debts owed him and saw to the care of his remaining slaves in his will. Surprisingly, he left the bulk of his estate in the hands of several friends who were directed to establish a trust. The funds received from the trust were to be used to bring religion to those who needed it, relief to those who could not help themselves, education to the public and to care for orphans. John Lambert's specific mention of orphans in his will lends credence to the story of his being abandoned as an infant. Provisions were made for the selection of other executors, if those men whom he had chosen declined the honor, none of the executors declined.

The trust established in the name of John Lambert is still active today. Much to the credit of Abiel Holmes, John Elliott, Gideon Dowse, Thomas Sumner, William Quarterman and Thomas Baker, named executors in the original will. These men and many more who have followed for more than 200 years, maintained the trust and used it for the purposes provided for in Lambert's will. Many Liberty County and Georgia residents owe a great debt of gratitude to a self made orphan who became a man of means and in turn, gave back to the community. Although John Lambert had no heirs to carry on his name, he left a legacy.

The old town of Sunbury, 11 miles East on this Road, was a leading port, said to rival Savannah in commercial importance. It was the first Seat of Justice of Liberty County. Sunbury Academy, established in 1788, was in its time the most famous School in South Georgia. The Rev. Dr. William McWhir, friend of George Washington, was Principal of the Academy for 30 years.

Fort Morris, about 350 yards south of Sunbury, was an important post during the Revolution. It was here that Col. John McIntosh sent his famous reply, "Come and Take it," to the British order to surrender the fort.

US 17/GA 25 at US 84 intersection
GPS Coordinates: N31.79937, W81.432628

In 1758, plantations and home sites began to become successful, the citizens decided they required a more convenient port rather than the arduous journey to Savannah. Sunbury plantations were producing rice, indigo, lumber and tar in greater quantities and it became apparent that a local port would serve their needs much more than traveling the distance north. Mark Carr chose 500 acres on the south bank of the Midway River as the site for the new settlement. The settlement was called Sunbury. It is speculated that the name was derived from an English town situated on the Thames or that simply, the settlement was located on a sunny spot along the banks of the Midway River. The Midway River is believed to be one of the deepest natural rivers south of the Chesapeake. The river was known to have depths of more than forty feet, making it ideal to port large ships. A road was established to the settlement of Midway by means of an old Indian trail, possibly the oldest in Georgia. The trail could be followed from the Midway River to the Georgia mountains.

The village consisted of 496 lots, having three public squares dubbed Kings, Church and Meeting and five wharves along the river. Soon the town began to prosper, surpassing Savannah. It is said that the residents of Sunbury controlled a third of the wealth in Georgia by 1772. However, records of 1773 show that Sunbury ported only one third the ships that Savannah claimed. Eighty home sites had been established by this time, along with a customs house, several businesses and a naval office. Sunbury realized the need for a fortification to protect them from Native American attacks and the Spanish to the south. A small battery was built on high ground to the south of the settlement also on the Midway River.

By 1776, the American Revolution was moving closer to Georgia and a new fort was constructed to protect the citizens of Sunbury from British invasion. Built by African American slaves of earth and wood, the fortification was called Fort Morris in honor of its first commander Captain Thomas Morris. Fort Morris garrisoned twenty-four cannons and sheltered 250 men and officers. A substantial barracks for the officers constructed of brick stood at the center of the fortification.

A British naval force under the command of Lieutenant Colonel L.V. Fuser had orders to attack Sunbury from the Midway River, while the land force would take the settlement of Midway, then proceed to Fort Morris and together the two forces would attack the fort; one from land, the other from the river. After the fall of Sunbury and Fort Morris, their orders were to proceed to Savannah.

Colonel John White commanded the Colonial troops at Midway and was determined to hold Lieutenant Colonel Prevost, who led the British land contingent. After several skirmishes, it became obvious to Colonel White that he was out manned at least four to one and he would not be able to hold the settlement. As he continued to fight Prevost, he dispatched Colonel John McIntosh and 127 militia to reinforce Sunbury and Fort Morris. Colonel White was forced to retreat. When the town was abandoned, White intentionally allowed a letter, detailing the Colonial Army's troop movements, to fall into British hands. The letter was intended to deceive Prevost into thinking the Americans had reinforcements on the way. Prevost was told that Fuser had delayed his attack on Fort Morris; not knowing what else to do, he had his troops burn Midway and retreat. He continued to burn and plunder plantations all the way back to the British stronghold in East Florida. Fuser had been taken aback when he demanded the surrender of Fort Morris and Colonel John McIntosh replied defiantly, "Come and take it!" Fuser chose to retreat and fight another day. The Fort was taken a few months later.

At the end of the Revolutionary War, Fort Morris was abandoned and the town of Sunbury was destroyed. Sunbury attempted to rebuild the settlement in 1782 and it was selected as the county seat for the newly formed county called, Liberty. The town of Sunbury never fully recovered the devastation left by the Revolution.

The Sunbury Academy was established in 1793 and became one of the finest schools in the south. Under the direction of Reverend Dr. William McWhir, Sunbury students excelled in many professions of Georgia and United States leadership. The Reverend Dr. McWhir, a friend of George Washington, was principal for thirty years. The Sunbury Academy was located in King's Square.

Liberty County rebuilt and was recovering. However, Sunbury was no longer an important seaport. Roads and bridges were being built making access to larger ports much easier and Sunbury's citizens soon began to abandon the settlement. The county seat was removed to Riceborough and it was the beginning of the end for Sunbury.

The War of 1812 brought some life back to the waning settlement. Fort Morris was again manned and now called Fort Defiance, in honor of the courage shown by Colonel McIntosh. The fort was manned by a body of students from the Sunbury Academy, commanded by their principal, the Reverend Dr. William McWhir. The boys held their ground and manned the walls against the British invasion that never came.

By the Civil War, the settlement of Sunbury was little more than a ghost town. Devastating hurricanes and yellow fever had taken their toll. The Union cavalry finished her off when they pillaged what was left of the settlement and burned their church to signal the Union Navy.

After the Civil War, any buildings left standing were moved to Dorchester. The only remaining structure today is Dorchester Presbyterian Church, built in 1854. The church's bell is originally from Sunbury. Sunbury was abandoned, left to be looted and worn down by mother nature. The property was purchased by the Georgia Historical Commission in 1968. The site was placed on the National Register of Historic Places in 1971 and in 1973, The Nature Conservancy helped the state acquire three more acres that contain the old Fort Defiance earthen works.

Fort Morris is one of the few remaining Revolutionary War era earthwork fortifications in the United States. The last patriot post to fall in the American Revolution, Fort Morris was surrendered to the British on January 9, 1779. The Fort Morris State Historic Site is open for self guided tours Tuesday through Sunday. A small admission fee is charged.

All that remains today of the settlement at Sunbury is a well maintained, peaceful cemetery. Embraced by towering oaks that shade its sleeping occupants who were all citizens of Sunbury.

South 0.3 miles from GA 38, 5.8 miles east of Midway Church
GPS Coordinates: N31.75896, W81.354661

Dorchester Presbyterian Church was founded in 1854. The church was established by the Midway inhabitants who traveled inland each year to their summer "retreats." E. A. Busbee donated the four acres of land for the construction of the church. Once completed, the sanctuary was named for the southern Carolina community that most of the Midway Church members once called home.

It is obvious from the donation list that membership at Dorchester was varied. The parishioners heralded from not only Midway but Sunbury as well. The bell, used to call the congregation to worship, once proudly hung in the now defunct town of Sunbury. Its resounding tones were silenced when Sunbury faded into history. The font[10] and communion service were used at Dorchester's sister church at Midway and the gift signified their unity.

The font was originally a donation from Dr. William McWhir, famed teacher and theologian, noted for bringing prominence to the Sunbury Academy. The facility was recognized as one of the leading academies of learning in the state. His contributions shaped the minds of numerous students, who eventually left distinctive marks not only on Georgia but in United States history.

A tankard, used for communion, was the bequest of John Lambert. One of the wealthiest men of Liberty County, who served his community well in life and left a legacy to her in death. His last will and testament provided for those unable to care for themselves. The trust, controlled by a group of notable executors passed the obligation along through the years to others of equally outstanding character. The trust continues to serve the community.

The communion service was an alm from Simon Munro, a Tory or British supporter who held so fast to his beliefs that he was forced from his home and family during the Revolutionary War.

The Dorchester Church still stands today. The strength of the church's many early supporters and benefactors remain a part of Liberty County citizens. As a group, Liberty Countians struggle to revive interest in the old Dorchester Presbyterian Church. The Dorchester Presbyterian Church has congregational meetings the first Sunday of every month.

GA 38, 5.8 miles east of Midway Church, Midway
GPS Coordinates: N31.76243, W81.352918

Dorchester Village was an inland settlement used during the sweltering months of summer by coastal Georgia inhabitants, located halfway between Sunbury and Midway and known only as a village, because it was never developed into a town. Generally, few people ever became permanent residents. The only major establishments in the village were the Dorchester Presbyterian Church and the notable Dorchester Academy.

In the days following the Civil War, persons representing the American Missionary Association (AMA) searched the southern states for opportunities to bring education to the former African American slaves. The Midway Church was discovered by the organization. The area had produced so many military, civic and political leaders that locating a school here was almost without question.

William Golden, a former slave himself, began a one room school. However, his lack of education doomed him to failure from the beginning. The AMA dispatched missionaries to assist in establishing an academy, but because of the hardships left as a result of the Civil War, the citizens were not pleased when northern, white women were brought in as teachers. The teachers were ostracized by the white community and forced to live among their students. The cultural changes were more than these women missionaries could bare and eventually, they returned home. The school was off to a rocky start.

Reverend Floyd Snelson stepped in and with funds from the AMA, he built a successful school. The term lasted six months and could educate 100 pupils. The students were required to grow vegetables and raise livestock as part of a vocational training program. The program produced not only food for the school, but revenues from products sold funded what the students and faculty could not produce themselves.

In 1896, the school could educate up to 500 students and had built dormitories for those pupils who were not local. The first graduation ceremony was held in 1896. Former African American slaves looked on in awe at the opportunities the young educated graduates had before them.

Dorchester Academy and likewise Dorchester Village would see many changes over the years. From the blossoming of Civil Rights Movement to the end of segregation. Dorchester Academy now serves as a community center. Dorchester Village no longer exists.

FORT MORRIS

Erected at the beginning of the Revolutionary War, to guard the Port
of Sunbury and St. John's Parish, Fort Morris was an enclosed
earthwork in the shape of an irregular quadrangle. Surrounded by a
parapet and moat. It contained a parade of about an acre. The fort
was defended by more than 25 pieces of ordnance of varied size. It
was named in honor of Captain Morris, who commanded the
company of artillery by which it was first garrisoned early in 1776.
Colonel John McIntosh commanded the garrison on November 25,
1778, when Col. L. V. Fuser, with 500 British ground troops,
supported by armed ships in the Medway river,
landed at Sunbury and
demanded the immediate surrender of Fort Morris. Colonel
McIntosh, with 127 Continental troops, some militia and citizens of
Sunbury, less than 200 men in all, replied, "Come and Take It!"
The enemy retreated to the South, and Continental troops held Fort
Morris until January 9, 1779, when it was captured by British forces.

Visitors Center, Fort Morris/Sunbury Historic Site
GPS Coordinates: N31.76172, W81.281946

Fort Morris, like many others in this area, was once a *Guale* Indian village. Built in the 1750s, it was not manned until 1776, as stipulated by the Continental Congress. The fort was garrisoned with 200 soldiers anticipating a British attack. Colonel John McIntosh was placed in command by his brother Lachlan, who was Commander of all the colonial forces.

Lieutenant Colonel L. V. Fuser, serving the Crown, approached Fort Morris in November 1778. Accompanying Lieutenant Fuser was Captain Roderick "Old Rory" McIntosh as Captain of the Light Infantry. Captain Roderick McIntosh was known as a Don Quixote[11]. Old Rory served with his Majesty's army for many years and refused to serve another, even for the independence of his adopted homeland. He was 65 years of age during the attack on Fort Morris but still ready, willing and more than aggressively able to storm any fortress. Tall with the ruddy complexion a Scotsman, glowing white hair that frizzed in the humid weather and stood straight out from his head, Old Rory was a sight to behold. Walking with a determined stride, it is said that his step covered four foot of ground at a pace.

Before the attack on Fort Morris, as the British troops surrounded the garrison, a figure approached the walls. Old Rory, deep in his cups[12] and very drunk, demanded, "Surrender, you miscreants! How dare you presume to resist his Majesty's arms!" Colonel John McIntosh recognized the voice immediately and commanded his men to hold all fire. Colonel McIntosh threw open the gates and responded "Walk in, cousin and take possession." Old Rory responded, all the while his manservant Jim was beseeching him to withdraw, "No, I will not trust myself with such vermin, I order you to surrender." A soldier, not recognizing the kinsman's banter, fired a shot. Old Rory was struck, the ball passed through his cheek and he fell to the ground but was quickly back to his feet. Jim pulling at his sleeve begged Rory to fall back to the rear. Rory, covered with blood brandished his sword and said, "Run yourself, poor slave, I am of a race that never runs." However, he did walk backward to the safety of the British lines, never turning his back on the enemy.

After several days of heavy bombardment, another demand for surrender was made to Colonel McIntosh. This time the summons was from Lieutenant Fuser, himself. As defiant as his voracious cousin, Colonel John McIntosh responded, "Come and take it!" Lieutenant Fuser did not advance, instead he retreated back to Florida. Forty-five days later, Fort Morris fell on January 9, 1779.

During the War of 1812, the fort was put to limited use once again as a remote guard post. In recognition of Colonel McIntosh's boldness and bravery, the fort was renamed, Fort Defiance.

Off GA 38, 1/2 mile past entrance to Sunbury Historic Site
GPS Coordinates: N31.45529, W81.16558

I magine a sea port bustling with activity, ships sitting low in the water heavy with cargo and sailors crowding the wharf after being long at sea. When the ships came in, the festivities began. Music filled the air, hawkers sounded out advertising rooms and bawdy women for hire, enticing patrons to try their luck in the gambling houses. The smell of the sea and the scent from the cook pots floated on the breeze from the east. The itinerant visitors sometimes led to trouble when their merry making rose to a crescendo in the crowded streets. For the most part, the town was a lively port of call. She was rich with commerce, trade and people. This was the port city of Sunbury.

For a time, Sunbury had only one rival to the title "Principal Georgia Port," Savannah. Much more than a port city, Sunbury's contribution to Liberty County, the state of Georgia and the American colonies can not be measured by its success. The city, by most standards, was very short lived, only viable for approximately fifty years and in existence for twenty years more. Sunbury's endowment can be measured by the quality of her citizens. There are many of citizens to which we, as a democratic society, owe the freedoms enjoyed in the United States today.

To name all of those hailing from Sunbury who shaped our great country, would be impossible without lengthy consideration. However, a great number of prominent names are forever linked with her history, including these:

Dr. Lyman Hall, signer of the Declaration of Independence, settled in Sunbury and practiced medicine there.

Richard Howley, a lawyer and native born Liberty Countian. He served as Governor of Georgia during the American Revolution and only narrowly escaped capture by retreating to northern Carolina.

John Elliott born in St. Johns Parish, served in many local capacities until elected to the Georgia Senate. He had a thriving law practice in Sunbury for a number of years and after having left for a number of years, Elliott returned to Sunbury to retire from public life.

Dr. Nathan Brownson, a physician from Liberty County, was an early supporter of the patriots cause during the American Revolution. He served as the chief surgeon for the Continental Army, delegate to the Continental Congress, Georgia Governor and a member of the State Senate, during his term the Georgia State Constitution was adopted.

Alfred Cuthbert, a lawyer, served two terms as state Senator and was elected a Georgia State Representative for five sessions of Congress.

Major John Jones settled with his family in Sunbury and established a plantation on Colonels Island. Jones served as aid de camp for Major General Nathaniel Greene during the Revolutionary War.

Lachlan McIntosh, soldier ascending to rank of Brigadier General, statesman and patriot. Numerous books have been written, totally devoted to his life and service to his county.

Button Gwinnett, noted statesman and signer of the Declaration of Independence, whose accomplishments are well documented.

George Walton, the third Georgia signer of the Declaration of Independence. Walton lived most of his life in Augusta, however, his connection with Sunbury stems from the American Revolution. Sunbury was used as a prisoner of war camp and Walton was held there for a time. Walton was a carpenter's apprentice at a young age, he aspired to become a lawyer and practiced law in Augusta, Governor of Georgia, Senator and Chief Justice of the Supreme Court. He was very involved in negotiating a peace treaty with the Cherokee in Tennessee.

James McKay McIntosh, grandson of the McIntosh Clan, joined the Navy as a young man and eventually attained the rank of Commodore. His service to his country against foreign enemies, pirates and slave traders won him the heart felt thanks of Congress.

Maria Jane McIntosh, sister of James McKay, found it hard as a woman to express the ideals of leadership bred into the McIntosh Clan. To make her voice heard, Maria Jane chose to become an author. Her articles, essays and novels as well as her children's literature carried the theme of moral responsibility and the rights of women as human beings. Her writings received much acclaim. Maria Jane McIntosh became a leader in the only venue available to her.

John Elliott Ward, a lawyer, Senator, Solicitor General, District Attorney, Representative, Lieutenant Governor of Georgia and Mayor of Savannah. John Elliott Ward's most noted position was his appointment as the first Minister to China.

The Honorable **William Law**, Liberty County Superior Court Justice of the Eastern Circuit.

The list of notable citizens, all patriots, continues. These are but a few of the names who throughout history have created settlements, churches and patriots who defended a nation at war. The patriots fought to gain freedom, valiantly protecting a way of life even though the battle was hopeless and mourned the losses of citizens and towns who were but a memory.

The city of Sunbury is today marked by a quiet cemetery representing over one hundred years of history. The earliest stone dates to 1788 and the latest, 1911. Once on the corner of Church Square in the bustling sea port. Today, Sunbury is but a page in history.

SUNBURY CEMETERY

In this Cemetery are buried men and women whose lives contributed much to the early history of Georgia. Among these were the Rev. Wm. McWhir, D.D., and his wife. The Rev. Mr. McWhir was for 30 years Principal of the famous Sunbury Academy. Born in Ireland, September 9, 1759, he was graduated from Belfast College and was licensed to preach by the presbytery of that City. He died in Georgia, January 30, 1851. Some burials were made in this plot in Colonial and Revolutionary Days, but most of the markers had been destroyed before the 1870s.

Left 0.2 mile from fork at Sunbury, left 0.1 mile, right 0.1 mile
GPS Coordinates: N31-77023, W81.284114

All that remains of the once lively port of Sunbury is the Sunbury Cemetery. The cemetery is believed to have occupied the southeast corner of Church Square. War brought some destruction and the elements of weather and time took care of the rest. Still those that remain today are well cared for and protected by century old oaks. Of the thirty-four markers that remain, the earliest is dated 1788 and the latest marked 1911. The peaceful little cemetery speaks volumes of history carved in stone.

Among those laid to rest here are Reverend and Mrs. William McWhir. Reverend McWhir was not only a man of theology, but a man deeply devoted to education. He was responsible for raising the standards of education in the institutions where he served to rival those of higher learning.

Reverend McWhir was of Irish descent, a graduate of Belfast College and granted a license to preach by the Presbytery of Belfast. He came to America in 1783, settling in Alexandria, Virginia. McWhir began teaching at the newly formed Alexandria Academy. It was there that he began his life long friendship with George Washington.

Washington assumed guardianship for his nephews, George Steptoe and Lawrence Augustine Washington and in November 1785, Washington enrolled the boys at the Alexandria Academy under the tutelage of Reverend McWhir. The boys, at ages ten and thirteen, were somewhat mischievous. Correspondence between Washington and McWhir became a regular occurrence, one they continued the remainder of their lives.

McWhir became headmaster at Sunbury Academy around 1790. The average enrollment was 70 students. He provided education in classical Greek, Latin and proper English as well as advanced mathematics and sciences. Under his direction, the Sunbury Academy had few rivals as a preparatory school. He firmly believed in the rod of discipline and used the birch freely on those that did not perform to the best of their ability or conducted themselves in an ungentlemanly way.

McWhir became mentor and guide to both his pupils and former pupils. During his thirty years as headmaster of Sunbury Academy, McWhir often found himself teaching the children of past alumni.

The Reverend Doctor William McWhir died January 30, 1851, at the age of 91. His teachings and influence did much to shape the course of history in Georgia.

COLONEL'S ISLAND

Until about 1778 this island was called Bermuda, but afterwards called Colonel's Island because of the large number of colonels having plantations here. Major plantations included "Woodville," "Herron's Point," "Maxwellton," "Suligree," "Maybank," "Black Rock," "Laws," "Cedar Point," "Hickory Hill," "Dunham's," and "Melon Bluff."
Rice and indigo were the principal money crops grown on Colonel's Island during the antebellum era. During the War Between the States the island was also a source of salt, an essential ingredient in the making of gunpowder. Long before European explorers reached North America Colonel's Island was a part of the Guale Indian kingdom of the Creek Nation.

GA 38 at Kings Road on Colonel's Island
GPS Coordinates: N31.85795, W81.60725

The expanse of land surrounded by water on all sides and located east of Sunbury was known as Bermuda Island. The *Guale* Native Americans had long since been pushed off their island home and forced to relocate to the mainland. Settlers from the island of Bermuda had settled there soon after the *Guale*; hence, the name Bermuda Island. The new inhabitants were quickly thinned with the onset of malaria. The survivors realized another bout of the fever would take them all and soon relocated to the mainland.

Eventually, Bermuda Island became a resort community. Residents of Sunbury began establishing plantations on the island to get away from the "city life" of the bustling port. The only means of reaching the island was by fording the inlets at the mouth of the Midway River.

One of first plantations was established by a Scotsman named Joseph Law. Law's plantation, Woodville, was the only one to grace the island for a long time. By the end of the Revolutionary War, retired military officers began establishing plantations on the island. The island became so populated with retired officers, the name was changed to reflect the new ownership. The island would now forever be known as Colonel's Island. Colonel Alexander Herron developed Herron's Point, Colonel Audley Maxwell built Maxwell Point, and later his grandson, James Audley Maxwell King, constructed Maxwelton.

The island proved to be an excellent location for livestock and the plantations prospered. Colonel's Island oysters were said to be the finest to be had along the Georgia coast. Hickory Hill Plantation became known far and wide for its hardwoods. The area known as the Hammocks produced cedar trees from which fence posts were made.

Another well known plantation was Melon Bluff. The Stevens family, who owned Melon Bluff, has a long and distinguished history in Liberty County. John Stevens received a land grant in the Midway District in 1752. He settled there a year later. The current owners of Melon Bluff are the Devendorfs. Mrs. Devendorf is a direct descendant of John Stevens. It was her father who began piecing the plantation back together, parcel by parcel, in the 1920s. Today, Melon Bluff Plantation is a 3000 acre privately managed nature preserve. The Devendorfs, along with their daughter, are tree farmers and ecotourism developers. They fiercely oversee the controlled cutting of the trees on their property.

The nature preserve features fifteen miles of trails, two lakes and beautiful saw grass marshlands. The property is a haven for bird watchers, hikers, cyclists and others who just like to explore. The forest is home to numerous native wildlife species including deer, coyotes, opossum, squirrels and a wide variety of birds. Kayaks are available for the spectacular view from the water, well marked trails through the dense vegetation provide a excellent and scenic hiking opportunity and the draft mules, Kit and Kate, pull a wagon for those less inclined to hike. Day passes are available for a fee.

The nature preserve is dedicated to the conservation of Liberty County's vast history. Keeping at least of portion of what was once the land of grand plantations from becoming a concrete jungle.

DORCHESTER ACADEMY

Formal education of blacks started with the Freedmen's Bureau in Liberty County. The Homestead School was continued with the aid of the American Missionary Association (AMA) and support of Reconstruction legislator William A. Goulding. The AMA started with one acre of land and 77 students in 1870. In 1874, the Reverend Floyd Snelson succeeded Goulding at the school. The AMA and Snelson built a new school and named it Dorchester Academy in honor of its Puritan lineage. In 1890, Dorchester Academy started a boarding school. By 1917, the school had eight frame buildings on 103 acres, 300 students, and become a fully accredited high school. The academic program ceased in 1940, with the construction of a consolidated public school for black youth at Riceboro. All academic equipment plus $8,000 were transferred toward that consolidation. Since, the facilities have served the community under the title Dorchester Cooperative Center, Inc. AMA continues financial report.

US 84/GA 38, 1.9 miles west of junction with US 17/GA 25
GPS Coordinates: N31.80137, W81.464739

Shortly after the Civil War, the Freedmen's Bureau sent the American Missionary Association (AMA) to find places where formal education could be offered to the now free African Americans. A missionary was traveling through Midway and by chance, visited Midway Church. After learning of some of the amazing historical figures and civic leaders who had been born and raised within this community, the missionary excitedly posted a letter to her home office. The letter raved of the attributes of Midway Church and Liberty County stating,

> "The influence of this old church on general intelligence, good morals, and genuine piety can hardly be paralleled in any other church in this country. At the breaking out of the recent war, it is said that three-forths of the white male adults of Liberty County were graduates of college."

She spoke of the untold number of teachers the county had produced, including the LeConte brothers who had a hand in the founding of the University of California at Berkley. She listed numerous attorneys, four Georgia governors, two judges and 83 ministers, although she did forget to mention two signers of the Declaration of Independence! Her recommendation was to proceed quickly with the establishment of a school for African Americans in Liberty County.

The first attempt to develop a school under the leadership of former slave, William A. Goulding, failed. The one room school was located on property donated by William B. Gaulden between Midway and McIntosh known as Goulding's Grove. The AMA next sent Rose Kenney and Eliza Ann Ward, white Massachusetts teachers, to teach at Goulding's Grove. The women did not last long, shunned by local whites, the teachers were forced to reside with African American families. The change in culture was just too much for the women to bear and soon they headed back to Massachusetts.

Reverend Floyd Snelson, a African American Congregationalist Minister and Missionary from Andersonville, can be credited with the success of the school. He moved to

Dorchester Academy

Liberty County to be near his brother and discovered the need of Goulding's Grove. He requested use of the AMA funds and was granted permission. Using the entitlements, he expanded the facility. The facility was to encompass 87 acres, a number of buildings and an expanded curriculum. Soon he was able to educate 100 students over a six month term. Snelson renamed the school Dorchester Academy to reflect the puritan beginnings of Liberty County and became its first principal.

Dorchester Academy continued to serve African American students of Liberty County until the outbreak of World War II. The establishment of a consolidated school for both African Americans and whites was built around 1940 at Riceboro. The supplies and part of the funds were transferred to the new public school. The Dorchester Academy facilities were utilized as the Dorchester Cooperative Center, Incorporated and the AMA continued to provide funds to assist the programs there.

DORCHESTER ACADEMY
BOY'S DORMITORY

This Georgian Revival building, built 1934 to replace an earlier structure destroyed by fire, was once a part of an extensive school campus begun in 1871 by the American Missionary Association. The school, founded to serve the educational needs of black children of Liberty County and coastal Georgia, closed in 1940 after public education became available to black children.

In 1948 the American Missionary Association, with the assistance of the local community, expanded the dormitory into a community center, which by 1961 would become the focus for many activities associated with the Civil Rights Movement. The Southern Christian Leadership Conference sponsored Citizen Education Workshops here (1962-1964), training over 1,000 teachers and leaders, who in turn educated over 10,000 in the basics of voter registration and non- violent social change. Dr. M. L. King, Jr. held a planning retreat here in 1962 to prepare for the 1963 Birmingham Campaign, one of the first major victories of the Civil Rights Movement.

US 84/GA 28, 1.9 miles west of junction with US 17/GA 25
GPS Coordinates: N31.80137, W81.464739

A frican American Georgia politician, William A. Goulding, died in Liberty County, where he was born 80 years earlier. Little is known about most of his life, other than the fact that he was a slave until gaining freedom at the end of the Civil War. Shortly after the war, he was elected to represent the Liberty Council at the convention that drafted the Georgia Constitution of 1868 and was among the first African Americans elected to the Georgia General Assembly. Goulding is better remembered for his work concerning the education of African American youth in Liberty County than his work as a civil servant. Goulding, though barely literate, recognized the importance of education and was a major factor in the creation of what would become Dorchester Academy.

The advent of World War II and the establishment of public schools allowing African American children to be educated alongside their white counterparts brought about many changes to Dorchester Academy. Its days of education were over. But were they?

Soon after the closure of Dorchester, the American Missionary Association (AMA) found another use for the facilities. The need for public adult education was great. The Civil Rights Movement was going into high gear and various leaders were searching for facilities to train those willing to learn about anything from voter responsibility to nonviolent protest.

Dorchester Academy hosted citizenship education workshops for the Southern Christian Leadership Conference (SCLC) during the 1960s. The SCLC trained close to 2,000 teachers and leaders, who in turn taught more than 10,500 others. Busloads of adult students arrived and in week long classes, were taught everything from basic reading, writing and math to portions of the state constitution. The classes would prepare the African Americans for the biased voter registration "tests" they encountered when exercising their Constitutional right to vote. The SCLC's leadership training was supported by a grant from the Marshall Field Foundation, which supported the Civil Rights Movement by steering its philanthropy into voter registration. Field Foundation representative Andrew Young, later the mayor of Atlanta, was the school's first director.

**FLEMINGTON
PRESBYTERIAN CHURCH**

Organized in 1815 as the Church and society of Gravel Hill, this was a branch of Midway Church. The Rev. Robert Quarterman was the first pastor. The first edifice was built in 1836 on land donated by Simon Fraser. This one was completed in 1852. Named Flemington in 1850 honoring William Fleming, it was separated from Midway in 1865. In 1866 it was admitted to the Georgia Presbytery with the Rev. D. B. Buttolph, pastor; W. E. W. Quarterman, Thomas Cassels, Ezra Stacy, James Laing, elders; S. A. Fraser, L. M. Cassels, deacons. Ezra Stacy was first Sunday School Superintendent. Bell and silver communion service are from Midway Church.

**Old Sunbury Road, 0.8 mile west of US 84 and Oglethorpe Boulevard, Fleming
GPS Coordinates: N31.86971, W81.570938**

William Fleming donated property for the construction of a church edifice at the settlement of Gravel Hill. The church, a branch of the Midway Congregational Church, was organized in 1815 and the Reverend Robert Quarterman was selected as minister. Quarterman was known as a superb theologian, possessing great zeal in his preaching. Eventually four of his sons would enter the pulpit, one son became a foreign missionary, both of his daughters married pastors, and one of the daughters served with her husband as a missionary in China for sixteen years. The Gravel Hill Civic Organization changed the name of the community and the church to honor William Fleming's generosity. The name was changed to Flemington.

Seventy members of the Midway Church, that resided in Flemington community, requested that their letter of membership be moved to Flemington Presbyterian Church in 1866. The church membership applied to the Presbytery of Georgia and on April 6, 1866, was duly elected as a Presbyterian church. The first official pastor of Flemington Presbyterian was Reverend D. L. Buttolph.

As for Flemington, a United State postoffice was established in 1869. By 1886, the town had numerous farms, naval stores[13], a railroad depot, a general store and a wheelright[14]. The railroad depot was an unmanned station where passengers could disembark and board, but could not buy a ticket.

Someone passed a rumor that the train, stopping briefly in nearby Ludowici on April 1, 1908, carried aboard it Georgia Governor Hoke Smith. The town bustled in preparation. The Mayor was dressed in his Sunday best, the Ludowici High School Band was spit polished and shined, and the local citizens gathered in droves to catch a glimpse of their esteemed Governor. Excitement abounded as the Georgia Coast & Piedmont Railroad Engine sounded her whistle trumpeting her imminent arrival. When the train arrived the conductor ceremoniously addressed the crowd, "the Governor will be unable to appear because today is the first of April." As the train pulled away from the depot and chugged into the distance, the town realized they had been duped, someone had staged an elaborate "April Fool's Day" joke.

Today, the Flemington Presbyterian Church is still active, although the settlement of Flemington has been absorbed as part of Hinesville.

SKIRMISH AT HINESVILLE

On Dec. 16, 1864, a detachment of the 7th Illinois Infantry (mounted) foraging near the right flank of Gen. Sherman's army which was then closing in on Savannah, met here in Hinesville a detachment of cavalry from Brig. Gen. Alfred Iverson's brigade of Maj. Gen. Joseph Wheeler's cavalry corps of the Army of Tennessee. Wheeler's corps and units of the Georgia Militia had offered steady resistance to Gen. Sherman's "March to the Sea" from Atlanta to Savannah.
After a sharp skirmish through the town, the Confederate detachment withdrew toward the Canoochee River to rejoin Iverson.

US 84/GA 38 near junction with GA 196, Hinesville
GPS Coordinates: N31.84091, W81.594375

Union troops arrived at Sunbury in December 1864. They set the Sunbury Baptist Church ablaze for no other reason than to signal their arrival to the federal gunboats anchored off St. Catherines Island. The gunboats had been unable to take the heavily fortified town alone, but with the additional help of land forces, Sunbury fell.

Brigadier General Alfred Iverson with his Army of Tennessee cavalry troops caught up with Sherman's army in Hinesville on December 16, 1864. A brief skirmish ensued between the two and although Sherman was delayed, his relentless "March to the Sea" could not be stopped. Iverson's men were forced to withdraw to the Canoochee River and search out the remains of Major General Joseph Wheeler's cavalry corp.

Sherman concentrated his foraging efforts along the Georgia coastline because of the vast plantations built there. The Union forces stripped any food, livestock and valuables they could steal. The provisions were stockpiled and a wagon train was formed to transport the goods to Savannah. The infantry guarded the wagons and if a Southern citizen came too close, they were shot on sight.

Many years after the war, a Confederate officer attended a reunion of Civil War veterans held in Ohio. The guest speaker for the evening was Senator John Sherman, brother of General William T. Sherman. The former Confederate officer sauntered to the Senator's table and began to closely examine the silverware displayed on the table. To answer the questioning stares, he stated, "I was just seeing if this was my wife's silver you Yankees carried off." He quietly put down the piece and walked away.

LIBERTY ARMORY SITE

Returning from the Revolution, the soldiers of Liberty County re-organized themselves into a troop of cavalry, known as the Liberty Dragoons, later the Liberty Independent Troop, the oldest cavalry company in Georgia. In continuous existence since that time, this military company has participated in every war in which this country has been engaged since the Revolution. As late as 1916 the troop served as a cavalry company on the Mexican Border.

When the company went to France in World War I, it was converted to Company B, 106th Field Signal Battalion. In World War II, it became Battery B, 101st Anti-Aircraft Artillery Gun Battalion and took part in the campaign in New Guinea. During the Korean conflict the battery served at Camp Stewart, Ga., and at Camp McCoy, Wisconsin.

At this armory site have taken place some of the most brilliant and colorful tournaments and parades of the Old South.

US 84/GA 38 at 101st Coast Artillery Drive, Hinesville
GPS Coordinates: N31.85016, W81.585658

L iberty County soldiers returning from the Revolutionary War banded together to form the "Dragons in the Liberty County Regiment of Military," known also as the Volunteer Troop of Dragoons. It is unclear in the Liberty Independent Troop minutes, meticulously kept by the detachment, which form of the name is correct, both forms were used. The regiment is the only volunteer militia unit of Liberty County still in existence.

During the early days of the troop, the men received no pay except when involved in active duty and even then no compensation was given for personal expenses. These expenses included necessities such as uniforms, equipment and horses, which they cared for personally. The state provided little more than weapons and ammunition.

The regiment became known as the Liberty Independent Troop in the late 1700s when they elected officers, noncommissioned officers and clerks. Captain John Berrien was elected Commander of the troop and served for six months when he was reassigned to a Savannah militia unit. William McIntosh, Jr. accepting the torch became the second Captain of the Liberty Independent Troop in August 1785.

The Liberty County Jockey Club, a horse racing track near Riceboro, was the first parade ground for the Troop. The regiment participated in various celebrations and events throughout the county. It spent each Independence Day at Sunbury until 1833, when the town had declined to a point where celebration was no longer possible.

The Liberty Independent Troop was granted a charter by the Superior Court of Liberty County, May 19, 1902. On March 14, 1918, the Troop adopted by-laws and guidelines, these were entered into the minutes. From the early 1700s until today, the Liberty Independent Troop has served in every war involving United States soldiers.

Although the gravestones have been destroyed by weathering and vandalism, it is believed that about a dozen people are buried in this family cemetery. William Harrison died March 30, 1883, in the 72nd year of his age. His wife, Sarah Sylvester Smith Harrison (born c. 1819) was born in Providence, Rhode Island. On January 4, 1886, Mrs. Sarah Harrison and six surviving children, heirs at law of the late William Harrison, agreed that part of the proceeds from collectible notes and accounts should be used for the purpose of erecting stones at the grave of William Harrison, deceased, and putting up a substantial enclosure around the family cemetery. Four of their children, William C. (born c. 1842), Nicholas F. (born c. 1844), Mary C. (born c. 1846), and Anna (born c. 1852), who apparently preceded their parent in death, may have been buried here. Their son, William L. Harrison (c. 1859 - 1890) is probably interred here also.

William Harrison operated one of the earliest mercantile stores in Hinesville and served as Hinesville postmaster and Liberty County treasurer.

Sherwood Drive, Hinesville
GPS Coordinates: N31.85308, 81.585975

William Harrison began his career as a postmaster and mercantile clerk in McIntosh County before the Civil War and continued his service during reconstruction. He moved to Liberty County in 1875, because of a boom in population in the Hinesville area. He built a store on the courthouse square and was a successful merchant. In 1881, William Harrison was elected Postmaster.

Mail delivery was suspended in Liberty County from the outbreak of the Civil War until February 28, 1882. Harrison located the small postal service in his general store, increased the delivery from once to three times per week and provided stamps for rural customers. Several other outlying areas established postoffices during this period including Fleming, Riceborough and Taylors Creek. J. M. Caswell followed Harrison as Hinesville Postmaster upon Harrison's death. The mercantile on courthouse square was purchased by J. R. Ryon.

Nothing remains of the Harrison family cemetery today. A vacant lot shaded by ancient oaks, which once shielded the etched stones of the Harrison family, is situated in the midst of a quiet Hinesville residential neighborhood. No trace of the stones remain, no indent in the ground marks a grave site and no granite monument to the first Postmaster of Hinesville can be found. The lone Georgia Historical Marker stands as the only reminder of the burial ground that occupies the barren lot.

THE BACON~FRASER HOUSE

The Bacon~Fraser House was built on a 23 acre tract situated on the eastern boundary of the town of Hinesville in 1839 by Mary Jane Bacon, widow of Major John Bacon. The house has been owned and lived in by their heirs until the present time.

The architecture is "plantation plain style" and its workmanship reflects the work of the best craftsmen of the day. The front and two-story section remains virtually unchanged. However, the two shed rooms and kitchen to the rear were removed and additional rooms added in 1923. The 1923 section was removed in 1979-1980 and replaced by shed rooms, porch, dining room and kitchen on the original foundation in the architectural style and interior design of the 1830 era.

A detachment of Sherman's army assaulted the plantation in December 1864, pillaging, looting and burning. The house was spared the torch, but the barn and all outbuildings were burned by the Northern troops.

208 East Court Street, Hinesville
GPS Coordinates: N31.84703, W81.593887

In 1824, William Fleming transferred ownership of many acres of property bordering his own to insure he had neighbors of his own choosing. Major John Bacon and Simon Alexander Fraser were considered friends of Fleming and in turn were given pieces of the property. In honor of William Fleming, the settlement was named Flemington. The first home was built in 1839 and belonged to Mary Jane Hazzard Bacon, the widow of Major Bacon.

The home, built in the architectural style known as plantation plain, was two stories with front columns and double chimneys. The features of this design, made popular in the south during the early 1800s, were of frame construction, gabled roof and exterior end chimneys. The interior layout consisted of two rooms of unequal size located on both floors with additional shed rooms and the kitchen in the rear. Due to open fire cooking during this time, kitchen fires were common, therefore kitchens were located at the end of an extended hallway or situated well away from the main house. Having the room separated from the house usually insured the house could be saved during a fire. Plantation plain houses of this period always featured a porch across the front. Houses were usually unpainted and raised on a rock foundation, a plantation plain style house had plastered interior walls or flush siding with chair rails. The houses contained hand carved woodwork, which would soon be a lost craft in America due to the Industrial Revolution. Mechanized wood working replaced the beautiful handwork formed by craftsmen of this era.

Homes of the plantation plain style were usually owned by the wealthiest of planters. The design divided public and private areas of the home, allowing invited guests into the private rooms whereas uninvited guests or business dealings were rarely allowed beyond the porch or front hallway. These protective devices were in place to protect the planter and his family from the uncertain intentions of callers, as well as demonstrate his wealth and high social standing.

In 1842, Simon Alexander Fraser married Mary William Bacon, daughter of Major John and Mary Jane Bacon. The home became known as the Bacon-Fraser House. The couple eventually had seven children and their descendants continue to distinguish themselves in Liberty County. Joseph Bacon Fraser Jr., their grandson, rose to the rank of Lieutenant General in the Georgia National Guard and was an early developer of Hilton Head Island, South Carolina and Chairman of the Board of Governors of the Sea Pines Plantation Company. Donald Hines Fraser, another grandchild, was a Hinesville attorney, member of the Hinesville City Council, Judge in Hinesville and Darien Courts, Solicitor General of Atlantic Judicial Circuit, assistant U.S. Attorney of the Southern District of Georgia and State Representative at his retirement from public service after 40 years. Another descendant, Virginia Fraser Evans, along with others, collected and wrote "A Pictorial History of Liberty County, Georgia" published in 1979.

The majestic southern plantation style home graces the oak lined street just beyond the Hinesville Courthouse Square. The Fraser family, to this day, own and reside in the house now listed in the National Register of Historic Places.

OLD LIBERTY COUNTY JAIL

While this building was not Liberty County's first jail, it served longer than any previous jail. When it was built in 1892 the jail had all the modern improvements and conveniences of a first class prison. Eighty years later it was condemn by Georgia Governor Lester Maddox as, "a rotten, filthy rathole."
Although there is no record of its construction or its architect, it is known that the contractor, a Mr. Parkhill, had completed the two story, three bay brick structure by October 1892.
The interior of the jail is divided by a brick wall into two sections housing a bull-pen (or drunk tank) and two cells downstairs and two cells and the upper part of the bull-pen upstairs.
A new county jail was opened in 1969 and the Old Jail was sold at auction on March 3, 1970 to the Liberty County Historical Society, which eventually donated the building to the City of Hinesville. The Old Jail is now on the Nation Register of Historic Places.

South Main Street, one block south of Courthouse, Hinesville
GPS Coordinates: N31.84599, W81.596822

The Liberty County Jail in Hinesville was completed in 1892. The modern structure was built of tempered steel crossbars, which were declared to be impervious to the saw blade and unable to be broken. The doors were said to be controlled by a three way locking system; a lever closed the cell door, which was bolted by a stout padlock that was encased in a locked box. The box was closed and locked with a key and for added security, a combination lock sealed the box.

Two cells were reserved for female prisoners and likewise, two cells held male inmates. The cells measured seven by ten feet and were designed for three to four captives each. Iron cots and swinging hammocks were the only sleeping arrangements. The only other accommodations were water tanks and a water closet for the females, while a water basin with "other fixtures for cleanliness"[15] were located down the corridor. Vents to the outside provided a system to disperse the noxious scents of sanitation and body odors. Amazingly, each cell and the jailor's office, all contained a fireplace. One wonders if the fireplaces within each cell were used. Heavy iron grating covered each portal and enmeshed in the window panes was wire netting. The walls were said to be 17 inches thick and the floor, a massive three foot thick slab of cement.

The most modern security measures were put into the construction of the Liberty County Jail. The strictest codes of precaution were observed. Yet, prisoners tested the system and on many occasions, the inmates escaped from confinement with little difficulty. A local man jailed for theft was able to escape from the Liberty County Jail five times.

Beyond the jail, between Courthouse Square and Washington Street, stood a giant oak, the Hanging Tree. The branches of the great oak bore the unfortunate souls meeting their last at the end of a rope. The sentences were handed down by the Liberty County Superior Court and usually carried out in a matter of months. The Savannah Morning News carried a story in its January 8, 1892 issue reading,

> "Will McCoy (colored) hangs today at Hinesville for the murder of John Bowie (colored) in Liberty County last September. Mr. Way presented a petition to Governor Northern in Atlanta this week asking that the sentence be commuted to life imprisonment. Judge Falligant, Solicitor General Fraser, and the prosecuting

attorney, W. W. Osborne, Esq., were requested to sign the petition, but refused, holding that the sentence was just. If nothing intervenes, he will expiate his sentence today."

Nothing intervened and McCoy "expiated" his sentence on schedule.

The Old Liberty County Jail, after almost eighty years of service, fell into disrepair. In 1969, a new jail was built and the old building was given over to the Liberty County Historical Society. Today, the jail is being completely restored and is listed as a historical site.

The Liberty Jail

BRADWELL PARK
1974

In memory of Samuel Dowse Bradwell
Founder of Bradwell Institute
on this site in 1871

Built by City of Hinesville
with assistance from HUD and
the Liberty County Garden Clubs

	Carl R. Dykes
Mayor	
	Ben Darsey
Mayor Pro-Tem	
	Frank Bagley
Councilman	
	Gene Mobley
Councilman	
	W. I. Stafford, Jr.
Councilman	
	Alonzo Walden
Councilman	
	Donald H. Fraser
City Attorney	

Commerce and Midway Streets, Hinesville
GPS Coordinates: N31.84719, W81.595314

Samuel Dowse Bradwell was destined to become an educator. His father, James Sharp Bradwell, an exceptional teacher and administrator, was first assistant headmaster of the McIntosh County Academy and later headmaster of Hinesville Academy.

When Samuel graduated college in 1860, the country was preparing for Civil War. He joined the Liberty Volunteers as an officer at the age of 21 and was known as the "Boy Captain" because his face still bore the youthful appearance of a child. His appearance was deceiving, Samuel Bradwell bravely led his men into battle.

Cannons belched and guns blazed during the Battle of Atlanta, the air was filled with acrid smoke and cries of the wounded. A Union mini-ball found its target in Samuel Bradwell and as he lay severely wounded on the damp red Georgia clay, he knew to survive he had to make it home. Sheer will carried Samuel the two hundred and fifty miles to Hinesville from the battlefield in Atlanta. He arrived half starved and feverish. As he recovered during the winter of 1864, Liberty County was over run with Union troops; Samuel Dowse Bradwell was hidden by family and neighbors to prevent his capture. He remained under their protective care until the end of the Civil War.

After the war was over, Samuel Bradwell and other Liberty County men established the Hinesville Educational Society, benefitting public education in Liberty County. They contracted the necessary repairs to the Poor School and Hinesville Academy, which were damaged during the war. Samuel Bradwell renamed Hinesville Academy, the Hinesville Male Academy, which defined the school's status as a tuition school solely for the education of boys. The Poor School relied on state and federal funds rather than tuition for operating expenses and its opening was delayed until those funds became available.

The Hinesville Male Academy was located at what is today known as Bradwell Park. The name was changed in 1872 to Bradwell Institute in honor of James Sharp Bradwell. All of Samuel's energy was encompassed in the success of Bradwell Institute and the *Hinesville Gazette*, a newspaper, which he established in his home in 1872.

The school flourished, assisted by both state and county funds. Samuel Bradwell eventually expanded the curriculum and allowed females to enroll. Students, who required boarding, leased rooms in private homes, avoiding the need for Bradwell Institute to build dormitory facilities. Bradwell Institute and the *Hinesville Gazette* remained Samuel's passion for the remainder of his life.

Samuel Dowse Bradwell died in 1903, however, his legacy lives on in the form of Bradwell Institute. The old building was razed in the late 1960s and a new more modern facility was built nearby. Bradwell Institute continues to provide a quality education for the youth of Hinesville today.

Bradwell Park was built as a town square on the former site of Bradwell Institute. The park is the center piece for the city of Hinesville and serves as the gathering place for community activities. The park was dedicated to Samuel Dowse Bradwell for his contribution to the educational development of Hinesville through Bradwell Institute, the *Hinesville Gazette* and his service to the community. The shaded benches provide a relaxing atmosphere for a quiet lunch or moment of reflection as water splashes in the nearby fountain. The park provides a proper memorial for Samuel Dowse Bradwell.

LIBERTY COUNTY

Liberty County, an original county, was created by the Constitution of Feb. 5, 1777 from Creek Cession of May 20, 1733. It had been organized in 1758 as the Parishes of St. John, St. Andrew and St. James. The theatre of many important events during the Revolution, Liberty County was named for American Independence. From it all of Long and McIntosh Counties were formed. Samuel Morecock was commissioned Sheriff in 1778, Wm. Barnard became Surveyor, Feb. 17, 1782, Francis Coddington in 1785 was made Clerk of Inf. and Sup. Courts of Liberty, Glynn and Camden Counties. John Lawson was sworn in as Coroner in 1790.

Courthouse, Commerce and Midway Streets, Hinesville
GPS Coordinates: N31.84719, W81.595314

There were eight original Georgia counties. Liberty County, founded in 1773, encompassed St. John, St. Andrew and St. James parishes. The Creeks claimed the land as their own until the arrival of Europeans, realizing that the white men were arriving in great numbers and agreed, with the Treaty of Savannah signed in 1733, to allow the whites to coexist on these lands. As the white population grew, the Creeks were pushed further and further west until nothing was left of their coastal Georgia settlements.

By 1752, a group of Congregationalists from Dorchester had settled in Liberty County. Southern Carolina had become overpopulated, disease was rampant, and crops continued to fail year after year. The group was granted 32,000 acres of land and began a settlement in the Midway District under the leadership of their long time minister, Reverend John Osgood.

The Revolutionary War struck the county hard and the settlements found that after the war much rebuilding had to be done. Many of the flourishing settlements before the war were left little more than ghost towns, most never recovered. Liberty County, so named because of the devotion to American Liberty displayed by its citizens, was created by the Constitution of Georgia in February 1777.

The development of counties and vice parishes ensured that the voters would have direct control over the local government. The Georgia General Assembly still elected the officials including sheriffs, tax collectors, justices of the peace and all worked directly for the state.

With the freedom of local government came responsibility. The counties were required to establish public schools that would be funded by the state. The United States Constitution protected the rights of individuals concerning political affiliation, allowing the known British sympathizers or Tories to reclaim confiscated property. The equal distribution of estates among heirs, freedom of the press, trial by jury, the principles of habeas corpus[16] and forbiddance of excessive fines or bail were all guaranteed under the new constitution. Provisions for the freedom to exercise one's choice of religion and prohibition of state religion were defining facts in the constitution, these amendments virtually abolished the Church of England in Georgia.

Liberty County has well deserved the name she carries. The county was home to a great number of patriots whose leadership shaped the future of, not only, the state of Georgia but the nation.

FORT MORRIS CANNON

This small cannon was a part of the armament of historic Fort Morris at Sunbury during the American Revolution. In November, 1778, a superior British force from Florida under Colonel Fuser of the 60th Regiment besieged the Fort. To the ultimatum to surrender the American Commander, Colonel John McIntosh, sent back the laconic reply: "COME AND TAKE IT." The enemy thereupon abandoned the siege and retired southward.

In January, 1779, the British returned to Sunbury by water. Fort Morris was then under the command of Major Joseph Lane of the Continental army. Ordered by his superiors to evacuate Sunbury following the fall of Savannah, Lane found reasons to disobey and undertook to defend the post against the overwhelming British force under General Augustin Prevost. After a short but heavy bombardment the Fort surrendered on January 9, 1779, with its garrison of 159 Continentals and 45 militia. This cannon, which was excavated at the site of the ruins of the famous Revolutionary fortification in 1940, stands here as a reminder of America's hard won struggle to achieve independence.

Courthouse, Main and Midway Streets, Hinesville
GPS Coordinates: N31.84719, W81.595314

I n January 1779, General Augustin Prevost attacked Fort Morris at Sunbury for the second time. Major Joseph Lane, who had taken over command from the defiant Colonel John "Come and take it" McIntosh, was given orders by his superiors to evacuate his post. British soldiers and their Native American allies overwhelmed the small American force. The British numbered over one thousand men and brandished several pieces of heavy artillery.

The first division of British forces arrived by land and the other navigated the Midway River. The troops converged on January 6, 1779 and immediately began to bombard Fort Morris. Major Lane knew well his responsibility to his two hundred men and the fortification. After three days of relentless pounding General Prevost demanded an unconditional surrender. Disregarding his orders, Major Lane refused.

General Prevost relentlessly fired artillery into the small fortification and Major Lane soon realized he was beaten. The soldiers of Fort Morris were captured and held as prisoners of war. The British confiscated twenty-four pieces of artillery, ammunition and supplies. American casualties were listed as one officer, three enlisted men and seven wounded. The British claimed only one fatality and three wounded. Sunbury became a prison camp for American officers and the British renamed the fortification in honor of King George III, calling it Fort George. Major Joseph Lane, who initially refused to surrender, was later court martialed for disobeying a direct order.

The cannon keeping a silent guard at the Hinesville Courthouse was recovered in 1940 during excavation of the Fort Morris site. The historic fort is now a state park open to the public for self guided tours and one of the few remaining Revolutionary War fortifications in the United States. The cannon is a remnant representing those patriots who fought and died for American Independence.

The Fort Morris Cannon

**HINESVILLE
METHODIST CHURCH**

The year 1837 marked the founding of Hinesville and the establishment of the Hinesville Methodist Church. For one hundred years this was the only church in Hinesville. The first services were held in a small frame building near the Bradwell Institute on Courthouse Square. A larger structure was later erected and used until 1942 when the church built a new edifice at the corner of Main Street and Memorial Drive. In 1985 a new building was completed. The first recorded trustees of the church Edward Way, E. O. Andrews, John Wells, Thomas Sheppard, and David Zoucks.
In 1987 the congregation celebrated one hundred and fifty years of doing the Lord's work in Hinesville

**At church, one block north of courthouse in Hinesville
GPS Coordinates: N31.84913, W81.595947**

L iberty Countians voted, by referendum in 1836, to move the county seat to a newly selected site. This site was named General Parade Ground and it was there that the population began to swell. General Parade Ground was also referred to as Azoucks' Old Field and was renamed Hinesville for the Georgia State Senator, Charlton Hines. Hines sponsored the legislation to change the Liberty County seat, honoring himself, in 1836 through the Georgia Senate.

One hundred years after John and Charles Wesley established the Methodist Church in Georgia, the Hinesville Methodist Church was founded in 1837. The church, whose teachings were based on the Wesleys' ministry, was located along side the Hinesville Institute on the courthouse square. The original building was a small wooden structure replaced by a magnificent brick building, which was constructed at corner of Main Street and Memorial Drive in 1942. That building housed the Hinesville Methodist congregation for over forty years. As their membership grew, a new sanctuary became necessary and an impressive edifice was constructed next door. The congregation moved to their formidable facility in 1985. Today, the 1942 sanctuary is the home to the Korean United Methodist Church congregation.

In 1968, Bishop Reuben Mueller of the Evangelical United Brethren Church and Bishop Lloyd Wicke of the governing Methodist Church joined together to become the United Methodist Church. The church at Hinesville followed suit. The two hundred year history of theological traditions are well observed in the Hinesville United Methodist Church. Recently the Hinesville Methodist Congregation celebrated more than one hundred and sixty-five years.

The Hinesville Methodist Church

CHARLTON HINES HOUSE

One of the first houses built in Hinesville after the town was established and became the county seat of Liberty County in 1837 was that of Charlton Hines, a state senator and for whom the town was named. This house, considerably altered, was built in 1837 on town lot number 33, which faced the Court House. Hines paid sixty-one dollars for this lot.

After Hines' death the house was occupied by his son and was later used as the Hines Hotel. In 1941 the house was moved from its location on Main (originally Market) Street to its present location and converted into apartments. Later it was completely remodeled and used as offices.

The house originally was much larger then it now is and had a plazza across the front. Only the central part of the original house is still standing. An interesting feature of the 1837 interior was a ceiling medallion in the parlor.

One half block west of Courthouse in Hinesville
GPS Coordinates: N31.84803, W81.596274

The Hines family moved from Effingham County, north of what is now Hinesville, to Liberty County in the late 1700s following the Revolutionary War. His parents, two sisters and Charlton were permanent residents as the turn of the century approached.

The town was established and called General Parade Ground. It became the county seat of Liberty County in 1837 and the name was changed to Hinesville in honor of Charlton Hines, their State Senator.

Hines was without question a prominent citizen; however, he was very unfortunate in matters of the heart. Hines married Mary "Polly" Quarterman in July 1806, two years later she died in childbirth. The child, Mary Elizabeth, died later that same year. In 1809, he married Ann Beard Bell, the couple had only one surviving child, Robert Charlton. Then, Ann Beard Bell Hines passed away. Hines then married Sarah June Way, a widow with two children, in 1855. Sarah was thirty-five years younger than Hines. Sarah and Charlton Hines had two children. At the time of his death, the children, Joseph Charlton "Charly" Hines, was two years old and his brother, James E. Hines, was less than a year.

Charlton Hines became a Georgia State Senator in 1828 and was reelected for eight terms during his tenure. During his reelection campaign of 1844, Hines was almost defeated when he was charged by a Savannah newspaper with cowardice and desertion from the Liberty Independent Troop in the War of 1812. Joseph Jones, Captain of the Liberty County Troop wrote a long letter to the Savannah newspaper detailing that Charlton Hines had indeed failed to appear when activated to full duty. Hines brought forth affidavits disproving the charge. The documents were successful and Hines was reelected. Hines later became Justice of the Peace for the district serving from 1884 through 1885. Obviously Hines was very successful, by 1860 he had amassed 22,500 acres of property in Liberty County and a vast number of slaves. His holdings in 1860 were estimated at $113,000.

The circumstances of Hines' death, who was almost 80 years old in 1864, are questionable. One account states that he died of a heart seizure in his home on the Liberty Courthouse Square, distraught as the Union Forces invaded Liberty County. According to another account, Hines was being taken to his son's estate, on the outskirts of Hinesville, when Union soldiers accosted the old

The Hines House

man and he died on the roadside. Some say his remains were interred on his son's estate and others that Charlton Hines is buried in the Midway Cemetery. In either case, the grave site is unmarked. The questions concerning the circumstance of Charlton Hines' death and the location of his remains will continue to be unanswered.

Sarah Jane Way died in 1903 at the age of 88. The home at Courthouse Square was inherited by Charly Hines. He built a general store next door to the home and converted the house into the Hines Hotel.

BRADWELL INSTITUTE

The town of Hinesville was established in 1837 and shortly thereafter, in 1841, the Hinesville Institute (or Academy) was established with Colonel James Sharpe Bradwell as the first headmaster. The first building was erected at a cost of $349.12 ½ and stood on the Courthouse Square where Bradwell Park is now located.

Hinesville Institute was closed during the War Between the States, but was reorganized and reopened in 1871 by Captain Samuel Dowse Bradwell, C.S.A., son of James Sharpe Bradwell. The name Bradwell Institute was given the reorganized school honoring Colonel Bradwell, the first headmaster of the Hinesville Institute.

Bradwell Institute was at first a boarding school and college preparatory, offering courses in Latin, Greek, chemistry and "other useful and practical sciences." At the turn of the twentieth century the school became a part of the public school system and was for many years the only high school in this section of Georgia, drawing students from surrounding counties.

Pafford Street, Hinesville
GPS Coordinates: N31.84997, W81.60371

The Bradwell family moved to the area, along with the Congregationalists from Dorchester, seeking better way of life. The adult male members of the family were granted 500 acres per man; the Bradwell grants were located in what is today the city of Hinesville. The town was founded in 1837.

The United States government, during this time, was a strong advocate of education and offered funding to promote the establishments of schools. The Hinesville City Council, shortly after its founding, created the Hinesville Institute and a number of "poor schools."[17] James Sharp Bradwell, who was the assistant headmaster for the McIntosh County Academy, was recruited and accepted the position as the first headmaster for the Hinesville Institute in 1840.

Liberty County began to take advantage of the government funds by establishing free schools and in 1840, twenty-five per cent of the male school age population was enrolled. The law specifically demanded that there should be no distinction "between rich and poor," although the free schools were regarded as "poor schools." Colonials, who could afford the cost, sent their sons to private schools such as Hinesville Institute. For the duration of the Civil War, the Hinesville Institute remained closed and the "poor school" continued to conduct classes.

Samuel Dowse Bradwell, son of James Sharp and Isabella Bradwell graduated from Oglethorpe College in 1860 at the brink of the Civil War. He willingly joined the Liberty Volunteers as a lieutenant, eventually attaining the rank of Captain, and then Commanding Officer. The troops playfully called him the "Boy Captain" because of his baby faced appearance. The nickname proved true, Samuel had yet to reach his 25th year. Samuel descended from a long line of soldiers, his father served in the Civil War and his grandfather the War of 1812.

Samuel served with distinction and during the Battle of Atlanta, he was severely wounded. He struggled with every ounce of energy he possessed to reach his home in Hinesville. The approximately 270 miles trip that would take a modern car about five hours, spanned almost a month for the critically wounded Samuel.

Samuel Dowse Bradwell continued his recovery in Hinesville. In December 1864, Union troops invaded the town. The only inhabitants, like those of any other during this period, were the women, children, the elderly and those who had returned from the bloody Civil War battles, so grievously wounded they were unable to meet the bugle call. Samuel's kinsmen hid him from sight of the Union regiment. Had he been found, he would have most likely been taken prisoner, even in his emaciated state or killed as a rebel officer.

At the conclusion of the war, during reconstruction, the Hinesville Educational Society was founded, of which Samuel Dowse Bradwell became a integral member. The devotion to education, inherited from his father, played a major part during the remainder of Samuel's life. The Society refurbished the tattered buildings of the "poor school" and readied the Hinesville Academy for reopening. Their efforts took five years to complete.

By 1870, Samuel opened the Hinesville Male Academy as a private tuition based school, where the students were boarded with local families. A short time later, when public funds became available, he then opened the "poor school." Samuel taught at all of the schools, alone.

1872 brought much change for the hard working Samuel. He changed the name of Hinesville Male Academy to Bradwell Institute, in honor of his father who had passed away ten years before. He requested and received a 20 year incorporation for the school from the Liberty County Superior Court. Samuel purchased a small printing press, constructed a building on the grounds of his home to house it and there he founded the *Hinesville Gazette*. The newspaper was the first of its kind in Hinesville. Samuel married Elizabeth Clifton; the couple would have two children and live with his mother just off the courthouse square. Samuel Dowse Bradwell gained the distinction of becoming the second Worshipful Master of Hinesville Masonic Lodge.

The student enrollment of the Bradwell Institute began to expand and Samuel was forced to recruit another teacher to be employed by the county and teach at the "poor school." Samuel devoted all of his time to the successful operation of both the school and the newspaper. Another major change occurred during this period, Bradwell Institute began to admit female students.

Bradwell Institute received operating funds from both county and state. Oddly enough, some of the funds were received from the sale of stray cattle rounded up by Liberty County Rangers.

Samuel Dowse Bradwell became a Georgia State Senator serving from 1888-89, State Commissioner from 1891 through 1895, President of Georgia State Normal College in 1895, superintendent of Georgia schools and President of Georgia State Teachers College, which is now known as Georgia Southern College at Statesboro. His distinguished public service as a soldier, educator, civil servant, newspaper editor and citizen make him one of Hinesville's most noted residents.

Today, Bradwell Institute continues to prosper. The public comprehensive high school has a curriculum geared to the needs and interests of its students' abilities and educational backgrounds. Bradwell offers a variety of student activities to match the varied interests of the student body. The school is continually upgrading facilities and equipment in order to keep up with the evolution of education. In the spirit of Samuel Dowse Bradwell, the school continues to thrive.

The *Hinesville Gazette* is now called the *Coastal Courier* and continues to bring the news to its subscribers today. The newspaper celebrated 130 years of continuous print in 2002.

**GA 196 at Gum Branch
GPS Coordinates: N31.8591, W81.72487**

Gum Branch Primitive Church was founded in 1833. The land was donated by Fanshaw Long, Jr., although no funds were available for the construction of a sanctuary. A brush arbor was built and for five years the church meetings were held there.

Brush arbors were typically simple structures. As the name implies, brush or hay was cut and woven into the framework of an arbor. The sides of the arbor were left open to the breeze with benches and pews beneath a foliage roof. The weave was loose enough to let the wind through, but thick enough for shade and to provide minimal protection from rain. As you might imagine, the roof leaked a little. The primary intent was to shade the congregation from the relentless southern sun. Many church services were held in such a setting, with the breeze blowing across the congregation and the brush filtered sunlight casting a yellowish green glow. Brush arbors were temporary structures, usually erected only for the summer. In a matter of days, the brush would be dried brown and would have to be replaced or the entire structure removed. Needless to say, this provided quite the fire hazard. By the cooler days of late autumn, brush arbors were no longer used and were removed.

Several congregations erected permanent "brush arbors" with shingled or tin roofs. Despite the lack of brush, they continued to be called "brush arbors" or simply "shelters." It is assumed because of the length of time, Gum Branch used the brush arbor, it probably began with a straw type roof and evolved into permanent shingled roofing.

The Gum Branch Primitive Church constructed their sanctuary in 1839, replacing the brush arbor. There was no music in the worship service and in 1858, the congregation was debating whether or not to adopt the primitive Baptist custom of "foot washing." The congregation split in 1925. The debate, resulting in the split, concerned the movement to a more moderate and modern doctrine.

The minority firmly held to the "old time religion," home missionaries and the values adhered to since the inception of Gum Branch Primitive Church. They withdrew from the congregation and founded a house of worship adjacent to the Gum Branch Primitive Church, known as Liberty Baptist Church. Both churches eventually became Baptist churches practicing moderate religious teachings.

**TAYLORS CREEK
METHODIST CHURCH
AND CEMETERY**

Taylors Creek Methodist Church was organized in 1807, by
the Rev. Angus McDonald, with seven members, including
James Darsey, Mrs. James Darsey and Robert Hendry.
A village soon grew up around the church, and was for many
years a trading center for the surrounding area. In the
cemetery adjoining the site of the church are the graves of
families of Bird, Daniels, Martin, Hendry and other who were
part of the Taylors Creek community and whose names have
been prominent in the history of Georgia.
The Taylors Creek Methodist Church edifice built here in
1841, was in use for 101 years, until in 1942 the site was
taken over by the United States Government to become a
part of the Fort Stewart Area.

**0.2 miles west of GA 119, 2.6 miles north of GA 144, at Fort Stewart
GPS Coordinates: N31.9349, W81.647993**

The Sunbury Road was a well traveled pathway, leading from the once bustling port city of Sunbury to its only Georgia rival port at Savannah. Along the route was an intersection; the crossing throughway was called Hencart Road because of the produce carried from the coastal settlements to interior regions for sale and trade. It was at this intersection that the Taylors Creek Methodist Church was established in 1807.

The Taylors Creek Village was built with the church at its center. The Methodist Sanctuary was constructed in 1841 and the settlement began to spring forth shortly thereafter. The community grew substantially and within ten years, a Baptist Church, stores and the Taylors Creek Union Academy had been built. In 1849, the Masons chose Taylors Creek as an appropriate location for Liberty Union Lodge Number 49. The Masons organized and began to meet on the second floor of the Academy. Their choice of sites would prove to be a saving grace for the Taylors Creek Methodist Church.

Like every other village or settlement during the Civil War, Taylors Creek was now a village of women, children, invalids and the elderly. Every able man, for the most part, was bravely attending his duty to the Confederacy with units such as the Liberty Guards, the Altamaha Scouts, the Liberty Mounted Rangers or the Liberty Independent Troop.

The unprotected citizens could only watch in horror as General Judson Kilpatrick's Cavalry Troop called "Kill Cavalry" approached. Kilpatrick was at the flank of General William T. Sherman catastrophic "March to the Sea." All of Sherman's generals had been given the same order, "all buildings were to be burned. Houses of worship were not to be spared the torch."

On that fateful day, Kilpatrick approached Taylors Creek Methodist Church, where he and his men would camp over the next few days. As he faced the well built wooden structure, a familiar emblem above the door caught his attention. The mark of the compass and square signifying the structure as a product of a Mason's hands. Kilpatrick, being among the brotherhood, admired the construction and did not have the heart to set the torch. The church escaped a devastating blow; however, the edifice did not go unmolested.

Kilcavalry's Troops stripped the pews and tables from the church and placed them by the Canoochee Creek. The troops passed the night comfortably seated in church pews along side the creek gambling by the light of their campfire. The desecrated sanctuary was used to store supplies stolen from the local residents and those taken in raids along the way. Taylors Creek Methodist Church, unlike so many, survived the war.

The ravages of the Civil War were not enough to deter Taylors Creek from becoming one of the largest communities in Liberty County. By 1886, several farms were located in the surrounding area; two lumber and two grain mills, a physician, a professional photographer, numerous business establishments and a post office occupied the village. The Methodist Church continued to hold services.

Taylors Creek Village was a progressive community until World War II. However, the little settlement was never incorporated as a town. Taylors Creek Methodist Church remained until 1941. One hundred years of history was torn down to make way for the construction of Camp Stewart, a United States Army facility. The families of Taylors Creek Village were forced to find new homes and those structures which could not be moved were destroyed.

Today ,all the remains of Taylors Creek Village and Taylors Creek Methodist Church is the cemetery. The Army, with the respect that is its due, takes excellent care of the sacred ground.

BLUE STAR
MEMORIAL HIGHWAY

A tribute to the Armed Forces
that have defended the
United States of America

In the park at the south entrance to Fort Stewart on GA 119
GPS Coordinates: N31.85795, W81.60725

A highway's course to the title "Blue Star Memorial" in Georgia is paved with General Assembly legislation. From acceptance of the local Garden Club, who superbly administers the program, to signature by the Governor, the process meets with many months of legislative traffic jams.

The route consists of the following waypoints:

A proposal is made by one of Georgia's esteemed Garden Clubs to bestow the "Blue Star Memorial" distinction on a certain thoroughfare. The proposal is accepted or rejected by the Garden Club committee, and if accepted, presented to the District's State Representative for legislative sponsorship. Again, the proposal is accepted or rejected.

If accepted, the legislative sponsor, and sometimes cosponsors, forms the proposal into a bill for presentation to the Georgia General Assembly. The proposal already has pretty high mileage, and the bill has only just begun its arduous journey. Once at the Georgia General Assembly, the bill is read before the House, then read a second time, and a report on the bill is given by the House Committee. The bill is read a third time, and then a vote is taken among the membership. The bill is adopted by the House, great you might think, have the plaque made, and let's have a ceremony. Well, not so fast. Next stop, the Georgia Senate.

The bill is read before the Senate and referred to committee. The Senate Committee reviews and reports on the bill to the membership. The bill is read a second time, then a third, and finally voted on. Once adopted by the Senate, the journey is almost at its end. The final stop on the trip is the Governor's office.

Once the Governor signs the bill, it becomes law. Now the plaque can be made and the ceremony planned. The highway will officially carry the title "Blue Star Memorial Highway" and proudly become a tribute to those that have and continue to defend our nation in the United States Armed Forces.

Endnotes

[1] The text is as stated from William Bartram's *Travels,* no corrections to grammar or usage have been made.

[2] The office of President of the Georgia Council of Safety eventually became the Georgia Governor.

[3] Small reed organ

[4] Leader

[5] Rosier, William. "Freemasonry in Liberty County."

[6] Donation

[7] A religious community.

[8] Political group favoring a limit to Royal authority

[9] City Councilman

[10] A receptacle for holy water.

[11] *Don Quixote* written in 1605 as a work of fiction by Miguel de Cervantes Saavedra, *a* Spanish novelist, depicting the escapades of a Spanish rogue.

[12] He drank whiskey all through the night.

[13] Naval stores are goods required in ship building and construction.

[14] Constructs and repairs wheels.

[15] *Hinesville Gazette*, October 18, 1892

[16] Innocent until proven guilty.

[17] Public schools funded by the state.

Bryan County

FORT MCALLISTER
10 Miles

Situated at Genesis Point, 10 miles east on the right bank of the Great Ogeechee River below the "lost town" of Hardwick, this fort was the right of the exterior line designed for the defense of Savannah. It denied the use of the river to Union vessels, protected King's Bridge (2.5 miles north) and the Savannah and Gulf (ACL) R.R. bridge 2 miles below, and preserved the river plantations from Union raids. Built in 1861-63 it repulsed with minor losses seven attacks by armored vessels, some mounting 15-inch guns.

Fort McAllister finally fell on Dec. 13, 1864, when attacked from the rear by Hazen's Division, 15th Corps, which passed this point about 7 A.M. and marched via Bryan Neck road (Ga. 63). Although its commander, Major George W. Anderson, refused to surrender, all resistance was smothered under waves of Union infantry which the small garrison of 230 officers and men could not long resist. The fall of Fort McAllister opened the Great Ogeechee River to Union supply ships and enable Gen. Sherman to establish a base at King's Bridge. From it, he could supply his whole army (about 60,000 men) which, after a 300 mile march from Atlanta, was then closing in on Savannah.

US 17 at junction with GA 144, Richmond Hill
GPS Coordinates: N31.94969, W81.31218

Fort McAllister was Savannah's most effective means of protection during the Civil War. Designed by Captain John McCrady, Georgia's Chief Engineer, the fort withstood six attacks from the Union Navy and did not fall. The packed earth ramparts were designed to absorb the impact of repeated mortar fire. Under the cover of darkness, Fort McAllister sent out a repair detail and when the sun cast its morning light, the ramparts appeared as if the siege had never occurred.

General Sherman found the fort's Achilles heel, when he suggested a land attack from the rear. On December 13, 1864, the seventh offensive waged against Fort McAllister was successful. Although the fort was taken, the brave Confederate soldiers never surrendered, they were merely outnumbered. General Hazen stormed the fort with 4,000 Union soldiers to Fort McAllister's 250. The fort held for fifteen minutes against the enormous odds.

Automobile millionaire Henry Ford purchased the fort site in the 1930s. Fort McAllister had deteriorated over the sixty plus years of its abandonment and the entrepreneur spent $200,000 to restore it. Unfortunately, the well meaning rescue work was badly done and a number of the artifacts so important to the forts history were lost. Although had the restoration not been attempted, many more artifacts would have been lost due to time and vandalism. The International Paper Company acquired the historic site in 1958 from Henry Ford's estate. In a gesture of goodwill, International Paper deeded the property to the state for the development of a historic park. During the late 1970s, International Paper entered into a substantial land preservation deal with the Nature Conservancy; thus deeding an additional 1,503 acres to the park. The Georgia Historic Commission continued the restoration began by Henry Ford. Fort McAllister was joined with Richmond Hill State Park in 1980 and together they became Fort McAllister State Park. Today, Fort McAllister appears much like it did in 1863.

The 1,700 acre park has much to offer. The Fort McAllister historic site will take you back to the time of antebellum Georgia when Confederate soldiers saw to their day to day duties and fought for a cause in which they believed. Fort McAllister State Park offers hiking, camping and boating, set against the beauty of maritime forests, salt marshes and the banks of Ogeechee River. The park is one of only four state parks located on Georgia's coast.

Labor Day 2001, Fort McAllister State Park opened a new facility housing the Visitor's Center and a museum dedicated to the impressive history of the site. Large artifacts of the sunken ship, the *Rattlesnake* formerly the *CSS Nashville,* were recovered in the 1960s. The salvaged machinery is on display beside the parking area. Recently the walking tour of the fort was improved with the addition of walkways made of shredded recycled tires. These paths give a spring to your step and make the tour around the historic site not only exceptionally interesting but a pleasure to walk.

Visitors are welcome to come for a day trip or stay for awhile, both camping and picnicking facilities are available underneath the shade of giant live oaks. The recreational facilities are located down a gated road near the park's Visitors

Center. A mile long causeway crosses a stream off of Redbird Creek and the salt marsh leads to Savage Island where camping facilities, a boat ramp and dock, and the Magnolia Nature Trail takes guests through the lush canopy filled with the voices of singing bird and scurrying squirrels. Visitors are invited to fish, crab or shrimp for their evening meal or enjoy the scenery of the sunset over the peaceful marsh.

Fort McAllister has something to offer everyone who visits. The magnificent view of the Georgia coastline to the century old oaks that have extended their vast branches over generations. Above all, Fort McAllister gives us a glimpse into 1863.

"DEAD TOWN" OF HARDWICKE
8 mi.

On May 10, 1754, GEORGE TOWN was established at the "Elbow" of Great Ogeechee River, eight miles east. In February, 1755, Gov. Reynolds, dissatisfied with Savannah as a capital and as a port, chose this new site because it "has a charming situation, the winding of the river making it a peninsular; and it is the only fit place for the capital." He preferred the deeper channel, the less lofty bluff, the more central location in the province, and the greater distance from the rival port of Charleston. He renamed it HARDWICKE in honor of his kinsman, the Earl of Hardwicke, Lord High Chancellor of England. Lots sold quickly, the plan's backers were granted 21,000 acres of land, and fortifications were planned; but the Home Government granted no funds and the project died, dooming Hardwicke (later HARDWICK) to obscurity.
In 1758, Hardwicke was included in the newly created Parish of St. Phillip. In 1793, Bryan County was created, with Hardwicke as County Seat. In 1797, the County Seat was removed to "Cross Roads" (Richmond Hill). By 1824, Alexander Netherclift was the sole resident. In 1866, an attempt was made to revive HARDWICK, but it failed; and so the town which might have become one of its capitals
became, instead, one of the "dead towns" of Georgia.

US 17/GA 25 at GA 144
GPS Coordinates: N31.94969, W81.31218

Hardwicke is a prime example of a grand idea gone awry. Governor Reynolds, with sound reasoning, was deeply dissatisfied with the capital city of Savannah. Savannah was located at the northernmost point of Georgia's coastline and in areas of trade, was forced to compete as a port with the more developed city of Charles Towne. Loading and unloading ships there was difficult at best with the steep shoals of Savannah's riverbanks. Charles Towne provided easier access; therefore, Savannah was not as popular a port of call. Governor Reynolds also liked the idea of his name associated with the founding of Georgia's capital, which is what he proposed, Hardwicke. He often grew jealous of the notoriety General Oglethorpe had gained and longed to have the Reynolds name noted in history, more prominent than simply on a listing of former Georgia Governors.

A number of lots had been granted by 1758, but only one structure had been built, a private residence. Public buildings like a courthouse, assembly house, church and jail were proposed, yet the funds were never forthcoming. Reynolds was unable to raise funds himself, so Hardwicke was doomed to fail. According to records, the vicinity of Hardwicke never claimed more than one hundred people at any given time. Reynolds was persistent and refused to provide the current capital, Savannah, with any funds for its maintenance or upkeep and his successor, Governor Ellis stated, "The Silk Filature[1]" is out of repair, the Church is so decayed that it is only kept from falling down by surrounding it with props and the prison 'is shocking to humanity.'" By order of Governor Ellis, the Hardwicke project was abandoned and the city founded by General Oglethorpe was not only restored but expanded.

An attempt was made to develop Hardwicke into an industrial area, that idea also died a quiet death when the Civil War brought a halt to any thoughts of expansion. At the end of the Civil War, in 1866, another attempt to revive the city was made; however, this to failed. It seems Hardwicke was doomed from the beginning. Today, it is but a footnote in history.

FORT McALLISTER
4.5 mi.

East 4.5 miles, on Great Ogeechee River, Fort McAllister was built 1861-62 to guard the "back door" to Savannah. During 1862-63, it repulsed 7 attacks by armored vessels, some mounting 15-inch guns. Dec. 13, 1864, its small garrison of 230 Georgians was over-whelmed by Hazen's Division, 15th Corps (U), which had marched via this road. Its fall opened the Ogeechee to Union vessels, which loaded with supplies for Gen. Sherman's army, had been lying in Tybee Roads and Port Royal Sound. A wharf and depot were built at King's Bridge (on US 17) from which these supplies were distributed to the invading forces.

Intersection of GA 144 and GA 144 Spur, 5.4 miles east of US 17
GPS Coordinates: N31.89007, W81.26588

Captain John McCrady, a Confederate engineer, was assigned the task of building a garrison that would withstand the attack of "modern" forces. General Robert E. Lee inspected the fort in 1861 during its construction and impressed with what he saw, made few suggestions to strengthen the works. Lee's ideas were quickly implemented, his suggestions included the addition of river pilings to thwart naval attacks.

Fort McAllister was the southernmost and most active Confederate fortification in Savannah's defenses. The fort consisted of seven gun emplacements separated by large traverses or trenches. The center bombproof shelter was used as a hospital and supply area, a barracks, officers' quarters, ten other cannons and several powder magazines. The mortar blasts of the ten-inch gun shook the earth with such force that the battery made of sand and marsh mud blocks began to crumble. Fort McAllister's earthen walls stood firm, largely due to their design. The impact of the heavier artillery was absorbed and slight repairs could be made during the night.

The fort was battered relentlessly by the Union ironclads before they began attacking Confederate defenses in Charleston harbor in March 1863. For almost two years, the fort's earthen walls withstood shelling by the warships; *Montauk, Passaic, Nahant* and *Patapsco*, wooden gunboats and mortar schooner.

When Fort Pulaski fell in 1862, the soldiers threw large logs, stones, iron scrapes, anything moveable into the river creating a blockade stopping the passage of enemy ships. Confederate vessels were given the route to navigate the channel.

The tedium of day to day garrison life at McAllister was broken in July 1862, when the blockade runner CSS *Nashville* arrived. The swift side wheeled steamer had failed in an attempt to run the Union blockade into Charleston, then escaped the Union Navy and navigated into the river arriving at Fort McAllister. The Union Navy quickly pursued the *Nashville* but was thwarted by Fort McAllister's guns. After four Union attacks, Fort McAllister stood strong.

January 27, 1863, the ironclad USS *Montauk* arrived with her revolving turret housing an 11 and 15 inch cannon. The 15 inch cannon was the largest used during the Civil War. The *Montauk* bombarded the fort with everything it had but caused no significant damage. The walls of earth absorbed each heavy blow. Fifteen direct hits by Confederate gunners caused little more than cosmetic damage to the *Montauk's* armor.

The *Montauk*, in February and March 1863, attacked again and again. The Union ironclad was still unable to take Fort McAllister. After the attacks, garrison life quieted until December 13, 1864. Union General William T. Sherman's army arrived on its way to the Georgia coast, leaving nothing but destruction in its wake. The fort defiantly stood before Sherman, blocking his supply lines and the long sought prize in his vicious "March to the Sea" and ultimate destination, Savannah. William B. Hazen's infantry division stormed the defenses. Despite Major George W. Anderson's valiant effort to defend the fort with only 230 men, Union troops overtook the Confederate forces in only fifteen minutes. Sherman watched the assault from the roof of a rice mill, two miles away.

Sherman marched his army into the defenseless Savannah with little effort. One week after Fort McAllister fell, Sherman's forces abandoned the fort and upon their departure, torched anything that would burn.

KILPATRICK ON BRYAN NECK

On Dec. 12, 1864, the 3rd Cavalry Division (U), Brig. Gen. J. L. Kilpatrick, USA, covering the right rear of Gen. Sherman's army which was then closing in on Savannah, crossed the Great Ogeechee River near Fort Argyle and the Canoochee River near Bryan Court House (Clyde) on pontoon bridges laid by the 1st Missouri Engineers (J) and moved down Bryan Neck.
That night, Kilpatrick made his headquarters at the plantation home of Lt. Col.
Joseph L. McAllister, 7th Georgia Cavalry (C),
which stood near the river immediately north of this site.
On the 13th, Kilpatrick sent Murray's brigade into Liberty County to scout the country to Sunbury. He ordered Atkins' brigade and the 10th Wisconsin Battery to camp at "Cross Roads" (Richmond Hill) then, with two of Atkins regiments, he moved down Bryan Neck. Approaching Fort McAllister, he skirmished with the Confederate pickets, driving them back to the fort. After examining the approaches to the fort, he moved on the Kilkenny Bluff (8 miles SE) where he was able to make contact with the *USS "Fernandian"* and forward dispatches to the flag-ship (U) reporting the arrival of Gen. Sherman's army at Savannah.
On the 14th, Kilpatrick moved with the balance of his command to Midway Church. After scouting the country and stripping it of livestock and provisions, he returned to Bryan County and went into camp at "Cross Roads" to picket the country to the south and west, and to protect the Union supply depot at King's Bridge.

Intersection of GA 144 and GA 144 Spur, 5.4 miles east of US 17
GPS Coordinates: N31.89007, W81.261588

Generale Hugh Judson Kilpatrick and the Union cavalry was ordered to ride down the coast to scout the area south of Savannah. He headed for the once prosperous port of Sunbury. While approaching the town of Dorchester, the Confederate cavalry accompanied by a Kentucky cavalry unit caught the Union cavalry unaware and attacked. The out manned Southerners were quickly forced back.

The Union troops continued on their mission to Sunbury, ringing of the Sunbury Baptist Church bell was the signal to the Union troops on Bryan Neck that the town had been secured. The town was all but deserted to begin with, little was left beyond the church but even that sacred building was not to be spared by General "Kill Calvary" Kilpatrick. General Kilpatrick was given his nickname by his own men, because he relentlessly drove the men and their mounts beyond all endurance.

Kilpatrick's calvary proceeded to nearby Midway. The Union Calvary set up camp around Midway Church. The high brick walls of the historic cemetery made an ideal corral to contain the confiscated livestock. After putting the torch to Midway

Church, the Union calvary raided the surrounding area.

HARDWICKE

This site on the Great Ogeechee, 14 miles from the Atlantic, was selected in 1755 by Governor John Reynolds for the capital of Georgia. He named it for his kinsman Lord High Chancellor of England, Philip Yorke Hardwicke. Reynolds said: "Hardwicke has a charming situation, the winding of the river making it a peninsula and it is the only fit place for the capital." In 1761, Sir James Wright, the Province Governor, determined against the removal of the capital from Savannah, Hardwicke then became little more than a trading village and it is now listed among "the dead towns of Georgia."

On GA 144 Spur, 2.1 miles north of GA 144
GPS Coordinates: N31.52588, W81.13480

The Georgia Trustees had no concept of the harsh conditions that General Oglethorpe and the Colonial settlers endured while trying to create towns from dense forest and marsh land. Most of the settlers were from cities and did not understand planting or harvesting crops for food and trade. By 1740, the settlers began to immigrate to established areas such as Charles Town to the north. In 1751, Parliament refused the Trustee's request for additional funds and the group was disbanded. Georgia became a Royal colony and Captain John Reynolds was sent to serve as the Georgia's first Royal Governor.

British Naval Captain Reynolds arrived on October 29, 1754, at the wharf in Savannah. He was greeted with enthusiasm from the local citizens, who felt that he brought progress and prosperity. Unfortunately, this was not the case. Captain Reynolds may have been an excellent Naval Commander, but he had little understanding of politics and public administration in a non-military world. By 1756, the citizens complained to the Board of Trade in London concerning the Governor's questionable land grants, dictator like rule and favoritism among the city officials.

Reynolds was unimpressed by Savannah as well. He saw the city as a miserable town of one hundred and fifty small, dilapidated wooden structures that shook with every wind and given a strong storm would be blown into sea. He feared that the French were winning the alliance of the Native Americans and that the bronzed people would eventually gather arms against the colonists. Governor Reynolds reported that he could not live in Georgia in the style to which he was accustomed, limited by his present salary and under horrid conditions. Tension increased between the Governor and his city councilmen. Controversy over government operations brought the opposing factions very close to physical violence; land grants by both the Trustees and the Royal Governor were carefully scrutinized for fraudulent dealings by the councilmen.

The Governor decided that his best course of action was to move the colony's capital fourteen miles inland to a small village situated on the Ogeechee River. So taken with the town, he named it for a relative the Lord High Chancellor of England, Philip Yorke Hardwicke. Reynolds felt that by moving the capital away from Savannah, he could start fresh without the influence of the old guard standing watch over local politics. Hardwick was surrounded by water on three sides, which Reynolds reasoned would make the town more defensible against what he felt were inevitable Native American attacks.

Governor Reynolds' actions were reported to the Board of Trade in London. The Board concluded that Reynolds had over stepped his authority and ordered an investigation. He returned to London to answer the charges. Henry Ellis was appointed Royal Governor during the interim. John Reynolds was forced to resign his appointment as Governor. Within a year, Hardwick was virtually deserted and only one small trader's tent remained. John Reynolds returned to naval duty and attained the rank of Admiral in the British Navy. Within a year, like Hardwick, John Reynolds died in London.

CAPT. JOHN McCRADY
Designer of Fort McAllister

Charlestonian, a student of Agassiz at Harvard, then professor of mathematics at the College of Charleston, he resigned his position at the outbreak of the war and became an officer in the Confederate engineers. Transferred to Savannah he spent his efforts surrounding that city with an extensive ring of defenses.

The rest of his life was academic. He returned to his old professorship in Charleston, later became assistant to Agassiz, then professor of zoology at Harvard, and finally professor of biology at the University of the South, Sewannee, Tennessee.

At Fort McAllister
GPS Coordinates: N31.53210, W81.11576

Little is known of Captain John McCrady's younger years, other than he was from Charleston, South Carolina, studied at Harvard under noted professor Louis Agassiz and eventually became a instructor of mathematics at the College of Charleston. McCrady resigned his position at the onset of the Civil War, using his degree in Engineering to aid the Confederacy.

Lieutenant John McCrady's first assignment was to design the defenses of Savannah. The Charleston Harbor Medical Department also received the benefit of his services along with other Confederate engineers. Their fortification withstood thirty-three hours of enemy fire without the loss of a single life and only four slightly wounded.

McCrady was recognized for his efforts and was named Chief Engineer for the State of Georgia, a promotion to Captain and led to what many believe was his greatest engineering success, Fort McAllister. The fort would survive seven attacks by Federal naval vessels, including the ironclads. The bombardment included the largest shells fired by a naval vessel in the Civil War.

Captain McCrady penned a report on March 8, 1863, to the Engineering Office of the Confederate States Army in Savannah following an attack on Fort McAllister, detailing the damage of a five hour shelling.

> "Earthwork.—- No material damage nor any that could not be repaired in one night. Guns.—One gun-carriage shattered; two traverse-wheels broken. Men.—Two men slightly wounded."

After five hours, the fort held and there were no casualties. The results of McCrady's work were astonishing, no other fortification held up under the same stress throughout the war. His services were requested throughout the south.

At the conclusion of the war, Captain McCrady returned to his professorship at the College of Charleston. Later, he accepted a position at Harvard in order to return to the side of his mentor, Louis Agassiz. McCrady assisted Agassiz with numerous projects including National Academy of Sciences and the Smithsonian Institution, of which Agassiz was named Regent in 1863. When McCrady denounced Darwinism, his popularity amid the scientific community dwindled and he received great criticism from his peers.

John McCrady returned to the land of his birth, where he spent the remainder of his life as professor of biology at the University of the South, Sewannee, Tennessee.

At Fort McAllister
GPS Coordinates: N31.53210, W81.11576

The defenses surrounding Fort McAllister were designed by Confederate Engineer Captain John McCrady. General Sherman was anxious to move into Savannah and the only obstacle to that goal was Fort McAllister. The fort stood guard over the Ogeechee River waterway to Savannah and if the Union failed to take the Fort McAllister, conquering Savannah would be impossible. The Ogeechee River flowing into Savannah was the key to opening the supply lines and feeding the hungry Union Army. Fort McAllister was garrisoned by little more than 200 men and General Sherman's Army numbered 4,000 Union troops. The determined Union forces stormed Fort McAllister by land on December 13, 1864; it was their only chance of success.

General Howard dispatched his best scout, Captain Duncan, several nights before to notify the Union fleet of the impending attack. Sherman chose a regiment that he was familiar with to lead the attack; now commanded by General Hazen, the Second of the Fifteenth Corps, the same division that Sherman had commanded at Shiloh and Vicksburg was called into action. Sherman briefed Hazen on the attack, warning him that Fort McAllister was heavily armed. The attacks from the sea had failed, but Sherman believed the fort was weak to the rear. Hazen's orders were to march quickly down the right bank of the Ogeechee River, assault and take Fort McAllister by storm. Sherman explained to General Hazen, that in his hands this day lay the safety of the entire Union Army and if he should fail, the campaign was lost.

Generals Sherman and Howard travelled down river along the left bank of the Ogeechee river to the rice plantation of Mr. Cheevea. A signal station had been established there to overlook the river and be on alert for Confederate ships. Former slaves aided the signal station by sending up rockets nightly and during the day, operating a steamboat up the Ogeechee River.

Two twenty pound Parrott cannons had been placed at the station and occasionally, a shot was fired toward Fort McAllister, three miles across the salt marsh. Fort McAllister's proud rebel flag could be plainly seen waving in the breeze. Other than the sporadic cannon blast and Fort McAllister's answering fire, the banks of the Ogeechee remained quiet and still as the Sabbath.

Fort McAllister

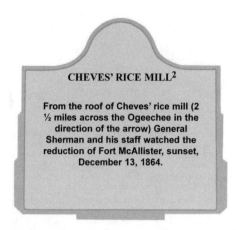

CHEVES' RICE MILL[2]

From the roof of Cheves' rice mill (2 ½ miles across the Ogeechee in the direction of the arrow) General Sherman and his staff watched the reduction of Fort McAllister, sunset, December 13, 1864.

By early afternoon, a small skirmish had taken place along the outer walls of Fort McAllister. Hazen signaled Sherman at his observation deck that all was in place. A faint cloud of smoke was noticed from an object gliding up the Ogeechee. A moments hesitation was broken when the Union flag of the United States came into view. Everyone was tense, holding completely still, waiting for the assault that could very well determine the success of this campaign.

Hazen's troops charged out of the dark fringe of forest and descended on the fort. The lines dressed in parade uniforms, their colors flying, moved forward at a quick, determined pace. The fort came alive in an instant, her large cannons firing with abandon; the air filled with noxious smoke, the yells of assault and screams of wounded and dying carried on the wind. Sulphurous white clouds blurred the view as shadowed ghostly figures fought the battle of their lives.

The Union assault was made using three lines, one from below, one from above and the third directly to the rear. All were simultaneous, the Confederate forces had little chance against the awesome force. The buried torpedoes killed more of the assailants than the heavy guns of the fort, which generally overshot their targets. After only fifteen minutes, Fort McAllister's garrison of two hundred and fifty Confederate soldiers were either captured, killed or wounded.

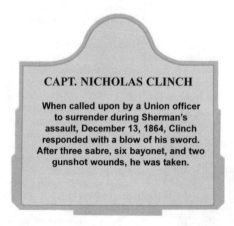

CAPT. NICHOLAS CLINCH

When called upon by a Union officer to surrender during Sherman's assault, December 13, 1864, Clinch responded with a blow of his sword. After three sabre, six bayonet, and two gunshot wounds, he was taken.

The cannons were silenced, the smoke cleared and the ramparts of the defeated Fort McAllister turned blue with Union troops. When Confederate Captain Nicholas Clinch was told to surrender his post, he responded with a blow from his sword. Hand to hand combat ensued and Clinch finally went down after three saber, six bayonet and two gunshot wounds.

Amazingly, Clinch survived, though he never surrendered his post. The Union soldiers fired their muskets in the air, their cries of victory travelled the three miles across the marsh to Sherman's ear. Fort McAllister had fallen, Savannah was within Sherman's grasp.

Sherman was anxious to get to the fort and congratulate Hazen on his victory. He and General Howard boarded a small skiff and were taken to the fort. On the way down river, they passed the remains of the *Rattlesnake*, her skeletal frame gleaming eerily in the moonlight. Hazen had already taken his leave of the fort and had commandeered the home of the overseer of McAllister's plantation. There Hazen had sat down to supper with his prisoner, Major Anderson, former Commander of Fort McAllister. Sherman and Howard joined in the meal.

During the meal, Hazen reported the details of the assault to his superiors and at the conclusion, the men walked nearly a mile from the house to the fort. Inside the fort lay the dead as they had fallen, they could hardly be distinguished from their living comrades, who slept in haunted silence, side by side in the pale moonlight.

The description of the attack in the words of General Hazen, leader of the assault:

> "....the line moved on without checking, over, under, and through abatis, ditches, palisading, and parapet, fighting the garrison through the fort to their bomb- proofs, from which they still fought, and only succumbed as each man was individually overpowered."

Major George W. Anderson reported the fall of Fort McAllister to General Beauregard, "The fort was never surrendered. It was captured by overwhelming numbers."

The Confederate losses were 48 killed and 54 wounded. The Union losses amounted to 134 killed and 110 wounded. The capture of the fort sealed the doom of Savannah, which was evacuated the night of December 19, 1864.

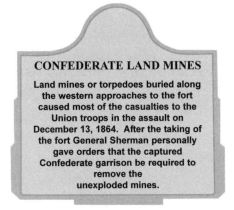

CONFEDERATE LAND MINES

Land mines or torpedoes buried along the western approaches to the fort caused most of the casualties to the Union troops in the assault on December 13, 1864. After the taking of the fort General Sherman personally gave orders that the captured Confederate garrison be required to remove the unexploded mines.

Sherman ordered the prisoners, armed with picks and spades, to march forward of the Union troops. The captured were to discover and remove their own planted eight inch shells along the road or explode them as they walked. Sherman observed,

> "They begged hard, but I reiterated the order, and could hardly help laughing at their stepping so gingerly along the road, where it was supposed sunken torpedoes might explode at each step."

Fort McAllister was attacked six times by Union ironclads, gunboats and mortars, each time repelling the enemy. Damage to the fort was never more than minimal, with repairs completed usually over the course of one night. Injuries were few and mortality much less. General Sherman's keen military eye saw their weakness to the ground assault from the rear. Fort McAllister fell December 13, 1864 and the road to Savannah was cleared for Sherman and the Union Army.

FORT McALLISTER
THE NAVAL BOMBARDMENTS

On July 1st and 29th, 1862, the fort was shelled by Union gunboats and on Nov. 13th by the ironclad *"Wissahickon"* and two escort craft. Hit below the waterline, *"Wissahickon"* withdrew after firing 17 11-inch and 25 other shells. The escorts withdrew later after firing 49 100-pdr. And 42 other shells.

On January 27, 1863, the armored monitor *"Montauk,"* Comdr. J. L. Worden, USN, anchored near the fort, leaving her escort of four gunboats one mile astern. She fired 61 15-inch and 35 11- inch shells, the first use of 15-inch shells against a land battery. On Feb. 1st, *"Montauk"* and her escort shelled for five hours, killing Major John B. Gallie, CSA, wounding 7 gunners, and disabling 1 gun. On Feb. 28th, while her escort shelled the fort, *"Montauk"* destroyed the *CSS "Nashville"*, aground 1400 yards NNW.

On March 3rd, the monitors *"Passaic," "Patapsco"* and *"Nahant,"* Capt. P. Drayton, USN, engaged the fort for eight hours with no more damage to either side than had been suffered in previous engagements. No further naval bombardments were attempted.

By act of the Confederate Congress, approved May 1, 1863, the defenders were thanked for their "gallantry and endurance."

At Fort McAllister
GPS Coordinates: N31.53210, W81.11576

OBSTRUCTION OF RIVER

To block the channel of the Ogeechee River, a double row of piling was placed across the river at a point opposite this marker.

F ort Pulaski, east of Savannah, fell to Union forces early in 1862. Savannah's southern protectors at Fort McAllister realized the need to prepare for an attack from the federal navy and obstructed the Ogeechee River. Only Confederate vessels would be allowed through the intricate maze of debris.

All was quiet at Fort McAllister. Young soldiers awaiting the fight grew tired of drilling, mundane duty and facing no other foe than disease carrying mosquitoes, biting flies and gnats. Boredom was quickly broken with the sight of the Confederate blockade runner *Nashville* steaming up the Ogeechee River to the fort. The Union blockade made entrance into

Savannah's Harbor difficult. Eventually, the side wheel steamer managed to escape the Union Navy pursuit, slip into the Ogeechee River and into the protection of Fort McAllister's armament. Union gunboats attacked twice in July and once again in November 1862. The Union failed to take the fort or sink the *Nashville*. Again, the fort grew silent but the calm would be short lived.

DAMAGE FROM NAVAL BOMBARDMENTS

The largest naval guns used against land fortifications were fired on Fort McAllister in 1863 from monitor-type Union ironclads. 15 in. shells penetrated 17 ft. of sand, digging craters 8 ft. in diameter and 7 ft. deep on exploding, but all damage could be repaired overnight.

January 27, 1863, the *Montauk*, a Union monitor class ironclad, led four gunboats, the *CPO Williams, Dawn, Seneca* and *Wissahickon* to within 1,500 yards of Fort McAllister. The *Montauk* opened fire using 15 inch shells, with the fort returning the assault. The barrage continued for five hours.

Captain John Worden, commander of the *Montauk*, was once in command of the first Union ironclad, the famed *Monitor*. Upon taking command of the ship, he was ordered to immediately take her underway. It is said Worden, showing his willingness for the fight, replied,

> "Sir, I will immediately adhere to orders and give it my best; although I have no provisions, men nor ammunition."

Needless to say, the *Monitor's* mission was delayed.

This day Captain Worden ordered the fire of 61, 15 inch shells. After the cannon blasts ceased and smoke cleared, enormous craters in the ramparts of Fort McAllister had left ugly scars and the *Montauk* showed signs of dimpled armor. Otherwise, little damage was caused by either side and no casualties were reported. That night, under a cover of darkness, a detail of Confederate soldiers crept away from their bomb proof fortification and filled the huge holes with sand making the ramparts good as new. Worden and his men, frustrated by their failure to take Fort McAllister, returned on February 1, 1863. The *Montauk* fired 48 strikes on the fort, but again did little damage to the Confederate battery.

HOT SHOT FURNACE

The hot shot oven was used to head cannonballs red hot to set fire to attacking wooden vessels.

C olonel R. H. Anderson reported to Brigadier General P. T. G. Beauregard the details of the attack. Beauregard had gained fame, if not, respect from the Union victory at Fort Sumter. The *New York World* said of him, in part,

> "Truly he is boastful, egotistical, untruthful, and wanting in tact, but he is certainly the most marvelous engineer of modern times. By his genius and professional skill he has erected batteries in Charleston Harbor that would sink all the wooden fleets of the world did they come under fire."

Again, the Union had attacked a fortification under Beauregard's command except Fort McAllister refused to be taken.

The battery was attacked at 7:45 in the early hours of February 1, 1863. The Union monitor, *Montauk* with one 15 inch and one 11 inch gun, three wooden gunboats and one mortar boat began to fire at will. The First Battalion Georgia Sharpshooters lined the riverbank to the west, ready to rain down an assault should the ships manage to breach the river obstructions. Martin's Light Battery was in reserve to the rear about one and a half miles and McAllister's troops were one mile out; all ready to spring into action should the fortification begin to fall. The *Nashville*, now known as the *Rattlesnake*, was moved upriver and ready to be scuttled, if necessary.

COLUMBIAD

This replica of a coast defense cannon known as the columbiad was manufactured, 1964, by Savannah Machine and Foundry Company as a public service. A similar cannon was positioned here during Union naval attacks, 1863. The columbiad fired 87-lb. Shells; its range was 2,500 yds.

T he *Montauk* focused her fire at the eight inch columbiad. The parapet in front of the gun was completely blown away, leaving it and the detachment who manned the gun, completely exposed. The men fought to the very end of the engagement refusing to be relieved.

MAJOR JOHN B. GALLIE

Killed in action
while commanding the fort
during the second attack of the
monitor
MONTAUK, February 1, 1863. The 32-
pounder beside which he was
standing was struck while Gallie was
going from gun to gun, encouraging
his men to calmness of aim.

Major John B. Gallie, Commander of Fort McAllister, paced from gun to gun. Gallie drove his men on, bolstering their courage. Even after taking a shell fragment to the face, with blood streaming down his cheek and pain creasing his forehead, Gallie refused to leave the line. With a jolt that shook the earth, the 32 pounder was hit. Major John B. Gallie was thrown to ground, this time he would not rise. His gallantry and unconquerable spirit gave his men the strength to continue. Captain G. W. Anderson, immediately assumed command and the fight continued.

**MAJOR
GALLIE'S GUN**

In this emplacement, chosen nearest
the enemy, was the gun, an 8-inch
columbiad,
commanded personally by Major
John B. Gallie.

After four hours of continuous shelling, the *Montauk* ceased fire and moved out of reach of Fort McAllister's guns. Her turret was damaged and would no longer revolve. Gallie was the only casualty of the day for the Confederates, seven soldiers were wound. The damage to the fortification would again be repaired during the night, although the 32 pounder was a complete loss and another would be brought from Savannah to replace it.

Beauregard reported the great loss of Major Gallie to his superiors. Upon learning of the noteworthy victory, the Georgia General Assembly expressed their appreciation. The following is their tribute to the fallen officer, in part,

"Resolved, that the determined bravery and resolute courage of the late Major John B. Gallie, the first
commander of that post, have written his name upon a lustrous page of Georgia's history, and his sublime

SINKING OF THE
CSS *"NASHVILLE (RATTLESNAKE)"*

In July, 1862, the CSS *"Nashville"*, Capt. Baker, ran the Union blockade and entered Savannah via Wilmington River with a cargo of arms. Loaded with cotton for Europe, she attempted to escape via Ossabaw Sound. Thwarted by the vigilance of the blockading squadron, she was withdrawn up Great Ogeechee River and refitted as a raider. Renamed *"Rattlesnake"*, her silhouette was lowered and she received heavier guns. In February, 1863, ready for sea, she dropped down-river to Fort McAllister to plan her escape.

On the 27th, she was forced to retire upstream upon the approach of the armored monitor, *"Montauk"*, Comdr. J. L. Worden, USN, and ran aground Seven Mile Reach a short distance above the fort.

Early on the 28th, *"Montauk"* anchored near the fort and within1200 yards of *"Nashville (Rattlesnake)"*. She opened fire will 11 and 15-inch guns while her escort shelled the fort. Fires broke out and shortly *"Nashville"* was aflame fore and aft. At 9:20 her pivot gun burst, at 9:40 her funnel went by the board, and 9:55 her magazine exploded, shattering her into smoking ruins.

Although damaged by direct hits from the fort's guns, *"Montauk"* struck a torpedo while dropping down-river which blew a hole in her bottom. She was beached in the mud for repairs.

At Fort McAllister
GPS Coordinates: N31.53210, W81.11576

The CSS *Nashville,* known then as the *Thomas L. Wragg*, was a 1221 ton side wheel steamer. She was built at Greenpoint, New York, originally for use as a passenger steamer, in 1853. The *Thomas L. Wragg* was seized by the Confederacy in Charleston, South Carolina, in 1861 and converted to the first vessel commissioned as a public armed cruiser of the Confederate States. She was renamed CSS *Nashville*. The original intent for the use of the *Nashville* was to convey the Confederate State envoys, Mr. Mason and Mr. Slidell, to Great Britain and France.

In October 1861, the *Nashville* was under orders to go to England. She captured and burned the merchantman sailing vessel *Harvey Birch* in the English Channel on November 19 and a like fate befell the schooner *Robert Gilfillan* on February 26, 1861, thus stopping English supplies to the Union. The *Nashville* ran the blockade into Beaufort, North Carolina, where she remained until mid March, when she steamed into Georgetown, South Carolina. She was fast for a side wheel steamer but was hampered because she had a very deep draft; she sat low in the water and was not as fast as most blockaders.

In July 1862, the *Nashville* ran the blockade into Savannah with a cargo of arms. She was identified by the Union Navy as a Confederate warship and was pursued relentlessly for the duration of her existence. The side wheel steamer managed to escape and slip into the river. The *Nashville* sought the protection of Fort McAllister's armament. By February 1863, the *Nashville,* now renamed the *Rattlesnake*, found herself bottlenecked down river on the Ogeechee. The *Rattlesnake's* haven had become a prison. Captain Baker, the Commanding Officer of the *Rattlesnake*, examined his options. He was given orders to escape with the ship intact, under no circumstances was he to let the *Rattlesnake* be taken. Baker was ordered to scuttle[3] the *Rattlesnake,* if capture was imminent. He believed to attempt an escape by means of the Savannah River was unsafe, because it was the busier of the two waterways available to him. Baker knew the only other alternative was the Ogeechee River; it was this course that he chose.

The *Rattlesnake* steamed up river and to his horror found the *Montauk* had already arrived. Too late to turn and make a run for the Savannah River, the *Rattlesnake* was forced to retreat. In her haste, she ran hard and fast aground at Seven Mile Bend on the Ogeechee River. The *Rattlesnake* could not be freed, she could but sit and await her fate.

death in that same engagement, has left a bright example of heroism to which every Georgian will always point with pride and admiration."

The *Rattlesnake*, on February 27, attempted to escape its bottled up position upriver on the Ogeechee. She was forced to retreat by the blockading Union navy and struck a sandbar at Seven Mile Bend. The *Rattlesnake* could not be freed. Captain Worden and the *Montauk* crew could not believe their good fortune. The *Montauk* navigated up the river and fired on the *Rattlesnake,* while two other Union vessels fired on Fort McAllister, simultaneously. The volume of cannon fire was deafening. The *Rattlesnake* caught fire and exploded. The impact shook windows twelve miles away in Savannah. The *Montauk* crew celebrated their long awaited victory. Returning downstream later that day, the *Montauk* struck a mine, causing yet another explosion and serious damage to the Union gunboat.

The Union attacked again on March 3, 1863. Nine vessels, three ironclads, three wooden gunboats and three mortar schooners made up the flotilla. The *Montauk* was so badly damaged that she was unable to join the assault. The nine ships fired 224 shots into the fortification, only fifty shots met their mark and of these only twelve actually exploded. No serious damage resulted from the onslaught that continued for seven hours.

Captain John McCrady, Chief Engineer, submitted the report to headquarters of the day's action. The earth work suffered no damage that could not be repaired through the night; one gun carriage was shattered and two traverse wheels were broken. Two men were slightly wounded and the fort suffered one fatality.

TOM CAT
Garrison Mascot

The sole Confederate fatality after seven hours of intensive bombardment on March 3, 1863, by the monitors *PASSAIC* (Capt. Percival Drayton), *NAHANT*, and *PATAPSCO*, supported by the *MONTAUK*, the *WISSAHICKON*, the *SENECA*, the *DAWN*, the *FLAMBEAU*, the *SERBAGO*, the *C.P. WILLIAMS*, the *NORFOLK PACKET*, and the *Para* was the garrison mascot. The death of the cat was deeply regretted by the men, and news of the fatality was communicated to General Beauregard in the official report of the action.

The one fatality was deeply felt among all the officers and soldiers of the camp. Tom Cat, the fort's mascot was killed during the fight. The soldiers gently laid him to rest with full military honors. During the night, the fort received much needed supplies including ammunition from Savannah. Fort McAllister was ready to resume the fight. The Union Navy chose to retreat.

The facts of this bombardment were diligently detailed by Assistant Engineer J. W. McAlpin. While under fire, McAlpin sketched the positions of each vessel, kept a tally of shots fired by the enemy and took notes of the engagement.

DESTRUCTION OF
THE CSS *NASHVILLE*

The swift Confederate blockade runner *NASHVILLE* (renamed *RATTLESNAKE*) was destroyed by the monitor *MONTAUK*, February 28, 1863, after she went aground on a sandbar in a hairpin bend of the Ogeechee River. The engagement was a three-way battle with the guns of the fort firing on the *MONTAUK*, and the *MONTAUK* concentrating on the *NASHVILLE*. The wreck of the *NASHVILLE* lies in the direction of the arrow, approximately 1200 yards.

February 28, 1863, the *Montauk* navigated up the river and fired on the *Rattlesnake,* while two other Union vessels bombarded Fort McAllister. The smell of gunpowder was pungent in air heavy with the early morning dew. The *Montauk* fired her 11 and 15 inch guns, the *Rattlesnake* was an easy target. The *Rattlesnake* caught fire, the flames quickly grew out of control. The pivot gun glowed red with heat and exploded, followed by a second explosion of the funnel and finally the powder magazine reduced the *Rattlesnake* to ruins. The deafening explosions shook windows twelve miles away in Savannah. All that remained above the waterline was the smoldering skeleton of the *Rattlesnakes*' side wheel.

MACHINERY FROM
THE CSS *NASHVILLE*

These portion of rotating machinery were removed, 1960, from the wreck of the Confederate blockade runner *NASHVILLE*, sunk in the Ogeechee River by shell fire from the USS *MONTAUK* in Feb., 1863. These relics give some conception of the power of the *NASHVILLE's* engine.

Captain John Worden and the *Montauk's* crew celebrated their victory, the first at Fort McAllister. The celebration would not last. The *Montauk* was about to meet her fate as well. While traveling down stream the *Montauk* struck a mine, part of the Confederate's river obstruction. A gaping wound was blown into the lower portion of her hull. Captain Worden was forced to beach his craft for repairs.

Captain George W. Anderson, named Commander of Fort McAllister upon the death of Major Gallie, related the circumstances involving the loss of the *Rattlesnake* to Brigadier General Beauregard. He implied that Captain Baker had needlessly scuttled the ship rather than fight. Anderson felt the circumstances did not warrant the destruction of the *Rattlesnake*. No proof was offered that the ship was intentionally disabled; nonetheless, Captain Baker did not deserve the implication contained in Captain Anderson's report.

On March 3, 1863, a Union squadron of three ironclads, three wooden gunboats and three mortar schooners relentlessly attacked Fort McAllister. The *Montauk* was unable to join the fight due to her damage. The flotilla fired on the fort for over seven hours in the heaviest bombardment the fort was ever to experience.

POSITION OF THE MONITORS

The monitors took positions against the far marsh in the direction of the arrow, between 900 and 1200 yards from the fort during the following series of attacks: by the *MONTAUK*, January 27, February 1, and February 28, 1863; and by the *PASSAIC*, the *NAHANT*, and the *PATAPSCO*, March 3, 1863.

Three ships of the Union fleet took positions off the battery, the *Passaic*, the *Nahant* and the *Patapsco*. The three opened fire at will for seven hours and twenty-four minutes. Another monitor ship lay in wait near the bend of the river. Three additional ironclads were at varying distances from 1,400 to 1,900 yards away from the Fort McAllister battery. The three ships off the battery fired 224 shots, of these only 50 met their mark and only twelve shells actually exploded.

Fort McAllister's guns concentrated on the three primary targets, the rest providing no immediate threat. The 42 pounder cannon and a rifle gun were principally used during the engagement. One of the ships was presumed badly injured when a shell from the 42 pounder struck near her turret and low on the her water line.

The specifics of this engagement are available due to the courage and calmness of Assistant Engineer J. W. McAlpin. While under heavy fire, McAlpin sketched the positions of each vessel, kept a count of the shots fired by the ironclads and took detailed notes as the action progressed.

During the night, as a detail repaired the day's damage to the fortification, a fresh supply of ammunition was received from Savannah. As a new day dawned on Fort McAllister, the Confederates were well prepared to renew the fight. The Union forces did not rise to the occasion, instead they decided to abandon their position and resume the fight another day.

For the next twenty-one months, life at Fort McAllister was quiet again. Then, there was General William Tecumseh Sherman's March to the Sea...

FORT ARGYLE

Near here, on the west bank of the Ogeechee River, Fort Argyle was built in 1733, to command one of the main passes by which enemy Indians had recently invaded South Carolina, and to give protection to the settlers of Savannah from anticipated
raids by Spaniards from Florida.
The fort was named in honor of John, Duke of Argyle, friend and patron of James Edward Oglethorpe, and was garrisoned by Captain McPherson with a
detachment of Rangers.

GA 144, 4.2 miles west of junction with US 17
GPS Coordinates: N31.97284, W81.37695

The colonists that General James Edward Oglethorpe recruited to begin the new settlement at Savannah had many fears, among them, the Spaniards to the south at St. Augustine. Oglethorpe was aware that the frightened coalition faced a number of difficulties including food, shelter and disease without the added worry of attack. To ward off such an attack, Oglethorpe had Fort Argyle built.

The garrison, constructed in 1733, was located near the nexus of the Canoochee and Ogeechee Rivers, high on a bluff where sentries stood duty, watching for the enemy's approach. In 1734, Fort Argyle was the only defensive outpost against the Spaniards. Oglethorpe manned the garrison with a detachment of Rangers. They guarded one of the main passes traveled by Native Americans, who had attacked southern Carolina only months before.

The outpost was named in honor of Oglethorpe's friend, the Duke of Argyle. The wooden stockade fort with its protective moat was built, not by militiamen, but by full time Rangers from southern Carolina under the command of Captain James McPherson. McPherson, a forty-five year old native of southern Carolina, had six years experience serving in the militia during the Yemassee War. The design of Fort Argyle was almost identical to others of its size such as Fort King George at Darien. Obviously, Oglethorpe found a plan he admired and its likeness would appear several more times along the Georgia coast in the coming years. It was described as 110 feet square with a moat that was four to five feet deep and fifteen feet wide. A berm[4] formed the inner wall, pointed logs formed the palisades or exterior walls. Bastions protruded out from each corner to allow cannons to be placed there on racks through the palisade walls. Twelve buildings were constructed inside the fortification.

Oglethorpe dispatched six families to complete work on the fort and farm the adjacent land. McPherson was ordered to split his 20 man ranger force and build a new fort further up the Ogeechee river. Only ten rangers and six militiamen were left to guard Fort Argyle against marauding Native Americans and the Spaniards. The fort remained in continuous use, although it was never fully manned, until the Battle at Bloody Marsh forced the cessation of hostilities in the latter part of 1746. By the mid 1740s, soldiering employed more men than any other occupation in Georgia. As the colonists increased their numbers and the people began to feel more comfortable in their surroundings, the men found serving in the militia a burden. The British government soon eliminated financial support to the militia, causing the local merchants to press for disbandment. The militia became unimportant, until England began imposing restrictive conditions and the Revolutionary War was on the horizon.

The Fort Argyle site is, today, a part of Fort Stewart Military Training Facility. Nothing remains of the old fort structure.

**HAZEN'S DIVISION
AT THE CANOOCHEE RIVER**

On Dec. 6, 1864, the 15th Corps (U), Maj. Gen. P. J. Osterhaus, USA, the extreme right of Gen. Sherman's army on its destructive March to the Sea, camped near Jencks Bridge, on Great Ogeechee River east of Blitchton. On the 7th, Oliver's brigade of Hazen's division was sent down the west bank of the Ogeechee to seize the bridge over Canoochee River, two miles southeast of Bryan Court House (Eden) (Clyde) and one-half miles northwest of this point. From Black Creek to the Canoochee, the advance was resisted by Confederate cavalry. After skirmishing most of the way, Oliver reached the bridge only to find it in flames and the south bank held by infantry and artillery (C) under Col. John C. Fizer. The position being naturally strong, with swamps along the river, Oliver withdrew to Bryan Court House to await Hazen's arrival.

On the 8th, Hazen reached Bryan Court House accompanied by Gen. Osterhaus and supported by Wood's division, which was posted near Fort Argyle on the Ogeechee. Learning of an abandoned ferry site downstream from the bridge, Hazen sent a party across during the night, flaked the position at the bridge, and forced the defenders to fall back toward "Cross Roads" (Richmond Hill). At dawn, the bridge was repaired and two brigades crossed. One moved to Station No. 2 (Way's), the other to Station No. 3 (Fleming), to break the Savannah and Gulf (ACL) Railroad at those points.

**GA 144, 4.2 miles west of junction with US 17
GPS Coordinates: N31.97284, W81.37695**

Many records were kept during this time, from individual diaries to formal field guides. The span of time between November 1864 until early December, when Savannah was actually taken, was spent by long hours of marching through rugged terrain and trying to survive. Sherman's troops were divided into right and left wings, leaving the devastated Atlanta to travel separate routes to the sea, the ultimate goal being Savannah.

The Confederates made this trek as difficult as possible. Their intent was to slow the Union Army as much as possible to give the noncombatants time to evacuate Savannah and the out manned Rebel Army time to prepare.

Major Generals Osterhaus and Hazen found it difficult to push their men beyond endurance, only to arrive at the river bank and find the bridges burned. Sherman had provided for these occurrences by having members of the engineering corps along to supervise the construction of temporary bridges, so that the divisions could ford the waterways.

The Union soldiers found themselves more times than not sinking ankle deep into the ooze of swamp mud that made a sucking noise as each foot was pulled from its sticky embrace. They lived in constant fear of the disease ridden mosquitoes that grew fat on their blood and the fevers that could bring death as well as a rebel musket.

Sherman's forces were converging on Savannah from all sides. Osterhaus was camped on the Ogeechee River at Blitchton. Oliver's brigade was ordered to take the Canoochee River bridge, but met Confederate Calvary along the way, and after a brief skirmish was forced to retreat to the Bryan County Courthouse. Confederate Colonel John C. Fiser, he changed the spelling of his name to Fizer after the war, held the south bank of the Canoochee and had burned the bridge. Hazen reached the courthouse and was joined by Osterhaus and Oliver.

Hazen's Divisions repaired the Canoochee bridge through the night and proceeded to their objective. The objective was the destruction of the Savannah and the Gulf Railroad at Way's Station and Fleming. With the supply lines broken, the South would either starve or surrender. Savannah surrendered December 19, 1864.

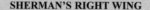

SHERMAN'S RIGHT WING

On Dec. 6, 1864, the 15th Corps (U), the extreme right of Gen. Sherman's army on its destructive March to the Sea, camped near Jencks Bridge on Great Ogeechee River, east of Blitchton. On the 7th, Oliver's brigade was sent in advance of Hazen's division to seize the bridge over Canoochee River east of Bryan Court House (Clyde). Beginning at Black Creek, his advance was resisted by Confederate cavalry. After continual skirmishing, Oliver's superior force reached the bridge only to find it in flames and the crossing strongly defended. Unable to advance, he returned to Bryan Court House to await Hazen's arrival.

US 280/GA 30 at Black Creek Church Road, 3.6 miles west of US 80
GPS Coordinates: N31.16657, W81.489287

The Federal Army consisted of 60 thousand seasoned veterans, of whom 5,000 were cavalry. During the march to Savannah, the army was to feed itself on the country. Each brigade had a detail of foragers, called "bummers," these men were instructed to take all necessary provisions, horses and mules, but were ordered not to enter dwellings nor insult the people and to leave enough food for each family, so that none would be destitute. Where the army met no resistance, Sherman ordered that mills, cotton gins and houses should not be destroyed; if the division or detail was attacked, all buildings were to be burned. For the most part, these orders were ignored and Sherman turned a blind eye to the atrocities. Sherman was noble in word, but in fact bringing the south, already obviously beaten, to its knees, meant that any action could be justified.

The march was first directed toward the Georgia capital, Milledgeville. Sherman divided his army into two divisions. The right wing under General Oliver Otis Howard followed the railroad to Jonesboro and McDonough with orders to stop at Gordon on the Central of Georgia Railroad. The left wing, under General Henry W. Slocum, marched by way of Decatur and Covington to Madison, and then on to Milledgeville. General Sherman accompanied the left wing. The movement from Atlanta began on November 15th and by the 23rd, Sherman and the left wing reached Milledgeville. The right wing invaded Gordon. Sherman did not destroy the capitol buildings at Milledgeville, his sights were set on Georgia's most important port, Savannah.

On November 24th, the march was resumed. Sherman's left wing left a path of destruction through Sandersville, Tennille, Louisville, Millen and other towns. Sherman's men held huge bonfires in front of each court house, burning the deed books stored there. Without these references, the southern owners of large plantations would be unable to prove ownership at the conclusion of the Civil War.

Small commands of Confederate Calvary ambushed the Union Army at every turn. These small forces had no hope of stopping Sherman's massive army, but their purpose was to keep it condensed so that the path of destruction was not so wide spread. No other campaign during all of the Civil War did more to encourage feelings of separatism between the northern and southern factions than Sherman's march through Georgia. The march began just as fall crops were being gathered. The foragers or bummers found food in abundance, even though Confederate troops on the field of battle were starving. The southern soldiers went hungry, not because there was no food, but because the supply lines had been cut with the destruction of the railroads, making it impossible to get provisions to them. Confederate forces had virtually nothing to keep them alive, except a willingness to fight for their way of life.

Sherman's army was not content to simply gather what food and supplies they needed, but destroyed everything they could not carry. Soldiers took everything of value that could be moved. Thousands of hogs, sheep and poultry were killed and left to rot in their pens. Dwellings were burned over the heads of women, children and the elderly without any justification.

Sherman's own memoirs relate the conduct of his men, estimating that they had confiscated and destroyed $80 million worth of property of which the Army could not use. This he described as "simple waste and destruction."

JENCK'S BRIDGE

On Nov. 15, 1864, after destroying Atlanta and cutting his communications with the North, Maj. Gen. W. T. Sherman, USA, began his destructive Campaign for Savannah–the March to the Sea. He divided his army (U) into two wings. The Left Wing (14th and 20th Corps), Maj. Gen. H. W. Slocum, USA, moved east from Atlanta in two columns which converged on Milledgeville, crossed the Ogeechee River near Louisville, then marched toward Savannah by two routes: the 14th Corps (Davis) on the old road near the Savannah River (Ga 24), the 20th Corps (Williams) via Springfield. Both corps approached Savannah via Monteith. Gen. Sherman accompanied the Left Wing as far as Sandersville. The Right Wing (15th and 17th Corps), Maj. Gen. O. O. Howard, USA, marched south via Gordon and crossed the Oconee River at Ball's Ferry. The 17th Corps (Blair) moved on roads south of the Central Railroad until opposite Midville, crossed the Ogeechee River there, and moved via Millen and Eden, destroying the railroad enroute. Gen. Sherman accompanied the 17th Corps from Tennille to the outskirts of Savannah.

The 15th Corps, Maj. Gen. P. J. Osterhaus, USA, moved in two columns, the right via Statesboro, reaching the Ogeechee River here at Jenck's Bridge on Dec. 6th. Finding the bridge burned, a pontoon bridge was laid. Rice's brigade crossed, drove back the defenders (C) with minor losses, and moved to Eden to join Woods' brigade, which had crossed 3 miles upstream at Wright's Bridge.

US 80 at the Ogeechee River
GPS Coordinates: N32.19705, W81.417913

General William Tecumseh Sherman began his "March to the Sea" in November 1864, with a list of Special Field Orders issued by his Aide de Camp, L. M. Dayton. Sherman selected for the flanking corps, the Fifteenth and Seventeenth commanded by Major General Oliver Otis Howard for the right wing and Fourteenth and Twentieth Corps commanded by Major General Henry W. Slocum for the left. The field orders provided instruction on how the corps would proceed and the rules for conducting their troops along the way.

Major General Oliver Otis Howard was a well seasoned veteran. He was severely wounded at the Battle of Seven Pines, where he lost his right arm. Howard soon rejoined the fight with an empty sleeve and eventually fought at Antietam, Fredericksburg, Chancellorsville and Gettysburg. His devotion to duty earned him the sincere thanks of the United States Congress.

Major General Henry W. Slocum was a Syracuse, New York attorney and graduate of West Point, when he joined the Twenty Seventh New York Regiment. The regiment was ordered to an encampment near Washington that his men jokingly called Camp Clara. Named so because Slocum's wife, Clara, accompanied her husband to Washington. Lieutenant Charles Baker graciously vacated his tent, so that the Slocums could have privacy.

The following was taken from General William Tecumseh Sherman's biography, written by his own hand. These are the Special Field Orders issued November 9, 1864:

1. For the purpose of military operations, this army is divided into two wings, viz.: The right wing, Major-General O. O. Howard, commanding, composed of the Fifteenth and Seventeenth Corps; the left wing, Major-General H. W. Slocum commanding, composed of the Fourteenth and Twentieth Corps.

2. The habitual order of march will be, wherever practicable, by four roads, as nearly parallel as possible, and converging at points hereafter to be indicated in orders. The cavalry, Brigadier-General Kilpatrick commanding, will receive special orders from the commander-in-chief.

3. There will be no general train of supplies, but each corps will have its ammunition-train and provision-train,

distributed habitually as follows: Behind each regiment should follow one wagon and one ambulance; behind each brigade should follow a due proportion of ammunition-wagons, provision-wagons, and ambulances. In case of danger, each corps commander should change this order of march, by having his advance and rear brigades unencumbered by wheels. The separate columns will start habitually at 7 a.m., and make about fifteen miles per day, unless otherwise fixed in orders.

4. The army will forage liberally on the country during the march. To this end, each brigade commander will organize a good and sufficient foraging party, under the command of one or more discreet officers, who will gather, near the route traveled, corn or forage of any kind, meat of any kind, vegetables, corn-meal, or whatever is needed by the command, aiming at all times to keep in the wagons at least ten days' provisions for his command, and three days' forage. Soldiers must not enter the dwellings of the inhabitants, or commit any trespass; but, during a halt or camp, they may be permitted to gather turnips, potatoes, and other vegetables, and to drive in stock in sight of their camp. To regular foraging-parties must be intrusted the gathering of provisions and forage, at any distance from the road traveled.

5. To corps commanders alone is intrusted the power to destroy mills, houses, cotton-gins, etc.; and for them this general principle is laid down: In districts and neighborhoods where the army is unmolested, no destruction of such property should be permitted; but should guerrillas or bushwhackers molest our march, or should the inhabitants burn bridges, obstruct roads, or otherwise manifest local hostility, then army commanders should order and enforce a devastation more or less relentless, according to the measure of such hostility.

6. As for horses, mules, wagons, etc., belonging to the inhabitants, the cavalry and artillery may appropriate freely and without limit; discriminating, however, between the rich, who are usually hostile, and the poor and industrious, usually neutral or friendly. Foraging-parties may also take mules or horses, to replace the jaded animals of their trains, or to serve as pack-mules for the regiments of brigades. In all foraging, of whatever kind, the parties engaged will refrain abusive or threatening language, and may, where the officer in command thinks proper, given written certificates of the facts, but no receipts; and they will endeavor to leave with each family a reasonable portion for their maintenance.

7. Negroes who are able-bodied and can be of service to the several columns may be taken along; but each army commander will bear in mind that the question of supplies is a very important one, and this his first duty is to see to those who bear arms.

8. The organization, at once, of a good pioneer battalion for each army corps, composed if possible of Negroes, should be attended to. This battalion should follow the advance-guard, repair roads and double them if possible, so that the columns will not be delayed after reaching bad places. Also, army commanders should practice the habit of giving the artillery and wagons the road, marching their troops on one side, and instruct their troops to assist wagons at steep hills or bad crossings of streams.

9. Captain O. M. Poe, chief-engineer, will assign to each wing of the army a pontoon-train, fully equipped and organized; and the commanders thereof will see to their being properly protected at all times.

By order of Major-General W. T. Sherman

BRYAN COUNTY

This County created by Act of the Legislature Dec. 19, 1793, is named for Jonathan Bryan, Revolutionary patriot and member of the Executive Council in 1777. The "lost town" of Hardwick on the Ogeechee River was the first temporary County Site. Laid out in 1755, it was named for Lord Hardwick, Lord Chancellor of England, a relative of the then Gov. Reynolds. Two Royal Governors recommended that it be the Capital of Georgia. An Act of 1797 designated a new County Site at Cross Roads, 2 miles from Ogeechee Bridge. The Site was later moved to Clyde and then Pembroke.

Courthouse in Pembroke
GPS Coordinates: N32.13329, W81.622088

Bryan County, the 16th Georgia County, was founded in 1793 following the Revolutionary War. The name was taken from a southern Carolina native, Jonathan Bryan, who accompanied General Oglethorpe to the fledgling colony and developed a settlement near Savannah. It was there that he built Brampton Plantation. Bryan soon noticed the ever increasing domination of England's King George and recognized that the intolerable acts imposed on northern colonies would soon reach Georgia. Jonathan Bryan served his newly adopted home as public treasurer, a member of the Council of Safety and as a Georgia Representative in Congress.

Bryan, having received large land grants from the crown, had his holdings scattered throughout the county. He counted among his friends, John and Charles Wesley, founders of American Methodism; James Whitefield, a marshal for the British who eventually joined the American Revolution as a Colonial; George Whitefield, who founded the first Georgia orphanage known as Bethesda; and of course, James Edward Oglethorpe, the founder of Georgia. The area that would become Bryan County was first a part of Chatham County, then the Midway District, and at last, it became the York district of the Great Ogeechee River. Ogeechee Neck was the first settlement, eventually becoming St. Phillip's Parish.

Georgia's 16th county was wedged between the great Ogeechee River to the east and to the west, the Cancoohee River. Hardwicke, for Lord Hardwicke High Chancellor of England, was developed with hopes of it becoming the first county seat. Cross Roads was chosen the county seat by the Georgia General Assembly in 1797, instead of Hardwicke. Cross Roads went through numerous name changes as did most Bryan County towns. The town became known as Ways Station, for the Way family and the fact that a railroad station was located there. As the population grew, the need for public buildings was realized. William Harn of Bryan County donated two acres of land in 1815 and a wooden courthouse was eventually built there in 1854.

Henry Ford sought refuge from his northern automobile manufacturing company and the town of Ways Station provided well. Ford established his plantation named Richmond Hill and eventually, Ways Station became known as Richmond Hill. Ford contributed much to the community. He donated money for health care, educational opportunities and even built St. Anne's Church. Rumor has it, that Ford would often visit the local places of business without a dime in his pocket and appear as an average citizen sharing a moment with his neighbors.

The Clerk of Court built a home across from the Courthouse in 1866 and believing the courthouse was a fire trap, moved a good portion of those records to his home. Two weeks later, his home burned to ground. Ironically, because of his safekeeping, most of Bryan County's records were lost forever. As history progressed, the population shifted further inland.

Pembroke was founded in 1892 as a railroad station on the South & Western line and the town was incorporated in 1905. Pembroke was named for Pembroke Whitfield Williams, a notable figure in both the development of the community and in education. A two-storied courthouse was built at Clyde in 1901 and it served as the county seat until the federal government annexed 105,000 acres of land from the middle of Bryan County. Clyde was named for Sir Colin Campbell, Lord Clyde, famed Field Marshal of Scotland.

In 1935, the County Seat was moved to Pembroke in the northern portion of the county. The Courthouse was completed in 1938, an annex was added in 1969 and the latest renovations were completed in 1990.

Fort Stewart, United States Army Training Facility, completely divides the northern and southern portions of the county. The northern portion of the county is served by the East West railroad line and Interstate 16, which leads northwest to Atlanta, Macon and Savannah. The southern part of the county is intersected by Interstate 95, which follows the coast from Florida to New York.

Endnotes

[1] A factory where silk was reeled.

[2] Both Georgia Historical Markers and Georgia Historical Charts are present at Fort McAllister. The marker represents the general history of a particular location or event, whereas the chart identifies a specific topic. The historical charts have been incorporated into the story to which it is most relevant.

[3] Intentionally sink her.

[4] A tightly packed mound of earth for protection from artillery fire.

Chatham County

THE 15TH CORPS AT THE
SAVANNAH AND OGEECHEE CANAL

On Dec. 6, 1864, the 15th Corps (U), Maj. Gen. P. J. Osterhaus, USA, the extreme right of Gen. Sherman's army on its destructive March to the Sea, forced a crossing of Great Ogeechee River at Jenk's Bridge (US 80 east of Blitchton) and drove the Confederate defenders toward Savannah. Corse's division crossed and occupied Eden. Smith's division remained on the west bank with the corps trains. With Hazen's and Woods' divisions, Osterhaus moved the west bank. Hazen to take the bridge over Canoochee River east of Bryan Court House (Clyde), Woods to prepare crossings over the Ogeechee at Fort Argyle (1 mile W. across the river) and on the charred ruins of Dillon's bridge, at the mouth of this canal.

On the 8th, Corse moved down the east bank to this point and found the bridge over the canal in flames. He rebuilt it, then camped here for the night. On the 9th, Smith arrived with the corps trains. Corse moved forward to the Darien road (*US 176), defeated a small confederate force entrenched astride both roads, and drove it toward Savannah. On the 10th, Corse moved north of Little Ogeechee River followed by Hazen who, having secured the bridge over the Canoochee, had crossed the Ogeechee at Dillon's Bridge. Smith moved north along the canal, followed by Woods who had crossed the Ogeechee at Fort Argyle. That night, Corse, Woods and Smith were in line facing the strong Confederate works along Salt Creek, with Hazen in reserve at the Little Ogeechee.

GA 204, 2.4 miles west of I-95 interchange
GPS Coordinates: N32.0837, W81.317062

The Savannah-Ogeechee Canal opened for transport in 1831 and soon became an important facet of the Georgia economy. The canal had an dramatic impact on the lumber industry of coastal Georgia due to the largest sawmill operations having direct access along the canal's basin. Locally grown commodities such as cotton, rice and peaches were shipped along the canal's waterways along with manufactured goods such as bricks and naval stores.

The canal began with a tidal lock at the Savannah River and continued through four lift locks as it traversed sixteen and a half miles before reaching the final lock at the Ogeechee River. Along the way, the canal passed through Savannah's industrial center, rice fields, tracts of timber, a lush tidal river swamp and the adjacent sand dune environment, which were all characteristic of the coastal Georgia landscape.

In December 1864, General Sherman's army plowed their way across the state. Major General P. J. Osterhaus led the right wing across the Savannah-Ogeechee Canal engaging a Confederate battalion and forcing the Confederate enemy back to the city. General Osterhaus was ordered to burn the railroad bridge over the Little Ogeechee, but by the time his men arrived at the bridge the Confederates had beaten them to the task. General Osterhaus strategically placed his men at various points along the canal to intercept Confederate troops being forced out of Savannah.

After the Civil War, the Savannah-Ogeechee Canal began its gradual decline. In 1876, heavy rains compromised the canal's embankments and its use in commercial ventures became almost nonexistent. A yellow fever epidemic struck the city that same year, taking over one thousand Savannah citizens; many believed that the stagnant waters of the canal had become a breeding ground for mosquitoes carrying the deadly disease and was public health threat. By the early 1890s, transportation along the canal ceased altogether. The Central of Georgia Railway bought much of the land surrounding the canal and the once prosperous transportation link died.

Today, the canal is undergoing a revitalization. Local citizens working with Chatham County's Department of Parks, Recreation and Cultural Affairs have banded together to form the Savannah-Ogeechee Canal Society. Work has begun to restore the waterway and its natural environment. Currently, most of the efforts have been directed toward the Ogeechee River terminus where a small museum and nature center has opened for visitors near Lock Five. The museum offers displays that emphasize both the canal's history and the natural history of the local area. A half mile of marked hiking paths allows access to the beautiful setting provided by this unique waterway.

White Bluff Road at Old Coffee Bluff Road, Savannah
GPS Coordinates: N31.96014, W81.136914

Nicholsonboro was a product of the Civil War, a community thrown together by necessity following General William T. Sherman's Special Field Order Fifteen. The order guaranteed forty acres of land and a government mule to the newly emancipated slaves; the freed men assumed that this was a permanent gift from the government. The government, knowing nothing of General Sherman's order, did not honor his promise. Many of the former slaves returned to the plantations of their birth and worked as sharecroppers. After the government rescinded the Sherman's order, others like the brave eighteen who founded Nicholsonboro made their own way in life.

The community at Nicholsonboro was founded in 1868 during the reconstruction period of the South. Two hundred former slaves left Catherines Island, led by its self proclaimed Governor Tunis G. Campbell and established their community on Cedar Groves Plantation. The land was previously owned by John Nicholson. It became a peaceful little community on the banks of the Vernon River about a quarter of a day's buggy ride from Savannah.

Like most communities one of the first tasks was to establish a place to thank God for his gifts. The Nicholsonboro Community built a temporary place of worship called a brush arbor but it was soon replaced with a little clapboard church. The sanctuary was furnished with a potbellied stove for heat and lanterns to light the scripture page.

Ten years later, the eighteen Nicholsonboro citizens signed a mortgage for the two hundred acre tract of John Nicholson's land. Accomplishing nearly the impossible, these remarkable people paid their mortgage of five thousand dollars in full within four years. In 1882, the title to Nicholsonboro was presented to her citizens.

The primary income was provided by fishing and farming; Savannah provided the market for its products. The Nicholsonboro community began to fade as fishing grew into a huge commercial endeavor. Without the large sea going vessels and modern day tackle, soon the fishing industry in Nicholsonboro could no longer compete. The city marketing laws became more stringent requiring that all farm grown food be inspected and properly treated. Nicholsonboro's citizens, family by family, moved to places called Sandfly, Pinpoint and Beaulieu. What did remain constant was their center, the heart of the community, the Nicholsonboro Baptist Church.

What the community members left behind inside the walls of their church was a tale of survival. The archives housed there include marriage licenses, birth records, baptisms and photographs. These records were all evidence of a good life that lasted only a short time, creating its legacy.

Nicholsonboro Baptist Church was constructed in 1890, adjacent to the original structure. The Church continues to hold services on Sundays and Thursdays. The original Nicholsonboro Baptist Church is Chatham County's oldest rural African

American church in its unaltered form. In 2000, the Georgia Department of Natural Resources' Historic Preservation Division granted $12,000 of the $20,000 needed for the restoration of this important historical site. The Cecil B. Day Foundation presented $4,000 from state Representative Burke Day of Tybee Island.

The little wooden clapboard church still opens her arms to the public, the church bell still tolls and Nicholsonboro Baptist Church remains a legacy to time long past and a hope for the future yet to come.

WHITE BLUFF MEETING HOUSE

Here meets the oldest congregation following the Reformed (Calvinistic) theological tradition in continuous service in Georgia. In 1737, 160 Reformed Germans came to Savannah seeking religious freedom. After working their terms as indentured servants the colonists petitioned the Trustees of the colony for a Reformed minister. In August, 1745 the Trustees acceded to the petition and granted a two-acre tract for the church and a glebe of land for the support of the ministry. The glebe land was officially granted by King George II in 1759. The first minister was John Joakim Zubly who also served in the Second Continental Congress.

White Bluff Presbyterian Church, White Bluff Road, Savannah
GPS Coordinates: N31.98614, W81.129109

White Bluff Meeting House was built on property granted by King George II to the Reformed Germans settling near Savannah. Two acres were granted in 1745 to the Germans seeking religious freedom to practice their Calvinistic religion. They arrived in Savannah in 1737 accompanied by their pastor, Swiss born John Joakim Zubly.

White Bluff settlement was established and the White Bluff Meeting House was built. The meeting house was a multipurpose structure, combining a place of worship, social center and community business office. It is the longest continually operating Reformed church in Georgia.

On December 16, 1945, the White Bluff Meeting House became a Presbyterian Church and joined the ranks of the Presbyterian Association of the United States; the name was officially changed to White Bluff Presbyterian Church. Today, the church has a congregation of 350 members locally and 3,000,000 within the United States association. The Presbyterian Association sponsors seventy-one universities and colleges and more than six hundred hospitals. The local ministry provides considerable community support in Savannah, including White Bluff Presbyterian's role as a founding member of the Faith Hospitality Network, which hosts homeless families and provides financial support for those requiring short term assistance in the community. Support is available for utility bills and food for those in need. Additional services consist of the Inner City Night Shelter and serves as a meeting place for outreach organizations such as Scouting and Alcoholics Anonymous.

The same goal exists today as it did over two hundred and sixty years ago; to promote the divine plan of Jesus Christ within the hearts and minds of each individual welcomed into the White Bluff Presbyterian Church.

CAPTURE OF THE USS "WATER WITCH"

In May, 1864, the USS "Water Witch" (80 officers and men and 4 guns), Lt. Comdr. Austin Pendergrast, USN, was on patrol duty in Ossabaw Sound. On the 31st, Flag-Officer Wm. W. Hunter, CSN, assigned Lt. P. Pelot, CSN, to command a boat expedition designed to surprise and capture the vessel. This expedition - 15 officers and 117 men, in 7 boats - arrived at Beaulieu Battery via Skidaway Narrows late on June 1st, only to find that "Water Witch" was cruising in St. Catherine's Sound. She returned to Ossabaw Sound next day and anchored for the night in the mouth of Great Ogeechee River, about 1 ½ miles SSE of Raccoon Key.

About 2 A.M. the 3rd - a dark and stormy night - the boat party muffled oars. When hailed, Lt. Pelot gave the order to board. The boats closed in, and the boarding parties cut through the nettings and swarmed over the rails. After a desperate fight with cutlass and pistol, in which Lt. Pelot - the first aboard - was killed, his men cleared the deck and the ship was theirs.

Lt. Jos. Price, CSN, assumed command. To prevent her recapture, he moved the ship through Hell Gate and up Vernon River to the protection of Beaulieu Battery, whose guns turned back such an attempt on the 5th. At Beaulieu, Lt. W. W. Carnes, CSN, reported on board, assumed command, and moved "Water Witch up-river to White Bluff to refit her and to receive her new crew.

Dancy Avenue, 0.1 mile from Davidson Avenue, ½ mile east of White Bluff Road
GPS Coordinates: N31.96693, W81.124415

The USS *Water Witch* was a Union vessel used at the beginning of the Civil War to blockade the mouth of the Mississippi River. The 378 ton side wheel steamer had a crew of sixty-eight officers and men commanded by Lieutenant Austin Pendergrast. In 1864, she served off the coast of Georgia blockading Savannah.

Confederate Lieutenant Thomas P. Pelot commanded the small steamer CSS *Firefly*. His orders were to take a small flotilla to Ossabaw Sound and capture the *Water Witch*. Lieutenant Pelot, on May 31, 1864, gathered a compliment of seven small boats manned with one hundred and thirty able bodied seamen. The Confederates sailed down the Savannah River to the Isle of Hope but when they reached Ossabaw, the *Water Witch* was nowhere to be found. Over the next few nights the Confederates would row out into the sound, but again, the *Water Witch* was nowhere to be found. Just before daylight the Confederate sailors would return to their camp on the shore.

However, on the night of June 2, the Confederate raiders ventured out into the sound once more. Flashes of lighting illuminated the Union ship in the distance and the Confederate sailors silently rowed toward her. At 2:00 a.m., five of the small boats touched the Union ship and the Confederates quickly scrambled up the sides. Lieutenant Pelot, reported to be the first aboard the *Water Witch*, was immediately shot through the heart; within fifteen minutes the remaining Confederates had subdued the Union crew and captured the ship. Five other raiders were killed during the ten minute fight, including the pilot, Moses Dallas, who had been brought along to navigate the ship back to the Savannah.

Moses Dallas earned his reputation as the best river pilot in the South. Strangely enough, the Confederate river pilot, who gave his life for the cause, was African American. The loss of Moses Dallas was unfortunate, his duties were given to another African American, who was not quite as adept, Ben Newell. The captured ship was grounded in the shallow sound three times and many of the captured provisions had to be jettisoned to lighten the vessel the last time it went aground. It took the entire day of June 4, 1864, for the Confederates to bring the USS *Water Witch* to the nearby coast. The USS *Water Witch* was conscripted into the Confederate Navy.

Note: The Confederate government purchased a casket for Moses Dallas and paid his funeral expenses. However, his story refused to die. A rumor persisted that Moses did not die on board the *Water Witch*, it was said that he faked his death and defected to the Union Navy. In truth, there were actually two men in Savannah during the Civil War with the name, Moses Dallas. The Confederate pilot, Moses Dallas was from St. Marys and was indeed killed during the capture of the USS *Water*

Witch. The Moses Dallas who defected to the federal navy was from Jacksonville, Florida.

**BLUE STAR
MEMORIAL HIGHWAY**

**A tribute to the Armed Forces
that have defended the
United States of America.**

Blue Star Memorial Markers

and By-Way Markers

The Garden Club of Georgia, Inc.

**Stephenson Avenue, entrance to Hunter AAF at White Bluff Road
GPS Coordinates: N32.01502, W81.136914**

Before World War II had ended, the Garden Club of New Jersey had a vision to perpetuate their appreciation to those who had served their country. From this vision the materialization of a war memorial came into being and in 1945, after the war's end, this movement became a priority.

The New Jersey organization, seeking a suitable means of honoring these men and women, took on a beautification project with the state highway department. Six miles of dogwood trees were planted on one of New Jersey's busiest highways and appropriately, the highway was named "Blue Star Drive." No billboards were permitted to deface this memorial span.

At the 1945 National Council of State Garden Clubs (NCSGC) annual meeting, Mr. Spence Miller, then New Jersey's state highway commissioner, suggested a similar project be adopted nationally. Hence, in 1946 at NCSGC's semi-annual meeting, it was adopted as a National Council project. The projection of the approved concept of Blue Star Memorial Highways was to have dedicated highways across the country with markers in appropriate locations. From this beginning, the Blue Star Memorial System has expanded to more than 100,000 miles of highway from coast to coast, including Alaska and Hawaii.

During World War II, almost every home window displayed the Blue Star service flag as a tribute to the family member who was in the service of our country. It seemed only fitting that the blue star be the symbol of the memorial marker. Thus, being representative of the star in the service flag, it was adopted as the uniform symbol to show memorialization. The official design was a gift from Mrs. Frederic R. Kellogg of New Jersey, the 1930-33 NCSGC President.

Of interest, the symbolic blue star of the Blue Star Memorial Highway program was at the crest of the original NCSGC President's pin, which was designed by Hessie Thompson Morrah of South Carolina in 1952. Featuring the seal in the center, it was surrounded by a laurel wreath and seven loops with the regional names on them. The pin was altered in 1961, when the South Atlantic Region was divided to form the Deep South Region and the eighth loop was added. The original President's pin with the blue star is now on permanent display at National Council Headquarters.

Today, the Blue Star Memorial Markers honor all men and women as a living legacy to all who have served, are now serving and will serve in our nation's armed forces. Currently, Georgia has a total of 67 Blue Star Memorial Markers, 53 highway markers and 14 by-way markers. It must be noted, however, that some markers are missing from their original sites and their whereabouts unknown. The costs of the memorial markers are $940 and the by-way markers are $235.

Helen Szmyd, 1999-2001 Chairman
Blue Star Memorial Markers

THE GEORGIA INFIRMARY

First African-American Hospital in the United States

Chartered by the Georgia General Assembly in 1832, the Infirmary was established "for the relief and protection of afflicted and aged Africans" under the provisions of the last will and testament of Savannah merchant and minister Thomas F. Williams (1774-1816). Originally located south of the city, it was moved here in 1838. Its fourteen acres included several single-story buildings and small farm tracts for vegetable gardens. In 1904, the Infirmary became one of the earliest training schools for African-American nurses. In 1975, it became Georgia's first day center for stroke rehabilitation.

1900 Abercorn Street, Savannah
GPS Coordinates: N32.03468, W81.05837

Thomas F. Williams was born shortly before the Revolutionary War in 1774 on Tybee Island. Although Thomas was African American, he was born without the bonds of slavery. He married a young woman called Hannah and with her established a home on Tybee Island. British soldiers, plundering the island, drove the couple from of their home and during their escape, Thomas and Hannah lost everything, including the all important papers acknowledging their freedom.

Noble Jones of Wormsloe Plantation wrote the following note:

"These are to Certify to my certain Knowledge that the Bearer by Name Thomas WILLIAMS and his Wife Hannah are both free born Blacks, but are Gone from tibe [sic—Tybee] to Savannah, got Cast away, but lost every thing they had, Likewise there free pass which I saw them with before.

W JONES J P
Alexander WHILEY"[1]

Thomas and Hannah moved to Savannah and it was there that he became a merchant and minister. Obvious by the contents of Thomas' will, he was very successful. Upon his death in 1816, Thomas bequeathed the sum of $1,000 to construct a hospital "for the relief and protection of aged and afflicted Negroes."

The Georgia Infirmary was chartered on Christmas Eve 1832 with Governor Wilson Lumpkin signing the act incorporating the facility. A Board of Directors was appointed consisting of Jacob Wood of McIntosh County and the Reverend Charles Colcock Jones of Liberty County. The hospital was located south of the city and in 1838, was moved to its current Abercorn Avenue address.

The Georgia Infirmary operated until the Civil War forced its doors closed. During General Sherman's March to the Sea, the hospital was not spared, all of its buildings were completely destroyed. Public donations and the Louisa M. Porter Aid Society made it possible for the hospital to be rebuilt in 1871. By the end of its first year, the hospital began to show a promising profit of $56.82. In 1904, the Georgia Infirmary served as a teaching hospital where African American women could earn a certificate in nursing.

Today, the hospital is a fully integrated facility serving the entire community. Known as the Georgia Infirmary Day Center for Rehabilitation, the hospital is a one of a kind facility working with stroke victims from all walks of life.

**AMERICAN GRAND PRIZE RACES,
1910 AND 1911
VANDERBILT CUP RACE, 1911**

On each side of Waters Avenue at this site stood the grandstands built for the famous Savannah automobile races in 1910 and 1911. The starting and finishing line was located in front of the stands.
On November 12, 1910, David Bruce-Brown won the American Grand Prize Race of 415 miles by only one and a half seconds, averaging 70.55 miles per hour in a Benz car. The Grand Prize Race held on November 27, 1911, was also won by Bruce-Brown, driving a Fiat, with an average speed of 74.45 miles per hour.
On November 27, 1911, Ralph Mulford, at the wheel of an American-made Lozier, was victor in the Vanderbilt Cup Race, averaging 74.07 miles per hour.
These races which were run over a course of 17 miles of fine roads in Chatham County are considered by authorities as the greatest automobile road races held in this country. Of international interest and importance, the event contributed their share in the development of the early automobile industry in America.

Waters Avenue at East 46th Street, Savannah
GPS Coordinates: N32.04574, W81.085995

In the early 1900s, the premiere international automobile racing event on this side of the Atlantic was the Vanderbilt Cup. Organized by Willie K. Vanderbilt to encourage American manufacturers to build a better car than the Europeans. The race was first held on Long Island in 1904. The top automobile manufacturers of the world were invited to compete. The race was a grand success. Crowds estimated at a quarter of a million turned out to watch the magnificent event. Crowd control was nearly impossible and during the 1906 race, one death and numerous injuries to spectators put the race in a precarious position.

The American Automobile Association (AAA), who sanctioned the event, withheld the race in 1907 until a viable crowd control plan could be established. The Savannah Car Club, in an effort to host future events, chose to organize a small race to prove that they could host an event that met AAA's standards of safety and notoriety. They staged a series of three races with Willie K. Vanderbilt acting as the honorary referee. Even though the festivities attracted the top car manufacturers and the best drivers, several of the fields had very few participants. The featured race of the day made the event a success and was quite popular with the fans, drivers and AAA officials. Louis Strang, winner of the featured event, called the race,

> "the best course I have ever raced. The only thing that equals it is the kind treatment I have received on every hand since I have been in Savannah."

AAA wanted to bring the race back in 1909, but concerns of crowd control still lingered. Savannah placed a bid to host the race, promising the use of the Georgia militia to conduct security. Although AAA preferred New York, Savannah was first choice if New York could not resolve the issues of safety. Long Island was able to convince AAA that their safety measures were sufficient and was chosen for the Vanderbilt Cup once again. Savannah settled for another big event. During this time, a rival group, the Automobile Club of America (ACA), had a precarious relationship with the newer AAA. It soon boiled over into a bitter debate over the direction the sport should take. The ACA elected to stage an international event that would surpass the Vanderbilt Cup in prestige. The American Grand Prize Race offered a sterling silver cup worth twice as much as the Vanderbilt Cup, the inaugural event was awarded to Savannah. The race was scheduled for Thanksgiving, November 26, 1908, with the preliminary race being the International Light Car Race.

Using convict labor, Savannah prepared the best race course possible taking painstaking care to build banks at every corner. The Governor issued an order allowing the State Militia to police the course. The Savannah Automobile Club promised that not one complaint would be heard. The event attracted the best drivers and cars from around the world.

The week began poorly when driver John Juhasz, while avoiding a dog in the middle of the road, crashed into a tree.

Juhasz survived, but his mechanic who was riding with him was instantly killed. The only injury to a spectator was received when a man received a bayonet wound for refusing to obey a soldier's warning. The competitors were not spared the unyielding control of the militia. The race's fourth place finisher had his tires and gas tank shot out when he refused to stop driving backwards on the front straightaway after the race was over. He later apologized for his misbehavior and in an appreciation for a job well done by the militia, he sent his gloves and goggles as a gift to the man who shot at his car! The races themselves ran without incident for both the competitors and fans.

The Grand Prize race was pure excitement with the closest top three finishers in the history of racing to date. The race, course, organization and everything connected with the event was highly praised by the worldwide press, manufacturers, drivers and racing officials. Not a single bad word or complaint was ever mentioned as promised by the Savannah Car Club. Savannah immediately sent a delegation to New York to plead their case. The Los Angeles Motordrome and Indianapolis Motor Speedway also bid for the race, the latter offering a $10,000 purse for the race, Philadelphia and Atlanta also considered applications. It wasn't a difficult choice, the memory of Savannah's success in 1908 had not faded. Savannah was awarded the rescheduled American Grand Prize Race for November 12, 1910.

The Grand Prize Race finish was breathtaking and was made all the more nerve wracking by the format used in those days. Cars were started in intervals similar to today's rally car events. Thus, when a competitor finished, he often had to wait for the actual time of another car even if it finished behind him. The race was determined by 1.42 seconds between the first and second place entries. Savannah's bid to host the Vanderbilt Cup was accepted without question.

Savannah began making plans to improve their course. The lanes were widened, oiled, repeatedly rolled, curves were lengthened and broadened and bad stretches were rebuilt to provide a safer surface. The grandstands were repaired and expanded; special trains and steamships were scheduled for additional transportation to the event and local auto clubs organized motorcades.

As the use of automobiles had become more popular, the ability to close the roads for practice days was impossible. This proved to be tragic, when one of the drivers was forced to take evasive action to avoid a wagon and was killed when his car hit a tree. Two other non-fatal accidents took place leading up to the race day. Suddenly, Savannah saw for the first time the problems Long Island had suffered.

The Vanderbilt Cup could not possibly produce a closer finish than the Grand Prize race the previous year, but it did produce more all around excitement. There were seven lead changes and with two laps to go, any one of four different entries were in place for the win.

The races of 1911 were the last held in Savannah. Despite accolades, there was, for the first time, a smoldering of complaints and discontent. Problems concerning price gouging of the race fans, the special trains were consistently late and poorly run. Meanwhile, the Savannah Automobile Club was running into some opposition. More private citizens were buying cars and it became difficult to justify closing the roads for practice runs for such long periods of time. There was a growing public protest over the use of convict labor to prepare the course and the militia to patrol the race.

Savannah remained out of the racing picture for over eighty years. A closed circuit road course was built nearby called Roebling Road but it never attracted any big time events. It was used by local car clubs and for marquee events. In May 1997, racing returned to Savannah and to a place that held the distinction of offering the greatest course of its era. Proud of the heritage in this sport, the brochure advertising this event proclaims,

See Racing History Being Made. Again.

LAWTON MEMORIAL
St. Paul's Greek Orthodox Church

This building was constructed in 1897-98 as a memorial to General Alexander R. Lawton (1818- 96) and his daughter Corrine (1844-77). It was used as a public space for cultural, educational and civic purposes until the 1930s. After serving in the Georgia House of Representatives and as president of the Georgia and Atlantic Railroad, Lawton served as Brigadier General and Quartermaster-General of the Confederacy, as ambassador to Austria-Hungary, and as fifth president of the American Bar Association. Chartered in 1907, St. Paul's Greek Orthodox Church acquired the building as its sanctuary in 1941.

14 West Anderson at Bull Street, Savannah
GPS Coordinates: N32.06241, W81.098274

Alexander Robert Lawton was born in 1818 at Beaufort County, South Carolina. Following in his father footsteps as a soldier, Alexander graduated from the United States Military Academy in 1839, was commissioned as a Second Lieutenant and assigned to the northern frontier until 1841. He eventually resigned from his artillery unit to study law at Harvard and was admitted to the bar at Savannah in 1843. There he established a law practice. Two years later, Alexander Lawton married Sarah Hillhouse Alexander and the couple had four children. Lawton was involved in a number of endeavors aside from the running of his plantation: In 1849, he accepted the position as President of the Augusta and Savannah Railroad, which he held until 1854, resigning when he was elected State Senator, he was then elected President of the Georgia Democratic Convention.

When Georgia seceded from the Union, Alexander resigned his seat in Congress to assist the organization of Georgia's militia. As Colonel of the 1st Volunteer Georgia Regiment, he seized Fort Pulaski under orders from Governor Joseph E. Brown. It was to be the first overt act of war in Georgia. In April 1861, he was commissioned Brigadier General and commanded Georgia's coastal defenses. Lawton was reassigned in 1862 to Richmond, Virginia, where he fought in the second battle at Manassas and was wounded at Sharpsburg later that same year.

Jefferson Davis appointed Lawton Quartermaster General in February of 1864. He accepted the position with reservations. Public doubt over the legitimacy of the appointment convinced him to resign in 1864. At the end of the war, Lawton returned to his law practice in Savannah and aided in the reconstruction of the defeated South. Lawton became involved once again in politics and from 1870 until 1875, he served in the State Legislature. In 1876, he chaired the State Electoral College and in 1877, acted as Vice President of the Georgia Constitutional Convention. President Cleveland wanted to appoint Lawton as Minister to Russia in 1885, but his heroic involvement during the Civil War led Congress to disapprove the appointment. Eventually, he was appointed as Minister to Austria and Hungary from 1887 until 1889.

General Alexander Robert Lawton died in Clifton Springs, New York, on July 2, 1896, he was 78. After his death, a building was erected on Bull Street and dedicated to the memory of Lawton and his daughter Corrine, who died during in a yellow fever epidemic in 1877. The reason Corrine Lawton was included in the memorial remains unknown.

The Lawton Memorial has served as an auditorium, where the public was entertained with musical recitals, lectures and political forums. The building was sold in the 1940s. Today, Lawton Memorial is home to St. Paul's Greek Orthodox Church.

Laurel Grove South Cemetery

In 1853, the city reserved 4 acres in the new Laurel Grove Cemetery for Savannah's African American community. This new burial ground replaced an older black cemetery located near Whitefield Square. Pastors Andrew Bryan (First Colored Baptist Church) and Henry Cunningham (Second Baptist Church) were among those whose bodies were moved to the new location. Here are buried many of Savannah's prominent black leaders—educators, civic/ community leaders, Masons, politicians, entrepreneurs, and religious leaders. Later increased in acreage by the city, it continues in use today.

Laurel Grove South Cemetery, 2101 Kollock Street, Savannah
GPS Coordinates: N31.99593, W81.269227

Lachland McGillivray, a Scotsman and Indian trader from Fort Augusta, established a plantation named Springfield in 1750. The four hundred forty-five acre tract bordered the Augusta and Ogeechee Roads on the outskirts of the Savannah settlement. Lachland McGillivray, a staunch loyalist during the Revolutionary War, abandoned his American property and fled to Scotland. Joseph Clay, Paymaster General of the American Army's Southern Department and a member of the Continental Congress, acquired Springfield Plantation in 1782. In 1806, Clay sold the property to his son-in-law, Joseph Stiles.

Joseph Stiles expanded the plantation until the total estate encompassed almost one thousand acres. In 1850, Stiles sold the property to the city of Savannah and one hundred acres was set aside to establish a new municipal cemetery. Colonial Park Cemetery had been closed due to overcrowding and Savannah required another burial place. James O. Morse, Savannah's City Engineer, was given the task of designing what was to become Laurel Grove Cemetery. The first burial took place on a dreary day in October 1852. On November 10, 1852, Mayor Richard Arnold dedicated Laurel Grove Cemetery. Henry Rootes Jackson was selected as guest speaker.

Four acres of Laurel Grove Cemetery was set aside in 1853 for African American interment. A number of noted African American leaders were moved from other locations into Laurel Grove at that time. The cemetery was expanded in 1857 and again in 1859 covering a span of thirty acres and including a caretaker's house.

An earlier African American Cemetery was noted as "Negro Ground" on a historical map of 1818. The plot was a good distance from the city and most graves were marked with simple wooden crosses or having no markings at all. The African customs of a dirt mound with various belongings of the deceased placed in remembrance was used in the earlier burial place and due to the lack of headstones many of the graves were lost over time. Laurel Grove South Cemetery eventually embraced the European custom of grand vaults and tombstones, replacing the tradition of plain dirt mounds.

In 1931, it was noted that time and the elements were slowly destroying Laurel Grove South and a movement was initiated to begin clean up. The Savannah Sugar Refinery donated wrought iron gates to the city of Savannah for use at the burial ground and the city, at the insistence of numerous African Americans, spent $3000 to clean and renovate the historic burial site. According to Charles Elmore, noted Laurel Grove historian, in the early 1970s W. W. Law,

> "almost singlehandedly led the movement to improve Laurel Grove Cemetery South and identified historically significant grave sites which led to the City of Savannah maintaining this venerable cemetery in a dignified manner by providing street names and markers to make it easy for citizens and historians to identify various burial places."

Laurel Grove South was recognized on a cold day in January 2000, as the most significant African American cemetery in the state. A Georgia Historical marker was placed as a result of the efforts expended by Mr. Charles Elmore and Friends of the Laurel Grove South Cemetery in cooperation with the Georgia Historical Society.

Laurel Grove South is the burial site of many who helped to shape Savannah and state of Georgia. A few of those who were laid to rest there are: Andrew Bryan who founded the First Colored Baptist Church on Jan. 20, 1788; Union soldiers Samuel Gordon Morse, John Nesbitt and Edward Wicks; Confederate veterans Alexander Harris and a man known only as "Old Tom." Educator Jane DeVeaux, who secretly taught slave children; and Raymond Snype, a jazz musician who organized The Golden Syncopators jazz band in 1929. May they all rest in peace.

**SAINT PHILLIPS
MONUMENTAL A.M.E. CHURCH**

The first African Methodist Church in Georgia was organized by the Rev. A. L. Stanford on June 16, 1865, at Savannah, Georgia and was given the name Saint Phillip African Methodist Episcopal Church. Two months and fifteen days later, the Sunday School had its beginning. Many great preachers have pastored this historic church. One was Bishop Henry M. Turner, a member of the state legislature during Reconstruction and a leader of the Back-to-Africa movement in Georgia, who pastored this church from 1870 to 1874. A storm demolished the church building in September 1896 and the Odd Fellow's Hall was secured for worship until the church could be rebuilt. The General Conference meeting in Waycross in 1897 renamed the church St. Phillips Monumental A.M.E. Church.
Memorial tablets in the church carry the names and dates of service of all the bishops in Georgia and all pastors serving this congregation since the church's beginning.
On May 7, 1961, the Church moved from Hall Street to its present location at Jefferson Street and Park Avenue.

**Jefferson Street and West Park Avenue, Savannah
GPS Coordinates: N32.06558, W81.100447**

The Civil War brought many changes, one of those changes was the public worship of African Americans in their own churches, not in the balconies of the white church. The first church was under the auspices of the Methodist Church South. Having no permanent pastor, William Bentley, C. L. Bradwell and William Gaines kept the congregation together and conducted services. The first visiting minister was Reverend James Lynch, who worked in secret with C. L. Bradwell to bring the church under the African Methodist Episcopal.

The first African Methodist Church in the state of Georgia was formed with Reverend Anthony L. Stanford as minister and named the Saint Phillips African Methodist Episcopal or AME Church. The church was officially founded on June 16, 1865. The first African American Sunday School met exactly two months and fifteen days later. Although every minister through the years has had a positive effect on the spiritual development of Saint Phillips, the following are noted:

Reverend Henry McNeal Turner was the first African American Chaplain to serve in the United States Army, appointed by President Lincoln in 1863. He was assigned as an agent of the Freedmen's Bureau in 1865 and from 1868 until 1870, as a delegate to the Georgia House of Representatives. At one time, Reverend Turner served as the Postmaster of Macon. He accepted the call to pastor Saint Phillips AME Church in 1870 and remained pastor until 1874. In 1880, he was elected as Bishop of Georgia and as Bishop was prominent in the Back To Africa movement where he led two expeditions from Savannah in the 1890s. His work in Africa led to the establishment and expansion of missionary work there.

Reverend J. B. Lofton served as pastor from 1887 until 1891 and it was during his administration that the church building was completed and cleared of all debts. In 1895, Reverend L. H. Smith, accepted the appointment. During his tenure a major storm struck in September 1896. Saint Phillips Church lay in ruins. The membership turned the disaster into an opportunity and chose this time of move the church to a more centralized location. During the interim the Odd Fellow's Hall was used for services until the property at West Broad and Charles Streets was purchased.

Reverend J. A. Lindsay took over leadership of the congregation in 1905 and began to lobby for the construction of a new sanctuary, it was not until 1909 and Reverend R. H. Singleton that the dream was realized. During his tenure the present sanctuary was constructed.

Possibly one of the most revered of Saint Phillips' ministers was the Reverend S. R. Dinkins. Dinkins served from 1937 until 1941 and just after his appointment the church building was advertised for public sale as a result of a past due mortgage. It seems the congregation was further tested when the north wall of the sanctuary collapsed on August 28, 1939 and if that was not enough the boiler exploded leaving the church completely without heat for the winter soon to come. Through all of the adversity the church and Reverend Dinkins stood firm. The money was found to bring the mortgage up to date, the wall repaired and the boiler replaced.

Reverend Henry W. Murph was called to serve Saint Phillips in 1941 until 1949, under his leadership the mortgage was paid in full and the membership was able to purchase an Austin Pipe Organ. Most amazing of all of Reverend Murph's accomplishments was his great success in getting the full cooperation of the entire membership. Reverend Murph went on to be elected as Bishop and served as Senior Bishop until his retirement in 1988.

The Reverend Doctor John Sterling Bryan took the church in 1949 and served until 1963. He initiated many major repairs to the Sunday School, adding a new roof and other renovations desperately needed at the time. Reverend Bryan became the Presiding Elder of the West Savannah District until his death in 1978.

In 1964, Reverend Doctor Benjamin Gay was selected to lead Saint Phillips. The church flourished like never before; a new parsonage was built and air conditioning was installed. Dr. Gay served the church for eighteen years, which was the longest term for any minister in Saint Philips history. Today, he serves as the Presiding Elder for the East Atlanta District.

Reverend Charles Wesley Purnell received the call to Saint Phillips on June 13, 1982. It was under his leadership that an elevator was installed to aid handicapped and senior citizens. A new Van Zoren Organ was purchased and a Kimball Viennese Edition Grand Ebony Piano. After eight years, Reverend Purnell went on to pastor the Bethel AME Church in Savannah.

Reverend Gregory Vaughn Eason, Sr. assumed the spiritual leadership of what is now known as Saint Phillips Monumental AME Church in June of 1990. At twenty-nine years of age, he was the youngest pastor in church history. His vision has brought Saint Phillips into the modern age with a Media Ministry, a Web Site Ministry, the enhanced Music Ministry includes a Praise Team and a Youth Liturgical Dance Group as well as an Outreach Ministry. He has initiated an 8:00 a.m. service for those finding the 11:00 a.m. service difficult when certain work hours interfere. Under his leadership, the parsonage was converted to a Child Development Center to serve the needs of the parents in the Saint Phillips community and a new parsonage was purchased. The Outreach of Faith, a television ministry, airs on cable three times per week.

Saint Phillips Monumental AME Church continues to flourish in the community and grow in spirit. The history of leadership and brotherhood has ensured that what Reverend Anthony L. Stanford began over one hundred and thirty years ago will continue to prosper in the future.

St. Phillips Church

**BIRTHPLACE OF
EIGHTH AIR FORCE**

On 28 January 1942, the Eighth Air Force was activated in the adjacent building, a National Guard Armory at the time.
Having moved to England, the Eighth was ready on 17 August to test the theory that daylight bombing raids could be made with profitable results. Twelve B-17's participated in this mission, striking the railway marshalling yards at Rouen, France, and returning safely back to their home base. This highly successful mission established the pattern for the strategic bombardment of Nazi Germany — the Eighth Air Force day and the RAF by night.
Under the leadership of Generals Carl A. Spaatz, Ira C. Baker and James H. Doolittle, it flew over 600,000 sorties delivering over 700,000 tons of bombs and destroying over 15,000 German aircraft.
On one single mission, December 24, 1944, it was able to send 2,000 B-17 Flying Fortresses and B-24 Liberators and nearly 1,000 fighters in the Battle of Germany.
The renowned winged-eight, the emblem of the Eighth Air Force, was designed by former Air Force Major Ed Winter, a native of Savannah.

**Old Chatham Armory, Bull Street near Park Avenue, Savannah
GPS Coordinates: N32.06449, W81.097367**

The Eighth Air Force was founded in Savannah in January 1942 during World War II. The Mighty Eighth's bombers and fighter planes carried the war deep into the enemy's territory and played a significant part in the defeat of Nazi Germany. Since World War II, the fighter squadron has provided their strength and skills to every major military engagement involving the Armed Forces of the United States. Its role in America's defense continues to be an important component of the United States Air Force's Air Combat Command. Roger Freeman, the foremost historian of Eighth Air Force, dubbed the unit, "The Mighty Eighth" when his landmark book was published by the same name in 1970. Freeman inadvertently bestowed a nickname, which has remained for more than thirty years.

The United States Department of War activated the Savannah detachment during World War II to support the invasion of North Africa, but its mission soon changed to carrying out the strategic bombings of German targets in the European theatre. The Squadron arrived in England in February 1942 and flew light bombers during its first mission on July 4. Six weeks later, on August 17, the fighters flew their first heavy bomber raid.

From 1942 until the end of the war in 1945, they piloted B-17 Flying Fortresses and B-24 Liberators in daylight bombing raids against Germany and Nazi occupied Europe. The Eighth's B-17s and B-24s suffered heavy losses over Europe, especially after the bombing of Germany began. These heavy bombers could carry enough fuel to reach almost any target in Germany, though there were no Allied fighters with enough fuel capacity to protect them. Once the Allied fighter escorts turned back, the Eighth's bombers were vulnerable to attacks by German Luftwaffe fighters. Defensive tactics pioneered by Colonel Curtis LeMay and others helped but could not dissuade the German fighters or the fierce anti-aircraft defense. During the spring, summer and fall of 1943, the Eighth Air Force losses reached unprecedented proportions, one in four airmen were lost. It became statistically impossible for a bomber crewman to survive a twenty-five mission tour of duty.

Losses escalated until long range P-51 Mustang fighters, effective external fuel tanks for P-47 Thunderbolt and P-38 Lightning fighters became available in the spring of 1944. After the fighters were modified losses slowly began to decline. The Eighth Air Force ended World War II with the highest casualty rates of any allied force.

The crews remained on constant alert during the long confrontation with the Soviet Union and during the Berlin crises in 1948, 1961 and the Cuban Missile Crisis in 1962. The bomber units were sent to forward areas to strike instantly with nuclear weapons in case of war. As weapons, strategies and tactics evolved with technology and geopolitics, the Eighth Air Force remained a major part of the United States' military strike force, often providing the "Big Stick" that stood behind peaceful diplomacy in difficult and threatening times.

In 1990, they played a significant role in the buildup of forces in Saudi Arabia for Operation Desert Shield. When the conflict became Desert Storm, B-52s were flown in spectacular record setting nonstop combat missions, flying from Barksdale Air

Force Base in Louisiana to positions in the Middle Eastern theater, launching their payload of cruise missiles and then returning to Louisiana. Other B-52s flying from bases in England, Spain, Diego Garcia and Saudi Arabia were largely responsible for weakening the Iraqi Republican Guard with low level carpet bombing attacks on their positions. Tanker aircraft from the Eighth supported all types of planes of the multinational forces during the Gulf War.

The Cold War came to a end with the collapse of the Soviet Union in 1992, deactivating the Strategic Air Command and the Eighth became part of the new Air Combat Command. In 1999, units of the Eighth were back in combat over Europe during Operation Allied Force, the NATO bombing campaign against Serbian operations in Kosovo.

Continuously active since 1942, today, the Eighth Air Force fulfills its strategic mission from a new headquarters at Barksdale and from bases around the American Midwest. The men and women of today's Mighty Eighth continue the heritage of dedication, vigilance and valor that began during World War II.

Eighth Air Force Commander Lieutenant General Thomas Keck had the following to say concerning the 2001 War on terrorism,

> "Let me reassure you that the airmen of the 'Mighty Eighth' are ready. They are highly trained professionals. They are ready to defend America and they are ready to go anywhere, anytime. As always, we stand ready to support whatever is asked of us by the national command authority. We are here to defend against countries, entities and people who actively oppose the United States and damage our interests by acts of violence and acts of war."

Birthplace of the Eighth Air Force

WARREN A. CANDLER HOSPITAL

Georgia's first hospital, this institution is believed to be the second oldest general hospital in continuous operation in the United States. It was founded in 1803 as a seaman's hospital and poor house and was incorporated in 1808 under the name of Savannah Poor House and Hospital Society. The hospital was removed to this site in 1819.

In 1835 a new charter was obtained for the institution.

During the War Between the States a portion of the Hospital was used for the care of Confederate soldiers. In the area to the rear a stockade was erected in 1864, around the great oak that still stands there, for confinement of Union prisoners.

After Sherman's occupation of Savannah and until 1866 the building served as a Union hospital.

The name was changed in 1872 to Savannah Hospital. From 1871 to 1888 the Savannah Medical College was located here.

In 1876 the building was completely renovated. However, the structure of the 1819 building was retained and remains as the nucleus of the present hospital.

In 1931 the facilities were acquired by the Methodist Church, and the name changed to honor Bishop Warren A. Candler.

Huntingdon Street off Drayton Street at old entrance, Savannah
GPS Coordinates: N32.06891, W81.094326

In 1803 Seaman's Hospital, reflecting the most prominent industry of the area, opened. The hospital was incorporated in 1808 and was renamed Savannah Poor House and Hospital Society. The name was changed again in the mid 1800s to the Central Cholera Hospital, although cholera was never a threat to the city of Savannah. In 1852, many changes were planned for the hospital complex enabling construction to begin on what is presently known as Forsyth Park. The hospital experienced dire financial problems and was eventually sold to the Marine Fire Insurance Company and the Planters Bank for $21,000. It was later returned to the city of Savannah for $7,000.

During the turmoil of the Civil War, the hospital was occupied under civilian administration as a Confederate Hospital and in 1864, a stockade was erected at the rear of the building. A large oak tree was encircled by a fence and used as a makeshift prison for Union soldiers. When General William Tecumseh Sherman moved into Savannah lock, stock and Union Army, the roles reversed, the facility became a Union Hospital and Confederate prisoners were held at the large oak. When the Union finally relinquished its hold on Savannah, the hospital was stripped. An African American doctor was left in charge and because none of the hospital facilities remained, the building became a haven for African American refugees. In 1866, the hospital was reorganized out of necessity when yellow fever ran rampant through the city. It is said that the administrators dug a cavernous underground morgue and autopsy room beneath the hospital to accommodate the dead.

The facility carries the distinction of the oldest United States hospital building in continuous use, it has operated for over 152 years. The Methodist, faithful to the healing ministry, took over in 1930. Savannah Hospital, as it was now known, would be operated on a much larger scale under the management of the Georgia General Hospital Board of the Methodist Episcopal Church. Renamed again Warren A. Candler Hospital, after the beloved Methodist Bishop, when the South Georgia Methodist Conference assumed control in 1931.

Southeast Georgia's two oldest health care institutions, St. Joseph's Hospital and Warren A. Candler Hospital formed a joint operating agreement and came together as one health system in 1997. The partnership made this the largest and most experienced health care provider in the region. Like any good joint venture, the health system builds on the strengths of each partner. Candler Hospital, maintained a strong reputation for providing the finest quality primary care, women's services and outpatient services, and formed a natural fit with St. Joseph's Hospital, recognized as a leader in the region with its Centers for Excellence in Heart Care services, Orthopedics and Neurosurgery.

The fundamental reasons for the consolidation agreement were to maintain local control and decision making of Savannah's healthcare system, as well as increase the services by reducing those that were duplicated. During the first year, St. Joseph's/Candler Health System generated over $13 million in operational cost savings, while expanding available health care benefits.

The network of healthcare offered by St. Joseph's/Candler Health System provides the community with expanded and comprehensive services. Now in almost every community in southeast Georgia and adjacent South Carolina, a St. Joseph's/Candler health system provider is conveniently available.

In May 1999, after two years of operations, St. Joseph's/Candler Health System was named to the list of the nation's Top 100 health systems as published in Modern Healthcare Magazine. In 2000, the health system repeated this accolade, ranking at number thirty-three of the nations Top 100 health care systems.

GEORGIA
HISTORICAL SOCIETY
Founded 1839

The Georgia Historical Society founded May 24, 1839, is one of the oldest historical societies in the country. Among its founders were I. K. Tefft, the noted autograph collector; William Bacon Stevens, historian, physician and prelate; and Dr. Richard D. Arnold, who as Mayor of Savannah formally surrendered the City to Gen. Sherman in 1864.

The Presidents of the Society have included John Macpherson Berrien, Attorney General under President Jackson and United States Senator, James M. Wayne, Associate Justice of the Supreme Court of the United States; and Henry R. Jackson, jurist, soldier, diplomat and poet.

Hodgson Hall, the home of the Society, is a repository for books, newspapers and manuscripts relating to the history of Georgia. Dedicated in 176, the building was a gift of Margaret Telfair Hodgson and Mary Telfair as a memorial to William Brown Hodgson, the distinguished scholar of Oriental languages and United States Dragoman and Consul to the Barbary States and Turkey.

Gaston and Whitaker Streets, Savannah
GPS Coordinates: N32.07046, W81.096745

The Georgia General Assembly granted a charter for the Georgia Historical Society on May 24, 1839. The Society was to be one of the first in the country and the first in the state of Georgia. During the years of 1874 and 1875, the present home of the Society was constructed through the generosity and long term support of Margaret Telfair Hodgson. Margaret Hodgson's only stipulation was that the building be named for her late husband, William Brown Hodgson.

William Brown Hodgson was an internationally known scholar and Middle Eastern diplomat. Hodgson spoke fourteen languages and for many years, served as an interpreter and counsel to the Barbary States and Turkey. His works concerning African Muslims, a sampling of which can be found in the Georgia Historical Society archives, remain the definitive reference on the subject today. Aside from his scholarly endeavors, William Brown Hodgson was an avid supporter of the Society and an active member.

The Telfair family was prominent in Savannah society. When Margaret Telfair married William Brown Hodgson, both were middle aged, and it was Margaret's family money that allowed Hodgson to realize a number of aspirations, that in turn benefited the community. It was Hodgson who created, what is today, one of Savannah's most beautiful and long featured areas Forsyth Park.

Margaret hired European trained and well known New York architect, Detlef Lienau to design Hodgson Hall. The interior high vaulted ceilings and decorative ironwork lend an air of comfortable surroundings. The engrossed researcher, amid thousands of historical documents, can pass an entire day without ever realizing the clock has dwindled to the five o'clock hour and closing time.

The Georgia Historical Society's dedication ceremony was a grand event with music and speeches, all praising the Society and the new building. Well, all praises except for one dissenter. Dr. Richard D. Arnold, formerly the mayor of Savannah, was one of the original three founders of the Society. Dr. Arnold was also the man who officially surrendered Savannah to General Sherman. He was very unhappy that the building would be named for William Hodgson and perhaps jealousy was the underlying factor. Dr. Arnold felt the honor had been purchased and that the person deserving the recognition was, in fact, Israel Tefft, another founder of the Society. Politics and personalities, it is said, should never be mixed. The membership paid little attention to Dr. Arnold's misgivings.

In truth, naming the building after Hodgson was a purchased accolade, but deservedly so. The Telfair family had given so much to the city of Savannah, including the very building that housed the Historical Society and due to the stipulation of construction placed by Margaret Telfair Hodgson the name was given and remains so to this day, Hodgson Hall.

True to Georgia's history, the Georgia Historical Society adopted the old Colonial seal and founders motto, *Non Sibi, Sed Aliis* or "Not for self, but for others," as its own. Throughout its history, the Society has collected, preserved and shared Georgia's most important documents, rare books, maps, photographs and artifacts that represent her growth throughout the years since her founding in 1733. Featured in the Society archives is a collection of unparalleled importance, the impressive group of manuscripts, rare books and research materials include diaries, personal letters, ledger books, books of recorded minutes, account books, church records and many other sources relating to Georgia and her history. The Georgia Historical Society also maintains and displays a wide range of Georgia artifacts from a Revolutionary War drum, a plantation medicine chest and military weapons to jewelry, snuff boxes, medals and badges, coins, seals and various items of historical significance.

When the azaleas begin to blossom and fragrant daffodils fill the squares with their bright yellow sunshine in April each year, the Georgia Historical Society holds its annual membership meeting. The Society hosts an impressive compliment of programs, publications, lectures and tours as well as providing statewide assistance to local historical societies through the Affiliate Chapter Program. The Society provides the Georgia Heritage education program and presents the annual Antiques Show and Sale.

In February 1997, the Georgia Historical Society assumed responsibility for the Georgia Historic Marker Program. Although the State of Georgia still maintains those markers erected prior to July 1, 1998, the Society has initiated a new statewide program. The new program has brought a number of changes to the face of the historical marker. No longer cast in dark green with gold lettering, new markers have black backgrounds with a silver seal and lettering. The seal has also been changed to bear the symbol of the Georgia Historical Society rather than the state seal. Several changes have been made to the sponsorship procedures and the Society will only approve twenty markers every fiscal year.

The Georgia Historical Society continues to provide, after one hundred and sixty years, a means of research, education and enjoyment of Georgia's diverse history. Today, the Society has over one hundred and seventy-five affiliate chapters dispersed throughout the state. The services provided by this not for profit organization are, without doubt, one of Georgia's most valuable assets.

The Georgia Historical Society

MOTHER MATHILDA BEASLEY. O.S.F.
GEORGIA'S FIRST BLACK NUN

Mathilda Taylor was born in 1834 in New Orleans, and came to Savannah as a young woman. She taught black children in her home before the Civil War, when it was still illegal. She married Abraham Beasley, a successful black businessman, in 1869. After the death of her husband in 1877, Mrs. Beasley journeyed to York England around 1885 to study as a nun, a Poor Clare, a branch of the Franciscan sisters. She returned to Savannah and established an orphanage in 1886 which became the St. Francis Home in 1892. In 1889, Sister Mathilda founded the first group of black nuns in Georgia which were of the 3rd order of St. Francis and became known as "Mother Mathilda". Under her direction, this small order ran the orphanage for several years until it dispersed, Mother Mathilda gained help from the Church for her orphanage and in 1899, took the habit of the Franciscans and continued working at the orphanage. In 1901, she was given a cottage near the Sacred Heart Church to which she had earlier given her husband's land holdings. She began to sew in her home and given the proceeds to poor blacks. On Dec. 20, 1903, the much beloved "Mother Beasley" was found dead, kneeling in the cottage's private chapel. Nearby were her burial clothes, funeral instructions and will.

Sacred Heart Catholic Church, 1707 Bull Street, Savannah
GPS Coordinates: N32.06002, W81.099315

Mathilda Taylor was born in New Orleans in 1834, the daughter of a Creole mother and African American father. Because of her mixed blood, Mathilda was shunned by the community of her Creole mother and considered an outcast among her father's African American relations. Nevertheless, Mathilda was orphaned at a young age and found herself adrift in a hostile world, she traveled to Savannah, seeking employment acceptable for a young free woman of color. She took in sewing and eventually found work in a restaurant owned by Abraham Beasley. During this time, before the Civil War, Mathilda secretly taught African American children to read and write, which was then against the law. Obviously the endeavor was of much importance to Mathilda, had she been caught the sentence would have been whipped publicly or possibly hanging.

Abraham Beasley, Mathilda's employer, was a financially secure, free African American during a time when most of his race was enslaved. He was a prominent widower, originally from Virginia with a young son. He had grown quite wealthy in Savannah pursuing various endeavors including that of grocer, saloon owner, restauranteur and slave trader.

Mathilda Taylor and Abraham Beasley were married on February 9, 1869. The newly weds began married life at 48 Harris Street. The first floor of their home was used as the Beasley's produce market, known as The Green Grocer. Abraham Beasley died on September 3, 1877 and was buried in the Catholic Cemetery on Wheaton Street. Mathilda inherited all of her husband's vast land holdings and wealth.

Mathilda Beasley was desperately troubled over the wealth she had inherited, which was the partially derived from the enslavement of others. She kept enough of the inheritance to support Abraham Beasley's son, giving him an inheritance when he came of age, and the remainder was donated to the Catholic Church. Mathilda's only stipulation was that part of the funds and property be used for an African American orphanage. Abraham's son was sent to live with relatives and Mathilda was free to pursue her true calling.

She journeyed to York, England, to serve as a novice, intent on taking her vows as a nun. In November 1884, Mathilda joined a group of Franciscan nuns arriving to work with the African American women of Savannah. The group was known as the "Poor Clares," their purpose was to establish a convent and school. The group of nuns did not adapt well to the foreign climate and were only in Savannah a short time. After the Clares' departure, it is obvious that Mathilda did considerable traveling. Father Oswald Moosmuller was left in charge of her financial accounts. Correspondence between the two, in 1885, indicates that he forwarded funds for Mathilda's travel and saw to repairs of a home on Skidaway Island set aside for the young son of Abraham Beasley.

By 1886, Mathilda was again settled in Savannah and working with African American orphans. The Colored Orphan Asylum was located at the intersection of 32nd Street and Habersham. This was the site of the first Sacred Heart Church. The first orphans were taken in during the spring of 1887.

Mathilda Beasley, then known as Mother Mathilda, founded the first group of African American nuns in Georgia called the 3rd Order of St. Francis, in 1889. Under her direction, the sisters ran the ever expanding orphanage for a number of years. In 1892, the name of the orphanage was changed to the St. Francis Home. Mother Mathilda repeatedly wrote to the Cardinal in Baltimore imploring him to send additional help and funding. Her concerns went unheeded.

In early 1895, several attempts were made to burn the orphanage. While authorities looked for outward sources, Mother Mathilda found the culprits from within. Several mischievous teenage girls living at the home had ignited the fires. According to records the young ladies were soundly dealt with and Mother Mathilda was certain the behavior would not be repeated.

The orphanage moved in the late 1890s to St. Benedict's Parish at East Broad Street. Finally, Mother Mathilda was able to meet a long awaited goal, the church and orphanage for the care of African American Catholic children finally occupied the same location. By this time, Mother Mathilda had reached her 60th year and was deeply concerned about the future of the orphanage upon her death. Again she sought the help of the cardinal. In 1898 three Franciscan sisters arrived, though after one year only one of the Franciscan sisters remained. One had died, another left Savannah to join a community in the north where African Americans were more freely accepted. That left only Mother Mathilda and one other to care for the children.

In 1901, at the age of sixty-seven, Mother Mathilda was given a cottage near the Sacred Heart Church. Located at 1511 Price Street, the property had originally been part of her husband's estate. Though she was aging and feeble, her eyesight failing, Mother Mathilda continued her work at the orphanage and to take in sewing, giving her last dime to the Church.

On December 20, 1903, eternal rest came to Mother Mathilda. She was found kneeling in the small chapel of her cottage, obviously observing her morning devotional as the angel of death came for her. Nearby, neatly arranged, were her burial clothes, funeral instructions and her will. The cause of death was listed as acute indigestion.

The Savannah Morning News carried an entire column dedicated to Mother Mathilda. The article read, in part,

> "By the Sacred Heart Clergy, Mother Beasley was held in the highest esteem and only words of warmest praise and eulogy were heard concerning her. Protestants speak in the highest terms of her life and character and among the negroes the feeling prevails that they have lost one of their best and truest friends and benefactors."

Mother Mathilda was buried along side her husband at the Catholic Cemetery. Following her death, the orphanage continued to operate under the direction of the Franciscan sisters. A day school was opened in 1907 in the basement of the church and was later replaced by a brick edifice built especially for the school. St. Benedict's school continued classes in Savannah until 1969. The orphanage was closed in early 1940; the children were transferred to Augusta.

On February 8, 1981, Mother Mathilda Beasley was honored during the Georgia Week Program at St. Benedict's Church. Under the direction of Sister Charlene Walsh, R.S.M., Mother Mathilda was heralded as a "role model from our roots, in our church, in our neighborhood."

In March 1982, a groundbreaking ceremony was held for a park funded by the city of Savannah in honor of Mother Mathilda. Sister Charlene and Mr. W. W. Law of Savannah were instrumental in having the park named for Mother Mathilda where children could happily play. Mother Mathilda would be pleased.

Mother Mathilda Cross

FORMER HOME HENRY R. JACKSON
UNION ARMY HEADQUARTERS, 1865

This building, now the quarters of a private club, was erected in 1857 for Edmund Molyneux, British consul at Savannah, and served as his residence and as the Consulate until Molyneux's return to England in 1863. In 1865 the Molyneux house was appropriated by the Union army as headquarters for General O. O. Howard and his successor, Gen. Wm. F. Barry. Representatives of the family claimed that furnishings valued at more than $10,000.00 including part of the famous Molyneux wine cellar, were damaged or removed during the Federal occupation.
The mansion was purchased from the Molyneux family in 1885 by Gen. Henry R. Jackson and was the home of that illustrious Georgian until his death in 1898.
Jackson equally distinguished himself as lawyer, soldier, diplomat and poet. He was Judge of the Eastern Circuit of Georgia (1849-'53) and in 1859 was special prosecutor for the United States in the celebrated case of the slave ship "Wanderer." He fought in the Mexican War and won distinction in the Confederate army as a brigadier general. He was ambassador to Austria (1854- '58) and minister to Mexico (1885-'86). A gifted poet, the best known of Jackson's poems is "The Red Old Hills of Georgia."

Bull and Gaston Streets at the Oglethorpe Club, Savannah
GPS Coordinates: N32.07044, W81.09535

The facts of Henry Rootes Jackson's life are quite straight forward. To discover his heart, the reader must follow through to the end. Jackson was the son of a revered Franklin College educator, he enrolled in Franklin College and eventually graduated from Yale University in 1839. Jackson received his law degree and was admitted to the Georgia Bar in 1844. He served as Justice of the Georgia Supreme Court from 1849 until 1853. Jackson was appointed to the Diplomatic Service as United States *Charge d'Affaires* in Austria and remained at that post for six years. Two urns from Austria can be seen today, along side the City Exchange Bell on Bay Street, donated by Jackson as gifts from his time in Austria.

During the Civil War, Henry R. Jackson served as judge of the Confederate Courts in Georgia. He left that position to accept the rank of Brigadier General and join the fighting. He led the Western Virginia and Cheat Mountain campaigns and in December 1861 was promoted to Major General commanding Georgia troops in defense of Savannah. It was during this time that he purchased a stately brick home on the corner of Bull and Gaston streets, formerly owned by the British Consul Edmund Molyneux.

In 1863, he joined the ill fated force at Atlanta opposing General William T. Sherman. After the devastating defeat, General Henry Jackson accompanied General Hood to Tennessee. Jackson and what was left of his division was captured at Nashville. He would remain imprisoned there until the end of war. While Jackson was in Tennessee fighting for the Confederacy, his home in Savannah became the Union Army Headquarters for General O. O. Howard. The Jackson family petitioned the victorious Union for years after the war to recover household furnishings taken during the Union occupation to no avail.

At the conclusion of the Civil War, Jackson resumed his law practice, served as Minister to Mexico, President of the Georgia Historical Society, a railroad executive and later a banker. Henry Rootes Jackson died in 1898 and was buried at Bonaventure Cemetery in Savannah.

Today, the Jackson House is home to Savannah's most exclusive private men's group, the Oglethorpe Club. Established in 1875, the Oglethorpe Club counts among its membership the leading citizens of Savannah.

Henry Rootes Jackson, distinguished public servant, accomplished soldier and barrister, will be noted in history, not for his political prowess, but for a more sentimental ideal. Henry Rootes Jackson was an accomplished poet. His expression of emotion was possibly the most noted in his day. The following stanza reveals his heart during the Confederate battles of the Civil War:

"Whatever fate those forms may throw,
Loved with a passion almost wild -
By day, by night - in joy or woe -
By fears oppressed or hopes beguiled -
For every danger, every foe
Oh! God! protect my wife and child!"

HENRY ROOTES JACKSON

**ARMSTRONG
JUNIOR COLLEGE**

Armstrong Junior College was founded on this site May 24, 1935 by the City of Savannah under the guidance of Mayor Thomas Gamble. The college was named for George Ferguson Armstrong (1868-1924), a native of Guyton, Georgia, who had this house constructed as his residence. Armstrong was nationally recognized for his maritime ingenuity at Strachan Shipping Company. He held membership in the Cotton Exchange and the Oglethorpe Club. He was a member of the First Baptist Church and was respected for his civic dedication and philanthropy. to honor him, Lucy Camp Armstrong Moltz and her daughter Lucy Armstrong Johnson gave Armstrong House to the City of Savannah.
This granite and glazed-brick, Italian Renaissance mansion was designed by architect Henrik Wallin and built 1916-1919. Olaf Otto was general contractor. Classes began in September, 1935 with 175 students in what The Atlanta Constitution called "the finest and most costly junior college in the United States."In 1959 Armstrong College became a part of the University System of Georgia and was designated a four-year institution in 1964. Two years later Armstrong State College moved to a new campus in south side Savannah. Historic Savannah Foundation preserved the property. The mansion was acquired in 1970 by members of the law firm of Bouhan, Williams & Levy.

**Bull and Gaston Streets, Savannah
GPS Coordinates: N32.07044, W81.09535**

Savannah's mayor, Thomas Gamble, conceived the idea for a city funded junior college in the spring of 1935. Mayor Gamble gained the support of the city aldermen and plans began to take shape. Interest in the project grew, the next step was to find a home for the fledgling institution. On May 27, the problem was resolved with the announcement of a significant donation from the estate of Savannah shipping magnet, George Ferguson Armstrong. Armstrong's widow and daughter made a presentation of the family home to the city of Savannah for use as the junior college. In honor of the generous gift, the college was named Armstrong Junior College.

Noted architect Henrik Wallin built the magnificent Italian Renaissance mansion, constructed of gray brick ,during the years of 1916 through 1919. The prominent historical district mansion was located at the head of Bull Street between Forsyth Park and Monterey Square. The imposing estate would be home for the junior college over the next thirty years and over time would see eight additional buildings constructed in the prestigious neighborhood.

Classes began in the fall of 1935, with 168 students and eight faculty members. The first president of the college was Ernest A. Lowe, formerly connected with the University of Georgia. Although the college was supported by the city, the University System offered counsel on curricular concerns. Ernest Lowe continued his tenure as President through 1941 and was briefly followed by Thomas Askew, who was called to military service. Foreman J. Hawes became the third president of Armstrong Junior College and remained so until his retirement in 1963.

The first commencement exercises were held in June 1937. Seventy-eight graduates received their two year degrees in various majors. The college had emphasized the two year liberal arts course of study from the beginning, however, the professional needs of Savannah demanded the addition of business courses and the initial classroom requirements of nurses for Savannah hospitals.

The city of Savannah found the financial constraints of supporting the junior college increasingly difficult and by the late 1950s, it became very evident that state funds were needed to continue college operations. Negotiations began with the University of Georgia in 1957 and Armstrong Junior College became part of the University System of Georgia in 1959. Armstrong was a city supported institution for twenty four years; the change would open the door for growth of the struggling college.

The 1960s brought tremendous change; in 1963, Otis Johnson became the first African American student to enroll. Johnson transferred from Savannah State College as a sophomore and graduated from Armstrong with the class of 1964. The increased student population spurred plans to expand the campus, another generous donation from a Savannah citizen, Mills B. Lane, Jr. a Savannah banker, made it possible. Two hundred and fifty acres on the southern outskirts of Savannah was purchased for the establishment of the new campus. The University Board of Regents approved the conversion of the college to a four year institution and the campus occupied the new residence in January 1966. The first four year degree class of 117 students graduated in June 1968.

The new four year institution status required a change of name to Armstrong State College. Under the direction of Henry Ashmore, the new President, Armstrong State would significantly expand its educational programs. The college offered degrees in dental hygiene and nursing, teacher education, and by 1971, would offer a Masters degree in Education, as well as a Bachelor of Business Administration. The faculty expanded to host numerous professors having Ph.D. credentials.

The civil rights movement in 1971, led to a program merger between Armstrong State and Savannah State College. As a result enrollment in both institutions suffered, over the next decade the idea of complete merger between the two colleges remained a prospect.

A movement began in 1996 by the Board of Regents, that all four year institutions would be considered "universities," leading to a name change, the second in Armstrong's history. This name change was to reflect the regional identification of the college. The suggestion met with vehement protest from college alumni and Savannah citizens against eliminating the Armstrong name. Armstrong Atlantic State University was the resulting compromise, although to this day, this college is still known as simply, Armstrong.

The changes since 1935 have been amazing. Today, Armstrong consists of a two hundred fifty acre campus with new facilities such as the Sports Center and University Hall, an eighty-five thousand square foot classroom and office building facility. Future construction is planned in the form of a $23 million ultra modern facility that will house Science Hall. The enrollment today numbers fifty-seven hundred with two hundred and fifty full time educators. A compass, the insignia adopted with the change to University status and new name as Armstrong Atlantic State University, signifies the bold course navigated toward a bright future.

Armstrong Junior College

MASSIE COMMON SCHOOL HOUSE
Savannah's Cradle of Public Education

Massie School is the only remaining building of Georgia's oldest chartered public school system. Constructed in 1855-56 and opened for classes on October 15, 1856, the Greek Revival building is listed on the National Register of Historic Places.

Peter Massie, a Scottish planter in Glynn County, Georgia. in 1841 bequeathed $5,000 "for the education of the poor children of Savannah." This donation was invested "until a large enough sum could be accumulated to build a school."

In 1855, the City retained John S. Norris to design and build Massie School. The center portion costing $9,000 is the original structure. The west wing was built in 1872 from plans by John B. Hogg, and in 1886 the east wing was erected.

The building was used briefly as a hospital by federal troops after Sherman's occupation of Savannah in December, 1864. Beginning May 1, 1865, it was operated for a few months as a school for the Freedmen, with teachers from the American Missionary Association.

Massie School became a unit of the Savannah-Chatham County Board of Public Education when that body was established in 1866. It was closed to regular classes in June 1874, having educated Savannahians for 118 years.

Calhoun Square, Abercorn and Wayne Streets, Savannah
GPS Coordinates: N32.0707, W81.092314

The Georgia State Legislature voted to create a system of public education starting with the appointment of a school commissioner in each county in 1837 and 1838. Georgia failed to provide any funding to support the state's proposal and the legislation failed. The State Legislature did manage to establish governing bodies for Savannah's public education system by establishing the Chatham County School Commissioners.

In 1851 the Justices of the Inferior Courts, acting as the County School Commissioners, decided to collect funds from the public and invest $10,000 of it in the construction of Georgia's first public school. Meanwhile, the city of Savannah planned to construct a public school using a bequeath of Peter Massie, a local plantation owner and planter. Peter Massie had willed $5,000 to be used for the purpose of educating Savannah's poor children. Savannah invested the monies in stocks of the Central Georgia Railroad and Banking and Savannah Gas Light Companies, the initial investment grew to $11,000. On March 3, 1852 at the Independent Presbyterian Church, Savannah citizens, the Justices of the Inferior Court and the Savannah City Council met and decided to merge their two funds. It was decided that two schools should be built, one on either side of Bull Street. Three school commissioners were appointed and plans for the schools were set. The schools were to follow the following guidelines:

> The buildings were to be built sixty by forty feet in outer dimensions and two stories high. Each story was to be divided into equal apartments capable of conversion into one room by means of folding doors and each apartment on both stories was equipped to accommodate fifty to sixty students. Each building was to have a suitable anteroom or foyer for entrance and storage of outer garments not worn in school. Each school was to have suitable yard rooms or gymnasium which were to be well enclosed. The yard rooms were to be outfitted with proper equipment for health and exercise. Both building were to be constructed of brick and fireproof.

The School Commissioner's mandate for construction was based on the ideas of Joseph Lancaster, an English educator, who supported the theory that teachers should address the student body as a whole and individual instruction should be among the more accomplished pupils, creating a reduced need for multiple teachers or assistants. This thrifty approach proved to be a economically viable option for providing public education to the children of the working class.

The first building was dedicated on February 6, 1855 and was simply known as the Barnard Street Public School because of its location at the corner of Barnard and Taylor streets. The construction, according to the School Commissioner's mandate, cost $7200 and was said to have been designed by well known Savannah architect, John Norris.

The Massie Common School, named for its benefactor Peter Massie, was slightly larger. The school, completed in 1856, was also designed by John Norris. The building rose to a gabled roof featuring open rafters supported by twelve to eighteen foot walls. The finishing was plaster applied over brick.

Children whose parents could not afford a private tutor were consider poor and were educated within the home. Male children were taught the basics of reading, simple equations and the facts of the Bible; girls were taught to cook, sew and tend a family. The Massie Common School offered much more in the way of public education than had ever been offered before, not only were they concerned with the standard educational requirements but introduced the sciences, physical education and also incorporated American and Western Civilization histories. The curriculum placed an emphasis on maintaining a healthy environment for learning and the importance of the child's physical development.

During the Civil War years, Georgia's government was in shambles, all public education was halted. An immediate effect of the Union occupation of Savannah was General Sherman's Order Number 29, which established a Board of Education. The board was comprised of eight persons, including the Mayor and Superintendent of Public Schools J. F. Cann, who was appointed for a two year term by Brevet Major General C. Grover.

After the Civil War, William Henry Baker, a Confederate soldier and graduate of Oglethorpe University was appointed Superintendent. During the twenty-eight years of Baker's administration, the Barnard Street Public School had a third story and two wings added, while the Massie Common School had two additional buildings constructed in 1872 and 1886, each accessible from the central structure and designed to match the original schoolhouse. The Massie Common School was closed in 1974, though the property remained a part of the Savannah, Chatham County Public School system.

Massie Common is today a resource center of living history, offering permanent exhibits of Savannah's City Plan, *Savannah in the Victorian Era* and *Elements of Greek, Roman, and Gothic Architecture*. The school is honored as Georgia's oldest school in continuous operation.

The Massie Heritage Interpretation Center is also the only remaining original building from Georgia's oldest chartered school. The Greek Revival structure is listed on the National Register of Historic Places and the facility provides an enrichment program, which is offered to increase students understanding of Savannah's historic and architectural heritage. The Heritage Center delivers system wide cultural diversity programs that are interdisciplinary in grades kindergarten through twelfth. The programs provide enrichment activities designed to enhance those of Savannah public school curriculum. Community studies, local urban environment and historic preservation receive special attention. In addition, emphasis is placed on providing experience, which enhances the understanding of Chatham County's cultural diversity. The center is open to the public from 9 a.m. until 4 p.m., Monday through Friday. Admission to the facility is free, but a donation is appreciated.

CASIMIR PULASKI

The great Polish patriot to whose memory this monument is erected was mortally wounded approximately one-half mile north west of this spot during the assault by the French and American forces on the British lines around Savannah, October 9, 1779. General Pulaski was struck by a grapeshot as he rode forward with customary ardor, from where his cavalry was stationed to rally the disorganized allied columns. The fatal ball which was removed from his thigh by Dr. James Lynch of South Carolina is in possession of the Georgia Historical Society at Savannah. Doubt and uncertainty exists as to where Pulaski died and as to his burial place. A contemporary Charlestown, S.C. newspaper item and other sources indicate that he died aboard a ship bound for that port. It was generally believed that he was buried at sea.

A tradition persisted, however, that General Pulaski died at Greenwich Plantation near Savannah and that he is buried there. When the monument here was under erection the grave at Greenwidh was opened. The remains found there conformed, in the opinion of the physicians, to a man of Pulaski's age and stature and were re-interred beneath this memorial in a metallic case in 1854.

Monterey Square, Bull and Wayne Streets, Savannah
GPS Coordinates: N32.07172, W81.094653

Casimir Pulaski was born in Warka, Poland on March 4, 1747. Pulaski's wealthy family educated him in the means consistent with those of his station. He learned numerous languages and manners be fitting a future count. Count Joseph Pulaski, Duke of Courland and Casimir's father, was among those opposing Russian interference in Poland. When Casimir was fifteen, he joined his father in the struggle. Casimir received his introduction to the horrors of war at the Confederation of Bar in 1768 and upon the death of his father, one year later, he became the leader of the military command. His crowning moment involved taking and holding Jasna Gora, the holiest place in all of Poland. Casimir's name was known throughout Europe; a short time later, he was implicated in a plot to assassinate the King of Poland and was forced into exile.

Count Casimir Pulaski's death was called for in Russia and his own homeland of Poland. He traveled to Paris in order to escape, meeting the very charismatic Benjamin Franklin. Franklin convinced Pulaski to join the American forces against England. Impressed with the ideals of the young colonies struggling against oppression, Pulaski volunteered. Franklin quickly penned a note addressed to George Washington extolling Pulaski's virtues.

Pulaski sailed to Philadelphia, in 1777, where he met General George Washington. He joined Washington's army at Brandywine and quickly proved himself to be a tremendous asset as military tactician. Pulaski discovered the British flanking Washington's army while scouting. Finding an escape route, he led the cavalry on a daring charge that allowed Washington's army to escape without a single casualty. Congress awarded Pulaski the rank of Brigadier General and named him Commander of Four Horse Brigades. Pulaski continued to distinguish himself at Germantown and Valley Forge.

In 1778, at Washington's insistence, Congress approved the establishment of the American Cavalry and named Pulaski its Commander. The Father of the American Cavalry was a strict taskmaster and demanded much of his men. He spent the winter months training and testing his men in cavalry tactics, using his personal finances when money from Congress was scarce in order to ensure his men had the finest supplies and safety equipment available.

By March, the rumblings of jealous officers grew loud. Pulaski refused to rise to their intrigues and requested that Washington approve the formation of an Independent Corp of Cavalry and Light Infantry made up of foreign volunteers; Washington agreed. Pulaski's Independent Corp of Cavalry became the training ground for all American cavalry officers. "Light Horse" Harry Lee, father of Robert E. Lee, was one of the officers trained under Pulaski as well as thirteen Polish officers serving in his legion.

In September 1779, Pulaski was instructed to assist in a joint operation with the French to recapture the city of Savannah. Against Pulaski's advice, the French commander ordered an assault at the strongest point of the British lines. Pulaski watching his troops falter from the onslaught of Red Coats, gallantly galloped forward to rally his men. Riding forward into battle, Pulaski was thrown from his horse and with a tremendous impact he fell to ground bleeding and obviously mortally wounded by a blast of grapeshot. The British had such respect for the General, they allowed him to be carried from the battlefield. Dr. James Lynch removed the fatal ball but to no avail. General Casimir Pulaski died two days later.

Pulaski is remembered brandishing a raised sword and responding to the trumpet's call to charge, thundering across the battlefield upon his trusted mount. The "Father of the American Cavalry" is an American Revolutionary hero.

PULASKI MONUMENT

The monument erected in this Square to the memory of General Casimir Pulaski, who fell at Savannah in the cause of American Independence, was completed in 1854. The corner stone was laid with impressive ceremonies, October 11, 1853. The 74th Anniversary of the traditional date of the death of the famous Polish patriot.

Dr. Richard D. Arnold was Chairman of the Commissioners in charge of the erection of the memorial for which $20,000 was collected by public subscription.

The designer of the monument, which is of Italian marble was the eminent Russian born sculptor, Robert E. Launitz of New York. At the conclusion of his explanation of the elaborate design and its symbolism Mr. Launitz stated:

"The monument is surrounded by a statue of Liberty embracing with her left arm the banner of the Stars and Stripes while in her right hand is extended the laurel wreath. The love of liberty brought Pulaski to America, for love of liberty he fought and for liberty he lost his life. Thus I thought that Liberty should crown his monument and share with him the homage of the free."

Monterey Square, Bull and Wayne Streets, Savannah
GPS Coordinates: N32.07172, W81.094653

A towering fifty-five feet, the Pulaski Monument stands majestically at the center of historic Monterey Square in Savannah. The architectural design of Robert Launitz, constructed of Italian Carrera marble, pays tribute to the memory of General Casimir Pulaski, the Polish patriot who sacrificed his life for American Independence.

General LaFayette, during his tour of the United States in 1825, laid the initial cornerstone marker for the monument. Financing began through the efforts of the Savannah Lottery Commission and funds were raised to begin construction of the monument in 1852. With great pomp and celebration the Pulaski Monument was placed on October 11, 1853. William Bowen delivered a stirring tribute to Pulaski that recognized his tremendous contributions, including his ultimate sacrifice.

Inside the cornerstone was a copper box used as a time capsule, the first in Georgia's history. George White, in his *Historical Collections of Georgia* published in 1855, stated that the box contained over one hundred items, including: Bank of Savannah notes in denominations of five, ten, twenty, fifty and one hundred dollars; engraved likenesses of Generals George Washington, Benjamin Lincoln and Robert Morris, Esquire, presented by I. K. Tefft; a medallion representing the Crystal Palace of New York, presented by W. A. Richmond; a piece of the oak tree from Sunbury, Liberty County, Georgia, under which General James Oglethorpe opened the first Lodge of Free Masons in Georgia; two Roman coins of the days of Constantine, Emperor of Rome, presented by Benjamin Arnold.

During the October 11, 1853 ceremony, Pulaski Monument architect Robert Launitz described his design and purpose, saying in part,

> "It is perceived at the first glance that the monument is intended for a soldier, who is losing his life fighting. Wounded, he falls from his horse, while still grasping his sword. The date of the event is recorded above the subject. The coat of arms of Poland and Georgia, surrounded by branches of laurel, ornament the cornice of two sides, or fronts; they stand united together; while the eagle, emblem of liberty, independence, and courage, rests on both, bidding proud defiance — the eagle being the symbolic bird of both Poland and America. The allegory will need no further explanation. The cannon reversed on the corners of the die, are emblematical of military loss and mourning, while they give the monument a strong military character."

The shaft of the statue was designed to have emblems of each state and territory with garlands and stars denoting that though they were young, the colonies would flourish. High atop the carving regally stands the Statue of Liberty holding her banner of stars and stripes. The monument as a whole represented, according to Launitz,

> "The love of liberty which brought Pulaski to America; for love of liberty, he fought; and for liberty he lost his life; - and thus I though that Liberty should crown his monument, and share with him the crown of victory."

Launitz estimated that the monument would take approximately two years for construction and delivery. The monument was completed a full six months ahead of schedule and ready for dedication in December 1853. The total cost was seventeen thousand dollars.

The monument now belongs to the City of Savannah and is managed by the Park and Tree Commission. It became apparent in the early 1990s that a problem existed as stones began to break loose from the structure and crash to the ground. The Monument was rapidly deteriorating and had become a safety hazard to those standing below the picturesque statue. A safety net was placed around the monument to catch falling debris, pending the much needed repairs. While examining the monument numerous surface cracks were observed and in 1995, Savannah allocated $100,000 toward its restoration. A study determined that nothing could be done with the statue still intact. The Pulaski Monument, revered centerpiece of Monterey Square, was disassembled in September 1996.

Problems began to raise their ugly heads from the beginning and costs continued to soar. The cost of repair was now topping $500,000 and only $265,000 had been raised. As the statue was taken apart, technicians realized that the Carrara marble was not of the finest quality, although beautiful it tended to be coarse and finely grained, this meant that pollution, rain and the elements had easily deteriorated the stone over time. The stone was stressed because as it was chiseled, utilizing a hammer and wedge, the vibrations of the implements weakened the stone's structure. Some of the blocks were laying at angles, causing an unbalanced distribution of weight resulting in instability. The most shocking of revelations came when it was found that the column blocks and foundation of the monument were hollow.

Questions were raised concerning why the monument's construction was so vastly inferior that it was at the point of ruin. Many factors came into play; to begin with the design of the monument and the stone used in its construction were not the quality used for structures of this size. Secondly, Launitz ordinarily restricted his carvings to marble mantelpieces and funerary art, that is headstones, crypts and such items associated with memorial stones; Launitz did not have the technical skills required to undertake the expansive fifty-five foot monument. The Pulaski Monument, when disassembled, revealed the same construction techniques used to create a fireplace mantel. The final flaw existed with the construction material, Carrera marble is known to be more susceptible to cracking.

The careful disassembly of the monument was at best a delicate task for technicians. The workers had to elevate the corners of the stone, which further accentuated the unequal distribution of weight throughout the monument, further weakening the marble. They were forced to keep compression on the structure in order to hold the monument together, otherwise, the marble would have shattered beyond repair. After disassembly was completed, the stones were stored at the Historic Railroad Shops on West Harris Street.

Further intensive examination revealed, that by sending a pulse of sound through the stone, the cracks went all the way through the marble. The Statue of Lady Liberty that graced the top of the monument was judged too brittle to be repaired. It was removed and donated to the Savannah History Museum. A replica of the statue was created by General Porcelain of New Jersey.

Another startling manifestation was discovered in the base of the monument, a vessel containing human remains. The remains were thought to be General Pulaski. The find was predicted by numerous historians; however, no proof existed that this was actually Pulaski. Legend has it that in 1853, Colonel William B. Bowen, owner of Greenwich Plantation, took three physicians to the supposed burial site of General Pulaski; a skeleton, believed to be that of Pulaski, was exhumed and placed in a metal box to be placed within the monument.

Ironically, during this time, a temporary monument was put in place by the strangest of sources, Hollywood. The movie version of *Midnight in the Garden of Good and Evil* was slated for production in Savannah. A portion of the scenes were to take place using Monterey Square as a location and the Pulaski Monument as a backdrop. When the movie was completed the stand in monument was removed.

The rededication and reinterment was originally scheduled for October 1999. Cost over runs and reassembly complications postponed the ceremony until 2000. The price tag now topped $865,000, more than fifty times the original construction cost in 1853. Savannah, her citizens, private benefactors, the Polish Legion of American Veterans, the Polish American Congress and numerous others raised the funds making the restoration of Pulaski Monument possible.

The mystery of General Pulaski's final resting place remains unresolved. It is a fact that Pulaski died on October 11, 1799, what happened after that is questionable. Various reports say he died at Greenwich Plantation and was buried there. Others say he died aboard a ship and was buried at sea. In 1834, the grave site at Greenwich was exhumed and professionals agreed that the corpse was consistent with that of Casimir Pulaski. Determining that those remains were the famed Cavalry General, they were encased in a strong box and placed underneath the Pulaski Monument. Speculation remains as to whether or not those were truly the remains of General Casimir Pulaski.

In September 1998, a private Pulaski Monument benefactor, Edward Pinkowski, and a group of Savannah researchers traveled to Promna, Poland, for the exhumation of the grave of Teressa Witkowska nee Brochocka, a grandniece of General Pulaski's. Her DNA was compared with that taken from the bones found interred in the monument at Savannah. Not enough DNA could be removed to provide conclusively that the remains are Pulaski's. Dr. Andrez Sikorski, a university professor in Warsaw, Poland, assisted local officials in tracking down the genetic trail. Sikorski's lab has made five unequivocal matches, but there has yet to be enough material to scientifically confirm Pulaski's identity.

The remains were studied by forensic anthropologist Dr. Karen Burns at the University of North Carolina. When viewing a portrait of Pulaski in Poland, she stated that the wide set eyes in the portrait were a match for the occipital holes in the disinterred skull. Although the clues seemed to be very strong, including the man's height and age at death, thirty-three years; the skeleton showed signs of a right hand that had been broken and healed, an old wound on the skull and a fused tailbone; all of these are in keeping with injuries Pulaski was known to have endured. Authenticity can only be determined though genetic research. A genetic match must be made with DNA taken from the remains buried in the monument and from that of a Pulaski relative. Experts continue the search in Russia and Poland, targeting other possibilities, such as the remains of Pulaski's youngest brother, Antonia Pulaski.

Even though the mystery of General Casimir Pulaski's final resting place remains ambiguous, his life is one to be revered without question. Pulaski paid the ultimate price in the fight for American Liberty and for that reason, his monument stands proudly in Monterey Square.

Pulaski Monument

COMER HOUSE
JEFFERSON DAVIS

Jefferson Davis, former President of the Confederate States of America was a guest in 1886 in the house on the northeast corner of Bull and Taylor Streets. The residence (built about 1880) was at that time the home of Hugh M. Comer, President of the Central of Georgia Railway.
Accompanied by his daughter, Winnie Davis, "the Daughter of the Confederacy," Mr. Davis arrived in Savannah, May, 3, 1886. He was escorted from Atlanta by a committee of Savannahians consisting of Hugh M. Comer, J. H. Estill, J. K. Garnett, George A. Mercer, J. R. Saussy, and Gen. G. Moxley Sorrel. The trip to Savannah has been described as a "continuous ovation."
The occasion of the visit of Jefferson Davis was the celebration of the centennial of the Chatham Artillery, one of the oldest and most distinguished military units in the United States. During his stay in Savannah the former President of the Confederacy received tributes of respect and affection from the local citizenry, visiting military organizations as well as from the thousands of visitors who attended the centennial festivities.

Across from Monterey Square, Bull and Taylor Streets, Savannah
GPS Coordinates: N32.07172, W81.094653

Former Confederate President Jefferson Davis was a much sought after speaker in the South during the spring of 1886. Atlanta wanted Davis to unveil a statue to the late Benjamin H. Hill, who had been among one of his loyal friends and allies. Savannah begged Davis to speak at the unveiling of the Nathanael Greene monument, a tribute to his heroism during the Revolutionary War. All requests were accepted and the offer of luxurious railway accommodations was very much appreciated.

Davis and his twenty-one year old daughter, Winnie, left home on April 27th, accompanied by the mayor and other prominent citizens. Davis' eldest daughter, Maggie, her children and Davis' wife had intended to make the trip as well; unfortunately Maggie's young son was stricken with scarlet fever and they were forced to stay behind.

Thousands gathered along the tracks and converged around the train car. Signs heralding "Our Hero" were held aloft in Davis' view. The train was decked with red, white and blue banners, his likeness bore one side of the train, while the name "DAVIS" embossed the other. A pullman berth was provided for his comfort and inside the coach, silver baskets hung from the ceiling filled with fragrant blossoms.

Along the track, people gathered and at every station Davis spoke for a moment or two, appeasing the eager citizens. The group arrived in Atlanta to find 15,000 people were in attendance to greet them and by the next day another 35,000 anxious Southerners swelled the city. The *Atlanta Constitution* reported the following,

> "at no period in her previous history (had the city) had within her borders such a host. From a score of states, including those of the far North, the people have come to do honor to the revered Davis."

Davis completed his tribute to Benjamin Hill in Atlanta and was once again on his way. The trip was a constant salute to the Southern hero. Savannah was no different. The citizens there met Davis with all of the enthusiasm due a former President.

Davis was the guest of Hugh Moss Comer during his visit. Comer's home was located on Taylor Street adjacent to Monterey Square and will forever be known as the Comer House, where Jefferson Davis once slept. Crowds surrounded the residence during his stay and several times Davis spoke from the iron balcony. His stay was especially pleasant and his hosts treated him with the utmost respect and courtesy.

Davis was to make two speeches on May 6, 1886. The first to celebrate the one hundredth anniversary of the Chatham Artillery and the other in tribute to Nathanael Greene. His first speech went without incident, yet during the second oration Davis's southern pride got the better of him. Davis noted a feeling of tension in Savannah's native citizens to tread lightly amidst their northern victors who had chosen to live in Savannah. This did not sit well with Davis who had no intension of bowing to pretense. His speech carried with it a note of defiance saying:

> *In 1776, the colonies acquired State Sovereignty. They revolted from the mother country in a desperate struggle. That was the cause for which they fought. Is it a lost cause now? Never. . . . The independence of these States, the Constitution, liberty, State Sovereignty, which they won in 1776, and which Nathanael Greene, son of Rhode Island, helped to win for Georgia, can never die.*

The crowd cheered his words as if the South was ready to rise again. The excited crowd lunged forward eager to touch the former President's hand. As the crowd pressed, Davis was forced back least he be crushed by the mob, finally a path was cleared and he was escorted to his awaiting carriage.

Northern reporters flocked to the telegraph office to file the stories of Davis' defiance. Advisors cautioned Davis to temper his remarks. Davis knew full well that it angered the Northern born citizens for a comparison to be made between the American Revolution and the Civil War. That very night at a banquet in his honor Davis, with intent to humble himself, said,

> "There are some, who take it for granted that when I allude to State Sovereignty I want to bring on another war. I am too old to fight again, and God knows I do not want you to have the necessity of fighting again."

He paused, again Southern pride and a refusal to accept defeat rose in his throat, he continued with

> "However, if that necessity should arise, I know you will meet it as you always have discharged every duty you felt called upon to perform."

Humility was not a part of the defeated President's temperament. His attempt to soothe Northern egos failed and his triumphant tour ended on a note of unvanquished belief in the right of the South's cause. His words had hit their mark and Northern newspapers crucified him on their pages. Many newspapers amazingly professed admiration for Davis' steadfast beliefs and the devotion with which the Southern people stood beside their fallen hero. The *Lowell Massachusetts Sun* reported,

> *Jefferson Davis suddenly emerges from his long retirement, journeys among his people and everywhere receives the most overwhelming manifestation of heartfelt affection, devotion, and reverence. Such homage is significant, startling. And it is useless to attempt to deny, disguise, or evade the conclusion that there must be something great and noble and true in him and in the cause to evoke this homage.*

Jefferson Davis died in New Orleans on December 5, 1889. He was 81.

CONGREGATION MICKVE ISRAEL
(Founded 1733)

The oldest Congregation now practicing Reform Judaism in the United States. Mickve Israel was founded by a group of Jews, mainly of Spanish-Portuguese extraction, which landed in Savannah, July 11, 1733, five months after the establishment of the Colony of Georgia.

The Congregation was incorporated in perpetuity by a special Act of the Georgia Legislature on November 20, 1790. After having worshipped in various temporary quarters for almost a century, in 1820 the Congregation built its own Synagogue - the first in Georgia - at the Northeast corner of Liberty and Whitaker Streets. The present Synagogue was consecrated on April 11, 1878.

In 1789 the congregation received a letter from President Georgia Washington which stated in part: "May the same wonderworking Deity who long since delivering the Hebrews from their Egyptian oppressors, planted them in the promised land - whose providential agency has been conspicuous in establishing these United States as an independent nation - still continue to water them with the dews of Heaven and to make the inhabitants of every denomination participate in the temporal and spiritual blessings of that people whose God is Jehovah."

East of Monterey Square, Bull and East Taylor Streets, Savannah
GPS Coordinates: N32.07172, W81.094653

A s General James Edward Oglethorpe prepared to establish the British colony of Georgia, he was approached by several affluent members of the Jewish community with a proposal. They offered financial support to Oglethorpe, who in turn would sponsor other Jews allowing them to establish a congregation in the New World.

Forty-two members, by far the largest group of immigrant Jews to travel to the New World, would establish the Congregation *Mickve Israel*. The trip on board the *William and Sarah* from London was horrendous, the ship ran aground in northern Carolina, through it all the determined settlers remained intent on their destination. Georgia offered a new start and opportunities unavailable in England. The Congregation *Mickve Israel* arrived in Savannah on July 11, 1733, with Torah firmly in hand, only five months following General Oglethorpe's arrival.

Unlike other Jewish communities, the priority for the Savannah settlers was to gather their congregation, establish a cemetery and then build a *mickvah*[2]. The first act of the Jewish community after landing in Savannah was divine services. The service was easily initiated because a *minyan*[3] was already in place and the Torah Scroll[4] was readily available.

Services were initially held in the various homes of congregation members. In 1735, the first synagogue was rented at Market Square, *Kahal Kodesh Mickva Israel,* which means Holy Congregational Hope of Israel.

The Ashkenazic Jews were appalled at the fact that the Sephardic Jews did not strictly adhere to dietary laws and other Jewish ceremonies, causing strife between the two factions. The Minis and Sheftall families joined with the Spanish Portuguese Jews[5], although other Germanic families or Ashkenazic Jews arriving in Savannah refused this union. The small congregation began facing internal struggles.

By 1742, the Spanish threat to the Georgia colony increased. The Spanish were established at St. Augustine and it was obvious that they intended to take Georgia then move up the coast to Carolina. The Sephardic Jews began to flee the Georgia colony. To protect themselves during the Spanish inquisitions, the Sephardic Jews claimed to follow the Catholic religion while in secret had maintained their Jewish heritage. Unfortunately, to do this made them guilty of Apostasy. If captured by the Spanish, their sentence was death. On July 5, 1742, the Spanish attacked and the Battle of Bloody Marsh ensued. Of the Sephardic Jews in Savannah, only the Minis and Sheftall families remained. By the eve of the Revolutionary War in 1774, enough Jews had returned to Savannah to reestablish the Congregation *Mickve Israel*.

During the Revolutionary War, Mordecai Sheftall became the highest ranking Jewish officer of the American forces. He rose to the rank of Deputy Commissary General of the Continental Troops in Carolina and Georgia. Mordecai Sheftall and his son, Sheftall Sheftall, were captured by British forces and imprisoned at Antigua. Eventually they were released in exchange for two captured British officers.

At the conclusion of the Revolutionary War, seventy-three members returned to the congregation. Governor Edward Telfair granted a charter to the congregation on November 20, 1790, to be held forever. The congregation's financial status and ability to maintain a meeting place was less than consistent. Membership rose and ebbed with the shifting population, when the congregation dwindled, so did the finances.

The fate of the Jewish congregation turned in 1818 and the need for a permanent Synagogue was recognized. Dr. Moses Sheftall and Dr. Jacob De la Motta undertook the task and found that the congregation possessed a lot given by the city of Savannah as well as several small buildings, which were rented. After meeting with the congregation, a bargain was struck with a respectable city mechanic, he would build the synagogue in exchange for the use of the small buildings at no charge.

On the corner of Liberty and Whitaker Streets, the first synagogue in the state of Georgia was consecrated by Dr. Jacob De la Motta on July 21, 1820. The small wooden edifice, only stood for nine years, succumbing to fire in 1829. The original *Torah* predating 1733 was saved. A sanctuary of brick construction replaced the wooden structure on the same site and was consecrated in 1841. It wasn't until 1853 that the congregation could pay for a permanent rabbi, Rabbi Jacob Rosenfeld was the first, serving until 1862.

A great influx of German Jews into Savannah began around 1874 and the congregation required a larger space to serve the swelling membership. A story is told, related in Tom Coffey's *Only in Savannah*, to save on architect fees, the congregation borrowed the plans for the new synagogue from a member of the congregation of the huge Cathedral of St. John the Baptist located on LaFayette Square. The plans were scaled down to fit their lot and the intriguing story relates that the first Jewish house of worship in Savannah was built in the form of a cross. *Mickve Israel* records state that the Monterey Square sanctuary, consecrated on April 11, 1878, was designed by New York architect Henry G. Harrison in the neo-Gothic style of the Victorian era.

Gradual changes began as the Reform movement swept Jewish congregation throughout America during the mid 1800s. The congregation of *Mickve Israel* was slow to adapt, many still clinging to the Portuguese *minhag*[6]. The members took their first small steps toward Reform in 1868 by omitting the celebration of the second day of festivals and admitting a choir with instruments. The Reverend Isaac P. Mendes, who served as the congregation's rabbi for twenty-seven years, cautioned against acceptance of Reform too quickly. In 1880, the use of the canopy in wedding ceremonies became optional; and in 1894, members were allowed to remove their hats during services.

Mickve Israel produced their own prayer books in 1895 and in 1902, the Union Prayer Book was accepted for use. In January 1904, the Congregation *Mickve Israel* was admitted into the Union of American Hebrew Congregations, then after thirty-six years, the transformation to Reform Judaism was complete. The congregation still maintains the Sephardic *El Norah Ah Lee Lah* melody sung during the closing hour of each Yom Kippur service. The congregation continued to grow. In 1902, the Mordecai Sheftall Memorial Hall was dedicated and used for a religious school and meeting facilities. The facilities were enlarged again in 1954 to keep pace with its ever expanding membership.

Mickve Israel's Archival Museum houses ten presidential letters, including a George Washington letter and others from Thomas Jefferson, James Madison and more recently, Presidents George Bush and Bill Clinton. The Torah Scroll, brought to Savannah in 1733, occupies a special place there.

The Congregation *Mickve Israel* continues to grow and prosper. The membership looks upon their rich heritage with pride tempered in humility. The congregation's wish for the future is that they be permitted to continue to serve equally well "One God and One Humanity."

The Congregation *Mickve Israel*

SAVANNAH VOLUNTEER GUARDS
Organized 1802

As infantry the Corps fought in the War of 1812, Indian Wars and as a battalion in 1861, serving with distinction in defense of Savannah and Charleston. In the spring of 1864 joined Lee's Army at Petersburg. On April 3, 1865 serving in the rear guard on the retreat to Appomattox having been reduced to 85 men, 23 were killed, 35 wounded and remainder captured. Reorganized in 1872. Served as infantry battalion in the Spanish-American War, as a battalion of the 61 C.A.C. in WW-I, and as 118th F.A. Battalion in WW-II where they were awarded 5 Battle Stars. Reorganized after WW-II and is now an active unit in the Georgia National Guard. This armory erected in 1892.

Near Madison Square at SCAD, Bull Street, Savannah
GPS Coordinates: N32.07316, W81.094031

The Savannah Volunteer Guards, like all other civilian militia units throughout Georgia history, can trace its roots to the first group of soldiers to set foot on Georgia soil accompanying General James Edward Oglethorpe. The Savannah Volunteer Guard separated from the original group, rather than become a part of the organized Army, becoming an independent unit in 1802. Men from this unit or reorganizations of this unit have fought in every American altercation since that date, under different names. It would be impossible to detail every battle they were involved in; this one was chosen because it was the last battle of the Civil War involving the Savannah Volunteer Guards and the last time the unit stepped into battle under the revered name of the Savannah Volunteer Guards.

The Savannah Volunteer Guards Battalion fought its last battle of the Civil War at Sailor's Creek. The Guards were known by the Confederate army as the 18th Battalion of Georgia Volunteers. They were commanded by the gallant Major William Starr Basinger, a distinguished lawyer and citizen of Savannah, who was later promoted to Colonel.

The battle of Sailor's Creek was one of the several battles, which took place after General Lee evacuated Petersburg and just before the surrender of the Confederate Army at Appomattox Courthouse. The Confederate Army was worn down and starving, bravely trying to make its way through the Union defenses of General Grant. The Guard was trapped in the attempt, every officer and man was either killed, wounded or captured.

When Lee evacuated Petersburg on the night of April 2nd, the Guards marched out with the rest of the army. It was an all night march and through the next day, then with only a few hours' rest, the march resumed before dawn. The march continued until April 6th, when Lee's retreating Confederate army was brought to task at Sailor's Creek. The army was trapped, but the men did not know it. They were fording Sailor's Creek, the color bearer in the middle carrying the staff inclined upon his shoulder, when a bullet split the staff, the ball lodged in the crack. The bullet was delivered from the front and the men saw that they were surrounded. The brigade was halted a few hundred yards from the creek, about half way up the slope of a long incline, the line formed and the Guards assumed a position on the extreme right of the line.

Eighty-five members of the Savannah Volunteer Guard went into battle that day at Sailor's Creek; thirty were killed, twenty-two were wounded and the rest were sent to northern prisoner of war camps. Every officer, save one, was killed or wounded. The year following, 1866, the bodies of the eighteen of the Guards who fell at Sailor's Creek were recovered from mass graves and returned to Savannah. Only seven of those could be identified. They were buried in the private lots. The remaining eleven were interred in the lot of the Guards at Laurel Grove Cemetery.

After the Civil War, the Savannah Volunteer Guards was disbanded. In 1872, they were again called to serve in the Spanish American War and again in World Wars I and II. The Guard eventually became a part of the Georgia National Guard and has bravely served each and every time their country has called them to duty.

POETTER HALL

Paula and Richard Rowan, along with May and Paul Poetter, founded the Savannah College of Art and Design in 1978. In March 1979, the college purchased it first building, this former Savannah Volunteer Guard Armory, built in 1892. The college named the building Preston Hall after its architect, William Gibbons Preston, and it has become the flagship building of an expanding campus throughout the Historic and Victorian districts of Savannah. The college's restoration, rehabilitation and adaptive reuse of this and numerous other historically significant structures have been recognized by the Historic Savannah Foundation, and the Georgia Trust for Historic Preservation. Preston Hall was renamed Poetter Hall to honor the invaluable contributions of May Poetter, who served as Vice President for Admission, and Paul Poetter, who served as Comptroller, from 1978 to 1997 when both were elected to the Board of Trustees.

Near Madison Square at SCAD, Bull Street, Savannah
GPS Coordinates: N32.07316, W81.094031

The Poetters retired, had built their dream house near Atlanta and planned a garden when their oldest daughter and son in law enlisted their services. May Poetter had worked as an Atlanta Public School teacher, English department supervisor and had written two textbooks for Houghton Mifflin Company. Paul was a research analyst working for the United States Bureau of Labor Statistics.

Paula and Richard Rowan, the Poetter's daughter and son in law, decided to open a four year school of art and design in 1978. The Poetters agreed to take some time from their well earned retirement to help get the school up and running. Little did they know that new careers were on the horizon. Getting started was more complicated than finding a place and holding classes.

Paula and May began working on the curriculum and concentrating on the educational aspects of the school. Meanwhile, Richard and Paul had their work cut out for them. They obtained the old Savannah Volunteer Guard Armory built in 1892 for the school, but before class could convene, restorations were required; painting, sanding, glazing and scraping consumed hour upon hour. During this time, Paul handled the funding and May began assisting Paula with recruiting the faculty and students.

The college began its first academic year with great success. On September 25, 1979, the Savannah College for Art and Design (SCAD) opened its doors. Seventy-one students in eight majors and eight faculty made up the full compliment of the school with May and Paul handling the administrative duties; Paula and Richard assumed leadership roles with the support of four staff members.

May and Paul lent credibility and stability to the school, considering that Paula and Richard were still in their twenties when the school first opened. May descends from a breed of 'Steel Magnolias' renowned in the South for a steel backbone encased in genuine warmth and graciousness. Meanwhile, Paul always had a ready smile and a word of encouragement for everyone: make no mistake, behind their impeccable manners and soft Southern accents lies an enormous capacity for hard work and the willingness to apply it to the cause of education and artistic vision that SCAD embodies.

They decided to end their tenures as Vice President of Admission and Comptroller, respectively, in 1998, but they are as busy as ever. May continues as a consultant to the admission department and both were elected to the college's board of trustees.

The Poetters were honored in 1998 with a painting of SCAD's flagship building, the old Savannah Volunteer Guard Armory, called Preston Hall. The painting was the work of SCAD Professor Sandra Reed and the building was formally renamed Poetter Hall. A portrait of the Poetters was done and presented to the couple by Professor JoAnn Eason, one of SCAD's first faculty members. The painting hangs in a place of honor in Poetter Hall.

Today, the Savannah College of Art and Design has grown to an enrollment of nearly 4,000 students, from eighty-four countries and all fifty states in seventeen different majors. The faculty and staff number close to five hundred. The physical facilities have grown to number forty-eight buildings, spread throughout Savannah's historic and Victorian districts.

MADISON SQUARE

Madison Square was laid out in 1839 and is named for the fourth president of the United States. Around the Square stand notable examples of the Greek revival, Gothic, and Romanesque architecture characteristic of nineteenth century Savannah.

To the west are St. John's Church (Episcopal), 1853, and the Green-Meldrim mansion, 1861, (Gen. W. T. Sherman's headquarters). To the north is the Francis Sorrel residence, 1840, which was visited by Robert E. Lee in 1862 when he commanded the Confederate coast defenses in this area. To the east is the Jewett house, erected 1842. The DeSoto Hotel and the Savannah Volunteer Guards' Armory, of a later period, are in the Romanesque style typical of their designer, William G. Preston, of Boston.

The central bronze monument commemorates the heroism of Sergeant William Jasper (2nd Continental Regt. of South Carolina) who was mortally wounded October 9, 1779, a short distance northwest of this marker, in the unsuccessful assault by the American and French forces upon the British lines, which ran immediately to the north of this Square.

Bull and Macon Streets, Savannah
GPS Coordinates: N32.07172, W81.094653

Madison Square was not one of General James Edward Oglethorpe's original squares. This square was laid out in 1839 and named in honor of the fourth President of the United States, James Madison. Featured at the center of the picturesque square is a statue of Sergeant William Jasper, a brave Revolutionary War hero who gave his life in 1779 during the Siege of Savannah. A granite marker on Madison Square was placed at the site of the lines of defense against the British during the Siege of Savannah. Commemorating Georgia's first two official highways are cannons to the south of Sergeant Jasper's monument.

Taking a stroll around the square beginning at its northwest corner you will find the Sorrel-Weed House, completed in 1841 and renovated in 1997 bringing back its original splendor. The southeastern rim of the square is shadowed by a huge red brick building that was once the Savannah Volunteer Guards Armory and presently houses the prestigious Savannah College of Art and Design. Across the street is the impressive Scottish Rite Temple also owned by the college. St. John's Church and Parish House adorn the western side of the square. St. John's, designed in the Gothic Revival style, was completed in 1853. The breathtaking stained glass windows relating the life of Christ are awe inspiring. The chimes, sounding on the hour, are truly melodious as the distinctive ring travels on a breeze for blocks around the sanctuary. The Parish House was originally known as the Green-Meldrim House and is noted as the captured headquarters of General William Tecumseh Sherman, marking the end of his March to the Sea.

Madison Square has also had its notable moments. It was there that *Midnight in the Garden of Good and Evil* author, John Berendt, met William Simon Glover the 86 year old porter who was paid to walk a dog that had been dead for over twenty years. The scene was eventually used in the film adaptation of the famous book. Another well known movie used Madison Square as a backdrop for filming several scenes, the movie *The General's Daughter*, filmed for about five weeks in the city of Savannah and Madison Square was the site of a pivotal segment between actors, John Travolta and John Benjamin Hickey.

Be it historical significance, architectural delight, general curiosity, Hollywood glitter or a moment of respite in beautiful surroundings, Madison Square has it all.

**Madison Square, Bull and Macon Streets, Savannah
GPS Coordinates: N32.07367, W81.094406**

It is believed that the Scottish Rite Masonry existed in Savannah as early as 1790 as a loosely organized group. The Ancient and Accepted Scottish Rites were first recognized as an established fraternity in the American colonies in Charles Towne, South Carolina in the early 1800s.

The Scottish Rite of Freemasonry is the educational organization of the Masons. It is comprised of twenty-nine degrees, which includes instruction in the history and lessons of the noble Fraternity, expanding the memberships' knowledge of history, legends, traditions and moral lessons. The Endeavors of the Rite are designed to build upon the initial lessons, while concentrating on individual worth, family values, patriotism and charities benefitting children. Perhaps the most recognized Scottish Rite charity is the Scottish Rite Children's Hospital, that was recently changed to the Children's Healthcare of Atlanta as a result of a merger with Egleston Children's Hospital. While the Scottish Rite never owned the facility, it has been maintained by the Fraternity since 1915. The merger allows the hospital to serve more children with less overhead costs without duplicating the services between the two independently run facilities.

More than 360,000 children received hospital services during the year 2000 and over $100 million in services were provided without reimbursement. No child is ever turned away, regardless of their ability to pay. Services include treatment of illnesses, trauma, birth defects and organ transplants without limitations. A child in need will be cared for, regardless of the situation presented.

There is also the National Scottish Rite Children's Learning Disability Clinics with twelve facilities in Georgia. These facilities assist children with visual, hearing and learning disabilities. Support for these clinics is obtained through the Georgia Chapters and the Supreme Council Fund of the Scottish Rite Foundation of Georgia. The foundation provides scholarships each year for deserving Georgia students who wish to continue their education following high school. One hundred scholarships were awarded last year to youth throughout the state.

The Scottish Rite services are so varied from Masonic education within the fraternity, to community service and charity that the Rite is not divided into local lodges, but rather, Valleys. Georgia is organized into six Valleys: Albany, Atlanta, Augusta, Columbus, Macon and Savannah with over 15,000 Master Masons who participate in these associations. Each member is proud of the fine tradition and history of the organization that espouses beliefs of strong moral character, community service, family values, civic responsibility and a deep abiding faith in God.

SERGEANT JASPER

Sergeant William Jasper, the famed Revolutionary hero, was mortally wounded a few hundred yards northwest of this spot on October 9, 1779, in the ill-fated attack of the American and French forces on the British defenses around Savannah. The monument to Jasper in this Square was unveiled in 1888 with great ceremony.

The 15 ½ foot bronze statue of Jasper was designed by the distinguished sculptor, Alexander Doyle of New York. The sculptor has depicted the heroic Sergeant bearing the colors of the Second Regiment of South Carolina Continentals during the assault at Savannah. His right hand, in which he holds a sabre, is pressed tight against the bullet wound in his side. Jasper's bullet ridden hat lies at his feet. His face, as portrayed by the sculptor, reveals intense suffering and resolute purpose. The bas relief panels on the north, west and east sides of the monument represent the sculptor's conception of three episodes in Sergeant Jasper's Revolutionary career - the ramparts of Fort Sullivan near Charleston where Jasper, under heavy fire, bravely replaced the flag; the liberation of Patriot prisoners by Jasper and a companion at what is now called Jasper Spring near Savannah; and the dying hero's last moments after the attack of October 9, 1779.

Madison Square, Bull and Macon Streets, Savannah
GPS Coordinates: N32.07367, W81.094406

Sergeant William Jasper was truly a Revolutionary War hero. His patriotism was without question, his bravery remained intact even in the face of tremendous odds and his valor endless until death finally claimed his resolve. William Jasper was a man willing to give all to a cause he believed in.

The sculptor, Alexander Doyle, captured the essence that was Sergeant Jasper in the bronze statue that graces Madison Square in Savannah. The tribute captures Jasper as he defiantly protects one of the symbols of his patriotism, the flag of his regiment, the 2nd South Carolina Continentals.

Sergeant Jasper's first known act of patriotism took place on a scorching June day in 1776 on Sullivan's Island near Charleston. The hail of British musket fire rained down on Americans holding a small piece of ground called Fort Sullivan. All day long the citizens of Charleston watched the battle from roof tops far away. They saw very little fighting, yet the distinct blue flag continued to wave and Charleston knew that the Americans still held Fort Sullivan.

A crack was heard in response to a shot, the 2nd South Carolina saw their flag go down, her staff shattered by the enemy's fire. Shocked they looked toward their commander, Colonel Francis Marion saying "Colonel, don't let us fight without our flag!" Marion replied, "Nothing can be done." Jasper, in an instant, leapt from the safety of the fort and ran to the spot where the flag had fallen, with no fear in his heart he tied the flag to a staff and spiked it into the wall. Defiantly, he gave three cheers and returned to his gun. The British and Americans alike stared with mouths agape at the fortitude of Sergeant William Jasper.

For his show of patriotism on that day in June 1776, President Rutledge presented Jasper with a dress sword, taken from his own scabbard. Jasper was bestowed an officer's commission, which he respectfully declined. Sergeant William Jasper could neither read nor write, he felt that others could better serve in an officer's position. Instead he accepted a promotion to scout for the American forces, a position well suited for him. He made several trips into enemy lines, always returning with valuable information.

During the siege of Savannah, the Second Regiment was in the thick of the fighting. Sergeant Jasper proudly carried the Regimental Colors. When he fell, mortally wounded, he handed the flag to a Lieutenant Bush. The lieutenant was killed immediately and fell into the ditch at Spring Hill along side Sergeant Jasper, the colors wrapped about his body. The enemy took the line within minutes and stripped the flag from the body of Lieutenant Bush. The flag was later carried to London and there it remained in the trophy room of the King's Royal Rifles.

The final resting place of Sergeant William Jasper is not known. It is believed that his body along with others slain in this, one of the bloodiest battles of the Revolutionary War, was interred in a mass grave near the Spring Hill fortification.

The monument to his bravery, patriotism and valor was unveiled with all of the ceremony due this hero in 1888. Forevermore, Sergeant William Jasper will hold aloft the flag so dear to his heart.

Sargeant Jasper Memorial

OLD SORREL ~ WEED HOUSE

A fine example of Greek Revival style, this building (completed in 1840 from the plans of Charles B. Cluskey, a well-known Georgia architect) shows the distinguished trend of Savannah architecture during the first half of the 19th century. The Mediterranean villa influence reflects the French background of the original owner, Francis Sorrel (1793-1870), a shipping merchant of Savannah who as a child was saved by a faithful slave from the massacre of the white colonists in St. Domingo. The antebellum tradition of refinement and hospitality associated with the residence was continued after its purchase in 1859 by Henry D. Weed. Here resided as a youth G. Moxley Sorrel (1838-1901) who achieved fame as one of "Lee's Lieutenants." Shortly after war broke out in 1861 Sorrel, a young bank clerk in Savannah, proceeded to Virginia where he obtained a place on Gen. Longstreet's staff. He served with conspicuous valor and zeal through the major battles and campaigns in that theater from the First Manassas to Petersburg and was thrice wounded. Sorrel became brig. general at the age of 26. Competent critics have called him "the best staff officer in the Confederate service," Gen. Sorrel's "Recollections of a Confederate Staff Officer" is an absorbing account of his war experiences.

Across from Madison Square at Bull and Macon Streets, Savannah
GPS Coordinates: N32.07367, W81.094406

Among the first members of the Sorrel family to reach the American shores was Frenchman, Antoine Sorrel des Rivieres. He served the French Army on the island of St. Domingo and it was there that his son, Francis, almost lost his life. Francis was rescued from certain death during an uprising of the Africans against the country who had enslaved them, after witnessing the massacre of his relatives and friends. His father's property was seized or destroyed and Francis barely escaped to Cuba with his life. His only saving grace was a benevolent family slave, who shielded the boy with his own body, refusing to allow Francis to be sacrificed. The experiences forever shaped Francis Sorrel's thoughts and actions.

In time Francis married and, with his new bride, made a home in Savannah. He became a merchant and developed a very lucrative business. The famed Irish architect Charles Blaney Cluskey was hired to design an elegant dwelling for the Sorrel family to be built at number 6 West Harris Street in 1840.

Charles Cluskey's love of Greek Revival design motivated him to design the impressive structure. Accented with Doric columns, a sweeping double entrance and marble floors, the home was a showpiece even then. In deference to the hot and humid Savannah summers, Cluskey drew plans for the main floor so that all the rooms opened onto a shaded veranda which embraced the home. Eventually, Francis' wife passed away but it is said his business, children and a host of friends sustained him. Although it is known that Francis fathered a number of children, only one name continues into history, that of his son, Gilbert Moxley Sorrel.

Gilbert was born February 23, 1838, in Savannah. Before the Civil War, he worked as a clerk in the Central Railroad banking house. He joined the Georgia Hussars with the rank of private, but was so impatient to actively participate in the war effort, he left the unit after serving only thirty days travelling to Virginia. In order to seek a prestigious assignment, Gilbert secured a letter of introduction from a family friend and high ranking Confederate officer, Colonel Thomas Jordon, who was Adjutant for Brigadier General Pierre Gustave Toutant Beaureguard. Private Gilbert Moxley Sorrel was assigned as volunteer aide-de-camp to General James Longstreet at Manassas on July 21, 1861.

General Longstreet was so impressed with young Gilbert's attention to detail that he requested a commission three weeks after the Battle of Manassas. Although Gilbert was young and had no formal military training, he received a captain's commission and an assignment as Adjutant General on Longstreet's staff. In his memoirs, he referred to the position as Chief of Staff, although there is no record of such a position existing in the Confederate Army at that time.

Sorrel was often described as a tall, slender and graceful young man with dark eyes and a friendly disposition. Opinions of Sorrel were mixed. Some describe him as very gallant and polished, where others found him to be demanding and overbearing. Captain Gilbert Sorrel, it seems, was ambitious and tolerated no blunders on his staff. Obviously, his work paid off. His superiors noted that he was the best staff officer in the Confederate Army, eventually rising to the rank of Brigadier General and on October 27, 1864, was given command of a brigade under General Ambrose Powell Hill's[7] Corps. At the time of his promotion to Brigadier General, Gilbert was twenty-six years old.

Brigadier General Gilbert Moxley Sorrel was wounded at Sharpsburg and again at Gettysburg when his horse was shot from underneath him. He took a shot in the chest, which penetrated a lung at Hatcher's Run in February 1865. Though never daunted, he was returning to his command when the war ended.

Gilbert returned to his Savannah home after the war and became the manager of the Ocean Steamship Company, then later moved to New York City. However, while in Savannah he was elected to city council and served as vice president to the Georgia Historical Society.

His wife, the former Kate du Bignon coming from a well placed Jekyll Island family, suggested he write his remembrances of the war during his convalescence after arriving home. Gilbert Moxley Sorrel died on August 10, 1901 at the home of his brother in Roanoake, Virginia. He was brought home to Savannah for burial in the Laurel Grove Cemetery. His *Recollections of a Confederate Staff Officer* was published in 1905, four years after his death.

Later the house at Number 6 West Harris Street was sold to the Weed Family, forever dubbing it the Sorrel-Weed House. The home continues to be a private residence, which at one time had a shop attached, that has since been removed. So it seems this would be the end of the story, not so with the Sorrel-Weed House.

Controversy over the home began in the mid 1990s. It seems the historic home was purchased by the family of Stephen Bader. Bader arrived in Savannah announcing his plans to renovate the Sorrel-Weed House. This announcement delighted the locals until Bader, according to newspaper articles, appeared to be interested only in the superficial image of the home. He failed to submit his plans to the Historic District Board of Review for approval, though nothing was said until the Sorrel-Weed House appeared with a fresh coat of paint in an orangish ocher.[8] Neighbors around the square were horrified and others rose up in support. The Historic Review Board issued an immediate stop work order, until the controversy was resolved.

To prove his point, Bader had hired a researcher out of Charleston and privately conducted a historic study. The research concluded that the orangish ocher color was the original paint scheme. After much deliberation on the part of the Historic Review Board, it was decided that the color would be toned down somewhat. Again, this should be the end of the historical Sorrel-Weed House controversy, well, not quite.

Lawsuits, historical debate and newspaper editorial battles raged on. Rumors abounded, some of them humorous in retrospect. A story was published that Bader had hired workers to tear down the shop attached to the home and in doing so a gray brick wall was removed. The wall, it seems, was also the common bedroom wall of his neighbor. Although the wall was eventually repaired by Bader, the neighbor held an expensive alabaster bust of Juliet Gordon Low hostage until "her" gray bricks were returned. The bricks were returned and the hostage was released.

Regardless of all the controversy on Madison Square, the Old Sorrel-Weed House appears to the untrained eye a beautiful structure. Its 1841, Greek Revival construction with picturesque porches are very pleasing, history lives on in this and other great houses. The only hope can be that those who are privileged enough to be the caretakers of a historic home treat them with the kindness and respect that is their due for surviving long enough to become a landmark.

Old Sorrel~Weed House

SHERMAN'S HEADQUARTERS
Green-Meldrim Mansion

General William Tecumseh Sherman used this house as headquarters from Dec. 22, 1864, until February 1, 1865. Charles Green offered the use of his home to General Sherman and his staff. Sherman's Chaplain conducted the Christmas services in St. John's Church. The house was built for Green, a British subject, residing in Savannah prior to 1854. The architect was John S. Norris of New York. The house is notable as one of the country's finest examples of residential Gothic Revival architecture, the detail of the interiors being as sumptuous as any to be found in America. Cost of construction of this house in the 1850s totalled $93,000. In 1892, it was acquired from the Green family as a residence by Judge Peter W. Meldrim, distinguished Georgia jurist and President of the American Bar Association (1912-1913).

St. John's Episcopal Church acquired the house from the Meldrim heirs in 1943 for use as a parish house and rectory. The house was purchased partly through public subscription by the citizens of Savannah. The house was declared a National Historic Landmark in 1976.

Across from Madison Square, Bull and Macon Streets, Savannah
GPS Coordinates: N32.07367, W81.094406

The Green-Meldrim House was built in 1850 as the lavish residence of Charles Green, noted Savannah lawyer and cotton merchant. Green, in an effort to exhibit his wealth, had his home constructed on one of the original Trust Lots on prestigious Madison Square. The grandeur of the home's Gothic Revival architecture completely overshadowed Green's efforts to display his wealth. John Norris, a well known architect from New York, was responsible for the magnificent structure.

A number of distinctive features set this residence apart from others built during the same period. One of the most unusual is the window shutters, which slide into pockets fashioned into the two foot thick walls, rather than the customary shutters attached by hinges. The interior of the home is almost garish in its opulence. Italian craftsmen in Savannah, who were contracted to construct the Cathedral of St. John the Baptist, were hired to lay in designs of molded plaster throughout the home in a manner befitting a royal palace. Two fireplace mantles carved from Carrara marble and custom made mirrors shipped from Austria are examples of Green's expensive tastes.

The home's link to historical prominence came in December 1864. General William Tecumseh Sherman ended his March to the Sea with the capture of Savannah and made the Green home his Savannah headquarters. It was from the Green mansion that General Sherman dispatched his now infamous telegram to President Lincoln, offering Savannah as his Christmas gift. Little actual damage was done to the home during General Sherman's stay, though a number of family belongings were taken from the house never to be seen again.

The house was sold in 1892 to Judge Peter W. Meldrim. Judge Meldrim made a name for himself as a state judge and President of the American Bar Association. Thus the mansion's name the Green-Meldrim House, the home had only these two owners during its history as a privately owned residence.

In 1943, the heirs of Judge Meldrim sold the home to St. John's Episcopal Church. Today, the Green-Meldrim House serves as the Parish House for St. John's and since 1976, is listed as a National Historic Landmark. The Green-Meldrim House is open to the public for tours.

Sherman's Headquarters

**FIRST GIRL SCOUT HEADQUARTERS
IN AMERICA**

The house adjacent to this building was the home of
Juliette Gordon Low at the time she founded Girl
Scouting in the United States, March 12, 1912. Formerly
the carriage-house and stable of the Low mansion,
this building became that year
the first Girl Scout headquarters in America.
At the death of Mrs. Low in 1927 the Founder of Girl
Scouts of the U.S.A. willed the original headquarters to
the Girl Scouts of Savannah (now The Girl Scout Council
of Savannah, Georgia, Inc.). This building has been
continuously used for Girl Scouting longer than any other
in this country.

**Drayton and Macon Streets, Savannah
GPS Coordinates: N32.07314, W81.092486**

Andrew Low at the age of thirty-five could look back upon eighteen successful years in Savannah. He arrived from his native Scotland, at the age of sixteen and worked in his uncle's cotton firm as a factor.[9] Andrew later became a partner and assumed control of the Savannah operation. In 1843, Andrew married Sarah Cecil Hunter and by the close of 1847, they had two daughters and a son.

The Lowes' classically designed home occupies the southwest Trustees lot on Lafayette Square in Savannah near the former site of the old jail. Architect John Norris was chosen to design the home in 1847. Unfortunately, while the house was under construction, Andrew Low's wife, four year old son and uncle died. The uncle willed his entire estate to Andrew, so it was a somber but wealthy Andrew Low and two young daughters who moved into the fine house at the close of 1849.

By 1850, Savannah had grown 14,000 citizens. A golden era began for Savannah during the years leading up to the Civil War. Andrew Low, acknowledged as the richest man in the city, owned ships that sailed the merchant routes between Savannah and Liverpool loaded with bales of cotton worth millions of dollars.

Five years later, "bright, gay, beautiful" Mary Cowper Stiles, daughter of William Henry Stiles, United States Minister to Austria, stepped through the elegant entrance as the second bride of Andrew Low. In time, three daughters and a son, William Mackay Low, brought new life into the home.

Andrew Low's most famous guest was General Robert E. Lee, a family friend whose association dated back to West Point, where Lee roomed with Mary Low's uncle, Jack Mackay. General Lee was a frequent guest at the Low's home while he was posted at Fort Pulaski. Upon Miss Mackay's marriage, General Lee gave her a gold brooch set with seed pearls and garnetts. General Lee was named godfather to Mary and Andrew Low's daughter, Jessie, on his last visit to Savannah in April 1870.

In 1886, William Mackay Low inherited his father's vast estates in England and America. Six months after the death of his father, he married Juliette "Daisy" Gordon. Daisy spent numerous summers in the home of her future husband's family in England during the summers and became great friends with William's sisters. It was in England that she and William fell in love. The couple used the Savannah house mainly as a winter residence and for a number of years made England their home.

William and Daisy's marriage, although it lasted for nineteen years, was an unhappy one. His consistent drinking and philandering led to divorce proceedings in 1904. Before the divorce was finalized, William Mackay Low suddenly died. Daisy was devastated at the reading of her husband's will to discover he had left the bulk of his estate to his mistress. The Low family home in Savannah was bequeathed to her.

After William's death in 1905, Daisy lived in Savannah year round. On March 12, 1912, she founded the Girls Scouts of America in the carriage house of her Low home. Daisy succumbed to breast cancer at her home in 1927. A year later, the house was purchased by The National Society of the Colonial Dames of America in the State of Georgia to be used as their state headquarters.

The First Girl Scout Headquarters building, formerly the carriage house of the estate, was willed to the Girl Scouts of Savannah, Inc. upon her death. The building was in continuous use for Girl Scout Troop activities, adult training and as administrative offices from 1912 until 1985, when the staff moved the Council office to 428 Bull Street. The Junior League of Savannah leased the building, while the Council determined how the property could be best utilized.

On January 15, 1996, the First Headquarters building reopened to the public with a threefold purpose. The building houses the Council's National Equipment Sales shop, Daisy's Garden and exhibits of historical Girl Scout memorabilia. The building serves as the Council's archive, holding records that are available for research purposes. Troops are invited to use the facilities for special ceremonies, although an appointment is necessary.

"JINGLE BELLS"

James L. Pierpont (1822-1893), composer of "Jingle Bells", served as music director of this church in the 1850s when it was a Unitarian Church located on Oglethorpe Square. Son of the noted Boston reformer, Rev. John Pierpont, he was the brother of Rev John Pierpont, Jr., minister of this church, and uncle of financier John Pierpont Morgan. He married Eliza Jane Purse, and served with a Confederate cavalry regiment. He is buried in Laurel Grove Cemetery. A prolific song-writer, his best known "Jingle Bells" is world famous.

**Across from Troup Square, Habersham and Macon Streets, Savannah
GPS Coordinates: N32.07255, W81.0897296**

There are as many stories about the life and times of James Lord Pierpont as there are versions of his most recognized tune. Most sources agree that he was born, wrote the song and later died, although that is the extent of any agreement. Whether or not this interpretation is completely factual is anybody's guess. These are the most popular notions concerning *Jingle Bells* and James Lord Pierpont.

James Lord Pierpont was born in 1822, the son of a minister, sometimes businessman other times politician who never quite found his niche in life. At the age of ten, young James was sent to school in New Hampshire. It seems, while there he wrote to his mother about riding in a sleigh through the December snow.

Pierpont ran away to join a seagoing ship at the age of fourteen and eventually followed the Gold Rush to San Francisco. In 1855, Pierpont is listed on the rolls of a San Francisco Unitarian Church as a member of the music committee.

Pierpont married Savannah native Eliza Purse in 1857. That same year Oliver Ditson and Company of Boston first published *One Horse Open Sleigh*. It is said that the song was written at his childhood home in Medford, Massachusetts and Mrs. Otis Waterman provided the first piano. Mrs. Waterman was known to be the only one in town to own a piano, which leads one to believe that this story is factual. The tune was played and Mrs. Waterman supposedly suggested that the song had a "merry little jingle" thus, the name *Jingle Bells*. The only thing we know for sure is that two years later the song was released again, under the name *Jingle Bells*. It has also been said that Pierpont wrote *One Horse Open Sleigh* for a Thanksgiving program for his church in Boston, it was so well received that the children were asked to repeat the performance at Christmas.

In 1862, Pierpont joined the Confederate Calvary much to the dismay to his seventy-seven year old father who had enlisted as a chaplain for the Union cause. Pierpont's greatest contribution to the war effort was several patriotic songs.

After the war, he tried his hand at the hardware business without much success. The South had very little money for things other than necessities and even occasionally, that was questionable. So none of Pierpont's songs ever made enough money to support his family. In 1880 James Pierpont's son, Juriah, renewed the copyright on *Jingle Bells* on the behalf of his father. Juriah spent the remainder of his life attempting to keep his father's name permanently attached to the song after the final copyright expired.

James Lord Pierpont died, in 1893, at the age of seventy. He is buried in Laurel Grove Cemetery. The infamous *Jingle Bells* lives on and is quite possibly the song most recognized worldwide. Strangely enough the tune that had become a treasured Christmas carol, isn't about Christmas at all.

FLANNERY O'CONNOR
CHILDHOOD HOME

Mary Flannery O'Connor, novelist and short story writer, was born in Savannah March 25, 1925. She grew up in this house and in later years she referred to it simply as "the house I was raised in." She lived here until 1938, attending church at the Cathedral across Lafayette Square and school at St. Vincent's Grammar School, the facing the square between Harris and Macon Streets. Flannery O'Connor thrice won the O. Henry award for best short story of the year. Her collected stories won the National Book Award in 1972. She died in 1964 at age 39.

207 East Charlton Street, Savannah
GPS Coordinates: N32.07255, W81.09144

Mary Flannery O'Connor was born in Savannah on March 25, 1925. Flannery, as she was called, was the only child of a middle class Catholic family. Her father, Edward, was a realtor, and later worked for a local construction company. Regina, her mother, came from a prominent Milledgeville family, where her grandfather held the mayor's office for many years.

The family home was quite large having three floors, although the third floor was never used, and included an unfinished basement. It was in the backyard of this house that young Flannery, at age five, taught a chicken to walk backwards. It was an amazing feat for a five year old.

Due to Edward's failing health the family moved to Milledgeville in 1938, where Edward O'Connor died due to complications of lupus[10] in 1941. Flannery attended Peabody High School while there she had her first taste of publishing. After graduation, she enrolled in the Georgia State College for Women. There she edited the college magazine until graduation. She earned a Bachelors Degree in 1945. Flannery attended the University of Iowa, where she signed up for every writer's workshop offered. It was at Iowa that she had her first short story, "The Geranium," was published in *Accent Magazine*. In 1947, Flannery graduated from the University of Iowa with a Masters of Fine Arts Degree in Literature and she then moved to New York to pursue her writing career. In 1948, the first four chapters of *Wise Blood* were published in the periodicals *Mademoiselle*, *Sewanee Review* and the *Partisan Review*. In 1952, *Wise Blood* was published as a novel. It would the first of two novels written by Flannery.

Wise Blood dealt with a young man striving to establish a church without Christ. Flannery's only other novel, *The Violent Bear It Away*, was written with much the same theme. Most of her works, especially the novels, had intensive theological backgrounds. Although her characters are deeply flawed and often violent, a number of them exhibit a caustic humor. Flannery used very descriptive text to highlight her characters and featured recurring cameos of flaming suns, mutilated eyes and peacocks in her stories.

Flannery suffered her first bout with disseminated lupus in 1950. She returned to Milledgeville, where she lived with her mother on a dairy farm. In spite of the illness, O'Connor continued to write and occasionally lectured about creative writing at colleges. Within five years, Flannery could no longer walk unassisted and relied heavily on crutches.

Flannery's short stories are considered to be her finest works. *When A Good Man Is Hard to Find and Other Stories* was published in 1955, she became known as the master of the short story. She was far from prolific publishing only thirty-one short stories and two novels, even so, her contribution to literature was vast. Flannery O'Connor is considered one of the most important voices in American literature. Her writing style is difficult to categorize, though it is often referred to as Southern Gothic. Her visions of comedy, tragedy, violence and religion combined, were not only intended to shock the reader but also to make the reader think.

After a short period of remission, an abdominal operation reactivated the lupus. Mary Flannery O'Connor died on August 3, 1964, at the age of 39. Her second collection of short stories was published posthumously in 1965 entitled, *Everything That Rises Must Converge*.

Flannery O'Connor's childhood home in Savannah is owned and operated by the Flannery O'Connor Home Foundation. They purchased the house in 1989 and it is maintained as a memorial to her, existing as a literary center. The parlor level consists of a large living room, kitchen, dining room and a sunroom. The top two floors and the basement have been converted into apartments that enable the foundation to pay expenses related to the home. A walled garden was added in 1993. The house is currently undergoing restoration work. The first floor is open to public free of charge on Saturdays from 1:00-5:00 and Sundays 1:00-4:00. The following is Flannery autograph, used by permission of the wonderful people of the Flannery O'Conner Home Foundation.

Cheers,
Flannery

REVOLUTIONARY WAR
BARRACKS AND FORTIFICATION

During the American Revolution the Military barracks, which were located a short distance south of Savannah, stood near here. Around this site heavy fighting took place in 1778 and 1779.

When Savannah was attacked by the British on December 29, 1778, a small contingent of Georgia militia was stationed east of the barracks. Col. George Walton, a signer of the Declaration of Independence, was severely wounded near here while attempting to rally his militia, following a successful flanking movement by Sir Jas. Baird's Light Infantry around the right of the Continental lines.

During the Siege of Savannah in 1779 by French and American forces the brick barracks were dismantled by the British defenders who left standing only the lower portion of the south wall. Under the direction of the famous British military engineer, Capt. James Montcrief, the remains of the barracks were converted into a strong fortification, known as hornwork, which dominated the center of the Royalist lines around Savannah.

In 1834 the Federal Governor built military barracks known as the Oglethorpe Barracks on the site. They were razed in 1889 when the DeSoto Hotel was erected.

In 1965 the DeSoto Hotel was razed to make way for the DeSoto Hilton Hotel and the main office of the Citizens and Southern Nation Bank.

DeSoto Hilton Plaza, Bull and Liberty Streets, Savannah
GPS Coordinates: N32.07449, W81.092829

The following poignantly eloquent article was printed in the Daily Georgian on December 30, 1842.

"Approaching the city, a short time since, by the Ogechee road, a few hundred paces in the rear of the old barracks, a small mound was pointed out to me, as one of the spots where the ashes of those heroes repose who fell, October 9, 1779, in the ever memorable siege of Savannah. The rude tumuli which was hastily erected over their remains, amid the gloomy silence which pervaded our stricken ranks, are now almost obliterated and levelled to the ground by the peltings of the thousand storms, which have beat upon them for more than sixty years. Citizens of Savannah, why do the bones of those gallant spirits whose lifeblood once watered your now prosperous soil moulder on without tablet or inscription, with no requiem but the signing of the mournful pines, and destined ere long to be lost in the tide of oblivion? The lofty column which rears its marble head, towering high o'er the summit of Bunker, tells truly where the gallant Warren and his brave compatriots fell, and proclaims the truth, that although long departed, still they live fresh in their country's memory. Did Jasper and the hundred who with him shared a bloody grave, fight in a less nobler cause, or come to a more inglorious end than they whose deeds that proud monument perpetuates? Every southerner will quickly answer no. Let us then as soon as the iron hand that fetters our energies is relaxed, and things glide on in their wonted channel, speedily erect a memorial worthy of their exalted fame, ere every landmark which shows their resting place be swept away by the corroding hand of time. There are many in the country who would, I am persuaded, contribute liberally to such an object at any time that a subscription may be opened; for surely there can be no project originated, calculated in such a degree to touch the chord of patriotism and make it to vibrate, as an appeal in behalf of those whose blood was shed freely as a ransom for our liberties. The Green and Pulaski monument is an evidence that our citizens are already imbued with this noble spirit; and we sincerely hope that in succeeding ages, the stranger's inquiry will not be in vain for the last home of the brave who died in battle beneath your walls. H."

In 1823, the site that the impassioned author spoke of was purchased by direction of the Secretary of War for the purpose of an army barracks. The United States government furnished the materials and soldiers supplied the labor. Oglethorpe

Barracks was completed in 1834 and ironically, the site was never used to house United States troops. The city of Savannah offered to buy Oglethorpe Barracks in 1852 and after a year without response, the government finally agreed. The local militia used the barracks until Sherman marched into the city and captured Savannah (these were not United States troops, but were Confederate).

Savannah sold the dilapidated barracks again in 1879. The property was much more valuable to the Savannah Hotel Corporation, who purchased the property for $75,000. The ruins that once was Oglethorpe Barracks was torn down. Construction of the elaborate Desoto Hotel began in 1888 and the upscale establishment held its opening in 1890. The Desoto was five stories tall with two hundred and six guestrooms. The hotel catered to the upper echelon of society and offered a solarium, barbershop, drug store and restaurant.

Today, the site is home to Savannah's Desoto Hilton. Overlooking Madison Square at the corner of Bull and Liberty streets, the luxury hotel offers beautiful historical surroundings with all of the modern conveniences.

CAPTURE OF SAVANNAH
DECEMBER 28, 1778

When the British attacked Savannah on December 29, 1778, the defending Continental forces, numbering about 650 men under command of Maj. General Robert Howe, were posted across Sea Island Road (now Wheaton Street) approximately 100 yards east of this marker.

The British army, 2500 strong, landed near Brewton Hill at daybreak on Dec. 29. It consisted of part of the 71st Highland Regt., New York Loyalists, and Hessians, and was commanded by Lt. Col. Archibald Campbell. The British promptly marched on Savannah. They halted on the road about 800 yards from the American battle line and deployed for attack.

Col. Campbell meanwhile learned of an unguarded pass through the swamp, which led around the right of the American line. He there upon detached the Light Infantry under Sir James Baird in an attempt, which proved successful, to flank the Continental position here.

Outflanked, the America position became untenable and Gen. Howe ordered Savannah evacuated. During the withdrawl, the Georgia brigade, commanded by Gen. Lachlan McIntosh, was cut off and suffered heavy casualties.

During the subsequent siege of Savannah by the French and Americans in 1779 the British line of defenses around the Town ran though this area.

Liberty and Randolph Streets, Savannah
GPS Coordinates: N32.07229, W81.084091

B ritish Colonel Archibald Campbell of Inverneill, Scotland, landed at the mouth of the Savannah River at Salter's Island leading a detachment of the veteran 71st Highlanders, their mission, the Capture of Savannah. Campbell was known to be an energetic and shrewd leader; as a tactician, he was without equal. His attention to detail ensured that each time his men took to the battlefield, every aspect and likely scenario had been thoroughly considered.

Savannah's American defense was led by General Robert Howe, recently appointed as Chief in Command of the Southern Department. Howe was forced to return with his troops to Savannah after a disastrous expedition into Florida. His command was decimated due to lack of supplies, insubordination and a yellow fever epidemic that left a weakened and defenseless troop to staggering back to Savannah.

Campbell's force arrived after a storm tossed passage; sea sick and debilitated. The men had a week to regain their composure and as the troops recovered, Campbell planned their attack. A British reconnaissance patrol managed to capture the

American soldiers who, under a threat of death, provided the British commander with information concerning the American troop movements. The remainder of the British fleet arrived on December 27, 1778. The prisoners informed Campbell that General Howe and his meager forces awaited reinforcements at Brewton Hall Plantation. Campbell had two corps of inexperienced Loyalist light infantry to bolster the 71st Highlanders and each corps was assigned to a company of veterans.

Colonel Campbell's orders were to combine forces with Major General Augustin Prevost and take Savannah. However, once Campbell realized that Prevost could only muster 1,500 men, he immediately decided that Prevost's forces were not necessary to reach his objective. Campbell ordered his men to board the naval transports and the small fleet sailed up river, arriving on the afternoon of December 28, 1778. Campbell, who excelled in troop movements and land attacks, lacked skill as a navigator. The British troops found themselves unable to disembark. Surrounded by swamps and creeks at high tide the area was too deep for his men to ford and when the tide ebbed, the small British fleet found themselves firmly grounded in the mud. The attack would have to wait until the following day.

Captain Cameron led the initial company ashore and immediately rushed the plantation house. Fifty patriots, who realized in an instant that they were defeated, met the company. The patriots retreated to the woods beyond the house. Captain Cameron was killed and seven of his men lay dead or wounded. The patriot pickets were no match for Campbell's superior force as they welded their claymore broadswords. He wasted no time in pushing forward to engage General Howe's American army.

Howe had deployed two divisions in a strong position across the main road into Savannah. The left wing was protected by the river, the right screened by the swamp. Colonel Eugee commanded two regiments of Carolina troops on the right covered by sharpshooters who hid in houses along the road. Colonel Elliot commanded three battalions of Georgia infantry on the left, two field cannons dominated their position.

Nearly half of Campbell's men remained onboard the transport. Howe, thinking he had seen the entire force was confident. He felt his position was strong, the swamp to his right was believed to be inaccessible. Campbell would have to attack from the left. Campbell's intelligence had paid off with Quamino Dolly; an escaped slave turned British scout. He informed Campbell of a hidden path that cut through the swamp to the American right wing. The plan formed in Campbell's mind instantly. A force sent along this path to right would enable his troops to surprise the unsuspecting Americans who were busily engaged with a decoy battalion on their left wing.

Colonel Campbell was heralded for his skillful tactics, meticulous planning and execution. General Howe, subsequently faced a Court of Inquiry as a result of the loss of Savannah. Howe was eventually cleared, "with highest honours." Unfortunately Howe's peers loudly criticized his actions, including General Gadsden with whom Howe later found himself facing in a duel of honor. Both men survived. Historians find that Howe was only partially at fault. Campbell's skill would have likely have won the day, regardless of the commander he faced.

Colonel Archibald Campbell, during the battle, revealed his improvisational skill and ability to exploit tactical weakness to gain maximum effect. These talents set him far apart from most of his peers. The Americans were completely unaware of their peril and according to Colonel Campbell, "continued to amuse themselves with their cannon."

Campbell managed, in less than a week, to recapture all of Georgia; the only exceptions being the towns of Sunbury and Augusta. He went on to secure military posts in southern Carolina and issued proclamations restoring the Crown's authority, requesting that all Georgia citizens take oaths of allegiance to the Crown and join its Loyalist regiments. The military prowess of Colonel Archibald Campbell and his magnificent victory was not enough to deter the brave Americans. The Revolution continued.

ST. VINCENT'S ACADEMY

The Convent and Academy of Saint Vincent dePaul was opened in June, 1845. Sisters of Mercy from Charleston, S.C., under the leadership of Mother Vincent Mahoney, began a boarding school, orphanage, day school and free school. St. Vincent's Convent became an independent Motherhouse within two years, and from here over 20 schools, hospitals, and orphanages were founded throughout Georgia. Early foundations continuing to give service include: St. Joseph's Hospital and St. Mary's Home. Savannah (1875), and St. Joseph's Hospital, Atlanta (1880).

Records attest to bravery and heroic service rendered by the sisters of Mercy during the yellow fever epidemics of 1855, 1876, and 1878, and to their care for the wounded and suffering during the Civil War.

Students at St. Vincent's included Winnie and Jeff Davis, children of Confederate President Jefferson Davis.

Noted architect, Charles B. Cluskey, designed the Convent and Academy building. The style is Greek Revival.

Heritage Hall in the original building recalls for today's young women St. Vincent's tradition of education excellence.

207 East Liberty Street at Abercorn Street, Savannah
GPS Coordinates: N32.07401, W81.091171

Reverend Jeremiah F. O'Neill, pastor of the Church of St. John the Baptist, requested the aid of the Sisters of Mercy in 1845. Sisterhoods were an important part of the church. They provided care for orphans, the elderly and the infirmed. Bishop England of Charleston had recognized the need of a sisterhood in the South years earlier and in 1829, established the Sisters of Charity of Our Lady of Mercy.

Six sisters were sent from Charleston to Savannah arriving on June 13, 1845 and moved into St. Vincent's Convent on Liberty and Abercorn Streets. The sisters wasted no time in attending the tasks at hand. Ten days after their arrival a boarding school for girls, an orphanage and a day school for both boys and girls were opened. The sisters began ministering to the sick and helped bury the dead during yellow fever epidemics. For years, the sisters divided their time between Macon and Savannah until the Columbus area sisterhood took over the academy in Macon in 1870.

In 1892, the Savannah Sisters of Mercy affiliated with Catherine McAuley who had established the first House of Mercy in Ireland. The House of Mercy in Ireland tended the needs of homeless and abused women and children from Dublin's slums. In Savannah, between 1845 and 1929, over 200 sisters called St. Vincent's Convent their Motherhouse. Today, all of Catherine McAuley's sisters in North and South America belong to the Sisters of Mercy of the Americas, which responds to the needs of the poor, especially women.

St. Vincent's Academy is, today, a Catholic college preparatory school for girls. It is owned and administered by the Sisters of Mercy and is the only private high school in Savannah's Historic District. The three main buildings of the school cover a city block on the south side of Liberty Street between Abercorn and Lincoln streets. While the Sisters of Mercy still maintain the school and its policies, the majority of today's faculty consists of professional lay teachers.

St. Vincent's instructs students in grades 9 through 12 and approximately two-thirds of the school's 400 students are Catholic. St. Vincent's is open to all young women, regardless of creed, race or socioeconomic status. Their classes average about twenty students with ninety-five percent of St. Vincent's Academy graduates attending college. The school administration believes the downtown location is an asset because it enables students to experience an urban environment and brings them into direct contact with Savannah's history and culture.

St. Vincent's places an emphasis on Christian values and moral character. This philosophy has led to a long tradition of graduates sending their daughters and granddaughters to their *alma mater*. The tradition has been carried on for four and five generations. At the same time, St. Vincent's cherishes the diversity of its student body and makes its services available to any young woman in Savannah.

St. Vincent's offers an extensive extracurricular program in visual arts and the school's chorus is known throughout the state. The Academy competes in eight varsity sports: volleyball, softball, basketball, tennis, track, soccer, riflery and swimming.

GERMAN MEMORIAL FOUNTAIN

This Fountain Commemorates The Religious,
Social, Agricultural, Economic, And Political
Contributions Of Early German Immigrants
To The Establishment And Growth
Of The Colony Of Georgia.
Erected And Dedicated In 1989
By Their Descendents

Members Of
GERMAN HERITAGE SOCIETY
GERMAN FRIENDLY SOCIETY
GEORGIA SALZBURGER SOCIETY

**Orleans Square east of Civic Center, Savannah
GPS Coordinates: N32.07655, W81.095554**

The German Memorial Fountain was placed at Orleans Square in tribute to the ancestors of the German Societies of Savannah. The fountain stands in honor and tribute to those who made the choice to immigrate to a new land of opportunity. It was because of their courage and sacrifice, as well as others like them, that the colony of Georgia has survived.

The beautiful bowl fountain sits at the center of Orleans Square, shaded by century old oaks trimmed in lacy Spanish moss. The setting provides a perfect place to spend an afternoon seated on a scroll backed bench quietly reading or enjoying lunch as a gentle breeze stirs the leaves and squirrels scamper across the grass and up a nearby tree.

German Memorial Fountain

DR. WM. A. CARUTHERS (1802-46)
Early American Novelist

One block west of this marker at the northwest corner of Bull and Whitaker Streets stood formerly the residence of William Alexander Caruthers. Virginia's earliest significant novelist. He resided in Savannah for several years before his death in 1846.

Dr. Caruthers, who married Louisa Catherine Gibson of Whitemarsh Island, Chatham County, moved in 1837 to this city where he successfully practiced medicine. He took a prominent part in affairs in Savannah as a realtor; was one of the founders of the Georgia Historical Society and while an Alderman, 1841-1844, was instrumental in giving Savannahians direct election of their Mayors.

As one of the South's pioneering historical romancers, Caruthers rewrote and first published at Savannah his last and finest novel, "The Knights of the Golden Horse Shoe" (1841), one of the earliest novels to be published in book form in Georgia. His first novel, "The Kentuckian in New York" (1834), contains an admiring description of Savannah. Dr. Caruthers died of tuberculosis at Marietta, Ga., 1846 and is buried there in an unlocated grave in St. James churchyard.

Chippewa Square, Bull and McDonough Streets, Savannah
GPS Coordinates: N32.07611, W81.093237

William Alexander Caruthers was a complex man. He was a well known physician, who practiced medicine in Virginia, New York and Savannah. Caruthers was also recognized as perhaps the "father" of the historical romance. Although most of his works have been forgotten over time, Caruthers was a great influence on authors of historical fiction and romance in the times to follow.

Little is known of his early life, other than he was quite proud of his Virginia heritage. In 1818, sixteen years old Caruthers witnessed a daring ascent of the Natural Bridge. He wrote his first work describing the events at the Natural Bridge, and *Knickerbocker Magazine* published his account. The records available list his first published works coming from New York in 1834.

Indications are that, by this time, he had already spent some time in Savannah because his book, *The Kentuckian in New York*, contains vivid details concerning the beauty of Savannah. He married Louisa Catherine Gibson in 1837. His bride hailed from Whitemarsh Island near Savannah and it was there that the newlyweds made their home. Late to marry, Caruthers was thirty-five at the time and was already experiencing symptoms of tuberculosis, which would eventually take his life.

His time in Savannah was spent pursuing Savannah real estate. His love of history and things historical led to his participation in the creation of the Georgia Historical Society and in 1841, William Caruthers was elected Alderman for Savannah. As a politician, he lobbied and won the right for Savannahians to elect the city's mayor.

Writing was a constant in William Caruthers life and by 1843, his work began to reveal a different element of his imagination. Basing his stories and novels on historical fact tinged with sidebars of mystery, suspense, romantic interludes and humorous lines, he brought a new form of writing called historical fiction to the south. The effects were intriguing and although Caruthers was never considered a great writer, his entertaining works have enormous appeal.

Only three of his published works: *The Cavaliers of Virginia*, *The Kentuckian in New York* and *The Knights of the Horse Shoe*, can still be found. An example of his writing style and gentle southern spirit is as follows in the exert was taken from an early edition of his work entitled *A Kitchen Fire-side in the Old Dominion*:[11]

"On the present occasion, though presumed to be not upon his dignity, the old major sat with folded arms and a benignant but yet contemptuous smile playing upon his features, illuminated as they were by the lurid fire-light, while Martin the carpenter told one of the most marvellous and wonder-stirring stories of the headless corpse ever heard within these walls, teeming, as they were, with the marvellous. Essex had often heard stories first told over the gentlemen's wine, and then the kitchen version, and of course knew how to estimate them exactly: now that before-mentioned incredulous smile began to spread until he was forced to laugh outright, as Martin capped the climax of his tale of horror, by some supernatural appearance of blue flames over the grave. Not so the other domestics, male and female, clustering around his chair; they were worked up to the highest pitch of the marvellous. Even old June ceased to twang his banjo, and at length got his eyes wide open as the carpenter came to the sage conclusion, that the place would be haunted."

William Alexander Caruthers succumbed to tuberculosis in 1846 and was buried at St. James Churchyard in Marietta, Georgia. Unfortunately his works are rarely known, which is a great loss to readers of historical fiction.

COLONIAL PARK

This cemetery, the second in colonial Savannah, was the burying ground for the city from about 1750 until it was closed against burials in 1853. Among the distinguished dead who rest here are Archibald Bulloch, first President of Georgia; James Habersham, acting royal Governor of the Province, 1771-73; Joseph Habersham, Postmaster General under three Presidents; Lachlan McIntosh, Major General, Continental Army; Samuel Elbert, Revolutionary soldier and Governor of Georgia; Capt. Denis L. Cottineau de Kerioguen who aided John Paul Jones in the engagement between the "Bon Homme Richard" and the "Serapia"; Hugh McCall, early historian of Georgia; Edward Greene Malbone, the noted miniaturist, and Colonel John S. McIntosh, a hero of the War with Mexico. The remains of Major General Nathanael Greene who died in 1786 reposed in the Graham vault until they were reinterred in 1901 in Johnson Square. The cemetery became a city park in 1896.

Colonial Park Cemetery, Abercorn Street and Oglethorpe Avenue, Savannah
GPS Coordinates: N32.07602, W81.090512

Colonial Park Cemetery was established in 1750, though it was not the first cemetery of Savannah. General James Edward Oglethorpe dedicated lots two and three of the Percival Ward in the area of York, Bull, Oglethorpe and Whitaker Streets as the original cemetery. This cemetery simply called the burial ground was only used for seventeen years when the city chose to establish another plot. All evidence of the original burial ground has disappeared through time, only a single plaque marks the location of those long forgotten graves.

The public burying ground was established in 1750 and located outside the city walls. The public feared, justifiably so, that the decaying corpses would bring disease into the city. Christ Church took over maintenance of the cemetery in 1758 and it remained a public burial ground for the next ninety-eight years, the cemetery was known as Christ Church Burying Ground.

After the British relinquished Savannah to the Americans in 1782, the old British earthworks around the cemetery were torn down. It was enlarged and the burying ground was incorporated into the city. Eventually funds were raised and improvements were made including: a brick wall, a gate installed at the intersection of South Broad and Lincoln Streets and a brick walkway was put in place to accommodate the horse drawn hearse bought by the city in 1803. A second gate was built in 1812 for the north end of the cemetery. A beautification project was undertaken in 1846. Trees and shrubs were planted to absorb the "poisonous effluvia" emitted from the cemetery that citizens believed brought yellow fever.

Colonial Park Monument

Laurel Grove Cemetery was opened in 1849 and Bonaventure later that same year. A Catholic cemetery opened in 1853. A number of remains were moved from South Broad Street, as the cemetery was then called. In 1853 the cemetery was officially closed to burials becoming a target for neglect and often, heinous vandalism. The decision was made to close the cemetery due to overcrowding and there was no surrounding area in which to expand.

When Union troops took Savannah in 1864 they used the cemetery to corral horses and assemble wagons. For entertainment, Union soldiers would alter the headstones or move them to different locations. After the Civil War, the cemetery continued to deteriorate.

In 1868, the Old Cemetery Association was formed to attempt preservation. The damaged brick wall was repaired and the gates, which the Union troops had nailed shut, were opened. However, money was in short supply, and further restoration was abandoned. The Georgia Historical Society assumed the preservation project in 1887 and attempted to record the markers and epitaphs. Over seven hundred epitaphs were gathered.

The city attempted to purchase the cemetery from Christ Church and was met with a lawsuit. The suit was settled by a compromise in 1895. The compromise stated that the city must forever preserve the site as a burial ground and was restricted from developing new streets through the cemetery. The area was to be designated as a public park and called Colonial Park. If the city violated the ordinances, the property would revert back to Christ Church. This stipulation was invoked in 1922 to prevent the city's plans to extend Lincoln Street through the cemetery.

Colonial Park Cemetery was now under the jurisdiction of the Park and Tree Commission of Savannah. The city demolished the surrounding brick walls but in 1897, completed a restoration, landscaping project and installed benches and trash receptacles, pathways and shrubs. Headstones were repaired and other stones, whose locations were lost over time, were mounted on the east wall to preserve them.

The Daughters of the American Revolution had the archway erected in 1913 at the northwest corner of the cemetery in honor of the American patriots who were interred there. The city erected the wrought iron fences on three sides in 1956 because of repeated vandalism. Another extensive restoration project was undertaken, the stones were cleaned and reset.

The Chicora Foundation did some historical and archaeological work in August of 1998. Their purpose was to identify graves sites lost over time and prepare a base map of Colonial Park Cemetery. According to *The Old Burying Ground: Colonial Park Cemetery*, an extraordinary book on the cemetery by Elizabeth Carpenter Piechocinski, over eight thousand unmarked graves were identified.

Some facts and myths concerning Colonial Park Cemetery include:

• The oldest marked grave is 1762, that of William Bowers Williamson.

• Some of General Sherman's men actually lived in some of the large family vaults in 1864 during the Union occupation of Savannah.

• Five Governors of Georgia are interred at Colonial Park including: James Habersham, Archibald Bulloch, Samuel Elbert, Button Gwinnett and Richard Howley.

• The majority of the graves in Colonial Park Cemetery lay on an east west line with the stones facing east. This custom is based on the idea that the resurrection of the dead will occur with the rising sun from the east. The dead were, therefore, interred facing east to await judgment day.

• It is believed that only one mass grave exists in the cemetery. The mass grave is said to be that of the 1820 yellow fever epidemic that claimed the lives of approximately one-third of the city. It is said to lie in the southern section of the cemetery.

Colonial Park Monument

JAMES EDWARD OGLETHORPE
(1696-1785)

The monument in this Square to James Edward Oglethorpe — the great soldier-philanthropist who founded the colony of Georgia — was erected by the State of Georgia, the City of Savannah and various Patriotic Societies. Impressive ceremonies marked its unveiling in 1910. The 9 foot bronze statue of Oglethorpe is the work of one of America's foremost sculptors, the celebrated Daniel Chester French. He has depicted the Founder of Georgia in the full dress of a British general of the period. Oglethorpe is portrayed with sword in hand: alert and ready for council or action. At his feet is a palmetto frond. The statue faces southward symbolizing the threat of Spain's imperial ambitions to the young colony. The pedestal and base of the monument were designed by Henry Bacon, the eminent New York architect whose collaborations with Daniel Chester French include the Lincoln Memorial. The four lions at the corners of the lower base hold shields on which appear, respectively, the coat of arms of Oglethorpe and the great seals of the Colony of Georgia, the State, and the City of Savannah. On the pedestal of the monument is carved a portion of the text of the charter which was granted by Parliament in 1732 to "the Trustees for establishing the colony of Georgia in America."

Chippewa Square, Bull and McDonough Streets, Savannah
GPS Coordinates: N32.07611, W81.093237

The monument that graces the midst of Chippewa Square is in the likeness of General James Edward Oglethorpe, founder of the colony of Georgia and responsible for the planning of beautifully designed cities such as Savannah and Darien. Oglethorpe is memorialized in bronze and continues to watch over his beloved colony.

Daniel Chester French was commissioned to sculpt the monument by the Georgia General Assembly in 1906, which had designated $15,000 for the construction. Henry Bacon, a New York architect, was commissioned to design the base. French carefully examined portraits and engravings of Georgia's founder and studied military apparel in keeping with the era in which Oglethorpe lived. He chose to portray the founding father as a soldier and leader, rather than that of a colonizer. Daniel French's interpretation is today, revered as the most handsome and heroic rendering of General James Edward Oglethorpe in existence.

The nine foot tall statue is depicted as standing proudly and defiantly looking southward toward the Spanish threat from Florida. Oglethorpe is adorned in full military regalia of the 1740s with shoulder and cuirass[12] armor, sword, waistcoat, high boots and tricorn hat. The pedestal has a portion of the charter of the Georgia colony carved into its sides. Lions holding shields bearing the Oglethorpe family Coat of Arms as well as the seals of the colony, state and city of Savannah are featured at each corner and a palmetto frond lies at Oglethorpe's feet.

French included much symbolism into this profound and exquisite work. The lions symbolize a complete victory over spiritual and secular rule, immortalizing Oglethorpe's ultimate purpose for the establishment of the Georgia colony; charity in its widest and most extended sense, the escape of the poor to a land of great opportunity. The motto on the seal of the Georgia colony spoke but the language of truth, *Non sibi sed aliis* or "Not for ourselves, but for others." A colony with fertile soil and a gentle climate, soon became an asylum for the oppressed of every land and every faith. The Oglethorpe crest carries the Latin motto, *Nescit Cedere* or "He who does not know how to give up."

The Great Seal of Georgia, adopted by the State Constitution of 1798, is embossed with three pillars supporting an arch, emblematic of the three branches of government; the legislative, judicial and executive. A man stands with a drawn sword defending the Constitution, whose principles are wisdom, justice and moderation. The reverse of the Seal shows a ship with cotton and tobacco and a man plowing, representing the agriculture and commerce of the Seal's motto, "Wisdom, Justice and Moderation." Finally, the palmetto frond symbolized victory in taming the wilderness.

Dignitaries and military units gathered to parade through the city ending at Chippewa Square on November 23, 1910 for the dedication ceremony of the Oglethorpe Memorial. Those in attendance included the Honorable Joseph M. Brown, Governor of Georgia, the British Ambassador and the Resident British Consul.

French and Bacon went on to produce another breathtaking monument, the Lincoln Memorial in Washington, D.C. Ironically, French carved the beloved Lincoln monument, dedicated to a Command in Chief who conquered the south, from Georgia marble.

WILLIAM STEPHENS

FIRST GRAND MASTER,
GRAND LODGE OF GEORGIA, F&AM

Born Jan. 1752 at Beaulieu (Bulie) Neck Savannah of distinguished English ancestry William Stephens was an eminent Lawyer and Jurist during and after the War for Independence.

Georgia's first Attorney-General, he was also Chief Justice of Georgia, Mayor of Savannah and held other important posts of honor. In 1802 President Thomas Jefferson appointed him United States District Court judge which position he held with distinction until just prior to his death on 6 Aug. 1819.

A dedicated Freemason, he was Worshipful Master of Solomon's Lodge at Savannah prior to 1783. In 1791, he was Worshipful Master of another Savannah Lodge, Union No. 10 (extinct).

When the Grand Lodge of Georgia, F&AM was organized at Savannah on 16 Dec. 1786 as the Independent and Sovereign Masonic Power in Georgia, William Stephens was elected Grand Master and he served through 1788. In 1793, he was re-elected Grand Master and served continuously through 1813. A record of longevity in that exalted Masonic office never since equalled.

The honored remains of Grand Master Stephens rest in the Colonial Cemetery of Savannah. His Masonic posterity, the nearly 100,000 Freemasons of Georgia will ever cherish his memory.

Colonial Park Cemetery, Savannah
GPS Coordinates: N32.07602, W81.090512

William Stephens was born to Georgia royalty. His grandfather, also William Stephens, was the first president of Georgia. In 1736, the elder Stephens were sent by the English Crown to meet General Oglethorpe and to evaluate his progress in the colony. The Georgia Trustees were concerned with General Oglethorpe's administration of the fledgling colony and the elder William Stephens was to keep the Trustees informed on military, civil and other concerns within the colony. In 1742, Stephens was named president of Georgia, a title that realistically should have been given to General Oglethorpe.

William Stephens was born in 1752 at his families' vast plantation called Bewlie or Beaulieu near Savannah. Carrying on the family tradition of public servitude, he grew to become a distinguished lawyer and judge. Stephens was Georgia's first Attorney General and in 1802, was named United States District Court Judge by President Thomas Jefferson.

Georgia claimed four lodges of Freemasonry during the late 1700s. William Stephens was Grand Master of the first masonic lodge, Solomon's Lodge at Savannah. On December 16, 1786, the four lodges met and together created the most Worshipful Grand Lodge of Free and Accepted Masons for the State of Georgia; William Stephens was elected and installed as

Grand Master of the State. He continued to be reelected in this position until illness forced his resignation in 1813.

Judge Stephens continued to serve the United States Court until shortly before his death. William Stephens died on August 6, 1819, he was laid to rest at Colonial Park Cemetery.

JAMES HABERSHAM

Here rests James Habersham - associate of George Whitefield and a leading merchant, planter, and public servant during Georgia's colonial era.

Mr. Habersham came to the colony in 1738 as a youthful follower of the Rev. Whitefield and collaborated with that eminent divine in the founding of Bethesda orphanage. He successfully administered the affairs of that institution during its early years. He established, in 1744, what developed into the most important commercial house in the Province, and became one of Georgia's largest planters.

During the colonial period he ably filled a number of important public positions, including provincial Secretary; President of His Majesty's Council for Georgia, and acting Governor of the Province during the absence of Sir James Wright, 1771-1773.

Though he disapproved Parliament's oppressive acts, Habersham remained firmly loyal to the Crown. Universally respected, he died, while visiting in New Jersey, August 28, 1775 - his last days darkened by the shadow of the impending Revolutionary struggle which arrayed, in his words and in his own case, "father against son, and son against father."

Colonial Park Cemetery, Savannah
GPS Coordinates: N32.07602, W81.090512

The Honorable James Habersham was born in Beverly, Yorkshire, England, in 1712 to noble parentage. When asked by his young sons what the term "Honorable" prefixed to his name meant, he explained that such titles were worthless in the Georgia colony, only promoting pride and unchristian feelings.

He arrived in the Georgia colony with his life long friend, the Reverend George Whitefield. It was with the encouragement of General Oglethorpe and the Wesleys that Whitefield, aided by Habersham, founded the Bethesda Orphanage. James Habersham was a practical schoolmaster and an able administrator, balancing Whitefield who tended to be a grandiose dreamer.

James Habersham became a merchant in 1744 and in 1750, was appointed Commissioner for the purpose developing the silk industry in the colony. He grew the first cotton in the state at Bethesda; the first few bales were exported to England. Habersham was appointed Secretary of the Province and later one of the Presidents of the Upper House of Assembly.[13] During the absence of Sir James Wright, Governor of Georgia, James Habersham was temporarily placed in the position until Wright returned from England.

Habersham was a staunch loyalist, completely allegiant to the English Crown. One of the greatest burdens of his life concerned his three sons, who all grew to oppose everything he believed. Each one joined the Friends of Liberty, later known as the Sons of Liberty supporting the revolutionary cause.

James Habersham, although he opposed British oppression, remained loyal to the Crown until the end of his life. His final days were spent in dismay of the coming Revolutionary War. James Habersham died in New Brunswick, New Jersey on August 28, 1775. He was buried at Colonial Park Cemetery in Savannah. His sons would eventually lie at his side, reunited with their father only in death.

GEN. LACHLAN MCINTOSH
(1727-1806)

Lachlan McIntosh, Georgia's ranking Continental officer in the American Revolution, was the son of John Mor Mackintosh who settled with a group of Highlanders on the Altamaha in 1736. Lachlan served as a cadet in Oglethorpe's Regiment and received part of his schooling at Bethesada. During the Colonial era he became a leading planter in Darien, accumulating a considerable property which he lost in the Revolution.

A firm supporter of American rights, McIntosh was commissioned colonel of the first Continental regiment raised in Georgia. A feud with Button Gwinnett, Signer of the Declaration of Independence, resulted in a duel fought near Savannah, May 16, 1777. McIntosh was transferred to Gen. Washington's headquarters after Gwinnett's death. He served with credit at Valley Forge and Washington, who described him as an "Officer of great worth and merit," later gave him command of the Western Department at Fort Siege of Savannah. His military career in the American Revolution, in which had shed his blood defending Georgia's borders, terminated with his capture when Charlestown fell in 1780.

In 1784 the continental Congress, promoted McIntosh to major general, vindicating him from his unjust suspension from command four years before as a result of representations to it by Gov. Walton. The patriot-hero lived out his remaining years at Savannah.

Colonial Park Cemetery, Savannah
GPS Coordinates: N32.07602, W81.090512

Lachlan McIntosh was born in Scotland and arrived with his family in the colony of Georgia with Oglethorpe. John McIntosh Mohr, head of the McIntosh clan and Lachlan's father, was a ranking member of the Scottish Highlanders recruited by Oglethorpe to defend Georgia against the Spanish threat to the south. The family settled at New Inverness, later to be known as Darien.

As a youth, Lachlan McIntosh spent several years being educated at the Bethesda Orphanage, along with his sister, Anne. The elder McIntosh Mohr was captured and confined in a Spanish jail. Mrs. McIntosh took the remainder of her children to Fort Palachacola on the Savannah River. Why Anne and Lachlan were singled out and left behind is a mystery. The McIntosh children were cared for at the orphanage for two years until Mrs. McIntosh returned.

Lachlan chose not to return with his mother, rather he decided to try his hand at business endeavors and moved to Charleston. There he met Henry Laurens and joined the Laurens' Counting House. Henry Laurens would remain a friend, advisor and confidant for the rest of his life. Through Laurens, Lachlan learned a great deal about British policies and their restriction. When the Revolutionary War began, he was ready return to Georgia and accepted an Army commission.

Lachlan had managed to secure property in Georgia and in 1775 was selected as a delegate for the Provincial Congress representing St. Andrew Parish. In January 1776, Lachlan was appointed Colonel of the Georgia troops and in September that same year, he was promoted to Brigadier General.

Impassioned disputes with a political rival, Button Gwinnett led to a challenge on the field of honor. When Gwinnett died as a result of the duel, McIntosh was charged with murder, brought to trial and acquitted. The fallout from the unfortunate situation left the patriots of Georgia with divided loyalties. Influential friends thought it best for McIntosh to transfer to General Washington's staff, removing him from the public eye until heated tempers cooled. McIntosh graciously accepted for no other reason except to maintain harmony within his home state.

Washington appointed General McIntosh commander of the northern Carolina Brigade at Valley Forge. According to General Weedon's Valley Forge Orderly Book, beginning on December 27, McIntosh was appointed a Brigadier for the day and was so appointed a successive fourteen times during the encampment.

Washington reassigned McIntosh to Fort Pitt at Yorktown on May 26, 1778. He remained in command there until May 18,

273

1779. He was then ordered south to participate in a campaign to recapture Savannah.

General McIntosh and French Naval Commander Count Charles Henri d'Estaing resolved to retake Savannah, which had been captured by British Colonel Campbell in late December 1778. General Lincoln was in command of all forces in Savannah, General McIntosh and Count Pulaski assembled ground regiments. On October 4, 1779, an intensive bombardment began and the American forces were well on the way to a victory. D'Estaing became impatient, fearing the possibility of an attack by the British fleet. He resolved to destroy the British and renewed the naval bombardment. Lincoln disagreed but it was too late. D'Estaing had already begun the assault with ground forces led by McIntosh, Hughes and Pulaski, which fought hard to no avail. In the foray, both d'Estaing and Pulaski were wounded. Pulaski died two days later.

D'Estaing recovered enough to request a truce to bury the dead and the British cautiously granted four hours. D'Estaing and Lincoln held a conference, after which d'Estaing abandoned the siege and sailed away as Lincoln protested. Lincoln ordered his troops to retreat to Charleston; McIntosh followed with his regiment.

The British fleet moved forward on April 9, 1780, managing to avoid fire from Fort Moultrie and anchored within cannons range of Charleston. Supplies were desperately low and the financial situation in Charleston was very poor. A forty day struggle ensued, finally due to the shortage of provisions and no reinforcements to aid them, Lincoln agreed to a surrender. The British took possession of the city on May 12, 1780. McIntosh was taken prisoner and was not exchanged until February 9, 1782. The confinement had left McIntosh a physically broken man; his health never recovered.

The British withdrew from Savannah in 1782. Georgia Governor Martin called a meeting of the state legislature, which met at the home of General McIntosh in order to reorganize the civil authority of the state. In 1783, McIntosh was promoted to Major General. He was elected to Congress in 1784 and appointed to assist in the organization of a treaty with the Indians that occupied the western section of Georgia. He continued to serve the state of Georgia until his death on February 20, 1806. Lachlan McIntosh was laid to rest at the Colonial Cemetery in Savannah.

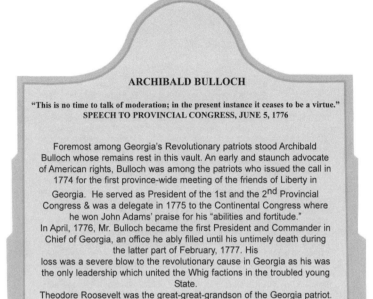

ARCHIBALD BULLOCH

"This is no time to talk of moderation; in the present instance it ceases to be a virtue."
SPEECH TO PROVINCIAL CONGRESS, JUNE 5, 1776

Foremost among Georgia's Revolutionary patriots stood Archibald Bulloch whose remains rest in this vault. An early and staunch advocate of American rights, Bulloch was among the patriots who issued the call in 1774 for the first province-wide meeting of the friends of Liberty in Georgia. He served as President of the 1st and the 2nd Provincial Congress & was a delegate in 1775 to the Continental Congress where he won John Adams' praise for his "abilities and fortitude." In April, 1776, Mr. Bulloch became the first President and Commander in Chief of Georgia, an office he ably filled until his untimely death during the latter part of February, 1777. His loss was a severe blow to the revolutionary cause in Georgia as his was the only leadership which united the Whig factions in the troubled young State. Theodore Roosevelt was the great-great-grandson of the Georgia patriot.

Colonial Park Cemetery, Savannah
GPS Coordinates: N32.07602, W81.090512

The year was 1730, the place was Charles Towne in southern Carolina; Archibald Bulloch, lawyer and statesman, is the subject. Bulloch benefited from the best liberal education available in the infant colonies and began to read the law at an early age. After passing the bar Bulloch practiced law in Charles Towne, for it was the law that he loved.

Bulloch accepted an officer's commission in a southern Carolina militia regiment in 1757 and moved to Georgia in 1762. Obviously, he quickly made a name for himself as an attorney and in 1768, was asked to correspond with the noted statesman, Benjamin Franklin. The letters concerned grievances against the Royal government. Rumblings of revolution were beginning to be heard in whispered tones when Bulloch was elected speaker of the Georgia Royal Assembly in 1772.

In 1775, Bulloch was elected to the Provincial Congress and was chosen by his peers as that assembly's President. He presided over the Second Provincial Congress and attended the Continental Congress in Philadelphia. These were exciting times, America was fighting for independence against her parental figure, the British king, and cries of liberty were heard in the streets. Bulloch was suddenly recalled to attend official duties in Georgia and missed his opportunity to sign the revered Declaration of Independence, though he was the first to receive a copy of the sacred document. He gathered the citizens of Savannah and publicly read its contents.

In early 1776, Bulloch led the Savannah militia to rid Tybee Island of the marauding British troops. In June was chosen the first Republican President of the colony of Georgia. Under his leadership, the first constitution of Georgia was approved. With much left to be done in the Georgia colony, Archibald Bulloch suddenly fell ill and died mysteriously in February 1777; he was 47 years old. As the ambitious Button Gwinnett succeeded to the office, accusations of poisoning and murder were heard throughout Savannah. Though nothing was ever proven, a cloud of distrust descended on Gwinnett.

Archibald Bulloch wielded great influence on the developing colony of Georgia. He had a one year old son at the time of his death, who would eventually become a United States Senator and Savannah mayor. Branches of his family tree spread downward several generations to a noted grandchild, President Theodore "Teddy" Roosevelt. Archibald Bulloch was, indeed, an American icon.

GEN. SAMUEL ELBERT (1740-1788)

Samuel Elbert, who became brigadier general in the Continental Army and Governor of Georgia, migrated to this Province from South Carolina as an orphan youth during the Colonial period. He prospered in mercantile pursuits and as an Indian trader; became a member of the Commons House of Assembly from Ebenezer, and was captain of a grenadier company prior to the Revolution.

A staunch patriot, Elbert served on the Council of Safety and commissioned (1776) Lieut. - Colonel of the first Continental regiment raised here. Col. Elbert participated in two Florida expeditions; gallantly commanded the Georgia Line at the fall of Savannah (1778); was captured by the British at Briar Creek (1779) and later took part in the Yorktown campaign. He was promoted to Brig. General in the Continental Army in 1783. He became Governor of this State, Sheriff of Chatham County and Grand Master of Georgia Masons.

Elbert died Nov. 2, 1788, and was buried at Rae's Hall Plantation near Savannah, in time, the burial place of the Revolutionary hero was forsaken and forgotten. During the early years of the 20th century the grave was desecrated and exposed when earth was removed from the Indian mound on which he and his wife, Elizabeth Rae Elbert, were buried. Following identification by acceptable evidence, the remains of the Revolutionary hero were rescued in 1916 by a committee of the Sons of the Revolution, headed by R. J. Travis. The bones of the patriot were reinterred here in 1924 with full military honors.

Colonial Park Cemetery, Savannah
GPS Coordinates: N32.07602, W81.090512

Samuel Elbert was born in 1740 at Prince William Parish, southern Carolina. He was orphaned at an early age and eventually wandered into the colony of Georgia. In Savannah, Elbert became one of the most successful merchants of the Georgia colony, owning a vast amount of property and operating a profitable import business. His commercial pursuits led to concerns about the increasingly restrictive British economic policies preceding the American Revolution.

Elbert joined the Friends of Liberty and began attending meetings held at Tondee's Tavern, plotting against the Royal Government. In June 1774, he was elected Captain of a Grenadier Company and later appointed to the Savannah Committee of Safety. He joined the Continental Army as a Colonel serving under General Lachlan McIntosh.

May of the following year, found Elbert in command of an expedition against the British in Florida, where he was captured at Fort Oglethorpe in April of 1778. A Charles Towne newspaper published a letter received from Elbert telling of his experiences, it read:

Dear General, Frederica, April 19, 1778

I have the happiness to inform you that about 10 o'clock this afternoon, the Brigantine Hinchinbrooke, the Sloop Rebecca, and a prize brig, all struck the British Tyrant's colors and surrendered to the American arms. Having received intelligence that the above vessels were at this place, I put about three hundred men, by detachment from the troops under my command at Fort Howe, on board the three gallies—the Washington, Capt. Hardy; the Lee, Capt Braddock; and the Bulloch, Capt. Hatcher; and a detachment of artillery with a field piece, under Capt. Young, I put on board a boat. With this little army, we embarked at Darien, and last evening effected a landing at a bluff about a mile below the town; leaving Col. White on board the Lee, Capt. Melvin on board the Washington, and Lieut. Petty on board the Bulloch, each with a sufficient party of troops.

Immediately on Landing, I dispatched Lieut. Col. Ray and Major Roberts, with about 100 men, who

276

marched directly up to the town, and made prisoners three marines and two sailors belonging to the Hinchinbrooke. It being late, the gallies did not engage until this morning.

You must imagine what my feelings were, to see our three little men of war going to the attack of these three vessels, who have spread terror on our coast, and who were drawn up in order of battle; but the weight of our metal soon damped the courage of these heroes, who soon took to their boats; and, as many as could, abandoned the vessels with everything on board, of which we immediately took possession.

What is extraordinary, we have not one man hurt. Capt. Ellis [of the Hinchinbrooke] is drowned, and Capt. Mowbry [of the Rebecca] made his escape. As soon as I see Col. White, who has not yet come to us with his prizes, I shall consult with him, the other three officers, and the commanding officers of the galleys, on the expediency of attacking the Galatea now lying off Jekyll. I send you this by Brigade Major Habersham, who will inform you of the other particulars. I am. & c.

SAMUEL ELBERT, Col. Commandant

Elbert was ecstatic. Two years earlier, the *Hinchinbrooke*, in the company of the twenty gun *Lady of Scarborough* and another vessel, sailed boldly up the Savannah River and under heavy rifle fire from the Americans, made off with several vessels laden with rice. Her capture was certainly a morale booster to supporters of the Revolution in the south who were struggling to turn the tide of war in their favor.

Being active in virtually all of the Georgia battles during the Revolution, Elbert was taken prisoner after the Battle of Briar Creek on March 3, 1779. He was exchanged for a British general two years later and promoted to Brigadier General. Elbert was immediately given orders to report to General George Washington and was on hand for the American victory at Yorktown. He was placed in charge of the large deposit of arms and military stores taken in the battle, eventually rising to the rank of Major General of the State Militia.

In 1785, the General Assembly elected Samuel Elbert Governor of Georgia, succeeding John Houston. Even though his health was beginning to fail, he accepted the honor and devoted much of his attention to something he already held dear, Georgia defenses and Creek Indian relations. During his term in office he signed legislation appointing the Board of Trustees, which chartered the University of Georgia. After his term, Elbert returned to his home in Savannah where he served one year as sheriff of Chatham County, but by then his health had noticeably deteriorated.

Samuel Elbert died November 1, 1788 and was buried on the grounds of his home in Savannah. Elbert's gravesite was neglected and forgotten over the years and in 1924, the mound in which both he and his wife were buried was desecrated. Their remains were reinterred in the Colonial Park Cemetery in Savannah. On December 10, 1790, the General Assembly named Georgia's 13th county in his honor, Elbert County.

JOSEPH CLAY, PATRIOT

A native of Yorkshire, Joseph Clay (1741-1804) settled at Savannah at the age of nineteen. His uncle, James Habersham, declared that his "industry" was "highly commendable" and "his Abilities for Trade unquestionable." Fulfilling his early promise, Clay prospered in Georgia as a merchant and rice planter.

He was a staunch supporter of American rights, served on the Council of Safety and in the Provincial Congress, and took part in the celebrated raid on the Royal powder magazine at Savannah in 1775. During the Revolutionary War Clay rendered efficient and faithful service to the American cause as deputy paymaster general of the Continental Army for the Southern Department. His career in the Revolution was distinguished by "Virtue & fortitude," said General James Jackson, who also paid high tribute to Clay's wife Ann (whose remains also lie here) for her beneficent care of the American wounded after the Battle of Camden.

In the years following the Revolution Joseph Clay held several positions of importance, including state treasurer and judge of the inferior court. He was one of the first trustees for the state college that later became the University of Georgia. He died Dec. 15, 1804. Joseph Clay's published letters (1776-1793) constitute a valuable historical source work for the period.

Colonial Park Cemetery, Savannah
GPS Coordinates: N32.07602, W81.090512

Joseph Clay at the age of nineteen, first stepped onto American soil in 1760, when he chose to join his uncle, James Habersham and cousins in Savannah. Habersham was very impressed with his ambitious young nephew until like Habersham's own sons, Clay joined the Liberty Boys to fight for American Independence. Habersham was a staunch Loyalist and refused to accept the path of his sons and nephew.

Clay and the Liberty Boys, in full view of the Royal Government, raided the powder magazine and stole six hundred pounds of gunpowder. Clay attained the rank of Colonel in the Continental Army during the Revolutionary War and was appointed Deputy Paymaster General in 1777. After the Revolution, he became a successful merchant.

Joseph Clay kept detailed correspondence with a number of friends and associates. His letters were eventually published and are available at the Georgia Historical Society in Savannah. It was in one of his missives to his friend Henry Laurens of southern Carolina that Clay expressed hope for his own and Georgia's recovery from the Revolutionary War. It read:

> "...Our State is setling again very fast, especially the back Country — a large Cession of land as far So'therly as the Oconees has lately been agreed to by the Creek Indians which will be setled immediately. Some valuable setlers have and are coming in from East Florida. Our Ports has been tolerably filled this Winter and though individuals will feel the effects of the War for many years, I may Say all their lives, yet the Country at large will soon recover. Nothing is wanting but hands to cultivate the earth. I have entered into business again with a hope by my Industry to retrieve past losses and with an expectation of being by that means more in the way of collecting my Old Debts; how far it may answer either of these purposes, time only can shew. . . ."[14]

Clay's hopes for a successful future were realized when he was elected to the Continental Congress, but for unknown reasons he did not attend. He became one of the original trustees of Franklin College, which later became the University of Georgia. In 1782, Clay was elected Treasurer for the state of Georgia and appointed Judge of the United States Court, the District of Georgia in 1786 until his retirement due to ill health in 1801.

Joseph Clay died at Savannah in 1804; he was sixty-three years old. His body was laid to rest near his uncle, James Habersham, in Colonial Park Cemetery.

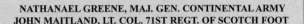

Colonial Park Cemetery, Savannah
GPS Coordinates: N32.07602, W81.090512

Graham's vault at Colonial Park Cemetery was the burial site for two revered patriots; General Nathanael Greene, who fought with conviction against the oppression of the British Crown, and Colonel John Maitland, who served the 7th Regiment of Scotch Foot with distinction against the American uprising to claim British territory.

Major General Greene rose in rank to become second only to George Washington, the only other Continental General to serve throughout the entire Revolutionary War. He attained this level from very humble beginnings. Greene initially entered the army as a lowly private. Well praised for his conduct on the battlefields of Trenton, Princeton, Brandywine, Germantown and Monmouth, he was later appointed the Quartermaster General at the personal request of General Washington and served until 1780. In July 1780, Greene returned to active service and in the fall, he presided over the trial of British spy, Major John Andree, who was convicted and hung.

Greene was chiefly responsible for the success of the American forces in the south. After General Gates was defeated at the Battle of Camden in southern Carolina, Greene was chosen to replace Gates as Commander of the Southern Theater of War. In December 1780, he assumed command of the defeated army, quickly reorganizing, and eight months later led his troops to victory over British control of the Carolinas. His men were defeated at the Battle of Guilford Courthouse with few losses, but British Commander Cornwallis was unable to recuperate due to lack of supplies, and he was forced to withdraw. Greene's strategic knowledge and defensive skills brought the war in the south to a successful end. Three years after having survived the American Revolution, Nathanael Greene fell dead of sunstroke near his Mulberry Grove Plantation in Savannah.

Lieutenant Colonel John Maitland was born the eighth son of the 6th Earl of Lauderdale and Lady Elizabeth Ogilvy in Haddington, Scotland. As a young man, he was commissioned Captain of Marines in 1757 and served in the Seven Years' War. It was there that he lost his right arm. After peace was declared, Maitland became the Clerk of the Pipe of the Scottish Exchequer and eventually was elected to Parliament in 1774. He returned to active military duty in 1777 and was sent to the American colonies. In 1778, now Major Maitland transferred to the Army and was again promoted to the rank of Lieutenant Colonel of the 1st Battalion of the 71st Foot of Fraser's Highlanders. He served with honor and on December 29, 1778, took part in the capture of Savannah.

In the fall of 1779, General Prevost established his headquarters in Savannah and was threatened by the French forces under the command of the Comte d'Estaing. French forces attacked from the Savannah River and the Continental troops from land. On September 16th, Admiral d'Estaing demanded Prevost's surrender "to the arms of the King of France." Prevost was given twenty-four hours to think it over. Meanwhile, British reinforcements arrived, including Maitland who had brought eight hundred men from Beaufort. Maitland and his men conducted a valiant march through the swamps to arrive at Prevost's side. Prevost decided to fight and the Continentals began a two week siege culminating in a major attack on October 9, 1779. The Americans suffered great losses, most of the casualties belonging to the French troops and included the Polish patriot, Casimir Pulaski. Lieutenant Colonel Maitland did not live to celebrate the victory.

Maitland believed that getting eight hundred men across the swamps was all but impossible and forcing his army through the enemy lines to join General Prevost was suicidal.   During the siege, Maitland's body was wracked with fever and chills, though his mind remained unabated; he lived only two days after the French took Savannah. He succumbed to malaria and died on October 22, 1779, at the age of 47.

Lieutenant Colonel John Maitland was buried in the Graham's family vault in Savannah's Colonial Park Cemetery. In 1981, led by distinguished Savannah pathologist, Dr. H. Preston Russell and the Georgia Historical Society, Maitland was iden-tified, presumably because of his missing arm. His remains were reinterred in a small box and placed in the family vault beneath the Lauderdale Aisle in St. Mary's Church, Haddington, Scotland and marked with a bronze plaque thanking the Georgians for his return. His name is inscribed on the board marking family burials. With the exception of the British spy, John Andréé, who was returned after his hanging in 1821, John Maitland is noted as the only other British officer to be returned to his homeland during the American Revolution. Unlike the United States, the tradition in Scotland is that a soldier is buried where he falls.

Major General Nathanael Greene lies beneath the obelisk in Johnson Square memorializing his contribution to the American Revolution. Lieutenant Colonel John Maitland lies among generations of his family, a patriot in his own right. Both men from opposing sides, shared in death what they fought for in life, a plot of American soil.

Colonial Park Cemetery, Savannah
GPS Coordinates: N32.07602, W81.090512

Denis Nicholas Cottineau de Kerloguen is truly an unsung hero. Born in Nantes, France, in 1745, his bravery and skill while serving in the French navy was recognized and he quickly advanced to the rank of Lieutenant. His reputation was called to the attention of famed American naval officer, John Paul Jones, who recruited Cottineau into the American navy during the Revolutionary War. Cottineau accepted the rank of Captain and served under Jones, taking command of the ship *Pallas*.

Today, few recall the story of John Paul Jones and the *Bon Homme Richard*, which quite possibly remains the greatest tale of daring attributed to an American naval officer. The converted merchant ship was old and slow sailing, her decks were virtually rotted through and she was armed with antique French cannons, which quite often exploded when fired. So armed, Jones sailed out of L'Orient in August 1779 on what was to be his most famous cruise.

Accompanying Jones was Captain Cottineau commanding the *Pallas*, Captain Landais commanding the *Alliance* and the smaller ship *Vengeance*, which played no part in battle. A cutter and two privateers made up the balance of the of the battle group, however, these three soon deserted. Their mission: to fire on the Scotch and English coasts, take the city of Leith, strike when possible at the British shipping fleet and take what cargo they held.

Jones commanded with a strong will and iron fist. The sailors he led were a motley crew; Portuguese, Malays, Swedes, French and even, English prisoners. When the time came to fight, the men under Jones' leadership distinguished themselves in battle. Jones' trouble came not with his crew but with an officer. Landais was insubordinate at every turn, he would sail off course with the *Alliance* only to return the next day to the squadron with utter contempt of any authority, especially Jones, of whom he harbored excessive jealousy.

At dusk on September 23, 1779, the American squadron faced a fleet of Baltic merchantmen, escorted by the newly constructed *Serapis* and the smaller but very powerful *Countess of Scarborough*. The *Serapis* fired on the old *Bon Homme Richard* relentlessly. The *Richard* was, quite literally, blown to bits. The old ship was taking on water, the crew was forced to man the pumps or drown, loud groans were heard from the *Richard*'s timbers and the decks began to buckle and collapse. The planks ran red with the blood of the dead and dying, yet through it all stood a defiant John Paul Jones.

Another blast shook his ship, this time from the opposite direction. Jones assumed the *Countess of Scarborough* was making herself known, but his attention remained on the *Serapis*. *Serapis'* Captain Pearson hailed Jones, thinking him about to surrender, "Have you struck?" he called, meaning have you struck your flag in defeat. Jones responded with his now famous words, "I have not yet begun to fight!" At the final surrender, it was Captain Pearson who surrendered.

Where, you might ask, was Cottineau during the battle? Cottineau, after an hour of hard fighting had taken the *Countess of Scarborough* and stood ready to aid Jones in his fight. Landais arrived and Cottineau called to him to take charge of the *Countess*, he would see to Jones. Landais, in an insane act, sailed around Cottineau and his prize, when he came into range Landais fired his cannons. You see, it wasn't the *Countess* who fired upon the *Bon Homme Richard* but the *Alliance* with Landais at her helm. Cottineau stared in disbelief.

Jones and the crew of the doomed *Bon Homme Richard* boarded the *Serapis*. They sadly watched as the old ship slipped beneath the waves to her watery grave. When told the story of Landais' treachery, Jones immediately brought charges.

After retirement, Cottineau and his wife moved to Santo Domingo where they purchased a coffee plantation. The couple had two sons, Achilles and Denis. When the slaves revolted and began to massacre the French on their island country, the couple escaped to Pennsylvania with their children and Reverend Antoine Carles.

In 1803 the Cottineaus' migrated to Savannah where Reverend Carles became the Pastor of the Church of St. John the Baptist. Captain Denis Nicholas Cottineau died five years later. The only notice of his death was posted in the mortuary reports at Savannah's City Hall, read:

> Denis Nichs. Cottineau, 63 years, native of France. Gentleman. From consumption. Died Nov. 29, 1808. Buried Nov. 30. Was afflicted three years. He died and was buried from the house of the Roman Catholic priest, Mr. Carles, on Broughton street.

The local newspaper made no mention of his death. Four years later his son, Achilles, died of yellow fever at the age of 22 and was buried beside his father. The younger son joined the American navy and was killed in a duel while trying to defend the honor of friend; he was shot through the heart and buried on foreign soil. His mother read the notice in the newspaper,

> "Two midshipmen on the *John Adams* fought a duel on the 3d inst., one of whom was killed the first fire."

Weeks later she was informed the slain duelist was her son. In 1825, Madame Cottineau returned to France and resumed her position in the court circle of the king.

The name Captain Denis Nicholas Cottineau has vanished from history. All that remains is a barely legible headstone in Colonial Cemetery. The epitaph has faded after two hundred years, yet Captain Cottineau has earned this honor:

**Sacred
to the memory of
Denis L. Cottineau de
Kerloguen
Native of Nantes (France)
Formerly a Lieut. in his late Most
Christian Majesty's Navy. Knight
of the Royal Military Order
of St. Louis. Capt. Commanding a
Ship of War of the United States
During their Revolution, and
a member of the Cincinnati
Society.
Obit. Nov. 29th 1808. Aged 63 years.**

JAMES JOHNSTON
Georgia's First Newspaper Publisher & Printer

Here repose the remains of James Johnston (1738-1808) - editor of Georgia's
first newspaper.
A native of Scotland, Johnston settled at Savannah in 1762, "Recommended as
a person regularly bred to and well skilled in the Art and mystery of Printing," he
was appointed public printer of the Province by legislative Act during the following year. The first issue of the GEORGIA GAZETTE appeared at Savannah on
April 7, 1763, and with some interruptions publication continued until 1802.
In the American Revolution Johnston sympathized with the royal government
and, in his words, "refused to admit to his Paper any of the Seditious publica-
tions then circulating thro' the different provinces." He closed his printing press
in February, 1776. When British rule was restored in 1779 he returned to
Savannah and resumed publication of the newspaper under the title,
ROYAL GEORGIA GAZETTE.
A good man and a skilled printer, Johnston did not lose the respect of the
Patriots. After the Revolution he was permitted to return. In 1783 he began
publication again under the style,
GAZETTE OF THE STATE OF GEORGIA.
He died in his 70th year, October 4, 1808.

Colonial Park Cemetery, Savannah
GPS Coordinates: N32.07602, W81.090512

J ames Johnston was born in Scotland, and at the age of thirty-four, settled in Savannah. He was a skilled printer and
eventually established the *Georgia Gazette* in 1763. The newspaper was the first of its kind in the Georgia Colony.
Johnston articles were biased, based on his loyalty to the English Crown. The *Gazette* printing house was located between
Abercorn and Drayton streets, where the Marshall House now stands. Johnston was appointed the official printer of the colony
and expanded his operation to include paper currency and government documents. He essentially became the Savannah mint
and printer.

The *Gazette* was published continually from April 1763 through November 21, 1765, when the British Stamp Act forced
all operations to halt for six months. Publication resumed in May 1766 under the name of the *Royal Georgia Gazette*, but less
than a year later with the Revolutionary War looming heavily on the horizon, Johnston was again forced to discontinue printing.

In 1783, at the conclusion of the Revolution, Johnston was allowed to remain in Savannah when so many loyalists were
pressured to leave, imprisoned or killed. Amazingly, Johnston even retained the respect of the colonists and began publishing
again. James Johnston was forced to change the name of the publication for a third time. The publication's name became
Gazette of the State of Georgia, which was published until his death on October 4, 1808. The tone of this last publication was
considerably more neutral.

Colonial Park Cemetery, Savannah
GPS Coordinates: N32.07602, W81.090512

J ames Habersham had three sons, James Jr., Joseph and John. The sons lay beside their distinguished father in Colonial Park Cemetery, much closer in death than they were in life. Where the elder Joseph was a devoted loyalist, his offspring joined the Sons of Liberty and served the American cause through both military and civic duties.

Joseph, the middle son, was by far the best known of the three. Born in Savannah on July 28, 1751, he was a founding member of the Friends of Liberty[15], accepting his first commissioned appointment in the organization, just short of his 23rd birthday. After receiving confidential information of the British skirmish planned for Lexington, Joseph accompanied the group on January 18, 1776, on a raid, which seized the gunpowder stored in the royal magazine. Joseph's leadership during the raid led to his appointment to the Council of Safety[16] in June of that year. In July 1776, he commanded the party that captured a government ship with several cannons and 15,000 pounds of powder.

Perhaps Joseph Habersham's greatest moment was when he raised a body of volunteers, who converged on the home of Royal Governor Wright. The governor was taken prisoner and held captive in his own home under armed guard. Joseph defended Savannah as Major of Georgia's 1st Battalion in March of 1776 and again in 1778, when the British captured Savannah. The fall of Savannah led Joseph to move his family to safety in Virginia, but he was unable to stay away. Joseph joined the Frenchman d'Estaing on the disastrous attempt to recover Savannah in 1779. By the end of the Revolution, Joseph had attained the rank of Lieutenant Colonel.

Joseph Habersham went on to become Mayor of Savannah and served in the State Assembly of Georgia in February 1795. Later that year, he was appointed Postmaster General of the United States. After his retirement, Joseph accepted the position of President of the United States Bank in Savannah, where he remained until the expiration of its charter in 1802. Joseph Habersham, soldier and statesman, died in Savannah November 17, 1815. Joseph was the last of the Habersham brothers to pass.

James Jr., the oldest Habersham son, was a leading merchant and planter. He was quite vocal during the Friends of Liberty gatherings concerning the restrictions and excessive taxation the British continually forced on the colonials. Taxation put a terrible strain on his business dealings. James was elected as Speaker of the Georgia General Assembly in 1782 and again, in 1784. He served on the Board of Trustees assigned to create a public secondary educational facility in 1785, resulting in the establishment of Franklin College, today known as the University of Georgia.

James Habersham Jr. died in 1799, but is said to still make his presence felt in what was once his home in Savannah. His home is today called the Olde Pink House Restaurant and Planters Tavern. His spirit seems to prefer quiet Sunday afternoons at home, which is when most of his visits are noted.

The youngest son, John was born in Savannah in 1754. Thanks to his father, John received a good English education and like his brother James, he pursued a career as a merchant. John's patriot blood ran hot; he assumed an active role in the Revolutionary War. He advanced to the rank of Major in the 1st Georgia Continental Regiment and earned the trust of the Native Americans. After the war ended, President George Washington appointed John as Indian Agent. He was a member of the Continental Congress in 1785 through 1786 and the Collector of Customs at Savannah in 1789 and 1799. John Habersham died near Savannah on November 19, 1799.

The Habersham children and grandchildren continued the tradition of civic service. John's son, Joseph Clay Habersham, became a physician and was appointed Health Officer of Savannah, President of the Medical Society of Georgia and was known throughout his life for his benevolence and his love of science. James's grandson, Richard Wylly, was elected to Congress in 1839 and continued until his death. While in office he enacted legislation and funding for the establishment of the first Norse telegraph line. His son, Alexander Wylly, was a naval officer. Upon his resignation from the Unites States Navy, he became a merchant in Japan. Alexander Wylly Habersham was the first to introduce Japanese tea into this country. In 1857, he published *My Last Cruise*, an account of the United States North Pacific exploration.

Obviously, the Habersham family has given much to Savannah, Georgia and the United States. May the Habersham name long be remembered!

The Olde Pink House

MAJOR JOHN BERRIEN
(1759-1815)

In 1775 John Berrien of New Jersey came to the province of Georgia, where one of his mother's kin had previously settled. His father, John Berrien (1711-1772), was a judge of the supreme court of New Jersey and a trustee of Princeton College. From the Berrien home at Rock Hill, N.J., General Washington issued his farewell address to the army in 1783.

At the age of 17 John Berrien was commissioned 2nd Lieutenant in the first Georgia Continental brigade (1776). A few months later he was promoted to 1st Lieutenant and the following year he was commissioned Captain. A firm supporter of General Lachlan McIntosh in the troubles that befell that officer after his slaying of Button Gwinnett in a duel. Berrien followed McIntosh to Washington's headquarters in 1777 and served as brigade major of the North Carolina troops at Valley Forge.

After the Revolution Berrien returned to Georgia with his family, which included his young son, John MacPherson Berrien, who was destined to become one of Georgia's most illustrious statesman. Active in public life in Georgia, Major John Berrien was for several years Collector of Customs at Savannah; served as an Alderman, and was State Treasurer at Louisville (1796-1799). Berrien died at Savannah on November 6, 1815.

Colonial Park Cemetery, Savannah
GPS Coordinates: N32.07602, W81.090512

John Berrien was exposed to politics and public service from birth. His father, also John Berrien, was Lord, Chief Justice of Trenton, New Jersey. It was through his father's political connections that young John first met George Washington, who gave his final address as General of the American forces from the Berrien home.

Berrien, the younger, had a sister called Valeria, who married Dr. Peter Le Conte and moved to his home in Georgia. John, at the age of fifteen followed, settling nearby in Savannah. He joined the Georgia militia as a Second Lieutenant under the command of General Lachlan McIntosh and was quickly noticed. Berrien was promoted to First Lieutenant in a battalion ordered to protect and defend the colony of Georgia. By 1777, he was commissioned as Captain and assigned to the Eighth Company of the First Battalion of Continental troops. Patriot John Hancock, who was very interested in the boy's progress, signed Berrien's commission. General McIntosh was reassigned after the fatal duel with Button Gwinnett, as a part of General George Washington's staff at Valley Forge. Captain Berrien resigned his commission and followed General McIntosh as a volunteer staff aid.

Captain Berrien was grievously wounded at Monmouth, struck in the head by a musket ball. The injury, although not fatal, would plague him with headaches for the remainder of his life. Toward the end of the Revolutionary War, his promotion to Major was signed by Edward Telfair, Captain General, Governor and Commander in Chief of the state of Georgia. Major Berrien returned to Savannah. It was there that he led a troop of Dragoons of the Georgia Militia commanded by Colonel James Jackson. The year was 1786 and the war was finished.

In 1787, he was appointed Collector for the Port of Savannah and after serving four years he was promoted to Inspector of Revenue for the port. George Washington and Thomas Jefferson signed his appointment. Berrien also served as Georgia State Treasurer and President of the Society of the Cincinnati in Georgia.

Berrien's patriot lineage continued through his son, John Macpherson Berrien. John Macpherson was known as the "honey tongued Georgia youth," and "the American Cicero." He completed his Bachelor's degree from the College of New Jersey[17] in 1796 and by 1799, was admitted to the Georgia bar reading law for Joseph Clay, then a federal judge. Although this was the usual progression, John Macpherson Berrien was a mere nineteen years old upon his admittance to the bar.

John Macpherson Berrien was selected by President Andrew Jackson to serve in his cabinet as Attorney General. Unfortunately, his tenure was short lived, strangely enough, because of a barmaid.

Peggy O'Neale was the daughter of Georgetown tavern owner. She was very attractive and eventually, became the mistress of John Eaton, a bachelor Senator from Tennessee. The problem was the liaison began while Peggy's husband was out to sea. When news of her husband's death arrived in Washington in January 1829 she wasted no time with mourning and married Senator Eaton rather quickly. President Jackson named Senator Eaton to the post of Secretary of War and had practically ordered the marriage in order to make an honest woman of pretty Peggy. The difficulty was that the other wives refused, including Mrs. John Macpherson Berrien, to have anything to do with Peggy. President Jackson was livid and ordered his cabinet to instruct their wives to be civil Mrs. Eaton. John Macpherson Berrien, who was about to be named Chief Justice of the United States, refused to make any excuse for his wife and would not instruct Mrs. Berrien on her behavior. In the face of the President's anger, John Macpherson Berrien resigned his post followed by most of President Jackson's cabinet.

John Macpherson returned to Savannah and resumed his law practice. He received honorary Doctor of Law degree from Princeton and the University of Georgia, where he served as Trustee for thirty years. John Macpherson Berrien's first wife, Eliza Anciaux died in 1828, leaving him with nine children. Eliza Hunter, his much younger second wife, died in 1852, this union had produced six children. John Macpherson Berrien died on New Years Day, 1856 at the age of 74.

The Reverend Charles Colcock Jones, famed Georgia historian, wrote of John Macpherson Berrien, "Few professional men die with so few enemies and so few faults."

HUGH McCALL (1767-1823)
EARLY GEORGIAN HISTORIAN

Hugh McCall who is buried here was the author of the first history of Georgia.

Forced by ill health into retirement, McCall, who was a brevet major, U.S. Infantry, became interested in the history of his adopted State. In spite of severe handicaps, he wrote a much needed history of Georgia. The first volume was published at Savannah, in 1811. The second volume, appeared five years later, carried his "History of Georgia" through the Revolutionary period. Time has not impaired the value and the usefulness of McCall's work.

His father, Colonel James McCall, played a heroic role in the Revolutionary War in the Carolinas. Hugh McCall passed his boyhood during those trying times. The closing words of the first history of this State are an ever timely reminder to posterity that

"The blood which flowed from the suffering patriots of that day, should never be forgotten; and the precious jewel which was purchased by it, should be preserved with courage and remembered with gratitude, by succeeding generations."

Colonial Park Cemetery, Savannah
GPS Coordinates: N32.07602, W81.090512

Hugh McCall was born a few scant years before the Revolutionary War in Carolina. His father, Colonel James McCall was a noted Revolutionary War hero serving in the Carolina militia. Little is known of McCall's younger years, yet what is known is that at the advanced age of 27, he became an ensign in the Third Sub Legion Army. McCall obviously served the army with distinction because by August 1800, he was promoted to Captain and Deputy Paymaster General. While serving as Deputy Paymaster, McCall wrote the first volume of *The History of Georgia*, published in 1811. In 1812, he was promoted to Major.

During the War of 1812, McCall was assigned as jailer of the British prisoners held in Savannah. Charges were filed against him before the City Council alleging that he conversed with the prisoners, which was illegal. It was the Savannah City Council's decision on October 24, 1814, that Major McCall was not guilty of the allegation and thereby, cleared of all charges. The accusation of wrongdoing seemed to sap the last bit of strength McCall possessed. Ill health forced his retirement from the army in 1815. A year later, the second volume of *The History of Georgia* was published.

The volumes dealt with the history of Georgia from its beginnings until the beginning of the Revolutionary War. Depending on the memories of elderly veterans as his primary resource, documentation was a rarity at that time, there are many inaccuracies in the text of his editions. Despite the obvious errors, the two volume set is very rare and a treasured item in historical circles.

By the time he retired, McCall was an invalid, unable to stand or walk. A specially built cart was constructed so that he could retain some sort of mobility. Cato, his manservant, remained a constant at his side, moving him sometimes cradled in his arms, from one location to another and attending to all of McCall's needs. He became the military storekeeper in Savannah in 1818 and in Charleston in 1821, a position he held very briefly. His health deteriorated rapidly and on June 10, 1824, Hugh McCall died at the age of fifty-seven.

His estate consisted of a grand pianoforte, backgammon table, mahogany furniture and two wheel chairs. McCall had a small library and wine cellar. Having never married, he left $200 and ten shares of Planters Bank Stock to his loyal companion, Cato. He made a generous contribution to the Union Society for the maintenance and up keep of the Bethesda Orphanage and anything remaining, he left his brother and two sisters.

Hugh McCall was buried in the Colonial Park Cemetery with full military honors.

WILLIAM SCARBROUGH
Promoter of the First Transoceanic Steamship

William Scarbrough (1776-1838) was the moving force among the enterprising business men of Savannah who in 1819 sent the first steamship across the Atlantic Ocean. The corporate charter which Scarbrough and his associates obtained from the Georgia Legislature in 1818 recited that "they have formed themselves into an association, under the style and name of the Savannah Steam Ship Company, to attach, either as auxiliary or principal, the propulsion of steam to sea vessels, for the purpose of navigating the Atlantic and other oceans..."

The side-wheel steamship "Savannah," a vessel of 350 tons, was built in the North under specifications of Scarbrough and his business associates. She steamed from Savannah May 22, 1819, on her epoch-making voyage to Europe, reaching Liverpool 27 days later.

William Scarbrough was the son of a wealthy planter of the Beaufort District, S.C. Educated in Europe, he moved to Savannah about 1798 and soon attained a leading place in the life of the community, becoming one of Savannah's so-called "Merchant Princes" of the era. The handsome Scarbrough residence, which still stands on West Broad Street, was a center of the social life of the city. There William Scarbrough and his vibrant wife, Julia Bernard Scarbrough (1786-1851), entertained President James Monroe as a house guest in 1819.

Colonial Park Cemetery, Savannah
GPS Coordinates: N32.07602, W81.090512

William Scarbrough was born in northern Carolina in the year of the Revolutionary War, 1776. He was educated in Europe at the University of Edinburgh and at the age of twenty-six immigrated to Savannah.

Everything Scarbrough touched seemed to turn to gold. He held a variety of positions including that of a bank director, manager of elections, member of the Board of Health, vestryman of Christ Church, Vice Consul of Denmark and Sweden and

Consul General of Russia. At the height of his fortune and popularity in the community, he became the principal investor and President of the Savannah Steamship Company.

The Savannah Steamship Company was about to launch the SS *Savannah*, a huge sailing ship supplemented by the use of a steam driven engine, even when the seas were at a dead calm the ship could still steam forward. The SS *Savannah* was the first steamship to cross the Atlantic. Despite the fact that the famed ship was received with much curiosity and interest, it was a financial disaster.

Scarbrough contracted architect William Jay to begin the design and construction of his home in 1819. He requested that it reflect his status in the community and the wealth he had amassed. Construction began on the Greek Revival home, which featured a grand entrance flanked by a pair of wrought iron lanterns. The impressive mansion listed a fashionable address on West Broad Street and Scarbrough referred to it as "the Castle."

The saying, "everything that rises must surely fall," most certainly applies to the Midas fortune of Scarbrough, his wealth was gained very quickly and just as quickly, it disappeared. In November 1820, Scarbrough at age forty-four was completely bankrupt. The courts declared him insolvent and seized his home and furnishings to be sold at public auction to satisfy his debtors. The home once called the "Savannah Whitehouse," because President James Monroe spent a good deal of time as a visitor there during his southern tour in 1819, was gone. Scarbrough had reached rock bottom. Not only had his finances completely disappeared, but he found himself on the verge of a complete emotional and physical collapse.

The house was purchased by Godfrey Barnsley and later the Dominick O'Byrne family. It eventually became a part of the Board of Education and was used as the West Broad Street in 1878 until 1962, when the school system abandoned the structure. The mansion was a dilapidated ruin due years of neglect and abuse. School children had left their mark and the Board of Education had painted the once opulent structure institutional green.

The Historic Savannah Foundation acquired the property in 1972 and began restoration with the help of Pennsylvania architect John Molner. The restorations were for naught, again the house was abandoned and left to stand idle for twenty years.

The Scarbrough House, as it was known, was obtained by the Ships of the Sea Maritime Museum. In 1995, another restoration began. The repairs included a new roof based on the documented design notes of original architect William Jay, a rear portico and an enlarged garden were all added. The restoration was completed in 1997 and the mansion museum was once again an impressive Greek Revival Castle.

The Museum houses a large collection of ship models, paintings and maritime antiques. Scarbrough, President of the Savannah Steamship Company, would have been proud. The Ships of the Sea Maritime Museum is located in the downtown historic district on what is now M. L. King, Jr. Boulevard. The museum is open Tuesday through Sunday from 10:00 a.m. until 5:00 p.m., admission is charged.

EDWARD GREENE MALBONE
(1777-1807)

Beneath this modest slab rest the remains of America's foremost
painter of miniatures.
Malbone, a native of Rhode Island, began his career in Providence
at the age of seventeen. He pursued his calling in Boston, New
York, Philadelphia, Charleston and in London, England.
Exacting and unceasing work undermined his constitution. Having
sought in vain to recover his health in the Island of Jamaica, he
came to Savannah in fore-knowledge of death and died here in the
home of his cousin, Robert MacKay, on May 7, 1807.
Though not yet thirty years of age when he died, he left no peer in
his art. Time has justified the statements you may read here in his
epitaph. Today, Malbone is acknowledged to be the finest miniaturist his country has yet produced, and among the greatest of all
time anywhere.

Colonial Park Cemetery, Savannah
GPS Coordinates: N32.07628, W81.090512

Edward Greene was born in Newport Rhode Island in August 1777, to humble circumstances. His grandfather, Godfrey Malbone, was a wealthy merchant and privateer. A run of bad luck, including the collapse of the slave trade and a fire that engulfed his lavish mansion, befell Godfrey. The misfortunes diminished his wealth so that two years later, Godfrey died penniless. His son and heir, John, was forced to make his way during the hard times following the British occupation of Newport. John Malbone never married the mother of his numerous children leaving Edward struggling to overcome the stigma to being born illegitimate. He won permission to use his father's family name by an Act of Legislature; thus, he became Edward Greene Malbone.

Malbone's youth was spent carefully studying the scene painters in the theatre of Newport. He looked for technique and style. Like a sponge, he soaked up the ambient talent of the painters around him. After selling his first landscape scene, Malbone was determined to give his life to art. He set off for Providence to seek his fortune as a portrait painter. Success came quickly for Malbone, he was 17 years old.

He remained in Providence for two years and began painting miniatures. He followed his art to Boston, New York, then Philadelphia, wherever a commission awaited his talent. In 1800, he accompanied his friend Washington Allston to Charleston, and in 1801, the two traveled to Europe.

Benjamin West, President of the Royal Academy of Art, pleaded with Malbone to remain in London. Malbone was anxious to return to America and eventually made his home in Charleston, though he often visited his family in the north. Malbone's health began to deteriorate and in an attempt to restore it, he sailed to the West Indies in 1806.

Realizing that death would take him soon, Malbone returned to America. He traveled to Savannah where he would spend his remaining days with a cousin, Robert McKay. Edward Greene Malbone died May 7, 1807, two months before his thirtieth birthday. He was buried in Colonial Park Cemetery.

Malbone's art has been said to be without peer. Based on the work of Robin Jaffee Frank in *Love and Loss: American Portrait and Mourning Miniatures*, Malbone's miniatures stand alone, not only in the United States, but throughout the world. He drew with the utmost of correctness, acutely endowed with the power of discerning character and the ability to delineate it. He possessed a fine, delicate taste which lent grace to his work, while being irresistibly charming; but his preeminent excellence was in coloring, creating perfect harmony with utmost delicacy and absolute truth combined. Malbone's work is displayed in such outstanding locales as the Corcoran Gallery in Washington, the Smithsonian, the Boston Museum of Fine Arts and the Pennsylvania Academy of the Fine Arts, to name but a few.

He was extremely prolific, more than two hundred of his portraits have been identified through painstaking research. In one burst of creativity, in the spring of 1801, he completed thirty-one miniatures in and of Charleston in only three months. During the winter of 1804 and 1805, Malbone painted seventeen portraits, while spending two months in Boston.

Edward Greene Malbone's friend, Washington Allston eulogized him saying,

> "Malbone had the happy talent of elevating the character without impairing the likeness. This was remarkable in his male heads, and no woman ever lost beauty under his hand. To this he added a grace of execution all his own."

COL. JAMES S. MCINTOSH (1784-1847)

James S. McIntosh achieved an immortal record of gallantry in the War of 1812 and in the War with Mexico. In 1814 he saw considerable action on the Canadian border, being severely wounded by bayonets at Resaca de la Palma in 1846. When a fellow officer, who found him on the field, asked if he might be of any service, McIntosh replied, "Yes, give me water and show me my regiment." Returning to combat the following year despite his wounds and advanced years, the brave Georgian was mortally wounded while leading his brigade at the bloody storming of El Molino del Rey, Sept. 8, 1847. His remains were brought home by the State of Georgia in 1848 and were reinterred in the McIntosh vault with military honors.

A native of Liberty County, McIntosh was one of the "fighting McIntoshes" who illustrated their country on many battle-fields. He was the great nephew of Lachlan McIntosh and his father was the Revolutionary hero, John McIntosh, who when the British demanded the surrender of Fort Morris at Sunbury sent back the defiant answer: "Come and take it." Col. James S. McIntosh's son, James McQueen McIntosh became a general in the Confederate Army and was killed in Arkansas while another son, John Baillie McIntosh served the Union cause well, losing a leg at Winchester.

Colonial Park Cemetery, Savannah
GPS Coordinates: N32.07602, W81.090512

Colonel James Simmons McIntosh was born to be a military leader. The blood through his veins was that of famed Scottish warrior John McIntosh Mohr, his great grandfather, who fought along side General James Oglethorpe repulsing the Spanish at the Battle of Bloody Marsh. General John McIntosh, his father, defended Fort Morris at Sunbury responding to the British demand for surrender with the immortal words, "Come and take it!" The list of heroic ancestors could extend for pages.

Colonel James McIntosh led his Georgia infantry regiment on May 9, 1846, into the Battle of Resaca de la Palma on the second day of fighting during the Mexican War. The following day saw the Mexican army forced to retreat at Palo Alto. The American troops were encouraged, commanded by Major General Zachary Taylor, and pursued the Mexicans only to find that Major General Mariano Arista, who commanded the Mexican forces, had established a new position in a *resaca*.[18] Resaca de la Palma crossed between Matamoros and Port Isabel, providing the Mexicans with a strong defensive position. General Taylor ordered the attack at 2:00 p.m. and after constant bombardment from Mexican artillery, the American Dragoons and Colonel McIntosh's light infantry forced the Mexicans out of the *resaca*. The Mexicans counterattacked and Colonel McIntosh lay wounded.

A Georgia infantryman tripped over his fallen Colonel and when he realized who lay on the blood soaked ground, asked if he needed anything. The soldier thought he was doing a last kindness for a mortally injured hero whom would never leave the battlefield that day. Much to his surprise, Colonel James Simmons McIntosh replied, "Yes, give me some water and show me my regiment." The soldier did as ordered and Colonel McIntosh rejoined the fight. It might interest you to know that during this time, Colonel McIntosh was sixty-two years old.

Twice, the Mexican army advanced and was beaten back. On the third attempt to regroup, the American artillery came at them full force with cannons blazing and musket balls whizzing through the air. The Mexican army fled in panic, leaving behind all manner of baggage. Among the items left were 474 muskets and carbines, eight pieces of artillery, General Arista's personal correspondence and a silver tea service. Of the 1,700 Americans engaged in the battle at Resaca de la Palma, thirty-three were killed and eighty-nine wounded. The Mexican Army brought an estimated force of 4,000 and official records show their losses at three hundred and fifty-nine killed or wounded. Most of the Mexican soldiers drowned trying the cross the Rio Grande at night.

Colonel McIntosh led his regiment into battle again on September 8, 1847, at Molino del Rey. Although the Georgia regiment emerged as heroes that day, having beaten back the Mexicans into a final retreat, their cost was high. The Mexican Cavalry attacked the Georgia column, fighting was heavy, smoke filled the air so thick that only the red orange fire seen spewing from the mouths of cannons marked the artillery line. Colonel McIntosh was hit in the chest and knocked to the ground, this time his wounds were fatal. The Georgia regiment fought on, not until the fighting was done and the smoke had cleared did they realize the loss. Colonel McIntosh's death was more tragic than losing the battle that day.

Colonel James Simmons McIntosh would now join brave ancestors and his name would forever be followed by "hero." His body was brought home to Savannah for burial and lay in state at the family home. The coffin was draped in reverence with an American flag upon which lay his sword and the bullet pierced uniform that he had worn when leading his men into battle. A grand procession escorted his body to the cemetery, where with full military honors, he was buried. Another Scottish Highlander was now at rest.

A fort was established by order of George W. Crawford, Secretary of War under President Zachary Taylor to protect the city of Laredo from further Mexican aggression. Initially, the fort was given the name Camp Crawford, however, in 1850 by Presidential decree, the name was officially changed to Fort McIntosh. President Taylor recognized the sacrifice of the brave officer serving under his command and bestowed the honor in memory of Colonel James Simmons McIntosh, a hero in the Battle of Molino del Rey. The site, which once was Fort McIntosh, is today the Laredo Community College.

JOSEPH
VALLENCE BEVAN
(1798-1830)
Georgia's First Official Historian

There was "None, No None!" reads the epitaph on this tomb, "Against
Whose Name The Recording Angel Would More Reluctantly Have Written
Down Condemnation."
Born in Dublin, Ireland, son of a Georgia planter, Joseph v. Bevan attended
the Univ. of Georgia for two years and graduated in 1816 from the College of
S.C. after which he enlarged his education in England. There he became
the friend of celebrated William Godwin who wrote the young Georgian a
widely-published letter suggesting a course of studies.
In 1824 Bevan became the first official historian of Georgia. The Legislature
empowered him to collect and publish the papers and documents in the
State archives. This he did with method and industry and was the first to
recognize the importance of copying
the Colonial records of Georgia in London.
Bevan served Chatham County in the Legislature in 1827. A former editor of
the Augusta Chronicle, he became in 1828 co-editor and co-publisher of the
Savannah Georgian. His projected history of Georgia was never completed,
death cutting short the career of the popular Savannahian at the age of thirty-two.

Colonial Park Cemetery, Savannah
GPS Coordinates: N32.07602, W81.090512

BELOW THIS STONE
REPOSE THE BONES OF
JOSEPH VALLANCE BEVAN
WHO WAS BORN
IN LIBERTY COUNTY, GEORGIA,
AND DIED IN SAVANNAH,
29TH MARCH 1830
AGED 32 YEARS

HIS MIND WAS ENLIGHTENED AND EDUCATED;
HIS MANNERS WERE SIMPLE AND UNPRESUMING;
HIS HEART WAS WARM AND AFFECTIONATE.
READER—
YOU MAY HAVE KNOWN A WISER MAN THAN
JOSEPH V. BEVAN, BUT YOU HAVE RARELY KNOWN
A BETTER, AND NONE, NO NONE! AGAINST WHOSE
NAME THE RECORDING ANGEL WOULD MORE
RELUCTANTLY HAVE WRITTEN DOWN
CONDEMNATION.

These are the words etched in the epitaph of Joseph Vallence Bevan. The carving contains two obvious errors one con-
cerning the spelling of Bevan's middle name and the other his place of birth. Joseph "Vallence" Bevan was born near
Dublin, Ireland, as the only child of Joseph and Avarina Elinor Bevan. In 1799, the family moved to Liberty County, where
Avarina died leaving her husband and two year old son to go on alone.

Bevan's father was deeply saddened by the loss of his wife and never married again. With a heavy heart, all of his energy was spent making a life for himself and his son in their newly adopted country. Joseph Sr. became a planter, merchant and was heavily involved in land speculation and amassed quite a fortune.

In 1811, Joseph Vallence Bevan entered the University of Georgia as a member of the Class of 1815. The university's academics were largely based on scientific teachings, greatly lacking in the humanities that he wished to study. In an effort to promote literature and humanities, the Demosthenian Literary Society was formed. Their purpose was to develop the University of Georgia's limited scholastic library. In 1813, the Dialectic Adelphic Society was created to encourage public speaking and literary pursuits. Bevan was active and served as an officer in each of these groups.

During his junior year at Georgia, Bevan became disillusioned with the school and decided to transfer to the College of South Carolina, later known as the University of South Carolina. He should have graduated the following year but was retained due to health issues and finally matriculated in 1816, among a class of thirty-one students.

Rather than return home, Bevan decided to travel to Europe until he reached his majority. While there, he met the most important influence in his life, English writer and philosopher, William Godwin. In December 1818, Bevan received word that his father had died of a severe fever at the home of John Bolton, a business associate.

Bevan returned to America and began writing and editing for a Savannah newspaper. He submitted a number of historical pamphlets and developed a reputation as a knowledgeable historian. When George Troup assumed the Georgia governor's office in 1823, he found that the state official records were in total disarray. It was at his suggestion to the Georgia legislature that Bevan be hired to publish an accounting of Georgia history. The legislature approved the appointment and Bevan was paid the sum of $400.

Until that time, Bevan had been making a meager living editing and reading the law. He found the work boring, mentally unstimulating and longed to research and write. He seized the moment and took on the immense task without a doubt in his mind. It was as if he found his intended purposes on the earth.

Bevan first prepared an outline and began to gather research materials based on a time line. His time line consisted of the Colonial Period, 1732 through 1754; Provincial, 1754 through 1775; Revolutionary, 1774 through 1783; the period of 1783 through 1802; and 1803 through 1825. He would examine the following points for each era:

1. The soil, together with the nature, quality and quantity of its produce.
2. Trade and manufactures.
3. Natural history, in a comprehensive sense.
4. Natural and artificial curiosities.
5. Internal improvements from one period of time to another.
6. Peculiar settlements, their origins and subsequent history.
7. Academics and other schools, together with the state of learning generally.
8. Various sects of religion, removed or existing.
9. Manners, habits and amusements of the people.

The materials Bevan gathered were the most extensive collection of Georgia historical data ever amassed. The collection consisted of the personal correspondence of various state leaders, manuscripts, military documentation and legislative papers. By the time he began organizing the data, a problem was very evident. Bevan had information and research materials on every era with the exception of the Colonial Period. He soon realized that to get that information, he would have to travel to England and visit the London archives.

He requested permission from the British government to view their historical documents and was quickly approved. When he approached the Georgia legislature for additional funds to cover research expenses and travel to London, they refused. Bevan had signed a horrible contract to write the Georgia history and now he was trapped in a bad situation. The contract made no stipulation for expenses, travel, supplies or publication. A flat fee of $400 was all that was promised and the legislature made it quite clear that no additional funds would be forth coming.

In 1825, Bevan wrote to Governor Troup advising him of the status of the Georgia history. The letter read, in part:

"I have the honor of transmitting to your Excellency a table of the Documents relating to the History of our State; having taken care to select such as I believe to possess real and intrinsic interest. Yet, you will discover, from their number, now presented, that they will form a much heavier and more expensive work, than either my finances or the patience of my readers will be likely to afford:-still it would seem desirable, that all our State papers, (exclusive of such as might be more technically termed the archaeologia of Georgia,) should be preserved and embodied in some permanent and durable form. -For, if they should once be scattered, it is not likely that they could ever be collected together again."

Bevan was finally forced to leave the Georgia history unfinished when funds sufficient enough to feed himself were expended. He had to take a salaried job, which provided for his support. The Georgia legislature continued to hound him for the remaining years of his life, the wanted manuscript which was never completed. When he died in 1830, $400 was taken from his estate and returned to the state of Georgia for a job left undone.

Bevan should be remembered, not for his inability to complete the Georgia history, but his integrity involving the work. His understanding of history, research methods and information reliability remain without equal. The name, Joseph Vallence Bevan, should forever be linked with Georgia history.

DUELLIST'S GRAVE

The epitaph of James Wilde on the nearby tomb is a melancholy reminder of the days of duelling and, particularly, of a tragic affair of honor fought January 16, 1815, on the Carolina side of the river near Savannah. Lieutenant Wilde was shot through the heart in a fourth exchange of fire by Captain Roswell P. Johnson, referred to in the epitaph, in bitterness, as "a man who a short time before would have been friendless but for him." The duellists were officers in the 8th Regt., U.S. infantry. The nature of their quarrel is unknown.

Richard Henry Wilde, the poet and statesman, was the brother of the young officer. Lieutenant Wilde had served in the campaign against the Seminoles and his vivid descriptions of Florida suggested to the poet an epic poem, which, like the life of James Wilde, was cut short by a fatal bullet.

The unfinished poem is remembered for the beauty of a single lyric.
The opening stanza of which is:
"My life is like the Summer Rose
That opens to the morning sky;
But ere the shades of evening close
is scattered on the ground - to die."

Colonial Park Cemetery, Savannah
GPS Coordinates: N32.07602, W81.090512

The headstone reads:

This humble stone records the filial piety fraternal affection and manly virtues of JAMES WILDE, Esquire, late District Paymaster in the army of the U.S. He fell in a Duel on the 16th of January, 1815, by the hand of a man who, a short time ago, would have been friendless but for him; and expired instantly in his 22nd year: dying, as he lived: with unshaken courage & unblemished reputation. By his untimely death the prop of a Mother's age is broken: The hope and consolation of Sisters is destroyed, the pride of Brothers humbled in the dust and a whole Family, happy until then, overwhelmed with affliction.

To this day, no one knows the reason why two friends drew weapons, walked ten paces and fired. The shots were fired not once or twice but four times until one of them lay dead on the cold January ground. Captain Roswell P. Johnson and Paymaster James Wilde must have had an intense disagreement to demand that blood be shed on the field of honor. Was it a woman, money, land or merely a ill timed insult that resulted in the former friends squaring off against each other? These are the usual slights of honor, still the reason for this duel will never be known.

Richard Henry Wilde, statesman and poet, was the brother of young James Wilde. He was so distraught over the senseless bloodshed, Richard Wilde expressed his grief using the only means at his disposal. The poem "Summer Rose" was written from that bereavement. The famed poet Lord Byron, upon reading the poem, commented, "No finer American poem has met my eye than Wilde's Summer Rose."

The only record of James Wilde's death was a brief death announcement on the yellowed pages of the burial book at Savannah's City Hall. The entry reads,

> "James Wilde, aged 23[19], native of Baltimore, died January 16, 1815, paymaster 8th Regt. U. S. Infantry; duel; buried 17th. He was shot through the heart at the fourth discharge by his antagonist, Capt. R. P. Johnson, of the 8th Regt. U. S. Infantry. His corpse was conveyed from the fatal spot, on the north side of the Savannah river in South Carolina, to Mrs. Wilson's Boarding House, facing the Baptist church, and thence buried with military honors."

The family felt that murder had been committed, but the more level headed United States Army Board of Inquiry found both men to be at fault. Unfortunately for Captain Johnson, Richard Wilde was not only a poet, but a United States Congressman and the Attorney General of Georgia. Though Johnson was acquitted of the charges, his career was in ruins. Captain Roswell P. Johnson died of yellow fever a short time after the duel. His death did not come as sudden nor as painlessly as a shot through the heart.

In this cemetery many victims of the Great Yellow Fever Epidemic of 1820 were buried.

Nearly 700 Savannahians died that year, including two local physicians who lost their lives caring for the stricken.

Several epidemics followed. In 1854 The Savannah Benevolent Association was organized to aid the families of the fever victims.

Colonial Park Cemetery, Savannah
GPS Coordinates: N32.07602, W81.090512

The year 1820 was a disastrous time for the citizens of Savannah. It began with a devastating fire of unknown origin that nearly consumed the entire city. Prevailing winds spread the fire and even with Savannah's two fire pump trucks the blaze continued for twelve hours and consumed an estimated four hundred and fifty buildings. An explosion of illegally stored gunpowder enhanced the blaze and hardly a business or home was left standing. The newspaper reported,

> "The town presents a most wretched picture. There is not a hardware store, saddler's shop, apothecary's (drug) shop, or scarcely a dry goods store left. There is no estimating the loss — it is immense."

The outpouring of support exceeded expectations, one large donation was given with a condition, that condition created a controversy that foreshadowed a crippling war. It seems New York sent $12,500 to aid in the rebuilding of Savannah, attached was the following:

> "Resolved, That it is the wish of the general committee that the money and goods to be remitted to
> Savannah be applied exclusively to the relief of all indigent persons, without distinction of color..."

In 1820, the first bitter debates over admitting states into the Union as either slave or free states were simmering, tension developed between northern industrialists and southern planters and Savannah received the New York dictate as an insult. The *Savannah Republican* made an attempt to balm the wounds by reporting that the needy of Savannah, both black and white, had been the first to receive relief. Savannah returned the donation to New York, the note simply said, "An injustice has been done our citizens by the direction of the Resolution."

Savannah thought she had seen the worst and was slowly rebuilding, when fate dealt another climactic blow. During the long hot summer and into the fall, yellow fever ravaged the city. From May until November, the fever raged and the city was in quarantine. Savannah was bordered on two sides with the standing water of rice fields; that which nourished Savannah both physically and economically also brought death. The flooded fields necessary for the production of rice was also the prime breeding ground for disease carrying mosquitoes.

Yellow fever is a blood borne disease, carried by body fluids, and the tiny mosquito is a prime delivery source. Mosquitoes were able to pass along the deadly disease to their eggs, which when hatched, carry the legacy of death. The name "yellow fever" results from advanced symptoms of the viral disease: yellow, because as the body begins to fail the skin takes on a sickening hue called jaundice caused by decreased liver function and the fever is usually severe in the later stages, thus the name. Mercifully at its worst, yellow fever claims its victims in approximately ten days.

Roughly seven hundred people lost their lives to this devastating epidemic. The city's population had dwindled to approximately 1,500. Dr. William R. Waring, whose family had provided Savannah three generations of doctors, wrote,

> "The scene of sickness, misery and ruin was awful, shocking and well-fitted to inspire a melancholy senti-
> ment of the shortness, uncertainty, and insignificance of life."

Two of the three generations of Waring's were lost to yellow fever, treating those they dedicated their lives to.

It is said that from 1807 until the epidemic in 1820, that 4,000 succumbed to the disease. Another bout with the deadly fever struck in 1876 and over one thousand people lost their lives. Dr. Waring criticized the standing water as unhealthy, but neither he nor any other man of science could prove the connection until 1898.

By the late 1920s, Dr. Max Theiler had conducted numerous years of research on the virus. In 1930, the vaccination was developed and included as part of the standard immunization schedule for children. Dr. Theiler was awarded the 1951 Nobel Prize in Medicine for his work in developing the vaccine for yellow fever.

Today, a Georgia Historical marker stands in Colonial Park Cemetery, in memory of those victims of the dreaded disease, yellow fever.

CONRAD AIKEN

Conrad Aiken, Poet and Man of Letters, was born in Savannah on August 5, 1889, and lived at No. 228 (opposite) until 1901. After the tragic death of his parents, he was moved to New England. Most of his writing career was divided between Cape Cod, Massachusetts and Rye, England. In 1962 he returned to Savannah to live and write in the adjoining house, No. 230 until his death August 17, 1973. Of his home here he wrote: "Born in that most magical of cities, Savannah, I was allowed to run wild in that earthly paradise until I was nine; ideal for the boy who early decided he wanted to write." Though he wrote novels, short stories and critical essays, his first love was poetry. His work earned many awards including the Pulitzer Prize (1930). National Book Award (1954), and the National Medal of Literature (1969). He was a member of the National Academy of Arts and Sciences and held the Chair of Poetry of the Library of Congress (1950 to 1952). Governor Jimmy Carter appointed him Poet Laureate of Georgia on March 30, 1973. Conrad Aiken is buried beside his parents in Bonaventure Cemetery.

Oglethorpe Avenue across from Colonial Park Cemetery
GPS Coordinates: N32.07628, W81.089712

Conrad Aiken's greatest influence was the life and death struggle of his parents. Their troubled life left an imprint on Conrad that he transformed into a successful writing career. The abundance of his work is dark and foreboding, though it is easy to understand his motivation. Therefore, his story is also that of his parents who created Georgia's Poet Laureate, Conrad Aiken.

William Ford Aiken, father of Conrad Aiken, was born in New York City in 1864. He graduated from Yale and attended Harvard Medical School, leaving to study at the European specialized eye and ear clinics in Vienna and Berlin. Shortly after returning to New York, Dr. Aiken suffered a nervous breakdown and at his doctor's suggestion, moved to Savannah for the milder climate. Anna Potter Aiken, Conrad's mother, belonged to a prominent New Bedford family. Although Anna Potter was born of Quaker stock, her father chose to become a Unitarian minister and his household was a somber place to grow up. Anna grew to be a vivacious young woman who loved the social life and her gaiety eventually won the heart of Dr. William Aiken.

Shortly after arriving in Savannah, the first of William and Anna's four children was born. A son the couple named Conrad on August 5, 1889. In November 1891, the small family leased an elegant Greek Revival home built in the 1850s from C. A. L. Cunningham at the exorbitant rent $100.00 per month. The first floor housed Dr. Aiken's offices, while the upstairs was the family's living space. Conrad described the home as,

> "And the brick stoop, which led to the second story, with its iron railing and brownstone steps, and little
> door under it which opened into the surgery's waiting- room...this was the real essence of the house, to
> begin with, this and the two immense trees which grew before it, above the rich dirt of the street, and
> which, whether in sunlight or moonlight, kept forever a moving pattern of leaf-shadow turning and revolv-
> ing over the serene house-front of tall windows and wrought- iron balconies, like an evanescent stencilling."

Though Conrad spent less than ten years living in the house at 228 Oglethorpe, the address would shape the remainder of his life.

Conrad's father was somewhat of a camera buff and founded the Savannah Camera Club. He took an interesting photo, which in later years haunted Conrad, of Anna Aiken seated on a tombstone at Colonial Park Cemetery surrounded by her four children and two African American servants.

The Aikens were described as "brilliant creatures," very attractive and intellectual. The couple was welcomed in Savannah society. The Aiken household became a very dark place by the turn of the century. Dr. Aiken's health, both physical and mental, had quickly deteriorated though the reasons are unknown. He was not heavily in debt, his career was a remarkable success and his family seemed ideal. Dr. Aiken began to exhibit very erratic behavior causing a colleague to question him, his reply was a cryptic "I haven't got time to answer that question, I'm in a hurry." Amazed by the response, the colleague posed the question again later that same day, this time Dr. Aiken replied, "Well, for an answer to that question I shall have to refer you to my lawyer." After pressing the question, Dr. Aiken poured out his troubles. He was being persecuted, Mrs. Aiken was plotting with her relatives and his to have him put in an insane asylum. His colleague warned that if he continued to display this conduct, people would begin to believe he was indeed crazy. Dr. and Mrs. Aiken began to have loud quarrels during this time and Dr. Aiken's paranoia intensified. Conrad would huddle with his siblings in the closet of his room, pulling his knees to his chest in terror while their parents had violent fights.

Dr. Aiken became obsessed with the belief that his wife was scheming against him and his absurd suspicions of her were manifested in many ways. Lizzie Wilkins, the African American housemaid, stated that he would not permit his wife to have conversations with the servants, when one of them left the house after speaking with her, the Doctor would subject them to rigid cross examination. Servants were not permitted to keep any scrap of paper; he counted Mrs. Aiken's stationery every night, requiring her to account for each and every sheet and envelope.

On another occasion, Dr. Aiken cautioned his wife about attending two social events in one week. She retorted, "Darling, I must have some recreation." Dr. Aiken accused her of neglecting her family and if she did not cease the endless gaiety, he would force her to have another child.

Accepting the advice of his doctor to get away and rest, Dr. Aiken traveled to Massachusetts in the late summer of 1900. Upon returning to Savannah in the fall, he seemed normal again, at least outwardly. The facade did not last. By this time, the Aiken children were terrified to their father. Conrad wrote later in life,

> "I suppose I liked him when I was very small, before the other kids were born- before I can remember...There was something angelic about him-later it became diabolic."

One night Mrs. Aiken awakened to the sound of heavy breathing. She found her husband virtually comatose. A note addressed to the coroner was pinned to the mantle. It stated he had taken morphine and atropine and wished to be buried as he was found. The doctor was summoned and eventually Dr. Aiken was revived. The note was later returned to him by his doctor expressing the hope that he would "never make such a fool of himself again." However, within weeks, Dr. Aiken attempted to take not only his life but also that of his wife's. He left the gas on in her room, informing her that they "would now see who would emerge from the apartment alive."

On February 22, 1901, Dr. Aiken traveled to St. Marys to make arrangements for a family holiday. He planned on a long rest at the coast and returned to Savannah. According to servants, he locked Mrs. Aiken in her room charging her with imaginary offenses. Throughout the night, the couple quarreled.

Conrad crept to his parents closed door as the angry voices rose again. Then there was silence. Conrad heard his father's voice counting, "One! two! three!," then a muffled cry followed by a pistol shot. Again, a count of three, another shot, a thud and silence. Conrad banged on the door, silence.

Conrad raced across the street to the police station. Patrolman J. Harry Lange was the first officer he found. He rushed with the officer back to his mother's room but stopped at the closed door. Patrolman Lange knocked then entered, Anna Aiken was lying on her bed in a very natural position, as if she were sleeping. Of course, Anna would never awaken again. A gaping wound to the right temple marred her porcelain skin as the crisp white sheets of her bed turned soggy red. Dr. Aiken had a similar wound, he lay face down on the rug. The 32 caliber pistol still clutched in his lifeless grip. Conrad lingered outside the door, while his siblings Elizabeth, Kempton and Robert cowered in terror in the adjoining room.

The burial services were held at Bonaventure Cemetery. Dr. and Mrs. William Ford Aiken were buried in a common grave. The four children were sent north to New Bedford after the funeral and reared by relatives of their late mother. The tragedy would mark Conrad for the remainder of his life.

Conrad grew to be a man in the chill of New England among his Potter relatives. He discovered a love for books and verse, leading to novels, short stories and poetry. His work was not well received by critics. One critic wrote,

> "Mr. Aiken's world is one of introspection, self-analysis, dreams, phantasy, hallucination, streams of consciousness, ambiguities, fragments of recollections and symbols and symbolism that escape the ordinary reader."

The review was not exactly a slight but hardly praise.

Later is a volume called *Blue Voyage*, Conrad said of his own work,

> "It is my weakness as an author that I appear incapable of presenting a theme energetically, and simply. I must always wrap it up in tissue upon tissue of proviso and aspect...turn laboriously each side to the light; producing in the end not so much a unitary work of art as a melancholy cauchemar of ghosts and voices, a phantasmagoric world of disordered colors and sounds; a world without design or purpose; and perceptible only in terms of prolix and fragmentary."

Even in those words, it is evident that the horrible legacy of his parents death marked his psyche and every aspect of his life.

Thirty-five years after that fateful shooting at 228 Oglethorpe Street, Conrad Aiken returned to face his demons. In 1961, Conrad took up residence at 230 Oglethorpe Street. He related, "An interesting experience, an eight inch brick wall now separates me from the past."

The passing years would bring Conrad to terms with his parents' grotesque end. He described their lives in one of his works, writing:

> "Two water snakes once inhabited a bowl. Of a sudden, obeying a simultaneous impulse, they had begun to eating the other's tail. They had thus formed a ring, which, as they devoured, became smaller. Smaller and smaller this ring of snake had become-until at last, as each snake performed the final swallow, they had both abruptly vanished. They were gone. Gone into the infinite. And here, of course, was the bowl of water to prove they existed."

Conrad Aiken remained in Savannah until his death, August 17, 1973. He was buried along side his parents at Bonaventure Cemetery. Governor Jimmy Carter named him Poet Laureate of Georgia on March 30, 1973.

1812
WESLEY CHAPEL

Savannah Methodism's first church building was erected on this corner of Lincoln and South Broad (now Oglethorpe) streets in 1812 by its first pastor, Rev. James Russell. Bishop Francis Asbury preached twice in Wesley Chapel on November 21, 1813. In 1819-20 under the preaching of William Capers the membership grew rapidly, and in 1821 John Howard enlarged the building to care for 100 new members. By 1848 this "good, neat house, sixty by forty feet", became too small; at a new location its successor, Trinity, was built. Among the early pastors of Wesley Chapel were James O. Andrew, George F. Pierce, Ignatious A. Few, and Thomas L. Wynn.

Oglethorpe Avenue and Lincoln Street, Savannah
GPS Coordinates: N32.07616, W81.085995

Truly, the "Mother Church of Savannah Methodism," Wesley Chapel was built in honor of John Wesley in 1812. In 1848, the chapel was moved from its location at Lincoln and Oglethorpe Streets to a new more elaborate building on Telfair Square. Since that time the church has been called the Trinity Methodist Church. By the time of Wesley Chapel was dedicated, John Wesley had been dead over twenty years.

No work concerning John Wesley would be complete without words from his own heart. Many times John Wesley preached on the meaning of the church; the following, in part, is his moving sermon entitled, "On the Church":

> "I beseech you that ye walk worthy of the vocation wherewith ye are called, with all lowliness and meekness, with long-suffering, forbearing one another in love; endeavouring to keep the unity of the Spirit in the bond of peace. There is one body, and one Spirit, even as ye are called in one hope of your calling; one Lord, one faith, one baptism, one God and Father of all, who is above all, and through all, and in you all."[20]

How much do we almost continually hear about the Church?!? With many it is matter of daily conversation. And yet how few understand what they talk of! How few know what the term means! A more ambiguous word than this, the Church, is scarce to be found in the English language. It is sometimes taken for a building, set apart for public worship: sometimes for a congregation, or body of people, united together in the service of God. It is only in the latter sense that it is taken in the ensuing discourse.

It may be taken indifferently for any number of people, how small or great, soever. As, "where two or three are met together in his name," there is Christ; so, (to speak with St. Cyprian) "where two or three believers are met together, there is a Church." Thus, it is that St. Paul, writing to Philemon, mentions "the Church which is in his house;" plainly signifying, that even a Christian family may be termed a Church.

Several of those whom God hath called out of the world, (so the original word properly signifies) uniting together in one congregation, formed a larger Church; such as the Church at Jerusalem; that is, all those in Jerusalem whom God had so called. But considering how swiftly these were multiplied, after the day of Pentecost, it cannot be supposed that they could continue to assemble in one place; especially as they had not then any large place, neither would they have been permitted to build one. In consequence, they must have divided themselves, even in Jerusalem, into several distinct congregations. In like manner, when St. Paul, several years after, wrote to the Church in Rome, (directing his letter, "To all that are in Rome, called to be saints") it cannot be supposed that they had any one building capable of containing them all, but they were divided into several congregations, assembling in several parts of the city.

The first time that the Apostle uses the word "Church" is in his preface to the former Epistle to the Corinthians: "Paul called to be an apostle of Jesus Christ, unto the Church of God which is at Corinth." The meaning of which expression is fixed by the following words: "To them that are sanctified in Christ Jesus; with all that, in every place," (not Corinth only; so it was a kind of circular letter) "call upon the name of Jesus Christ our Lord, both theirs and ours." In the inscription of his second letter to the Corinthians, he speaks still more explicitly: "Unto the Church of God which is at Corinth, with all the saints that are in all Achaia." Here he plainly includes all the Churches, or Christian congregations, which were in the whole province.

He frequently uses the word in the plural number. So, Gal. 1:2, "Paul an apostle, — unto the Churches of Galatia;" that is, the Christian congregations dispersed throughout that country. In all these places, (and abundantly more might be cited) the word "church" or "churches" means, not the buildings where the Christians assembled, (as it frequently does in the English tongue) but the people that used to assemble there, one or more Christian congregations. But sometimes the word Church is taken in Scripture in a still more extensive meaning, as including all the Christian congregations that are upon the face of the earth. And in this sense we understand it in our Liturgy, when we say, "Let us pray for the whole state of Christ's Church militant here on earth." In this sense it is unquestionably taken by St. Paul, in his exhortation to the elders of Ephesus: (Acts 20:28) "Take heed to the Church of God, which he has purchased with his own blood." The Church here, undoubtedly, means the catholic or universal Church; that is, all the Christians under heaven.

Who those are that are properly "the Church of God," the Apostle shows at large, and that in the clearest and most decisive manner, in the passage above cited; wherein he likewise instructs all the members of the Church, how to "walk worthy of the vocation wherewith they are called."

John Wesley's full sermon, "On the Church."

INDEPENDENT
PRESBYTERIAN CHURCH

The Independent Presbyterian Church was organized in 1755. The first meeting house stood facing Market Square in Savannah, between what are now St. Julian and Bryan Streets, on property granted by King George II for the use and benefit of those dissenters who were professors of the doctrines of the Church of Scotland agreeable to the Westminster confession of Faith.

The original church building erected on the present site was designed by John H. Greene, a gifted Rhode Island architect, in 1819 it was dedicated with impressive services which were attended by President James Monroe. The church was destroyed by fire in 1889.

The present church building was completed in 1891. The architect, William G. Preston, followed the general plan of the former structure. It is regarded as a notable example of American church architecture.

Among the distinguished ministers of the Independent Presbyterian Church since its founding have been John Joachim Zubly, 1758-1781; Henry Kollock, 1806-1819; Daniel Baker, 1828-1831; Willard Preston, 1831-1856, and I. S. K. Axson, 1857-1891.

Ellen Louise Axson who was born in the manse of the Independent Presbyterian Church in 1860 was married in 1885 to Woodrow Wilson, later President of the United States, in a room in the manse.

Bull Street and Oglethorpe Avenue, Savannah
GPS Coordinates: N32.07672, W81.092759

The Scotsmen who arrived with General James Edward Oglethorpe in 1733 and remained in Savannah, founded the Presbyterian Church of Savannah about 1755. The first sanctuary was built on a lot issued by Royal grant for the purpose of a Church of Scotland adhering to the Westminster Confession of Faith.

The initial structure at Market Square was used as a powder magazine and stable during the British occupation at the time of the Revolutionary War. Fire destroyed the first edifice in 1790 and the second sanctuary built in 1800 on St. James Square, which was damaged by a hurricane. The swell in membership led to a third site constructed at Bull Street and Oglethorpe Avenue.

Plans were solicited from all over the United States and it was those of John Holden Green that were accepted. The Columbian Museum and Savannah Daily Gazette remarked upon the consecration of the new facility in 1819,

> "From grandeur of design and neatness of execution, we presume this church is not surpassed by any in the United States."

The ceremony was widely attended, including guests as prominent as President James Monroe and John C. Calhoun.

Before the completion of the edifice, many of the pews were sold at public auction, the average bid brought $1,140. Family pews went to some of the most prestigious members of Savannah as well as the colony of Georgia.

Lowell Mason, known as the father of public school music programs and composer, served as the church organist. Many of his works echoed through the Independent Presbyterian Church before they were released publicly. Strains of *Blest Be the Tie That Binds* and *Nearer My God to Thee* still resound from the choir today.

The edifice went untouched during the ravages of the Civil War. During this time some of the state bank currency was embossed with an engraving of the Independent Presbyterian Church. Ellen Louise Axson, whose grandfather was minister of the church, was born in the manse or clergy's residence. In 1885, she was also married there to future United States President Woodrow Wilson.

The Independent Presbyterian Church included in its membership some of the most prominent in Savannah society, including the Telfair family. When Mary Telfair, who was heir to the Telfair fortune, passed away in 1875 she bequeathed a considerable amount of money and property to the church. One of the Telfair gifts included a substantial and most lovely mahogany pulpit. Miss Telfair stipulated that if the church ever ceased to use the pulpit, her endowments would be transferred to an alternate charity.

The church caught fire in 1889 and as firefighters fought the vicious blaze, word of the disaster spread throughout Savannah. Many of the parishioners gathered and despite the warnings of firefighters, plunged into the burning sanctuary and within minutes emerged carrying the awesome pulpit. The baptismal font and flagstones were also saved. Why did these dedicated Presbyterians enter the burning church? The membership was not sure if a destructive fire would exempt them from the exception in Mary Telfair's will. The parishioners were taking no chances. It was immediately decided to rebuild the edifice.

Plans for the new sanctuary were found at the Boston Public Library. *Harper's Magazine* printed the following in the February 1919 issue:

> "In architecture the primacy must be yielded above every other edifice in Savannah to the famous Independent Presbyterian Church. The structure on the outside is of such Sir Christopher Wrennish renaissance that one might well seem to be looking at it in a London Street, but the interior is of such exquisite loveliness that no church in London can compare with it. Whoever would appreciate its beauty must go at once to Savannah and forget for one beatific moment in its presence the walls of Tiepolo and the ceilings of Veronese."

In 1928, the Axson Memorial Building was built on the site of the manse and houses the Mary Telfair Chapel, educational facilities, a reproduction of the 1885 manse parlor and the Wilson-Axson Room. The 1819 church facade was excavated and reconstructed as a wall in 1980, it stands on the church's property on West Hull Street across from the present day sanctuary as a reminder of the vast history of the church. The Independent Presbyterian Church continues to grow and the wonderful gift of Mary Telfair, the mahogany pulpit remains the focal point of the sanctuary today.

Independent Presbyterian Church

Bull Street and Oglethorpe Avenue, Savannah
GPS Coordinates: N32.07672, W81.093237

Richard Wayne, father of James Moore Wayne, hailed from Yorkshire, England. At 19 years of age, he sailed to the New World landing at Charles Towne in 1759. It was there that he met and married a woman of considerable wealth, Miss Elizabeth Clifford. Her family had been among the first settlers of Carolina and were extremely well connected.

Wayne was appointed to the Carolina General Assembly in 1777 and his loyalties remained with the Colonies although after the British took Charles Towne in 1780, Richard's sentiments began to change. He was taken prisoner at his Goosecreek Plantation home but released after taking the oath of allegiance to the English crown. Wayne was branded a Tory by the Carolina General Assembly and banished from the state, if he returned to the Carolina colony he would be put to death. He fled with his family to Savannah. In 1782, his wife's family interceded on Wayne's behalf and his name was removed from the banishment list.

Wayne purchased a Back River plantation in 1789 and opened a shop in Savannah dealing in the Factorage and Commission Business.[21] The business, first called the Subscriber was later known as Wayne's Wharf; and in any event the business was a success. It is said that Wayne often dealt in the slave trade, he held public offices such as Justice of the Peace, Alderman, Mayor Pro Tem and Chairman of the Commissioners of Pilotage.

In 1790, the last of the Wayne's thirteen children was born in Savannah, a son named James Moore Wayne. James grew up at West Broad and Indian Street in an area known as Pepper Hill. He studied under a private tutor and eventually attended Princeton Law School. He graduated in 1808 and return to Savannah to clerk for a Savannah lawyer. The elder Wayne died in 1810 and it was that same year that James was admitted to the Savannah bar.

After serving in the War of 1812, James entered politics. In 1814, he was selected as a Representative to the Georgia General Assembly, then Mayor of Savannah in 1817, a position he resigned in 1819. The ambitious James Moore Wayne was elected to the bench of the Superior Court in 1819.

He sold the Savannah home in 1831 to William Washington Gordon, grandfather of Juliette Gordon Low. The imposing Regency mansion was done in shades of brown and designed by famed architect, William Jay.

James served in Congress from 1829 until 1835 and accomplished much in his time there. He worked toward free trade; assisted in drafting legislation to push the Cherokee Indians beyond the Mississippi River, ensuring additional land for settlers; presided over two Georgia Constitutional Conventions; President of the Georgia Historical Society; and a trustee for the

University of Georgia. James Moore Wayne's crowning achievement came in 1835, when upon the death of Justice William Johnson, President Jackson appointed him to the bench of the United States Supreme Court. He held this office for thirty-two years, until his death in 1867.

Like his father before him, James Moore Wayne found himself in a quandary during the Civil War. He was staunchly opposed to cessation but was fiercely devoted to Georgia and the south. During the war, he chose to remain in Washington D.C., this decision was criticized by many. Even his own family was divided, his son chose to resign his commission in the United States Army and fought as a Confederate. James Moore Wayne died in 1867 at the age of seventy-seven in Washington D.C. He body was brought home for burial at Laurel Grove Cemetery.

One hundred and twenty-four years after the death of James Moore Wayne, the second Savannah citizen to gain an appointment to the United States Supreme Court was sworn in. Clarence Thomas was born in Pinpoint, Georgia near Savannah.

James Moore Wayne Monument

LOWELL MASON
(1792-1872)

Lowell Mason, noted composer of sacred music, was organist of the
Independent Presbyterian Church (1820-1827) and Superintendent of
its Sunday School (1815-1827).
A native of New England, Mason moved to Savannah at the age of
twenty. He resided in this city for approximately fifteen years until his
return to Massachusetts in 1827. He was active in the civic and religious life of his adopted city. He served as Secretary of the Savannah
Missionary Society; was an organizer of a school for the instruction of
sacred music, and was Superintendent of the inter-denominational
Savannah Sabbath School.
While Mason was the organist of the Independent Presbyterian Church,
he set to music Bishop Reginald Heber's hymn, "From Greenland's Icy
Mountains." In the church that then stood on this site the now famous
hymn was sung for the first time.
Among later well known compositions by mason was the music for the
great hymn, "My Faith Looks Up to Thee" and "Nearer, My God, to
Thee."

Bull Street and Oglethorpe Avenue, Savannah
GPS Coordinates: N32.07672, W81.092759

L owell Mason, born in the town of Medfield, Massachusetts in 1792, displayed a talent for music at a very young age.
Even so his parents discouraged him, believing that music would never gain him a respectable living. Mason appren-
ticed in a banking firm and eventually moved to Savannah to accept employment. While working as a bank officer in
Savannah, Mason pursued music in the only forum he knew, the church. He became the organist for the Independent
Presbyterian Church.

Mason began to study music with F. I. Abel and as his talent and confidence grew. He began to compose works of his
own. Still working at the bank by day, composing by candlelight at night, Mason would perform his pieces for the church congregation on Sundays. It was this group of parishioners who first heard Heber's hymn *From Greenland's Icy Mountains* sung to
music of Mason's composition. Mason gathered his courage and began submitting his work to publishers in Philadelphia and
Boston and with every rejection, his courage withered. Finally in 1822, the Handel and Hydn Society of Boston,
Massachusetts, offered to publish his works, under one stipulation: the collection would not carry Mason's name. Anxious to
have his work published, Mason agreed.

Mason's work was published as The Boston Handel and Haydn Society's Collection of Church Music. Little did anyone
realize that the much rejected collection would eventually be reprinted seventeen times and sell over fifty thousand copies and
be used in numerous schools and church choirs all over New England.

In 1826, Mason returned to the land of his birth. Still doubtful of the reliability of music as a vocation, Mason took a position as a bank teller at American Bank. He became Director of Music at Hanover Green and Park Street Churches. Mason then
accepted a permanent position with the Bowdin Street Church, while maintaining his day job. He became President of the
Handel and Haydn Society in 1827.

Mason compiled the first Sunday School collection of music in 1829 with the *Juvenile Psalmist*, followed by the *Juvenile
Lyre* written in 1830 and 1831. His work was in demand and Mason now knew where his true calling lay. In 1831, Mason quit
his job at American Bank and began to teach music in private schools and vocal classes at Bowdoin Street Church in Boston.
Along with George J. Webb, Mason founded the Boston Academy of Music in 1832. He was the first to introduce the
Principles of Pestalozzi in public schools. The Principles of Pestalozzi teach that children should learn through activity, should
be free to pursue their own interests, draw their own conclusions and to learn through repetition. The purpose of the Boston
academy was to bring music education to those who could not afford private lessons and tutors, as well as to raise the standard
of music used by churches.

Through the efforts of the Boston Academy, music was taught on a contingency basis in four Boston public schools in 1837. Mason, himself, taught at one of these schools without compensation. The success of his teachings led to the inclusion of music in the curriculum beginning in 1838. Mason was appointed Superintendent of Music in the Boston schools in 1837 and became a staff member of the teachers' institute of the Massachusetts State Board of Education, where he was involved in state sponsored music teacher training in 1845.

Lowell Mason influence on music education in the United States was enormous. Through his efforts, music became a required course of study in public schools. In 1853, Mason and his assistant at the Boston Academy, George F. Root, founded the first Normal Musical Institute in New York, it was here, that teachers from across the United States came to be trained in the instruction of music education. Although the institute was only in existence for six short years, the idea of training music teachers through Normal Institutes and conventions, not only prospered, but expanded in the years to come.

Mason had four sons, all encouraged to be musically active. The two elder children, Daniel Gregory and Lowell, formed a publishing company in New York City. Henry, the third son, and Emmons Hamlin founded Mason & Hamlin, a firm that first made organs and later, pianos. The youngest son, William was a distinguished concert pianist and teacher. He studied in Europe with Liszt.

Lowell Mason reached the end of his musical journey on August 11, 1872, at the age of 80. He was buried in the Rosedale Cemetery in Orange, New Jersey. During his life, he penned over 1,200 compositions and set to music more than 400 others.

BIRTHPLACE OF JULIETTE LOW
(1860-1927)
FOUNDER OF THE GIRL SCOUTS OF THE U.S.A

In the house that stands opposite this marker Juliette Gordon Low, founder of the Girl Scouts of the United States of America, was born, October 31, 1860. It was her girlhood home until her marriage there in 1886 to William Low, an Englishman, then residing in Savannah.

As a friend of Lord Baden-Powell, founder of the Scout Movement, Juliette Low became active in Girl Guide work in England and Scotland in 1911. It was at his suggestion that she started Girl Scouting in America.

On March 12, 1912, at the Louisa Porter Home in this city, Mrs. Low founded the first Girl Guide troop in the United States. Her niece, Daisy Gordon, of Savannah, was the first member enrolled. Through Mrs. Low's energetic and determined leadership the movement spread rapidly under the name "Girl Scouts."

Mrs. Low died in Savannah, January 17, 1927. In n 1953 her birthplace was acquired by the Girl Scouts of the United States of America, and funds for its restoration were raised by the 2,500,000 members. The property is now maintained by the Girl Scouts as a memorial to their founder and as a center of activities for all Girl Scouts.

Bull Street and Oglethorpe Avenue, Savannah
GPS Coordinates: N32.07672, W81.092759

T he Wayne-Gordon house exudes a feeling of Victorian family life as visitors enter the dwelling. Built in the early 19th century for Savannah Mayor James Moore Wayne the house features Egyptian Revival and classical architecture popular during the period of its construction. In 1831, James Moore Wayne sold the home to his niece Sarah and her husband, William

Washington Gordon I, Juliette Low's grandfather. The house was the family estate for four generations of Gordons and carries, not only the story of a prominent southern family, but the history of Savannah as well.

It was in the Wayne-Gordon House that Juliette Magill Kinzie Gordon was born on October 31, 1860. Her father, William Washington Gordon II was a Confederate General during the Civil War and her mother, Nellie Kinzie Gordon, was a socialite. Little Juliette from her earliest years felt the tension between social appearance and harsh reality. Both parents wanted their second child to be a boy, however, when little Juliette was born her Uncle George Magill peered at her and said, "I bet she's going to be a Daisy." The name stuck and for the remainder of her life she was known by the childhood nickname.

Just months after Daisy's birth, the United States erupted into Civil War. Daisy's father, joined the Savannah militia and was soon promoted to General. It was an unusual time in the life of Daisy and her older sister, Eleanor. They rarely saw their father or any other male member of their family. In spite of the scarcity of food and clothing, the Gordon family did not lack for much during the war. Their grandmother in Chicago continually sent boxes of supplies.

Like most Confederate war veterans, William Gordon returned to his family with little means of supporting them. This meant that Daisy and her sister spent their early years in a frugal environment. To be rich in the war ravaged South would have been more of an embarrassment than acknowledging the fact that money was scarce. The family moved into a smaller house next door to their cousins, though the Gordon children seemed blissfully unaware of any financial difficulties.

At the age of 13, Daisy was sent to Stuart Hall, a boarding school in Virginia. There she discovered English poets and novelists and found an outlet for her interest in drama and theatrics. She continued her education at Edge Hill and at Mesdemoiselles Charbonnier's School in New York City. Unlike her mother or her sister Eleanor, Daisy was awkward and uncomfortable in social situations. Throughout her life, Daisy exhibited a rebellious streak that kept her from entirely fitting the conventional image of the aristocratic Southern Belle. She was described as plain, having not yet developed into the beautiful young girl that was eventually introduced into Southern society. Her wit and charm added to her allure, making Daisy one of the prettiest girls in all of Savannah. In the summer of 1882, at the age of 21, Daisy was sent abroad to spend time with friends of her parents in England, the Low family. The Lows were happy to receive her and she remained with them until 1884.

William Gordon wished for his daughters to find husbands who supported themselves through hard work. Always different, Daisy found herself falling in love with William Mackay Low, the heir to a family fortune. Her feelings were kept secret until January 1885, with her mother and siblings away, Daisy was left with her father to run the household. She threw elegant parties to impress her love and was delighted that he would see her in a local play. Her father knew immediately that his second child was in love.

William Low's visit to Savannah was disrupted by a medical problem befalling Daisy. She experienced excruciating pain in her ear and sought the help of a physician. Having read about a new procedure in a New York newspaper to heal abscess of the ear drum, Daisy requested that the doctor make use of it. The operation entailed injecting silver nitrate into her ear drum by way of the nasal passage. Immediately after the injection, her pain increased and the ear bled frequently. The ear drum had ruptured, it is not known whether the damage was a direct result of the injection or if the ear was already damaged. In either case, over the next year the hearing in both of Daisy's ears diminished almost to complete deafness.

By early 1886, the couple had their parents' permission to wed and the ceremony took place on December 21 of that year. The Lows moved to England and Daisy was welcomed into English society. Whether viewing her beautiful artwork, fishing with her in full evening attire or listening to her talk of her travels throughout the world, Daisy's audiences were enthralled by her wit and enthusiasm. Her deafness did not affect her acceptance.

Although the couple maintained appearances for a number of years, the marriage was not a happy one. William Low was spoiled and self centered, spending a good deal of time drinking and chasing women. Daisy was in the process of divorce when William Mackay Low suddenly died of paralysis in 1905. Shocked over the sudden demise of her husband, Daisy was devastated to learn during the reading of his will, that William Low had left the bulk of his vast estate to his mistress. Embarrassed and dejected, Daisy spent the next several years traveling throughout Europe and India.

Daisy was in Scotland in 1911, when she met Lord Robert Baden-Powell, founder of the British Boy Scouts. It was through Baden-Powell that she became keenly interested in the scouting movement. Like others of his time, Lord Baden-Powell could not see girls learning to live outdoors or endeavoring to become civic leaders, never mind learning to follow careers outside the home. He would not permit girls' groups to be called "scouts" at all, although he authorized a few troops of Girl Guides under the direction of his sister. Daisy Low did all she could with the troops of Girl Guides in England but found the program too restricted for her high hopes.

In 1912, she returned to Savannah determined to put everything she had into making Girl Scouts a reality. On the night of her return, she called an old friend and said, "I've got something for the girls of Savannah and all America and all the world and we're going to start it tonight!" On her own property and using her own funds, Juliette "Daisy" Gordon Low began Girl Scouts, United States of America. Her first troop consisted of eighteen Savannah girls. On a tennis court shielded by curtains, Daisy put them in bloomers and put them through a physical fitness program. She trained them in the basics of independent living and service to others, preparation for careers as well as for home and family. She broke the traditional walls that restricted the life of the Southern lady, prepared girls to compete and succeed in any endeavor they chose.

The movement spread like wildfire across the country, she directed it into the paths of community and national service. In the early days, Daisy Low shocked her fashionable contemporaries by decorating her hat with parsley and carrots. When asked about the wilting vegetables, she would use the opportunity to solicit funds for her girls. During World War I, she had Girl

Scout troops working with the Red Cross, raising vegetables in their backyard gardens and selling Liberty Bonds. Presidents and other national leaders showered her with honors.

Daisy devoted her time, energy and finances for fifteen years to the scouting movement. She elicited major support and contributions from communities all around the world and was a frequent speaker at various events. In an attempt to expand her organization, she tried to merge with the Campfire Girls. A joining that failed due to administrative disputes. Daisy oversaw the compilation of the Girl Scout handbook *How Girls Can Help Their Country*, and in 1919, she was present at the first international meeting of Girl Scouts and Guides.

In 1923, Daisy was diagnosed with breast cancer. She kept her illness a secret and dauntlessly continued her efforts with scouting. She was instrumental in organizing the world Girl Scout camp in the United States in 1926. Less than a year later, on January 17, 1927, "Daisy" Juliette Magill Kinzie Gordon Low died of cancer in Savannah, at the age of sixty-six. The membership in the Girl Scouts by this time numbered 167,000. She was buried in the uniform representing the organization she founded, which to this day continues to change the world. In her breast pocket was placed a note from the head of the Girl Scouts, United States of America, reading: "You are not only the first Girl Scout but the best Girl Scout of them all."

The Girl Scouts purchased the Wayne-Gordon house from the Gordon estate in 1953. It was opened in October 19, 1956, as a program center and historic house museum. The house has been elegantly restored to reflect the 1880s and furnished with period antiques. The house is decorated with artwork by Juliette "Daisy" Gordon Low. Located in the heart of the Savannah Historic District, "the Birthplace," as the Girl Scouts commonly call it nationwide, was the city's first National Historic Landmark.

By their eightieth anniversary in 1992, the Girl Scouts had an estimated fifty million members worldwide.

Birthplace of Juliet Lowe

TRINITY METHODIST CHURCH
Mother Church of Savannah Methodism

Trinity Church is the oldest Methodist Church in a city whose intimate association with John Wesley and George Whitefield gives it a unique place in the history of Methodism.
The cornerstone of the building was laid February 14, 1848, in a ceremony presided over by the Reverend Alfred T. Mann, Pastor. The edifice, which was completed in 1850, is in the Corinthian order of architecture and was designed by
John B. Hogg of Savannah.
Prior to the erection of Trinity Church the Methodist congregation in Savannah worshipped in Wesley Chapel on South Broad Street. Among the great preachers of the Methodist Church whose names are associated with the Chapel are Francis Asbury, William Capers, John Howard, James C. Andrew, Ignatius Few, Elijah Sinclair and George F. Pierce. Through their faith and service others have lived more valiantly.

Next to Telfair Square, Barnard and President Streets, Savannah
GPS Coordinates: N32.07887, W81.094943

The Trinity Methodist Church, located at 127 Barnard Street, holds the distinction of the oldest Methodist church in Savannah; today, known as the Trinity United Methodist Church due to the merging of both modern and traditional factions within the Methodist religion. It carries the honored title of the "Mother Church of Savannah Methodism" from the day when the church was known as Wesley Chapel and located on Lincoln and Oglethorpe Streets.

The church was built for an expanding congregation in 1850 and the design was the creation of John B. Hogg, a Savannah architect. Hogg used the Corinthian style of architecture to create the magnificent sanctuary. The Corinthian style is very decorative, having very simplistic lines. The capitals or tops of the columns are crowned with ornate leaf carvings. Typically, Corinthian roofs are flat, however, it appears in Hogg's design some deviation was used with Doric style cornice or roof, which are customarily slanted.

The interior of the church was taken from the design of the Wesley Chapel in London. Georgia pine was hand hewn for the interior framing, flooring and wainscoting. The walls of the church memorialize past ministers who have died while in her service. The outer walls of the church were constructed of Savannah grey brick and finished with a stucco exterior.

The Trinity United Methodist Church has recently celebrated one hundred and fifty years of service to their Savannah congregation. The church tragically sustained damage as a result of fire in 1991, but has recently moved back into their home edifice on Telfair Square. Historically resilient, the Trinity United Methodist Church continues to serve her Savannah congregation.

Trinity Methodist Church

TELFAIR FAMILY MANSION
(1818 - WILLIAM JAY, ARCHITECT)

This building is one of the city's outstanding examples of Regency architecture. The main floor and basement kitchens are maintained as a historic house museum. The rotunda and west wing are later additions. It
was left by Savannah's outstanding philanthropist, Mary Telfair (1789-
1875), relative of William Gibbons, friend of Peter Cooper, last surviving
child of Edward Telfair (Revolutionary patriot and early Governor of
Georgia) to house the Telfair Academy of Arts and Sciences which was
formed under her will. Notable among her other public bequests are the
Telfair Hospital, the interiors of the Independent Presbyterian Church, and
(with her sister) Hodgson Hall.
In the Colonial and Revolutionary periods "Government house", the residence of the Royal Governors of Georgia, stood on this site. Here on the
night of January 18, 1776, in one of the dramatic episodes of the
American Revolution, Major Joseph Habersham, commanding a small
force of patriots walked alone into the chamber where Governor Wright
was conferring with his Council and announced, "Sir James, you are my
prisoner." Habersham later became Postmaster General of the United
States.

Next to Telfair Square, Barnard and President Streets, Savannah
GPS Coordinates: N32.07887, W81.094943

The site of the Telfair Family Mansion was historic long before Edward Telfair contracted William Jay as architect to build his family home. The lot was the original site of the Savannah Government House at a time when Savannah was the capital city of the Georgia colony and all the government offices of the time resided there.

It was on that lot that the Government House stood when, Liberty Boy Major Joseph Habersham burst in on Royal Governor James Wright and proclaimed him a prisoner of the Revolution. Governor Wright was held prisoner for a short time until his escape, making his way to the safety of England. When the Siege of Savannah was over and the British again controlled the colony, Governor Wright returned. When the Revolution concluded and the British were forced back onto their ships and across the sea, Governor Wright was again driven away.

In 1817, William Jay, a youthful lad of twenty-four, arrived in Savannah and one of his first projects was the Telfair Family Mansion. Although he was touted as "the famed architect from England," few in his homeland even recognized his name, most associated the name with his father or perhaps his grandfather, who were both renown ministers. When young Jay arrived in Savannah, working as an architect was the last thing on his mind, he had many wild oats to sow and threw himself into that endeavor.

Jay's actions spurred his father to write the following:

> "My son, besides professional talent and cleverness, had a large share of wit and humor, qualities always dangerous and commonly injurious to the possessor. So it was, alas! here, His comic powers drew him into company not the most friendly for youthful improvement. He was led into expense by his admirers and flatterers, and for awhile left the path in which he had been taught to go."

Jay loved the ladies, gaming tables, the theater, horse racing and other sports in which one could drop a dime[22], most of all, it is said, William Jay loved to drink and Savannah was a hard drinking town. Even for his love of the drink, Jay's actions were put aside as youthful folly and no harm to his reputation was ever apparent.

He had arrived in Savannah at a most opportune time. Rapid population expansion accompanied the boom in internal and foreign commerce. Wealth was quickly accumulating as a number of Savannah merchants seized the moment to expand into the export trade, which resulted from the War of 1812. From 1810 until 1820, Savannah's population doubled and her wealth seemed limitless. With accumulating riches came the desire for expensive and impressive homes to reflect the newly acquired lifestyles. Public buildings had to convey a sense of prosperity. Jay was the up and coming name in architecture and Savannah citizens clamored for his name to be attached to their homes or business.

The Telfair Family Mansion was completed in 1819 and was, indeed, a sight to behold.

Today, the mansion is the home of the Telfair Academy of Arts and Sciences, the building bequeathed by Mary Telfair. The Telfair family's benevolence reached beyond the artistic with the donation of the Telfair Hospital, interior furnishings of the Independent Presbyterian Church and along with her sister Margaret, Hodgson Hall, the home of the Georgia Historical Society.

Examples of William Jay's architecture can still be seen around the historic squares of Savannah, such as the Scarborough House on West Broad Street and the Owens-Thomas House on Abercorn, both as impressive today as they were over one hundred and fifty years ago.

TELFAIR ACADEMY OF ARTS & SCIENCES
OPEN TO THE PUBLIC —

Created under the Will of Miss Mary Telfair (c. 1789-1875, the Telfair Academy of Arts & Sciences opened as the first public art museum in the Southeast with a preliminary private showing, February 12, 1885. After extensive remodeling and additions, with Detlef Lienau of New York as architect, the building was formally dedicated May 3, 1886. Among the prominent persons who attended the dedication were: Jefferson Davis and his daughter, Winnie Davis; Charles C. Jones, historian; Gen. A. R. Lawton; Gen. Henry R. Jackson; Gen. G. Moxley Sorrel; Col. John Screven and Col. Charles Olmstead. Carl L. Brandt, N. A., served as Telfair's first Director, 1883-1905.

Next to Telfair Square, Barnard and President Streets, Savannah
GPS Coordinates: N32.07887, W81.094943

The Telfair patriarch was former Georgia Governor and Revolutionary War hero Edward Telfair. It was his bequeath that made it possible for son Alexander to have the extraordinary mansion built, which would be the family home until 1875. The present day face of Telfair Academy of Arts and Sciences is bedecked with statues of the great masters; Phidias, Raphael,

Rubens, Michelangelo and Rembrandt. The life size figures are but a introduction to the glorious treasures held safely within her walls. The mansion houses examples of fine art including the Telfair Family collection.

Construction began in 1818 and was completed a year later. The famed English architect William Jay was commissioned to design the structure. He selected a neoclassical Regency design. The design was elegantly portrayed by the rectangular porch crowned by a semicircular window, the porch is supported by four Corinthian columns. The interior spaces have been restored to their original elegance. The period rooms provide a splendid setting for the Museum's decorative arts collection, including American and European objects from 1790 until 1840. The center pieces of the opulent collection are the Telfair family furnishings, including a rare Philadelphia suite of maple furniture and an unusual dining table with two sets of semicircular leaves.

Alexander Telfair only lived in the mansion for twelve years when he died unexpectedly. The home was willed to his sister, Mary. Mary Telfair was an avid art collector and patron of the arts. She, along with her sister, Margaret Telfair Hodgson, donated funds to build Hodgson Hall, home to the Georgia Historical Society and named for William Hodgson, Margaret's late husband. Upon her death, Mary bequeathed the Telfair Family home, its furnishings and her notable art collection to the care of the Georgia Historical Society. Mary's intent was that the Telfair mansion be used as an art museum.

Adhering to the wishes of their patron, the Telfair home became known as the Telfair Academy of Arts and Sciences in 1886. Architect Detlef Lienau was commissioned to convert the family home into a museum. Lienau, who was a great admirer of the original architect William Jay, was extremely careful to preserve Jay's classical Greek design, while expanding the spaces for exhibits and special events held in the museum. Lienau enlarged the Telfair mansion, added a Sculpture Gallery and Rotunda. Strangely enough, Lienau duplicated the rotunda of his most famous design the Lockwood Mansion in the Telfair Academy's main room. The formal opening in 1886 of the Telfair Mansion and Art Museum was attended by dignitaries from all over the United States, including former Confederate President, Jefferson Davis and his daughter, Winnie.

Today, the Telfair Academy of Arts and Sciences features an extensive collection of art, furnishings, as well as the Owens-Thomas House Museum. The museum features special showings, events and the grand Telfair Ball and Auction each February. The Telfair Academy of Arts and Sciences is open for the public to view its magnificent collection for a small admission.

Telfair Academy of Arts and Science

WRIGHT SQUARE

This Square, which was laid out in 1733, was originally named for John Percival, Earl of Egmont, who played a large part in founding the colony of Georgia. Its name was changed around 1763 to Wright Square in honor of James Wright, royal governor of the province of Georgia (1760-1782). In the Town Hall which was located on the present site of the Chatham County courthouse George Whitefield, Church of England minister at Savannah, preached to large congregations in early colonial days.

In 1739 Tomo-chi-chi, the Chief of the Yamacraw Indians who befriended the early Georgia colonists, was buried with ceremony in the center of this Square. Gen. Oglethorpe acting as one of the pallbearers. The monument to William Washington Gordon (1796-1842) commemorates the founder and first president of Georgia's earliest railroad, the Central Railroad and Banking Company — an enterprise which greatly promoted the economy of this State. Designed by the distinguished architects, Henry Van Brunt and Frank M. Howe, the handsome monument to Gordon symbolizes the progress and prosperity of the world by means of commerce, manufacture, agriculture, and art. It was completed in 1883.

Bull and President Streets, Savannah
GPS Coordinates: N32.07809, W81.091939

Originally known as Percival Square, the square was named in honor of the Georgia colony's staunchest supporter in the British Parliament, the Right Honorable John Lord Viscount Percival, Earl of Egmont and President of the Georgia Trustees. It was the second square designed and was laid out by General James Oglethorpe. In 1763 the square was renamed Wright Square, in tribute to Royal Governor James Wright.

When Governor Wright came to Savannah in 1760, he was not exactly welcomed. Although he was true to his office and not unpopular, Governor Wright's first duties were to the King of England and to that end supported the Crown's unfair taxation policies. The Revolutionary War was on the horizon, troubles had already began in the northern colonies and the southern colonies were soon to follow.

Savannah fell in to the British in 1778 and Governor Wright was allowed to return to his post in 1779. Savannah remained in the hands of the British throughout the Revolution. At the war's end, Americans returned to Savannah in triumph. Governor Wright was forced to flee the Georgia colony, this time he would never return. Governor James Wright died in 1785, only three years after leaving the Georgia colony. He was buried at Westminster Abbey.

The squares of Savannah present a beautiful picture of the old city, although Oglethorpe's intent was much more practical. The squares "made the town more compact and easier to defend," according to the Historic Savannah Foundation. Each square consisted of ten lots for private residences on the northern and southern sides, the eastern and western sides were reserved for public buildings and churches. Oglethorpe believed this led to a balanced community. If attacked, the colonists could bring their families and livestock into the interior of the square and be able to defend it from all sides.

Oglethorpe laid out six squares or wards in 1733, of those six, four still remain. Johnson, Wright, Ellis and Telfair were laid out in that order and later Reynolds and Oglethorpe squares were added. The squares eventually numbered twenty-four, unfortunately two of the squares have been partially obliterated. Montgomery Street runs through both Elbert and Liberty Squares dividing them into half squares, one half a park and the other is occupied by public buildings. The third square 'lost to progress' was Ellis Square. The once historic park has been replaced by a public parking garage.

Wright Square is the site of two monuments. One tucked away in the southeast corner is a granite boulder donated by the Colonial Dames in remembrance of Tomo Chi Chi, the great Native American Chief. Tomo Chi Chi contributed immeasurably to the colonization of Georgia and was said to have been buried at the center of the square. It was his request to be interred along side his Savannah brethren. General James Oglethorpe was one of the men to carry his body to the site in 1739.

The other monument stands impressively at the center of the square, in honor of William Washington Gordon. The substantial memorial was built with four columns of pink Georgia marble. Throughout his lifetime, Gordon pursued a number of careers: military, legal, political and private. During his military career, he graduated from United States Military Academy at West Point and as a soldier served with the Georgia Hussars. William Washington Gordon's legal career, found him apprenticed under James Wayne and later practicing, in his own right, from 1819 until 1836. As a politician, Gordon was Alderman of Savannah, Mayor of Savannah, served in the House of Representatives and the Georgia Senate.

However, it was his private endeavors where he made a name for himself. William Washington Gordon was founder and organizer of the Central of Georgia Railroad and Banking Company. For those accomplishments, Gordon earned a place in the history of Georgia.

Upon the death of William Washington Gordon, the Chief Engineer of the Central of Georgia Railroad, Mr. Reynolds stated,

> "the steadiness and determination with which he pursued the great objects of benefiting his native state and this city, and the most distinguished of publics benefactors."

The Central of Georgia Railroad and Banking Company dedicated the Wright Square memorial to their first president and founding father on June 25, 1882.

TOMO-CHI-CHI'S GRAVE

Tomo-Chi-Chi, Mico of the Yamacraws, a tribe of the Creek Indian Nation, is buried in this Square. He has been called a co-founder, with Oglethorpe, of Georgia. He was a good friend to the English, a friendship indispensable to the establishment of the Colony as a military outpost against Spanish invasion. He negotiated with Oglethorpe the treaty formally ratified on May 21, 1733, pursuant to which Georgia was settled. Mary Musgrove, half-breed niece of Emperor Brim of the Creek Indians, acted as interpreter between Oglethorpe and Tomo-Chi-Chi and lent her great influence to the signing of that treaty and to the treaties negotiated by Oglethorpe with other tribes of the Creek nation.

In 1734, at the age of 84, with his wife Senauki, Tomo-Chi-Chi visited the English Court and was received by the King and by the Archbishop of Canterbury. He was a man of fine physique, tall and of great dignity. He died October 5, 1739 at Yamacraw Indian Village, and at his request was brought to Savannah to rest among his English friends. He was buried here with military honors.

Wright Square, Bull and President Streets, Savannah
GPS Coordinates: N32.07809, W81.091939

Tomo Chi Chi was General Oglethorpe's greatest ally when he arrived at the Georgia colony and he made peaceful relations with the Native Americans possible. He was known as the great Yamacraw Mico[23] in the Creek Nation and shared the dream of the Georgia colony with Oglethorpe. He knew that the white race held a superior power and struggled to maintain an alliance that would benefit both the white and Native American cultures. Tomo Chi Chi prophesied that if the Creek fought against the white settlers, it would be the end of civilization as they knew it. Unfortunately, regardless of his admirable works and those of Oglethorpe, the great people have been virtually vanquished.

Having served his people and the Georgia colony with fidelity, sincerity and generosity; Tomo Chi Chi died at the age of 97 years. His passing was observed as any great leader of the Georgia colony could expect and Oglethorpe saw to it that his friend was buried in a manner benefitting one of his stature. At his request, Tomo Chi Chi was buried among his white brethren. The following was written as his obituary and published in the *Gentleman's Magazine* in 1749[24]:

"SAVANNAH IN GEORGIA, Oct: 10, 1739.

King Toma-chi-chi died on the 5th, at his own town, 4 miles from hence, of a lingering Illness, being aged about 97. He was sensible to the last Minutes, and when he was persuaded his death was near he showed the greatest Magnanimity and Sedateness, and exhorted his People never forget the favours he had received from the King when in England, but to persevere in their Friendship with the English. He expressed the greatest Tenderness for Gen. Oglethorpe, and seemed to have no Concern at dying but its being at a Time when his Life might be useful against the Spaniards. He desired his Body might be buried amongst the English in the Town of Savannah, since it was he that had prevailed with the Creek Indians to give the Land, and had assisted in the founding of the Town. The Corpse was brought down by Water. The General, attended by the Magistrates and the People of the Town, met it upon the Water's Edge. The Corpse was carried into Percival Square. The pall was supported by the General, Coln Stephens, Coln Montaigut, Mr Carterat, Mr Lemon, and Mr Maxwell. It was followed by the Indians and Magistrates and People of the Town. There was the Respect paid of firing Minute Guns from the Battery all the time during the Burial, and funeral-firing with small Arms by the Militia, who were under arms. The General has ordered a Pyramid of Stone, which is dug in this Neighbourhood, to be erected over the Grave, which being in the Centre of the Town, will be a great Ornament to it, as well as testimony of Gratitude.

Toma-chi-chi was a Creek Indian, and in his youth a great Warriour. He had an excellent Judgment and a very ready Wit, which showed itself in his Answers on all Occasions. He was very generous, giving away all the rich presents he received, remaining himself in wilful Poverty, being more pleased in giving to others, than possessing himself; and he was very mild and good natured."

Although no great imposing monument stands in honor of Tomo Chi Chi in the city of Savannah, the area believed to be the site of his grave does hold a marker. A massive granite boulder, taken from Georgia's Stone Mountain in Atlanta, commemorates Tomo Chi Chi's burial in 1739. The granite stone lays at the southeast corner of Wright Square. Tomo Chi Chi would have appreciated the simplicity of this marker, but possibly we owe much more to a man that contributed so much to the founding of the Georgia.

Tom-Chi-Chi Monument

LUTHERAN CHURCH
OF THE ASCENSION
(Founded, 1741)

On April 14, 1741, John Martin Bolzius, who as Pastor of the
Salzburgers at Ebenezer was in charge of Lutheran work in the
colony of Georgia, founded the congregation now known as the
Lutheran Church of the Ascension.
In 1756, members of the congregation purchased for one hundred
and fifty pounds the lot upon which the present church building
stands, directly East of this marker. Around 1772 a nearby building which had formerly served as a court house was acquired at a
cost of seventeen pounds and was moved to this site, becoming
the first church building of Lutherans in Savannah.
The present church was erected in 1843. Extensive remodeling
was completed in 1879 and at that time it was dedicated as "The
Evangelical Lutheran Church of the Ascension." The choice of the
name is connected with the beautiful stained glass window behind
the altar, portraying the Ascension of Christ into heaven.

Wright Square, Bull and President Streets, Savannah
GPS Coordinates: N32.07809, W81.091939

The Salzburgs, a group of German immigrants, arrived in the Georgia colony in 1734. General Oglethorpe granted them fifty acre lots for each family, in a village called Ebenezer. When bouts of malaria and flux threatened the health of the settlement, the Salzburgs requested that they be relocated. Although Oglethorpe disagreed, he did not forbid the people from moving. The Salzburgs realized that the majority of their population would not survive the summer at Ebenezer and decided to move with the support of their two Lutheran Ministers.

John Martin Bolzius, one of the Lutheran Ministers, sought the aid of John Wesley to hold a Communion Service for the Salzburgs because they had not yet built a church. The pious Wesley refused communion to Bolzius and his flock because they had not been baptized by an ordained Episcopal minister. Bolzius, always the exemplary Christian, did not think ill of Wesley, quite the contrary; he wrote to Wesley an extremely warm letter thanking him for ministering to the Salzburgs. The letter was entered into Wesley's journal, after which Wesley noted,

"Can any one carry High Church zeal higher than this? And how well have I been since beaten with my own staff!"

Bolzius began conducting services in a building used to house visiting Salzburgs organized in 1741. Thirty years later, a lot was deeded to the Lutherans, and in 1772, the first wooden framed Lutheran church was built in Savannah. A devastating fire took the church in 1797 and another was constructed in its place. This edifice was used until 1843 when a sturdier building of brick was erected.

The present sanctuary was designed by George B. Clarke and construction began in 1875. As the Norman and Gothic shape began to take form, it was quite

The Lutheran Church of the Ascension

obvious that this would be a substantial structure. The magnificent stained glass pictorial of *The Ascension* arrived from Philadelphia in 1878. The Lutheran Church of the Ascension was dedicated in 1879.

Today, as you enter the church, the effect of the stained glass depicting the Ascension of Christ to heaven is quite possibly the most dramatic of any in Savannah. The window is framed by a fresco of terra cotta and gold, engraved in a delicate design of interwoven vines and symbols. A Thorvalden[25] statue of Christ adorns the lower narthex[26], the windows of the nave[27] tell the sixteen episodes of the history of the Church and a rose window displays Martin Luther's[28] coat of arms. The beauty culminates with a carving of Da Vinci's[29] Last Supper aptly done on the marble altar.

The church is located on Wright square and designated as a National Historic Landmark. The congregation remains very proud of its more than 250 years of history.

OWENS ~ THOMAS HOUSE
MARQUIS de LAFAYETTE

This residence is the outstanding monument to the architectural genius of William Jay who completed his designs for its construction prior to his twenty-first birthday. Supervision of the work brought Jay to America in 1817. Its period is English Regency. Its style is known as Greek Revival. Its interiors are particularly notable and, in many features, unique. Of its style and period it is Savannah's finest and among the nation's best.

The mansion was built 1816-1819 for Richard Richardson, a Savannah merchant. The basement, of "tabby" construction, is of much earlier date, and contains the original trim of the de Brahm house which once occupied the site.

General LaFayette was quartered here as a guest of the City when he visited Savannah in 1825. He addressed the populace from the south balcony. The mansion was left in trust to the Telfair Academy of Arts and Sciences in 1951 by Margaret Gray Thomas whose grandfather, George W. Owens, distinguished lawyer and Member of Congress, acquired the property from the Bank of the United States. It is now a historic house museum.

Across from Oglethorpe Square, Abercorn and President Streets, Savannah
GPS Coordinates: N32.07772, W81.089712

The Owens-Thomas House is considered by some, "the Most Beautiful House in America." The home graces Oglethorpe Square at 124 Abercorn Street. Construction began in 1816 and was completed three years later for the home's original owner, cotton merchant and banker Richard Richardson.

The home was designed by Richardson's brother in law, famed English architect William Jay, when he was just beginning his career as one the first professionally trained architects in the United States. The home continues, to this day, to be considered the finest example of English Regency architecture in America by architectural historians. The design was considered so beautiful, Jay's reputation as an architect was sealed for the remainder of his life.

The Richardsons' lived in the house for three years until Richard suffered grave financial loses. The Bank of the United States foreclosed on the splendid home. For the next eight years, Mrs. Mary Maxwell operated an elegant and exclusive boarding house in the residence. Among her most notable guests was the Revolutionary War hero, the Marquis de LaFayette. LaFayette, who stayed at the home in 1825 was said to have given two separate speeches from the ornate cast iron balcony on the southern facade of the home. Such speeches were an expected tradition and it is said that a throng of adoring Savannah citizens gathered to hear the famous Frenchman speak.

George Welchman Owens, a lawyer, congressman and former mayor of Savannah, purchased the home from the bank in 1830 for $10,000. The home remained in the Owens family until 1951, when his granddaughter, Margaret Thomas willed the property to the Telfair Academy to be used as part of the Telfair Museum of Art. Thus, the name of the home became the Owens-Thomas House.

No mere description of the residence could possibly do justice to the beauty that is the Regency design of the home. The home is constructed mostly of tabby and finished with a patina colored stucco. Many elaborate features of the home separate it from others, notably the brass inlaid staircase, the bridge spanning the stairwell and the amber glass used in the dining room, creating a romantic effect.

Jay introduced two design innovations never before seen in any Savannah home. The first of which was the Grecian inspired veranda on the south side of the home made of painted cast iron. The second astounding feature was the installation of an elaborate plumbing system allowing for the convenience of running water, a water closet[30] and baths. The innovation was noted as the most sophisticated domestic sanitary system in 19th century America. Jay and Henry McAlphin established a foundry for the production of the cast iron to be used in the construction of the home in an effort to promote a fireproof structure.

The basement area had a more industrial feel, housing, what is today, the remains of the plumbing system, kitchen, laundry, wine cellar and ice chamber. Only two major alterations have been made to the original structure in the over one hundred eighty year history of the home. In 1830, a second story was added to the rear of the structure and in 1950, an English garden was added in what was the carriage turn around. The Carriage House, which includes one of the earliest complete slave quarters, also houses a stable which today serves as the Museum Shop and Regional Art Gallery.

The Owens-Thomas House contains an outstanding collection of decorative arts, most of which belonged to the Owens family. Only a few of the furnishings belonging to the original owner, Richardson, remain in the home which includes three marble top tables.

The Telfair Museum of Art developed a three phase preservation project for the Owens-Thomas House in 1992. The first of which entailed transforming the carriage house into a visitor's center and museum shop. The second phase was much more extensive consisting of cleaning and repairing the stucco and stone; conserving and painting of the windows and blinds; repair of the wrought and cast iron fencing, railings and balcony; and major structural repairs including the removal of a modern exterior staircase and replacing the roof, gutters and climate control system. Phase three, which is ongoing, concerns the interior furnishings and interior design of the home.

The Owens-Thomas House is open to the public, Tuesday through Saturday, 10:00 a..m. to 5:00 p.m. and on Sundays, 2:00 p.m. until 5:00 p.m. A small fee is charged.

COLONIAL TOWN GATE
DAVENPORT HOUSE

In 1757, during the administration of royal Governor Henry Ellis, a line of earthwork defenses, including a palisade, was erected around Savannah. Immediately west of this marker was located Bethesda Gate, one of six entrances into the town. Through Bethesda Gate passed the Sea Island Road connecting Savannah and the tidewater settlements to the east and southeast.

This square, known as Columbia Square, was laid out in 1799. Facing it on the north is the "Davenport House," one of the handsomest examples of Georgian architecture in the south. This finely proportioned dwelling, completed in 1820, was designed and built by its owner, Isaiah Davenport (1784-1827), one of Savannah's outstanding builder-architects.

In 1956 the "Davenport House" was restored by Historic Savannah Foundation as the first preservation project of that organization. It is open to the public at certain times during the week.

Columbia Square, Habersham and State Streets, Savannah
GPS Coordinates: N32.07719, W81.089729

Located at the picturesque Columbia Square, the Colonial Town Gate is known as the Bethesda Gate. The Colonial Town Gate once guarded the eastern entrance into the city of Savannah. Today, the square features a fountain at its center that once adorned the landscape of Wormsloe Plantation.

The north side of Columbia Square is graced with what is one of the most impressive successes of historic preservation seen in Savannah, the Isaiah Davenport House. The restoration of this structure served as the catalyst for the restoration of historic homes throughout Savannah, the Historic Savannah Foundation was established as a result of the Davenport House restoration and is the reason so many of Savannah's historic homes are available for public tours today. These homes echo the footsteps of our forefathers and tell priceless stories of our history that we can hardly afford to lose.

Isaiah Davenport moved to the port city of Savannah at the age of twenty-three, where he used his skills acquired as a carpenter's apprentice in 1808 and began to build houses. He married Sarah Rosamund Clark and built the first of their homes in 1812. Davenport was noted as a superb builder but also became involved in civic endeavors. He was appointed Fire Marshal for Greene and Columbia Wards in 1810, then Alderman and finally, Constable. As a builder, he was contracted to build fencing around each of the city squares and built homes for several prominent Savannah families. During this time Davenport's wealth increased enough to hire skilled workers, in addition to the slave labor he used for less detailed work. It was during this time that he began to purchase and resale properties as well.

He purchased a prestigious lot at the corner of State and Habersham Streets around 1813 that included a house only partially built, the structure forever known as the Davenport House was completed in 1820. The house was built in the Federal or Adam style in a neighborhood considered to be conservative middle class. The interior design reveals the influence of Greek Revival architecture and the more formal public rooms of the house, the office and parlor, were built to impress those who might visit.

After only seven years of occupancy, Davenport contracted yellow fever. Sarah Davenport was unable to care for her contagious husband due to the pregnancy of their tenth child, three of which had died in infancy and with a nurse at his side, Davenport died at the age of forty-three. Sarah Davenport was left with little cash on hand and was forced to sell some of their property, furnishings and slaves. She considered selling the Columbia Square home but instead opened her home to boarders. Finally selling the home in 1840, she operated several boarding houses, first on Jones, then Broughton Street. Sarah Davenport died in Savannah in 1869 at the age of eighty-one.

William Baynard purchased the Davenport House in 1840 and his family resided there until 1890 when downtown Savannah became a less than desirable address. The house was carved into apartments and from the 1890s through 1950 between nine and thirteen families occupied the property at one time, most in one room apartments. The beautiful home created by Davenport eventually fell to ruin.

Katherine Summerlin purchased the Davenport House in 1955. Summerlin's intent was to demolish the house to add parking space for her funeral home next door. However, public sentiment was changing and historic preservation was becoming more popular. That same year, the City Market had been demolished for parking and citizens recognized the loss of a historic site, unfortunately too late.

Anna C. Hunter, who conceived the idea of saving the Davenport House, discussed the thought with six other ladies and the Historic Savannah Foundation was born. The foundation met with Summerlin several times and finally, persuaded her to sell the property for $22,500. The funds were raised only hours before demolition was to begin.

Like most projects when the initial need is resolved, support disappears. This left the foundation trying to determine what was to be done with the Davenport House. Making the most needed repairs, the foundation leased the house to an organization for use as office space. The rent helped to pay the mortgage on the property and after a few years the foundation decided to renovate the entire building. In 1963, the Davenport House was opened to the public as a house museum and quickly became a popular Savannah attraction.

The house as presented was filled with antiques and that were not in keeping with those that might have originally been used to furnish the home. Many of furnishings were of the wrong period or too ornate for a 1800's middle class dwelling. In the 1990s, Davenport House was refurnished piece by piece in keeping with the appropriate adornments of Davenport's time.

The Davenport House stands today as an excellent example of 1800s middle class Savannah living. The Historic Savannah Foundation's attention to detail and exemplary research has created much more than a museum to the past but an accurate picture of life during the time of Isaiah and Sarah Davenport. The Davenport House museum is open to the public daily from 10:00 until 4:00, a small fee is charged that in turn supports maintenance of the historical site.

The Davenport House

JOHNSON SQUARE

Johnson Square is named for Governor Robert Johnson of South Carolina who befriended the colonists when Georgia was first settled. It was laid out by Oglethorpe and by Colonel William Bull in 1733, and was the first of Savannah's squares. In early colonial days the public stores, the house for strangers, the church, and the public bake oven stood on the trust lots around it. Events of historical interest are associated with Johnson Square. Here in 1735, Chekilli, head Chief of the Creek Nation, recited the origin myth of the Creeks. In 1737, the Rev. John Wesley, after futile efforts to bring to trial certain indictments against him growing out of his ministry at Savannah, posted a public notice in this Square that he intended to return to England. The Declaration of Independence was read here to an enthusiastic audience, August 10, 1776. In 1819 a ball was given for President James Monroe in a pavilion erected in the Square. Eminent men who have spoken here include the Marquis de LaFayette, (1825); Henry Clay (1847), and Daniel Webster (1848). Beneath the Nathanael Greene monument rest the remains of the famous Revolutionary general and his son.

Johnson Square, Bull and St. Julian Streets, Savannah
GPS Coordinates: N32.07979, W81.091778

Founder General James Edward Oglethorpe designed Savannah as the first planned city in much the same pattern used in Washington D. C.'s planning sixty years later. Oglethorpe's methodical plan was based on a grid pattern of streets and alleys surrounding open spaces called squares. The northern and southern lots of each square were reserved as housing lots; the eastern and western sides were reserved for public buildings. In 1733, there were only four squares but eventually twenty-four were created, of the original squares twenty-one still exist today.

Each square remains a home for a monument, fountain, historical marker or a combination of each. The squares are individually landscaped and all have their own unique style, charm and beauty. Oddly enough, the name for each square is in conflict with the monument erected on it. For example, the Nathaniel Greene Monument is located Johnson Square rather than Greene Square and the Oglethorpe Monument is on Chippewa Square.

Johnson Square was the first to be designed and was named for Robert Johnson, Governor of South Carolina. The featured obelisk in the center of the square is a tribute to Nathanael Greene. Greene was a New England born Revolutionary War General and devoted member of General George Washington's staff. General Greene was rewarded for service to his country with the grant of Mulberry Grove Plantation. He died there in 1786 of sunstroke, at the age of 44. Both General Greene and his son are buried beneath the monument. Two fountains grace each side of the monument.

Massive ancient oaks with a beautifully entwined network of expansive branches shade Johnson Square. Surprisingly, a feature you won't see at Johnson Square is Spanish moss. The oaks are completely free of the gray draped fringe, eradicated as a result of pollution from nearby buildings. Savannah citizens often call the square, Bank Square, due to the large banking companies that surround it.

In 1735, Chekilli, Chief of the Creek Nation recited the origin of the Native tribe on Johnson Square saying,

> "At a certain time the earth opened in the west, where its mouth is. The earth opened and the Kasihtas (Creeks) came out."

John Wesley publicly issued notice here of his return to England, the future Father of Methodism left in failure but would eventually return and spread his message throughout the colony.

Johnson Square remains a popular lunch retreat due to its centralized location, live music and food carts often found on the square. Nearby is Churchill's Pub, it was here that many of the bar scenes featured in the film, *Midnight in the Garden of Good and Evil* were staged.

CHRIST CHURCH
The Mother Church of Georgia

This Episcopal church was the first house of worship established with the founding of Georgia in 1733. Early rectors included the Rev. John Wesley (1736-37), who began the earliest form of Sunday school and published the first English hymnal in the colonies, and the Rev. George Whitefield (1738-40), founder of Bethesda Orphanage. The cornerstone for the first building on this site was laid in 1744. James Hamilton Couper designed the current and third structure in 1838. The 1819 Revere & Son bell continues in use today. One of many prominent members was Juliette Gordon Low, founder of the Girl Scouts of America.

Johnson Square, Abercorn Street, Savannah
GPS Coordinates: N32.07979, W81.091778

General James Edward Oglethorpe designed the city of Savannah with a vision that on each and every square a place of worship would be prominent. When he landed at Savannah with his storm tossed group of colonists, he employed spiritual leadership to help guide the struggle to carve a settlement from the wilderness. Oglethorpe brought the most devout ministers of the gospel he could find, John and Charles Wesley. The first services were held in General Oglethorpe's tent along side the Savannah River. The Wesleys thanked God for the colonists' safe passage and prayed for continued guidance during the hard times to come.

The first church of Georgia, Christ Church, was founded in 1733 and graced Johnson Square. The church was founded as an Anglican house of worship, although after surviving the ravages of the American Revolution, the congregation voted to become Protestant Episcopal. A bell was purchased from the Boston firm of Revere & Son in 1819 and through the years has sounded during times of joy, sadness and alarm. Revere is known in history as Paul Revere, famous for his midnight cries of British invasion.

By 1823, a small diocese emerged with three parishes and in 1838, the present edifice known as Christ Episcopal Church was built at the same location. Over the next year, six churches and six parishes were added to the Georgia Diocese and the first Georgia bishop was elected. Today, the diocese extends throughout southeast Georgia, over 32,994 square miles. The first church of Georgia still sounds her Revere bell and calls all those who will, to worship.

Christ Church

NATHANAEL GREENE MONUMENT

Beneath the monument in this Square repose the remains of Maj. Gen. Nathanael Greene, of Rhode Island, who died near Savannah on June 19, 1786, at Mulberry Grove Plantation which had been granted to him by this State in appreciation of his services in the Revolution. The 50 foot, white marble obelisk, designed by the well-known architect, William Strickland, was completed in 1830. The original cornerstone was laid here on March 21, 1825, by Greene's old friend, the Marquis de Lafayette. At the dedicatory ceremony General Lafayette said:

"The great and good man to whose memory we are paying a tribute of respect, affection, and regret, has acted in our revolutionary contest a part so glorious and so important that in the very name of Greene are remembered all the virtues and talents which can illustrate the patriot, the statesman, and the military leader. . . "

General Greene's remains were originally interred in the burial ground now known as Colonial Cemetery. His exact resting place was a matter of doubt and speculation for many years. The remains of the famed Revolutionary hero were found in the Graham vault in 1901, and were reinterred beneath this monument the following year.

Johnson Square, Bull and St. Julian Streets, Savannah
GPS Coordinates: N32.07979, W81.091778

To say Nathanael Greene was beloved would be an understatement. His dedication to the cause of Liberty and in support of the Revolutionary War effort was untiring; his devotion to General Washington was unquestionable; his courage in the face of the enemy was unwavering and his commitment to those in his command was unfailing. Nathanael Greene died of sunstroke, at the age of forty-four, only three years after the Revolutionary War ended. His loss was grieved by the nation.

Greene's last years were spent in happy leisure. Although troubled by his financial losses during the Revolution, he pursued the life of a planter with abandon on his Mulberry Grove Plantation, along with his charming, if not somewhat overly flirtatious, wife Catherine and their brood of five children. Greene was constantly approached to enter the governmental arena as a statesman and had his life not been so tragically cut short, he quite possibly would have ascended to the highest government office.

Alexander Hamilton spoke of Nathanael Greene to the Society of the Cincinnati saying,

"What he might have done on a greater scale and with more ample resources, it is, of course, impossible to say; but the intellectual qualities that he showed were precisely those that have won distinction for the foremost strategists of modern times."

George Washington, it has been said, was grooming Greene to succeed him.

Nathanael Greene was laid to rest in the Graham vault of Colonial Park Cemetery. Later his son, named for Greene's friend and mentor, George Washington, was placed beside him after drowning at Mulberry Grove. In 1825 a corner stone was laid by Greene's friend and fellow patriot, the Marquis de LaFayette, as a memorial in his honor. The fifty foot white marble obelisk was completed in 1830 and the magnificent monument is located in Johnson Square.

Over time General Greene's final resting place came into question. The atrocities of the Civil War further exacerbated the confusion when Union troops stooped to grave robbing. According to Web Garrison's *Treasury of Civil War Tales*, Sherman's men showed no deference to the gallant patriots who had died for American liberty and the oppression of northern men as well as southern.

Seventy years after the monument was erected, Nathanael Greene's remains were located. In 1901, both he and his son were reinterred beneath the protective sphere of the Nathanael Greene Monument.

Washington's Southern Tour

During his Southern tour of 1791, President George Washington attended services at the original Christ Church on Sunday, May 15. While in Savannah from May 12-15, Washington lodged at a house on the corner of Barnard and State streets on St. James (now Telfair) Square, dined at Brown's Coffeehouse with the Society of the Cincinnati, toured the ruins of the Revolutionary earthworks with General Lachlan McIntosh, was entertained at the Silk Filature on Reynolds Square, and attended a large public dinner. After Sunday services, Washington dined with Catherine Greene (widow of Nathanael Greene) at Mulberry Grove plantation north of the city before departing for Augusta. Erected by the Georgia Historical Society, the Society of the Cincinnati in the State of Georgia, and the Sons of the Revolution in the State of Georgia.

Johnson Square on Bull Street, Savannah
GPS Coordinates: N32.07979, W81.091778

President Washington arrived at the road to Purrysburg, Carolina, along the Savannah River on May 12, 1791. He was met by Noble Wimberly Jones, Colonel Joseph Habersham, John Houston, General Lachlan McIntosh and Joseph Clay, the men escorted the weary President to the home of his long time friend, Catherine Greene. The visit was more a ruse than social, the committee wanted to delay Washington's arrival in Savannah until preparations could be completed to greet him in fine fashion. Although months had been spent in anticipation of the President's calling, no one knew for sure when he would arrive. No one, of course, except Washington.

The President had prepared a detailed itinerary of his southern tour in which he noted each stop and how long he would remain, then calculated the distance to the next stop and how much travel time should be allotted, taking into consideration weather, rough traveling conditions and unanticipated meetings. Washington had allowed three days for his visit to Savannah and then planned to proceed on to Augusta.

The welcoming committee surely must have been on their toes, for when Washington arrived at the designated meeting place at 6:00 a.m. they were there to greet him. Although it was stated that the President only stopped for a short time to inquire as to Mrs. Greene's health, he did not arrive in Savannah, twenty-five miles by water, until 6:00 p.m.

Washington arrived at the Mulberry Grove Plantation of Mrs. Greene by horse drawn coach and the group traveled on the Savannah by way of the Savannah River. According to the President the "winds and tides" were against them. The usual four hour trip turned out to be a seven hour ordeal.

The late arrival did little to dampen the spirits of the excited crowd. Washington was rowed to shore by eight captains dressed in light blue silk jackets, black satin breeches, white silk stockings and round felt hats with black ribbons lettered in gold reading, "Long live the President." A procession of boats met the President, ten miles out and escorted his party the remainder of way. As the President stepped from the ship a band played and the crowds sent up deafening cheers at his approach.

Senator James Gunn and Congressman James Jackson introduced Savannah's Mayor Thomas Gibbons and the city Aldermen. After a salute of twenty-six guns by the Chatham Artillery, Washington was finally taken to his lodgings on St. James Square. A long procession trailed behind including the city officials, the welcoming committee, the artillery company, the local light infantry, officers of the militia, members of the Cincinnati Society and Savannah citizens.

Dinner was scheduled to be a private affair at Washington's lodgings, but ended up as a formal dinner at Brown's Coffeehouse. One hundred of Savannah's most esteemed individuals attended and after sixteen toasts, all accompanied by resounding artillery fire, the evening finally came to an end, much to the relief of an exhausted President Washington. Savannah presented a beautiful picture on the stroll back to President Washington's accommodations. The city was lighted with over three hundred candles, fifteen of which were placed in the formation of a "W".

May 13th was filled with speeches in the President's honor. The Society of Cincinnati, a patriotic society founded by officers of the American Revolution of which General George Washington was the first President, presented an address; the citizens of Savannah; the Congregational Church; the Society of Midway, a nearby community; the Savannah Mayor and Aldermen; the Freemasons; and Reverend John Earnst Bergman of the German Congregation at Ebenezer. Washington responded to each and every address with the exception of Reverend Bergman. The good Reverend chose to speak in Latin and Washington didn't understand a word of the two hour address.

A grand ball was held that evening in the Long Room of the Filature, where silk was once manufactured. The President made his appearance at 8:30 p.m. and was personally introduced to each of the ninety-six ladies in attendance that evening. By 11:00, an exhausted President Washington made his excuses and returned to his rooms for a much deserved rest. The President's departure did not put a damper on the party, dinner was served at midnight and dancing continued until 3:00 a.m.

At 6:00 a.m. on Saturday, May 14th, Washington walked about Savannah. Generals McIntosh and Wayne relived the defense of Savannah in 1779 during the procession. Many Americans and French allies lost their lives during the siege and although that battle was lost, the war was won.

Washington dined that night with no less than two hundred Savannah citizens underneath a beautiful arbor supported by three rows of pillars covered in laurel and bay leaves. The site was chosen for its view of the city, the harbor, the river and the rice fields. A concert and fireworks display completed the evening. That was the last night Washington would spend in Savannah.

After attending church services at Christ Church on Sunday, May 15th, Washington took his leave of Savannah. He was escorted out of Savannah by the city gentlemen and a detachment of Dragoons led by Major Ambrose Gordon. Thirty-nine artillery discharges and thirteen volleys were fired in salute.

Stopping off once again at Mulberry Grove, this time the visit did not include all of the pomp and circumstance surrounding the President. The two old friends managed to share the afternoon. Washington was then on way, as scheduled, to Augusta.

The following was President George Washington's impression of Savannah[31]:

"Savannah stands upon what may be called high ground for this Country. It is extremely Sandy wch. makes the walking very disagreeable; & the houses uncomfortable in warm & windy weather as they are filled with dust whensoever these happen. The town on 3 sides is surrounded with cultivated Rive fields which have a rich and luxurient appearance. On the 4th. or back side it is a fine sand. The harbour is said to be very good, & often filled with square rigged vessels but there is a bar below over which not more than 12 Water can be brot. except at Spg. tides. The tide does not flow above 12 or 14 miles above the City though the River is swelled by it more than dble, that distance. Rice & Tobacco (the last of wch. is greatly encreasing) are the principal Exports. Lumber & Indigo are also Exported, but the latter is on the decline, and it is supposed by Hemp & Cotton. Ship timber-viz-live Oak & Cedar, is (and may be more so) valuable in the expt."

Although George Washington could have quite easily retained the office of the Presidency for the remainder of his life, he asked to be released from bonds of public office at the end of his second term in 1797. He longed to return to his farm at Mount Vernon and retire from public life. Washington left the Presidency feeling discouraged over the constant political bickering between the parties supporting Thomas Jefferson and those of Alexander Hamilton. George Washington's retirement was to be short lived, he died at his beloved Mount Vernon on December 14, 1799. The nation mourned a great man, "the Father of our Country."

Reynolds Square, Abercorn and St. Julian Streets, Savannah
GPS Coordinates: N32.0796, W81.089498

A monument in the likeness of John Wesley stands in Reynolds Square, the embodiment of the Christian Perfection that Wesley preached. His stern expression reveals the intensity of his message, the Bible clutched firmly in his left hand reflects the strength of his convictions and the right hand extended, offers the path to enlightenment.

Wesley preached, in 1742, about Christian Perfection. Admitting that no life was without flaw, even his own. Perfection implies good deeds, obeying the edicts of God and the avoidance of ignorance, mistakes and temptation. He recognized that no one would ever attain perfection and to do so would not be human.

During this time, Wesley preached a series of sermons detailing the ideals of Christian Perfection. These sermons included God's Preparing, Accepting and Sustaining Grace; Spiritual Disciplines: Works of Piety; Mission: The Works of Mercy and finally, Christian Perfection. On God's Grace, Wesley preached the following:

"The grace or love of God, whence cometh our salvation, is FREE IN ALL, and FREE FOR ALL.... It is free in all to whom it is given. It does not depend on any power or merit in man; no, not in any degree, neither in whole, nor in part. It does not in anywise depend either on the good works or righteousness of the receiver; not on anything he has done, or anything he is. It does not depend on his endeavors. It does not depend on his good tempers, or good desires, or good purposes and intentions; for all these flow from the free grace of God; they are the streams only, not the fountain. They are the fruits of free grace, and not the root. They are not the cause, but the effects of it."

He defined piety as,

"The chief of these means are prayer, whether in secret or with the great congregation; searching the Scriptures; (which implies reading, hearing, and meditating thereon;) and receiving the Lord's Supper, eating bread and drinking wine in remembrance of Him: And these we believe to be ordained of God, as the ordinary channels of conveying his grace to the souls of men."

Wesley taught that people must be Christians in both word and deed, which were to be used to express a love of God. He believed that Christians must grow in God's grace, which first prepares us for belief, then accepts us when we respond to God in faith. Wesley believed that God's grace sustains us as we do good works and participate in his mission. He not only preached about works of mercy, he was said to have "practiced" what he preached.

This was truly a man of God. Although his frailties as merely a man were often a source of discontent within himself. Wesley believed in the message of which he spoke. He devoted a lifetime, bringing the message public so that all who might hear his voice or read his works would find peace in God.

John Wesley Monument

JOHN WESLEY'S
AMERICAN PARISH

John Wesley, an Anglican minister, served as the religious leader of the Georgia colony from February 6, 1736 to December 2, 1737. His inclusive ministry sought to embrace both Native Americans and colonists. In 1976, The United Methodist Church declared this, the site of their founder's American ministry, a Nation Historic Landmark encompassing

1. His new world landing site at Cockspur Island on U.S. 80 E.
2. The site of his first sermon at Bull St. and Bay Lane.
3. The Wesley monument on Reynolds Square.
4. Site of his parsonage and garden at Congress and Abercorn.
5. Site of Wesley's first permanent worship place at York & Whitaker.
6. And in 1995, Trinity Church on Telfair Square, "The Mother Church of Savannah Methodism."

Reynolds Square, Abercorn and St. Julian Streets, Savannah
GPS Coordinates: N32.0796, W81.089498

General James Edward Oglethorpe invited young controversial evangelist, John Wesley to travel to Georgia as the colony's religious leader in 1735. A proposal that Wesley refused unless accompanied by his brother Charles. Oglethorpe agreed, the Wesleys set sail on board the *Simmonds* on October 13, 1735. Charles was to serve as Oglethorpe's private secretary and religious counselor at Frederica, while John would provide religious leadership throughout the colony.

School friends and members of The Holy Club, Benjamin Ingham and Charles Delamotte also traveled with the Wesleys. The Holy Club was a group of like minded students at Oxford who were all very devoted in their beliefs. The group was led by John Wesley. The club eventually evolved into the religion of Methodism. The group arrived at Pepper Island, presently Cockspur Island, on February 6, 1736. John Wesley uttered his first words of prayer in the newly founded colony at this site. On March 7th, Wesley preached his first sermon at the courthouse in Savannah in a tent erected as Oglethorpe's temporary home.

Charles had trouble adjusting as Oglethorpe's secretary and he was ill suited as parish priest. Charles' over zealous style of preaching was extremely unpopular with the colonists. They did not understand his aggressive approach and Methodism was an entirely new concept. These people had uprooted themselves from the land of their birth, were struggling to survive in a harsh new land and wanted the comfort of a spiritual leader offering familiarity. Charles, in his exuberance, did not see or understand the needs of his parishioners and after six months of constant strife, returned to England.

John Wesley was involved in troubles of his own. Along with the spiritual unrest came scandal. John became somewhat romantically infatuated with a young woman, Sophy Hopkey. The situation became heated, John turned away. The rejected Sophy let it be known far and wide that she had been betrayed. After her marriage to another man, John refused her communion and she registered charges of defamation.

Although the situation was eventually resolved, John like his brother before him had come to his final straw. He began to question himself and his mission. No strides had been made to bring the Native Americans to Christianity and he felt that his mission had failed. This led John to note in his journal, "I came to convert the Indians, but, oh, who will convert me?" John Wesley, utterly defeated, returned to England on December 2, 1737.

Of course, his time in Georgia had not been wasted. John had learned a considerable lesson and during a religious service at Aldersgate Street Meeting House in England in May of 1738, he had an epiphany. He knew that God called him to return to Georgia, his initial stay had been but an apprenticeship for what would be his life's work for the next fifty years.

Many points of interest lay in and around Savannah telling the story of John Wesley's life and ministry there. Mentioned previously is the site of his first prayer at Cockspur Island, a monument was placed there to mark the occasion. The John Wesley statue reverently stands with one hand reaching out to his congregation and in the other he holds a Bible in his steely grip. The statue graces Reynolds Square and facing the statue is the parsonage and garden where John resided. The Oliver Sturges house now occupies the site of the parsonage. John Wesley's first sermon was heard at the corner of Bull Street and Bay Lane where today, the United States Customs House proudly stands. The United States Post Office at Wright Square is the site of Wesley's regular services and Trinity Church on Telfair Square is known as The Mother Church of Savannah Methodism. John Wesley's voice continues to echo throughout Savannah.

ITALIANS IN GEORGIA'S GENESIS

When James Oglethorpe left England to begin the new colony of Georgia. In 1732, one of the passengers was Paul Amatis, an Italian artisan, skilled in producing silk. He was later placed in charge of Trustees Garden. Later, more Italian families came to pursue the task of producing silk. Joseph Ottolenghe is responsible for erecting a public filature in Savannah, on what is now Reynolds Square. It was at this filature that a one time record number of 15,212 pounds of cocoons was delivered for processing into raw silk. High hopes for success in this undertaking is exemplified on one side of the original Georgia Seal which depicts a mulberry leaf, a silkworm, and a cocoon, with the encircled words "Non sibi sed aliis," "Not for ourselves, but for others."

Reynolds Square at Abercorn and St. Julian Streets, Savannah
GPS Coordinates: N32.0796, W81.089498

The *Ann*, sailed from Gravesend, England and safely tucked on board was most important cargo, the future of a colony to be called Georgia. One hundred and twelve passengers, including General James Oglethorpe, arrived in Georgia on January 31, 1733, after a brief stop in Charles Towne for supplies. The conditions were appalling, settlers lacked basic survival skills and combined with the harsh surroundings, many died within months of arrival. Salt poisoning from the brackish water, disease and no means of sanitation quickly took its toll.

Oglethorpe divided the families into various villages based on like ethnic backgrounds and situated in strategic locations for the defense of the main settlement at Savannah. Among those first colonists were a small band of Italians seeking freedom to worship as they wished and an opportunity for a brighter future.

Paul Amatis, an Italian, was among the first to arrive with Oglethorpe. He brought with him the knowledge and skills to produce silk. Within weeks, the next group of colonists arrived and Paul Amatis was there to greet the newly arrived settlers. General James Oglethorpe, along with Tomo Chi Chi served as the diplomatic welcoming committee when two young Italian boys and their father arrived, they were called Tondee.

Within two months the Tondee brothers, Peter and Charles, were orphaned when their father succumbed to malaria. Paul Amatis graciously took the boys in, providing a temporary home. Paul Amatis never achieved the great silk production he imagined and within three years he too succumbed to the harsh conditions.

The Tondee brothers were again uprooted and sent to live on the farm of Henry Parker, one of four Civil Magistrates for the infant colony. Peter, the oldest of the Tondee brothers, was sent to work the fields of Parker's farm on the bluff at the Isle of Hope. When Peter was sixteen years old, the brothers were sent to the newly founded Bethesda Orphanage. Peter was apprenticed as a carpenter there and during the construction of the Great House, he learned his craft very well.

Joseph Ottolenghe, an Italian Priest, was another determined to make the silk industry prominent in the colony. Ottolenghe was sent to the colony at a time when slavery was legalized and his mission was to bring the Christian faith to the slaves and masters living in the coastal swamplands. Although Ottolenghe failed miserably in his efforts to bring Christianity to the colonial South, he was extremely successful in his silk endeavors. Directing his own slaves in the cultivation of silk for profit in the transatlantic market. Ottolenghe was responsible for the first Georgia filature or silk manufacturer in the colony and was memorialized on the original Georgia state seal.

Italians Ottolenghe, Tondee, Amatis and others like them, were responsible for weaving the fabric and building for future generations settlements bravely defended for all ethic cultures. The entrepreneurial spirit was born in 1733 and today, remains based on the foundation established so long ago.

**THE
OLIVER STURGES
HOUSE**

This house, built in 1813 by Oliver Sturges, successful Savannah merchant, occupies the site of the parsonage of John Wesley, minister of the Church of England in Georgia 1736- 37 and founder of Methodism.
Mr. Sturges was a two-fifths owner of the Steam Ship SAVANNAH, first steamship ever built and first to cross the Atlantic. The SAVANNAH'S historic voyage was planned in the Sturges House, which was one of a pair of brick Federal-style residences located on Trust Lot T, Reynolds Ward, Mr. Sturges partner, Benjamin Burroughs, lived in the other residence, where the John Wesley Hotel is presently located.
Morris Newspaper Corporation, owner and operator of newspaper throughout the United States, purchased the Sturges House from Historic Savannah Foundation in 1971 for conversion into corporate headquarters. The careful restoration of the house was completed in 1973.
The Oliver Sturges House has been entered on the National Register of Historic Places.

**Next to Reynolds Square, Abercorn & St. Julian Streets, Savannah
GPS Coordinates: N32.0796, W81.089498**

Oliver Sturges was a successful merchant in Savannah and when he made the decision to build a home, he faced a family dilemma. Resolving his problem, he did not build one but two houses. Why two? Well, the two homes were identical, like his twin daughters and when each came of age they would have identical homes.

The homes were located at 27 and 29 Abercorn Street and were built in 1812, taking a year to complete. The beautiful red brick structures featured elegant marble stairs flanked by wrought iron hand railings. The interior was set apart from other structures of the day by featuring unusually high ceilings and intricate plaster work.

In the 1890s, earthquake tremors were felt throughout Savannah and it was during this time that tie rods were put through many of the old historic buildings. They have become a badge of antiquity today and the Oliver Sturges homes plainly show tie rods on the front and side facades.

The home known today as the Oliver Sturges house, 27 Abercorn Street, was saved from destruction by the Historic Savannah Foundation. The Morris Newspaper Corporation purchased the home and it was under their careful attention that a full restoration and remodeling project was undertaken. The home was transformed into the executive offices of the corporation.

The Oliver Sturges twin house, 29 Abercorn Street, was the site of the first parsonage of John Wesley. The historic building was damaged by fire in 1913, during this time the former Sturges house was known in whispered circles as Savannah's premier brothel. After the fire, the house became the John Wesley Hotel and in 1982, the house again fell victim to fire. In 1983, the house was purchased and renovated to become the lovely property known as the Planter's Inn.

It is said the image of a woman dressed in a gown moves about the floors, rearranging pictures and wandering around the lobby late at night. Speculation says it is perhaps one of the Sturges twin who lived in the home or possibly, the spirit of one of the ladies of the evening who once entertained there.

The Oliver Sturges House

THE GEORGIA
MEDICAL SOCIETY

The first Medical Society in Georgia, sixth oldest in America, was organized June 28, 1804, and continues to be active in Savannah today. Dr. Noble Wimberly Jones, first President, was the son of a member of General Oglethorpe's first settlers of 1733.

Dr. Samuel Roberio Nunez, first practicing physician, arrived July 10, 1733, with the second expedition to the new colony. He arrived in time to treat successfully a raging epidemic of dysentery.

In 1740, the first clinic for the poor opened at nearby Bethesda under Dr. John Hunter and Reverend George Whitefield, who previously had founded America's oldest orphanage there.

The Georgia Medical Society adopted the state's first Code of Medical Ethics, achieved a program of systematic vaccination against smallpox, carried out health surveys of Savannah and surrounding counties, founded a Medical Library, formed the first systematic anti-malarial effort begun in the United States, and conducted extensive studies of Savannah's major epidemic diseases — malaria, yellow fever, and smallpox.

Washington Square, Houston and St. Julian Streets, Savannah
GPS Coordinates: N32.07846, W81.085099

Only a few scant months after General Oglethorpe landed in 1733, the colony was in danger of complete devastation. Dysentery spread in epidemic proportions through the colonists already struggling to survive harsh conditions. The entire colony might have succumbed to the disease had it not been for Dr. Samuel Nunez.

Nunez was a Portuguese Sephardic[32] Jew, escaping the Spanish Inquisition, was permitted by General Oglethorpe to settle in Savannah. Nunez, with forty-two others, was given permission to establish home sites around Ellis Square. The arrival of the Portuguese people was met with suspicion among the other colonists. The English feared that the Portuguese would align themselves with the Spanish in Florida. Nunez was the only physician in Georgia and he possessed the knowledge to treat the fever that raged through the infant colony. The epidemic was alleviated, the English colonists had no choice but to accept Nunez and his people considering, in General Oglethorpe's words, he "saved the colony."

Dr. Noble Jones was an early Georgia settler who established a thriving plantation called Wormsloe. It was his son, Dr. Noble Wymberley Jones, who served as the first president of the Medical Society at Savannah in 1804.

In 1849, the Savannah doctors and others across the state converged in Macon to form the Medical Association of Georgia. Their purpose was set forth in a list of goals guiding the membership, including:

1. The advancement of medical knowledge.
2. The elevation of professional character.
3. The protection of the interests of its members.
4. The extension of the bounds of Medical Science.
5. The promotion of all measures adapted to relieve suffering in humanity.
6. To protect the lives and improve the health of the community.

Today, the Medical Association of Georgia still exists and claims more than 7,000 members. The goals are much the same as they were over one hundred and fifty years ago. Though the Association has remained largely the same in its purpose, the organization has become the voice of medicine in Georgia. Government, business and citizens alike all look toward the Association for answers to questions concerning the medical profession in Georgia.

ATTACK ON BRITISH LINES
OCTOBER 9, 1779

Over this ground hallowed by the valor and the bravery of the soldiers of America and of France was fought October 9, 1779. It was one of the bloodiest battles of the Revolution when Savannah was taken by the British and possessed for several months. It was eventually retaken by American and French forces.

A short distance west of this marker stood the famous Spring Hill Redoubt and along here rant he line of entrenchment built by the British around Savannah. After a three weeks siege, the British stormed the enemy works in this area early on October 9.

Arrayed in the opposing armies that day were soldiers of many American Continentals, Grenadiers of Old France, Irishmen in the service of King Louis XVI, Polish Lancers, French and Negro volunteers from Haiti, Scotch Highlanders, Hessians, Royalist provincials from New York Tory militia, armed slaves, and Cherokee Indians.

After a heroic effort to dislodge the British and the Allies three with heavy losses. Thus the siege was lifted and the French fleet sailed from Georgia, an episode of far reaching significance in the American Revolution.

Visitors Center, West Broad and Liberty Streets, Savannah
GPS Coordinates: N32.07634, W81.099379

The early years of the American Revolution were quiet in Georgia. Orders were issued in 1778, bringing the main concentration of the Revolutionary War to the South. British warships sailing off of the New York Harbor were redirected to the southern Carolina and Georgia coasts.

Major General Augustine Provost captured Savannah with very little resistance, returning control to the British and for a brief time the Georgia assembly met under the authority of the British Crown. Provost expanded his control of Georgia to Augusta and Sunbury, aligning with the Cherokees' in northwest Georgia. He effectively controlled the entire state.

Southern Carolina General Benjamin Lincoln put together a small force of locals to drive the British out. On May 18, 1779, General George Washington ordered General Lachlan McIntosh to return to Georgia in support of General Lincoln.

In the summer of 1779, French Admiral Valerie d'Estaing arrived with twenty ships and eleven frigates from the French West Indies and joined General Lincoln. Their combined land and water forces formed a plan to take back Savannah. By September, d'Estaing entered the mouth of the Savannah River; his troops landed without opposition and probably could have walked into the city unopposed. Instead, d'Estaing had sent a demand for surrender to Provost, who responded by secretly quickening the pace at which the British troops were strengthening the city.

On October 9, 1779, Generals Lincoln and McIntosh, Admiral d'Estaing and Polish Count Casimir Pulaski led troops into Savannah, attacking with heavy artillery bombardment. Provost's men held the line and the attack was repelled. The British troops turned and advanced on the retreating army, eight hundred of the initial force of five thousand French and American soldiers lay dead by the end of the day. Count Pulaski and Admiral d'Estaing were both wounded, Count Pulaski was moved to the American ship, the *Wasp*, where his wounds proved to be fatal[33], d'Estaing's injuries were not serious. D'Estaing returned to the sea, Generals Lincoln and McIntosh led their forces on to Charles Towne reasoning that the British would likely attack there next, they did. On May 12, 1780, General Lincoln surrendered Charles Towne and his army to the British.

Ironically, d'Estaing survived the American Revolution only to fall victim to the political revolution of his native France. Called as a character witness for Marie Antoinette during the French Revolution, he was condemned to death and beheaded on April 28, 1782. The sixty-four year old nobleman remarked when the sentence was rendered, "When you cut off my head, send it to the English; they will pay you well for it!"

Among the soldiers who fought in this battle are: Samuel Davis, father of future Confederate President Jefferson Davis and Major Pierce Charles L'Enfant, future architect of Washington D.C.

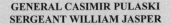

GENERAL CASIMIR PULASKI
SERGEANT WILLIAM JASPER

Near this spot two notable heroes of the American Revolution were
mortally wounded in the ill-fated assault by the American and
French forces upon the British lines here on October 9, 1779.
Brig. Gen. Casimir Pulaski, the famous Polish patriot was fatally
wounded by a grapeshot as he rode forward into the heavy fire
from the British defenses located in this area.
Sergeant William Jasper fell a short distance west of this marker
while attempting to plant the colors of the 2nd Regiment of South
Carolina Continentals upon British entrenchments.
To their memory and to the memory of the hundreds of gallant sol-
diers of America and France - including the French commander-in-
chief, Count d'Estaing - who shed their blood here in the cause of
Liberty, this marker is erected.

Visitors Center, West Broad and Liberty Streets, Savannah
GPS Coordinates: N32.07632, W81.100452

The battle plan of September 8, 1779, called for allied forces to join American troops and converge on Savannah from the north and west. The combined American and allied armies would lay siege to the British defensive position known as the Spring Hill Redoubt, which was the outskirts of Savannah. The bombardment lasted for three weeks. It is written that the artillery barrage killed or injured numerous civilians, demolishing homes in Savannah. Part of the blame for the collateral damage and death was placed on errant artillery shells fired by soldiers who had consumed too much rum. Today, the area is the site of the Savannah Visitor's Center.

The Siege of Savannah began on October 9, 1779 and the field of battle was shrouded by fog in the early morning hours. The Americans, joined by the French soldiers led by Count d'Estaing, appeared ghostly in the lifting mist. The sun would set this day on a battlefield amassed with the dead of those fighting for American independence. The struggle ensued at Spring Hill Redoubt as planned. French and American forces numbering approximately 5,500 clashed with 2,630 British soldiers. The British were aided by two hundred armed slaves and eighty Native Americans. Less than one hour later more than three hundred officers and soldiers lay dead and the cries of the wounded echoed across the battlefield, moaning in agony. The British claimed a loss of eighteen men.

Among the dead were Sergeant William Jasper and Count Casimir Pulaski. Sergeant William Jasper died protecting the flag of his regiment while Count Casimir Pulaski was mortally wounded by grapeshot.[34] Polish Count Casimir Pulaski was probably the best known European to give his life in the assault. He recruited his Polish Legion and financed their involvement in the American Revolution out of his own pocket. These battles marked the first time that American and French forces fought side by side.

Count d'Estaing was wounded in the arm and calf of his left leg. He recuperated at Greenwich and Bonaventure Plantation despite the objections of their British loyalist owners. The movement of the wounded from Spring Hill to Bonaventure and Greenwich occurred without retaliation from the British. In fact, the British loaned two carriages to convey them, many of these men never left the make shift hospitals. Their bodies lie in unknown graves on the grounds that are today, Bonaventure and Greenwich Cemeteries.

The withdrawal of French troops began four days later on October 13th under the direction of d'Estaing. Count d'Estaing commented that the troops returned on board the vessels without being attacked, annoyed or even followed. The British were content with the fact that the French were leaving.

British soldiers occupied Savannah until its liberation on July 11, 1782, by Colonel James Jackson and his Georgia Legion.

October 9, 1779 was described by an eye witness as follows,

"Such a sight I never saw before. The ditch was filled with dead, and in front, for 50 yards, the field was covered with slain. Many hung dead and wounded on the abattis[35]; and for some hundred yards without lines, the plain was strewed with mangled bodies, killed by our grape and chain shot".

ANDREW BRYAN

Andrew Bryan was born at Goose Creek, S.C. about 1716. He came to Savannah as a slave and here he was baptized by the Negro missionary, the Reverend George Leile, in 1781. Leile evacuated with the British in 1782 at the close of the American Revolution and Bryan took up his work. He preached at Yamacraw and at Brampton Plantation. On January 20, 1788, the Reverend Abraham Marshall (White) and the Reverend Jessie Peter (Colored) ordained Andrew Bryan and certified the congregation at a Brampton barn as the Ethiopian Church of Jesus Christ. The Reverend Bryan moved from place to place with his congregation and was even imprisoned and whipped for preaching during a time when whites feared any slave gathering as a focus for rebellion. He persevered and finally bought his and his family's freedom and purchased this lot for his Church. Andrew Bryan pastored until his death, October 6, 1812. He is buried in Savannah's Laurel Grove Cemetery.

West Bryan Street, west of West Broad Street, Savannah
GPS Coordinates: N32.08238, W81.099057

Andrew was born on a plantation near Charles Towne, southern Carolina in 1737. He was born the property of Jonathan Bryan, the namesake of Bryan County; thus, his given name was Andrew Bryan. Jonathan Bryan was not a typical slave owner. He and his brother Hugh, were arrested on one occasion for ministering to their slaves. The Bryan plantation became known for teaching the ways of God to those in bondage, much to the dismay of others that believed this type of education was wasted on slaves and only served to incite disruptions.

In 1782, Andrew heard a sermon led by George Liele, the first African American licensed to preach to slaves along the Savannah River. Andrew and his wife Hannah requested baptism and Reverend Liele complied. Liele returned to England with the British in 1782 and Andrew assumed the role of lay pastor for Liele's congregation.

Andrew built a chapel for his small flock with the full support of his master and brought droves of slaves and white planters alike into the small shack used for his services. Hundreds of others were denied because of vicious threats from their masters. The rapid growth of the congregation caused a great deal of apprehension among the slave owners. Slaves were severely punished by their masters for attending these services and some were cruelly dealt with by the Georgia militia. Andrew and his brother Sampson, were lashed and imprisoned.

The case was brought before Chief Justice Henry Osborne of the Savannah district court. The ruling was made that Andrew and Sampson Bryan and their congregation could hold religious services unmolested at any time between sunrise and sunset. Jonathan Bryan defended Andrew and Sampson and gave them the privilege of worshiping in the Brampton plantation barn. At first, the congregation was small, mainly due to the fear of reprisal from slave owners. In 1788, Reverend Matthew

Marshall ordained Andrew Bryan as a minister with the full authority to preach the gospel and to administer the ordinance of the Baptist Church.

After the death of Jonathan Bryan, his son William, sold Andrew his freedom. Andrew began buying property in the Savannah area and in 1793, he purchased the lot on which First Bryan Baptist Church now stands. Reverend Bryan sold the property to a board of white trustees for The First African Baptist Church. At the time it was unlawful for an African American to own a house of worship. Reverend Andrew Bryan served as pastor for over nine years.

The church merged with the Savannah Baptist Church and the Newington Church; forming the Savannah Baptist Association in 1802. It was during that year that the First African Baptist Church was recognized by the Georgia Baptist Association as the first African American church in the state. By the winter of 1802, the Second African Baptist Church was organized to accommodate the rapidly growing membership, due to the efforts of Reverend Bryan. On January 2, 1803, the Ogeechee African Baptist Church was organized.

Reverend Andrew Bryan died October 12, 1812. His body was interred at the Laurel Grove Cemetery in Savannah. It is said that his memorial service had more than 500 people in attendance.

> "And it came to pass afterward, that he went throughout every city and village, preaching and shewing the glad tidings of the kingdom of God."[36]

JOHN RYAN'S EXCELSIOR BOTTLE WORKS

On this site in 1852 stood the Excelsior Bottle Works operated by John Ryan for the manufacture of soda water and other carbonated beverages. Ryan's soda, in colorful bottles embossed with his name and location, was known throughout Georgia. His operations expanded to Augusta, Columbus and Atlanta. Today, Ryan's bottles are prized by collectors nationwide. John Ryan with his contemporaries, Thomas Maher and James Ray, is commemorated for his pioneer contribution to the soda water industry in Georgia and the United States. Ryan retired from business in 1879 and passed away in Savannah on March 23, 1885.

Bay and Montgomery Streets, Savannah
GPS Coordinates: N32.09426, W81.135058

John Ryan had, to be politically correct, a colorful background. He was born in New York and married there. Five daughters and two sons were born to the Ryan clan, sadly, only one of the sons survived. Ryan and his family moved south prior to 1856 and it was that year he was listed as a member of the Board of Health in Savannah. He was a member of the Democratic Nominating Committee for Mayor and Alderman, treasurer for the Hibernian[37] Society, the Young Men's Literary Association and a committee member for the Defense of Savannah. John Ryan served on the board of directors of the Georgia Mutual Loan Association for a number of years as well. Ryan boasted that he was a Confederate Officer, although his name never appeared on any list of Confederate soldiers though it is possible that he served in a limited capacity. In 1852, Ryan opened a soda water business in Savannah, located on the corner of Taylor and West Broad streets. It was the largest soda water bottler in Georgia.

Unfortunately, from the start one especially unnerving problem plagued him, people refused to return his bottles. Ryan began running newspaper ads in 1860, encouraging patrons to return the bottles and cautioning others in the bottling business against buying his bottles for reuse with their products. The returnable bottle was born during this time. Bottles, returned for pennies, were sterilized and reused.

In 1860, in order to boost sales, the ever enterprising Ryan began selling pharmaceuticals and elixirs. His ad read,

> "Southerners will buy Northern manufactured articles, when such can be had of home production, of good quality and on as good terms. The following home made articles will compare favorably with the best importations, and can be had in any desired quanity - - syrups, raspberry, strawberry, gum, lemon, etc.; cordials - rose peppermint, essence of peppermint; Stought on bitters, etc., Philadelphia and Imitation London Ports and Scotch Ale; soda water superior to any ever bottled before in this city. All articles warranted to give satisfaction or the money refunded, John Ryan, N. E. corner Bay and West Broad streets, Savannah, Georgia."

Ryan's Irish temper led him to appear in front of a judge quite often; though he appeared in all capacities, as a plaintiff, defendant, administrator and petitioner of the court. In April 1865, Ryan was accused of treason; David R. Dillon, who was Ryan's agent, brought the charge. The case was heard in the United States Court Room at the Customs House Building in front of a Special Military Commissioner. The charge was treasonable practices and the accusation was that Ryan leased emancipated slaves in his employee as workers for the Confederate Army. People gathered at the Customs House, all trying to hear and see the proceedings. The trial caused a moment of excitement in Savannah, although the moment was soon dashed when on April 18, 1865, all charges were dismissed against Ryan for lack of evidence. It is very possible the charges were brought because of a business dispute between Ryan and Dillon, no proof was ever introduced to substantiate the allegations. Ryan's reputation was certainly damaged, which was perhaps the intent all along, though Ryan was unfazed by the gossip.

In 1869, Ryan moved his business to Broughton Street, described as the "first house east of Masonic Hall." However, darker times were about to follow. Ryan was summoned to court again in 1875. The charge was assault against an apprentice in his employee named Daniel McSweeney. Dr. Robert P. Meyers made a statement after examining the boy saying; McSweeney was beaten unmercifully, inhumanly and seriously. Ryan delivered affidavits to Magistrate Abrams from his employees stating that he never beaten or abused the apprentice. On November 2, 1875, an Ordinary[38] determined that Daniel McSweeney's allegation lacked sufficient evidence and he was returned to the care of Ryan.

He continued to expand his soda water business until 1878, when he went into partnership with John Ray. The partnership did not last and later that same year Ryan sold the Savannah Excelsior Bottle Works to Fredrick Meincke. Ryan continued to be listed on the city register as owner of the bottle works until 1881, possibly as a result of an owner financing arrangement. Ryan opened bottling businesses in Columbus, Augusta and Atlanta from 1882 to 1885.

On March 22, 1885, John Ryan died. He was buried in an isolated plot at the Catholic Cemetery. His grave remains unmarked. All of his properties were sold and the assets were given to his wife, Margaret.

EVACUATION OF SAVANNAH

On Dec. 14, 1864, Fort McAllister having fallen the day before, opening the Great Ogeechee River to Union shipping and rendering Savannah untenable. Lt. Gen. W. J. Hardee, CSA, decided to evacuate the city to save it from a destructive bombardment and to extricate his besieged army. River craft being unequal to the task, and no pontoon bridging being available, an engineering expedient was adopted. Directed by Lt. Col. B. W. Frobel, CSA, pontoon type bridges were laid by sailors of the CS Navy and details from the Georgia Militia. Using large "cotton flats" for boats, car wheels for anchors and planks from the city wharves for flooring, a bridge was laid from the foot of West Broad Street to Hutchinson Island, another across Back River to Pennyworth Island, and a third across Little Back River to the South Carolina shore.

On the 19th, orders were issued giving priorities and times of withdrawal. The heavy guns were spiked and carriages and ammunition destroyed. At dark, the garrisons of Whitemarsh Island were withdrawn into the city and evacuated via the bridges.

At dark on the 20th, the garrisons of Causton's Bluff, Thunderbolt and the Savannah River batteries gathered at Fort Jackson and were transferred by steamer to Screven's Ferry; but the main garrison "infantry, cavalry, light artillery and wagons" crossed on the bridges well before dawn, the rear-guard had cleared Hutchinson Island, the bridge from West Board Street had been cut adrift, and the troops were marching via the Union Causeway to Hardeeville.

In park at Bay and Jefferson Streets, Savannah
GPS Coordinates: N32.08169, W81.094208

T he following appeared in the Savannah Republican as an editorial on December 21, 1864. The day that Savannah fell.

To the Citizens of Savannah:

By the fortunes of war we pass today under the authority of the Federal military forces. The evacuation of Savannah by the Confederate army, which took place last night, left the gates to the city open, and General Sherman, with his army will, no doubt, to-day take possession.

The Mayor and Common Counsel leave under a flag of truce this morning, for the headquarters of Gen. Sherman, to offer the surrender of the city, and ask terms of capitulation by which private property and citizens may be respected.

We desire to counsel obedience and all proper respect on the part of our citizens, and to express the belief that their property and persons will be respected by our military ruler. The fear expressed by many that Gen. Sherman will repat the order of expulsion from their homes which he enforced against the citizens of Atlanta, we think to be without foundation. He assigned his reason in that case as a military necessity, it was a question of food. He could not supply his army and the citizens with food, and he stated that he must have full and sole occupation. But in our case food can be abundantly supplied for both army and civilians. We would not be understood as even intimating that we are to be fed at the cost of the Federal Government, but that food can be easily obtained in all probability, by all who can afford to pay in the Federal currency.

It behooves all to keep within their homes until Gen. Sherman shall have organized a provost system and such police as will insure safety in persons as well as property.

Let our conduct be such as to win the admiration of a magnanimous foe, and give no ground for complaint or harsh treatment on the part of him who will for an indefinite period hold possession of our city.

In our city there are, as in other communities, a large proportion of poor and needy families, who, in the present situation of affairs, brought about by the privations of war, will be thrown upon the bounty of their more fortunate neighbors. Deal with them kindly, exercise your philanthropy and benevolence, and let the heart of the unfortunate not be deserted by your friendly aid.[39]

SAVANNAH WATERFRONT

The colony of Georgia began on Savannah's waterfront in 1733. The riverfront has always played an important role in Georgia whether as colonial port, exporter of cotton, or tourist destination. The first commercial house below the bluff opened in 1744. Cotton dominated Savannah's exports throughout the nineteenth century. Construction began in the early 1800s for the multi-storied warehouses and "Factor's Walk," named for the cotton brokers whose offices were in the upper floors. River Street was created in 1834 and cobbled with ballast stones. The last cotton office on the waterfront closed in 1956. River Street's revitalization began in 1977.

River Street at Visitor's Center behind City Hall, Savannah
GPS Coordinates: N32.08153, W81.091166

General James Edward Oglethorpe first arrived on Georgia soil, February 12, 1733. It was on the banks of the Savannah River, where the Savannah City Hall building now stands and with a prayer from John Wesley, the land became the thirteenth colony. Oglethorpe, true to his military background, immediately began to plan the layout for his newly founded city.

Oglethorpe knew the power of trade could make or break his fledgling endeavor, by 1739, he had created a substantial wharf along the riverfront. The Savannah River became the major port for Georgia goods bound for European markets. The following years were kind to Savannah's shipping industry and the port became the most important exporter of New World lumber and cotton. Only briefly eclipsed by Sunbury to the south, Savannah maintained her status for almost one hundred years.

Imagine, if you will, a sea port bustling with activity. Great mountains of white gold[40] stacked high waiting to be loaded on ships bound for foreign ports. The smell of cook fires burning to feed the hungry dockmen, the sounds of men singing and slaves chanting their ancient gullah verses; the sight of tall masted ships sometimes three deep at the wharf patiently anchored, waiting to dump their ballast and receive the valuable cargo. Cotton was king in Savannah, the wealth that it brought her can be seen in the magnificent historical homes throughout the city. Savannah enjoyed the finest of everything. River Street, as the wharf lane is known today, was the richest place in the Georgia colonies.

The ships ballast became a problem for the city fathers. Ballast were stones used to maintain the stability of the ship and control the draft. Once the ship arrived at the wharf the ballast stones were removed, the weight of the cargo provided the same service. Ballast were being unloaded in the lane and eventually the huge piles of heavy stones impeded the horse and wagon traffic delivering goods. Something had to be done.

An enterprising Irish immigrant proposed that, for a price, he would remove the ballast. The officials gladly accepted the offer and paid the Irishman handsomely. Later, so the story goes, the Irishman noted that when it rained the wharf lane became so sodden with mud that the wagons with their heavy loads were constantly being stuck in the quagmire. Not only were the wagons a problem but if a businessman had dealings on River Street, the mud and mush caked ones shoes. Again our enterprising Irishman approached the city fathers. He proposed that, for a price, he would pave the street and eliminate the waterfront problem. What materials would he use, you ask? Why the ballast stones he had only recently removed, of course. Again the city fathers paid him well, the Irishman got rich, and Savannah's wharf lane was paved.

In 1818, the bottom dropped out of Savannah's economy. The cotton market fell to rock bottom. Savannah was placed under a yellow fever quarantine. Ships' courses were altered and most never returned to Savannah's wharf. The riverfront began to decline, over the next century, the wharf became only a shadow of its former glory. The wharf was quiet, it would be over one hundred years before Savannah's Waterfront found her voice again.

The Savannah Commercial Wharf has been revitalized and is now the largest foreign commerce port of the South Atlantic Coast. The City of Savannah undertook a massive urban renewal project in the 1970s to restore the Savannah Waterfront. The program involved converting over 80,000 square feet of abandoned cotton warehouses into spaces for shops, restaurants and art galleries. By June of 1977, the project was completed and Old River Street sang again. This time the voices of tourists from all parts of the world could be heard, wandering from shop to gallery and stopping in for the excellent cuisine offered at the restaurants along the wharf still paved with the Irishman's ballast.

Today, River Street is home to over seventy businesses. The area is known world wide for the spectacular St. Patrick's Day celebration staged each year in March. River Street is lined with street performers, candy shops and kite stores; shops with everything from vacation mementos to fine art; restaurants featuring specialties from barbeque to bisque and some of the finest seafood around. Beautiful parks along the riverside with bubbling fountains and brick benches also provide a place for a quiet lunch or a moment of reflection along the banks of the Savannah River. Savannah has truly earned the title, "The Hostess City of the South."

River and Barnard Streets, Savannah
GPS Coordinates: N32.0823, W81.092872

John Bartram was appointed Royal Botanist in America by King George III. Accompanying him along his travels was the third of nine children, William. Together, father and son explored the flora and fauna of southeastern America and Spanish Florida. It was on this trip that the Franklin tree or *Franklinia alatamatha* was discovered and named for their good friend, Benjamin Franklin. Over three hundred specimens were taken over the course of their travels and returned to England. Many of these original samples remain, to this day, a part of the British Museum of Natural History.

Upon the Bartram's return to Philadelphia, William worked on a farm, while John cultivated what was to be the most expansive garden in America. William had a talent for sketching the different species of plant and animals, his drawings were brought to the attention of famed English botanist, Dr. John Fothergill. Fothergill was so impressed by William's rough sketches, he offered to finance another southern expedition. Wanderlust, it seems, was inbred in William and he accepted Fothergill's proposal and in exchange, William was to return collected seeds and specimens of native flora and send them to England. This was much the same arrangement as his father had before him. John Bartram was now nearing the end of his life and too feeble to accompany his son.

William Bartram traveled by schooner from Philadelphia to Savannah, where he disembarked on his southern tour. From Savannah, he traveled with John McIntosh to the Indian Congress in Augusta. It was there that he observed the following during treaty negotiations:

> "…the negotiations continued undetermined many days; the merchants of Georgia demanding at least two millions of acres of land from the Indians, as a discharge of their debts, due, and of long standing. The Creeks, on the other hand, being a powerful and proud spirited people, their young warriors were unwilling to submit to so large a demand. However, at length, the cool and deliberate counsels of the ancient venerable chiefs, enforced by liberal presents of suitable goods, were too powerful inducements for them any longer to resist, and finally prevailed."

The young warriors were ready to wage war with the greedy white settlers, though more mature minds prevailed and the treaty was signed. William Bartram later assisted surveyors in marking Georgia's new borders resulting from this treaty.

Bartram also saw great beauty in the Georgia landscape. He noted the dangers of the wilderness land, so much of which had yet to be tamed. He recorded the influence of man on the environment and how some animal species were being hunted to extinction.

> "…the land rises very sensibly, and the country being mountainous, our progress became daily more difficult and slow; yet the varied scenes of pyramidal hills, high forest, rich vales, serpentine rivers, and cataracts [waterfalls], fully compensated for our difficulties and delays. The buffalo once so very numerous, is not at this day to be seen in this part of the country; there are but few elks, and those only in the Appalachian mountains. The dreaded and formidable rattlesnake is yet too common, and a variety of other serpents abound. The alligator, a species of crocodile, abounds in the rivers and swamps, near the coast, but is not seen above Augusta. Bears, tigers, wolves, and wild cats are numerous enough…."

Bartram's travel led him through Georgia, Carolina, Florida and Alabama. Sometimes with the company of fellow travelers and other times were spent alone with his thoughts. He was seen so often about the Native American lands that he became readily accepted. His description of Native Americans and their lifestyles is said to be the definitive view without the bias of stereotypes. The Native Americans dubbed him Puc Puggy or the Flower Hunter, certainly a name well suited from Bartram.

Should Bartram be remembered for something other than his explorations, it must be the description of people, places and features of travels without embellishment. The picture he painted was so accurate that his words influenced settlers to chose a place in which to settle based on his observations.

He predicted that the region would be excellent for the cultivation of corn, grains, indigo, grapes and various fruits, as well as raising silkworms. He foresaw that the many "delightful glittering streams of running water" would eventually lead to water powered mills to grind the grain. Although his predictions were not always accurate, Bartram captured an excitement many came to share about the Georgia colony. In his writings, Bartram left us a chronicle of what the colony once was.

He returned to Philadelphia in 1777 and found his father in great distress concerning the Revolutionary War which was blazing all around Philadelphia. The elder Bartram feared that the British would destroy his beloved garden. John Bartram died in late 1777, his garden was left intact.

William Bartram died in 1822 at the age of 83. He continues to live through his descriptive writings and startlingly accurate sketches. Today, many of William Bartram's published writings and numerous drawings are on display at the Exposition Center in Savannah.

LANDING OF OGLETHORPE AND THE COLONISTS

James Edward Oglethorpe, the founder of Georgia, landed with the original colonists, about 114 in number, at the foot of this bluff on February 1 (February 12, new style), 1733. The site where he pitched his tent is marked by the stone bench located about 100 feet west of this marker. Savannah was for more than 100 years built according to Oglethorpe's unique city plan. Bull Street, the principal street of the city, is named in honor of Colonel William Bull of Charleston, S.C., who assisted Oglethorpe in laying out the city. The colonists sailed in the ship Anne from Gravesend, England, November 17, 1732; landed at Charles Town, S.C., January 13, 1733; proceeded later to Beaufort, S.C., and thence, in small boats, through the inland waterway to Yamacraw Bluff. The town site had already been selected by Oglethorpe in friendly negotiation with Tomo-chi-chi, Mico of the Yamacraws, and with Mary Musgrove, the English-speaking, half-breed Indian princess who later, as niece of Emperor Brim of the Creek Nation, claimed sovereignty of southeastern Georgia.

Next to City Hall at Bull and Bay Streets, Savannah
GPS Coordinates: N32.08124, W81.091585

General James Edward Oglethorpe had two major concerns, those of poverty and unemployment. His solution to the problems of England was the founding of the colony of Georgia. Three years before sailing, his friend, the Earl of Egmont wrote,

> "The scheme is to procure a quantity of acres either from the Government or by gift or purchase in the West Indies (by that he meant the New World) and to plant thereon a hundred miserable wretches who being let out of gaol by last years's Act, are now starving about the town for want of employment; and that they should be settled all together by way of colony, and be subject to subordinate rulers, who should inspect their behavior and labour under one chief head; that in time they with their families would increase so fast as to become a security and defense of our possessions against the French and Indians of those parts; They should be employed in cultivating flax and hemp, which being allowed to make into yarn would be returned to England and Ireland and greatly promote our manufactures."

Egmont speaks of the West Indies meaning the New World or American colonies. During that time the lands were vastly unexplored and colonies were only just beginning to be developed. Little was known in England about this far away land. The "last year's Act" he refers to is English prison reform, many people were released from debtor's prison during this time. The remainder of the quote is self explanatory and quite succinctly details Oglethorpe's intent, although not his sentiments.

The society petitioned the Privy Council, requesting permission to seek one hundred volunteers among the indigent people and their families wishing to pursue opportunities in a New World colony. They would be provided with passage, land and the supplies needed to survive and in turn they would plant hemp and flax, returning the raw materials to England for manufacture and export. Timber and raw silk were also mentioned as items to be cultivated and shipped to England. The Crown was elated with the idea of enriching the Royal coffers and fully approved the plan. England would be relieved of some of their less than desirable countrymen and if they did not survive the travel or harsh conditions it was of little concern.

King George II issued a royal charter to twenty-one trustees for the new colony in 1732. The charter would last for twenty-one years after which Georgia would become a royal colony. No trustee would receive compensation or be allowed to own property in the infant colony in order to insure the charitable nature of the venture. No family was allowed to own more than 500 acres of land, which was substantially more than the average colonist already there. For example, Carolina colonists owned little, if any land. The trustees designed a seal which was inscribed in Latin *"Non sibi, sod aliis,"* or "Not for themselves, but others." Georgia was to be the only colony that existed for the benefit of the people and Oglethorpe, as a Georgia trustee, never received any monetary consideration for the endeavor.

The royal charter granted lands to extend from the mouth of the Altamaha River to the South Seas, now known as the Pacific Ocean. The area was so vast, that even today, Georgia is the largest state east of the Mississippi River. The charter further promised that the colonists would be endowed with all the rights of the English including freedom of worship with one exception, Roman Catholicism was banned. The Crown felt that the Roman Catholic religion would challenge the men's allegiances drawing them toward Spain, which was firmly entrenched at St. Augustine.

One hundred and fourteen charter colonists were selected for the upcoming voyage. The ship *Ann*, 200 tons of cargo, commanded by Captain John Thomas and owned by a Charles Towne merchant, Samuel Wragg, was chosen for the journey. Ample supplies were amassed. Four days each week the passengers ate beef, two days they had pork and one day fish. One quart of water was allowed "whilst the beer lasted" and two quarts thereafter. No hard liquor was allowed either on board the ship or in the Georgia colony although beer and wine were permissible.

The *Ann* sailed from England on November 17, 1732, arriving in Charles Towne on January 13, 1733. She sailed on to Beaufort arriving on January 20. The colonists were left there to enjoy a few days on shore while Oglethorpe and Lieutenant Colonel William Bull of Carolina selected a site for the settlement. Once the site was chosen, a sloop and five smaller boats delivered the colonists to their new home. They arrived on February 1, 1733 and upon leaving the ship, John Wesley led the colonists in a prayer of thanksgiving for their safe arrival and success in surviving the wilderness. Many more prayers would be issued up in the coming months and years. Life in the infant Georgia colony was difficult at best and many colonists did not live to see the spring.

Oglethorpe established a friendship with the Chief of the Yamacraw, Tomo Chi Chi that lasted the remainder of his life. When Oglethorpe returned to England in 1734 Tomo Chi Chi, his wife Scenawki, his nephew and adopted son Toonahowi and six other chieftains accompanied him. After arriving, the Native Americans were entertained at great expense to the Crown; King George and the Archbishop of Canterbury received them. Scenawki, who had been blinded in one eye, was fitted with a glass eye and it is said to have greatly improved her appearance. Tomo Chi Chi and his wife were eternally grateful.

Treaties of peace and friendship were signed. Oglethorpe and his Native American companions returned to the Georgia colony. After a year, Oglethorpe returned to England to solicit funds for the colony. The Spanish felt that Oglethorpe was a great threat to their tenuous hold in Florida and petitioned the Crown, demanding that he not be allowed to return. The English government refused their request. Oglethorpe returned with a regiment of six hundred men, most of which were the brave and fearless Scottish Highlanders. He knew that war with Spain was eminent.

In 1740, Oglethorpe led a raid into Spanish Florida. Although he managed to take St. Augustine, Castillo San Marcos, the Spanish Fort was never taken. The Spanish retaliated by invading Georgia at St. Simons in 1742. The Highlanders and Oglethorpe's British regulars stopped the Spanish invasion and soundly defeated them at the Battle of Bloody Marsh. Georgia was safe and Spain would never be a threat to her again. George Whitefield, founder of the Bethesda Orphanage, wrote,

> "The deliverance of Georgia from the Spaniards is such as cannot be paralleled but by some instances out of the Old Testament."

General James Edward Oglethorpe was promoted to the rank of Brigadier General. After spending ten years in the Georgia colony, he returned to England in 1743. General James Edward Oglethorpe never saw the Georgia colony again.

SS SAVANNAH AND SS JOHN RANDOLPH

The first steamship to cross the Atlantic Ocean, the SS SAVANNAH, sailed from this harbor on May 22, 1819 and reached Liverpool 27 days later. The anniversary of her sailing, May 22, is celebrated as National Maritime Day. Captain Moses Rogers was her master. James Monroe, President of the United States, inspected the vessel here and was taken on a trial excursion on May 12. The Savannah Steamship Company (of which William Scarbrough was principal promoter,) fitter her with a 90 H.P. engine and boiler. She was of 330 tons burden, 98'6" long, 25'2" breadth, 12'11" draft, equipped with paddle-wheel, spars, and sails. She depended primarily upon sail power in the open seas. Before returning to Savannah she visited St. Petersburg, Crondstadt, and Stockholm.

The SS JOHN RANDOLPH, American's first successful iron steamship in commerce, was launched in this harbor July 9, 1834. Prefabricated in Birkenhead, England for Gazaway B. Lamar of Savannah, she was shipped in segments and assembled here. She was 100' long 22' breadth. Unlike the SS SAVANNAH, she was an immediate commercial success in the river trade, and was the first of a great fleet of iron steamboats on the rivers of America.

City Hall, Bull and Bay Streets, Savannah
GPS Coordinates: N32.08103, W81.090903

The SS *Savannah* was built in New York, where its revolutionary design sparked much interest. The question on everyone's mind seemed to be, "Was this the dream boat of the future or a steam driven coffin? Many people thought that Davy Jones's Locker[41] was the only destination for the SS *Savannah*. Yet, the elegant ship would make history as the first steam powered vessel to cross the Atlantic and return without incident. The voyage excited the interest of various world leaders including; the King of Sweden and Norway; the Czar of Russia and the fifth President of the United States, James Monroe. It caused envy in the British Navy and fooled several worthy captains into thinking it was a vessel on fire. The ship's daring commander was Captain Moses Rogers.

She was without equal for her time, a sailing vessel with an auxiliary steam engine that operated by means of paddle wheels. When the weather was unfavorable for sails, the engine was available to continue the journey. For use under steam, she had a seventeen foot bent smokestack that could be swivelled in any direction according to the direction of the wind, this prevented the deck area from being inundated with the thick, black smoke that belched from the boilers. On each side, she had a wheel made of wooden paddles linked by iron chains; when used as a sailing ship, the paddles could be compressed like a fan and the side wheels were secured on the deck.

The paddle boxes were made of canvas to avoid interference with the wheels' movement. The copper boilers were laid in a horizontal rather than a vertical position to distribute their weight evenly on the ship. The boilers had a secret design to prevent the salt from the boiled water from leaving deposits on the sides. The anchor had iron chains instead of rope, an improvement in shipbuilding that had only recently began to appear.

Though the exterior smokestack and paddle wheels were unfamiliar to most, the interior design was lavish and received universal praise. No expense had been spared for the passengers' accommodations. The state cabin had mahogany, rosewood and brass decorations, full length mirrors were carefully placed to create the illusion of space. The SS *Savannah* resembled a pleasure yacht more than a transatlantic ship.

The SS *Savannah's* maiden voyage sailed from New York on March 28, 1819 and arrived at her namesake port on April 26. Crowds gathered to stare at the wondrous ship as she sailed into the Savannah harbor. President James Monroe boarded her to make a final inspection cruise of the city's forts and defenses along the Savannah River, accompanied by Secretary of War, John C. Calhoun. The delighted President suggested that the government should purchase the *Savannah* and put her into service along the coast of Florida, which was being plagued by pirates from Cuba.

Despite the extensive favorable publicity, ticket sales for her upcoming ocean voyage were slow and efforts to convince merchants to entrust their cargo to SS *Savannah* was completely unsuccessful. At first, it was also impossible to assemble a crew. No doubt, both potential passengers and crew noted the heavy black coal smoke emitted from the stack and feared the sparks from the soft pine wood used to start the boilers. Some believed that the paddle wheels would be hazardous in a storm even if lashed to the deck; others feared the engine would break loose. In the end, Stevens Rogers, sailing master and first officer, no blood relation to Moses but later a brother in law, had to find a crew in New London, where he and the Captain had been born and were trusted.

Finally on May 22, 1819, the SS *Savannah* "put to sea with steam and sails" on a historic journey that would take her to England, Sweden and Russia with stops in Norway and Denmark before returning to Savannah. Captain Rogers well understood the reaction of the uninformed populace witnessing for the first time the *Savannah* sailing with bare poles under steam. He eagerly awaited the first European reaction, which happened off the coast of Ireland. An attendant at a signal station spotted the *Savannah* and immediately assumed she was on fire.

The speedy British revenue cutter *Kite* was dispatched to the rescue. However, the Kite found herself chasing the SS *Savannah* for five hours before she caught up to her, enabling the "rescuing" Lieutenant Bowie to board her and discover the incredible truth. As one could imagine, the newspapers told and retold the story to delight their readers, ever expanding on the length of the chase and the prowess of the American vessel and her captain. Actually, the most amusing part of the incident was not revealed until years later in separate accounts by Stevens Rogers. The only way the *Kite* could stop the SS *Savannah* was by firing several warning shots across her stern!

For all the lavish praise and her innovative design, the SS *Savannah* was a financial failure. Not until 1838, when the British *Sirius* and *Great Western* crossed the Atlantic under continuous steam would the public trust themselves or their cargo to this new type of ship. No other American steamship attempted the voyage until the *Massachusetts* in 1845.

Moses Rogers tried to sell the SS *Savannah* in Washington, but the government was no longer interested. Although President Monroe had been enthusiastic the year before, his desire to have the ship had waned. The Savannah Steam Ship Company was in severe financial difficulties and after Savannah was nearly completely destroyed by fire in 1849, the SS *Savannah* was stripped of all her steam related machinery. Ironically this refurbishment released much more space for cargo and the ship was sold. Under the command of a new captain, she became a successful commercial venture, then the SS *Savannah* came to a tragic end. After only two years, she ran aground off Long Island and broke into pieces.

The SS *John Randolph* was among the first iron clad steamships and unlike the SS *Savannah*, she was a commercial success from the start. So successful, in fact, that she was enlisted in the United States Navy to serve her country during World War II.

The SS *John Randolph* was one of the first Liberty class ships to make the Russian run. They set out for Murmansk in the early convoys of 1942. The SS *John Randolph* and SS *Richard Henry Lee* were the only Liberty ships in the convoy. On May 24th, the *Lee* reported floating mines while the convoy was steaming through patches of thick fog. The mine warning instantly put everyone on the alert and made it especially tough for the watch standers. As soon as the fog lifted, German bombers hit the convoy.

On the morning and forenoon watches of May 25th, about a dozen bombers and torpedo-bombers attacked. One plane was shot down by the *Lee's* navy gun crew. Like most ships making the run at that time, the SS *John Randolph* fired at will, although armed only with light machine guns. That evening her log recorded:

"Air battle on again. All driven away. This is no child's play. Battling is furious. Fog banks save the day. Convoy fighting ice, mines, bombs, torpedoes and submarines."

The SS *John Randolph* continued the fight until July 5, 1942, when she struck a mine. The Liberty class ironclad steamer was lost.

T he United States Customhouse sits atop hallowed ground, sacred in that it was on this lot that the small wooden framed house that was General James Edward Oglethorpe's first home in the American colonies. Also revered because it was here in 1736, that John Wesley first held prayer in the New World with his Bible firmly held in one hand and his eyes raised to the heavens.

The cornerstone was laid in 1848 and the design of John H. Norris began to take shape. The granite for the structure was shipped from Massachusetts, the building was noted as the "handsomest public building" to be constructed during that era. Six magnificent granite columns, weighing fifteen tons each, graced the entrance. It must have been a sight to see the huge granite columns on board a sailing ship traversing the Savannah River.

The impressive Greek Revival structure's interior matched the opulence of its outer shell, the most noted feature was the marble staircase. The stairway ascends half way to the first story where it divides forming a circular stairwell. The marble stairs appear to have no support except the wall to which they are attached, however each step interlocks with the next to form the incredible illusion.

The building has always been primarily used by the United States Customs Service though it has housed a number of other federal agencies during its long history as well. The United States Post Office and Federal Courthouse once made their homes in the substantial building.

The third floor court room was the scene of the trial of Charles Augustus Lafayette Lamar in 1859 and 1860, owner of a yacht used for slave running called, the Wanderer. Lamar was tried before Judge James Moore Wayne, who was an Associate Justice of the United States Supreme Court. The case of the *Wanderer* was the last trial ever to come to court involving a violation of the law against the importation of slaves, Lamar was acquitted on a technicality. The slight was that Lamar was not personally on board the *Wanderer* when slaves were transported.

In 1918, the Savannah Laboratory was established to analyze raw sugar to be imported by the Savannah Sugar Refining Corporation at Port Wentworth. The operation initially was conducted in one room of the Customhouse, however today the Savannah Laboratory consists of a 20,000 square foot facility. They are a full service facility with the capability to conduct chemical and physical testing of all types of commodities, narcotics and controlled substances.

Laboratory specializations are generally related to textile and apparel analyses. The laboratory is designated as the Customs' testing facility for wool which includes determining clean content and wool grade. Further, the laboratory is uniquely capable of determining if upholstery fabrics meet taxation requirements and addresses country of origin issues. The Savannah Laboratory is actively developing a trace element profile.

The Savannah Laboratory provides technical instruction for the Customs Agents in training at the Federal Law Enforcement Training Center in Brunswick, Georgia. The Laboratory also provides specialized technical training to customs import specialists, inspectors and special agents; it provides support to the agency's International Customs Training program. It also operates a mobile laboratory to meet the onsite testing needs of southeastern United States ports. The unit is a state of the art, custom built vehicle capable of simultaneously housing all manner of highly technical testing apparatus.

CHATHAM ARTILLERY'S "WASHINGTON'S GUNS"

These cannon, which were captured when Lord Cornwallis surrendered at Yorktown in the American Revolution, were a gift to the Chatham Artillery by President George Washington — a mark of his appreciation for the part the local military company played in the celebration of his visit to Savannah in May, 1791. Washington commended the Chatham Artillery in "warmest terms" and at one of the functions in his honor (which took place on the river bluff east of this spot) proposed a toast "to the present dexterous Corps of Artillery."

The "Washington Guns" have thundered a welcome to many distinguished visitors to Savannah, including James Monroe, the Marquis de Lafayette, James K. Polk, Millard Fillmore, Chester A. Arthur, Jefferson Davis, Grover Cleveland, William McKinley, William H. Taft, and Franklin D. Roosevelt. During the War Between the States the historic cannon were buried for safety beneath the Chatham Artillery armory and were not removed until 1872 when the Federal occupation troops had departed. The "Washington Guns" were taken to Yorktown in 1881 by a contingent of the Chatham Artillery and led the parade at the centennial celebration of Cornwallis' surrender.

In park at Bay and Drayton Streets, Savannah
GPS Coordinates: N32.08095, W81.089707

O ctober 19, 1781, General George Washington and his Continental Army with the invaluable assistance of the French, commanded by Comte de Rochambeau, forced the surrender of the British army under the command of Lord Cornwallis. This defeat, at Yorktown, marked the end of the American Revolution. The British lacked the finances and the fortitude to continue. They were forced to negotiate for peace, recognizing American independence.

Almost ten years later, on May 12, 1791, Savannah was dressed in her finest to receive the most venerated hero of the American Revolution, President George Washington. He was welcomed with all of the honors his position demanded. His visit was arranged as part of his tour of the southern states and was celebrated in true patriotic fashion; including a parade, dinners and a ball in his honor.

Washington was the guest of an inn on Telfair Square for the duration of his visit to Savannah. He toured the site of the 1779 battlefield, bloodied by the Siege of Savannah. Washington commented on the change in Savannah, since that fateful day, to Lachlan McIntosh, who had served with Washington at Valley Forge. Washington had on numerous occasions sided with McIntosh when his exuberance exceeded his senses, including the ruinous duel with Button Gwinnett. Washington noted his observations of Savannah in his diary, writing,

"It is extremely sandy (which) makes the walking very disagreeable & the houses uncomfortable in warm &

348

windy weather ... The town on 3 sides is surrounded with cultivated Rice fields which have a rich and luxuriant appearance."

The Filature, a long hall once housing the silk industry of Savannah, was the site of Washington's departure dinner. After his four day visit, Washington continued his journey to Augusta, stopping only to see the lovely Caty, widow of Nathaniel Greene. The Greenes had been long time friends to the President. Months later a gift arrived intended for the city of Savannah, from none other than President Washington. He called it a "bread and butter" gift, thanking the city for their hospitality. The two cannons surrendered by Cornwallis at Yorktown continue to be treasured mementoes of Washington's visit and from that point forward were referred to as Washington's Guns.

The guns were given a place of honor until war again threatened Savannah. As Sherman steadfastly marched to the sea, Savannah rushed to hide her most precious gift. The cannons were buried beneath the Chatham Artillery armory where they remained until 1872, when Federal troops finally released the city from its choking hold.

Before and since that time, the guns have sounded the welcome for numerous prominent figures. Presidents to War Heroes, have heard the voices of Washington's Guns as they have bid, "Welcome to Savannah."

CHATHAM ARTILLERY'S
"WASHINGTON GUNS"

These bronze cannon were presented to the Chatham Artillery by President Washington after his visit to Savannah in 1791. Of English and French make, respectively, they are excellent examples of the art of ordnance manufacture in the 18th century. An inscription on the British 6 pounder states that it was "surrendered by the capitulation of York Town Oct. 19, 1781."

The English cannon was cast in 1783 during the reign of George II and the royal insignia and motto of the Order of the Garter appear on its barrel. The French gun was manufactured at Strasburg in 1756. On its elaborately engraved barrel appear the coat of arms of Louis XIV: the sun which was the emblem of that monarch, and a Latin inscription (which Louis XIV first ordered placed on French cannon) meaning "Last Argument of Kings." The dolphins were emblematic of the Dauphin of France. The gun was individually named "La Populaire." Reminders of America's hard-won struggle for Independence and of the great man who led the Continental forces in the Revolution, the historic "Washington Guns" were placed on public display here through co-operation of the Chatham Artillery and the City of Savannah.

In park at Bay and Drayton Streets, Savannah
GPS Coordinates: N32.08095, W81.089707

In 1998 Savannah citizens showed their parental concern of the city's historical monuments. A pickup truck with a flatbed trailer pulled up beside Washington Guns, donated by President Washington after his southern tour of Savannah in May 1791. The mysterious truck's occupants dismantled the black wrought iron fence surrounding the cannons, in broad daylight, these men were about to make off the guns. Frantically, civic minded citizens called the Savannah Police Department.

The police investigation identified the culprits, the case was quickly solved. The Coastal Heritage Society had removed one of the guns to Fort Jackson and would return for the second very soon. Of course, there was no need for alarm, the cannons were returned in due time and looking as good as new.

The Chatham Artillery, who owns the guns, enlisted the aid of the city of Savannah for periodic maintenance work on the cannons. Washington Guns experienced an extensive cleaning and examination, including the search for rot that would eventually deteriorate their wooden carriage. After replacing the rotted wood and painting the cannons, they were safely returned to the park at Bay and Drayton Streets.

The first cannon, much more ornate of the two, was manufactured in France in 1756 and called, La Populare. The intricate design work on this cannon resulted in an extended cleaning process, according to John Roberson, the Fort Jackson artificer, who completed the work. The smaller, English cannon is of a simple design making the process much easier.

Chatham Artillery funded the restorative work and obviously, as the caretakers to the Washington Guns, takes their responsibility well to heart. Today, the Washington Guns remain impressively displayed for tourists as well as local citizens to admire. The cannons represent an American victory, with liberty and independence as the prize.

BIRTHPLACE OF
THE UNIVERSITY OF GEORGIA
MEETING PLACE OF LEGISLATURE IN 1785

Directly across Bay Street from this marker formerly stood the brick building, built in the late Colonial days and known as the "Coffee House," in which the Legislature of Georgia met in 1785. Owned by Thomas Stone, it was described in a newspaper advertisement in 1785 as having "ten large, cool, elegant rooms" and as "not equalled by any other house in the state" for "business, and conveniency of a large family."

While meeting in the house owned by Thomas Stone the House of Assembly of Georgia enacted on January 28, 1785, an act for the "establishment of a public seat of learning in this state" - the preamble reciting that it was "among the first objects of those who wish well to the national prosperity, to encourage and support the principles of religion and morality, and early to place the youth under the forming hand of society, that by instruction they may be moulded to the love of virtue and good order." The charter granted to the Board of Trustees of the University of Georgia in 1785 the first charter issued in the United States to a state university.

In park at Bay and Drayton Streets, Savannah
GPS Coordinates: N32.08064, W81.090206

The University of Georgia was incorporated by an act of the General Assembly on January 27, 1785, creating the first state chartered and state supported university. At the first meeting of the Board of Trustees, held in Augusta on February 13, 1786, Abraham Baldwin was selected president. Baldwin drafted the charter that was adopted by the General Assembly.

The University was legally established in 1801 when the trustees selected a land site. John Milledge donated 633 acres on the banks of the Oconee River in Athens, Georgia. Josiah Meigs replaced John Milledge as University president, when Milledge was elected Governor of Georgia and work began on the first building. Originally called Franklin College, in honor of Benjamin Franklin, the building is now known as Old College. The first class graduated in 1804.

The curriculum of traditional classical studies was broadened in 1843 to include a Juris Doctorate[42] and again in 1872 to include agriculture and mechanical arts. Today, thirteen schools and colleges with auxiliary divisions, carry on the University's programs. The University System of Georgia is now governed by the Georgia Board of Regents. The Board of Regents' Chancellor, exercises a general supervisory control over all institutions of the University System, though each institution has its own executive officers and faculty.

In 1858, the University of Georgia commissioned the Athens Foundry to build a new wrought iron gate and fence to replace the battered wood fence that surrounded the campus. The money for the project was raised by selling the original botanical gardens, which were located west of the campus. Serving as the entrance to the campus from the City of Athens, the Arch is located on Broad Street on the north side of the campus.

The Arch was patterned after the great seal of Georgia, which appeared on the state flag. The Arch itself represents the state constitution and the three columns supporting it represent wisdom, justice and moderation. Originally, the Arch held heavy gates that were once locked to secure the campus, but they disappeared sometime around 1885. In 1946, two electric lights were added and the Arch was moved about six feet away from the street. Today, the Arch has become the official university logo, its image can be found on everything from T-shirts to staff business cards.

The traditions of the University of Georgia run deep. The legend of the Georgia Arch is repeated to every freshman who dreams of becoming a Georgia alumnus. Georgia student, Daniel Huntley Redfearn class of 1910, vowed never to walk beneath the hallowed wrought iron Arch until he held the sacred parchment of graduation in his hand. Redfearn stuck to his pledge even though during hazing he was forced to run the gauntlet beneath the Arch with his classmates, clothed only in his underwear. Redfearn ran with his classmates, but went around the Arch. Professors, hearing rumors of Redfearn's vow, announced the tale to classes. The tradition of Georgia's Arch was born. Redfearn never forgot the day he held his diploma aloft and walked through the Arch of Georgia. He provided in his will that $1,000 be donated for the maintenance and care of his inspiration.

Other fine traditions continue to hold true in the hearts of Georgia students but probably none more dear than the Georgia football mascot, Uga. Uga is a white English bulldog, whose caretakers and spokesmen are Savannah attorney, Frank "Sonny" Seiler and his wife Cecelia. I hesitate to use the word "owner" because it is uncertain who the master would be. Since 1956, Uga has proudly led the team onto the field at Sanford Stadium for the contests between the hedges. There have been five massive, white English bulldogs in the Uga line since that first appearance in 1956. The mascot has appeared at the 1943 Rose Bowl, in the movie *Midnight in the Garden of Good and Evil*, graced the cover of *Sports Illustrated*, invited to the Downtown Athletic Club and escorted through the banquet hall to dinner by none other than the President. Uga has also been photographed with Heisman Trophy winner, Herschel Walker.

The Georgia "G" signifies the beloved university; the chapel bell rings signifying the victory of every proud Georgia athlete; the Redcoat Band is the "heart" of Bulldog spirit; and strains of *Glory, Glory*, the Georgia fight song, echo in Sanford Stadium between her historic hedges. But each and every fall Georgia hearts beat a little faster as the air cools and the leaves bring vivid color, the battle cry sounds once again, "How 'Bout Them Dawgs," the football season at Georgia has begun.

In park at Bay and Drayton Streets, Savannah
GPS Coordinates: N32.08087, W81.090002

Eli Whitney was a born inventor and entrepreneur. In his teens, Eli became a blacksmith, making nails on a machine that he invented at home, later he became the country's only manufacturer of ladies hatpins. However, young Eli had his goal set high and was determined to enroll at Yale College. Eli's parents never took his little inventions seriously and squashed his plans for Yale. He had no inclination to practice law or study theology, so a higher education would be wasted on their son, the dreamer. Determined, Eli was twenty-three before he earned enough money for his tuition, twenty-seven before he graduated. His classmates saw him as middle aged. Eli was faced with a new problem, no profession existed for a man of invention and Eli had to earn a living. He decided to teach.

He accepted a position as a tutor for a Carolina community in 1793, his salary was set at one hundred guineas per year, about $500.00. Southern planters were at their most desperate during this time; crop failures and an economy still recovering from effects of the Revolutionary War led to hard times for the planters. Eli was about to come to their aid. Harvests would soon amount to vast proportions the likes of which the south had never seen.

Sailing south, Eli happened to meet the beguiling Mrs. Greene, the widow of Revolutionary War hero Nathanael Greene. The two quickly became friends, Mrs. Greene or "Caty" as she was known, was rumored to be quite friendly.

Unfortunately, when the ship arrived at Charles Towne, Eli found that the promised salary would be cut in half. Eli refused to take the post and decided teaching was not what he wanted to do after all. The always persuasive Caty convinced Eli to accompany her to Savannah, allowing him to board at her plantation and barter his board by assisting the plantation manager, Phineas Miller. Phineas was a Yale alumnus only a few years Eli's senior. Eli accepted the proposal.

Caty loved to entertain. One evening while neighboring planters visited, the conversation turned to crops. The green seed cotton the planters grew required ten hours of grueling hand work to remove the seeds from only three pounds of cotton. Caty suggested that Eli might try his hand at devising a machine to do the work.

Eli watched the process and studied the hand movements. One hand held the seed while the other teased out the short strands of lint. His machine would duplicate the motion. To take the place of a hand holding the seed, he made a sort of sieve of wires stretched lengthwise. To do the work of the fingers which pulled out the lint. Eli had a drum rotate past the sieve, almost touching it. On the surface of the drum, fine, hook shaped wires projected which caught at the lint from the seed. The restraining wires of the sieve held the seeds back while the lint was pulled away. A rotating brush which turned four times as fast as the hook covered drum cleaned the lint off the hooks.

He gave a demonstration of the machine before a few of the planters. Within an hour, Eli did what amounted to a full day of work of five slaves. Eli promised to patent the machine and to produce a few more. With that promise, the planters ordered cotton be planted across their entire plantations. Within weeks so much cotton was planted that Eli would never be able to gin all of it. It was about that time that Eli's workshop was broken into and the plans for his invention were stolen.

Before Eli had the chance to register his patent to protect his idea, the prematurely planted cotton came to maturity. The crops were ready to harvest, the planters had no time for the fine points of law or ethics, so Eli's machine was copied without a thought to legalities.

Eli had entered into partnership with Phineas Miller by this time. The agreement was that Eli would go to New Haven to secure his patent and begin manufacturing machines, while Phineas remained in the south and distributed the machines. The partnership between Phineas and Eli gave no thought of royalty arrangements, their first plan was that no machine was to be sold, but simply installed for a percentage of the profit. Since the two had no idea that cotton planting would take place in massive proportions, Eli and Phineas did not realize that they were asking for an agreement that could have reasonably earned them millions of dollars a year. It was Phineas' idea to take one pound of every three of cotton instead and the planters were furious. Cotton, one of the easiest growing crops, was now being harvested in white floods that threatened to drown everyone. By the time, Eli and Phineas were willing to sell the machine outright or even for a modest royalty on each machine manufactured with Eli's pirated plans, the amount of money due them was astronomical. The planters never paid their debts so the partners were in deep financial trouble. Their only recourse was to go to court but every court they approached was in cotton country. In 1801, the partners were willing to settle for outright grants from cotton growing states, in return the cotton gin would be public property within the state. Only one state agreed and even they made a counter offer for half the asking price. Eli accepted $50,000 for which he received a down payment of $20,000. The balance was never paid.

In 1803, the states disregarded their agreements and sued Eli for all the money paid to him and his partner. That year alone the cotton crop earned close to ten million dollars for the planters. The price of slaves had doubled and planters no longer troubled themselves with guilt over having stolen Eli's invention. Eli was forced to appeal to Congress for debt relief in 1804 and by one vote was saved from total ruin. He was broke, his patent was worthless, he was thirty-nine years old and the past ten years had been wasted either in courtrooms or traveling from one court to another.

Eli turned his back on the cotton gin and the south forever. Phineas and Caty Greene married and lived the remainder of their lives on Cumberland Island. In 1805, Eli returned to New Haven and vowed to start over.

**OLD SAVANNAH
COTTON EXCHANGE**

The Savannah Cotton Exchange building was completed in 1887 during the era when Savannah ranked first as a cotton seaport on the Atlantic and second in the world. In its heyday as a cotton port over two million bales a year moved through Savannah. The Cotton Exchange was the center of activity in the staple which dominated this city's economic life before its evolution into a leading industrial seaport.

The Exchange was designed by the nationally-known Boston architect, William Gibbons Preston (1844-1910). His design won out in a competition participated in by eleven architects. The Exchange is believed to be one of the few structures in the world erected over an existing public street.

The beautiful iron railing around this grass plat, with panels featuring medallions of famous statesmen, authors and poets, once graced the ante-bellum Wetter House in Savannah.

The former Cotton Exchange is now the headquarters of the Savannah Chamber of Commerce, which cordially invites you to stop in for a visit.

**Park at Bay and Drayton Streets, Savannah
GPS Coordinates: N32.08087, W81.090002**

Eli Whitney's cotton gin, invented almost one hundred years before on Mulberry Grove Plantation near Savannah, had revolutionized the cotton industry. Cotton could be processed on a large scale and at tremendous speed compared to doing it by hand. Eli Whitney's cotton gin made cotton "King in the South." Savannah was a bustling port city and the cotton exchange would be a lucrative business.

The Savannah Cotton Exchange, established in 1872, did not have a permanent home until 1886, when the directors decided that its location had to be central to the port. The only site considered was on Bay Street in the heart of the port district, nothing else would suffice. Unfortunately, there was no property available on which to build.

The directors of the Cotton Exchange had an idea. An application was placed before the General Assembly of Georgia for permission to construct a building, of all places, above the Drayton Street slip. An ordinance was passed in November 1885, awarding the Savannah Cotton Exchange "air rights" on the condition that the building would not interfere with the public use of the Drayton Street slip. As plans were made for construction, the directors knew the building would serve as the focal point for the city's economy. The resulting structure would have to be impressive. The directors went shopping for an architect. Who could design something so spectacular that it would eclipse the buildings surrounding it?

The complicated task was awarded to Boston architect, William Gibbons Preston. The site was unique in that the building would have to be designed to stand above an existing boat slip, that later would become a city street. Preston resolved the dilemma by designing a building that would be perched upon five pairs of iron columns, calling his design "Devonshire," his was selected from a panel of sixteen entries in an open competition.

Old Savannah Cotton Exchange

Preston was a student of the fashionable Queen Anne style, which is prevalent in a majority of his work. The design utilized red brick, stubby pilasters or columns, intricate classical detailing, low relief decorative terra cotta work and steep gables. Preston primarily used northern materials, which he was familiar with such as: Boston Terra Cotta Company trim, Quincy granite, red northern bricks and a small relief panels representing the trade of Savannah cotton between the New World and the Old. The Savannah Cotton Exchange was known to the city as "King Cotton's Palace." Savannah flourished under King Cotton's rule and it was this city that set cotton prices for the world. The waterfront warehouses were filled with "white gold," bringing in a considerable amount of money. During this time the *per capita* income of Savannah exceeded that of most cities in all of America.

The Savannah Cotton Exchange was the first building in America to be constructed entirely above a public street. This left the tax collector in a quandary, how could the property be taxed when it did not, in fact, occupy any space of property? Of course the government found a way around the issue, built using the principle of Air Rights, the exchange was taxed for the space underneath the building as if it actually touched the earth, but at a lower rate.

The building housed the Cotton and Naval Stores Exchange until 1952, when it became the headquarters of the Savannah Chamber of Commerce. Since 1974, the Savannah Cotton Exchange building has served as a meeting place for the membership of Solomon's Lodge No. 1 of Free and Accepted Masons.

OLD
CITY EXCHANGE BELL

This bell, which is believed to be the oldest in Georgia, bears the date 1802. Imported from Amsterdam, it hung in the cupola of the City Exchange from 1804 until a short time before that building was razed to make way for the present City Hall. In its day, the bell signalled the closing timed for shops and was rung by a watchman when fire broke out. Its rich tones were heard in celebration of American victories during the War of 1812. It pealed a welcome of such distinguished visitors to Savannah as Monroe, LaFayette, Polk, Fillmore, Clay and Webster and it tolled tributes for America's illustrious dead. The tower of the City Exchange, where the bell hung, was a favorite resort of those anxious about the arrival of vessels. The replica of the tower in which the historic bell presently reposes was erected in 1957 through the combined efforts of the Savannah Chamber of Commerce, the Pilot Club of Savannah and the Savannah-Chatham Historic Site and Monument Commission.

In park at Bay and Drayton Streets, Savannah
GPS Coordinates: N32.08076, W81.089707

The Old City Exchange Bell has the distinction of being the oldest public bell in Georgia still in use. Generations of Savannahians have been born and died since its arrival from Amsterdam and installation in 1802. All the while, the bell remains a symbol of significant happenings in the city of Savannah. When the Exchange was originally constructed no appropriation for a bell was made, no tower was in the plans. In 1802, when plans to install a clock for public use in the Independent Presbyterian Church steeple were rescinded, one thousand dollars was given to Robert and John Bolton to import the clock and bell.

A belfry was constructed on top of the Cotton Exchange at the expense of the city of Savannah. Robert and John Bolton provided the clock and bell at their cost, a total of $990.63, returning the remaining funds to the city treasury. It took two years for the work on the Exchange to be completed and the bell and clock were not in place until 1804.

A resolution was made by the City Council on May 28, 1804, that from March 31 until September 22, the bell would be rung at 9:00 p.m. each evening and at 8:00 p.m. the remainder of the year. The ringing would signify the closing of the shops in Savannah for the day. For years, a church bell was rung to give notice to the public that city council was about meet, now the Exchange bell took over those duties as well. Whenever fire threatened the city, the loud clear tones of the bell would reverberate throughout the city. When America reigned victorious in the War of 1812, the bell could be heard for miles.

When the Old City Exchange was torn down to make way for a new city hall, the bell was transferred to the tower of John Rourke and Son's Foundry at Bay and East Broad Street, where it continued to peel the hour. In 1957, a replica of the belfry was built in the park at Bay and Drayton Street and the bell was placed there. The Savannah Chamber of Commerce, the Pilot Club of Savannah and the Savannah Chatham Historic Site and Monument Commission, in a combined effort, hung the bell in a place of distinction for the enjoyment of citizens and tourists alike.

The Old City Exchange Bell has sounded its rich reverberation during times of joy and sorrow, in welcome and departure, as well as the sounds of everyday life. Its soothing tone was like a friend. Savannah grieves its silence.

The Old City Exchange Bell

SALZBURGER MONUMENT
OF RECONCILIATION

The nearby Salzburger Monument of Reconciliation was dedicated to The Georgia Salzburger Society and given to the City of Savannah in 1994 by the State of Salzburg Austria, in memory of the Lutheran Protests of Salzburg who were denied religious freedom and expelled from their homeland.
The first thirty seven Salzburger to come to Georgia landed at this site on March 12, 1734. They were welcomed by James Edward Oglethorpe, founder of the Georgia Colony and given temporary shelter before moving to their new home, Ebenezer, in what is now Effingham County. Additional colonists from Salzburg and other Germanic people continued to settle at Ebenezer until 1752.

Abercorn at Bay Street, Savannah
GPS Coordinates: N32.08068, W81.089192

I n 1734, thirty-seven industrious Lutheran Germans fled Salzburg, Austria, in search of religious freedom and became known in the new Georgia colony as Salzburgers. General James Edward Oglethorpe was there to meet them and after a consultation, it was decided that they would make their home at the settlement of Ebenezer.

Conditions were harsh, eventually the Salzburgers decided to relocate their community in 1736. Moving thirty miles up the Savannah River and again calling the settlement New Ebenezer. The town was surveyed and laid out by Wormslow Plantation owner, Noble Jones. Georgia's first public school was created here in 1736, as well as the colony's first orphanage. The community eventually expanded to a population of more than 1,600 members.

Each Salzburger had been given a white mulberry tree in which to begin the production of raw silk. Overall, the silk industry failed in the new colony, except at New Ebenezer. The resilient Salzburgers gained much success and a bustling silk culture was born. Soon, New Ebenezer was known as the "Silk Capital" of the New World.

The Jerusalem Lutheran Church was built in 1769. Georgia clay fired in a nearby kiln provided brick for twenty-one inch thick walls. The community's women and children hand carried the brick from the kiln to the construction site. It is reported that some of the brick to this day bear the fingerprints of Salzburger children. A swan featured on the steeple comes out of the legend of John Huss. Huss supported church reform, which was illegal during his time, he was accused and sentenced to be burned at the stake. His dying words were reported to have been, "You may burn this goose but out of these ashes will be a swan."

Colonel Archibald Campbell led British troops into New Ebenezer during the Revolutionary War and ordered that the town to be set to the torch, the possessions of the Salzburgers' seized and the white mulberry groves destroyed. New Ebenezer became a prisoner of war camp, the church a British hospital and storehouse. Later after the British moved their wounded, the Jerusalem Lutheran Church became a horse stable. General Anthony Wayne of the Continental forces arrived in 1782 and drove the British out of New Ebenezer. Unfortunately, the damage had already been done. New Ebenezer was left in ruins and most of her citizens never returned.

Today, all that remains of the proud New Ebenezer community is the church and cemetery. Although the community has been incorporated into Effingham County, its ties to Savannah and Chatham County are very strong. The Jerusalem Lutheran Church still remains active and is the oldest facility of its kind in America. The cemetery has memorials to Israel Christian Gronau and John Martin Bolzius, the two ministers who led their Lutheran congregation from Austria to the New World, though time and war have erased their actual burial sites. The grounds have been restored to much the way they would have appeared in 1755, a Salzburger home was built as a reproduction of a house built by the early settlers of this time. In 1971, a two story brick museum was constructed on the site of the first orphanage. A monument near the church pays homage to John Adam Treutlen, one of the original Salzburgers who became the first Georgia governor. Governor Treutlen was killed in 1782 by the British in Carolina.

Salzburger descendants gather each year on March 12 to celebrate their ancestor's arrival in the Georgia colony. The huge family reunion consists of religious services and the retelling of Salzburger history. A Family Retreat and Conference Center was built to feature the life style that must have existed during the eighteenth century. The facility is available for church groups, family reunions, school groups and scouts. The church, cemetery and Georgia Salzburger Society Museum are open for public tours.

Albert Winter from Salzburg, Austria, visited Savannah and Ebenezer for the 250th Anniversary celebration in 1984. It was then that he noticed that no memorial for his kinsmen stood in Savannah. He solicited the assistance of the Austrian State of Salzburg for the placement of a monument dedicated to the Georgia Salzburgs. Dr. Hans Katschthaler, Governor of Salzburg, commissioned noted sculptor Anton Thuswaldner to create a monument. The beautifully carved monument was brought to Savannah and dedicated on Labor Day 1994. The monument stands gracefully in a park on Bay Street near the Lincoln street ramp and is known as the Salzburger Monument of Reconciliation. The small lot where the monument sits was officially designated as Salzburger Park. The monument is a fitting memorial to those who added to the patchwork of humanity that became the Georgia Colony.

THE GEORGIA HUSSARS
Organized 13 February 1736

This Troop of Mounted Rangers was raised by Gen. Oglethorpe to patrol and protect the Colony of Georgia from the Spaniards and Indians. It fought at Bloody Marsh in 1742 and at the Siege of Savannah in 1779. Its record during The War 1861-65 is unsurpassed as was its service in Mexico, World War I, World War II and Korea. It remained Horse Cavalry until October 1940. From Colonial times to Vietnam Hussars have represented Savannah in all our wars. It is still an active unit in the Georgia Army National Guard.

In park at Bay and Lincoln Streets, Savannah
GPS Coordinates: N32.08006, W81.088066

General James Edward Oglethorpe had plans for the defense of the Georgia colony before sailing in 1733. Convincing a group of fearless Scottish Highlanders to settle in the infant colony along with the British regulars that accompanied him, he would have his army. The militia was first called to war against Spain near Fort Frederica at the Battle of Bloody Marsh in July of 1742. Oglethorpe's militia, including the Georgia Hussars, soundly defeated the Spaniards, who would never be so brave as to attack the colony again.

The Hussars joined General George Washington during the Revolutionary War. It was one of those men, General John McIntosh, who commanded a small post at Sunbury called Fort Morris. He stated when faced with a call to surrender:

"We would rather perish in a vigorous defense than accept your proposal, sir. We, sir, are fighting the battle of America and therefore disdain to remain neutral til its fate is determined. As to surrendering the Fort receive this reply, Come and take it!"

General McIntosh was one of those fearless Scotsmen.

Men of the Georgia Hussars fought side by side with Texans in their struggle for independence against Mexico in 1836. Later that same year, they banded with the Macon Volunteers and helped to remove the Seminole Indians from Florida. They were first to engage Osceola at the Withlacoochee swamp during the second Seminole uprising.

The Georgia Hussars saw action during the Civil War. They responded to the call by joining volunteer regiments, battalions and batteries. The Hussars fought bravely to deter Sherman's March to the Sea, although the effort was valiant, they were no match for Sherman's forces.

After the Civil War, the Georgia Hussars aided in Reconstruction and the reestablishment of a state military force. They trained extensively and served both on American soil and abroad. They raised over 3,000 soldiers for the Spanish-American War, which was the last effort that the Hussars would fight under the name given to them by their founder, General Oglethorpe.

The twentieth century brought the establishment of the National Guard. The Georgia Hussars were absorbed into the National Guard, whose troops were called to settle domestic disputes usually associated with labor strikes, court ordered death sentences and during natural disasters during peace times. In 1916, the Georgia National Guard was activated to the Mexican border under the command of General John J. Pershing. Their target was the Mexican bandit, Pancho Villa, responsible for repeated raids on American settlements. Villa continued to fight until 1920, when he finally surrendered his troops to Adolfo de la Huerta. He eventually went into seclusion but was found and killed in July of 1923.

By 1917, the Georgia National Guard was fighting "over there" in World War I, participating in the European theatre. They joined the 42nd Rainbow Division and were involved in combat for 167 days. They were called to arms again in 1940. Every state in the Union provided National Guard troops, which mobilized for one year of training. The popular song of the day was *Goodbye Dear, I'll Be Back in a Year* and was written as a reflection of Guardsmen bidding a tearful farewell to their wives and sweethearts. Unfortunately, it turned out to be much more than a year in World War II. The Japanese bombed Pearl Harbor and the United States entered World War II. The Georgia National Guard became part of the 30th and 8th Infantry Divisions, serving in France arriving shortly after D-Day, in Italy, Guadalcanal, New Guinea and the list goes on. Following the war, the Georgia Army and Air National Guard was reorganized and the men were activated for the Korean Conflict, then in the 1960s and 1970s they were airlifted into South Vietnam.

The Georgia Army and Air National Guard mobilized more than five thousand men and women during Operation Desert Shield and Operation Desert Storm. More than seven hundred were assigned to Saudi Arabia, while thousands of others manned stateside posts.

After the attacks of terrorism on September 11, 2001, President Bush called to active duty the National Guard. The Georgia Army and Air National Guard continues to heed the call. They are trained to fight with modern technology and weaponry and are proud to carry on the tradition of Georgia's militia and National Guard. Whatever the call, be it natural disaster or foreign threats, the Georgia National Guard stands ready.

**Bay Street between Habersham and Lincoln Streets, Savannah
GPS Coordinates: N32.21738, W81.087148**

Prince Hall Masonry in Savannah received sponsorship from the Most Worshipful Prince Hall Grand Lodge, State of Massachusetts, on February 4, 1866. Reverend Anthony L. Stanford, James M. Simms, Barcus S. Davidson, King S. Thomas and Stephen Johnson were the first members. The charter was eventually surrendered and on June 24, 1870, Eureka Lodge No. 11 became Eureka Lodge No. 1 under the jurisdiction of the Most Worshipful Prince Hall Grand Lodge of Georgia.

The Eureka Lodge was the first recorded Black secret organization to be founded in Georgia. The Civil War had not yet ended when the lodge was organized by free men of color. At that time, the only gatherings allowed to African Americans were religious services, President Lincoln's issuance of the Emancipation Proclamation freed the restraints and the Masonic brethren began to hold meetings.

The meetings were initially held at the home of Stephen Johnson, who served as treasurer, he resided on Pine Street in a house which adjoined the West Broad Street School. Several attempts to organize the lodge failed. The formation of the lodge required twelve Masons to be in attendance and it was not until 1866 that the stipulation was met. One additional person was required to establish the lodge in 1866, when James Jackson heard of the dilemma, he volunteered to serve as the last man. He was the first Senior Stewart and was initiated as a Mason in Philadelphia. Named the Eureka Lodge, these men were among the leading and most prominent African American men in the city of Savannah. James Jackson, was the only Caucasian in the group. They met in what is today, the Chatham Bank and Trust Company, west of Johnson Square.

James Merilus Simms was the first Grand Master and founder of Eureka and Prince Hall Masonry in Georgia. Simms was born in Savannah on December 27, 1823, his mother was a slave owned by the Potter Family, his father was the Potter family patriarch. In the days of his youth, it was a crime to teach slaves to read and write, though it was commonplace that when an owner's child was tutored, their slave playmates often were allowed to join. Therefore when James' white father hired a French tutor for his children, James attended classes along with his half siblings. He was a good student, not only did he learn to read and write, but to speak a number of foreign languages as well. James was also a talented musician and played for both white and African Americans at social gatherings. He in turn passed his knowledge on to other slaves, when caught, he was publically whipped for his transgression. Eventually his mother saved enough money and purchased her son's freedom, from his father, for three hundred dollars.

When the Civil War reached Savannah, James sailed to Trinidad and then to Boston; during his time in Boston, he became a Mason. He also became an ordained Baptist Minister and returned to Savannah in February 1865. James joined the Union

Army and served as the Chaplain for Army posts in Florida and Georgia. He was given a Union Army pension as a war veteran, which he received until his death.

During the South's Reconstruction, James Simms represented Chatham County in the Georgia Legislature and was later appointed Judge of the Senatorial district by Governor Bullock. He served as the Customs Inspector and diligently worked for the Freedmens Bureau in Savannah. James Simms became the District Deputy Grandmaster for the Most Worshipful Prince Hall Grand Lodge of Massachusetts, which covered Georgia, Florida and Alabama in 1866. He became the first black Masonic Grand Master in Georgia's history.

By 1871, he left the congregation at First African Baptist Church and joined First Bryan Baptist Church where he became a deacon and trustee board member. In 1888, James Simms wrote *The First Colored Baptist Church in North America*, which detailed the history of the First Bryan Baptist Church. He was a newspaper editor, owning the *Southern Radical* and *Freedmens Journal*. James played an important role in the movement to bring the Georgia State Industrial College to Savannah, presently known as Savannah State University.

Reverend James Simms died on July 9, 1912. The funeral was conducted at the First Bryan Baptist Church. The Most Worshipful Prince Hall Grand Lodge of Georgia placed a monument at Grand Master Simms grave in June 1920. Over five hundred Masons marched from the old Masonic Temple on Gwinnett Street near West Broad to Laurel Grove Cemetery South to dedicate the monument.

OLD HARBOR LIGHT

This beacon light was erected by the federal government in 1858 as an aid to navigation of the Savannah River. Standing 77 feet above river level and illuminated by gas, it served for several years as a guide to vessels passing over the hulls of ships that the British scuttled in 1779 to close the harbor to the French naval forces. During the Siege of Savannah that year by the French and Americans the warship Truite, commanded by the Count de Chastenet de Puysegur, shelled this area of Savannah from her anchorage in Back River opposite this point.

The development of this portion of Emmet Park as a garden area was a project of the Trustees Garden Club during the centennial year of the erection of the "Old Harbor Light."

In park at Bay and East Broad Streets, Savannah
GPS Coordinates: N32.07935, W81.08416

The Old Harbor Light has stood the watch during the night, while Savannah slept for one hundred and forty-two years. The Harbor Light technically a beacon range navigation light was placed seventy-seven feet above the Savannah River by the United States Lighthouse Board in 1858. The gas powered lamp atop an ornate twenty-five foot cast iron post was used to pilot ships into the precarious Savannah harbor. No one really knows who constructed the light, but it has is likely that it originated from England or perhaps, France.

The British Navy scuttled six ships in the Savannah harbor during the Revolutionary War and the Siege of Savannah. Their intent was to congest the Savannah River waterway so that the French Navy would be unable to come to the aid of their American allies. The Old Harbor Light provided an essential guide through the treacherous waters.

The gradual deterioration in the Old Harbor Light became painfully apparent in 1998. While examining the light, which is considered a historical monument and treated as such, the city discovered that rust and corrosion were slowly taking their toll on the structure and it was gradually becoming unstable. Cables were attached to the light to secure it in position and ensure that the light did not plunge into the Savannah River. For safety reasons and with sadness, the gas lamp was extinguished.

A general contractor, TIC Company, was hired to carefully disassemble the historic light. The one hundred and forty-five year old structure was taken down in six parts and gently lifted onto a flatbed truck with the assistance of a crane. The Old Harbor Light was then removed to the city fabrication shop. Amazingly, it took less than five days to complete the removal process and move it to the location where the light was to be restored.

The restoration process included removing all signs of rust and corrosion, the surface metal was treated and the Old Harbor Light received a fresh coat of paint. The outer surface was given a special coating that will inhibit future rust. Repairs were made in places where the iron had weakened and corroded, some areas grown thin over time, had to be reinforced. The lenses were cleaned and the gas system flushed to ensure there were no obstructions.

The cost for restoration, which included consultation work, design, planning and actual restoration was a hefty $200,000. Savannah's Park and Tree Service, a part of the city Facilities Maintenance Department, funded a little over one third of the cost while the *Savannah Morning News* and CSX Corporation each donated $62,500 to the project.

The light was reignited in March 1999. The Old Harbor Light continues to stand the watch.

Old Harbor Light

THE TRUSTEES' GARDEN

At this site was located the first public agricultural experimental garden in America. From this garden was disseminated the upland cotton which later comprised the greater part of the world's cotton commerce. Here were propagated and from this garden distributed, the peach trees which gave Georgia and South Carolina another major commercial crop. The garden consisted of ten acres. It was established by Oglethorpe within one month after the settlement of Georgia. Botanists were sent by the Trustees of the Colony from England to the West Indies and South America to procure plants for the garden. Vine cuttings, flax, hemp, potashes, indigo, cochineal, olives, and medicinal herbs were grown. The greatest hope was centered in the mulberry trees, essential to silk culture. In the early days of the Colony, Queen Caroline was clothed in Georgia silk, and the town's largest structure was the filature. The silk and wine industries failed to materialize. The distant sponsors were unable to judge of the immense importance of the experiments conducted in other products, in 1755 the site was developed as a residential section.

Pirate's House parking lot, Bay and East Broad Streets, Savannah
GPS Coordinates: N32.07843, W81.083661

Within a month of General Oglethorpe taking his first step onto Georgia soil, he had not only laid plans for the city but also located a spot to be the first experimental garden in America. He dubbed the ten acre plot, the "Trustees Garden," in honor of the English Trustees of Georgia.

Oglethorpe's plan for the garden was based on London's famed Chelsea Botanical Garden. Botanists were dispatched far and wide to retrieve plant cuttings; fruit trees, flax, hemp, spices, cotton, indigo, olives and medicinal herbs began arriving in droves and soon the plants began to take root.

England had placed great hopes that Georgia would provide a great wine industry and that vast mulberry tree groves would result in abundant exports of raw silk. Neither of these dreams materialized. The soil and weather conditions were not suited for the growth of either grapes or mulberry trees, the crops failed. However, peach trees flourished, and the Trustees Garden provided the initial groves that eventually dubbed Georgia, The Peach State. Peaches, quite literally, grew into a major commercial crop.

Green seed cotton was also grown in the garden. Some of the plants were distributed among the colonists, massive rivers of white were the eventual result. Georgia could later lay claim as the leading exporter of cotton to the world. Cotton was king for a time.

A small building was erected in 1734, for the use of the gardener. The structure was built from Savannah brick made only a short distance away on the Savannah River. The rooms consisted of an office, tool room, stable and hayloft. By 1753, Georgia no longer needed the experimental garden and the Trustees Garden became a residential area.

Savannah became a well known seaport. An inn for transient seamen was built on the garden site. Only a block from the Savannah River, the inn became a popular spot for sailors as well as pirates. It was here that the unsavory lot traded sea stories and drank to their adventures. Legend has it that a tunnel existed beneath the rum cellar leading to the port, through which ship's masters would carry unsuspecting drinking men aboard their ships to complete their crews. It is said that many a man awoke aboard a tall masted ship bound for foreign ports.

Today, the old inn is the site for one of Savannah's most unique restaurants, The Pirate House. The property is owned by the Savannah Gas Company and has been recognized by the American Museum Society as a validated historic tavern and house museum. The old brick gardener's room houses two of the fifteen dining rooms. The restaurant has wonderful atmosphere intended to transport guests back in time to the days of tall masted ships, pirates and old salts.

The Captain's Room and the Treasure Room feature framed pages of an early edition of *Treasure Island* written by Robert Louis Stevenson. It is said that parts of the book were to have taken place at The Pirates House. In the story, Captain Flint lay in an upstairs room when he breathed his last, some say that he's still there. The Jolly Roger Room pays tribute to the Trustees Garden with a diagram of London's Chelsea Botanical Garden as Oglethorpe might have seen it. And if you ask nicely, the hostess will show you the entrance to the tunnels that led to waiting ships at the wharf. A word of advice, don't drink too many of the Pirate's Punches, least you find yourself, on a rolling sea when you wake.

FORT PULASKI

Named for General Casimir Pulaski, the Polish hero who was mortally wounded at the Siege of Savannah, 1779. Fort Pulaski was built in accordance with plans by General Simon Bernard, formerly chief engineer under Napoleon. Begun in 1829 and completed in 1847, the fort was constructed principally under Lt. J.F.K. Mansfield. There Lt. Robert E. Lee saw his first service after his graduation from West Point. Pulaski was never garrisoned until its seizure by Georgia troops in January, 1861, to prevent occupation by Federal forces. On April 10, 1862, Federal batteries on Tybee Island commenced the bombardment of Fort Pulaski. After 30 hours of bombardment as a result of which the walls were breached and its guns disabled, Col. Charles H. Olmstead surrendered the Fort. The bombardment marked the first effective use of rifled cannon against a masonry fortification and constituted an epoch in military history.
Abandoned by 1885, Fort Pulaski became a National Monument in 1924 and was placed under the National Park Service in 1933.

US 80 near the entrance to Fort Pulaski
GPS Coordinates: N32.01876, W80.899565

Fort Pulaski was built in the 19th century military architecture style called the Third System. Construction began on the fort in 1829 as a part of the United States' plan to build a series of nearly two hundred fortifications along the Atlantic and Pacific coasts in answer to the depletion of coastal defenses caused by the War of 1812. Although Fort Pulaski was one of these forts, the plans were never completed largely due to Fort Pulaski's untimely demise.

A young West Point graduate named Lieutenant Robert E. Lee was stationed near Savannah at Cockspur Island and given the task of designing earthworks and canals to aid in the construction of Fort Pulaski. The construction site was largely underwater, a complicated system of canals drained away the excess water. This provided a stable mass of land on which to build the fort's foundation. Land maps of 1862 show the area inside the canals as the only dry land around.

Fort Pulaski was the first of its kind. Planned and built at a leisurely pace during peacetime by a commission appointed especially for planning the construction. Construction began with seventy foot long pilings driven into the mud that would support a fort built of twenty-five million bricks. The wood subflooring, consisting of two layers of timbers, would be used to support the brickwork. Military servicemen, skilled masons and carpenters, battling the intense Georgia summer sun and disease carrying mosquitoes, did the construction. Work was not always steady because of the environmental hazards; completed construction took almost eighteen years. The massive two storied fort rose from the mud and murk of Cockspur Island in 1847. Slaves from surrounding plantations were hired out by their owners as cheap labor in addition to the skilled workers and military men. Ironically, it was the children of these very slaves that were to become the first African American soldiers recruited during the Civil War, fighting to bring down the fort their forefathers helped to build.

The two tier structure was completed under the command of Major General David Hunter. The hexagon shaped edifice faces east and includes a moat, two powder magazines and a large parade ground. Locally made brick called "Savannah Grays" were used in the lower portion of the walls, while the much harder "rose red brick" from Baltimore, Maryland and Alexandria, Virginia comprised the upper walls and doorways. The red brick has passed the test of time. Visitors often think that massive restoration has been done and that these are modern day brick.

The fort was christened "Pulaski" in honor of the Revolutionary War hero, General Casmir Pulaski who valiantly gave his life on soil that was not his homeland for a cause he desperately believed in. General Pulaski was wounded and died during the siege of Savannah. Fort Pulaski lay silent for fourteen years until the dawn of the Civil War. During that span, the citizens of Savannah felt protected from foreign invasion; all the while, the enemy lie in wait on a common shore.

Union troops constructed eleven sand batteries on the northwest end of Tybee Island under the command of Captain Quincy A. Gilmore. Four of the batteries were built on the site of the Lazaretto, used in the 1770s to quarantine newly arriving slaves to avoid the infiltration of epidemic disease. The work was completed under a cover of darkness and communication was limited to soft whistles and hushed tones. Before the sun illuminated the nights work, the troops camouflaged their handiwork with sea oat plants and driftwood.

Even the Union soldiers efforts to conceal the thirty-six guns, magazines and bombproof shelters was for naught, Fort Pulaski realized almost immediately that the Union planned an attack. Although Confederate officers were curious, none placed too much importance on the bunkers almost two and half miles in the distance. It was commonly known that no armament manufactured at that time had an accurate or effective range from that distance.

The rifled cannon was an experimental gun field tested by Union and Confederate troops. The weapon's actual power and accuracy was unknown, both sides had discarded the weapon as untried. Union Captain Quincy A. Gilmore, an astute materials science engineer, believed that the rifled cannon would quickly render the fort indefensible and eliminate an extended siege sparing the lives of countless men. Captain Gilmore's peers did not share his faith in the experimental weapon and all but laughed as he trudged the heavy weapons over the marsh nearly a mile. Captain Gilmore did not believe Fort Pulaski was impenetrable and literally stuck by his guns.

On April 11, 1862, Union troops directed their rifled cannon at Fort Pulaski. For thirty hours the bombardment continued, smoke filled the air and the walls of the southeast angle of Fort Pulaski began to crumble. Rifled cannon pieces threw heavier loads with greater accuracy and higher velocity than smooth bore guns traditionally used. The quick success of this experimental cannon surprised military strategists. Fort Pulaski surrendered to Union forces. The fort would remain under Union control for the duration of the Civil War. By October 1864, Fort Pulaski would be used against the Confederacy. The accuracy and range of the rifled cannon rendered brick fortifications obsolete.

Major General David Hunter, who at one time commanded construction of Fort Pulaski, now stood against her as a Union Officer. Almost immediately after Fort Pulaski was taken, General Hunter, known as Lincoln's Abolitionist General, issued General Order #7, stating:

> "All persons of color lately held to involuntary service by enemies of the United States in Fort Pulaski and on Cockspur Island, Georgia, are hereby confiscated and declared free, in conformity with the law, and shall here after receive the fruits of their own labor."

From this order, General Hunter recruited the newly freed slaves for the formation of the First South Carolina Volunteer Regiment. The regiment was used largely for manual labor.

Edwin M. Stanton, Federal Secretary of War, received a post relaying that Confederate Major General Samuel Jones held six hundred Union officers prisoner at Charleston and that the General had placed these officers in the direct line of fire from federal artillery. In effect, the Union was killing its own officers. In retaliation, Edwin Stanton ordered six hundred Confederate prisoners of war be positioned on Morris Island in the Charleston harbor in direct line of sight of the Confederate guns of Fort Sumter. The standoff continued until a yellow fever epidemic threatened the city of Charleston and General Jones was forced to evacuate the prisoners from the city. Edwin Stanton responded by moving the six hundred prisoners of war to Fort Pulaski. These prisoners of war will be forever known as the Immortal Six Hundred.

By October 23, 1864, when the weary and sick prisoners arrived at Fort Pulaski, only five hundred fifty remained. They were promised wool blankets and clothes, some were almost bare skinned, however, due to limited supplies the prisoners went without sufficient food, blankets or clothes. Captain J. Ogden Murray, Staff of the Virginia 7th Cavalry stated,

> "After picking out the lumps, bugs, and worms in this rotten corn meal there was not more than seven ounces of meal left fit for use. About December 10th scurvy made its appearance in our prison amongst the weakest of the prisoners. Most every man in the prison was suffering more or less with dysentery and a large majority were from the starvation diet, unable to leave their bunks."

Miraculously, only thirteen deaths were recorded during the Immortal Six Hundred's incarceration. The dead were buried in unmarked graves on Cockspur Island, most succumbing to dehydration as a result of dysentery. In March 1865, the surviving prisoners were sent to Fort Delaware where conditions, although deplorable, were somewhat better.

Fort Pulaski now stands as a National Monument and exists as one of the best preserved forts along the Atlantic seaboard. The park includes scenic marshes and uplands that support a variety of animals indigenous to the southern barrier islands. White tailed deer, alligators, raccoons, armadillos as well as resident and migratory birds can be observed at any given time throughout the park. Self and ranger guided tours are available. Fort Pulaski provides a picturesque setting for other activities such as fishing, boating and picnicking. A small fee is charged.

JOHN WESLEY
(1703-1791)

On February 6, 1736, John Wesley, the founder of Methodism, landed at Peeper (now Cockspur) Island near here and there preached to his fellow voyagers his first sermon on American soil. A monument has been erected on Cockspur Island to commemorate the event.
Sent to Georgia by the Trustees as missionary, Wesley was the third minister of the Established Church in the colony. He preached in the scattered settlements of Georgia, journeying thither by boat and over Indian trails. Wesley returned to England in 1737 after differences with his parishioners. "I shook off the dust of my feet and left Georgia," he wrote, "having preached the Gospel, there (not as I ought, but as I was able) one year and nearly nine months."

Fort Pulaski near the Visitor's Center
GPS Coordinates: N32.02748, W80.892388

To believe John Wesley more than a man would be a dire mistake. Although he devoted his life to Methodism and spreading the word of God, John Wesley was a man with human weaknesses, desires and frailties. Though none of these characteristics could possibly cast a shadow over his pious works as a servant of God. These normal human traits were aspects of the man as well.

John Wesley was ahead of his time in many ways. The most controversial, perhaps, was in regard to his thoughts concerning women. He believed that women had certain rights, such as spreading the word of God. He expressed the belief saying,

> "May not women as well as men, bear a part in this honorable service? Undoubtedly they may; nay, they ought; it is meet, right and their bounden duty. Herein there is no difference, 'there is neither male nor female in Christ Jesus."

Possibly, his opinions were formed at a young age. His mother, Susanna, was not only a strong willed woman but very vocal in her opinions. Although quite pious throughout his life, John Wesley had a healthy view of the feminine sex.

Grace Murray was one of John Wesley's spiritual children. She was a young widow who was quite beautiful and had obtained a superior education. John Wesley appointed her Matron of the Orphan House at Newcastle Upon Tyne in England. Later, at John Wesley's request, she traveled through the northern counties to meet and regulate the female classes. Like other traveling pastors of those days, she traversed on horseback. No one would contest, nor does it lessen the memory of John Wesley, to say he loved Grace Murray and had a wish that she would become his wife.

The couple was engaged to be married; but John's brother Charles and long time friend and fellow preacher, George Whitefield, were opposed to the his marrying at all. The two conspired and convinced Grace to marry another. The man they had in mind was John Bennet, one of John Wesley's early pastors. Charles and George were successful. John Bennet, after his marriage to Grace and fully aware of the severed engagement, separated from John Wesley, became a Calvinist and the pastor of a church in Cheshire, England.

John Bennet had been easily convinced to marry Grace; he had once been sick of a fever and she had tenderly nursed him back to health. From that point on he knew she would one day be his bride. She had been persuaded that her marrying John Wesley would in all probability lessen his usefulness in the church.

John Wesley was heartbroken. He poured out his sorrows in prose and verse. He laments in a letter,

"The sons of Zeruiah were too strong for me. The whole world fought against me, but above all my own familiar friend. Then was fulfilled, 'Son of man, behold I take from thee the desire of thine eyes at a stroke, yet shall not thou lament, neither shall thy tears run down.' The fatal, irrecoverable stroke was struck on Thursday last. Yesterday I saw my friend that was and him to whom she is sacrificed."

Nearly thirty years after her husband's death, John Wesley, who had never spoken her name again, was summoned to Grace's side by the lady herself. He spent a short time with her, though nothing is known of what was said, and after this interview, did not speak of her again until her death.

In 1803, Grace Murray Bennet died. John Wesley's only comment upon hearing of her death was,

"I saw the work of God prosper in her hands. She was to me both a servant and friend, as well as a fellow-laborer in the Gospel."

THE WAVING GIRL

For 44 years, Florence Martus (1868-1943) lived on nearby Elba Island with her brother, the lighthouse keeper, and no ship arrived for Savannah or departed from 1886 to 1931 without her waving a handkerchief by day or a lantern by night. Throughout the years, the vessels in return watched for and saluted this quiet little woman. Few people ever met her yet she became the source of romantic legends when the story of her faithful greetings was told in ports all over the world. After her retirement the Propeller Club of Savannah, in honor of her seventieth birthday, sponsored a celebration on Cockspur Island. A Liberty ship, built in Savannah in 1943, was named for her.

Fort Pulaski near the Visitor's Center
GPS Coordinates: N32.02748, W80.892388

The story of Florence Martus was known far and wide as one of the most romantic tales ever told. During the late 1800s and early 1900s a sea story was passed from ship to ship about the mysterious "Waving Girl" of Elba Island. Was she a mirage seen only by eyes too long at sea or an actual woman waving a welcome to passing ships; a white handkerchief by day and lantern by night?

Florence Martus was very real. She was born on Cockspur Island in 1868. Little is known of her younger years, the first known record is when Florence, along with her family, escaped the devastation of the Great Hurricane of 1881. She would have been thirteen at the time her family sought the protective shelter of Ft. Pulaski, while raging winds and tidal surges ripped apart buildings and entire homes were washed away.

Florence's brother accepted the position of lighthouse keeper on Elba Island and she accompanied him. Life as a lighthouse keeper was lonely and monotonous work. There are stories of many a keeper's wife eventually going mad as a result of the isolation. What life must have been like for 19 year old Florence?

Legend has it that young Florence was engaged to a sea going man. She stood at the shore on a high bluff by day waving her white handkerchief in the wind and by night, young Florence would greet the passing ships with her lantern held high. Florence vigilantly stood her post so she would be the first to welcome her suitor home. Alas! the young lad never returned, yet Florence continued to stand the watch.

Yet whether the legend be true or only a romantic sea tale, Florence steadfastly stood for over forty years. Most likely she greeted the passing vessels only to relieve the intense boredom of a remote lighthouse station. Still the legend remains today.

To honor "The Waving Girl," the Altrusa Club of Savannah commissioned a statue by Felix de Weldon and thus Florence continues to stand her watch at the east end of River Street. Weldon later attained world wide acclaim for his Iwo Jima Memorial, in Washington, D. C. depicting Marines raising the American flag on Iwo Jima during World War II.

TYBEE LIGHTHOUSE

A lighthouse on Tybee was one of the first public structures in Georgia. Completed in 1736 by William Blithman of cedar piles and brickwork, its 90 foot height made it the loftiest in America. Destroyed in a storm, it was replaced by another built by Thomas Sumner in 1742 which Oglethorpe called "much the best Building of that kind in America." It was almost entirely rebuilt in 1757 by Cornelius McCarty and James Weyms. In 1773 John Mulryne built the third lighthouse on a third site. The Mulryne lighthouse forms the base of the present structure, making part of it of Colonial construction. In 1791 Georgia ceded it with 5 acres of the Federal government. Partially destroyed by the Irish Jasper Greens of Savannah during Union occupation of the island. It was repaired and today is one of the famous lighthouses on the Eastern seaboard.

Lighthouse near Fort Screven, Tybee Island
GPS Coordinates: N32.02234, W80.844424

The Tybee Island Light Station is historically one of the most complete stations in America, complete in the sense, that the buildings used in support of Tybee's beacon are still in place. The majestic lighthouse that stands watch over the Savannah River entrance dates back to 1773 and continues to this day as an operating lighthouse. The first lighthouse was completed in 1736, under the direction of General James Oglethorpe, who recognized the need for coastal protection. The light would serve to warn mariners of shallow waters, mark the waterways and be a lookout post for Spanish troops attempting to attack Savannah. The structure was initially made of wood and stood an impressive ninety feet tall. The Tybee lighthouse was the tallest building of its kind on American soil.

The lighthouse had problems from the beginning. It became quite obvious shortly after construction was completed that the light had been built too close to the waterway. Beach erosion, gale force storms and tidal wash threatened the foundation. Work began on a new structure in 1741. In August 1741, a severe storm claimed the Tybee Lighthouse. The beacon was extinguished for more than six months.

The second tower was completed in March 1742. Made of stone and wood, this tower stood a total of one hundred and twenty-four feet including the thirty foot flag pole placed at her crown. Oglethorpe noted the structure was "the best" in America. However, like the first tower, this structure was also built dangerously close to the shore. In 1768, a third lighthouse was proposed and construction began.

The third and final site was chosen and remains the location of the lighthouse today. Construction of the brick structure was completed in 1773. The interior consisted of wooden stairs and landings, the lighthouse stood one hundred feet tall. In 1790, the Tybee lighthouse as well as all other lighthouses in America, came under the care of the United States Lighthouse Establishment.

The lighthouse was illuminated, during the late 1700s, by large candles with metal discs placed behind them to reflect the light. Later sixteen lamps burning whale oil replaced the candles. An eight foot tall, French made, 2nd Order Fresnel Lens replaced the whale oil lamps in 1857 in the lighthouse lantern room. The lens was molded glass prisms in brass frames and magnified to such high intensity that only one whale oil lantern was needed.

Confederate troops worried about the brilliant light and for only the second time since its construction, the light was extinguished. The wooden stairway leading to the lens was destroyed to prevent the invading Union troops from using the light. Their efforts resulted in little deterrence other than delay. Union troops repaired the damage and the tower was used as a lookout for Confederate forces approaching Fort Pulaski until the garrison's surrender in 1862.

A fourth tower was completed in 1867. The new reinforced structure was built atop the existing structure using sixty feet of the old lighthouse as a foundation. The lighthouse was built of brick and cast iron, added to the sixty foot base was an additional ninety-four feet and a nine foot tall 1st Order Fresnel Lens. The lighthouse was an amazing one hundred and fifty-four feet tall. The lighthouse was reclassified and announced as a major aid in navigation and the light station required the service of three light keepers to work the facilities. The fourth and final lighthouse was illuminated on October 1, 1867, her guiding beacon could be seen for eighteen miles.

Modernization caught up with the Lighthouse Service in 1933 and the beacon was converted to electricity. Three lighthouse keepers were no longer needed. George Jackson became the last lighthouse keeper at Tybee Island, serving until his death in 1948. The United States Coast Guard took over responsibility of the Lighthouse Service in America in 1939 and occupied the Tybee Island Light Station until 1987. Age and high costs prompted the Coast Guard to relocate to Cockspur Island and the Tybee Island Historical Society took over the lighthouse. A lease agreement was established through the Coast Guard and the Historical Society continues to this day the care and restoration of the Tybee Light Station. The Coast Guard still maintains the light itself.

The Tybee Light Station consists of the following historic structures: The Head Keepers House, built in 1881 for the head lighthouse keeper and his family. The structure includes a livingroom and bedroom with two additional bedrooms on the second floor. The building is currently under restoration and will serve as a museum dedicated to the Jackson family upon completion. The Summer Kitchen, the oldest of the buildings was constructed around 1812. To avoid prevalent kitchen fires this structure was built away from other structure and served the lighthouse keepers until 1910, when it became a store room. The 1st Assistant Keeper's House, was built in 1885 on site of the original keeper's home which burned in 1884. The 2nd Assistant Keeper's House, was built as the confederate barracks in 1861. Union troops occupying the Tybee Light Station during the Civil War used the building as Union Headquarters on Tybee Island. Currently, this is the home for the Tybee Island Historical Society. The Fuel Storage Building was built in 1890, soon after kerosene replaced whale oil as the fuel source for the lighthouse. The building was designed to be fireproof constructed with brick walls, a concrete floor and a tin roof. A diesel powered generator was housed here at one time to provide power to the lighthouse. Finally, the three car garage, built around 1930, is today home to the Tybee Light Station Gift Shop.

For twelve years the Tybee Island Historical Society has worked tirelessly, without government assistance, to raise funds for the restoration of the Tybee Light Station. The volunteer based organization has collected funds from public and private groups, noted contributions were received through Harbour Lights and their Collectors Society. The descendants of Tybee Lighthouse Keeper George Jackson have played an integral part in raising funds as well. The Society hired a well known lighthouse restoration firm, International Chimney Corporation of Buffalo New York, as the general contractor to restore the Tybee Island Light. Like the original structure, Scottish masons, Irish painters and local craftsmen were used to supplement their own skilled crew, which brought a nostalgic feel to the project.

February 28, 1999 was chosen for the relighting ceremony. The windy February day was filled with excitement and anticipation. Historical reenactors added to the significance of the occasion and as the sun began to set over the water, fireworks erupted from the tower. A fully costumed Scottish bagpiper belted out a rendition of *Amazing Grace* as Grace Jackson Weaver, daughter of George Jackson, threw the switch, which brought the Tybee Island Lighthouse to life once again.

Today, the beautiful black lighthouse with the white band stands its post, where it has remained for over two hundred years. A tribute to the past and a light to guide the future.

TYBEE ISLAND

Tybee Island was named by the Indians who came from the interior to hunt and fish. Settled since the beginning of the colony of Georgia, it was the scene in 1775 of the first capture by the first Provincial vessel commissioned by any Congress in America for naval warfare in the Revolution, when a Georgia schooner captured an armed British vessel laden with military stores, in 1776 the royal Governor, Sir James Wright, broke his parol and escaped to a British man of war in Tybee Roads. The Council of Safety ordered all Tybee houses sheltering British officers and Tories destroyed and a raid on the island by the Patriot forces accomplished this purpose.

In 1779 a large French fleet under Count d'Estaing anchored off Tybee for two months during the siege of Savannah by the French and American forces. In the War Between the States, Federal troops erected batteries here for the reduction of nearby Fort Pulaski. Troops were trained on Tybee Island during both World Wars.

Tybee Museum, Fort Screven near the lighthouse, Tybee Island
GPS Coordinates: N32.02154, W80.844135

Tybee Island is possible the most eclectic beach community short of Key West. Everything about the island is diverse, including its history. Once believed to be a harsh environment for an established community, Tybee Island is now the most densely populated of any island on the Georgia coast. Originally, the island was home to the Guale Indians, who lived at one time on all of Georgia's barrier islands from Cumberland to Tybee, later the land was used as a camping ground for the Yamacraw, who fished and collected salt there. Over the next two hundred years, Tybee would be the temporary host to Native Americans, Spanish, French and eventually, the British laid claim to the land as part of the colony of Georgia.

Eventually the Spanish landed, Francisco Gordillo is thought to be the first around 1520. His purpose was believed to be gathering Native Americans as slaves, however, he sailed in disappointment. He left a knife and rosary on the island to mark his presence. Twenty years later another Spaniard, Hernando Desoto found the items while charting the island. Archeological explorations have noted the existence of a Spanish settlement once occupying the island. In 1733, Oglethorpe landed with his first one hundred colonists and developed the first Georgia city a short distance from the island at Savannah.

John Wesley took his first steps on American soil on Tybee Island and it was here, in 1736, that he knelt on the sandy shore and said a prayer of hope and well being for the colony. It was that same year that General Oglethorpe ordered a lighthouse erected on the north end of the island. Built on cedar piles with a brick base, the lighthouse was twenty-five feet square at the bottom and rose to a height of ninety feet. The light was fueled with whale oil. It had double duty as a lookout tower for Spanish invaders sneaking their way up the coast line to the Savannah River.

Men of honor used the remote location, before the Revolutionary War, as a dueling ground. These men were mainly Carolinians, who sought to avoid their state's anti-dueling laws. British regulars were used to construct a garrison called Fort Tybee in 1750, the fort was eventually rebuilt and called Fort Screven.

French Admiral D'Estaing used Tybee Island as his staging ground in 1779 during the Siege of Savannah to reclaim the city from the British. Admiral D'Estaing's attempt failed miserably and he sailed away leaving the Americans alone in their defeat. During the British occupation, loyalists used the island for a base of trade with merchant ships and in defiance, the Americans staged an attack and burned the Tory settlement to the ground. At the Revolution's end, it was from Tybee Island that loyalists escaped capture, fleeing to Canada and the West Indies.

Tybee Island was completely leveled in 1804 by to a violent hurricane. Every standing building lay in ruins as well as a two storied fortification that had been built on the adjacent Cockspur Island. During the War of 1812, Tybee's lighthouse was used as a signal tower to warn of attack by the British and although no attack ever came, another tower was built as a lookout post to guard the Savannah River. A lazaretto was built on the western tip of the island to hold slaves and other immigrants in quarantine to guard against contagious disease. Mass graves of the dead go unmarked on that end of island, many remain undiscovered to this day.

Twenty-five years later, in 1829, construction on Fort Pulaski began. Robert E. Lee was assigned as one of the military engineers to undertake its design and construction. During this time the island had few permanent residents and was only used for fishing and camping when weather permitted. In 1854, another hurricane pummeled the area. The forces of rain, wind and water were so strong that the courses of several area creeks were altered forever.

By the outbreak of the Civil War, Tybee would play an important military role in United States history. The first Confederate troops occupied the island in December 1861, the rebel forces would withdraw to Fort Pulaski under orders from Robert E. Lee to defend Savannah and the Savannah River. Union troops under the command of Quincy Adams Gilmore took control of Tybee and began constructing cannon batteries on the westside of the island facing Fort Pulaski about one mile away. Those batteries fired a new weapon called the rifled cannon at Fort Pulaski and changed forever the way coastal areas were protected. On April 11, 1862, after thirty hours of constant fire from the devastating rifled guns, Fort Pulaski surrendered and all bricked forts from that point on were considered obsolete.

After the Civil War, Dr. James P. Screven bought most of the island, but he failed to develop any of it. Large lots were eventually sold and by 1875, five people owned ninety percent of the island. It is thought that the other ten percent was owned by river pilots and their crews. In 1875, the United States Government leased 138 acres from the Screven estate and other landholders. The arrangement continued until 1946 when the lease was turned over to the Municipal Government of Savannah Beach.

The Tybee Improvement Company was formed in the early 1870s to promote the building of a seaside resort area on the island. A daily steamship service was established and in 1876, The Ocean House, Tybee's first major hotel was constructed. A wooden tramway was laid to transport hotel guests from the steamship pier on the north end to the resort along the oceanfront. A horse railway continued along Main Street to the inlet in order to provide guests with the option of bathing in the calm waters of the Back River. By the 1880s, the development of Tybee as a seaside resort was a great success; bathhouses, dancing pavilions, boarding houses and summer cottages were erected along the beachfront close to the hotel.

In 1885, the Tybee Beach Company obtained a controlling interest in the island with the intent to bring the resort into greater popularity and encouraged the sell of lots for permanent and seasonal residents. A railroad to Tybee was a necessity for further development and in 1887, the Savannah and Tybee Railroad was completed. The train not only cut the traveling time to the island in half, from an hour and a half to forty-five minutes, it also made the entire island accessible by offering eight stops between the north end and the inlet on Back River. The railroad continued to offer service until 1933, when U.S. Highway 80 was completed and made railroad passage a thing of past.

The last significant hurricane came ashore in 1898, over eighty percent of Tybee's structures sustained major damage. Although the exact number of dead is not known, the number is assumed to be quite high. Most were killed by the intense storm surge and flooding. The exact eye of the hurricane was to the south at Brunswick.

Today, Tybee Island offers the quiet surrounding of an old time beach community. As you cross the Lazaretto River bridge, a different feeling envelopes you, "Tybee time" has begun and the world slows. Tybee Island offers a wide range of amenities with hotels, restaurants and even the historic T.S. Chu's.

Although I hesitate to advertise, Chu's deserves a slight mention. T. S. Chu immigrated from China in the early 1900s, and it is said he slept in the dunes until he could afford better and things did get better for Chu. He began with a small market, that is, today, described as a retail empire consisting mostly of convenience stores and gas stations. T. S. Chu's first store remains open on the island and the store motto says it all "Anything you use, you'll find at Chu's." The store sells everything from tourist souvenirs to hammers and anything you can think of in between. Chu's is definitely a Tybee Island historic location.

Tybee Island has much to offer. The remaining historical sites include Fort Screven, the Tybee Island Lighthouse and Museum and nearby Fort Pulaski to name but a few. But most of all Tybee offers a feeling. The beach, the sea oats swaying in the breeze and smell of the salt sea spray from which, it is said, Tybee Island received her name: *tybee*, the Native American word for salt.

Tybee Museum, Fort Screven near the lighthouse, Tybee Island
GPS Coordinates: N32.02154, W80.844135

In 1872, President Cleveland commissioned Secretary of War, William C. Endicott to submit a plan for the protection of the United States Coast. After a year of travel and examination, Endicott submitted a four hundred page report calling for the construction of concrete and granite fortifications and requesting funds totaling ninety-seven million dollars to defend the coast. Congressional approval was slow due to the enormity of the plans and the massive amount of money required for the effort. In 1896, the contracts were finally approved and construction could begin on a new fort to be constructed on Tybee Island.

The fort was first dubbed Fort Tybee for obvious reasons, later called Camp Graham and then in April 1899 by Presidential Proclamation the name was officially changed to Fort Screven. The name was derived from General James Screven, who bravely gave his life during the Revolutionary War near Midway, Georgia, in 1778.

By the late 1800s, America was being drawn into war with Spain. Americans were incensed over Spain's treatment of the Cuban people. The Spanish government, in an effort to control guerrilla forces, herded the Cuban citizens into concentration camps. The conditions were deplorable, the very young and very old began to die.

Georgia coastal defenses were strengthened as war drew eminent. Temporary fortifications were constructed to guard entrances to Savannah, Darien, Brunswick and St. Marys. All but one of these was abandoned soon after the Spanish American War ended. The Savannah harbor was monitored by the USS *Amphitrite*, home based in Port Royal, South Carolina. She kept watch from Charleston to Savannah. The USS *Amphitrite* was a 262 foot long, double turreted monitor with a beam 55 feet wide. She was armed with four ten inch guns, two mounted forward and two aft. Originally built in 1874, she was refurbished in 1895. The *Amphitrite* carried a crew of two hundred men and thirteen officers.

In February 1898, the United States battleship *Maine* suddenly exploded and sank to the bottom of the Havana harbor. Two hundred and sixty-six American men were lost and although the sinking was ruled an accident, Americans believed that Spain had deliberately attacked the ship. American citizens demanded retribution. Theodore "Teddy" Roosevelt and his Rough Riders became famous for their charge up San Juan Hill during the four month war with Spain. Roosevelt returned a hero and was eventually elected to the highest office in the land. A total of four hundred sixty Americans were lost in what Roosevelt called, "a splendid little war."

Fort Screven's six batteries went to full alert, although they never saw any action, the fort was ready and willing. The fort was an active military base from the Spanish American War of 1898 through the end of World War II. The Coastal Artillery occupied the fort until 1929, when it was taken over by the famous 8th Infantry.

During the Great Depression, Fort Screven was commanded by Lieutenant Colonel George Catlett Marshall, who went on to command the entire United States military during World War II and authored the Marshall Plan. His efforts were rewarded with the Nobel Peace Prize in 1953.

In 1940, the Coastal Artillery Corps took over again. During the years of World War II, a diving school was established to train engineers for underwater salvage operations and to repair bomb damaged ports. The United States Army Engineer Diving and Salvage School became the only school of its type operated by the Army in the United States. At the end of World War II, the fort was declared surplus and sold to the City of Savannah Beach, now Tybee Island, for $200,000, which in turn auctioned it off to the public.

In 1961, Battery Garland, the former gun battery and magazine for a twelve inch, long range gun became the Tybee Museum. Rooms, which once stored six hundred pound projectiles and two hundred pound bags of gunpowder, are now home to the collections and exhibits telling the story of over four hundred years of Tybee Island history.

Fort Screven

Between February 21 and April 9, 1862, Federal troops under Gen. Quincy A. Gillmore erected 36 guns in 11 batteries, extending eastwardly on Tybee Island from Lazeretto Creek opposite Fort Pulaski. Two of the Federal batteries consisted of rifled cannon. The work was carried on under cover of darkness and was concealed by day behind camouflage of branches and brushwood. The Fort was defended by a garrison of 385 men under Col. Charles H. Olmstead of Savannah. Twenty of the 48 guns faced the Federal batteries, but when the bombardment of the fort began from the shore the defenders of the Fort found that they were of insufficient range to damage the attackers. After a continuous bombardment of 30 hours the walls were breached and the Fort was surrendered. It was the first effective use of rifled cannon against a masonry fortification and thus marked an epoch in military history.

US 80 east of Lazaretto Creek, Tybee Island
GPS Coordinates: N32.01526, W80.875935

Joseph Brown, Georgia's Governor in 1861, issued an order to Colonel Alexander Lawton in command of the 1st Volunteer Regiment, to take Fort Pulaski. Colonel Lawton and his men boarded the side wheel steamboat *Ida*, for the journey down river. Marching boldly into the fort with drums tapping in unison and colors flying, they found that there were no Union troops garrisoned at the fort.

Union forces did plan to retake the fort. In October 1861, Captain Samuel F. DuPont commanded a fifty-one ship flotilla, manned with 12,500 troops in all. The troops were commanded by Brigadier General Thomas Sherman[43], who sailed under sealed orders from Hampton Roads, Virginia to South Carolina. Hilton Head and Bay Point were taken on November 7, 1861, and Port Royal followed a few days later. The Union used these beachheads as headquarters, while preparing to take Fort Pulaski.

Meanwhile at Fort Pulaski, Confederate Colonel Charles Olmstead was appointed to command the garrison of three hundred eighty-five officers and men, who had forty-eight guns between them. The Confederates connected a telegraph line between the fort and Savannah so that immediate communication for supplies and reinforcements could be established. General Robert E. Lee arrived in Savannah to reinforce its coastal defense in the fall of 1861. The residents of the sea islands had evacuated, so Lee ordered the troops to remove the guns from the batteries and return to Fort Pulaski.

Tybee Island was abandoned in November and all guns were ferried to Fort Pulaski. The Confederate troops placed submerged mines on the river channels as protection against Union gun boat attacks. Facing Cockspur Island, McQueens Island was predominantly marsh and not suitable for the placement of an artillery battery. The distance between the fort and Tybee Island was more than one thousand yards. Tybee and McQueens Islands were considered one continuous land mass, separated only by a small creek called Lazaretto. The longest firing distance of smooth bore guns and mortars, during that time, did not exceed seven hundred yards. Fort Pulaski was considered to be quite safe. In fact, General Lee remarked to Colonel Olmstead, "Colonel, they will make it pretty warm for you here with shells, but they cannot breach your walls at that distance." Even the United States Chief of Engineers, General Totten had said before the war, "you might as well bombard the Rocky Mountain."

General Thomas Sherman's Chief Engineer, Captain Quincy A. Gillmore had another thought. Advanced technology in weaponry was of great interest to Captain Gillmore and he remembered an 1859 experimental rifle cannon the United States Army had toyed with and then discarded. This was to be his "Secret Weapon." Risking the ridicule of his superior officers and colleagues, Captain Gillmore proposed the use of the rifle cannon and much to his surprise, General Thomas Sherman agreed. Captain Gillmore began working on a plan. He well understood the art of war, where secrecy, surprise and ingenuity were paramount.

From February 21 until April 9, 1862, materials, supplies, ammunition and guns were unloaded through the breaking surf and then transported long distances across the sand and marsh. Roads were built, gun emplacements, magazines and bomb proof shelters all were constructed. Gun crews were trained. Fording the last mile of shoreline was the most difficult; the shore was nothing more than an open marsh and worse yet, in full view of the fort as well as within range of the Confederate guns. Captain Gillmore ordered his men to work only at night and to speak in whispered tones. Before dawn, evidence of the night's work was camouflaged by building sand dunes in front of the works. The cannons were hauled across the marsh on sling carts, each cart requiring the strength of two hundred and fifty men to move it. At various distances, thirty-six cannons and mortars were positioned in eleven batteries.

General Thomas Sherman was replaced by General David Hunter in March 1862, but Captain Gillmore retained command of the post. The Confederates followed General Lee's instructions at Fort Pulaski, piling sandbags between the guns and digging "rat holes" in the terreplein[44] for the protection of the gunners. The Confederate soldiers cut the fort's interior ground into wide traps and trenches to prevent Union cannon balls and shells from rolling into the structure of the fort. On the evening before the battle, a large audience in Savannah, attended a concert performed by a famous African American pianist, Blind Tom, who played his original composition, *The Battle of Manassas*. Everyone enjoyed the evening with no knowledge of the battle yet to come.

The Union dispatched Lieutenant James H. Wilson, under a flag of truce, to Fort Pulaski with a formal demand to surrender on April 10, 1862. Colonel Olmstead replied that his duty was to defend the fort. Union guns opened fire at 8:10 a.m. It was time for Union soldiers to avenge Fort Sumter, two days shy of the first anniversary of the beginning of the Civil War.

The guns from Fort Pulaski returned fire. Soon the exchange fire from each side was rapid and increasingly accurate. The Union rifle guns performed as expected and their shells penetrated the thick wall of the fort. The southeast side of the fort began to flake away to the depth of two to four feet. The shots from the fort began to waver, the batteries on Tybee were nearly all masked behind a low sand ridge and were protected by heavy sandbags; General Gillmore's plan was ingenious.

When the projectiles from the rifle batteries began striking the walls of the north magazine, where 40,000 pounds of gunpowder were stored, Colonel Olmstead knew the fort was in danger of exploding. It was too late to wire Savannah for reinforcements, there was not enough time to organize a rescue effort. In an act of bravery, Colonel Olmstead decided to surrender the fort to save the lives of his men. At 2:30 p.m. on April 11, 1862, after thirty hours of Union bombardment, Fort Pulaski surrendered. It was an unconditional surrender.

Meanwhile, Union General Henry Benham made ready to storm the fort with his 10,000 troops in direct assault, if the Confederate continued to resist. The Union continued to hold Fort Pulaski until the Civil War came to an end.

US 80 west of Lazaretto Creek, Tybee Island
GPS Coordinates: N32.0136, W80.890757

Native Americans first inhabited the tiny island called Tybee. The island, a mere two and a half miles long and only two-thirds of a mile wide, was named for the Native American word for salt. During the 1500s, the Spanish settled on Tybee but the effects of brutal storms and malaria soon drove them away. The Spanish believed Tybee to be an unhealthy place. The Spanish surmised that diseased vapors were emitted from the marsh grasses and flowed on the wind. The Native Americans had a different view, they believed the sea air at Tybee had healing properties. General James Edward Oglethorpe arrived at Tybee two hundred years after the Spanish first claimed the land. Oglethorpe began developing the colony he called Georgia, now claimed for England.

General Oglethorpe insisted on an anti-slavery provision in Georgia's original charter. Planters concluded that the only way to make cultivation successful was with the use of slave labor. Using the example of their Carolina neighbors, in 1749, the Georgia colonists repealed Oglethorpe's provision and passed an act allowing for the use of slave labor. The act was passed with an amendment. In order to allow slavery, a Lazaretto[45] Station was required. Tybee Island was chosen for the sight due to its remote location away from Savannah proper. In 1767, one hundred acres were purchased from Josiah Tattnall on the extreme western tip of the island bordering a waterway that became known as Lazaretto Creek.

Several hospital buildings with wards for the sick were completed during the next year. All ships were required to make port at the Lazaretto Quarantine Station before being allowed to enter the Savannah Harbor. Slaves were automatically detained for four months in an attempt to avoid the spread of contagious disease. When a person died, they were buried on the island in an unmarked grave.

The station was used continuously until 1785. Harsh weather and salty breezes took their toll on the buildings, with the hospital in a state of complete state of disrepair, it was decided that a new quarantine station would be built on Cockspur Island. The Lazaretto Quarantine Station at Tybee Island was abandoned.

ROGER LACY (LACEY)

Roger Lacy (Lacey) arrived in Savannah in 1734. While a resident of the Georgia Colony, he spent most of his time at a trading post in Augusta. There he gained employment as a trader and served as the post commander. Roger Lacy (Lacey) was a member of Masonic Lodge No. 44 at Swan Tavern in Long Acre, London. He received an appointment as a Steward of the Grand Lodge of England, January 29, 1731. Thomas Thynne, Viscount Weymouth, Grand Master of the Grand Lodge of England, granted a deputation to him for constituting a lodge at Savannah. This lodge, now known as Solomon's Lodge No.1, Savannah, Georgia, was one of the lodges which created the Grand Lodge of Georgia, December 16, 1786. Roger Lacey Lodge No. 722, F. & A.M., Savannah, Georgia, is named in honor of Roger Lacy (Lacey).

One half block south of Victory Drive on River Drive, Thunderbolt
GPS Coordinates: N32.0327, W81.050086

Freemasonry actually began when General James Edward Oglethorpe stepped off the *Ann* onto the shores of the Georgia colony. Oglethorpe organized the first lodge in Savannah in 1734 and was the first Master of the Lodge. In December 1735, the lodge was registered with the Grand Lodge of England as The Lodge at Savannah in Ye Province of Georgia.

Recorded in the annals of the Grand Lodge of England is this notation, indicating that numerous Masons were traveling to the New World and the Grand Lodge, intended to aid in their support,

> "collect the Charity of this Society towards enabling the Trustees (of Georgia) to send distressed Brethren to Georgia where they may be comfortably provided for...that it be strenuously recommended by the Masters and Wardens of regular Lodges to make a generous collection amongst all their Members for that purpose..."

Roger Hugh Lacey arrived in the Georgia colony in 1736 and carried a Deputation from the Grand Master of Masons in England to establish a Savannah lodge. The Lodge at Savannah changed its name in 1770 to Solomon's Lodge No. 1 and it remained under the leadership of the Grand Lodge of England until the Grand Lodge of Georgia was created, December 16, 1786.

Two short lived lodges were created in Savannah during the late 1700s, Unity Lodge and the Grenadiers. Except for these two instances, Solomon's Lodge was the only Georgia Lodge from 1734 until 1785. Solomon's Lodge is known as the Mother Lodge of Georgia, the second lodge to be constituted in North America and is now the oldest continuously operating lodge in the Western Hemisphere.

A faction of the Freemasons broke away from Solomon's Lodge in 1784, over a disagreement in the direction of the lodge. The two factions soon overcame their differences and with the addition of lodges in Augusta and another in Washington, Georgia, the four lodges banded together to become the most Worshipful Grand Lodge of Free and Accepted Masons for the State of Georgia on December 16, 1786. Over the next thirteen years, eight more Georgia lodges were created. With the exception of Solomon's Lodge, no other lodge has endured.

By late 1958, the membership of Solomon's Lodge had grown to such proportions that the wait to rise in the ranks was considerable. It was decided that another lodge would be formed thus the Roger Lacy Lodge was constituted on December 6, 1958. Roger Lacy Lodge and Solomon's Lodge are identical in both ancient works and rituals. Though the Roger Lacy Lodge had only a forty-five year history, its membership has grown to 181 strong. Though only chartered for forty-five years, the roots of the Roger Lacy Lodge have been firmly set since 1735 with the formation of Solomon's Lodge.

Today, Georgia claims 451 Lodges and boasts over 70,000 members.

SAVANNAH STATE COLLEGE

This state college was established in 1891 as the Georgia Industrial College for Colored Youths as an outgrowth of the Second Morrill Act of 1890 and an Act of the Georgia General Assembly, November 26, 1890, creating this institution as one of the original Negro land-grant colleges. The initial session was held at the Baxter Street School in Athens from June to August, 1891. In October of the same year, the school sessions began on the present site. Its initial educational program was agricultural, mechanical and literary, and by 1898, the college was able to award its first degree.

It was the first public institution of higher learning to be established for Negroes in the state and now is a part of the University System of Georgia.

The first president (1891-1921) of the college was Major R. R. Wright who, when just a lad, was asked by General O. O. Howard of the Freedman's Bureau what message should he take back to the people of the North, Young Wright's famous answer was, "Just tell them, we are rising." His answer inspired the poet, John Greenleaf Whittier to write the poem, "The Little Black Boy of Atlanta."

Near Colston Administration Building, B.J. James Drive, Savannah
GPS Coordinates: N32.02363, W81.055879

The Second Morrill Act of 1890 stated that Congress would appropriate funds for the establishment of colleges providing education in agriculture and the mechanical arts. The legislation went on to specify that no college would be granted funds, if a distinction of race or color was made in the admission of student and allowed that separate colleges for white and African American students to be established and funded only if the grant money was divided equally between the two.

It was under this act that Georgia State Industrial College for Colored Youth was founded in 1890. The college is the oldest college dedicated to the education of African Americans in Georgia. The school was originally located in Athens and by October 7, 1891, the Georgia State Industrial College moved into its permanent home on La Roche Avenue in Savannah. The college has remained in this location since that time.

Major Richard R. Wright Sr. was named the first president in 1891 and continued his tenure until 1921. It was under the administration of the school's third president, Benjamin F. Hubert, that the college in 1928 was granted permission to issue formal degrees at graduation. In 1932, Georgia State Industrial College for Colored Youths became simply, Georgia State College.

Dr. William K. Payne, the college's fifth president, saw the name of the school change again. The school would now be known as Savannah State College. In 1996, the Board of Regents of the University System of Georgia granted Savannah State College status and the school became Savannah State University.

As of July 1997, Dr. Carlton E. Brown assumed leadership of Savannah State University. The University is located on one hundred sixty-five acres of beautiful salt marsh. The latest enrollment was 2,200 students with an overwhelming majority of them from Georgia. The University offers twenty-five undergraduate programs and three graduate degrees.

Savannah State University offers a wide range of collegiate sports for both men and women as well as a variety of extracurricular activities, including the Wesleyan Gospel Choir, Student Government, the school newspaper, a number of performing arts groups, academic clubs, fraternities and sororities. The school can claim more than 20,000 living alumni throughout the world and in every imaginable career endeavor. There are approximately fifty alumni chapters nationwide. Savannah State University continues to provide a quality education and bright future for its students. Words quoted from Savannah State University's first president, Major Richard R. Wright, from poet John Greenleaf Whittier's, "The Little Black Boy of Atlanta", "Just tell them, we are rising."

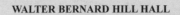

WALTER BERNARD HILL HALL

This is the oldest building on the Savannah State University campus. It was constructed in 1901 by the students and faculty of then Georgia State Industrial College during the administration of the college's first president, Richard R. Wright, Sr. It is named for the chancellor of the University of Georgia at that time. President William Howard Taft visited Hill Hall in 1912 and African American soldiers trained here during World War I. The building has served as a dormitory, library, classroom and administrative building, student center, bookstore, and post office.

Alexis Circle, Savannah State University, Savannah
GPS Coordinates: N32.02415, W81.056534

S avannah State University moved to Savannah after its brief beginning in Athens on October 7, 1891. Major Richard R. Wright, Sr. was the first president. Architectural plans for a new building were drawn in 1900 and soon construction began on the building to be named for Walter Bernard Hill, then chancellor of the University of Georgia. The building would forever be known as Hill Hall.

Said to be the oldest building on the Savannah State campus, this is most likely incorrect, since the college occupied the location for nine years preceding Hill Hall's construction. The building was constructed utilizing student and faculty labor and upon completion in 1901, the building was to be a men's dormitory.

Over the years, Hill Hall served a variety of purposes including that of a library, classroom, administrative building, student center, bookstore and post office. The grand three storied brick building was the center of campus activity for many years. The heart pine staircase served as a natural setting for students posing in their caps and gowns before they took that momentous walk to receive their diplomas and go out into the world. When first built, the kitchen and dining room occupied the first floor while the second and third floors were open, like a general ward or barracks. Later the larger rooms were partitioned, two boys to a room and a library replaced the dining room.

Hill Hall, a place of history, not only sheltering young students as they grew into educated men but the building was also refuge for African American soldiers as they trained to meet their country's call to arms in World War I. By 1966, Hill Hall began to show its age of sixty-five years. Students banded together, staged a strike and sit in over the deplorable conditions of the aging building. Little but cosmetic improvements were made at that time.

Hill Hall was recognized, in 1992, as a historic site and placed on the National Register of Historic Places. This distinction qualified the building to receive restoration funding from the Black College Initiative of the Department of the Interior. Hill Hall was one of only eleven buildings chosen throughout the country. Unfortunately, it took four years for Savannah State University to receive the funding and by the time money was released, it had become necessary to close Hill Hall.

The floors that born the weight of thousands of students over the years began to sag and school officials feared for the stability of the ninety-five year old building. The Black College Initiative grant amounted to $625,000 and would be enough to begin restoration, although much more money would have to raised before the needed repairs could be completed. The students and faculty took an active role in raising funds, though a much needed boost would come from an unlikely source. In 1998, Hill Hall was leased for use in the John Travolta movie, *The General's Daughter*.

The rehabilitation effort would require $2.5 million to complete. A benefit gala raised $75,000, the University of Georgia Board of Regents pledged $395,000 and incredibly, Paramount Pictures donated $50,000 to the project. By the end of the year, phase one, including roof repairs and asbestos removal was under way. Then tragedy struck.

On May 8, 2000, flames poured out of the upper stories of Hill Hall. Black smoke filled the air as firefighters rushed to the scene to do what they could to save the building. Firefighters were unable to enter the building due to the intensity of the heat, instead they kept a steady stream of water on the structure. The students, faculty and alumni of Savannah State University were devastated. Hill Hall suffered extensive damage, the roof collapsed in several places but Hill Hall stood fast and refused to fall. The cause of the fire was believed to be electrical.

Hill Hall is currently undergoing restoration.

MERCER AUTO CAMP

In 1910 and 1911 the Mercer Automobile Company of Trenton, New Jersey made entries in the Great Savannah races. Washington Roebling II, the only company owner who drove in the races, and driver Hughie Hughes led teams in several light car and grand prix events. Hughes won the 222.82 mile 1911 Savannah Challenge Race, running at an average speed of 70 mph. The camp, built on this site along the race course, provided housing for team members; garage space; and storage space for spare parts, fuel and other necessities. It was destroyed by Hurricane David in 1979.

103 LaRoche at Majestic Oaks Drive, Savannah
GPS Coordinates: N31.98204, W81.070288

The Mercer Automobile Company was founded in May 1909, located in Mercer County, Trenton, New Jersey. The company was a consolidation of the former Walter Automobile Company and Roebling Planche Cars, which were built in an old brewery. The first Mercers were loud, thundering machines with a monocle windshield, a round gas tank and two bucket seats wedged in between. The body consisted of a hood with arched fenders, usually painted bright canary yellow and understandably, called Raceabouts.

The first Mercer ever assembled rolled out in 1910. By 1911, Mercers were entered in six major motoring events and were victorious in five. The light weight, eager Beaver L-head and 300 cubic inch piston displacement T-head engines helped Mercer set World Class records, eight of which were set by racing legend, Ralph DePalma.

The biggest races during this time were held in Savannah. In 1910 and 1911, the American Grand Prize Race and the Vanderbilt Cup were both held there and a Mercer was entered in each race.

Life around the race course was a city unto itself. The Mercer Automobile Company sponsored housing for drivers, mechanics and what we would think of today as pit crews; buildings were constructed for garage space and storage for parts, tools and all of the elements required to keep an automobile running well on the course. However after 1911, cars no longer raced in Savannah. Mercer Auto Camp, once filled with the excited voices of greasy mechanics and adrenaline filled drivers, was an abandoned village.

The remnants of Mercer Auto Camp remained over time, a virtual ghost town of long forgotten races that were seldom mentioned, if they were acknowledged at all. Savannah citizens driving down LaRoche Road sometimes noticed the old weather worn shacks but assumed they were old slave shanties. Most people speeding by in their cars, barely noticed the old stick shacks at all.

In September 1979, Hurricane David wiped away the last reminder of racing in Savannah. David blew in with ninety-two mile per hour winds off Ossabaw Sound. The hurricane made landfall south of Savannah and circled up the coast on a destructive path toward New England. When he left David took with him the old stick shacks that had once been Mercer Auto Camp. Savannah survived the hurricane and suffered for a week or two without power as downed lines were repaired.

Strangely, the area around LaRoche Road and Majestic Oaks Drive seemed desolate. Perhaps when all is quiet and still, the thunderous roar of a Mercer still bellows in the distance and the laughter of mechanics and drivers can be heard drifting across the marsh.

ISLE OF HOPE
NATIONAL HISTORIC DISTRICT

In 1736, Noble Jones, John Fallowfield and Henry Parker settled this important outpost on the colony's inland water-way to the south and named it Isle of Hope. Jones' Wormsloe Plantation was fortified and armed against Spanish attack until 1742. The Island developed peacefully through the Revolution, still important as an inland port. The 1800s brought more residents and farms. Although strongly armed during the Civil War, no action took place. By 1870 daily trains served the growing interest in the island as a resort. Barbee's Pavilion, at the river terminus of the railroad, became world renown in the 1920s. Activity centered on the river and many large homes were built. Isle of Hope continues today as a tranquil outpost of coastal life.

LaRouche Avenue before Tuten Fish Camp at Isle of Hope[46]
Skidaway Road 1/4 mile from entrance of Wormsloe
GPS Coordinates: N31.99488, W81.057268

Southeast of Savannah, where Laroche Avenue meets Bluff Drive, is the historic village known as the Isle of Hope. The name is deceptive in that the Isle of Hope is not an island at all, but a peninsula or sandy beach head. The Isle features areas of high bluffs with magnificent views of Skidaway Island across the Intracoastal Waterway to Skidaway Narrow and the Isle of Hope River.

The Isle of Hope was established as a retreat for Savannah's most prominent citizens in the 19th century. The cool breezes brought relief from the intense summer heat. The Isle provided a safe haven from the malaria outbreaks so common in the summer months.

The distinctive community was first settled in 1736 by Noble Jones, John Fallowfield and Henry Parker, although the land was originally deeded to Henry Parker alone. It was thought in 1736, that the Isle would provide an important defensive out-post to lend added protection of Savannah to the south. A fort was established at Wormsloe Plantation owned by Noble Jones, in 1742, as a defense against the Spaniards attacking from their base at St. Augustine.

The land was divided into lots and sold in the 1850s and 1860s. The population began to grow and a small community known as Parkersburg was created. The Isle of Hope was never seriously threatened by either the American Revolution or the Civil War. Although a Confederate hospital was established there during the Civil War and General William T. Sherman briefly visited. The Isle of Hope was never the site of any significant battle.

In 1871, a railroad was built to connect the city of Savannah with the Isle of Hope and daily commuter service was estab-lished at the requests of wealthy land owners. The Isle of Hope was, by the early 20th century, not only a popular resort escape but residents began establishing permanent homes in which they lived year round. By 1920, the Barbee Pavilion, where the river and the railroad met, became a world renowned retreat.

The houses built from the middle 1800s until the turn to century ranged from Greek Revival, Victorian and Neoclassical architecture to Craftsman Bungalows constructed for the use of the working class. Most of the residences had formal and informal gardens, while the landscape was graced by ancient live oaks dripping with gray streamers of Spanish moss.

Today, visitors to the Isle of Hope have many options for sightseeing. Wormsloe Plantation is open to the public for tours as a state park; the Bethesda Orphanage, the oldest still operating orphanage in America, has a museum dedicated to the long and distinguished history of facility; and the Isle of Hope Marina offers boating charters for outdoor enthusiasts. Isle of Hope has beautiful historic homes and old summer cottages adding seaside charm to the picturesque community.

NOBLE JONES' "WORMSLOW"
1736-1775

This 1 1/2-mile oak avenue leads to the tabby ruins of Noble Jones' colonial fortified plantation. Jones and his family were original settlers in Georgia, arriving in Savannah with founder James E. Oglethorpe on February 1, 1733. As a middle-class carpenter from England, Jones would perform a variety of roles in the new colony of Georgia including: constable, physician, surveyor, Indian agent, soldier, member of the royal council, treasurer, and senior justice of the province, in 1736, Jones leased 500 acres from the Trustees of Georgia and in 1745, finished construction of the fortified home he named "Wormslow". From this outpost, Jones commanded a company of marines charged with patrolling the inland water route and alerting Savannah of any Spanish attack. Wormslow was also well known for its horticultural efforts. Indigo, rice and silk were all cultivated here by Jones, his indentured servants, and later slaves. Following generations of the Jones family lived at Wormsloe for over two centuries, building on their ancestor's prominent role in Georgia history. The tabby ruins of the original "Wormslow" home survive as the last architectural remnant of Savannah from the Oglethorpe era (1733- 1743).

Wormsloe at museum parking lot, Savannah
GPS Coordinates: N31.9633, W81.069859

Noble Jones arrived among the first one hundred in the Georgia colony with General James Edward Oglethorpe. In 1736, he leased five hundred acres of property from the Georgia trustees on the Isle of Hope about ten miles south of Savannah. Wormslow was the name he chose for the plantation created there. John Fallowfield was allotted the adjoining property, though eventually Jones expanded his holding to include that land as well.

In 1739, Jones began to build his home made of fortified tabby. The construction was interrupted on two different occasions during the War of Jenkins Ear, an altercation with Spain concerning claim to the Georgia colony. After the Spanish were defeated at the Battle of Bloody Marsh, invasive threats were no longer uppermost in the colonists' minds and construction resumed on Jones' plantation home.

The house was one and a half stories with four bastions for protection against attack from all sides. Clearing land, Jones began cultivating cotton, rice and mulberry trees for the production of raw silk and he owned cattle as well. In 1756, Jones received a royal grant and his ownership was finalized.

During this time, Noble Jones commanded a company of Marine boatmen who patrolled the waters near Savannah's port, serving as constable, soldier and Indian agent. He was appointed to governmental positions as Royal Council member, treasurer and assistant to the President of the Colony and Justice of the Province. Noble Jones died in 1775, on the eve of the American Revolution. Wormslow Plantation was bequeathed to his daughter, Mary Jones Bulloch until her death in 1795, when the property passed to her brother, Noble Wimberly Jones.

While the father had remained a loyalist, Noble Wimberly (N. W.) Jones was a patriot and noted Georgia statesman. He was elected to the Commons House of Assembly during its first session and attended the First Provincial Congress in 1775. He was elected to the Council of Safety and became the friend and confidante of Benjamin Franklin.

N. W. was with the Liberty Boys when large quantities of gunpowder was stolen from the Royal Powder Magazine and later used against the British in Boston. When the British took Savannah in 1778, N. W. fled to Charles Towne where he was promptly captured and imprisoned. After his release at the end of the Revolution, N. W. gave up public service and practiced medicine. Although he had received no formal training, N. W. had apprenticed under his father becoming a very well known and respected physician. In 1804, he helped organize the first Georgia Medical Society and served as the society's first President.

Noble Wimberly Jones was never a permanent resident at Wormslow during his adult years. He did live there for a short time during 1796, after the death of his sister to ensure that the property was taken care of. After his death in 1806, Wormslow declined. When his son, George, moved there in 1828, the original tabby house was in such a sad state that he was forced to abandon it. George built a two storied frame house to the north of the original structure on a waterway called Jones Narrows.

As the Civil War approached, earthworks were built along the river at Wormslow. The fortification was known as Fort Wimberly. The fort was never manned and saw little, if any, fighting. Union troops seized Savannah in 1864 and in December of that year, raided Wormslow and ransacked the house, though the dwelling was not burned. Wormslow was confiscated but in 1865, the plantation was returned to the Jones family.

In 1880, the property was willed to George's son. He changed his name from George Frederick Tilghman Jones to George Wymberley Jones De Renne and the spelling of Wormslow became Wormsloe. De Renne made a number of changes and improvements to the plantation. Today, visitors enter the grounds of the plantation beneath the branches of four hundred ancient oaks planted along the roadway on the ocassion of the birth of his son, Wymberley Wormsloe De Renne. The drive is quite possibly one of the most pleasant to be found. The overlapping live oak branches let in only mere beams of light that dapple the unpaved road. The entrance to Wormsloe is marked by an impressive masonry arch that was erected when young Wymberley came of age. Two dates are engraved in the massive structure, 1733, the date of Noble Jones arrival in the New World and 1913, the date that the arch was put in place.

On the left of the road traveling down the shaded drive is the 1828 Jones family home and further down is a silo left from the dairy operation which was in use in 1910 for about thirty years. This was the last agricultural endeavor of Wormsloe Plantation. The tabby ruins of Noble Jones' first home can be seen, as well as the family cemetery.

Noble Jones was originally buried here in the family cemetery alongside his wife, Sarah and their young son, Indigo. Jones was eventually moved to the Colonial Park Cemetery and later, his great grandson, George Wymberley Jones De Renne, had him disinterred and placed at Bonaventure. In 1875, a stone monument was placed in his memory at the Wormsloe family cemetery.

The ruins of Noble Jones' 1737 home are the only remains of the colony's first structures. After the construction of the 1828 house, the Jones family continued to make it their primary residence. The 1828 house and over sixty-fives acres of the original Wormsloe Plantation still remains in the Jones family to this day.

The Jones family donated 822 acres of the historical plantation to the Nature Conservancy in 1972. The Conservancy eventually turned the property over to the state of Georgia. Today, the historic site is part of the Georgia State Parks system and is opened to the public Tuesday through Sunday. A small fee is charged to visit the historic Wormslow Plantation.

ISLE OF HOPE
METHODIST CHURCH

The Isle of Hope Methodist Church was organized in 1851. The first Trustees were George w. Wylly, Simeon T. Murphy, John B. Hogg, William Waite, Theodore Goodwin, Thomas J. Barnsley and the Rev. William S. Baker.

The church building that stands here was erected in 1859 on land given by Dr. Stephen Dupon. Its architecture is similar to that of the early churches at Midway and Ebenezer. The gallery at the rear of the church was built primarily for the accommodations of slaves.

Symbolic of the hospitality extended by the Church to all faiths is the large key that hangs outside the entrance.

During the War Between the States a Confederate battery stood on the church lot, mounting two 8-inch columbiads and two 32-pounder cannon. The church was used as a hospital for Confederates stationed in the area, the pews (still in existence) serving as beds. Thirty-three Effingham County soldiers sleep in the adjoining churchyard.

Parkersburg Road at church, Isle of Hope
GPS Coordinates: N31.98197, W81.058953

The Isle of Hope Methodist Church was erected in 1859 on the eve of the Civil War. As the area developed the need for a Methodist place of worship was recognized. Under the direction of a board of trustees, the first edifice was built. The Reverend William S. Baker served as the first minister for the Isle of Hope congregation. The church was a typical 1700 ecclesiastical sanctuary; a wooden, whitewashed structure with a gallery so that slaves could attend services.

The churchyard was utilized as a Confederate battery in 1863 and by 1864, the edifice was converted into a Confederate hospital. The wooden pews were used as makeshift beds, many of which can still be found inside the church. The names of Confederate soldiers injured during battle are still evident in their carvings on the pews. Many of the pews bear the names of southern soldiers, who spent their last moments leaving a permanent mark of their existence.

Although the church was spared General Sherman's torch, the church bell was melted and formed into cannonballs.

Today, the Isle of Hope Methodist Church is still active, holding regularly scheduled services at 412 Parkersburg Road. Alongside the church is the historic cemetery, which provides the final place of rest for thirty-three Confederate soldiers from Effingham County. Perhaps their names could be found scratched on pews inside.

Isle of Hope Methodist Church

BETHESDA: ITS FOUNDING

The idea of establishing an orphanage in Georgia was suggested by Charles Wesley and James Edward Oglethorpe. Enthusiastically embraced by the Reverend George Whitefield, he labored toward that end after his arrival in Georgia in 1738.

Through his efforts substantial sums were raised and a grant of 500 acres obtained in 1739 from the Trustees of the Colony. Site of the Orphan House (far removed from "the wicked influence of the town") was selected by Whitefield's faithful co-worker, James Habersham, who wrote, "The boys and girls will be taught to labor for their souls as well as for their daily bread."

March 25, 1740, Whitefield laid the first brick in the Orphan House to which he gave the name Bethesda, hoping it would ever prove what the word imported, "the House of Mercy", November 3, 1740, 61 children took up residence at the "Great House", described by an English traveler of the period as a "square building of very large dimensions, the foundations of which are of brick, with chimneys of the same; the rest of the superstructure of wood".

Since then hundreds of young people have gone forth from Bethesda's sheltering arms to make their mark in the world, among them Governor John Milledge and General Lachlan McIntosh.

Bethesda, Ferguson Avenue off Whitfield Avenue
GPS Coordinates: N31.96075, W81.096193

The new millennium brought about many firsts, however, the year 2000 also celebrated the 260th anniversary of Reverend George Whitfield's dream, the Bethesda Home for Boys. The Bethesda Orphanage, translated means "the House of Mercy," lays claim to the original five hundred acres of land deeded by General James Edward Oglethorpe.

America's oldest home for children opened in 1740. Oglethorpe and brothers, John and Charles Wesley, originally conceived the notion after being faced with an abundance of children, whose parents had been lost due to disease and the harsh living conditions. The prominent clergy approached colleague, the Reverend George Whitefield with the idea; embracing the project, he worked tirelessly for the remainder of his life to provide for his beloved Bethesda. Many notable Savannah citizens joined in the quest including James Habersham, a lifelong friend of Whitefield's.

The children of Bethesda began their day at 5:00 a.m. with morning prayers. Their daily routine consisted of picking cotton, spinning, knitting, kitchen chores and caring for the animals. When the sun dropped low in the sky, oral examinations were given on what the students had learned through their labors. After evening vespers, the exhausted students had no complaint about a 9:00 p.m. bedtime. Whitefield believed in the adage, "An idle brain is the devil's workshop."[47] Whitefield was quoted as having said,

> "No time is allowed for idleness or play, which are Satan's darling hours to tempt children to all manner of wickedness, as lying, cursing, swearing, uncleanness."

Today, the Bethesda Home for Boys continues in the tradition of Reverend Whitefield. Boys aging from six to fourteen experiencing difficulties at home, in school or in society, are guided by a professional staff of teachers, social workers, counselors, ministers and house parents. Bethesda provides counseling and life skills education to the boys enrolled in either a residential or day program.

Bethesda opens her arms with an impressive brick archway that frames a lane of ancient live oaks. A sense of peace overwhelms, as if the comfort of Whitefield still lingers. Gently rolling pastures embrace either side of the oaks leading to the heart of Bethesda and the marshlands beyond.

Nature's beauty extends as far as the eye can see. Bethesda provides a calming effect to youths who have experienced some of life's harder lessons. The natural environment provides an opportunity for fishing, animal care and forestry studies.

The grounds feature a causeway through marshland that leads to a covered dock, a gift from the graduating class of 1996, as well as the Mallory Boush Nature Trail dedicated in 1993.

Historical remnants include the old Bern bell, which has awakened thousands of boys for morning prayers and called them home each evening. The Whitefield Memorial Chapel, a tribute to Reverend Whitefield, provides a place for spiritual direction. The Cunningham Museum exhibits artifacts revealing the stories of Bethesda's history.

Reverend George Whitefield's dream not only became a reality but continues to provide a "House of Mercy" after more than 260 years.

Bethesda Home for Boys

BETHESDA:
HIGHLIGHTS OF ITS HISTORY

The interest of George Whitefield in the institution he founded here never flagged. During his lifetime he paid frequent visits to what he called "my beloved Bethesda, surely the most delightful place in all the southern part of America."

Whitefield's will left Bethesda in trust to Selina, Countess of Huntingdon. In 1773 lightning and fire damaged the main building, enlarged 4 years previously by the addition of two wings. Repairs were made as a result of her benevolence.

Her plans to establish a college at Bethesda were thwarted by the American Revolution. During that struggle the Georgia House of Assembly appointed trustees to manage the property.

In 1788, under the patronage of the Countess of Huntingdon, Bethesda was opened as a college. Following her death in 1791 the existing Board of Trustees was incorporated by Act of the Legislature and the State assumed control of the property.

During the next ten years Bethesda fell into decay. Revived in 1801, the school was closed 4 years later following a disastrous fire. In 1855 the Union Society acquired the property and recommenced the great work begun by the Reverend Whitefield.

Bethesda, Ferguson Avenue off Whitfield Avenue
GPS Coordinates: N31.96075, W81.096193

The life long passion of Reverend George Whitefield began at the request of General James Edward Oglethorpe and the Wesley Brothers. Reverend Whitefield along with his friend, James Habersham, were quickly enticed to bring to fruitation the vision of a Georgia orphanage. Oglethorpe procured a land grant of 500 acres for this purpose and in 1738, the first bricks were laid for the construction. Whitefield purchased a supply ship called the *Savannah* to serve the facility and supervised the construction of a road leading to Savannah. It is said that his was the first road of any length built in Georgia.

Bethesda was built with enough distance between the children and Savannah to ensure the children were, to quote Whitefield, away from the "wicked influence of the town." He tirelessly traveled to gain support for his beloved Bethesda, it is rumored that in a time when crossing the Atlantic was not an easy venture, Whitefield made the trip thirteen times.

Whitefield was a convincing and gifted orator, he is credited with delivering over 18,000 sermons, many of which resulted in collections destined for the orphanage. During a trip to Philadelphia, Whitefield managed to garner support from an unlikely source, Benjamin Franklin. The usually tight fisted Benjamin Franklin noted in his autobiography,

> "I happened...to attend one of his sermons, in the course of which I perceived that he was going to finish with a collection, and I silently resolved that he would get nothing from me. I had in my pocket a handful of copper money, three or four silver dollars, and five pistoles[48] of gold. As he proceeded I began to soften and concluded to give the coppers. Another stroke of his oratory made me ashamed of that and determined me to give the silver, and he finished so admirably that I emptied my pocket into the collector's dish, gold and all".

Benjamin Franklin, it seems, having softened even more, eventually became a trustee of the orphanage.

James Habersham served as the practical schoolmaster, while Whitefield was a visionary and expansive dreamer. Habersham's skill as an able administrator guaranteed immediate success for the orphanage. The children created an almost entirely self sufficient utopia; they raised their own vegetables and tended their own livestock.

During his later years, Whitefield envisioned a college established at Bethesda, the attempt failed miserably. Reverend George Whitefield died in1770, after thirty two-years at Bethesda. The story of Bethesda was just beginning. Whitefield bequeathed his entire estate, including Bethesda, to an English friend, Lady Hastings, the Countess Dowager of Huntingdon. Whitefield had been her private minister for many years.

The year of Whitefield's death brought the first of many disasters to the orphanage. Bethesda was struck by lightning and as a result, burned to the ground. Hardly defeated, Lady Hastings sold some of her jewels to rebuild. A portrait of her was commissioned upon the rededication and lovingly displayed in the great hall.

Then came the British. Troops were poised and ready to sack the defenseless orphanage. When the doors to the great hall were thrown open, their plans were dashed; upon encountering the life sized portrait of the countess was revealed. It was mistakenly assumed that the orphanage was loyal to Crown. The soldiers left without disturbing a thing.

At the end of the Revolution, Lady Hastings again attempted to realize Whitefield's dream of a college at Bethesda, again the venture failed. Mismanagement eventually brought the orphanage to the gates of destruction, until Henry Laurens assumed leadership. Laurens' leadership restored Bethesda, when the death of Lady Hastings brought unsuspected changes.

The Countess died in 1794 and the Georgia legislature confiscated the orphanage. Management was reorganized, creating a board of thirteen Trustees. The establishment of the Savannah Home for Girls, in 1801, brought another change, Bethesda was restricted to males. After a second devastating fire and a hurricane, the Georgia legislature sold Bethesda; dividing the proceeds between Savannah's poorhouse and hospital, the Union Society and the Chatham Academy.

The Union Society, so named because its founding members consisted of a Catholic, a Protestant and a Jew, turned out to be Bethesda's saving grace. Richard Milledge, Peter Tondee and Benjamin Sheftall, as the founding members, continued to use Bethesda's endowment for the relief of distressed widows and the education of poor children. Prior to the Civil War, the Union Society recovered most of the original Bethesda land. During the Civil War, orphans were safely cared for, while a portion of the campus was used as a hospital for the 7th Georgia Battalion.

Bethesda was saved from the ravages of war again, as General Sherman concluded his vicious March to the Sea. Union troops converged on Bethesda and as the Yankee soldiers approached the main hall with torches lit, preparing to burn all that stood, the caretaker appeared. The scene that took place, like that of the Revolutionary War, could have but one explanation, Divine Intervention. When asked to whom the property belonged, the man responded that Bethesda remained in the care of the Union Society. Although the commander was surprised to find Union sympathizers this far South, he ordered that Bethesda be spared. The Union troops marched away, leaving Bethesda untouched once again by the ugly hand of war.

The beautiful gateway arch was constructed in 1938 and officially dedicated on the 200th anniversary of Reverend George Whitefield's founding of Bethesda. The portrait of Lady Hastings, that once stopped an army, has been restored and now adorns the Bethesda Cunningham Museum.

The continued existence of Bethesda is, as always, dependent upon alumni and donor support. Their goal is to turn the rich heritage of Bethesda's history into the clear vision of its future. Their moto:

"Bethesda - fostering the children of tomorrow--today."

THE UNION SOCIETY
AND BETHESDA

In 1750 the Saint George's Club, a benevolent organization, was founded in Savannah. Of its 5 original members Peter Tondee and Richard Milledge had attended Bethesda. At some time prior to 1765 its name was changed to the Union Society. The organization from its beginning took a deep interest in Bethesda.

The Union Society continued in existence during the American Revolution. While prisoners of the British at Sunbury 4 members of the Society, Mordecai Sheftall, Josiah Powell, John Martin and John Stirk, held a meeting April 23, 1779. The Union Society was incorporated by the Legislature in 1786.

After Bethesda was discontinued in 1805 the Society carried, along with other charitable work, a considerable share of the burden of educating orphan children in the community. In 1854 it purchased 125 acres of the original Orphan House Tract for $2500.00. Buildings were erected and furnished at a cost of $4700.00. The children under the charge of the Society were removed to Bethesda that year.

Past Presidents of Union Society include Mordecai Sheftall, George Houstoun, Noble W. Jones, Joseph Clay, Joseph Habersham, David B. Mitchell, John Macpherson Berrien and Richard D. Arnold.

Bethesda on Ferguson Avenue near Whitfield Avenue
GPS Coordinates: N31.96075, W81.096193

The Saint George's Club was founded in 1750 for the purpose of supporting the working men of the Georgia colony after slavery was legalized. Originally, General Oglethorpe had prohibited the existence of slavery by means of the Georgia charter. However, as planters began building vast plantations with hopes of exporting crops, they realized that the cost of white labor was exorbitant and would seriously undermine their profits. Planters represented the wealth of the colony and slavery was eventually admitted.

The majority of the Georgia colony men were what we would think of today as blue collar workers. They were not wealthy and did not want slavery allowed in the colony. Slavery took away the working man's jobs, many were forced into share cropping, soldiering or indenture to pay their debts and feed their families. The Saint George's Club could do little to help relieve the burdens of the working man.

The name of the group was eventually changed to the Union Society. The term "Union" represented the founders who were a Catholic, a Protestant and a Jew that had bonded together to form what is believed to be the first charitable organization in America. The founders were Peter Tondee, Richard Milledge and Benjamin Sheftall. The society continued through the Revolutionary War, Benjamin Sheftall even conducted a meeting with other members while a prisoner of war at Sunbury. After the war, the Union Society was incorporated by an Act of the Legislature in 1786.

Following the Revolutionary War, the society was left to decide what contribution they were to make to the community. At the suggestion of Peter Tondee and Richard Milledge, it was decided that they would assist in the relief of distressed widows of the Revolution and the schooling and maintenance of poor children. Tondee and Milledge had both spent time as children at Reverend Whitefield's Bethesda Orphanage and the Union Society chose it as the recipient of their charitable works.

The Bethesda Orphanage had fallen on hard times and the Union Society spared nothing to restore the worthwhile facility. Pieces of the property had been sold to pay taxes, bit by bit the Union Society bought back each parcel until 1854, when Bethesda was whole once again. Buildings were rebuilt, furnished and others were restored. Then, as fate would have it, war again reared its ugly head.

The Civil War brought a halt to the rebuilding process, but for the most part, Bethesda remained untouched. When news of Sherman's March to the Sea arrived at Savannah and then the orphanage, the children were spirited away to safety. Bethesda

Orphanage was spared the torch, largely because of the Union Society. When a Commander from the North asked to whom the property belong, the caretaker responded, "the Union Society." Assuming "Union" meant northern sympathizers, the Yankee troops left the orphanage unmolested.

Bethesda continues to survive to this day under the care of the Bethesda Union Society Endowment Trust Committee and other organizations devoted to making a difference in these children's lives. The mission statement of Bethesda says it best,

"Bethesda Home for Boys is committed to equipping the boys under our care with the tools necessary to build character based on education, spiritual guidance, and personal integrity."

**SITE OF
COLONIAL SHIPYARD**

Approximately 300 yards northeast of this marker there was located in colonial days a shipyard where at least one vessel capable of engaging in overseas trade was built. The creek on which it stood is known as Shipyard Creek.

The site of the shipyard was on the Beaulieu (or Bewile) plantation of John Morel and was favorable for shipbuilding activities because of its accessibility to the Vernon River and the plentiful supply of live oak in the vicinity.

Here, in December, 1774, Daniel Giroud, shipbuilder, constructed the brig "Bewile," a vessel of 200 tons burden. In reporting the launching of the ship the "Georgia Gazette" stated that "those who are judges say she is well built and of the best materials, particularly her frame." During the American Revolution Giroud assisted in the construction of several Continental row galleys which saw service in Georgia waters.

**Shipyard Road, 0.2 mile east of Ferguson Road, Savannah
GPS Coordinates: N31.94225, W81.107174**

During the late 1700s, Savannah colonists found a new endeavor to supplement the agricultural exports they chiefly relied on. The abundance of hardwood all about the settlement, not only, provided wood for their homes, churches, public buildings and schools but would also supply raw materials for shipbuilding.

Colonists soon discovered that the live oak tree provided excellent shipbuilding timber. In 1794, timber from Georgia was shipped to Boston for the use as the frame of the war ship, USS *Constitution*. Nicknamed "Old Ironsides," the *Constitution* was often heralded as being impervious to cannon balls. The Georgia oak construction was so resilient that when cannon balls were fired at her they seemed to bounce harmlessly away. According to the United States Navy, the only metal in the USS *Constitution*'s construction was castings, spikes, bolts and a hull sheathing made of copper from Paul Revere's foundry.

Cedar timber was used because of its resistance to mildew and the natural scent kept insects at bay. The most useful of all the Georgia timber was white pine, it normally grows very tall and its branches sprout only from the upper most part of the tree, these trees made excellent masts. The pine also provided pitch and tar used in waterproofing the hull and kept the ship watertight.

Before the Revolutionary War, England had vigorously encouraged colonial shipbuilding. Most of the forest in England had been harvested to the point that little building materials were available. By the end of the colonial period, England still relied on America to build over a third of her merchant ships.

Savannah had become the regional shipbuilding center by the early 1800s. Two and three masted schooners, brigs and merchants ships were being constructed for regional use and many found their way to England. Locally built ships were used for coastal trading between Charles Town, Darien, Brunswick and further south into Florida.

The SS *Savannah* was built in 1819, a Coastal Georgia steamboat that made the first transoceanic voyage. Small inland steamers were locally built at the Colonial Shipyard at Beaulieu Plantation. These steamers were used to navigate the rivers and sounds that are all about Savannah. Larger coastal steamers were built to transport passengers from Savannah to the nearby coastal cities.

While steamers usually carried passengers, sailing vessels carried bulk supplies and cargo. The introduction of the railroad in the middle 1800s brought a decline in both passenger traffic and cargo transport. Travel by rail was a much faster means of transportation and it was not hampered by weather conditions as sea travel was.

By the early 1800s, Beaulieu Plantation owner, John Morel, had died and most of his property, including the plantation, had been sold to pay outstanding debts. With the advent of the railroad shipbuilding declined and soon only the small ships used locally were built. Modernization brought the end to the construction of tall masts and steamer ships built from Georgia timber.

MODENA

This location first appears (1734) in Georgia's history as a Savannah outpost. An original settler was Thomas Mouse who is remembered for his description of early hardships here. An evangelical visitor in 1736 was John Wesley. By 1740 the settlement was abandoned. The Island revived when the Georgia Trusteeship ended in 1753, and Colonial Government established. An early grantee was John Milledge, whose plantation at this site was called "Modena." He was the orphaned son of one of the "First Hundred," the youthful protege of Oglethorpe, Captain of the Rangers, and member of First Commons House of Assembly. His son and successor, John, Jr., was a leader in the American Revolution. He was appointed State Attorney General at the age of 23 when still in uniform, and later became U.S. Representative, Governor, and U.S. Senator. As Governor he helped found the University of Georgia (Originally Franklin College). Modena was an active plantation until Mid-Nineteenth Century. The name is thought to come from Modena, Italian seat of silk culture; an industry envisioned for early Georgia, but which did not flourish.

Skidaway Institute of Oceanography, Skidaway Island
GPS Coordinates: N31.98588, W81.022829

General James Edward Oglethorpe assigned five families and six single men to Skidaway Island in 1734. The colonists built a small fort at the northern end of the island at the river with one carriage gun and four swivels. Despite attempts to tame the area, by 1740, the island was abandoned. The pioneers realized that the sandy soil was unfit for farming and the conditions were much too harsh. The next period of settlement began in 1754, when twenty-nine land grants were issued to settlers who were determined to be more successful. One of the grantees was John Milledge, who was among the first one hundred settlers of the Georgia colony. John Milledge established the plantation Modena, which is believed to be named for the Italian town that was the premiere of the silk culture. Silk production was one of the first industries attempted on the Georgia coast. Modena Plantation survived until the middle 1800s.

The Revolutionary War had little impact on Skidaway Island and its struggling inhabitants. One small skirmish occurred when a party of British Marines landed to forage the island, the patriot settlers made short work of the group driving the unwanted invaders off the island. The period between the Revolutionary War and the Civil War was a prosperous one. The population on the island expanded to approximately 2,000 settlers. Modena Plantation began successfully producing sea island cotton, indigo, corn, cattle and hogs.

The good times were in grave peril as the Civil War threatened. The settlers of Skidaway built solid earthen batteries to defend against attack and the 4th Georgia Battery was posted there. Unfortunately, the success of the Union blockade in 1862 cut off all supply lines to the island, eventually Skidaway was abandoned again. The South was a conquered land, slavery was abolished and Modena fell into ruin.

During the South's Reconstruction, southerners had only their property and natural resources to climb out of poverty. The industrialized North had the financial and political advantage over its impoverished southern neighbors and used the advantage to force their way into property ownership across the South. Skidaway was no exception, various northern interests gained control of the island in the late nineteenth and early twentieth centuries. The largest of these, Union Camp, which was then called Union Bag and Paper Corporation, consolidated its holdings and used Skidaway for pulpwood production in the 1940s. By 1964, Union Camp had designs to develop residential properties on the island, but Skidaway lacked a bridge that would provide easy access for cars. Union Camp offered to donate five hundred acres to the state, if Georgia would build a bridge to the island. The land was donated in 1967, which became the site of Skidaway Island State Park.

By this time, the Milledge estate was forced to sell their Skidaway Island holdings including Modena to the Roebling family of Trenton, New Jersey. The Roebling family was made infamous during the middle 1800s when John A. Roebling designed and eventually began construction on the Brooklyn Bridge in New York. John Roebling lost his life to the bridge, shortly after construction began his foot was crushed on the job site and tetanus set in. John Roebling was dead within days. John's son, Colonel Washington Augustus Roebling, took over his father's dream and eventually finished the bridge in 1883. The cost of building the bridge to Colonel Roebling was high as well, his health suffered to an extent that for the remainder of his life he was virtually bedridden. This was not the first experience with the Savannah area for the Roeblings, Washington Augustus Roebling II had found fame during the early 1900s racing automobiles here, unfortunately, the Roebling family seemed to be cursed. He was lost during the terrible tragedy of the SS *Titanic.*

In 1967, the Roebling family agreed to give Modena Plantation to the state of Georgia. The bill authorizing the Oceanographic Research Center was passed by the Georgia legislature during the 1967 through 1968 session, setting in motion a series of significant events. Other donors gave access routes and most importantly, the local government, working with the State, committed to building a bridge required for easier access. The bridge was completed in 1971.

Located only four miles from downtown Savannah, the 700 acre tract features a deep channel on the Wilmington River leading to the open Atlantic Ocean only six miles downstream. Early efforts were directed toward learning more about ocean currents along the Georgia coast, the adjoining Blake Plateau and the barrier islands, which extends from the Carolinas to Florida. The Coast Guard coast used the studies of ocean currents for salvage and recovery off of the coast of Georgia. Eventually there was significant work in the fish farming industry, seaweed by products and the development of the sea clam. The site was given to the University System of Georgia, which launched a program of academic and environmental studies.

Skidaway Marine Science Complex, on the grounds of the former Modena Plantation, consists of Skidaway Institute of Oceanography and the University of Georgia Marine Extension Center. The complex has a 14 panel, 12,000 gallon aquarium with marine and plant life of the continental shelf. Other exhibits highlight coastal archaeology and fossils of the Georgia coast. Nature trails overlook marsh and water. Skidaway remains a substantial research center valued at $10 to $20 million. The Complex is opened to the public for a small fee.

Union Camp subsequently developed a gated, residential golf community called, The Landings, which today, features six 18 hole golf courses. Despite Union Camp's extensively developed property, the island today has one of the most beautiful state parks in Georgia. The features include two scenic nature trails and a full complement of facilities.

Locals still refer to the area as Modena.

JASPER SPRING

On this spot, according to long and persistent tradition, occurred one of Sergeant William Jasper's most famous exploits during the American Revolution. Here, in 1779, at the spring then located along the road to Augusta, Sergeant Jasper and Sergeant John Newton ambushed a detachment of ten British soldiers and liberated several Patriot prisoners who were being taken to Savannah.

While no contemporary confirmation of Jasper's feat exists (it was first publicized by Parson Weems in 1809 in his life of Gen. Francis Marion), the exploit was in every way characteristic of the immortal sergeant. An illustration of his courage and resourcefulness is found May 15, 1779; "The brave serjeant Jasper ... has lately given a new proof of his courage and address: He, with another serjeant, a few days ago, crossed the Savannah river, took, and brought to Major General Lincoln's headquarters, two Captains, named Scott and Young, of the British troops in Georgia."

Sergeant Jasper was mortally wounded, Oct. 9, 1779, while heroically bearing the colors of the 2nd South Carolina Continental Regiment in the assault on the British entrenchments at Savannah.

August Avenue at I-516, Savannah
GPS Coordinates: N32.08971, W81.128025

Sergeant William Jasper, a member of the 2nd South Carolina Continental, felt restless as his regiment waited for the arrival of General Lincoln in the spring of 1779. The regiment was assigned to assist in the retaking of Savannah, which had fallen to the British. Jasper had a brother, who had taken the Tory side, stationed at Ebenezer only a short distance from the American entrenchment and decided to visit him there.

Jasper's brother was shocked to see him walk into the encampment and warned him away. To cover himself, Jasper lied and said he had deserted the Americans. He was offered a commission to join the Tories but declined saying that even though he left the service of America, he would never take arms against her. The pretense was accepted. Jasper remained with the Tory detachment for several days. He was careful to absorb any information he managed to overhear during his visit. After two or three days, Jasper embraced his brother and went on his way. After backtracking and traveling in round about directions, Jasper returned to his regiment and reported all that he had overheard to General Lincoln.

Several weeks passed and the regiment remained entrenched. Jasper decided to entertain himself with another visit to his brother. This time, another sergeant by the name of Newton accompanied him. Jasper and Newton strolled into the enemy camp like old friends, the soldiers there had no suspicions attached to the mild mannered Jasper.

After several days among the British, a number of American prisoners were brought into camp. When Jasper inquired he was told that the group had deserted from Savannah and in their flight, had stolen from the King. Jasper was told the prisoners were to be hung in Savannah.

The sad looking group, shackled hand and foot, was caked with mud and clearly frightened for their lives. Among them was the sorrowful figure of a woman and her small son. The woman had refused to leave the side of her captive husband, determined to stand with him to the last. Her love for him was obvious and overshadowed any concern for herself or her child, for what lives could they have without him? The woman sat alternating between pitiful moans of grief and the vacant stares of acceptance.

Jasper was so touched by this outpouring of emotion, he knew something had to be done, even if it meant his own life. Jasper and Newton took their leave. Jasper knew that he might risk his own life, but never his friend's. He explained his thoughts to Newton saying, "I must rescue these poor prisoners or die with them; otherwise that woman and her child will haunt me to my grave." Newton agreed and the two pledged one to the other to rescue the prisoners or die trying.

After the departure of the prisoners, guarded by ten British soldiers, Jasper and Newton tracked the group. Of course,

Jasper and Newton were only two unarmed men against ten British soldiers fortified with loaded muskets and bayonets. They knew the odds were against them, but still they watched and waited for the perfect place to stage an ambush.

Two miles west of Savannah was a well known spring, locals called the Spa. Travelers often stopped there for a respite before continuing on their journey. The soldiers selected the spot for a moment of rest and had a refreshing drink from the cool, clear water. Jasper and Newton lay in wait.

Four of the soldiers rested by the road, while the others accompanied the prisoners. Two soldiers kept guard, while two others filled their canteens. The two filling their canteens rested their muskets against a tree, as they knelt by the spring. Quickly, Jasper and Newton leapt from their hiding spot and seized the muskets. With hearts pounding in their throats, Newton and Jasper shot dead the soldiers standing guard. The momentarily panicked soldiers at the spring, lunged for their fallen comrades' muskets. Jasper and Newton struck using their unloaded muskets as clubs and bashed in the skulls of the British soldiers. They grabbed the unused muskets and leveled the barrels at the five remaining soldiers and demanded their surrender. The British soldiers instantly laid down their arms. Jasper and Newton had taken the ten British soldiers without assistance.

During the commotion, the lady had fallen in a swoon and the boy wailed over her unconscious body. Jasper and Newton released the men from their bondage using the points of the bayonets. The men gathered around the mother and child, when she regained her senses, all were safe. Her cries of joy filled the air, as she clutched her husband and son, then fell to her knees before Jasper and Newton kissing their hands in gratitude.

Realizing that surely other soldiers had heard the shots, Jasper and Newton knew they had to immediately depart. The Americans with their recent captives crossed the Savannah River and rejoined the American army at Purysburgh. The British prisoners were turned over to General Lincoln.

Sergeant Jasper would never see the end of 1799. On October 9, 1799, during the Siege of Savannah, Sergeant William Jasper gave his life for the cause of America's liberty.

OLD JEWISH
BURIAL GROUND

Established by Mordecai Sheftall on August 2, 1773 from lands
granted him in 1762 by King George III as a parcel of land that
"shall be, and forever remain, to and for the use and purpose of a
Place of Burial for all persons whatever professing the Jewish
Religion."
During the ill fated attempt of the French forces under Admiral
Charles Henri, Comte d'Estaing, and the American forces under
General Benjamin Lincoln, to recapture Savannah from the
British. General Lincoln's Orders of the Day of October 8, 1779
stated that "The second place of rallying, or the first if the redoubt
should not be carried, will be at the Jew's burying ground, where
the reserve will be placed."
According to the account of Captain Antoine-Francoise Terance
O'Connor, a military engineer servicing with the French forces, on
October 8, 1779, shortly after 4:00 AM. "The reserve corps, com-
manded by M. le Vicomte de Noailles, advanced as far as an old
Jewish cemetery, and we placed on its right and a little to the rear
the four 4-pounders."

Off Cohen Street, off West Boundary, Savannah
GPS Coordinates: N32.07236, W81.103494

J uly 31, 1787, the 16th day of Ab[49], a society called the Mashebet Nafish laid the foundation for the stone wall surrounding the Jewish Burial Ground. The property was donated for that purpose by Mordecai Sheftall, who set the first stone.
The deed to the burial ground was issued in the names of various men who shared the Jewish faith. The burial ground completed the circle, which began by the establishment of a synagogue the preceding year.

Services were performed regularly on the Sabbath and holidays and on one occasion there were seventy-three members in
attendance. The elderly were the main support of the synagogue, having retired from their labor.

For years, there was no permanent location for public worship, however, the need to teach the doctrine of their ancestors
necessitated a temple in Savannah. A synagogue was erected and consecrated on July 21, 1820, unfortunately, the temple was
consumed by fire on December 4, 1829.

Dr. Moses Sheftall, President of the congregation, found that the temple did not have enough funds to rebuild the synagogue and solicited subscriptions from a limited number of the congregation to defray the cost of rebuilding.

The synagogue was constructed of brick, on a lot granted by the city of Savannah to the Hebrew congregation. Mordecai
Sheftall was responsible for the preceding information in a letter to the editor dated August 24, 1843 to a Savannah newspaper.
It closed with the following:

> "I have, Mr. Editor, brought the history of ourselves to a conclusion. It might probably serve to beguile
> some leisure moments of your distant readers. It will, I am convinced, convey a proud and elevated interest
> to many of those who reside in the city of Oglethorpe, particularly the descendants of the settlers of 1733,
> whose adventurous grandsires left their homes for the more perfect enjoyment of religious liberty in the
> untried clime of the new world, and whose fathers, born upon the genial soil of Savannah, now quietly
> repose within its bosom."

The following letters were written to Dr. De la Motta congratulating him on consecration of the synagogue in Savannah.
The first was written in the name of Thomas Jefferson and the second, James Madison. The letters are self explanatory, therefore I close with the words of two great men:

To Dr. Jacob De la Motta, Savannah, Ga.

Th. Jefferson returns his thanks to Dr. De la Motta for the eloquent discourse on the consecration of the Synagogue of Savannah which he has been so kind as to send him. It excites in him the gratifying reflection that his own country has been the first to prove to the world two truths, the most salutary to human society, that man can govern himself, and that religious freedom is the most effectual anodyne against religious dissension: the maxim of civil government being reversed in that of religion, where its true form is "divided we stand, united we fall." He is happy in the restoration, of the Jews particularly, to their social rights, and hopes they will be seen taking their seats on the benches of science, as preparatory to their doing the same at the board of government. He salutes Dr. De la Motta with sentiments of great respect.

Thomas Jefferson

To Dr. Jacob De la Motta, Savannah, Ga.

Montpellier, August, 1820.

Sir——

I have received your letter of the 7th inst., with the discourse delivered at the Consecration of the Hebrew Synagogue at Savannah, for which you will please accept my thanks.
The history of the Jews must for ever be interesting. The modern part of it is at the same time, so little generally known, that every ray of light on the subject has its value.
Among the features peculiar to the political system of the United States, is the perfect equality of rights which it secures to every religious sect; and it is particularly pleasing to observe in the good citizenship of such as have been most distrusted and oppressed elsewhere, a happy illustration of the safety and success of this experiment of a just and benignant policy. Equal laws protecting equal rights are found as they ought to be presumed, the best guarantee of loyalty and love of country, as well as best calculated to cherish that mutual respect and good-will among citizens of every religious denomination, which are necessary to social harmony, and most favourable to the advancement of truth. The account you give of the Jews of your congregation brings them fully within the scope of these observations. I tender you, sir, my respects and good wishes.

James Madison.

Mary Musgrove was born at a time when the land served only to nourish and nurture the Native American tribes. Mary was born Cousaponokeesa in 1700 at the settlement of Coweta, near what is today, Macon. She descended from the Wind Clan of the Creek tribe, her mother was sister to Hoboyelty, Civil Chief of Coweta, called Emperor Brim or Bream by the Europeans. Mary's father was thought to be a white trader, perhaps Scottish or English. Her patriarchal lineage was of no consequence to the Creek. Native Americans only recognized the maternal line, her mother's royal blood established Cousaponokeesa's place within the Creek Nation.

Cousaponokeesa was taught the ways and language of her mother's people until she reached the age of ten years. Then she was sent to live among her white relatives near Charles Towne in southern Carolina. It was among her father's people, that Cousaponokeesa became Mary. She was baptized and educated as a Christian, something very foreign to the young Indian girl. Mary absorbed everything she was taught until again the child's world was upended. The Yamasee revolted in 1715 against the unfair trading of the Carolinians. Mary was returned to Coweta that year as a result of the revolt. The double alliance of the Creek Nation and English education would serve her well in the coming years.

Colonel John Musgrove, thought to be the son of a Carolina landowner and a Native American woman, was solicited by the Carolina governor to visit the Creek Nation with an offer of peace. It was there that he met Mary and the couple were soon married. Mary and John established a trading post at Yamacraw Bluff in 1732. Savannah would be located at this site only one year later. Theirs was the only post available to Charles Towne merchants to trade with the Native Americans to the south.

General James Edward Oglethorpe arrived to claim the land for the English Crown in 1733, fully aware that to have any success in this endeavor, he would first have to win the favor of the Creek Nation. Oglethorpe sought a negotiator who could communicate with the Creek Nation. Mary Musgrove was the perfect candidate.

The opportunity ideally suited Mary, who was ambitious. She immediately saw this as a means to advance her fortunes, both socially and financially. The idea of becoming an important person in the eyes of the Creek Nation and the colonists appealed to her. Mary was tireless and fearless in the missions she undertook, although she insisted on a fair wage for her work.

The Musgroves kept the struggling colonists supplied with meat, bread and liquor. They soon established a trading post called Mount Venture on the south side of the Altamaha River in order to keep an eye on the Native Americans and the Spanish.

Mary put the traders and Indian couriers in her employ at the disposal of Oglethorpe. John Musgrove died in 1734.

Mary promptly married John Musgrove's indentured servant, Jacob Matthews. Public opinion of Matthews was mixed. Some believed him to be power hungry and a drunkard, while others saw him as hardworking. Apparently Matthews worked hard but aligned himself with the malcontents in Georgia and was the self appointed chief critic of the authorities within the infant colony.

Mary made numerous trips between Savannah and Frederica to spy on the Spanish and to assure the support of the Creek tribes for the English garrison. Due to May's absences, Matthews was placed in charge of defending Mount Venture with a force of Georgia Rangers. When fighting broke out between Spain and Britain in 1742, the Creeks sided with the British due to Mary's influence and the joint Creek-Georgian Army successfully pushed the Spaniards back at the Battle of Bloody Marsh.

Mary's landholdings increased significantly when her Native American kinsmen transferred their holdings to her. She now owned thousands of miles of land along the Savannah River and the islands of Sapelo, Ossabaw and Saint Catherines. The British refused to recognize the legality of these land transfers to Mary, although they saw no problems with transfers made by Native Americans to the British crown. The reluctance of the British to honor Mary's land transfers, who was by now the oldest living woman in the clan, infuriated the Creek Nation. The Creeks saw this as an attempt by the Savannah authorities to cheat the Native Americans out of their holdings.

Jacob Matthews died on May 8, 1742. Mary's third and final husband, was a renegade Anglican minister, Thomas Bosomworth. Bosomworth arrived in Georgia during 1741 and was appointed Secretary of Indian Affairs. This position was not important enough for Thomas, so he determined to be a warrior and traveled to Frederica to help Oglethorpe defeat the Spanish.

He soon tired of camp life at Frederica and had attempted to write essays on religion. Thomas Bosomworth next felt a call to preach and went to England for Holy Orders in March 1743. He was appointed minister to Georgia for a term of three years on July 4th and returned to Georgia on December 2nd. He soon tired of preaching and Mary. Bosomworth returned to England in 1745 without notice to his wife or providing for his church in Savannah, declaring that he would not return. The Trustees ignored the complaints Bosomworth attempted to bring to their attention. Bosomworth again decided to become a soldier but was back in Georgia in early 1746. He was, however, no longer the minister. One report was that he cast aside his Sacerdotal[50] but another related that the Trustees had torn them from him.

Bosomworth lost no time in hatching a new scheme. He and Mary set up a trading post at the Forks, where the Ocmulgee and Oconee Rivers merged. Mary and Thomas secured a grant of St. Catherines, Sapelo and Ossaba Islands from the Creeks in addition to a tract of land lying between Savannah and Pipe Maker's Creek. Mary continued to pursue having her property ownership recognized by the Crown and was unsuccessful at every turn. The fact that a woman, let a lone a Native American woman, assumed ownership of property was not possible in the eyes of the Crown.

Bosomworth supported Mary's claim to the lands because it profited him to do so, although he was accused of high treason against the Crown for his trouble. Mary, Bosomworth and numerous Indians were outraged by the British refusal to recognize Mary's claims and in summer of 1749, a parade into Savannah turned into protest. Mary was placed under arrest but was soon released for fear of a larger revolt by the Native Americans. She was allowed to travel to London with her husband to argue her case before the British Board of Trade. In London, she accepted a compromise where the islands of Ossabaw and Sapelo were to be sold by the British at a public auction and Mary would receive the proceeds. She was to retain St. Catherines Island, but only "in consideration of services rendered by her to the province of Georgia," rather than because she was the rightful owner.

Mary "Cousaponokeesa" Musgrove Matthews Bosomworth died five years later. All of her property passed to her English husband and his heirs according to the English law, not to Mary's female relatives as was the Creek custom. Mary was buried at St. Catherines Island; today, the island is a wildlife preserve.

During the next one hundred years, the lands that were once claimed by Mary Musgrove became Colerain Plantation. The owner, James Potter, was a very successful planter and almost all of the land was cultivated in rice. James Potter died when Sherman's troops marched on Savannah and for many years after, the Plantation lay in ruins.

In 1916, the property was purchased by the Savannah Sugar Refining Company. A manufacturing plant for processing and distributing refined sugar was built and remains in operation today.

BATTLE BETWEEN CONFEDERATE GUNBOATS
AND UNION FIELD ARTILLERY
(December 12, 1864)

In December, 1864, was fought on the Savannah River near here one of the few battles in which Confederate gunboats and Union field artillery were engaged against each other.

Colerain Plantation, as these lands were then known, had been occupied on December 10, 1864, by units of Sherman's army. Anticipating an attempt by a Confederate naval flotilla, which had been engaged in protecting a railroad bridge further upstream, to return to Savannah, Captain C. E. Winegar's battery was posted on a bluff about one mile East of this marker.

Early on the morning of December 12, 1864, the CSS Sampson and Macon and their tender, the Resolute, attempted to run past the Federal battery. There was a "terrific fire" from both sides, according to John Thomas Scharf, a midshipman of the Sampson who later became the well-known historian of the Confederate States Navy. The gunboats were struck several times.

Unable to get past the battery, the vessels turned about. In doing so the Resolute collided with the gunboats and drifted helplessly upon Argyle Island where she was captured by troops of the 3rd Wisconsin Regiment. With the aid of barrels of bacon thrown in their furnaces, the two gunboats were able to steam out of range. They escaped to Augusta.

US 17 at the Savannah Sugar Refining Company, near Port Wentworth
GPS Coordinates: N32.14134, W81.157138

It was December 1864 when General William T. Sherman achieved his objective, capturing Savannah during his arduous March to the Sea. The war dividing a nation was coming to an end and the South had been thoroughly defeated. On December 10, General Sherman's troops occupied Colerain Plantation near Savannah. He ordered a battery to a bluff overlooking the Savannah River, commanded by Captain C. E. Winegar, his orders were to prevent the destruction of a railroad bridge that was the supply route between Savannah and Charleston.

Initially built in Savannah, the *Resolute* was to be used as a tugboat on the Mississippi River. Confederate Captain J. E. Montgomery selected her to join his River Defense Fleet in 1861 and began to convert her into a cotton clad ram on January 25, 1862. A four inch oak beam with a one inch iron covering on her bow and double pine bulkheads filled with compressed cotton bales completed her transformation from tug to cotton clad. The CSS *Resolute* was put into Confederate service as a side wheel gunboat ram. In December 1864, the CSS *Resolute*'s orders were to escort the Confederate gunboats *Macon* and *Sampson*. The *Sampson*, also a tugboat turned gunboat, was mustered into Confederate service in 1861 under the command of Captain W. W. Hunter. The *Macon*, with Lt. J. S. Kennard in command, was placed into service in August 1864 although still lacking her full complement of artillery.

The CSS *Sampson* and *Macon* were ordered to proceed to the Charleston and Savannah Railway bridge spanning the Savannah River and destroy it. The CSS *Resolute* took heavy fire as she sailed passed the Union field artillery. Guns blazed from both sides, the Confederates from the north side of the Savannah River and the Union from the south. The *Resolute* was hit once, her deck shuddered from the impact, her planking held. She was hit a second time with the same result. As the flotilla of three neared the obviously fortified bridge the captains realized their only hope was to make a run for it, hoping the Union blockade was unable to close off their only escape. The *Resolute*, *Macon* and *Sampson* began their turns in the river to effect the retreat.

As the turns were made the *Resolute* suddenly realized that the river channel was not wide enough for her to turn and before she could adjust her course, the sickening sound of rendering timber could be heard. Damaged, the CSS *Resolute* ran aground on Argyle Island, her crew watched as the CSS *Macon* and *Sampson* sailed on without incident.

The CSS *Resolute* was captured by Union soldiers under Colonel William Hawley. Her crew would spend the remainder of the war in a prison camp and the *Resolute* was made a part of the Union fleet. The CSS *Macon* and *Sampson* were taken up the Savannah River to Augusta where both remained until the end of the war. The CSS *Resolute*, although she was taken by the Union, did her job well and those under her care were safe.

**MULBERRY GROVE
PLANTATION**

Mulberry Grove which is located approximately 3 miles northwest from this marker is one of the most historic of the old Savannah River plantations.

In early Colonial days mulberry trees were cultivated at Mulberry Grove for use in Georgia's silk industry. Later it became one of the leading rice plantations of Georgia. At the end of the Revolution the plantation, which had belonged to Lieutenant Governor John Graham, a Royalist, was granted by the State of Georgia to Major General Nathanael Greene as a reward for his military services. General Greene was residing at Mulberry Grove at the time of his death on June 12, 1786.

In 1793 Eli Whitney, who was the tutor of the Greene children, invented the cotton gin at Mulberry Grove. The following year a large ginning machine was erected at the plantation. Its foundation still stands there.

US 17 at City Hall, Port Wentworth
GPS Coordinates: N32.14683, W81.161317

Mulberry Grove Plantation once covered an expansive 2,141 acres in, what is today, western Chatham County. The plantation has a wonderful history filled with noted historical figures and events of historical significance.

In 1733, when General Oglethorpe first arrived the area was known as Joseph's Town. Property at the site was granted to John Cuthbert, Patrick Mackay and George Dunbar, all Scottish Highlanders. John Cuthbert is possibly the first to enlist the services of indentured servants in order to fulfill his obligations to the Crown for the land grants he had received. Cuthbert soon fell victim to the unmerciful conditions of the young colony and the land was inherited by his sister, making Ann Cuthbert quite possibly the first colonist woman to own property in the New World. This fact was not popular with the English trustees who did not subscribe to the Scottish tendency toward female equality.

Dr. Patrick Graham, President of Georgia and eventually a member of the Royal Governor's Council, married Ann Cuthbert in 1740. Dr. Graham interests lay in planting and he began to grow mulberry saplings to sell to the Georgia colonists, hence the plantation name of Mulberry Grove. Dr. Graham expanded his planting operating in 1749 to include the cultivation of rice. He recognized the importance of mass labor to ensure a fruitful harvest and even though slavery was forbidden by the Georgia charter, Graham brought in slaves. Other planters began to realize that the only way to plant and harvest vast quantities was to have cheap labor. Thus the Georgia charter was amended to include slavery. Dr. Graham died in 1758 and Ann Cuthbert Graham married planter James Bulloch of Carolina.

Ten years after the death of Ann Cuthbert Graham Bulloch, in 1774, Royal Lieutenant Governor John Graham purchased Mulberry Grove Plantation. Governor Graham had a new home and out buildings constructed on the property. However, Governor Graham's enjoyment of his new home would not last long. Sparks of the Revolutionary War could be seen on the horizon and in 1776, the Liberty Boys began conducting raids on plantations owned by loyalist supporters. Royal Governor John Graham was forced to flee for his life back to England, Mulberry Grove was confiscated as loyalist property.

After the war, loyalist properties were divided among heroes of the Revolution. The plantation had been abandoned for almost ten years and had deteriorated into a state of disrepair; even in this condition, it was a much coveted piece of property and was awarded to Major General Nathanael Greene who served valiantly in the Continental Army. Greene had purchased a half interest in Cumberland and Little Cumberland Islands several years earlier for the purpose of growing oaks for ship building but decided that the location was too remote to bring his family. In October 1785, Greene moved his family to Mulberry Grove.

Greene had hardly settled in when he died of a sunstroke while visiting a neighboring plantation in 1786. He was interred with full military honors in the Graham Vault at Colonial Park Cemetery, alongside Lieutenant Colonel John Maitland who was killed during the Siege of Savannah. Greene's son, George Washington Greene, was also placed in the vault after his tragic drowning in the Savannah River in 1793.

Catherine, Nathanael Greene's widow, was widely known for her beauty and charm. She was known to entertain lavishly and after the death of her husband, assumed the role of host for a number of distinguished visitors. President George Washington, long time friend of the Greene family, visited Mulberry Grove twice during his Southern Tours. George Washington had said of the lovely Mrs. Greene, "She's the best dancing partner I've ever had."

Catherine Greene had been left virtually destitute after the death of her husband. It was said that he had lost most of his money during the Revolution. He supported his men from his own pocket, when unable to obtain funds from the Continental Congress. Webb Garrison, in his *A Treasure of Georgia Tales* related that many high placed men came to the aid of Caty Greene; Alexander Hamilton, Henry Knox and of course, her old friend George Washington; the Marquis de LaFayette financed the education of one of her sons; and Jeremiah Wadsworth loaned Mrs. Greene a considerable sum of money to meet her continuing debts. According to Garrison, "Caty could only offer her charms as repayment. The liaison, continued until Mrs. Wadsworth discovered some of their letters."

Mrs. Greene hired Eli Whitney, a young visitor from Massachusetts, to tutor her children on a temporary basis. It is said Whitney was so enamored with Caty's charms, he remained at Mulberry Grove for over a year. While there he invented and developed the cotton gin. A monumentous event that would eventually bring great changes to the South.

In 1796, Catherine Greene married Phineas Miller, who once served as her late husband's secretary. Still in dire financial straits, the couple moved to Cumberland Island. It was there that they built the estate of Dungeness in 1802.

Mulberry Grove changed hands a number of times during the years. By 1856, the property was owned by Zachariah M. Winkler and expanded into an even larger rice plantation. Threats of Civil War now loomed dark on the horizon. In 1864, General William T. Sherman's army was tearing its way through the South to Savannah. Although Savannah was never burned, Union soldiers took no pity on Mulberry Grove. The once affluent plantation was burned to the ground. This was the end of Mulberry Grove as a large agricultural plantation.

Even though General Sherman's orders were to leave Savannah untouched, the Union troops did considerable damage nonetheless. With no respect for the Revolutionary War dead, the troops desecrated the Graham vault among others, in search of valuables. They amused themselves by destroying gravestones and altering the epitaphs written in tribute to fallen heros and statesmen. As a result the location of the Graham vault was lost.

Eventually, the vault was found, and the bodies of Nathanael Greene and his son were removed to lie beneath the beautiful marble obelisk at Johnson Square. The cornerstone was laid on March 21, 1825 and presided over by the Marquis de LaFayette, a memorial to Nathanael Greene and his enormous contribution in the cause of Liberty.

Catherine Greene Miller suffered another devastating loss when Dungeness, at Cumberland Island burned in 1866. Catherine and Phineas Millers' remains lay buried on Cumberland Island. Thomas Carnegie purchased the property and rebuilt Dungeness in 1884; this house burned in 1959.

Mulberry Grove was commemorated by a state historical marker in 1938, although little was left but ruins by this time. In the 1970s, the Georgia Port Authority bulldozed what was left of the estate and the Winkler family, who had owned the property for more than one hundred years sold Mulberry Grove Plantation to BASF-Wyandotte Corporation.

The Georgia Ports Authority purchased Mulberry Grove in 1985 and efforts to preserve and restore the historic site began. In 1999, Mulberry Grove was approved for membership in the National Trust for Historic Preservation, however, the efforts have met with numerous complications. Hugh Golson, a Winkler descendant, and the Bluffton Historical Preservation Society continue their untiring struggle on behalf of Mulberry Grove Plantation.

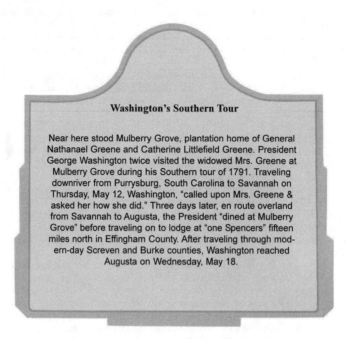

Washington's Southern Tour

Near here stood Mulberry Grove, plantation home of General Nathanael Greene and Catherine Littlefield Greene. President George Washington twice visited the widowed Mrs. Greene at Mulberry Grove during his Southern tour of 1791. Traveling downriver from Purrysburg, South Carolina to Savannah on Thursday, May 12, Washington, "called upon Mrs. Greene & asked her how she did." Three days later, en route overland from Savannah to Augusta, the President "dined at Mulberry Grove" before traveling on to lodge at "one Spencers" fifteen miles north in Effingham County. After traveling through modern-day Screven and Burke counties, Washington reached Augusta on Wednesday, May 18.

GA 21 north just south of I-95, Port Wentworth
GPS Coordinates: N32.17936, W81.161317

President George Washington both began and ended his Savannah tour with a visit to his long time friend, Mrs. Catherine Greene. President Washington had known Mrs. Greene and her deceased husband, General Nathanael Greene, for well over fifteen years. General Greene once noted that obviously Washington was enchanted by his lovely wife saying,

> "...at a little dance in 1779, His Excellency (Washington) and Mrs. Greene danced upwards of three hours without once sitting down."

Mrs. Greene was likewise taken with Washington, promising to name her first born son for the President; George Washington Greene was, in fact, named for Mrs. Greene's dancing partner. Later, after the death of General Greene, Washington offered to give his namesake "as good an education as this country will afford at my own cost and charge." However, the Marquis de Lafayette made the same offer and the young man was sent to Paris rather than Mount Vernon. Unfortunately, George Washington Greene, upon his return from Paris drowned at Mulberry Grove and was buried with his father at Colonial Park Cemetery. His body along with General Greene's was removed to the location of the Greene Monument in 1901.

President Washington was said to have stopped only briefly to inquire about Mrs. Greene's health, though that statement was not altogether true. President Washington's intent was a brief visit to his friend, but his Welcoming Committee had other plans. They needed a little time for the crowd in Savannah to gather and final preparations to be set into motion for the President's grand arrival into the city. While he was being distracted by Mrs. Greene, a feat easily accomplished by the charming lady, a horseman was sent ahead to warn the town of the President's imminent arrival.

The President again paid a visit to Mrs. Greene, upon his departure of Savannah enroute to Augusta. This time the meeting was a little more intimate and the friends were able to share a quiet repast. President Washington then took his leave and traveled on the Augusta.

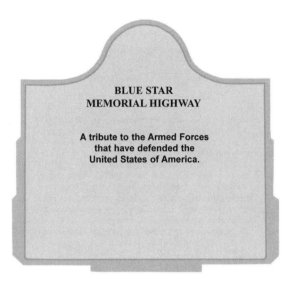

**BLUE STAR
MEMORIAL HIGHWAY**

**A tribute to the Armed Forces
that have defended the
United States of America.**

**I-95 at the Georgia Welcome Center
GPS Coordinates: N32.21.738, W81.174229**

Each Blue Star Memorial Highway marker is dedicated by a state recognized garden club and assigned to a particular stretch of road. The designation is formalized in a Resolution presented at the Georgia Legislature. The following example was chosen as a prime representation of the true spirit of Blue Star Memorial Highway legislation and the Georgia program, which is a invaluable asset to the National Garden Clubs Association. The following is an actual approved and presented Resolution:

A RESOLUTION

Designating the Heritage Trail as a part of the Blue Star Memorial Highway; and for other purposes.
WHEREAS, from the northern to the southern border of Georgia, U.S. Highway 441 is one of the few areas remaining in the United States where there are miles of scenic landscapes, historic small towns, cultural experiences, and abundant recreation facilities; and
WHEREAS, the promotion of tourism represents a readily available and effective tool with which to spur economic development; and
WHEREAS, Highway 441 travels through miles of scenic Georgia, containing several beautiful mountain lakes and numerous sparkling streams, as well as attractive rural landscapes; an abundance of state, federal, and local recreation facilities; many historic sites; museums; mom and pop businesses; and cultural centers; and
WHEREAS, designation of this route as a historic and cultural highway will promote economic well being through tourism.
NOW, THEREFORE, BE IT RESOLVED BY THE GENERAL ASSEMBLY OF GEORGIA that U.S. Highway 441 from the North Carolina state line to the Florida State line is designated Heritage Trail as a part of the Blue Star Memorial Highway.
BE IT FURTHER RESOLVED that the Department of Transportation is authorized and directed to place appropriate signs at appropriate locations designating said highway as provided in this resolution.
BE IT FURTHER RESOLVED that all signs erected on state rights of way must meet the department´s design specifications and be approved for content by the department.
BE IT FURTHER RESOLVED that the State Department of Transportation will be responsible for and fund the development of the sign plan, furnish posts and hardware, and erect route signage.
BE IT FURTHER RESOLVED that the Clerk of the House of Representatives is authorized and directed to transmit an appropriate copy of this resolution to the commissioner of transportation.

THE VILLAGE OF ABERCORN

Near here the Village of Abercorn was laid out, in 1733, and ten families assigned to it. In 1734, when the Salzburgers arrived in Georgia, many of them were stationed in Abercorn to wait for their homes to be built in Ebenezer and a road cut through to that place. Their pastor, the Rev. John Martin Bolzius, remained with them during the months of waiting. The location of the Village proved unsuitable for permanent settlement, and in a few years Abercorn was abandoned, to take its place among the Dead Towns of Georgia - only the creek that runs beside the site still bears the name.

A half mile south of Effingham County line at County Road 3
GPS Coordinates: N32.2304, W81.193777

General James Edward Oglethorpe arrived in the Georgia colony in 1733 with one hundred anxious and apprehensive families. His military organizational skills quickly rose to the occasion and Oglethorpe arranged living arrangements just as he would assigning duty stations. The one hundred families were divided into groups, ten families each. Each group was assigned a location in which they were to develop a settlement. One group, in particular, was assigned a lovely place on the Savannah River about fifteen miles north of the main settlement at Savannah. This location was considered important because it allowed a way point in communication between Savannah and Charles Towne in southern Carolina.

The settlement was divided into twelve lots, a lot was approximately fifty acres. One lot or fifty acres was allowed for each family. A lot at the northern and southern ends of the settlement was to be used as public property for the construction of a meeting house and church. The colonists named the village Abercorn and quickly built shelters to house themselves. They began to plant crops to feed their families and generally went about making a life at Abercorn.

Illness struck the village. The most susceptible, the children and elderly, grew weak; then fevers and chills convulsed their bodies. Many began showing signs of flux, which resulted in blood loss through the bowels. Flux was deadly and malaria, from the disease infested mosquitoes, was just as deadly. The colonists believed they were doomed. The Salzburgers, of German descent, arrived about six months later and were also assigned to Abercorn with the promise that they would eventually have homes at Ebenezer. During their short stay in the village, only a matter of months, the majority of the Salzburgers began experiencing intestinal problems.

A road was completed between Ebenezer and Abercorn. The Salzburgers gratefully move to their new home. The road facilitated the delivery of supplies to Ebenezer and was essential to the survival of the settlement. As the colonists of Abercorn continued to suffer the effects of disease, they were unable to work the land. By 1737, only four years after Abercorn's establishment, the village was all but abandoned.

In December 1739, Misters Stephens and Jones were sent by Oglethorpe to evaluate the failed settlement. Stephens castigated the early settlers by reporting that never had he seen such a more pleasant place, further that the settlers were lazy and had no desire to develop the beautiful settlement beside the Savannah River. Of course, during the winter months, the disease carrying insects were nowhere to be found and only delivered their deadly stings during the long summer and fall. Stephens' criticism failed to bring civilization back to Abercorn. When Georgia legalized slavery another attempt was made to establish plantations and cultivate the land. The attempt met with some success, until the advent of the Civil War, when slavery was no longer an option: Abercorn was doomed to failure.

By 1780, when William Faden published maps of the area, Abercorn was noted as "an early settlement fifteen miles from Savannah where no memorial of its former condition can be seen." The area is, today, known simply as a boat landing on the waterway between Savannah and Augusta.

SHERMAN AT POOLER

On Dec. 9, 1864, troops of Mower's division, 17th Corps, of Gen. Sherman's army (U), which was closing in on Savannah, advanced to Pooler after suffering losses through the day from artillery mounted on a RR flat car, torpedoes planted on the roads, and the stubborn resistance of Confederate infantry. By evening, Pooler had been seized and a strong line had been established astride the RR, on the road passing by the depot. An advance line was constructed about 300 yards farther east. That night, Gen. Sherman and Gen. Blair (17th Corps) established headquarters in Pooler, about 300 yards west of the depot, the former on the north side of the road.

US 80 at the First Baptist Church, Pooler
GPS Coordinates: N32.116, W81.249122

The calendar read December 1864, as General William Tecumseh Sherman marched more than ten thousand Union troops toward Savannah. By the 9th of the month, his men had only ten miles left to travel before General Sherman could complete his Christmas list by presenting the city of Savannah to President Lincoln.

During the long march from Milledgeville, the Union troops had met with no opposition. Occasionally, they would capture a war wearied soul trying only to make his way home from a war long since lost by the South. As Sherman's men approached the Central of Georgia Railway at Pooler Station on the outskirts of town, it was a cold winter day and Confederate soldiers silently lay in wait as the Union troops grew near the station. Two hundred Confederate soldiers attacked. The Union troops made short work of the Confederates, those who were not killed were taken prisoner. General Sherman ordered that camp be made near the site of the railway depot.

General Sherman led his troops into the small impoverished community of Pooler. He approached a group a men huddled in the road, in the midst of the huddle he found a young Union officer, whose foot had been virtually blown to bits by a torpedo planted in the road. The young soldier waited his turn, with beads of sweat across his forehead and pain evident across his mouth pulled into a sickening grimace, for a surgeon to amputate his leg in an effort to save his life.

The young officer was riding along with the rest of his brigade, when his horse triggered a torpedo buried in the road. The horse was immediately killed and the young officer gazed in horror at the protruding bone stump where his boot once been. General Sherman's skin turned ashen as he noticed the terrible wound. Years later in his memoirs General Sherman related, "This was not war, but murder, and it made me very angry."

General Sherman ordered the Confederate prisoners forward and armed them with picks and spades. They were made to march in close contact along the road to locate and remove the eight inch shells buried in the road or die as they exploded beneath the prisoners feet. General Sherman was said to have laughed as the prisoners begged to be relieved of this order and as they carefully tiptoed through the prospective mine field. Fortunately no more bombs were found.

From the opening of his tent near the Pooler Station, General William Tecumseh Sherman gazed down the straight path of rails. He imagined the city of Savannah, only eight miles away, falling at his feet. President Lincoln would have Savannah by Christmas.

Endnotes

[1] The text has not been altered in any way including obvious spelling or grammatical errors.

[2] Ritual bath

[3] The gathering of ten men

[4] The first five books of the Bible

[5] Sephardic Jews

[6] Traditions

[7] Commonly known as A. P. Hill

[8] Pumpkin color

[9] Merchant

[10] According to the Center for Disease Control in Atlanta, lupus is a chronic inflammatory disease that can affect various parts of the body, especially the skin, joints, blood, and kidneys. The immune complexes build up in the tissues and can cause inflammation, injury to tissues, and pain.

[11] The text has not been altered in any way including obvious spelling or grammatical errors.

[12] Breastplates

[13] Preceding the Georgia General Assembly

[14] No changes or corrections have been made to grammar or content.

[15] The organization was also known as: Sons of Liberty, Liberty Boys or the Liberty Society.

[16] Evolved to become the Georgia General Assembly

[17] Princeton

[18] A dry river bed.

[19] This is incorrect, James Wilde was actually only 22 years old at the time of his death.

[20] The Bible, Ephesians 4:1-6

[21] An 18th Century Pawn Shop and Consignment Store.

[22] Betting

[23] Chief of the Yamacraw

[24] No changes to the article regarding spelling, capitalization or word usage will appear. The article is noted, in its entirety, as it was published in 1739.

[25] Sculptor, Bertel Thorvalden (1770-1884) of Denmark

[26] Entry

[27] Main sanctuary

²⁸ Founder of the Lutheran Church

²⁹ Artist, Sculptor, Inventor, Leonardo Da Vinci (1452-1519) of Italy

³⁰ An indoor toilet

³¹ Taken from Washington's Southern Tour Diary. The text is noted with out changes to spelling or format.

³² A Member of the European Jews settling in Spain and Portugal.

³³ Another story contends that Pulaski was taken to a nearby plantation, where his wounds proved fatal.

³⁴ Fragmented shrapnel encased within a musket or cannon ball.

³⁵ A clearing or valley

³⁶ The Holy Bible, King James Version, Luke 8:1.15

³⁷ A society of Irishmen.

³⁸ Local judge.

³⁹ No changes in content or grammar were made to this article. It appears as published in 1864.

⁴⁰ Cotton

⁴¹ The bottom of the sea.

⁴² Law Degree

⁴³ No relation of General William T. Sherman

⁴⁴ The level space behind the walls, where guns are mounted.

⁴⁵ quarantine

⁴⁶ There are two historic markers entitled Isle of Hope, National Historic District. Both markers contain exactly the same wording, therefore, I have elected to write only one article. I have listed the locations of each marker, although the GPS Coordinates will lead you only to the first marker. Each marker has a beautiful view of the marsh from slightly different angles.

47 John Ray's "Compleat Collection of English Proverbs," 1670

⁴⁸ Gold coins

⁴⁹ The 5th month of the ecclesiastical year on the Jewish Calendar.

⁵⁰ Powers of a Priest.

Bibliography

"About North Georgia." Publisher Randy Golden, 2000.

Adams, Henry. *The Education of Henry Adams*. University of Virginia, Boston and New York: Houghton Mifflin Co., 1918.

"Amidst the Ashes." Student Media Department. University of Alabama Press, 1996.

Anderson, Sue. "Romance and Elegant Leisure," *Official Guide to Southeast Destinations*.

Bartram, William. *Travels of William Bartram.* Layton, UT: Peregrine Smith, 1980.

Bell, Malcolm, Jr. *Major Butler's Legacy: Five Generations of a Slaveholding Family*. Athens: University of Georgia press, 1987.

Biographical Directory of the American Congress 1774-1961. U.S. Government Printing Office, 1961.

Bridges, Edwin. *George Walton: A Political Biography*. PhD dissertation, University of Chicago, 1981.

Brunswick and the Golden Isles Visitors Bureau. *African American Heritage Highlights Display*, 2001.

Bryant, Pat. *Georgia Counties: Their Changing Boundaries*. Atlanta: State Printing Office, 1983.

Camden County Marriages 1819-1865. Camden County Official Records.

Carl Vinson Institute of Government, University of Georgia.

Clifford, Rev. Dr. Alan C. *Atonement and Justification: English Evangelical Theology 1640- 1790: An Evaluation.* Oxford: Clarendon Press; New York: Oxford University Press, 1990.

Coleman, Kenneth. *Colonial Georgia: A History*. New York: Charles Scribner's Sons, 1976.

Coulter, E. Merton. *Georgia: A Short History*. Chapel Hill: University of North Carolina Press, 1960.

Corruth, Gorton. *Encyclopedia of American Facts and Dates*. New York: Harper and Collins Publishers, 1997.

Danford, Beth. *Pecans and Georgia: A Historical Match*. Georgia Pecan Commission. 2000.

Dengler, Sandy. *Susanna Wesley*. Chicago: Moody Press, 1987.

Dove, Sue K. *Pecan History*. University of Georgia Coastal Plain Experiment Station, 1997.

Epworth By The Sea. St. Simons: 2001.

Eubanks, Thomas A. *Sugar and Tabby: The McIntosh Sugarhouse, a Special Building on the Georgia Coast*. Department of Natural Resources. Atlanta: 1985.

"Evergreen Explorer," *Newsletter Evergreen Presbyterian Church*, vol. 4.3, June 2000.

Foner, Eric. *Reconstruction: America's Unfinished Revolution 1863-1877*. New York: Harper and Row, 1988.

Games, Gwylim. *Overview of World Religions*. Lancaster University, 1995.

Gannon, Michael. *Operation Drumbeat*. New York: Harper & Row, 1990.

Gardner, Robert G. *A History of the Georgia Baptist Association, 1784-1984.* Atlanta: Georgia Baptist Historical Society, 1988.

Georgia Beer Wholesellers Association, 2001.

Georgia House of Representatives, Public Affairs, 2001.

Georgia Visitors Information, Atlanta: 2001.

Golden Isles Chamber of Commerce. Brunswick: 2001.

Henduck, Bill. "Close to Home," *Atlanta Journal Constitution*, February 1999.

Hickox, O. Jonathan. *4th Georgia Calvary*. 1998.

"Historic Valley Forge," *Independence Hall Association,* Philadelphia: 1995.

"History." National Oceanic and Atmospheric Administration, vol. 1, no. 1, January 1971.

Hopper, Ree. *Hopper-Pratt Family Reunion*. 2000.

Howels, John. *Georgia 1793-1799.* Special Collection 846, Box 4. Georgia Historical Society. Savannah: 1970.

Jackson, Harvey H. *Lachlan McIntosh and The Politics of Revolutionary Georgia*. Athens: University of Georgia Press, 1976.

Jackson, Michelle. *Forty Acres and a Mule Promised by General Sherman*. World African Network, 1998.

Jurick, John T. *Georgia Treaties, 1733-1763*. Vol. x1: pp. 15-17 in Alden T. Faughan (gen ed.), *Early American Indian Documents: Treaties and Laws, 1607-1789*. Frederick, Maryland: University Publications of America, 1989.

Kemble, Francis Anne. *Journal of a Residence on a Georgia Plantation in 1838-1839*. University of Georgia Press, pp. 219-221, 1984.

Lamplugh, George R. "George Walton, Chief Justice of Georgia, 1783-1785." *Georgia Historical Quarterly*, Vol. 65, 1981.

Lanning, John Tate. The Spanish Missions of Georgia. Chapel Hill:1935.

Lenz, Richard J. *Longstreet Highroad Guide to the Georgia Coast and Okefenoke*. 2001.

"Letters by Henry J. Osborne." Georgia Historical Quarterly, December 1969.

Lear, Tobias. *Last Words of General Washington*. Philadelphia, 1892.

Matthews, Marguerite Marree' Evans. *The Floyd's of Camden County*. 1999.

"Men of Mark in Georgia." ed. by William J. Northern. Spartanburg: Reprint Company, 1974.

Miller, Michael W. *Tabby Resources in Georgia*.

Mims, Edwin. *Sidney Lanier*. Port Washington, NY: Kennikat Press, 1905.

Moore, Steve. *Frederica, Fort and Town: Historical Background*. Fort Frederica National Monument, 1997.

"Oh Susanna: Model of a Christian Mother," *Glimpses*, Issue 77. Christian History Institute.

Patterson, Ni'cole. *Digs Done on Hamilton Place Slave Plantation*.

Phillips, Dan K. "Hermit of the Essex Coast," *Coast Guide*, 1995.

Rhyne, Nancy. *Touring the Coastal Georgia Backroads*. Winston-Salem: John F. Blair Publisher.

Rodgers, Thomas G. "Colonials Collide at Bloody Marsh," *Military History*, October 1996.

Ross, Kathy W.; Stacy, Rosemary. *John Wesley and Savannah*. Armstrong Atlantic State University, 1999.

St. Simons Island Trolley Company, 2000.

Salzer, James. "Georgia Once had 3 Governors," *The Augusta Chronicle*.

"Savannah Daily Advertiser." Pg 1, col. 2. September 1872.

"Secrets of Gascoigne Bluff, The," Golden Isles Navigator, 2001.

Shepherd, Victor. *The Life and Art of Charles Wesley*, 1998.

"Signers of the Declaration of Independence." Independence Hall Association. Philadelphia: 1995.

Smith, Julia Floyd. *Slavery and Rice Culture in Low Country Georgia 1750-1860*. Knoxville: 1985.

"Stagecoaches and Public Accommodations in Antebellum Georgia." *Chattahoochee Refugee Society*, Atlanta: 2001.

"Stagecoach Etiquette." *Omaha Herald*. Nebraska: 1867.

Stiles, R. M. *Letter Book 1808-1809*. pp. 293-295.

"Stockman Family Newsletter, The" Vol 8, no. 1. March 1993.

Storer, Charles S. *Reminisences of Elizabeth 1845-1886*. C. S. Storer, 1983.

Sullivan, Buddy. "Touring Coastal Georgia, *The New Georgia Guide*, pp. 594-619. Athens: University of Georgia Press.

Talmadge, Herman. *Talmadge: A Political Legacy, A Political Life*. Atlanta: Peachtree Publishers, 1987

Thompson, Eloise. *History of St. Marys United Methodist Church*. 2000.

Whitelaw, Ralph T. *Virginia's Eastern Shore*. Richmond Virginia Historical Society. 1951.

Travel Notes

Travel Notes